DOING RESEARCH ON CRIME AND JUSTICE

DOING RESEARCH ON CRIME AND JUSTICE

Second Edition

EDITED BY

ROY D. KING

AND

EMMA WINCUP

OXFORD
UNIVERSITY PRESS

OXFORD

UNIVERSITY PRESS

Great Clarendon Street, Oxford OX2 6DP

Oxford University Press is a department of the University of Oxford.
It furthers the University's objective of excellence in research, scholarship,
and education by publishing worldwide in

Oxford New York

Auckland Cape Town Dar es Salaam Hong Kong Karachi
Kuala Lumpur Madrid Melbourne Mexico City Nairobi
New Delhi Shanghai Taipei Toronto

With offices in

Argentina Austria Brazil Chile Czech Republic France Greece
Guatemala Hungary Italy Japan Poland Portugal Singapore
South Korea Switzerland Thailand Turkey Ukraine Vietnam

Oxford is a registered trade mark of Oxford University Press
in the UK and in certain other countries

Published in the United States
by Oxford University Press Inc., New York

British Library Cataloguing in Publication Data

Data available

Library of Congress Cataloging in Publication Data

Data available

Typeset by Newgen Imaging Systems (P) Ltd, Chennai, India
Printed in Great Britain
on acid-free paper by
Ashford Colour Press, Gosport, Hampshire

ISBN 978–0–19–928762–8

1 3 5 7 9 10 8 6 4 2

Dedication

To my wife, Jan
Roy King

To my son, Ben
Emma Wincup

Preface to the second edition

The suggestion that a second edition of *Doing Research on Crime and Justice* should be produced was made at the 2003 British Society of Criminology Conference hosted by the Centre for Comparative Criminology and Criminal Justice at the University of Wales, Bangor. Flattered by the acknowledgement from Oxford University Press that the first edition had already proved to be successful but surprised that a second edition was being discussed so soon after the first had been published in 2000, we began to consider what form a new edition might take. To assist us in our task Oxford University Press supplied comments from academics who had requested inspection copies of the first edition. The feedback was overwhelmingly positive and it quickly became apparent that whilst *Doing Research on Crime and Justice* was developed as an honest guide to criminological research, principally for doctoral students, in practice it was being used by a much wider audience. Similarly, whilst it was conceived as a text mainly for UK students, the sales figures supplied by the publishers suggested its actual readership was more geographically dispersed.

Following consultations with our original contributors we submitted a proposal to Oxford University Press for a much-expanded new edition. We planned to retain our original aim of bringing together the accumulated wisdom of some of the leading and best-established criminologists practising in Britain with the fresh experiences of a new and rising generation of scholars. At the same time we hoped to address some of the areas we had neglected in the first edition, to recognize some of the key developments that had taken place in criminological research in the intervening years, and to produce a text which would continue to appeal to a diverse market. We set out the changes between the two editions in our editorial introduction.

We are grateful to Sarah Hyland for making the initial suggestion that a new edition might be appropriate and to Rachael Willis and Nicola Haisley who worked with us efficiently to ensure that it was brought to fruition. We greatly appreciated their understanding and patience as we experienced the inevitable delays which accompany projects of this scale. Peter Herbert gave valuable technical assistance in the final stages of preparing the manuscript. Once again, however, we owe our greatest debt to our contributors whose collective wisdom and expertise in criminological research is here distilled. We thank them all.

ROY D. KING   EMMA WINCUP
Cambridge, January 2007   Leeds, January 2007

Preface to the first edition

The idea for this book was conceived when we were colleagues together at the Centre for Comparative Criminology and Criminal Justice at the University of Wales, Bangor. In one of our regular meetings to discuss research agendas one of us remarked on how little guidance there had been when she was a PhD student about the real process of doing criminological research. Somehow the insights of even the most knowledgeable and experienced supervisors, thrown into discussions during supervisions or thesis committee meetings, do not have the same gravitas as words on the printed page, and yet the words on the printed pages of methodology textbooks and research monographs made all too little reference to the lived experience of researchers doing their research. Indeed all too often the textbooks are written as though research is not a lived experience at all, but simply the application of techniques developed by others and which have been deemed right for one or another style of research.

Emma's remarks reminded the other editor of his first experience of social research: examining the case records of probationers vaguely searching for clues as to possible explanations for their delinquency, in fulfilment of the undergraduate dissertation requirements for a sociology degree at the University of Leicester. Indeed he was not much wiser when subsequently invited by his eminent PhD supervisor, the late Jack Tizard at the MRC Social Psychiatry Research Unit, to study patterns of long-stay hospital care for children. Being parachuted in to fieldwork situations can be an extremely daunting business—and no amount of reading can fully prepare one for it. That sense of wondering what one has embarked on, and how one is going to go about it, indeed why one is there at all, has probably beset generation after generation of research workers. The strong will always survive, but it was a long time before he realized that at bottom the research process was essentially about finding things out and trying to understand what it is that one has discovered. Research methods and techniques are an aid in that process but are sometimes wrapped in mystique and it is easy to believe that they should be used like a recipe book. There are, of course, circumstances in which a rigorous application of technique is essential. But there are others where improvisation is the order of the day. The measure of the good researcher comes in judging the difference between these situations and having the flexibility to deploy the best approximation one can find to make the maximum possible use of what, in the social world, are always unique circumstances and opportunities.

The original title for this volume was going to be *The Honest Criminologist's Guide to Doing Research on Crime and Justice* (in homage to Norval Morris and Gordon Hawkins). Hardly any of the established authors contributing to Parts One, Two, and Three of this volume had a formal research training. Most had learned what they know through trial and error in the school of hard knocks and some of them are battle-scarred. When they were invited to contribute to this volume in ways which got beyond the conventional accounts in methodological appendices and in ways that also reflected some of their own real experiences of the research process, most readily embraced the idea of expressing themselves as 'honest criminologists'. All of these authors, some now approaching the end of their careers, are actively involved in passing on what they have learned either to graduate students or to younger colleagues, or both, in their respective fields of expertise. However, there seemed much to be gained from bringing that wealth of expertise together in a single volume for the benefit of those approaching criminological or criminal justice research for the first time, be they undergraduates taking their first fumbling steps on the road to discovery, or one of an increasing number of practitioners in the criminal justice field who are becoming both research-literate and research-active, or perhaps especially graduate students or neophyte professional researchers.

By contrast most of the authors contributing to Part IV will have had some formal research training as part of their doctoral studies. Some of these authors are already on their third or fourth post-doctoral research projects, whereas others have only recently emerged from their *viva voce* examinations—in one case since writing the first draft of his chapter for this book. The careers of these contributors have been forged in a very different political, economic, and social climate from that in which their supervisors started out twenty or thirty years earlier. And they work within a discipline which has changed almost beyond recognition. Among these contributors will be some of the movers and shakers of criminology in the coming years: and the sharpness and recency of their experience can be expected to resonate with those of the generation to come. If we are right, then there will be everything to be said for revisiting these areas in subsequent editions: to create periodic benchmarks on the state of the discipline.

In editing this volume our biggest debt, of course, is to our contributors. The volume stands or falls on what they have had to say. Many produced their chapters under enormous pressure, not least the pressure of the research process itself: the need to manage research centres and institutes, the continuing need to compete for research funds, and, for the authors in Part IV, the need to establish independent research careers. Given the level of commitments it is not surprising that the process was more time-consuming than our original schedule proposed. It is sometimes hard to know who feels guiltier in this process: editors for nagging people about deadlines or contributors for missing them. But we hope the task has been worthwhile and we are grateful to Michaela Coulthard and Myfanwy Milton at Oxford University Press for having confidence in the project and being patient with the delays.

Several others have contributed to the shaping of this volume in various ways, sometimes without knowing it. Some of these are acknowledged in the dedication (fittingly in a book that deliberately spans the generations to Emma Wincup's grandparents and Roy King's grandchildren). Others include colleagues at the Centre for Comparative Criminology and Criminal Justice, especially Claire Davis our Research Administrator who organized an initial conference of the contributors in Bangor in September 1998 and has worked closely with the editors throughout. And, of course, our students, especially our graduate students.

Thanks also to our copy editor, Kate Elliott, who reminded us of the importance of grammatical correctness and produced many improvements.

ROY D. KING   EMMA WINCUP
Bangor, July 1999   Cardiff, July 1999

Outline contents

Detailed contents

PART II THEORY, DATA, AND TYPES OF CRIMINOLOGICAL RESEARCH

3 The relationship between theory and empirical observations in criminology   75

Anthony Bottoms

4 In search of causes and explanations of crime   117

Per-Olof Wikström

PART III RESEARCH ON CRIME, CRIMINALS, AND VICTIMS

9 Researching 'street criminals' in the field: a neglected art?

Mike Maguire

10 Mission impossible? Researching organized crime

Patricia Rawlinson

PART V SOME RECENT CASE STUDIES

Notes on contributors

John Baldwin is Professor of Judicial Administration in the School of Law at the University of Birmingham.

Anthony Bottoms is Emeritus Professor of Criminology at the Institute of Criminology at the University of Cambridge and professional fellow in Criminology at the University of Sheffield.

Manuel Eisner is Reader in Criminology at the Institute of Criminology at the University of Cambridge.

Philip Hadfield is Univeristy Research fellow in the School of Law, University of Leeds.

Joel Harvey is a Researcher in the Academic Division of Clinical Psychology at the University of Manchester.

Frances Heidensohn is Visiting Professor in the Department of Sociology at the London School of Economics and Emeritus Professor of Social policy, University of London.

Mike Hough is Professor and Director of the Institute for Criminal Policy Research in the School of Law at King's College London.

Darrick Jolliffe is Senior Lecturer in Criminology in the Department of Criminology, University of Leicester.

Roy King is Emeritus Professor of Criminology and Criminal Justice at the University of Wales, and Senior Research Fellow at Bangor the Institute of Criminology at the University of Cambridge.

Alison Liebling is Professor in Criminology at the Institute of Criminology at the University of Cambridge.

Friedrich Lösel is Professor and Director of the Institute of Criminology at the Unviersity of Cambridge.

Mike Maguire is Professor of Criminology and Criminal Justice of Cardiff University and Univeristy of Glamorgan.

George Mair is Professor of Criminal Justice in the School of Law at Liverpool John Moores University.

Pat Mayhew is Director of the Crime and Justice Research Centre in the School of Social and Cultural Studies at Victoria University of Wellington.

Rod Morgan is Professor of Criminal Justice and Visiting Professor at the Land on School of Economics at the University of Bristol.

Tim Newburn is Professor of Criminology and Social Justice in the Department of Social Policy at the London School of Economics.

Alpa Parmar is a PhD student at the Institute of Criminology at the University of Cambridge.

Patricia Rawlinson is Lecturer in Criminology in the Department of Criminology at the University of Leicester.

Robert Reiner is Professor of Criminology in the Department of Law at the London School of Economics.

Sandra Walklate is Eleanor Rathbone Chair Sociology in the School of Sociology and Social Policy, University of Liverpool.

Per-Olof Wikström is Professor of Ecological and Developmental Criminology at the Institute of Criminology at the University of Cambridge.

Matthew Williams is Lecturer in Criminology in the School of Social Sciences at Cardiff University.

Emma Wincup is Senior Lecturer in Criminology and Criminal Justice in the School of Law at the University of Leeds.

List of tables

List of figures

Introduction

Roy D. King and Emma Wincup

We opened the introduction to the first edition of this book by remarking that problems of law and order, crime, and the criminal justice process had never had so much attention as in the last few years and by arguing that if they were to be properly addressed, they must be effectively researched in ways that are theoretically grounded, methodologically secure, and practically based . In the six years or so that have elapsed since then much has happened. And much of what has happened is rather depressing for researchers. In that time the promise of a New Labour government to be 'tough on crime, tough on the causes of crime' has strangely metamorphosed into recent plans to deliver 'smarter justice' which aims to 'rebalance the criminal justice system in favour of the victim'.

For those readers who entertain a healthy scepticism about political rhetoric it will have come as no surprise that New Labour has found it much easier to be tough on crime than on the causes of crime. The pressure from the media and opposition parties had long since led here, as in the United States, to a bidding war in which politicians competed to show that each is tougher than the next and none dared to advocate a more reasoned approach for fear of being branded as 'soft on crime'. And it is hard to be tough on the causes of crime when so little is known about the specific causes and when policies that would impact effectively on the known correlates—inequality, poor housing, poor parenting, and so on—would either be extremely costly or else have so far defied our capacity to devise them. Certainly even the vast expenditures on punishment—uneconomic, inefficient, and ineffective as they mostly are, thus contravening an earlier political mantra of the Thatcher era that might have presaged a change of direction— seem cheap by comparison, at least in the short run. In the long run, things might be different, but politicians have never been notably interested in the long run.

What may be harder for the dedicated criminological researcher to take is the way in which politicians, in spite of the commitment to evidence-based policy, have been reluctant to use that evidence in a genuinely open debate about criminal justice, have introduced programmes in advance of, or in defiance of, evidence as to their effectiveness, and have been less than enthusiastic about the publication of research findings even in the limited arena of academic conferences. It is, to say the least, surprising that, according to poll evidence, the public continues to believe that crime rates are going up when in fact they have, overall, been falling for a decade according to both official statistics and the British Crime Survey[1]. It is true that there have been other genuine areas of concern, including worrying increases in low-volume violent crime, but it is even more worrying that these have not been placed in a context that relates them to risk or to violent crime rates elsewhere. It continues to be the case that many of those most worried by the phenomena remain least at risk of becoming a victim—and *vice versa*. And whilst the total

---

[1] Though as we go to press the veracity of some claims are being called into question.

level of crime in England and Wales remains high, there are certainly many other juris-dictions in which levels of violence are far worse. Several chapters in this book bear testi-mony, albeit muted in the context of considerations of future research funding, to the often poor fit between the rolling out of new policies or programmes and the evidence on which they are ostensibly based, as well as to difficulties over the timing and form of publication. In 2003 we were involved in the organization of the British Society of Criminology Conference. One of us, then from the host university, acted as Chair and felt bound to draw attention in his summing up to his concern that three sets of researchers, engaged on research projects funded by the Home Office, had been required to withdraw their papers. But there was worse to come as projects have been terminated early and some research reports have simply failed to materialize.

By the time this new edition appears in print the Government will have introduced yet another Criminal Justice Bill—the sixtieth Home Office bill since Tony Blair came to power—designed to implement the Prime Minister's pledge to 'rebalance the criminal justice system in favour of the victim' and to introduce new powers of instant civil justice for dealing with antisocial behaviour, as well as further restrictions on violent offenders following the expiry of their sentences and requiring unanimity in parole board deci-sions to release life-sentence prisoners which will take risk aversion to new heights. It is likely to be accompanied by three other bills introducing new powers to tackle organized crime, to scrap the use of juries in serious fraud trials, and to open up the probation service to competition through the abolition of local probation boards, thereby giving the National Offender Management Service the statutory backing it currently lacks, and allowing regional offender managers to commission probation services from the volun-tary and private sectors. This welter of legislation has, according to some counts, created over 3,000 new offences since 1997.[2] Moreover, it is not lost on opposition parties, not to mention criminal justice professionals and academic criminologists that successive bills sometimes reverse recently implemented legislation and that over fifty sections of the 2003 Criminal Justice Act had not been put into effect before proposals for the new Criminal Justice Bill had been announced.

In these circumstances it is sometimes hard to remember that the Government has made a number of genuine attempts to make criminal justice more of a system than once it was, and there is little doubt that practitioners at many levels are seriously disillusioned, none more so than in a beleaguered probation service which has undergone more changes in a shorter space of time than any public service could be expected to survive. In criminal justice as in other areas of public service the drive towards marketization serves more to undermine the professional commitment that has underpinned British public life than it does to improve efficiency. Meanwhile, reconviction rates remain stubbornly unaffected, the prison population continues to rise, and the public remains unconvinced as the currency of criminal justice initiatives becomes devalued. And while those of us at the empirical end of the spectrum of criminology voice concerns at the way in which evi-dence-based policies have been interpreted, those at the philosophical end wish to remind government just why 'justice' as a process implemented by disinterested parties under the watchful eye of independent judges came to replace the central role played by victims in the righting of wrongs.

---

[2] ' "Smarter justice" plans aim to rebalance system in favour of victim', *The Guardian*, 16 November 2006.

Perversely, these developments have taken place alongside considerable developments in the knowledge base accumulated through high-quality research—achievements that have been won in an increasingly difficult research climate which has become progressively more subject to government control. We argued, in the first edition, that how well the problems of crime and justice will be tackled in future will depend upon new generations of criminologists able to learn from what has gone before. That remains our message. But one of the most important lessons to be learned is that if criminological research is to have any impact, it is criminologists themselves who must enter the political arena to get across their findings directly and to address the policy implications. The time has surely come for media-savvy criminologists to take a leading role in the political debate—not by taking sides but by directly persuading politicians, but above all the press and the public about the real state of crime and the real policy choices available, each with their attendant positive and negative consequences. In the prevailing climate, that may not be easy for young scholars whose careers may be dependent upon the next research grant. It may be the case that some of the elder statesmen and stateswomen of the field, many of whom are represented in this volume and whose active research careers may be nearing an end, need to take on a concerted role in that regard—an unofficial advisory council on criminal justice policy.

The structure of the second edition

We were encouraged to produce a second edition of the book by the many favourable comments from those teaching research training courses in universities around the country for whom it filled a gap, and by our own growing sense that the research community had moved on in a variety of ways with a growing importance for some research styles which had not been reflected in the first volume. We therefore wished to produce an enlarged and more rounded collection that repaired some of the omissions of the first edition whilst nevertheless building upon what we were told were its strengths. The rationale for the book remains broadly the same: to produce a blend of chapters by, on the one hand, some of the most successful and distinguished researchers who could reflect upon their considerable experience of the research process in their substantive areas to the benefit of new researchers; and on the other by some of the most promising recent doctoral students thereby capturing their first experiences of doing research.

In producing an enlarged, more comprehensive volume, which includes one substantial new section, the balance between those two objectives has changed. In the first edition nine of the nineteen chapters were by 'new' researchers. In this edition the additional chapters by several more distinguished researchers has left space for only four contributions by new researchers whose work is showcased here both for its quality and for its capacity to round out the volume either with innovative methodology or an application to a newly emerging field of study. All the established contributors to the first volume were invited to update and rethink their contributions for the second edition. We were delighted that all accepted the invitation, although subsequently Dick Hobbs had to withdraw, thus providing an opportunity for Paddy Rawlinson—a 'new' researcher last time—to join the ranks of more senior authors. Rod Morgan, Robert Reiner, and

Roy King all took the opportunity to produce a new version in collaboration with distinguished colleagues—respectively, Mike Hough, Tim Newburn, and Alison Liebling—largely because of a belief that the better way of updating an essentially reflexive and methodological account was through an additional 'take' on what was the current state of the field.

Parts I and II

The main differences between the two editions occur in Parts I and II. In the original edition Part I comprised two chapters, by Tony Bottoms on the relationship between theory and research, and by Rod Morgan on the politics of criminological research. Both chapters transcended the various subdivisions of the field into substantive areas which provided the organizational structure for most of the rest of the book. Several teachers and students had remarked that the first edition lacked any overarching view of the research process itself. In this edition Part I begins with a new chapter by the editors which is intended to go some way towards filling that gap and we hope it gives at least an orientation to the new researcher as to what to bear in mind when embarking on a research project for the first time. We have deliberately avoided any sense that research is a matter of taking one or another 'method' from a methodological textbook and applying it to a problem, preferring to stress that research is a lived activity, in which it is constantly necessary for the researcher to look backwards and forwards as he or she progresses through, and tries to make sense of, several analytically distinct but necessarily interrelated stages. It should be read prior to dipping into more conventional textbooks on the subject.

In **Chapter 2** Rod Morgan and Mike Hough provide a substantially updated account of the changing political context within which criminological research has taken place over the last several years. They report on the trials and tribulations of researchers pressed for 'quick wins' and reflect on the 'short and unhappy life' of the Crime Reduction Programme and its aftermath. What they believe began as a sincere attempt at basing policy on evidence turned out to be a triumph of hope over experience. And they note that the raft of initiatives introduced to deal with antisocial behaviour have been largely exempt from any requirement to be evidence-based. Though their critical assessment of the political influence on recent research is carefully balanced, coming as it does from two leading researchers who have been at the heart of policy based research, we think it should provide very sobering and challenging reading for politicians, civil servants, and researchers alike.

Part II is essentially a new section on theory, data, and types of criminological research. In **Chapter 3** Tony Bottoms effectively starts from our assertion that research is a lived activity which moves back and forth between the various analytical stages and gives an impressively thoughtful account of the dialogue between theory and empirical observations that ought to exist, and sometimes does, in criminological research. It provides a subtly nuanced reconsideration of the issues he addressed in the first edition, and culminates in the presentation of the evolving work of Sampson and Laub as an exemplar of Layder's adaptive theory at work. In particular he argues that their work shows that it is possible to unite explanatory and causal theories on the one hand with theories which stress interpretive meaning from the point of view of the actor on the other. Co-existence between 'cause' and 'agency' is possible, he suggests, but 'only if we develop a concept of *explanation* which does not make *prediction* its central characteristic'.

Thereafter all the other chapters in this section have been newly commissioned and the contribution by Per-Olof Wikström in **Chapter 4** follows on naturally from where Bottoms leaves off. Like Bottoms he too discusses the relationship between cause and prediction but draws attention to the confusion that has arisen around them in a research and policy agenda that has been dominated by 'risk factors'. His richly detailed reconsideration of the often ignored complexities of the search for causes and explanations in criminology—which he sets out with rare clarity—provides a timely reminder of the need to revisit the origins of the criminological enterprise and to provide convincing theoretical explanations that would specify how 'causes' produce their purported 'effects'. He points out that the government is not 'tough on the causes of crime' precisely because it does not know enough about the causes or how to manipulate them, and concludes that if it were serious about crime prevention one would expect major investment of resources in long-term fundamental research on causality rather than a succession of attempted 'quick fixes'.

In **Chapter 5** Friedrich Lösel discusses the many ways in which evaluation research has evolved and argues that if we are to balance scientific and practical demands in the real world, it is essential to develop realistic expectations and to take a broader and longer-term view of the potential impact of research upon policy. There is no doubt that evaluation research has become extraordinarily complex as researchers have sought ways to describe and take account of the many possible factors operating not just in the treatment groups but also in the control groups, which could provide threats to validity. As a result, much of Lösel's chapter is probably more directed towards the professional researcher since many evaluation studies are likely to be beyond the resources of doctoral candidates. But there are many important lessons along the way. Whilst Lösel believes that criminologists should implement randomized field trials wherever possible, he has little patience with endless controversies about experiments as the 'gold standard' or indeed the relative virtues of quantitative versus qualitative research . Instead he recommends that criminologists should *both* promote randomized control trials *and* make the best use of available data, recognizes that experimental designs are not limited to research using statistical analysis, and notes that at all levels of methodological rigour, 'sound theories make interpretations of outcomes more robust'.

Manuel Eisner and his research student Alpa Parmar, a partnership wholly in keeping with the spirit of this volume, provide a carefully argued case in **Chapter 6** for the need for much more complex research designs to take account of issues of cultural diversity in criminological research and then present two case studies. In the first Eisner discusses the, admittedly expensive, Zurich Project on Social Development of Children in which 50 per cent of the respondents had a first language other than German. Interviews were conducted in a total of ten languages and great attention was paid to considerations of cross-cultural equivalence. In her smaller-scale study of perceptions of criminality in a British Pakistani community, Parmar addresses, among other things, the issue of ethnic matching of researcher and respondents in a more qualitative research context. They conclude that it is hard to imagine how criminological research in any large city could avoid paying close attention to ethnic and cultural diversity, and that researchers should not expect methods developed in monocultural settings to produce valid results. The detail of their research will surely embarrass those who, for whatever understandable reasons, may have taken a far too tokenistic approach to these issues.

In **Chapter 7**, Frances Heidensohn, one of our leading comparative researchers, whilst recognizing that all research is, or should be comparative, reviews and classifies the burgeoning number of international and comparative studies on crime and justice under the headings of case studies and what she calls multistudies and according to the research style of the comparative researcher. Just as questions of cross-cultural equivalence were at the heart of Eisner and Parmar's account of research in settings of cultural diversity, so they dominate (or should dominate) research which deliberately sets out to cross national and cultural boundaries. Despite the many problems, she shows that internationally comparative research can pay rich dividends in the insights it provides.

We hope that these new contributions in Part II go some way towards redressing the first edition's emphasis on qualitative, and to some extent parochial, research and thus give the reader a more rounded overview of the range of research 'out there'.

Parts III and IV

Part III, on 'Research on Crime, Criminals and Victims' and Part IV on 'Research on Criminal Justice Agencies and Institutions' remain broadly the same in their scope as their counterparts in the first edition. We probably need to say rather little about these chapters here because each seems to have earned an established place in the relevant literatures on the subject. For this edition most contributors, either singly or in combination with their new co-authors, provide a finely detailed review of the developments in the last few years together with a critical assessment of the current state of play, whilst retaining the essential structure and the strengths of the original essays.

In **Chapter 8** Pat Mayhew reports on the major hike in sample size to 40,000 for the British Crime Survey which took place immediately after the first edition was published, and the move to continuous rolling fieldwork to facilitate this. She notes how the victim survey has itself 'fallen foul' of administrative criminology in that a substantial part of it now provides 'performance indicators' for the forty-three police forces in England and Wales—although the increased sample size was also intended to provide a more reliable measure of violent crime. In addition to reviewing the latest methodological developments—and the dilemma of whether to embrace them or to maintain comparability with earlier sweeps—she revisits some of the predictions she made in the first edition as to the role local victim surveys might play in the audits which local partnerships were required to undertake following the implementation of the Crime and Disorder Act 1998.

Mike Maguire notes that there have been welcome signs of change in researching street criminals since the first edition was published, sufficient for him to turn his subtitle for **Chapter 9**—a neglected art—into a question rather than a statement. He then gives an elegant review of the state of that art. Nevertheless, he argues, despite the growing number of interview-based and ethnographic studies of street criminals, research involving interaction with offenders still remains the exception rather than the rule. He goes on to echo the sentiments expressed by Wikström that there is an urgent need for studies about how and why offenders make decisions to commit crime in that only if we are in a position to 'explain' the causes of crime will we be in a position to reduce or prevent it. As things stand, too many theories remain at best inadequately tested.

Patricia Rawlinson provides a rather different reflexive account of researching organized crime from that offered by Dick Hobbs in the first edition. In **Chapter 10** she begins by discussing the *Mafia mystique* which surrounded much of the early work on organized crime, before addressing the current interest in the phenomenon of people-trafficking following the collapse of the Soviet Union. She builds upon her previous contribution by providing two case studies from her own recent work and reminds us of the need to harmonize the different aspects of what it means to be a researcher—not just investigating organized crime but also in other settings. It helps, (see Eisner and Parmar, and Heidensohn above) if, like Rawlinson, one has the linguistic facility to operate in a cultural setting different from one's own (although she provides some entertaining examples where the right words evaded her!)

In updating her contribution to the first edition Sandra Walklate explores the impact of government attempts to rebalance the criminal justice system in favour of the victim and comments on the growth of restorative justice measures in **Chapter 11**. Whilst the basic structure of her chapter remains broadly the same she has taken the opportunity provided by the new edition to develop further her arguments on feminism and victimology. The case study she described, though now ten years old, remains sufficiently relevant to be worth repeating here.

In **Chapter 12** Robert Reiner and Tim Newburn's review of policing research embraces, among other things, the various studies of discrimination and effectiveness of the policing of minority ethnic groups which followed in the wake of the Macpherson Report which had been published shortly before the first edition went to press. Whilst the driving force behind much police research has remained the government's priority of crime control and a concern for measures of police performance, Reiner and Newburn argue that a return to fundamental and theoretical research on policing and the police, including replication of some of the classic observational studies, is needed if our understanding of police practice and police culture is not to get increasingly out of date.

John Baldwin, in **Chapter 13**, argues that the climate in which empirical research on the criminal courts is pursued has changed since the publication of the first edition. In part this is because of the enactment of the Freedom of Information Act, 2005, which has opened up new possibilities, and in part because of heightened concerns about justice in the wake of some high-profile miscarriages of justice as well as the failure to bring successful prosecutions for the murder of Stephen Lawrence. In light of Macpherson's findings about institutional racism across the criminal justice system, he adds a new section to his review which discusses studies of discrimination and differential treatment. The classic case study, with its cautionary tale about the politics and ethics of research remains as pertinent for this edition as it did before.

George Mair has probably undertaken the most daunting task for our contributors of documenting the changes which have taken place in the nature of community penalties and the way they are administered—changes which he rightly describes as 'momentous'. In **Chapter 14** he argues that although the politicization of community penalties has led to an explosion of research studies, most of them have had a negligible impact on policy or practice—because too often the research has been fragmented, time-limited, badly focused, concentrating solely on outcomes, and poorly integrated into the policy process despite direct or indirect Home Office involvement. Mair cites several examples of censorship—delays in publication, spin of the results, termination of projects—which ought to have no place if an evidence-based approach to policy or practice is to have any real meaning. He concludes with a plea to rethink the policy–research relationship, with more independence for researchers and greater clarity in reporting results, targeted to particular audiences so that they can have a greater impact upon practitioners. Above all, perhaps, what is needed is greater stability in the way services are organized and delivered so that the results of research can be applied to a 'recognizable landscape'.

The research scene in prisons is probably somewhat healthier than in other areas of the criminal justice system, in part because the results of research on matters such as order, legitimacy, staff and prisoner cultures and so on have been of obvious practical interest to managers as well as academic interest to researchers. In **Chapter 15** Roy King and Alison Liebling, argue that whilst some difficulties remain, the procedure for gaining access has become more formalized, funding sources have become more varied, prison staff have become more 'research-literate', and both at establishment and headquarters levels there is a greater openness to research. Perhaps as a result, they are able to draw upon their combined experiences to produce a long list of agreed 'dos and don'ts' for the different stages of the research process which builds upon the ten nostrums discussed in the first edition. They also identify some areas where new researchers may face genuine dilemmas.

Part V

Part V contains case studies by four 'new' scholars at the beginning of their independent academic careers. These reflect both the interdisciplinary nature of criminological research and the importance of keeping abreast of cutting-edge methodological developments. Their contributions are very different from one another but each shows the kinds of methodology that can be deployed in doctoral research in their respective settings and we expect new doctoral students will be able to glean much of comfort from what they say here.

Matthew Williams, in **Chapter 16**, raises intriguing issues about the ethical and methodological problems encountered in researching cybercrime. In particular he extends the boundaries of participant observation to online contexts—though the need to understand the culture if one is not to make mistakes is as true in the virtual world as it is in the real world. This is a research area which will surely engage the attention of future generations of criminologists.

In **Chapter 17** Philip Hadfield discusses the conduct of ethnographic research on the licensing courts whilst also acting as an expert witness. This unusual dual role provided an experience of courtroom drama quite different from that described by previous non-participant observers, and one which posed both personal challenge and concern for, and changes in, personal identity.

Joel Harvey demonstrates in **Chapter 18** what Wickström pointed out in **Chapter 4**, namely that longitudinal work doesn't have to involve long-term commitments. He was able to pursue short-term longitudinal as well as cross-sectional work in his multi-method approach to the study of how young men survive in prison, which also embraced social network analysis.

Finally, in **Chapter 19,** Darrick Jolliffe gives an account of the research process which demonstrates the value of systematic review and meta-analysis in defining and refining research problems—in his case on empathy, self-reported offending and school bullying. He also shows the need for both persistence and adaptability in gaining access to research sites—which could very well provide the moral underpinning of this book: 'If, at first, you don't succeed, try, try and try again.'

PART I
PRACTICE AND POLITICS IN CRIMINOLOGICAL RESEARCH

1

The process of criminological research

Roy D. King and Emma Wincup

Introduction

In this chapter we seek to provide an overview of the research process for individuals doing research on crime and justice for the first time, whether they be new research students or one of the increasing numbers of practitioners encouraged or required by their employers to undertake research. In truth, although the circumstances in which research into crime and justice will be carried out, the risks, even dangers, and ethical considerations associated with it may have their own particular features and peculiarities, as revealed in later chapters of this book, the research process itself does not differ significantly from other forms of research in the social world. The process we outline here, then, has a wider application.

It is important at the outset to say something about what this chapter does *not* attempt to do. First, we do not seek to be comprehensive—a glance at the second edition of Colin Robson's (2002) text which is also aimed at both social scientists and practitioners and which runs to almost 600 pages should be enough to demonstrate that we could not hope to cover the same ground in about one-twentieth of that space. Second, we make no pretence, and for much the same reasons, to deal with any of the matters we raise in sufficient detail to send the reader out with competence to deal with them. Third, and above all, we do not seek to offer what George Mair in **Chapter 14** of this volume describes as 'bloodless prescriptions' to be 'followed to the letter in order to produce a perfect piece of research'. There is, in our view, no such thing as a perfect piece of research and there is no one best way of carrying it out. But there are certainly many examples of research that are a lot less perfect than they could have been and so it did seem important, in the second edition of this volume, to provide for the reader what we regard as some common-sense guidelines for understanding the research process. We have deliberately adopted a broadbrush approach to dealing with what we take to be the main steps and some of the big issues in a simple, straightforward, and largely non-technical way. In our efforts to demystify the research process we hope we have not strayed too far in the direction of dumbing things down. Our hope is that by making things simple, more researchers will be encouraged down the avenues that we have found exciting to explore.

It may be helpful to begin by thinking of the research process as rather like climbing a mountain—it is certainly very daunting at the outset, there are many opportunities for making serious mistakes, and there are many occasions when you think you have reached the top only to find that the peak is beyond yet another ridge. Before embarking on a mountaineering expedition it is important to plan it as thoroughly as you can in advance. It would make sense, for example, before leaving base camp, to plan the most likely inter-mediate bases *en route* to the top, but also to be prepared for any contingencies which might lead you to take a somewhat different path. You would certainly need to ensure that you kept to a timetable, bearing in mind the provisions you could carry and the prospects of inclement weather delaying your progress. It would be foolhardy, and perhaps fatal, in the absence of a map, to go wandering off in the mist. Like the wandering mountaineer, too many researchers, criminologists included, have lost their way through bad planning, poor time-keeping, or inexperience (see in **Chapter 9** the refreshingly honest reflections of Mike Maguire, one of the most successful and distinguished of British criminologists, on his first untutored forays into conducting criminological research). Fortunately criminological research much more rarely leads to fatalities than mountaineering (for exceptions, however, see Hobbs' (2000) discussion in the first edition of this book, of researching serious crime although note the more qualified take on this by Patricia Rawlinson in **Chapter 10** of this edition). It does, however, often involve encountering risk and danger in the process of collecting data (Ferrell and Hamm 1998; Linkogle and Lee-Treweek 2000; see also the reflexive accounts by Hoyle, Sharpe, and Wardhaugh in the first edition of *Doing Research on Crime and Justice* (2000)). Risks of a different kind can follow when the writing up of good criminological or sociolegal research which upsets establishment figures endangers the careers of researchers (see John Baldwin in **Chapter 13** of this volume).

It is important for the serious mountaineer to make use of the best available equip-ment. The kind of equipment used in Lord Hunt's first successful assault on Everest in 1953 has since undergone endless refinement using new materials. When embarking on an expedition, the mountaineer should be satisfied that the chosen equipment, though it might not have been used on this particular mountain by this particular mountaineer, will have been tried and tested on many other mountains by many other mountaineers. Likewise the researcher will be able to take advantage of the equipment used by other researchers in other settings, involving a whole battery of research strategies, tools, and techniques, each designed and developed to perform a particular role in a particular way. But there is no tool better adapted for the research process than the human mind with its ability to think, plan, check progress, analyse data, and to make records—and where necessary to change direction. Good researching, like good mountaineering, depends upon knowing where you are in relation to where you have come from and where you want to get to. Even the least well-equipped mountaineer probably has a compass and a watch with which to take bearings so that it is possible to monitor the current position in relation both to base camp and to the summit, but sometimes survival in the field will depend upon making good judgement calls on what to do next when faced with unfore-seen obstacles. We cannot stress enough that ingenuity and resourcefulness in the field can be the key to success as a researcher. One of us recently supervised a research student with a well-planned research design, and some reasonably well-rehearsed techniques, for a study of all the corrective labour colonies in the Ryazan region of Russia. The study had been approved by the local authorities and preliminary pilot work had been carried out. By the time she arrived to enter the field proper, and some 1,500 miles from home, how-ever, the political mentors had changed jobs, rendering the original plan impossible.

Decisions had to be made on the hoof. She ended up with an entirely different research design, in which she spent her time comparing two colonies in each of two other regions: and far from the relative comfort zone of the Golden Ring found herself alone in some penal colonies in Siberia. It meant a radical rethink of the research objectives, but it produced a relatively powerful research design, and her eventual book on the research went on to win the British Society of Criminology annual book prize (Piacentini 2004).

One can only push a simile so far before it breaks down, but before we move on to the research process proper, we want to reiterate the importance of the compass and the ability to take a bearing. Time and again in the research process it is essential, like *Janus*,[1] to be able to look both ways: to look forward focusing on the summit or research objective and even the eventual research report, and to look back on the starting point, and to know where you are in between.

The research process

We address the research process in seven analytically separable stages:

(a) initial ideas and implicit theories;

(b) interrogating the literatures;

(c) turning initial ideas into researchable problems;

(d) developing the most powerful research design;

(e) choosing the most appropriate methods;

(f) ruthlessly analysing the data;

(g) publicly presenting the results.

Though the stages are analytically separable they are logically interconnected and at least some of them may, in practice, proceed side by side. In any event, like *Janus*, the researcher must constantly look backwards and forwards, striving for consistency between the stages.

Initial ideas and implicit theories

Research must begin with an idea. Sometimes the idea comes from within the prospective researcher, sometimes it is implanted, for example by a potential supervisor, and sometimes it is dangled like a carrot by a funding agency often with a vested interest in the outcome. In the first of these instances the idea may be intuitive, inchoate, no more than a gut feeling about something or other. In the second the idea may well carry some baggage, perhaps a loose end left open from a supervisor's previous research to be tackled from within the same theoretical perspectives of the supervisor. In the third the idea may come prepackaged with strict limits as to how far the idea can be

---

[1] In Roman mythology, *Janus* was the God of doorways and passageways and the patron of the beginning of the day, month, and year. In both space and time he looked both backwards and forwards.

pursued and gift-wrapped with a methodological straitjacket (see, especially, the discussion by Rod Morgan and Mike Hough in **Chapter 2**, but also other chapters in this volume, for concerns about this issue, particularly in relation to Home Office funded research).

In any of these situations, but especially the first, the initial task is to interrogate *oneself* about why one has the idea. This is particularly important for doctoral research as a favoured opening question in oral examinations is to ask why the topic was chosen. When one has answered that question, it is necessary to ask oneself *why* one gave *that* particular answer and not another, and so on in a kind of infinite regression until one runs out of questions or answers. The next thing to do is to write it all down: question, answer, question, answer. This process of self-interrogation is not easy and can often be embarrassing and sometimes even painful. But it is necessary and it is enormously useful. Necessary, because the chances are that it will reveal an embryonic theory. I want to study this *because of* or *in order to do* that looks rather like a theoretical statement or at least a potential hypothesis. This can then be developed and related to other theoretical ideas which may already exist in the literature, and indeed from one of which it may turn out to have been derived. Theory is, or should always be, an essential ingredient of the research process, though it is often rather neglected or even completely ignored (see Bottoms, this volume). The process is also enormously useful because setting out one's ideas at the outset constitutes the starting point to which one may look back and, reassuringly, from which one may measure progress.

Faced with a blank sheet of paper, novice researchers may find it difficult to think of a topic. There are many tried and tested strategies for generating ideas. For example, one may look to the media for inspiration. At the time of writing (December 2006) several of the recent stories in the newspapers (now easily accessible on the Internet) could inspire possible research projects. It was recently reported that the prison population in England and Wales has reached 80,000 and that prisoners are being held, once again, in cells in nineteen police force areas. This opens up important issues to consider about the causes and effects of prison overcrowding, not least in a situation where a welter of different legislative acts have interacted with media reporting to impact upon sentencing policy. Similarly the trial of the five men accused of the murder of Sharon Beshenivsky, a West Yorkshire Police Officer shot whilst responding to an armed robbery, might lead to questions relating to the availability of firearms, the apparent growth in gun crime, and whether police officers should be armed. Press reports that the recipients of antisocial behaviour orders (frequently referred to as ASBOs) regard them as a badge of honour rather than stigmata might draw attention to the unintended consequences of intended human action and the need to understand the meaning of criminal justice sanctions from the point of view of those on the receiving end.

A second source of ideas is to consult previous research studies. Research almost always opens up more questions than it answers and the concluding sections within academic articles or the final chapters of research monographs and research reports often provide suggested topics for future research. Similarly, textbook chapters reviewing the current state of knowledge about a particular issue frequently identify gaps in knowledge. As editors we asked the authors of the chapters in Parts II, III, and IV of this volume to provide brief reviews of the styles of research relating to their chosen area and their achievements. In so doing, many have identified criminological questions which have yet to be posed elsewhere and may provide inspiration for those whose sheet of paper remains stubbornly blank.

Further ways to think of a research topic might be to draw upon your own experiences. Numerous research studies have been conducted by professionals working in the criminal justice system on topics that are closely related to their work environment, and specialist texts exist to guide those who have to manage their roles as *both* researcher and practitioner: Robson (2002) is particularly recommended for those who occupy these dual roles. Potential practitioner researchers should note carefully that by suggesting that the workplace can provide inspiration for a research topic, we are not advocating covert research and we believe that research should *normally* be undertaken with the full consent and knowledge of participants. Practitioners may have ready access to organizational data and documents which can be analysed, activities which can be observed, and colleagues and clients who can be interviewed but their normal access is *not* for research purposes. Profound ethical considerations enter into the equation when practitioner researchers seek to use their privileged access to their clients for research purposes. Whilst some criminological studies have been conducted *covertly* by criminal justice professionals (for example, Holdaway's (1983) study of the occupational culture of the police rank and file), generally they are best avoided because of the ethical difficulties they produce (see Zeni (2001) for a detailed discussion). This need not preclude practitioners from *overtly* researching issues closely related to their own work situation providing certain safeguards are followed. It will be helpful for the reader to look at Reiner and Newburn's exposition of research into the police by insiders and outsiders in **Chapter 12** of this volume, and their analysis could, of course, be applied to other areas of the criminal justice system.

Some students may be fortunate enough to draw inspiration from either paid or voluntary work for criminal justice agencies. Others may have to think more imaginatively about whether their own workplace can provide suitable ideas. For example, students working in pubs or clubs may use this opportunity to address important criminological questions relating to, for example, policing of the night-time economy, recreational drug use, or binge-drinking and its links with violent crime. An intriguing merging of roles is explored in **Chapter 17** of this volume where Philip Hadfield pursued his research on drinking habits whilst acting as an expert witness before the licensing courts. Such a merging of roles, however, can involve the researcher in walking a tightrope. Experiences beyond the workplace can also produce ideas which merit further consideration. For example, being an avid football supporter and frequently attending games could inspire an examination of the management of football hooliganism or, for those who are truly armchair-bound, a fascination with crime programmes on television could translate into research on their possible impact on public perceptions of crime and justice.

Finally, one possible way forward is to replicate the work of earlier researchers. This is an important part of the development of scientific knowledge, and it is certainly not to be despised, though it may be less fun and less exciting than being the first to conquer the mountain or to open up a new route to the summit. Students, even those with limited time and resources, may find that it is possible to replicate a published research study on a smaller scale. For example, this might involve using a selection of questions from the British Crime Survey to find out more about the impact of crime on a particular group such as international students.

Interrogating the literatures

Having interrogated oneself about the research idea, the next step is to interrogate the literature. There are, typically, a number of literatures one needs to review: substantive, theoretical, methodological, policy related, and so on, and it can be easier to think of the task as a series of reviews. For example, one of us supervised a doctoral student researching young offenders' experiences of referral orders.[2] In addition to reviewing existing studies on the referral order, she also explored the literature on restorative justice theory, qualitative research in general, and her chosen methods (interviews and observation) in particular, as well as youth justice policy. The scope of this review may sound daunting but there are strategies for keeping the task focused and manageable, which we will explore below.

Time and again new researchers (and, we surmise, some established researchers) are aware that 'doing a literature review' is part of the 'research process' yet do little more than go through the motions. The reality is that reviewing the literature, or more precisely literatures, has to be done with a clear sense of purpose. In each and every case the key question to pose must be what relevance does this have for my research? An appropriate review of the literatures *excludes* those pieces of work which do not bear directly on the emerging research question. The *real* secret of a good literature review is that it is well targeted to the purpose at hand and not a scattergun approach to work in that general area without any obvious indications of the directions for future research.

One of us looks back with a complete sense of embarrassment at the untargeted nature of the literature review which nevertheless passed muster for his own Ph.D.

The review should be comprehensive but when the literature on the topic is voluminous it does not need to include absolutely everything written about the topic or matters closely related to it. In these circumstances it would be reasonable to set some parameters at the outset; for example, focusing on the literature from England and Wales or literature from a particular time period. This strategy is used by George Mair in **Chapter 14** of this volume. Without these parameters the task could become unmanageable, delaying later stages of the research process, and thus they should be strictly adhered to unless it becomes obvious that they are unnecessarily restrictive. The parameters used need to be made explicit when writing up the literature review and justifications for their usage offered.

There is another sense in which the literature review can become unmanageable. In reviewing the available literatures there is rarely time to read books from cover to cover. Judicious use of the index, the preface, and the introductory and concluding chapters may enable one to gut and fillet the essence of most contributions. Whatever one reads, it is always important to record exact bibliographic details (perhaps by using specialist software such as EndNote), and when taking notes to make it clear what is a direct quotation with the appropriate citation and what are the note-takers' paraphrases of the original. Herein lies the difference between research and plagiarism.

For some innovative research subjects there really may not be much in the way of literatures available. In such cases one cannot be faulted for not reviewing what is not

---

[2] Since April 2002 offenders aged 10–17 appearing for the first time before the youth courts in England and Wales who plead guilty are referred to a youth offender panel. This panel comprises of members of the community who aim to bring together the victim and offender to discuss the offence and determine appropriate remedies.

there. But the researcher would be wise to think laterally. If there is no research in my subject area, is there research in a relevant and related subject area? One of us recently supervised a student studying death row in the United States and suggested that although there may not have been much research on the management of death on death row, the literature on the management of terminal illness in hospitals and hospices may throw up suggestive ideas. This example reminds us that criminologists need not confine themselves to literature from within the discipline.

The literature review is often perceived as a stage to be completed at the beginning of the research process. In one sense this is correct. Reviewing the relevant literature can help to identify a topic or if a topic has already been chosen, to determine whether the topic is sufficiently original to merit further research. The sad fact is that few ideas are completely original. In a world where there have probably been more practising researchers in criminology and criminal justice during, say, the last twenty years than there have been in the previous two-hundred-year history of the discipline, it would be surprising if no one had already addressed the issue in which one is interested. But we would contend that reviewing the literature is an essential element of the *entire* research process and should not be limited to its initial stages. The main reasons for this are twofold. First, given the rapid growth of criminological research and ongoing changes to criminal justice policy, criminological researchers need to be alert at all times to new publications and policy developments so that the literature review is only completed once the final report or equivalent is complete. Second, when analysing the findings, most researchers will find themselves offering comparisons between their own findings and those of others and so there may almost certainly be a need to revisit work already reviewed in light of one's own findings.

When reviewing the available substantive literature, it is important to focus not just on the findings of previous research studies but on their theoretical and methodological orientations. This may pay dividends in identifying appropriate theoretical frameworks or methodological approaches, either because the conclusion reached is that following in the steps of others appears to be the best way to proceed, or that a different path needs to be taken to overcome theoretical and methodological deficiencies inherent in previous studies.

In most cases the findings of the literature review need to be shared with others. For those preparing literature reviews for research degrees, the so-called 'write up'[3] tends to be in the form of a self-contained chapter included early in the dissertation or thesis (normally the second chapter) and for an empirically-based project it is likely to occupy 10–20 per cent of the available words. Sometimes, depressingly, such a chapter is limply titled 'Literature Review'. It is almost always better to use a title that relates to some essential finding or conclusion to be drawn from the literature which has excited you—especially if you wish your readers to stay awake. However, it is important to emphasize that academic literature should not be confined to a self-contained chapter in the dissertation or thesis. Instead almost all the other chapters should refer to the literature whenever and wherever it serves to illuminate the findings, or to draw comparisons with the work of others with regard to aspects of research design or methodological issues.

---

[3] We have drawn attention to this term by placing it in inverted commas because it is somewhat misleading as we believe that writing should not be delayed until the final stages of the research process.

When research is conducted for purposes other than securing a research degree, the final 'write up' rarely includes a detailed literature review: the exceptions here tend to be books which started life as Ph.D. theses. Instead, a brief literature review is often incorporated into a background section or chapter but as before, it is, or at least should be, referred to throughout the publication.

Most literature reviews conducted by researchers have taken the form of *narrative* accounts. One of the weaknesses of many narrative literature reviews is that they comprise little more than detailed descriptions of particular studies. Whilst a useful starting point is to prepare short summaries of these, the literature review should go beyond this and be both critical in orientation and synoptic in its structure. The researcher should aim to offer a discussion which identifies the main themes that have emerged, evaluates the strengths and weaknesses of the current knowledge base, and frames the study she or he has conducted by emphasizing what contribution it has made to advance an academic understanding of the topic.

In more recent years, especially where the research questions posed are about the effectiveness of one or another criminal justice intervention, so called *systematic* reviews of the literature have been deployed. The Home Office has recently funded a number of such reviews on topics as diverse as closed circuit television (Welsh and Farrington 2002), the impact of street lighting on crime (Farrington and Welsh 2002) and the effectiveness of criminal justice and treatment programmes in reducing drug-related crime (Holloway *et al.* 2005). Recent US examples can be found on the web pages of the Campbell Collaboration's Crime and Justice Co-ordinating Group (http://www.campbellcollaboration.org/CCJG). Succinctly defined by Welsh and Farrington (2002: 3), systematic reviews 'use rigorous methods for locating, appraising and synthesising evidence from prior evaluation studies, and they are reported with the same level of detail that characterises high quality reports of original research'. In practice this means that the review is guided by explicit objectives, studies from across the globe are sought and are included or excluded according to predetermined criteria, and the report provides details of both the findings of the review and the methods deployed to reach them. Darrick Jolliffe, in **Chapter 19** of this volume, provides an example of how systematic reviews can be incorporated into doctoral research projects—in this case on bullying in the classroom. Another excellent example of the use of systematic reviews in doctoral research is by Cheliotis (under review) who adopted this approach to explore the effectiveness of temporary release schemes for prisoners.

We hope we have conveyed clearly the message that conducting a literature review is more complex than it might appear at first sight. For those requiring further advice, specialist texts have been produced, for example, Hart (1998), which are recommended for novice researchers, and more experienced researchers seeking guidance on systematic reviews should see Farrington and Welsh (2005) and Petticrew and Roberts (2005).

Turning initial ideas into researchable problems

In this section we draw upon our extensive experience of working with students designing a research study for the first time, either as a required assignment for a research training module or one they intend to carry out in order to prepare a dissertation or thesis. Often, students do not struggle to think of ideas for potential projects but face difficulties at the next stage when they need to turn their initial idea into a researchable problem.

Perhaps one of the greatest challenges faced by novice researchers is to develop a research question that will establish a central direction for their study. One of the major pitfalls at this stage is to write a research question which is too broad, and this is particularly problematic given that the time available for student research is limited and financial resources are non-existent. These practical constraints aside, it is important to emphasize that some research questions (for example, the causes of youth crime) are simply too big to be answered through a single study and instead need to inform a programme of work (for example, focusing on different forms of youth crime or different groups of young offenders). Less frequently, in our experience, do students prepare research questions that are too narrow in scope but this does happen, more often by practitioners whose employers, who may also be funding the research, might want them to focus on some of the minutiae of criminal justice practice within their bailiwick. Whilst the proposed research study might be useful for the organization concerned, its contribution to academic knowledge may remain unclear unless it can be cast in some wider theoretical context. Imaginative thinking, guided by an experienced academic supervisor, can usually produce a proposed topic which satisfies both the employer and the requirements of the degree. For instance, an interest in the impact of a specific training programme for police officers might be transformed into a broader project on the occupational socialization of new recruits.

If politics is the 'art of the possible', then science, according to Sir Peter Medawar (1967) is the 'art of the soluble'. There is simply no point in asking questions which by their nature are not capable of being answered through the scientific instruments at our disposal. 'Why is the world?' and 'What is the meaning of life?' are not scientific questions because they cannot be answered through observation or experiment and there are no criteria against which we could judge the answers to be 'right'—or, more importantly, 'wrong'. Karl Popper (2002), most famously, has adumbrated the view that the essential feature of a scientific proposition is that it is capable of being falsified and that science advances through a process of falsification of some hypotheses and the provisional verification of others. Verification of an hypothesis is always, in principle, only provisional because one can never rule out the possibility that the next replication might falsify it, but in practice there are many scientific propositions that 'for all practical purposes' can be regarded as 'true'. Without such trust in their veracity, none of us would get on a plane again.

In passing, we might note that Kuhn (1962) and indeed others have taken a different view from Popper as to the process of scientific advancement, but that does not detract from the points we make here. Whilst we might measure and record what some people believe to be the reason the world exists, or the meaning which they find in life, the views which we measure and record have no particular scientific merit in themselves, although the nature and distribution of such views might in turn help us to explain how and why people behave in some situations. W. I. Thomas (Thomas and Thomas 1929: 572) has argued this point most convincingly when he proclaimed that 'if men (sic) define situations as real they are real in their consequences'. Which is not to say that the situations *are in fact* real—indeed they may be patently absurd and easily shown to be false—but if the actor believes them to be real, then he or she will act in accordance with that belief.

Misunderstandings of the world in which we live can thus be powerful explanations of the way in which we behave—as many star-crossed lovers have found out for themselves.

Sometimes the questions we are interested in may be *capable* of being answered scientifically, but for one reason or another it may not be practicable to ask them. This may be because the answers to those questions might be politically sensitive—one of us once wanted to do research on the impact of the Irish 'troubles', and in particular the imprisonment of Republican and Loyalist paramilitaries, on the nature and size of the high-security prison estate of England and Wales, but at the time no Home Secretary would countenance it. Such questions might now be asked of the Irish—but probably not in relation to Islamic terror suspects. Sometimes, the subjects of research will not be keen to have their activities exposed—organized criminals, corrupt politicians, and what Howard Becker (1963) called 'secret deviants' of one kind or another. Sometimes the questions in which we might be interested might be too traumatic for either researcher or respondents to handle—many students over the years have approached us wanting to research issues surrounding either serial killers or children convicted of murder but have had to be deflected into other areas of related interest for want of a plausible research design.

Sometimes the hypothesis to be tested may be derived deductively from a body of theory already well established in the literature. Sometimes the hypothesis may be developed inductively from the naive and somewhat inchoate ideas with which we initially approach the field, although having interrogated *both* ourselves *and* the literature we might have come up with a more nuanced hypothesis. Indeed in some cases we might develop a hierarchy of hypotheses, one derivable from the other, and each of which must be 'true' if the hypothesis from which it is derived is 'true'. In all cases our research questions remain the same: what do we need to know in order for us to be as sure as we can be that this hypothesis is, or is not, false. The search is on, or should be on, for a critical case or situation (within the plausible remit of one's research) in which the hypothesis is most likely to founder. If it passes that test it is likely to pass all lesser tests. Providing one stays focused on that, one will not go far wrong.

Not all research, however, will take the form of asking questions which relate to the testing of hypotheses. In many situations the state of current knowledge may not have advanced sufficiently even to formulate hypotheses, let alone to test them, and in these situations the researcher may be concerned with a mapping of the terrain and an exploration of possible themes and relationships between events which might become suggestive of hypotheses to be tested in the future. Such exploratory studies have played, and continue to play, an important part in the growth of knowledge on crime and justice, though it is important that researchers have a mind to linking their findings to the existing literature and where possible to help build a more integrated and cumulative picture of their chosen topic. It is important to stress that the first task of all scientists is *description:* to describe accurately both what they have seen and what they have done. It is perhaps extraordinary, but nevertheless true, that there have been studies which have purported to test the effectiveness of a particular intervention programme without ever providing a detailed description of what the programme entails but instead assuming that 'everyone knows' what, say, 'intensive supervision' means. In such circumstances, even if the programme was shown to be effective it could not easily be replicated for want of that basic description. George Mair (this volume) reports in a somewhat similar vein that he could not get on with a Home Office study of the effectiveness of probation day centres without first gathering the simplest information about how many such centres actually existed.

In our experience, the stage in the research process of moving from initial idea to research problem can appear to take a disproportionate amount of time and students can get bogged down as they write and rewrite their questions and hypotheses. However frustrating it becomes to produce multiple drafts, time spent at this stage will reap dividends later but only if the researcher remains attentive to the lessons learned. Once the data collection stage is underway it is all too easy to become distracted and lose sight of those lessons, resulting in an unfocused research study which fails to answer the initial research question.

At the risk of repeating ourselves the choice of research questions should look backwards to the literature and forwards to issues of research design. The researcher should be as certain as possible that each question is capable of being answered empirically, and that the answer will make a contribution, however small, to academic knowledge. This means ensuring that potential barriers—practical and ethical—can be overcome and that the degree of risk and danger can be minimized. We are aware that we have moved here towards a counsel of perfection which we know none of us will actually achieve.

Developing the most powerful research design

Arguably the most important stage in the research process is the choice of research design. It is here, essentially, that any piece of research stands or falls. Or to put it in military terms where the battle is won or lost. It is important to differentiate between research design and research methods—they are not the same, but all too often new researchers make a serious mistake by moving straight from deciding the research question to choosing between methods, usually presented as a choice between quantitative methods, which produce data capable of being manipulated statistically, and qualitative methods, which are designed to elicit the meaning of events to the people who experience them rather than the frequency with which those events occur. In our view decisions about what methods to deploy should only be taken after the greatest possible thought has gone into the research design.

To pursue our new military analogy, research design is akin to military strategy determined at headquarters, research methods are the military tactics to be used in the field. A good research design is produced by asking oneself what kinds of data would I need to collect in order to provide the maximum possible leverage in answering the research question, and from what sources should I collect it? Only once those decisions are made does one go on to consider the detailed methods through which the data will be collected. Within the research literature there are examples of many different research designs and methodology texts often provide typologies. Rather than perplex the novice researcher further by adding yet another typology, we instead provide a series of questions which might be posed before determining the appropriate research design. Once answered, the most appropriate research design should follow. The real *eureka* moment for most research is when one comes up with the right *design* rather than any particular *result*. If the design is right, the rest more or less follows, and at least one is bound to come up with some meaningful result. Get the design wrong and it does not much matter what happens next; the results will still not have much bearing on the research problem one set oneself.

Is the aim of the research to test a hypothesis or to develop theory?

We have already touched on these issues to be raised here in the preceding section but we need to explore them further. Theory is the means through which one can explain and understand phenomena scientifically. It enables one to place the findings of research within a conceptual framework which makes 'sense' of the data (May 2001). Many criminologists, including Tony Bottoms who nevertheless writes eloquently about the relationship between theory and data in **Chapter 3** of this volume, would hesitate to call themselves theorists, yet recognize that theory informs all that we do as we move through the different stages of the research process (Holdaway and Rock 1998). The term theory in this instance is not reserved solely for grand theories such as the dialectical materialism and its derivative conflict theories associated with Marx (1906), or social system theories of twentieth century American functionalists such as Talcott Parsons (1951), but applies also to what Robert Merton (1957) called middle-range theories which attempt to explain aspects of the social world such as crime or victimization as well as microlevel or 'grounded' theories (Glaser and Strauss 1967) which have been developed to try to understand the emerging data in the course of the research process itself.

For pedagogical purposes, we can make a distinction between research which is *deductivist*, i.e. which starts by accepting (or formulating) a theory, then proceeds from this general proposition to consideration of particular cases in order to test the theory, on the one hand, and research which is *inductivist*, i.e. which starts by drawing inferences from particular cases, then proceeds towards the development of general theoretical propositions, on the other. In practice the distinction outlined is too crude and projects may move from being inductivist to deductivist and back again as researchers struggle to make sense of the world they are exploring. In addition, we can question whether research can ever be truly inductivist because researchers never begin with a clean sheet: as we hope we have made clear, at the start of the research process is an idea and interrogating that idea provides one with at least an embryonic theory with which one starts to make sense of things. Despite these limitations this distinction encourages researchers to consider the role theory will play in their proposed research project and to select an appropriate research design. As we will now consider, experimental and quasi-experimental designs are best suited to deductivist research projects.

Is the research study aimed at finding causes or considering whether 'something' works?

Time was when criminologists were mainly concerned with discovering the causes of crime. One of us, many years ago, pursued an undergraduate dissertation that sought evidence from juvenile probation files that might substantiate or refute one or other of the 'causes' of delinquency discussed by Barbara Wootton (1959) in her book *Social Science and Social Pathology*. Unravelling causal relationships, in the sense of what causes crime or delinquency, is a matter rarely discussed in the literature these days. It is a subject too complex for us to discuss further here (but see the elegant clarification of the issues in **Chapter 4** of this volume by P-O Wikström and also Wikström and Sampson 2006). Nowadays criminologists more often concern themselves with whether a particular intervention is effective in reducing offending and sometimes they are required to do so by virtue of a given research contract. Interventions might include an offending behaviour programme, a new approach to policing, or a technological innovation for preventing crime. Effectiveness can be defined in multiple ways but typically refers to a reduction in the level or severity of crime committed by an individual and usually deploys reconviction rates as a proxy measure for reoffending (see Lloyd *et al.* 1994, for a detailed discussion of the problems associated with this approach) or crime rates in a specific area (see Maguire 2007) for a thorough overview of the limitations of official crime statistics and **Chapter 8** of this volume on the advantages and disadvantages of alternative sources of data). Alternative measures might include reductions in the level of drug use amongst individual offenders or fewer instances of antisocial behaviour in an area. (See also Friedrich Lösel's discussion of evaluative research in **Chapter 5** and Brambring and Lösel 1990)

Some researchers choose to conduct experiments, or quasi experiments, to allow them to draw inferences about the causes of crime or the impact of an intervention programme on offenders, and experimental approaches—which are the stock in trade for natural scientists—are understandably perceived to be the most powerful research design for uncovering such relationships. Indeed, in the criteria for inclusion in systematic reviews, to which we referred earlier, there is a controversial hierarchy of research designs—known as the Maryland Scale—in which the random allocation of subjects to experimental groups (who receive the treatment or intervention) and control groups (comparison groups who receive nothing), and which thereby mimic clinical trials in medicine, is regarded as the 'gold standard' for testing effectiveness and causal relationships. Experiments which involve randomized allocation of cases to experimental and control groups, raise important ethical problems and in practice are very difficult to conduct (see de Vaus 2006 and Tilley 2006 for a summary of the main difficulties). Researchers may therefore opt for a quasi-experimental approach which is not reliant upon random allocation but rather upon the matching of subjects in the experimental and control groups.

Rarely are criminological studies in the UK based on a purely experimental research design but such designs are sometimes deployed in other countries, particularly the United States. However, as discussed in **Chapter 2**, some Home Office researchers searching for definitive answers to the question 'What works?' have increasingly advocated the use of experimental designs reliant upon random allocation. Nevertheless, questions have been raised as to whether they should be regarded as the 'gold standard' which some researchers and funding agencies claim (Wilcox *et al.* 2005). And some writers have argued that ascertaining whether or not something works can be determined through the collection and analysis of more qualitative data (Greene 2005; Shaw 1999).

Our own view is that randomized trials and quasi-experimental studies have an important role to play in research on crime and justice, but there are vast tracts of the field for which they are not yet appropriate and others where they are simply not appropriate at all. It would be a pity if, in the official pursuit of 'tested' results, the many possibilities for other kinds of research were squeezed out for lack of government or Research Council funding.

Is it necessary to take a long-term view of the problem or is taking a 'snapshot' sufficient?

The vast majority of criminological research adopts a cross-sectional design, in which data are collected laterally, to capture the situation as it was at a specific point in time.

This is analogous to the way that a still camera records the scene that was in view at the moment the shutter closed. In reality, of course, cross-sectional research is not instant-aneous and may take several months to complete. But so long as changes in that time are small, or irrelevant to the research question, then for all practical purposes the analogy with a camera holds. There have, however, been a comparatively small, but nevertheless significant number of longitudinal studies, where criminologists have been concerned to plot changes with the passage of time—rather in the way that a cine-camera records mov-ing images. Once again longitudinal research does not quite measure up to the analogy with the movie camera, because instead of clips per second that produce an appearance of movement, the longitudinal researcher most frequently takes a series of snapshots with so-called follow-up studies of the same group of subjects at well-spaced intervals—extending over years or even decades—to reveal how things have changed or developed.

The best-known criminological example of longitudinal research is the *Cambridge Study of Delinquent Development* established by Donald West and continued by David Farrington. They studied 411 males born in South London in 1953 and 1954 and have repeatedly followed them up from the age of 8 into late middle age (http://www.scopic. ac.uk/studies.htm#Cambridge). A more recent example is the Edinburgh study of Youth Transitions and Crime (http://www.law.ed.ac.uk/cls/esytc/). This is a programme of research which aims to address a range of fundamental questions about the causes of criminal and risky behaviours in young people. The core of the programme is a major longitudinal study of a single cohort of around 4,000 young people who started second-ary school in Edinburgh in the autumn of 1998. These two studies have prioritized collecting quantitative data, although the Edinburgh study does have a qualitative component. Others have focused on gathering qualitative data exclusively and as a con-sequence have been smaller in scope. For example a longitudinal study conducted by researchers at University of Teeside provides an insight into young people's transition into adulthood, including their involvement (if any) in criminal activities and drug use (see Webster *et al.* 2004 for the latest report). Others still have obtained both qualitative and quantitative data; for example, the work by Howard Parker and his colleagues (Parker *et al.* 1998) on young people and drug taking. These latter two examples both used face-to-face interviews to collect data and appear not to have been designed originally as longitudinal studies but to have benefited from successful funding applica-tions that subsequently enabled them to answer questions which emerged from the original study.

The principal, and of course obvious, advantage of longitudinal studies is that, as gen-erally conceived, they can provide a long-term view. This makes them ideally suited to answer research questions about the range of factors which influence an individual's pathway into and out of crime and which could not be satisfactorily answered in other ways. These factors might include individual, family, and social matters but also the impact of participating in interventions designed to prevent crime and antisocial behaviour. The main disadvantages of these long-term follow-up studies are that they are highly resource-intensive—both in terms of time and money—and there can be major problems of attrition in the size of the original cohort as researchers gradually lose touch with participants. The latter problem can be particularly difficult for some crimino-logical studies because offenders and ex-prisoners are less likely to be living in stable accommodation (Social Exclusion Unit 2002 and see Lewis 2003 for an example of a study of ex-prisoners which failed to obtain data from a sufficiently high proportion of the sample).

It is worth mentioning, however, that longitudinal work does not have to be long-term. As Wikström has noted in this volume some developments in an offender's life may take only a short while to have an impact. The decision to commit a burglary may take only minutes in the making, or to plan an armed robbery a few weeks, the main impact of imprisonment on a first offender may take effect in the first few days, and the days immediately before and after release from custody may be extremely anxiety provoking. Designing independent research to capture these changes over brief periods may not be easy, although some of these topics may be well-suited to small-scale studies by practitioners. Joel Harvey, in **Chapter 18** of this volume was able to incorporate a short-term longitudinal study within his multimethod approach to his doctoral research in prisons.

It should also be noted that it is possible to obtain a view of changes over time by taking repeated snapshots at intervals using similar, but not the same, individuals as participants on multiple occasions. The most obvious criminological examples are the British Crime Survey and the International Crime Victim Survey (see the discussion by one of the founders, Pat Mayhew, in **Chapter 8**) but other government surveys also collect data of interest to criminologists (for example, the British Social Attitudes Survey and the General Household Survey). These surveys are generally on such a large scale that the costs can only be undertaken by government departments, but in principle there is no reason why the design should not be adapted for use on much smaller projects. Access to data from some of these surveys can be obtained via the UK data archive (http://www.data-archive.ac.uk/) which allows students and other researchers without generous budgets to pose and answer research questions which require a long-term view provided they possess the necessary skills to analyse large-scale sophisticated datasets.

Finally, it is possible to collect data that approximates to longitudinal data, but much more cheaply, by simultaneous cross-sectional surveys with different, but perhaps to some degree matched, samples of, say, prisoners at the beginning, middle, and end of their sentences.

Does researching the selected problem require an emphasis on breadth or depth of understanding?

Research designs vary in the extent to which they prioritize breadth over depth and *vice versa*, and a useful approach is to place them on a continuum. At one end is the single case study which aims to establish an 'intensive examination' (Bryman 2004: 49) of a single case, which might be of an individual, event, social activity, group, organization, or institution (Keddie 2006). Cases might be selected because they are thought to be typical or atypical or, indeed for other reasons to which we will return shortly. Criminological examples of single-case studies are numerous and range from classic studies of individual criminals or institutions by researchers belonging to the Chicago School in the 1930s (see Deegan 2001, for an overview) through to more recent studies of criminal justice institutions (for example, studies of individual prisons by Morris *et al.* 1963, or by King and Elliott 1978, or Rock's (1993) case study of an English Crown Court). At the other end of the continuum lies the large-scale social survey involving the collection of data from nationally representative samples (see Pat Mayhew's account in **Chapter 8** for details of criminological examples including the British Crime Survey).

The choice between these two types of research design depends upon the nature of the research problem you have set yourself. Criticisms of both approaches are legion but in a sense are beside the point: each has advantages or disadvantages; or rather, they each play a different part in the wider research process. Case studies in some sense narrow the focus, by concentrating on a small number of examples, often only one, of the phenomena under study. But in another sense they provide a greater 'depth of field' revealing in some detail many aspects of the phenomena at the same time as well as the context in which they are found. Case studies allow the researcher 'to deal with the subtleties and intricacies of complex social situations'; in particular, 'to grapple with relationships and social processes' (Denscombe 2003: 38). In so doing they enable the researcher to gain an understanding of what makes people tick, how an organization works, and how one event may lead to another. Surveys, on the other hand, broaden the focus, to include all the possible cases available (as in a census) or, more usually, sufficiently large randomly selected samples of cases to represent the total population about whom one is interested. Providing certain rules are followed, and which are set out in methodology textbooks, it is possible to make generalizations about the total population based on the survey findings, with measurable degrees of confidence as to the margins of error. But at the same time that the focus is broadened, so depth of field and especially context is lost: surveys typically provide data on particular selected attributes or variables which have been abstracted from the wider whole.

Case studies are in some ways attractive for research students, because they require fewer resources, and for practitioners, because they may have privileged, but essentially local access. In fact they are far more difficult to bring off successfully by novitiate researchers. For one of us, the first exposure to professional research involved a case study of a hospital for handicapped children in Surrey. Dropped into an environment he scarcely understood, he asked naive questions of consultants, nurses, and patients, observed what went on in a persistent but unfocused fashion, read voraciously all the available documentary sources, and spent much time on Epsom Downs reflecting on what it all meant with embarrassingly little result. Of course, he learned a great deal from that experience and the next case study was much more successful, but the reality is that case studies by their very nature are best done by more sophisticated researchers capable of making connections both between the many events they see and with the literatures on related matters. Above all, case studies require mature judgements about the meaning of the events one observes and a capacity to think about them in theoretically meaningful ways. Ironically, surveys, though sometimes more expensive, are relatively straightforward to undertake, in that they start from taking existing theoretical propositions for granted. There are, unfortunately, as many surveys that have been conducted which have taken a scatter gun approach in ignorance of accepted or emerging theory as there are case studies where the researcher failed to make good sense of their data—but we had best draw a veil over those, whilst nevertheless drawing attention to the dangers.

Critics of the case study approach often argue that it is not credible because it is not possible to generalize from the findings gathered in this way. But this is to miss the point, and in any event is not always true. There is a sense in which case studies and surveys stand at opposite ends of a *temporal* spectrum. There are many situations where we simply do not know enough about the field to decide which are the crucial attributes or variables whose relationships we want to examine in a survey. In a situation where we know little, exploratory case studies offer the only sensible way forward. The case study researcher will typically adopt a 'grounded theory' approach formulating potential hypotheses which, for the time being at least, make the most sense of the emerging data. At the end of the case study there may be a number of plausible hypotheses which seem to have some kind of explanatory power and which *then, and only then*, might be worth testing in a large-scale survey. As Keddie, (2006: 21) has argued, generalization 'involves the statement of a theoretical position, which in turn will be tested through the use of further case studies and other methods'. Surveys come into their own when testing theoretical propositions derived from the emerging literature—and many of those propositions will have emerged as a result of case studies.

We have said above that it is not true to say that it is not possible to generalize from case studies. We defend that position by reasserting our insistence that all research has to be theoretically informed. On the basis of existing theory it is perfectly possible to select a *critical* case which would provide the Popperian test of falsifiability for any particular hypothesis. One asks oneself what would be the circumstances in which a theoretical proposition could be unambiguously falsified, and then chooses a case in which those circumstances are most likely to be fulfilled. If the case does indeed falsify the theory, then it has at least to be revised. But if, in this worst-case scenario, the case study does not refute the theory, then this may be extremely powerful evidence for its provisional verification. Since, in the Popperian world at least, science progresses through the falsification of propositions, *critical case studies* can be a great, and extremely parsimonious, contributor to the general state of our knowledge.

We have identified the extreme ends of the continuum, but there are many intermediary places upon it. Somewhere in the centre are research designs which utilize both case-study and survey strategies, and towards one end are designs that adopt carefully selected comparative case studies (see Frances Heidensohn's discussion of international and comparative criminology, for example, in **Chapter** 7 of this volume) and towards the other may be a variety of local surveys or surveys focused upon very limited and particular objectives (see Mayhew, this volume).

Space precludes a more detailed discussion of case studies and surveys and interested readers are directed to the classic texts in the field: Yin (1984) on case studies and Marsh (1982) on surveys. And while there is tendency to identify surveys with questionnaires and interviews which pose questions with precoded answers that can be subjected to quantitative analysis, and case studies with qualitative methods involving observation, less structured interviews, and documentary sources, in fact both approaches can, and sometimes do, deploy mixed methods—of which more below.

How involved will users be in the research process?

The involvement of users in research is increasingly encouraged. In fact, many funding bodies require their grant holders to outline ways in which user involvement can be encouraged at different stages of the research process from design through to dissemination. For example, the Economic and Social Research Council encourages applicants to identify potential users outside of the academic community, consult them when preparing the research bid, and arrange for their continuing involvement in the research process in an appropriate way. Similarly, the Joseph Rowntree Foundation insists that all projects have advisory groups made up of academics and users, providing separate funding for this purpose. User involvement is perceived as a means of ensuring that all forms of research, whether theoretical or empirical, are policy relevant although, as we will explore later in this chapter, the relationship between research and policy is far from simple. Depending upon the extent to which users are to be involved, the research strategy may have to take account of this.

Whilst user involvement tends to be confined to the inclusion of users in steering groups and/or ensuring that research findings are disseminated to the key user groups, sometimes the extent of involvement can be far greater. Users may be involved at the data collection stage; often through deploying users as interviewers. This is based upon the premise that using interviewers who can forge a special relationship with the research participant can generate the best data, and it can be particularly appropriate for so-called 'hard-to-reach' groups. There are few examples of criminological research which have taken full advantage of this approach. A rare exception is Fountain and Howe's (2002) study of the nature and extent of substance use among homeless people which used experienced outreach workers rather than social researchers to conduct interviews with homeless people. Researchers interested in this approach would do well to draw lessons from research on children and disabled people (see the Joseph Rowntree Foundation website—www.jrf.org.uk—for recent examples).

It should be evident from the discussion above that the research design which emerges will be shaped not only by intellectual considerations but also practical ones. Availability of resources, financial and human, and the time available to produce the 'results' are key determinants. When designing research studies a useful starting point is to outline the best research design possible and then to reflect upon what *actually* can be done. Conducting research is a dynamic process and further refinements may need to be made once the research is underway if it becomes evident that the selected approach can no longer be pursued. It is necessary to remember that all research designs are ultimately a compromise between what one would like to do and what is possible within the inevitable constraints. Of course, there have to be limits because the data gathered must be capable of answering the research question posed, and ultimately this may mean going back to the original research idea and asking a different question or indeed starting with a fresh idea.

Choosing the most appropriate methods

A brief examination of the academic literature on research methods reveals even greater confusion than that relating to research design. First, sometimes references are made to criminological research methods. Let us be clear: no such methods exist. As we made explicit at the beginning of this chapter, the social science research process is similar, regardless of the topic under consideration. Criminologists, therefore, have to choose from the same menu of research methods as sociologists, psychologists, and other social scientists. The main research methods available to social scientists are questionnaires, interviews, observation, and documentary analysis. Second, there is a tendency to distinguish between qualitative and quantitative methods but, as we have argued, this is misleading because all the methods listed above can be used to obtain quantitative and/or qualitative data or indeed both, depending upon how the method is utilized. For instance, we can ask open questions in interviews to collect complex answers that require sensitive qualitative analysis and sometimes interpretation, to reveal intended meanings, or we can ask closed questions in which the interviewer checks one of a number of pre-determined possible answers, the frequencies of responses then being subjected to statistical analysis. We do not attempt here to explore in full each method. There are multiple examples of good texts aimed at novice researchers, which provide an introduction to each method and we direct readers below to our own favourites. Instead, we will briefly describe each method and identify the key factors which are crucial to obtaining good data from its use. Space precludes a detailed exploration of the relative advantages and disadvantages of each method. Every way of seeing is also a way of not seeing and it pays to be aware of the nature of the lens through which you are trying to capture the real world. Reading widely about the chosen method and thinking through why using other methods would be less preferable is absolutely essential.

Questionnaires

Questionnaires describe a written list of questions which have been carefully designed to collect information about a particular topic and are sent to participants by post or, increasingly, electronically, but which may occasionally, usually when they are used in case studies, be handed out directly to participants by the researcher. Participants are required to complete and return the questionnaire themselves, although it is sometimes possible for the researcher to collect them from a central point after they have been completed. Sometimes, and incorrectly in our view, the term questionnaire is also used to refer to what are more properly regarded as interview schedules. Questions tend to be closed, thus facilitating statistical analysis of the answers. Potentially they offer an economical and effective way of collecting large amounts of data but their ability to do this hinges upon good questionnaire design (see Oppenheim 2000, for guidance) which should always be developed after extensive pilot work, to encourage a high response rate to questions that are known to be meaningful and capable of producing responses which can be analysed easily.

Interviews

Interviews are a favoured method of criminologists but there are several different styles of interview. At one extreme there can be highly structured interviews where interviewers rigidly adhere to a schedule as they invite participants to answer questions for which the interviewer has a number of predetermined responses which can be ticked off. In effect this is the same as a self-completion questionnaire—except that the interviewer has the opportunity to explain things that may not be clear and also to record information that may speak to the perceived seriousness with which the respondent answered the questions. At the other extreme unstructured interviews may simply give the respondent free reign to develop a conversation on a number of particular topics in whatever way s/he chooses and regardless of the prior judgements of the researcher. This may seem deceptively simple but can involve considerable skills (see Parker and Morris 1999, for guidance). The resulting materials from such interviews are much harder to analyse and require the subsequent sorting of themes, and categorizing the modalities of response to those themes by the researcher. Since an accurate record of exactly what was said and how it was said, including the pauses, may be essential to understanding the meaning of the exchange it is usual to use a recording device, which these days, fortunately, are a good deal less obtrusive than once they were. Even so, it is necessary sometimes to turn off the machine, and to remember what the respondent says 'off the record' which may qualify things in important ways. Between the totally structured and the completely unstructured interviews there are various hybrids—either semistructured in which the interviewer retains a degree of control over the topics discussed, the time devoted to them, and is free to offer prompts, or interviews which involve various combinations of techniques.

Interviews are normally conducted on an individual basis in face-to-face situations, but can also be conducted by telephone, and with or without the aid of computers. Interviews can also be conducted with small groups[4] of respondents though these are more difficult to control. We have used most types of interviewing technique in a variety of settings. Once again there is no one best way, but rather, it is a matter of horses for courses. In the initial stages of a research project, in an area relatively under-researched, more open-ended techniques are likely to help map the terrain and throw up ideas for theorization. In the latter stages, or where one wants to test hypotheses on the basis of evolving or established theories, one is more likely to close things off in a more structured manner. Interviewers may be hired for the purpose, in which case they will need to be trained, or may be integral or sole members of the research team. Regardless of the form the interview takes, the keys to successful interviewing are the ability to establish rapport with the research participant and to listen carefully to the responses.

Observation

Observation involves witnessing events at first hand in order to capture what actually happens. Researchers vary in the extent to which they choose to participate in the social setting they seek to observe, ranging from complete participant through to complete observer with varying roles in between (Gold 1958; Junker 1960). In fact, this is not quite such a self-conscious choice as it might sound because any researcher involved in an observational role has to 'participate' in the situation to some degree if only to explain why s/he is there, but in practice will always be drawn into discussions. Whether consciously participating or striving not to participate, the presence of an observer will always change the situation to some degree and it is always necessary to use other methods to try to assess how far that presence might have made a difference.[5]

Early observational studies were conducted covertly, where for example a researcher entered say a mental hospital as a 'patient' with the research identity known only to the medical superintendent (Caudill 1958). Such studies are not recommended for two reasons. First, there are ethical objections relating to the impossibility of gaining informed consent from participants if they are unaware that there is a research project going on. Second, what can be observed is necessarily constrained by the normal limits of whatever

---

[4] Group interviews are not synonymous with focus groups. Focus groups require a critical mass of participants, usually between six and eight and the researcher occupies the role as moderator. See **Chapter 16** by Matthew Williams for an interesting example of doctoral research incorporating the use of focus groups—in this instance online.

[5] Our experience is that however obtrusive the presence of the observer, the longer s/he is there the more that presence is taken for granted and the more 'normal' becomes the behaviour of those observed. It is not easy for researchers to sustain a role over time. It is far harder for respondents to 'play' a role for the benefit of the observer, and sooner or later the daily exigencies of work and the normal routine take over. To an astonishing degree observers come to be seen as 'one of us' rather than a threatening presence.

covert role is adopted. Nevertheless, there may be some situations where covert observation might be the only way of getting data. Mike Maguire discusses some studies where such covert methods were used in **Chapter 9** of this volume as do Reiner and Newburn in their discussion of 'inside insiders' in **Chapter 12**. Even when the observer is not acting covertly participation can be taken too far to the point where the essential scientific purpose of the observation is lost. In the first edition of this book one of us described the situation where a research student was openly introduced as a participant observer and undertook the initial training for prison officers, but who 'went native' to such a degree that he became more prison officer than researcher (see King 2000)

At the opposite end of the spectrum from the covert participant observer is the observer who comes in as a complete outsider focusing on some particular aspect of activity to be observed and measured. The archetypal situation is that of the 'time and motion' study designed to fix the rate of return for some industrial process which is to be carried out in an ergonomically preferred fashion. Most social scientists embarking on observational studies will have experienced jibes about 'where is your stop watch?' or 'writing it all down in your little black book are you?' One of us, once, in a follow-up to that study of the hospital for handicapped children already referred to, did observe staff at two-minute intervals recording (with surprisingly successful results) how many times they spoke to the children in their care (King and Raynes 1967).

As with interviews, choice of observational style will depend on how much is known about the situation in advance. The less one knows in advance, the more open- ended the observational style, with the observer hanging around for as long, and as unobtrusively, as possible. The more reason one has, theoretically to watch out for some particular behaviour, the more tightly focused become the observations. With focused observations the observer may well have a recording schedule to note each occasion a behaviour is observed. With more open-ended observations the observer will write up as detailed notes as possible, immediately after the observation period has ended.

Documents

Documents come in many forms including the written word, visual images, and statistical data. What they have in common is that they pre-exist as part of the setting one is studying and they frequently provide the legal, organizational, or cultural context for the phenomena under review, or some institutionalized monitoring or audit of those phenomena. Depending upon the form in which the document appears and the analytic approach selected, they can provide researchers with qualitative and quantitative data. Technological developments have added to the amount and number of forms that documents take (Wharton 2006). As Morgan and Hough in **Chapter 2** of this volume have noted 'the great fortune of the British criminologist is that he or she inhabits a domain in which there is more than enough data available for secondary analysis' (p. 70). Readily accessible documents for criminologists include annual statistics and reports produced by criminal justice agencies, statutory instruments, and White Papers, parliamentary debates, and newspaper reports. Furthermore, access may be negotiated to others such as files belonging to criminal justice agencies and court transcripts. In addition to using documents gathered for other purposes, researchers can request that documents are created specifically for their own research; for example, by asking criminal justice professionals to keep diaries. There is a consensus in the literature on documentary research that its value as a research method hinges upon evaluating carefully the sources to be used rather than simply accepting them at face value (see Scott 1990 for a more detailed discussion).

Researchers do not have a free choice of methods. The methods chosen derive from the research design which in turn was determined in relation to the research question. The choice of methods also has to look backwards to one's theoretical perspective within which the research question has been framed and be consistent with that. For example, a research question that has been framed within a perspective that focuses upon a process of interaction is unlikely to be answered by research methods that fail to observe that process in action. Some theorists, who take a rather purist approach, might insist that certain methods are actually incompatible with a particular theoretical perspective and so should not be contemplated on epistemological grounds. Others, amongst whom we number ourselves, are prepared to be more pragmatic. Whilst we would utterly resist a totally eclectic approach that tackles a problem by leaving no stone unturned, we take the view that the development of methods within any particular theoretical perspective has not reached the stage where one can afford to be exclusive. And for reasons we address shortly—that triangulation of method enhances our confidence in validity—we are, within theoretically reasonable limits, perfectly prepared to adopt a multiplicity of methods and to see advantages in that.

The expertise of the researcher is also a key consideration when weighing up the advantages and disadvantages of different methods. One's choice of method has to look forward to considerations of analysis. There is no point whatsoever in using methods which run beyond one's powers of analysis. If you do not know how you are going to analyse the data, it is probably not worth collecting them. Moreover, the ethical stance of the researcher can be influential. Individual researchers may judge particular approaches to collecting data as unethical. An obvious example here is conducting covert participant observation, which most ethical codes explicitly discourage. Finally, the availability of resources plays an important role in influencing the choice of method or methods. Some methods, for example, participant observation, will be costly in terms of time whilst others, for example postal questionnaires, may require considerable financial investment in order to generate a sufficient sample for quantitative data analysis.

Increasingly, researchers may select a range of different methods, known as method or technique triangulation (see Noaks and Wincup 2004, for a more detailed discussion). For example, one possible design might start from some preliminary observations in the field, then proceed through interviews in which the researcher gains a better understanding of what she or he has seen from the point of view of the subject, and in a final stage asks well-targeted questions in a questionnaire used with a much larger sample—this time to test an emerging hypothesis. Whilst a multimethod approach can be beneficial (see **Chapter 18** for Joel Harvey's account of the advantages of using multiple methods to study one criminological issue; namely, self-harm amongst prisoners), there are dangers in assuming that this is always the best approach to adopt as one of us has argued elsewhere:

We would like to advocate that researchers adopt a pragmatic and theoretically coherent approach to data collection, using appropriate methods to answer their research questions. The latter is important because researchers need to guard against the tendency to keep adding research techniques to their research design in an eclectic manner with the blind hope that it will produce a better thesis, report or other publication. A multi-method approach should only be pursued if it adds value to the study by enhancing understanding of the criminological issue of interest ... combining methods does not automatically enhance validity (Noaks and Wincup 2004: 10).

Ruthlessly analysing the data

It is not our intention here to explore in detail how to analyse data. Once more there are detailed texts which serve this purpose: for qualitative data, Coffey and Atkinson (1996) is highly recommended and for quantitative data, Bryman and Cramer (2004). Instead we are trying to pass on 'a feeling' for the process. It cannot be stressed too much that research is an art (or at least a craft) as well as a science and a great deal depends upon the professional judgement and experience of the craftsperson. Many experienced researchers, at least if they are honest, will be able to recall the feeling of sitting at their desk (or on the floor!) surrounded by interview transcripts, field notes, or questionnaires and not knowing quite how to proceed. Whilst the move from data collection to data analysis can be daunting, especially for those attempting it for the first time, we outline some basic rules below which should ensure that it does not become overwhelming.

Rule No 1. Never ask questions you do not know how to analyse.

Rule No 2. Pilot your research instruments so that you can test not only their reliability and validity but also the analysis that can be carried out on the data.

If these rules are followed, then the movement from data collection to analysis should be a smooth transition. If they are not, then problems at the data collection stage will be compounded when it comes to the analysis.

Rule No 3. Keep the analysis simple. There is nothing to be said for pursuing an over-elaborate analysis from the outset. As a rule of thumb, the more complex the analysis, the more the original data gets distorted for the purpose, and the less meaning it may have either to the researcher or to anyone else.

Rule No 4. Pursue the analysis ruthlessly, step by step. This is not incompatible with the preceding rule, providing the analysis is pursued stage by stage. If the first analysis poses further questions, then pursue those questions ruthlessly so far as your data will allow—but no further.

Data analysis takes time. Despite the availability of a wide range of data analysis packages (for example, SPSS for quantitative data and NUD.IST and Atlas/ti for qualitative data) to assist researchers with this task—and we must emphasize assist rather than conduct—findings do not emerge readily from the data. The first stage, and this can be the most time-consuming one, is to get a feel for the data. For quantitative data this means ensuring that the data are 'clean'; in other words, input errors have been corrected and the data make sense. Running frequencies for each variable in the database can help to identify anomalies. Good researchers should have an eye for detail and be prepared to apply common sense. For qualitative data the initial task is to read (and read again) interview transcripts, field notes, and other forms of data and to be alert to emerging themes. One important point to consider is the distance between the researcher and the data. As a rule of thumb the closer the researcher is to the data, the more s/he is likely to develop 'a feel' for it and what it means. Large-scale studies, where the data are often collected by 'hired hands', entail particular problems. In part these can be alleviated through reaching a consensus as to how to record data and putting procedures in place to share data but the best advice we can offer is to encourage active discussion about the data throughout the research project.

When we introduced the different stages in the research process we noted that although they are analytically separable, they are logically interconnected and at least some of them may, in practice, proceed side by side. Data analysis is often relegated to the end of a research project but as we have argued here, it can and should begin much earlier in the research process.

There are two general questions to which all researchers must pay attention in the analysis of data—questions about the *reliability* and the *validity* of the data—if they wish to convince their audiences about the value of their findings. The questions are not synonymous but they are related. *Reliability* broadly refers to the degree to which a research instrument—or indeed a whole segment of research conducted through one of the methods discussed above—produces the same results, for all practical purposes, when conducted in the same way by two or more researchers or on two or more occasions. It is essentially about consistency. In practice there can be real problems about interpreting whether or not measures are reliable, especially when checking the use of measures on two separate occasions—so-called test–retest reliability. This is because different results might reflect real changes over time rather than the unreliability of the instrument. *Validity* of a research construct or a research finding refers to the extent that the construct actually measures or reflects the phenomenon we have conceptualized, or the finding accurately represents what is, in some sense, 'really there'. It is essentially about, for want of a better word, the truthfulness of the results.

Data may be obtained reliably but need not necessarily be valid. Valid data, on the other hand are normally capable of being shown to be reliable. One of us now regularly commutes between North Wales and Cambridge and the difference between reliability and validity can perhaps be demonstrated by reference to two sets of bathroom scales, one in each residence. The scales in North Wales always weighs the author at 160 pounds but the scales in Cambridge always weighs him at 165 pounds. Both scales seem to be reliable—in the sense that they repeatedly measure the same subject at the same weight. But they cannot plausibly both be valid—at least one of them, and quite possibly both, will be giving the wrong weight. We would test the validity of the two scales by triangulation of method—that is, by looking for other sources of data that would give us more confidence that one or another scale is correct. In this instance the check is much simpler than it would be in a real criminological research situation since the Department of Weights and Measures has standard weights we could use to check the two scales for accuracy. But the importance of looking back to theory can also be demonstrated by this example. Since the scales are in two separate locations some distance apart, it might be 'theorized' that the subject gained or lost weight during the intervals between weighings. But if, obsessively, the subject weighed himself immediately before leaving one address and on arrival at the other, one might have to abandon that theory in favour of one that somehow a metabolic change takes place on the five-hour journey between locations. If either of these theories were 'true', then our earlier assumptions about reliability and validity might change. Both scales might be unreliable, repeatedly giving the same weights despite weight gains or losses by the subject: or both scales might be both reliable and valid, accurately picking up the weight changes of the subject between the two locations. To get a clearer idea about which was the right interpretation, and to convince our readers of it (assuming for the moment that there were no standard weights to resolve the matter), we would triangulate by using other data. Had the subject's eating habits changed, or had calories been burned through exercise which might account for the different measures? Was there other evidence of weight gain or loss—dropping a jean size, or tightening or loosening of the belt? For some types of research, especially those reliant on quantitative scaling devices, there are standard procedures to be used for expressing confidence in reliability. Ultimately, however, questions about the reliability or validity of measures, or whether genuine change has taken place, are down to the judgment of the researcher, and eventually the reader, and will depend upon the power of the findings to explain the issues which the research set out to address.

Publicly presenting the results

There is not much point in doing research unless it makes a difference: we believe strongly that research should not be undertaken just for its own sake. As one of us argues (King and Liebling in **Chapter 15** of this volume), researchers should aim to make a modest impact on society. It would, however, be naive of us to assume that research inevitably informs criminal justice policy in a direct and immediate fashion and indeed, as we noted in our introduction, the years since the first edition of this book was published have given few grounds for optimism that politicians pay much heed to research, despite the stated preference for evidence-based policy. The extensive literature on the relationship between research and policy identifies a range of more complex relationships (see Young *et al.* 2002 for a recent review), and the experience of the Crime Reduction Programme (see Morgan and Hough, as well as Mair, this volume and the Special Issue of *Criminal Justice* published in 2004) reminds us that even research commissioned to evaluate new criminal justice initiatives may fail to have the desired impact. Whilst it is easy to be pessimistic about the potential of criminological research to influence policy, it is important to remember that one study alone is unlikely to have a major impact. Rather, a coherent and cumulative body of knowledge on a criminological issue is likely to be far more influential. As a result, researchers have a responsibility to make their findings widely available and will often be required to do so.

Doctoral students will be expected to present their results in the form of a thesis and most universities lodge these in their libraries unless the subject matter is sufficiently sensitive to render this impossible. Researchers who have received funding to enable them to conduct research will be required to produce a report, which the funders may decide to make available. Prior to the production of a thesis or report, initial ideas might be tried out in the form of a conference paper. These papers may be developed into further academic publications including book chapters, journal articles, and research monographs.

For criminological research to achieve its potential to challenge the wilful misrepresentations about criminal justice policy which appear in the tabloid press, and to keep politicians honest when they participate in the ensuing debates, academic research needs to be disseminated in the widest possible way so that key audiences get to know about it. Those involved in criminal justice as policy-makers or practitioners may not read publications intended predominantly for academics. Researchers who seek to make a difference need therefore to explore alternative ways of conveying their research findings. At its simplest this may mean including executive summaries of lengthy reports, publishing short briefing documents (known as *Findings* by the Home Office) alongside reports, although George Mair's strictures in **Chapter 14** about the effectiveness of these vehicles for communicating complex results should be heeded. There is everything to be said for researchers to write articles for specialist audiences in practitioner journals and magazines such as *Police Review, Prison Service Journal,* or *The Magistrate* as well as speaking at professional conferences, and there is considerable scope for researchers to be more imaginative when disseminating their findings.

Arguably, given the level of public ignorance and the ways in which politicians of all stripes submit to the 'law and order' agendas of tabloid press proprietors, the popular audience may be much more important than the academic one, though much more difficult to access. Many of us, over the years, have cultivated journalists in the print and broadcast media, only to find that even the responsible end of the spectrum sacrifice 'truth' for 'a good story' and in any case they impact on only a small section of the reading, watching and listening public. Many academics are reluctant to engage, fearing that their findings are likely to be distorted, but the time is coming for some stars of the criminological community with media savvy to strut their stuff on the wider stage.

As we have made explicit above, researchers need to become skilled at writing for a range of different audiences. Here, as elsewhere, it is a matter of horses for courses and a rather different approach is required for different audiences. We provide some general guidance below, based on our experience as authors, editors of books and journals, and supervisors of students.

1. Writing is not as straightforward as it first appears: novice researchers should seek as much help as possible by consulting the available literature (Richardson 1990; Woods 2005), consulting experienced researchers and others who may be able to help (for example, university press offices), and reading good examples of the type of publication they wish to produce.

2. Writing is a time-consuming process and you should adopt an approach to writing which works best for you. Some authors feel that they can only write if they have substantial chunks of time to work on a draft. Others, and perhaps these are the most productive, seize whatever opportunity they can to write. A further point of variation is that some authors will spend a great deal of time carefully writing each sentence so that it requires only 'polishing' once completed while others will write quickly and produce multiple drafts until they have achieved a satisfactory final version.

3. Familiarize yourself with any conventions you are expected to adhere to. Often these are made explicit; for example, journal editors prepare notes for contributors

which can usually be found in the inside of the back cover and/or on journal web sites. Sometimes, and especially for non-academic publications, would-be authors need to work out what the conventions are by looking at material which has already been published.

4. It is important to make what you write interesting, and so it pays to spend time thinking about how you are going to tell your story to best effect. To go back to what we said at the very beginning of this chapter it is often a good idea to think about what, in principle, your finished product will look like from the outset of the research process and consider the research process in reverse order: if those were to be the results, this is the kind of analysis I would have to have done, those are the data I would need to have collected, which could only have been achieved through this research design.

5. Write clearly in an appropriate way for your intended audience. It is not necessary to 'dumb down' to reach a lay audience but technical concepts should be explained.

We have focused in this section on writing because as others have argued (Blaxter *et al.* 2006) it remains the primary means by which researchers communicate with each other and with interested parties about their work. New technology has made the written word available more quickly, to a wider audience and in different formats.

Concluding comments

We began this chapter by emphasizing that the research process is in broad terms the same for all social researchers, regardless of their particular focus. As such, criminologists embarking on their research careers can make good use of the ever-growing number of relevant texts and we offer recommendations in the following section. Whilst neophyte criminological researchers may share many experiences with their peers working within other social science disciplines, they will also face challenges which stem from their subject matter: negotiating the politics of law and order; being party to knowledge about illegal acts and exposure to personal risk are some of the more obvious examples. Later chapters in this book provide the opportunity to learn from the experiences of others as they lay bare their, sometimes painful, experiences of conducting criminological research. However, there is no better way to learn about criminological research than to conduct it oneself and so we must end with encouraging our readers to rise to the challenge of designing and carrying out their own study.

Suggestions for further reading

There is an abundance of texts which provide a more detailed discussion of the research process than our allocated space in this edited collection has allowed. Those listed below are particularly recommended for novice researchers, especially postgraduate students completing dissertations and theses for masters and doctoral degrees respectively.

Blaxter, L., Hughes, C., and Tight, M. (2006) *How to Research* (3rd edn), Buckingham: Open University Press. Focusing on the practice and experience of doing social science research, this introductory text provides useful guidance for less experienced researchers involved in small-scale research projects. Bell, J. (2005) *Doing Your Research Project* (4th edn), Buckingham: Open University Press. This text describes itself as something of a 'bible' for first-time researchers in social science. It assumes no prior knowledge of research methodology or experience of carrying out research.

There are numerous texts which provide an overview of the range of research designs and methods. Two which appear most frequently on reading lists are May, T. (2001) *Social Research: Issues, Methods and Processes* (3rd edn), Buckingham: Open University Press, and Bryman, A. (2004) *Social Research Methods* (2nd edn), Oxford: Oxford University Press. Becker, S. and Bryman, A. (eds) (2004) *Understanding Research for Social Policy and Practice*, Bristol: The Policy Press. Comprehensive in scope, and written by experts in a thoroughly accessible and engaging style, the book combines theoretical and applied discussions to provide the essential one-stop guide to research for social policy and practice. Robson, C. (2002) *Real World Research* (2nd edn), Oxford: Blackwell, is comprehensive and is intended to be a resource for both social scientists and practitioner researchers.

Learning from the experiences of others is one of the most effective ways to find out more about the research process. Subsequent chapters of this book provide an insight into the realities of conducting criminological research. Further honest accounts of the research process can be found in the first edition of *Doing Research on Crime and Justice* published by Oxford University Press in 2000; in particular, it includes nine chapters detailing the first forays of researchers into topics as diverse as organized and corporate crime, domestic violence, prostitution, and women's imprisonment. Similar discussions can be found in Hobbs, D. and May, T. (1993) *Interpreting the Field: Accounts of Ethnography*, Oxford: Oxford University Press; Jupp. V., Davies, P., and Francis, P. (2000) *Doing Criminological Research*, London: Sage.

References

BECKER, H. S. (1963). *Outsiders*. New York: Free Press.

BLAXTER, L., HUGHES, C., and TIGHT, M. (2006). *How to Research* (3rd edn). Buckingham: Open University Press.

BRAMBRING, M. and LÖSEL, F. (eds) (1990). *Children at Risk: Assessment, Longitudinal Research and Intervention*. Berlin: Walter de Gruyter.

BRYMAN, A. (2004). *Social Research Methods* (2nd edn). Oxford: Oxford University Press.

—— and CRAMER, D. (2004). *Quantitative Data Analysis with SPSS 12 and 13*. London: Routledge.

CAUDILL, W. (1958). *The Psychiatric Hospital as a Small Society*. Cambridge, Mass: Harvard University Press.

CHELIOTIS, L. (under review). 'Reconsidering the Effectiveness of Temporary Release: a Systematic Review'.

COFFEY, A. and ATKINSON, P. (1996). *Making Sense of Qualitative Data*. London: Sage.

Criminal Justice (2004). Vol. 4, No. 3, Special Issue on the Crime Reduction Programme.

DE VAUS, D. (2006). 'Experiment' in V. Jupp (ed.), *The Sage Dictionary of Social Research Methods*. London: Sage.

DEEGAN, M. (2001). 'The Chicago School of Ethnography' in P. Atkinson, A. Coffey, S. Delamont, J. Lofland, and L. Lofland (eds), *Handbook of Ethnography*. London: Sage.

DENSCOMBE, M. (2003). *The Good Research Guide* (2nd edn). Buckingham: Open University Press.

FARRINGTON, D. and WELSH, B. (2002). *Effects of Improved Street Lighting on Crime: A Systematic Review*. Home Office Research Study 251, London: Home Office.

—— (2005). *What Works in Preventing Crime: Systematic Reviews of Experimental and Quasi-experimental Research*. London: Sage.

FERRELL, J. and HAMM, M. (1998). *Ethnography at the Edge: Crime, Deviance and Field Research*. Boston, MA: Northeastern University Press.

FOUNTAIN, J. and HOWES, S. (2002). *Home and Dry? Homelessness and Substance Use in London*. London: Crisis.

GLASER, B. and STRAUSS, A. (1967). *The Discovery of Grounded Theory*. Chicago: Aldine.

GOLD, R. (1958). 'Roles in sociological field observations', *Social Forces* 36(3): 217–23.

GREENE, J. (2005). 'Understanding Social Programs through Evaluation' in N. Denzin and Y. Lincoln (eds), *The SAGE Handbook of Qualitative Research* (3rd edn). Newbury Park, Ca.: Sage.

HART, C. (1998). *Doing a Literature Review: Releasing the Social Science Imagination*. London: Sage.

HOBBS, D. (2000). 'Researching Serious Crime' in R. King and E. Wincup (eds), *Doing Research on Crime and Justice*. Oxford: Oxford University Press.

HOLDAWAY, S. (1983). *Inside the British Police: A Force at Work*. Oxford: Blackwell.

—— and ROCK, P. (1998). *Thinking about Criminology*. London: Routledge.

HOLLOWAY, K., BENNETT, T., and FARRINGTON, D. (2005). *The Effectiveness of Criminal Justice and Treatment Programmes in Reducing Drug-related Crime: A Systematic Review*. Home Office Online Report 26/05, London: Home Office.

HOYLE, C. (2000). 'Being a "Nosy Bloody Cow": Ethical and Methodological Issues in Researching Domestic Violence' in R. King and E. Wincup (eds), *Doing Research on Crime and Justice*. Oxford: Oxford University Press.

JUNKER, B. (1960). *Fieldwork*. Chicago: University of Chicago Press.

KEDDIE, V. (2006). 'Case Study Method' in V. Jupp (ed.), *The Sage Dictionary of Social Research Methods*. London: Sage.

KING, R. D. (2000). 'Doing Research in Prisons' in R. King and E. Wincup (eds), *Doing Research on Crime and Justice*. Oxford: Oxford University Press.

—— and ELLIOTT, K. W. (1978). *Albany: Birth of a Prison—End of an Era*. London: Routledge & Kegan Paul.

—— and RAYNES, N. V. (1967). 'Some Determinants of Patterns of Residential Care' in *Proceedings of the First International Conference of the International Association for the Scientific Study of Mental Deficiency*. Montpellier, 12–20 September 1967, Michael Jackson.

KUHN, T. (1962). *The Structure of Scientific Revolutions*. Chicago: Chicago University Press.

LEWIS, S., VENNARD, J., MAGUIRE, M., RAYNOR, P., VANSTONE, M., RAYBOULD, S., and RIX, A. (2003). *The Resettlement of Short-term Prisoners: An Evaluation of Seven Pathfinders*. RDS Occasional Paper No. 83. London: Home Office.

LINKOGLE, S. and LEE-TREWEEK, G. (2000). *Danger in the Field: Ethics and Risk in Social Research*. London: Routledge.

LLOYD, C., MAIR, G., and HOUGH, M. (1994). *Explaining Reconviction Rates: A Critical Analysis*. Home Office Research Study 136, London: Home Office.

MAGUIRE, M. (2002). 'Crime Statistics: the "Data" Explosion and its Implications' in M. Maguire, R. Morgan, and R. Reiner (eds), *The Oxford Handbook of Criminology* (3rd edn). Oxford: Oxford University Press.

MARSH, C. (1982). *The Survey Method: The Contribution of Surveys to Sociological Explanation.* London: Allen & Unwin.

MARX, K. (1906). *Capital.* Chicago: C.H. Kerr.

MAY, T. (2001). *Social Research: Issues, Methods and Processes* (3rd edn). Buckingham: Open University Press.

MEDAWAR, P. (1967). *The Art of the Soluble.* Harmondsworth: Penguin Books.

MERTON, R. K. (1957). *Social Theory and Social Structure.* Glencoe, Ill: The Free Press.

MORRIS, T., MORRIS, P., and BARER, B. (1963). *Pentonville: A Sociological Study of an English Prison.* London: Routledge & Kegan Paul.

NOAKS, L. and WINCUP, E. (2004). *Criminological Research: Understanding Qualitative Methods.* London: Sage.

OPPENHEIM, A. (2000). *Questionnaire Design, Interviewing and Attitude Measurement* (2nd edn). London: Continuum International Publishing Group.

PARKER, H., MEASHAM, F., and ALDRIDGE, J. (1998). *Illegal Leisure: The Normalization of Adolescent Drug Use.* London: Routledge.

PARKER, T. and MORRIS, T. (1999). *Criminal Conversations: An Anthology of the Work of Tony Parker.* London: Routledge.

PARSONS, T. (1951). *The Social System.* Glencoe, Ill: The Free Press.

PETTICREW, M. and ROBERTS, H. (2005). *Systematic Reviews in the Social Sciences: A Practical Guide.* Oxford: Blackwell Publishing.

PIACENTINI, L. (2004). *Surviving Russian Prisons: Punishment, Economy and Politics in Transition.* Cullompton: Willan.

POLSKY, N. (1971). *Hustlers, Beats and Others.* Harmondsworth: Pelican.

POPPER, K. (2002). *The Logic of Scientific Discovery.* London: Routledge.

RICHARDSON, L. (1990). *Writing Strategies: Reaching Diverse Audiences.* Newbury Park, CA: Sage.

ROBSON, C. (2002). *Real World Research: A Resource for Social Scientists and Practitioner-researchers* (2nd edn). Oxford: Blackwell Publishing.

ROCK, P. (1993). *The Social World of an English Crown Court: Witnesses and Professionals in the Crown Court at Wood Green.* Oxford: Oxford University Press.

SCOTT, J. (1990). *A Matter of Record.* Cambridge: Polity Press.

SHARPE, K. (2000). 'Sad, Bad and (sometimes) Dangerous to Know: Street Corner Research with Prostitutes, Punters and the Police' in R. King and E. Wincup (eds), *Doing Research on Crime and Justice.* Oxford: Oxford University Press.

SHAW, I. (1999). *Qualitative Evaluation,* London: Sage.

SOCIAL EXCLUSION UNIT (2002). *Reducing Re-offending by Ex-prisoners.* London: Office of the Deputy Prime Minister.

THOMAS, W. I. and THOMAS, D. (1929). *The Child in America.* New York: Alfred Knopf.

TILLEY, N. (2006). 'Quasi-experiment' in V. Jupp (ed.), *The Sage Dictionary of Social Research Methods.* London: Sage.

WARDHAUGH, J. (2000). ' "Down and Outers": Fieldwork amongst Street Homeless People' in R. King and E. Wincup (eds), *Doing Research on Crime and Justice.* Oxford: Oxford University Press.

WEBSTER, C., SIMPSON, D., MACDONALD, R., ABBAS, A., CIESLIK, M., SHILDRICK, T., and SIMSPON, D. (2004). *Poor Transitions: Social Exclusion and Young Adults.* Bristol: The Policy Press.

WELSH, B. and FARRINGTON, D. (2002). *Crime Prevention Effects of Closed Circuit Television: A Systematic Review.* Home Office Research Study 252, London: Home Office.

WHARTON, C. (2006). 'Document Analysis' in V. Jupp (ed.), *The Sage Dictionary of Social Research Methods.* London: Sage.

WIKSTRÖM, P. O. and SAMPSON, R. J. (2006). *The Explanation of Crime: Context, Mechanisms and Development.* Cambridge: Cambridge University Press.

WILCOX, A., HOYLE, C., and YOUNG, R. (2005). 'Are Randomised Controlled Trials Really the "Gold Standard" in Restorative Justice Research?', *British Journal of Community Justice* 3(2): 39–49.

WOODS, P. (2005). *Successful Writing for Qualitative Researchers* (2nd edn). London: Routledge.

WOOTTON, B. (1959). *Social Science and Social Pathology.* London: Allen & Unwin.

YIN, R. (1984). *Case Study Research: Design and Methods.* Beverly Hills, CA: Sage.

YOUNG, K., ASHBY, D., BOAZ, A., and GRAYSON, L. (2002). 'Social Science and the Evidence-based Policy Movement', *Social Policy and Society* 1(3): 215–24.

ZENI, J. (2001) (ed.). *Ethical Issues in Practitioner Research.* New York: Teachers College Press.

2

The politics of criminological research

Rod Morgan and Mike Hough

Preamble

This chapter offers an unashamedly personal view of criminological research and its complicated relationship to criminal and social policy. We should say at the outset that we are by no means disinterested parties. We have both had a long involvement with criminological and criminal policy research. We have done a great deal of research for government—and a great deal of research independently of government. One of us worked for several years as a Home Office researcher and research manager. We have both worked as either civil servants or Whitehall appointees with responsibilities for policy, and in this capacity we have been users of research. We have both been closely involved in the process of commissioning research. Depending on the reader's viewpoint, this may make us uniquely qualified to write on the topic—or, by virtue of our involvement in the research process, uniquely disqualified from doing so. We simply make this warning at the outset.

Introduction

At the time of writing (July 2006) New Labour, under Prime Minister Blair, had been in office for nine years. New Labour gained power in May 1997 in part by persuading the electorate that it, and not the Conservative Party, could successfully deliver 'law and order'. It promised to be 'tough on crime, tough on the causes of crime' (Labour Party 1997). The Manifesto, on the basis of which the Party won a third term in May 2005, made clear the importance of this 'tough' statement, which has become New Labour's 'law and order' mantra. 'We banished', the Manifesto confessed, 'Labour demons', of which three were admitted. One of the three was crime, which the Government now boasted it had cut. 'We proved our competence' (Labour Party 2005: 6).

The importance of this admission and claim can scarcely be overestimated. When the Labour Party gained power in 1997 it had spent eighteen years in the political wilderness and it is significant that the Conservative Party began their long period of rule on the basis, in 1979, of the most radical election manifesto of recent times. At the heart of it also was an undertaking to be tough on crime. The Conservatives made 'restoring the rule of law', which they claimed the preceding 'Old Labour' Government 'had undermined', one of their five major tasks. They said they would do so by implementing specific 'law and order' policies. They proposed spending more on law and order services while economizing elsewhere. They would pay the police better. They would introduce tougher sentences for violent offenders. They would introduce 'short, sharp, shock' custodial regimes 'for hooligans' (Conservative Party 1979). All the psephological evidence suggested that they gained considerable advantage over Labour by these means, particularly among working-class voters. Thus were constructed the Old Labour demons that New Labour successfully sought to exorcise, both when preparing for their ascendancy while in Opposition during the mid-1990s, and thereafter in power since 1997 (Downes and Morgan 2007).

The first version of this essay (Morgan 2000) was written at a time when the Labour Government was preparing to launch the largest programme of criminological research ever undertaken in the UK. It was part of their Crime Reduction Programme. They had promised 'law and order', historically their Achilles heel. Now they had to deliver it. They needed to establish their governmental credentials and claimed they would do so on the basis of 'evidence-based policy', for which criminological research was pressed into service. Today, almost a decade later, we can scrutinize the nature of that research programme and the use that was made of it. We shall also consider what other criminological research was being undertaken, by other means. The lessons, we suggest, will show that policy can shape what counts as research and as evidence, just as much as evidence can shape policy. Criminological research—how and what work does or does not get commissioned, and how ultimately that work is used—is necessarily a political project and process. During the course of our account we shall draw on our own experiences, both as research providers and as consumers.

Setting the criminological scene

Whatever criminology is about, it is inescapably about crime. It is a hardy perennial that much criminological work is theoretically impoverished, and that crime is best contemplated within broad horizons—political economy, social stratification, socialization and role theory, social justice, culture-related, and so on. Over the years many critics have suggested that the study of crime and our responses to it should be part of a broader commitment to the development of fundamental social or normative theory, and as part of that ambition have disclaimed the title criminology (in favour, for example, of a sociology of deviance or broader feminist studies) because of its typically narrow, technicist limitations or its infusion with prevailing political, legal, or social assumptions. Yet criminology, as entrepreneurial gambit, occupational title, and disciplinary descriptor, thrives despite the predilection of its practitioners to claim for their own contribution some prefix—*new, radical, left, critical, realist, left-utopian*—signifying enquiring purity, theoretical significance, and social relevance while attaching to the work of others a label—*positivist, administrative, jobbing, right, right-utopian*—signifying political subservience or corruption, theoretical impotence, or social irrelevance. Why? The answer is that because criminology is inescapably about crime, and thus uniquely has a social problem and a negative label at its heart, it is unavoidably normative in orientation. For this reason any account of current criminological research must at some point grapple with the socio-economic and political context within which criminology as it is taught in places of higher education continues to burgeon.

At the beginning of the new millennium Britain was arguably a more fractured society than at any point since the Second World War. This is the consequence of a paradox. Modernity has increased the degree to which we share a common politicocultural infrastructure, the language of which endorses citizenship, democracy, public accountability, equality of opportunity, collective and individual justice, and so on. Almost everyone: has the vote; has access to elementary education, free at the point of delivery; derives information and entertainment from national mass media; benefits from the state-provided safety net of a National Health Service; and, if unemployed, sick or of pensionable age, has the assurance of transfer payments which will minimally provide shelter, put clothes on backs, and food in bellies. Moreover, we are all citizens of a state that has signed up to international human rights conventions and, in the Human Rights Act 1998, has incorporated those obligations into domestic law. It was not so previously. Yet whereas two-thirds to three-quarters of us live comfortably or luxuriously, enjoying unprecedentedly high incomes and a cornucopia of consumer choice—new and more powerful cars, second holidays and homes, electronic gadgetry, designer fripperies, and prepackaged all-the-year-round exotic foods brought to our out-of-town supermarkets from every corner of the globe—the other one-quarter to one-third of the population live in poverty and insecurity which in the latter decades of the twentieth century grew, in relative terms, progressively more acute (Hutton 1996).

Our unprecedented prosperity was less equally shared in the mid-1990s than twenty years previously, a situation marginally redressed since. During this period income inequality grew in Britain more than in almost all other developed countries, including the USA. According to the latest government statistics the proportion of the population today living in households with income at or below 60 per cent of the median household income—the most widely accepted definition of low income—is 11.4 million, a reduction of 2.5 million on 1996/7, but a figure still much higher than in the early 1980s (see Hills 2004; Glennerster *et al.* 2005). This relative poverty is both persistent—families are trapped within it—and geographically concentrated. It is explained largely by technological change and shifting labour market conditions, combined with demographic changes and the determination of successive governments to control or cut public expenditure and to minimize redistributive fiscal policies. New Labour's fiscal policy has not actually been regressive, but the structural pressures in the global economy towards inequality have offset their good intentions. The aim was to reduce child poverty—and some progress has been made. But in 2004/5 there were still 3.4 million children living in low-income households, a high proportion of them in single-parent households and more than half of them in workless households.

Unemployment is today lower than for twenty years, but there is less and less call for unskilled workers and their relative earnings have declined. Long-term unemployment has increased, as has low-paid, temporary, and part-time employment. New Labour has introduced the minimum wage and tax credits, but the number of households in need of such provision has increased: more than three times as many people are in receipt of tax credits as were in receipt of Family Credit a decade ago. Children brought up in relative poverty are significantly more likely to fail at school and the absence of educational qualifications is the greatest handicap for those entering the more competitive labour market. Twelve per cent of young people leave school with fewer than five GCSEs (4 per cent with no grades at all) and one in four 19-year-olds still fail to achieve a basic level of qualification (NVQ2 or above).

Some of these themes are the enduring stuff of social stratification. However, being unemployed and living in relative poverty in the twenty-first century is not the same experience as it was at the end of the nineteenth century or in the Great Depression of the 1920s. Today virtually every household and child's head has images piped into it of what one writer has termed the 'carnival of wealth and self-indulgence' (Davis 1998: 175) which a majority of the population takes for granted. The cultural and political solidarity of the working classes—a term now considered quaint—has all but evaporated. The nuclear family, let alone the extended family, has for a large proportion of households fallen apart. Young mothers struggle alone to bring up a growing proportion of children in relative poverty and more and more old people live out their days in uncared-for solitude. Poverty today is concentrated in several thousand sink estates, the residual legacy of our post-war commitment to public housing. Both in these areas, and in the new city centre, night-time economy, entertainment zones where the relatively affluent and the clamouring young gather, the informal social controls of yesteryear, based on the lifetime knowledge of neighbourliness backed up by traditional petty officialdom (concierges, park keepers, shop assistants, bus conductors, station porters, and so on) have declined in potency or have been rationalized out of existence in the interests of alleged efficiency.

The precise implications of these fundamental structural and cultural shifts for the incidence of crime is difficult to gauge. We saw some of the steepest increases in crime—whether measured by police statistics or the British Crime Survey—in the late 1980s and early 1990s, at a time when the gap between rich and poor was growing at its fastest. Since the mid-1990s, levels of crime have declined by about two-fifths (Walker *et al.* 2006), and there have been steeper falls in many forms of crime, notably burglary and vehicle crime. Whilst Labour has been quick to point to these falls as evidence of governmental competence, they are better understood as a consequence of long-run trends that counterbalance the growing social inequalities that we have described above. The technologies of crime control have improved. Houses are better protected now than at any time since the Victorian era, and car design has finally caught up with the challenges posed by vehicle crime. The police can now deploy a range of surveillance and detection technologies—such as CCTV, DNA analysis, and Automatic Fingerprint Retrieval—that in combination make many crimes more risky to undertake. Desire for popular consumer durables motivates much volume crime but, paradoxically, their low cost, high quality and availability means that, when set against the risks involved in illicit acquisition, the pay-offs from crimes such as burglary are much lower than two or three decades ago.

If we take the long view, we remain a high-crime society. More than ten times as much crime is today recorded as in the immediate post-war period. This is unsurprising given the vast increase in the amount of desirable, stealable, and relatively anonymous property in circulation (Maguire 2007). The recent falls are hard to interpret as an indication of a society that is at growing ease with itself; it is more plausible that we have simply become more efficient at managing the tensions and discontents that are associated with an economy premised on the idea that the 'winner takes all'. And whatever the successes in containing 'volume crime', anxieties remain—or indeed burgeon—about less serious but more visible forms of low-level disorder—badged by New Labour as antisocial behaviour.

Leaving aside the swirling entertainment and shopping zones that are obvious 'crime attractors', it is generally the sites repeatedly identified by studies of socio-economic disadvantage where crime and disorder most flourishes. These are the geo-coded hot spots identified by the new generation of local authority planners preparing the crime and disorder audits required by the Crime and Disorder Act 1998. The poverty indicators correspond with the community safety alarums—high police-recorded crime, high incidence of domestic violence, evidence of alcohol and illicit drug abuse, many addresses of known offenders, permanently excluded school pupils, children on the at-risk register, and attenders at hospital accident and emergency departments. Every major city has its stigmatically deprived 'symbolic location'. But the major conurbations in the rust-belt zones have swathes of housing, mostly owned, or previously owned, by local authorities where hopelessness thrives. Becoming the victim of crime and disorder is a major social concern much represented in politicians' surgeries and political analysts' focus groups.

We live with some uncomfortable political truths. Property crime affects the whole country, but it is most prevalent for those city dwellers most beset by multiple disadvantage. Serious violence is also concentrated in these areas: whilst homicide has risen by almost two-thirds nationally since the mid-1990s, the extra crimes are concentrated almost entirely in the poorest third of the country (Dorling 2005). Britain is now a more unequal and insecure society than was the case a few decades ago and crime and disorder is the generally recognized, principal symptom of our social disarray. The widespread incidence of predatory property crime and the thankfully less common incidence of predatory violent crime is symptomatic of a slow-burning socio-economic civil war. It is the flip side of the complacent acceptance by the majority of the population of a prosperity based on inequality and the progressive marginalization or social exclusion of those who are least equipped to flourish in a market economy.

This state of affairs is partly the consequence of global technological change bearing down on a nation that was the crucible of the industrial revolution. Traditional sources of employment—agriculture, fishing, mining, and large-scale manufacturing—have massively declined and large sections of the workforce have almost literally been thrown on the scrap-heap. Successive governments have pursued polices which, depending on one's viewpoint, have exacerbated the strains of this transition or have radically made the British economy more adaptable. The Conservative governments of the 1980s proudly boasted of leading Europe towards privatization, deregulation, and the creation of a more 'flexible' labour market—that is, a labour market in which the workforce is less protected, less well trained, and less invested-in. New Labour have pursued the privatization–deregulation path even more radically, albeit, in recent years, alongside greater investment in public services. Fiscal policies have been adopted based on the proposition that whereas the already well-rewarded apparently need the *incentive* of greatly increased incomes (both earned and retained after tax), the disadvantaged need the *discipline* and *spur* of modest or reduced state benefits in order that the dependency culture be undermined. The wealthy become more wealthy and the poor relatively poorer. Those with jobs work longer and longer hours while those without jobs, particularly the rising generation of long-term unemployed youth, have time to kill.

It is to middle-income Britain, relatively thriving, but nevertheless anxious about the pitfalls and tensions abounding in the new deregulated market place, that the major political parties make their pitch. This was the constituency to which New Labour promised to be 'tough on crime' and initially undertook not to reverse the reduced taxation policies to which the Conservatives had moved during the course of eighteen years. On the one hand New Labour has used the language of social inclusion and restorative justice, and preached the virtues of public services and holistic social policy. They have greatly extended investment in public services, notably education and health, even if the returns on this investment have been slower and less certain than expected. On the other hand they have pursued the marketization of public services with a vigour that is reminiscent of the Thatcher administration, and in controlling the socially troublesome, they have significantly shifted the balance away from welfare measures in favour of criminal—and civil—justice measures. That is, New Labour has been willing to pursue a pathway from modernity—assimilation and incorporation—to post-modernity—separation and exclusion (Young 1998).

Law and order politics

The strength of the Conservative Party has traditionally been its capacity to signify oneness with the bastions of British sovereignty—the monarchy and the aristocracy, property, the armed forces, the institutions of the educated elite, the land, and the law (Parkin 1967; see also Honderich 1990). By contrast the Labour Party has traditionally grounded its appeal on cautiously challenging these institutions and assumptions: it has laid claim to the values of community and redistributive justice. After the Second World War this cleavage offered distinctive choices in most areas of social policy—taxation, education, health, housing, and so on. One could vote for progressive taxation and high-quality, more-or-less-free-at-the-point-of-delivery, comprehensive public services: or for self-reliance within the competitive market place backed up by basic, selective, and means-tested state provision. Throughout most of the twentieth century the pursuit of Labour Party ideals meant activists, or groups closely allied to the Labour Party, from time to time becoming involved in skirmishes with the law, the police, and the courts. This was necessary, for example, to achieve recognition of trade unions more than a century ago and again during the 1980s to defend their rights and interests, most conspicuously during the miners' dispute of 1983–4. Parallel acts of civil disobedience periodically engaged Labour Party supporters pursuing protest or reformist agendas ranging from the Campaign for Nuclear Disarmament in the 1960s to poll-tax resistance in 1989–91.

Although the Labour and Conservative parties have seldom taken radically distinctive policy stances on 'law and order' issues, their general ideological positioning has meant a tendency to different explanations of crime and disorder. Conservatives have typically assumed crime to be the product of individual pathology and the breakdown of established patterns of authority. Labour has tended to assume that crime is the product of structural forces, in particular inequality and lack of legitimate opportunity. Thus Conservative and Labour Party projects have been different. For Labour the task has been to *connect* the phenomenon of crime to socio-economic policy: the Conservative Party

has been keen to *disconnect* these phenomena (Downes 1989). For Labour these connections provide *explanations*, whereas for Conservatives they provide *excuses* and serve to
undermine the rule of law itself.

During the 1970s and 1980s, a period during which there was growing public concern
about crime, the Conservatives were able rhetorically to underline their commitment to
the rule of law, accusing Labour of unreliability in this sphere by recording and trotting
out a catalogue of incidents illustrating the willingness of Labour Party supporters to
break the law or speak ill of it and its enforcement agents. It is this aspect of Old Labour
on which the Conservatives successfully capitalized in the 1979 election and which New
Labour strove, again successfully, to put behind it in 1997. New Labour wishes to be seen
as the party that will best protect citizens against crime—to be the *real* party of law and
order—and, given that the 1980s was a decade of inexorable growth in recorded crime
and almost unprecedented civil disorder (industrial disputes, inner-city riots, and public
protests), the better guarantor of the Queen's Peace. This is best exemplified by: their
backing while in Opposition, and implementation since coming to office, of the key provisions of the Crime (Sentences) Act 1997 providing presumptive minimum sentences
for particular convictions (thereby effectively endorsing Conservative Home Secretary
Michael Howard's claim that 'prison works'); their adoption of a series of tough and
'responsibilizing' measures, particularly in relation to young offenders and their parents,
in the Crime and Disorder Act 1998; providing the police with a range of new powers
allowing them to dispense 'on the spot' summary justice, for example through Penalty
Notices for Disorder; and their vigorous pursuit since 1998 of antisocial behaviour and
'respect' agendas backed up by a raft of new legislation to tackle 'yobs' (see Morgan 2006).
These measures are increasingly justified as a much needed exercise in 'rebalancing' the
system in favour of the 'law-abiding majority'.

It is true that the Crime and Disorder Act 1998 and subsequent statutes and initiatives
have incorporated measures opening up crime prevention in a holistic sense. The
Morgan Report (Home Office 1991), whose key recommendations the Conservative government rejected, was dusted off and local authorities statutorily required to prepare
Crime and Disorder Strategies based on a partnership approach between all the key agencies. But it is noteworthy that having initially adopted the all-encompassing language of
community safety (see Hughes 1998: ch. 6), New Labour in the end preferred the narrower, tougher term of 'crime and disorder'. Further, when most local authorities failed
initially to make use of antisocial behaviour orders (ASBOs), it was Prime Minister Blair
who personally intervened and repeatedly kick-started the initiative, so successfully that
being 'ASBO'd' has become a colloquialism (Morgan 2006). Likewise No 10's intervention to promote the 'street crime' initiative against robbery in 2001–2 and the *Respect
Action Plan* of 2006 (Home Office 2006).

New Labour has put in place measures structurally to address socio-economic disadvantage—Sure Start, tax credits, the urban regeneration programme and so on—but as
far as the causes of crime and disorder are concerned, tough love is to be applied in a
largely individualistic sense according to tough-minded criteria. The policy language
relentlessly contrasts the 'law-abiding citizen' with 'criminals', and elevates the protection
of the former to the central purpose of the criminal justice system. Proposals to deal with
the latter are couched entirely in terms of managerial control rather than social equity or
collective justice. This reflects the application by New Labour of their approach to the

management of the public services generally (Hutton 2005), rather than any specific commitment to criminal justice principles (see Faulkner 2006). Crime *hot spots* are to be identified and short-term *risk assessments* made so that there can be *targeted interventions* subject to *cost-benefit evaluations* of effectiveness.

This highly instrumentalist approach to criminal justice policy has been accompanied increasingly by governmental critiques of a 'human rights culture' that places greater weight on the protection of the accused than on the safety of the public. The argument, at its most explicit in a speech made by the Prime Minister at the launch of the 'Respect' programme for tackling antisocial behaviour, is that we are fighting twenty-first-century crime with nineteenth-century methods (Blair 2006); the protection of suspects afforded by full due process, the argument goes, has become too expensive and too cumbersome in relation to the challenges of modern crime. In its place the Government advocates forms of civil law remedy such as the ASBO and forms of summary justice, with the right of appeal to a full court hearing. The aim, as the Prime Minister said in his speech, is to make enforcement easier and to reverse the burden of proof; if offenders wish to challenge on-the-spot fines, for example, the choice is theirs.

The Government has had a complex and often ambiguous attitude to research into crime policy. After a decade of New Labour it is clear that some of the central pillars of criminal policy, such as the move towards civil law measures and to summary justice, have been constructed in a research-free zone. On the other hand, the Crime Reduction Programme, launched in 1999, and several other initiatives had evaluation built into their design from the start—on a scale that was impressive, if not unique. But as we shall see, it was to be research that conformed to the prescriptions of New Labour governance.

The criminological enterprise

In 1993–4 one of us was jointly responsible for putting together a criminological reader which has become a standard text in the UK. In the preface to the first edition (Maguire, Morgan, and Reiner 1994) we noted the extraordinary development during its relatively short life of criminology in higher education as a taught subject and research enterprise. This extraordinary development has continued. In the space of little more than half a century, criminology has been transformed from being the focus of a few, lone, pioneering figures to a major academic industry, large-scale and organized as far as teaching is concerned and expansive, though still largely cottage, with respect to research. In the 1950s there were virtually no undergraduate courses, and those who began to teach the subject at postgraduate level had remarkably little research material on which to draw in preparing their courses. Today virtually none of the more than 130–40 universities in the UK is without undergraduate options in criminology (or some application of criminology or criminal justice) and many now have specialist taught postgraduate courses. There are a score or more criminology-related university research centres avidly competing for the funds available from the Home Office, the Economic and Social Research Council (ESRC), the major charitable research foundations, and, increasingly, the local authorities and statutory services. The *Howard Journal* and *British Journal of Criminology* have been joined by about a dozen other journals whose content is largely or partially devoted to criminology articles. Several leading publishers and one or two small, specialist publishers carry substantial lists of titles devoted to criminology.

This extraordinary growth is not surprising. The 'law and order' services—police, the Crown Prosecution Service, the courts, the youth offending teams (YOTs), probation, and prisons—have grown enormously in terms both of personnel and budget. In 2006–7 total government expenditure on the criminal justice system will approach £20 billion. The police service alone now employs approaching 200,000 personnel; the prison, probation, and youth justice services around another 85,000. The official budget and headcount does not tell anything like the full story, however. The burgeoning commercial security industry is estimated now to be significantly larger than that of the state police (Jones and Newburn 1998) and the senior ranks of the security services are drawn substantially from the state police and other law and order services. The latest recruits to this expanding *corps* of 'law and order' players are the YOTs and the local government Crime and Disorder Reduction Partnership (CDRP) officers. More and more short or distance-learning courses have been organized by the universities to meet these new market opportunities.

Criminology is an intrinsically attractive subject as far as an expanding proportion of social science and law students is concerned. It addresses questions of general public interest. It covers incidents and processes—crime and punishment—that provide the subject matter of a high proportion of news coverage and popular entertainment. And criminology has become of straightforward utilitarian career value. Recruits to the law and order public services are increasingly expected to have some familiarity with the criminological theory and practice that informs practical crime prevention, social work, policing, sentencing, and so on. Criminology is the product of contemporary governance and increasingly services it through the recruitment and training of personnel. It was ever thus, but has become more so. Much of the debate in criminological texts about the shifting contours of criminology represent real changes of theoretical emphasis and substantive interest in what and how academic criminologists teach and undertake research. But it has always been the 'government project' (Garland 2002) that has driven the expansion of the discipline, even though the 'government project' marginally changes from time to time in tone, method, and direction. Nowhere is this more apparent than in the funding of criminological research.

Criminological research for government

If size and influence are the criteria then any institutional account of criminological research in Britain must begin with the Home Office Research, Development and Statistics Directorate (RDS, as the former Home Office Research Unit and other more specific research groups within the Home Office are now known). RDS is the largest single employer of criminological researchers in the UK. At any one time there are in the region of 85 researchers and 40 statisticians, together with support staff. Not all researchers are graduates who have studied criminology either as an undergraduate option or as a postgraduate specialism. Several have backgrounds in a variety of social sciences ranging from economics to geography and psychology and are new to the areas of crime prevention, policing, and criminal justice on which most RDS work is focused. Moreover, because RDS has the largest criminological research budget in Britain, a budget used both in-house and to commission research from the academic community, market research companies, and, increasingly, private sector consultants, the Directorate intermittently funds the work of outsiders, including a considerable number of academic criminologists based in universities. It exercises the natural influence of paymaster, actual and potential—grants hoped for as well as received.

Until 2003 RDS was organized as a single directorate within the Home Office, largely co-located in its own offices. The majority of staff are now 'embedded' in five policy directorates, with only a small central core. The embedded staff are probably less independent of their policy customers than hitherto. Although RDS's research staff and statisticians continue to be centrally recruited and managed, decisions about the content of the research programme, and to an increasing extent about the research budget, are made within the five policy directorates, and then agreed with ministers. Nor is ministerial oversight simply a question of rubber-stamping officials' recommendations. Leaving aside the need for research, the potential visibility of criminal policy research means that there is close political scrutiny of the programme. These changes reflect wider shifts in the way that government departments operate, with a progressive reduction of officials' discretion, and a tighter harnessing of their work to political imperatives.

In 2005–6 RDS's total budget, including staff costs, stood at £24.4 millions of which £16.2 millions were spent on research contracted out. Like all institutionally powerful paymasters RDS inspires both sycophancy and disdain. Especially during the period of expansion of research that occurred in New Labour's first few years, there was—depending on one's perspective—considerable academic interest in making a contribution to policy development or in securing a place at the feeding trough. The criminological fraternity is, at best, insecure about its identity as impartial scholar, and some sections like to see themselves as spokespersons of the oppressed caught in the expanding trap of criminal justice. Not surprisingly, academic reactions to RDS, and those who are funded by it, can sometimes be extreme. Those academic researchers, and criminological centres, who regularly undertake contracts for the Home Office are sometimes the object of scarcely disguised contempt from other criminologists who wear their radical-critical pretensions conspicuously on their sleeves.

It is widely contended, and not just by the radical outsiders, that most Home Office-funded criminological research is:

i.   almost entirely atheoretical *fact gathering*—how many crimes are not reported? How many crimes probably are committed by persons arrested (or probably not committed by persons imprisoned)? What drugs are consumed by young people arrested and not arrested? What is the level of compliance of offenders sentenced to one court order as opposed to another? And so on;

ii. is *narrowly focused*—generally on a recent spending or administrative initiative or piece of legislation;

iii. and is designed to be, and in its final product invariably is, *policy-friendly*.

Which is to say that it is: *empirical*; generally *quantitative* (the emphasis being on measuring the easily measurable); increasingly incorporates a *cost-benefit* assessment;

overwhelmingly *short-termist*—designed to answer the question whether whatever is being evaluated is having an immediate impact; and *uncritical*, in the sense that it does not question general government policy but merely reports whether the evidence collected supports the continuation of one policy tactic as opposed to another.

To the extent that this typification is correct—and we suggest that though it largely is, it is nonetheless not the whole story—it should not be a cause for surprise and is certainly no scandal. It was ever thus. The Home Office serves an elected government more or less carrying out manifesto commitments. RDS's customers are the Home Office policy divisions serving political masters whose primary interest is confirmation that the policies they are pursuing are working so that the public at large, given whatever hopes and fears they entertain, can be persuaded that they made the correct choice at the last General Election and will make the same choice at the next.

This is not to say that the RDS criminological research programme is a political charade. It is not. Its design and delivery are methodologically demanding and professionally competent—indeed it enjoys a substantial international reputation in that regard—and it is characterized by a high level of integrity with respect to reliability and validity. RDS has over the years been an unrivalled source of apprenticeship for leading researchers, many of whom have since left the Home Office, taken up senior academic posts in university departments of criminology and, coincidentally, contributed to this volume. Moreover, a significant proportion of the research undertaken *within* RDS, as well as *for* RDS, is published in the same academic journals which carry the work of scholars not aspiring to Home Office funding. Nevertheless, the RDS research programme is ultimately managed for political ends—to enhance the reputation of the political party in government. That means that at best it aims at the fine-tuning of policy, not challenging it and certainly not discrediting either it or the agencies that deliver it and for which the government is responsible to Parliament. This is a fact of Home Office life.

Only when the ministerial thumb is pressed too firmly on the RDS programme is the discomfort within RDS as palpable as that more generally felt without. This tends to occur either when an administration has accumulated an extensive policy record to defend, or when it feels itself under threat by the Opposition. These conditions were certainly met in the last years of the Conservative administration, from 1992 to 1997, when Michael Howard was Home Secretary. He arguably exercised a baneful hands-on influence, and at one point even considered disbanding the Directorate. This stimulated an unprecedented exodus of research staff, including one of the authors of this chapter. The arrival of New Labour in 1997 was greeted largely with a sense of relief by the criminological community, although, as we shall discuss, it became clear within a short time that Conservative politicians held no monopoly on the desire to exercise a tight grip on their policy research.

RDS research under New Labour

In the early years of New Labour, the political commitment to 'evidence-led policy' and to partnership between policy and research was very evident—and to our minds, sincere. Governments that have been out of office for almost two decades tend to be hungry for new ideas and usually want support in implementing them. Many academic criminologists found this new relationship not simply lucrative and flattering, but refreshing and interesting. In 1999 the Government launched its very visible £250 million *Crime Reduction Programme*—for which a separate evaluation budget of £25 million was nominally attached for the first three years of its projected ten-year lifespan. Many other criminal justice initiatives were also launched—and evaluated—in the early years of New Labour. The latter include: the youth justice provisions in the Crime and Disorder Act 1998 and the work of the Youth Justice Board established to oversee the working of those provisions (an overall budget of £85 million over three years); the drugs prevention programme in both prisons and the community (a budget of £211 million over three years); additional resources for the Probation Service (including £56 million to pilot, evaluate, and implement the Drug Treatment and Testing Order); and additional resources for the Prison Service to provide prisoner programmes, resources which the then Director General of the Prison Service, Martin Narey, said would substantially be devoted to developing the literacy, numeracy, and employment skills of young offenders in the Young Offender Institutions (YOIs).

At the same time, the British Crime Survey (BCS) was greatly extended in size—with a sample of 40,000—and converted into a continuous rolling survey. A range of other surveys were also launched, including the Citizenship Survey, the Offending and Criminal Justice Survey and the Commercial Victimization Survey. In aggregate these surveys added substantially to the amount of criminologically relevant information about crime and justice.

This volume of research activity, supported by a £40m annual budget, represents a step-change from the period 1991/2–1996/7 when the total Home Office research budget ranged between £11 and £15 million *per annum*. The RDS budget has always been split between external research and in-house research officers who both carry out research and supervise projects contracted to external researchers. For most of the 1990s the balance tipped in favour of in-house work. The expansion of research under New Labour resulted in a shift towards external work. Most of the evaluations of the Crime Reduction Programme, for example, were contracted out, and we were both involved in several of these evaluations as academic researchers.

Evaluating the Crime Reduction Programme

The Crime Reduction Programme had a fairly short and unhappy life, and it was at this time that the honeymoon relationship between a new administration and the cadre of academically-based policy researchers began to sour. The basic idea was that the programme would be rolled out in phases over a ten-year period. Each phase would be evaluated, and the lessons learned from evaluation at each phase would be incorporated into the design of the next phase. This process would result in an upward spiral of effectiveness.

In hindsight, the programme has to be regarded as the triumph of hope over experience. Many things went wrong (see Maguire 2004; Hough 2004; Hough *et al.* 2004). Little control was exercised over the content of projects in the programme, which was funded in response to bids from local Crime and Disorder Reduction Partnerships. Evaluators were typically faced with a multiplicity of disparate initiatives implemented in parallel in the same areas. Implementation failure was widespread, partly because timescales were tight, and partly because it is in the nature of innovation to prove problematic. Agencies under evaluation underestimated the demands that evaluation would make on them, and found it difficult to comply with demands for data; some of the poor performers probably judged that it would in any case be better for them if they dragged their heels.

The political pressure for 'quick wins' also meant that Phase 2 of programmes were introduced before Phase 1 was fully evaluated, and the idea of phased learning was dropped. The evaluations produced some positive results, but more often inconclusive findings reflecting implementation failure, on the one hand, and methodological limitations, on the other. Evaluators fed back news of endemic implementation failure to their policy paymasters, but these found themselves in an impossible position. Operating in an increasingly demanding 'can-do' work ethos, they were reluctant to admit failure to ministers. The Crime Reduction Programme, and the evaluations, carried on for three years, before there was a silent retreat from the initiative.

The overall learning from the Crime Reduction Programme was extremely disappointing. In one of the bigger evaluations that we directed, one of us spent £1m of Home Office money to document the fact that well co-ordinated, well-implemented multimodal burglary prevention schemes could have a modest impact, but that achieving this co-ordination was an uphill struggle. Results were finally published in a very low key way in late 2004 (Hough *et al.* 2004)—long after the Home Office had published a much more positive four-page summary of the results of this and two other evaluations—a point to which we shall return. Maguire (2004) has discussed how the Crime Reduction Programme came into being as a result of an unusual 'window of opportunity' when such a programme appeared attractive to politicians, administrators, practitioners, and researchers alike, resulting in a level of funding for pilot projects and evaluation which in the UK was unprecedented in the crime reduction field. It was understandable why we collectively seized the rare opportunity of major funding, but as Maguire (2004: 213) suggests, 'the ideal of "evidence-based policy" may be more effectively pursued as a quiet, iterative process over the longer term, than through a risky investment in one high profile and rapidly implemented "programme" which promises more than it can guarantee to deliver'.

The aftermath of the Crime Reduction Programme

Funders' and contractors' experience of the Crime Reduction Programme prompted several reactions. Perhaps the most important of these was a rethink within RDS of the approach to evaluation. It was decided to target evaluation resources more intensively on fewer research questions—a sensible response, given that the evaluation resources had clearly been spread too thinly in many of the CRP programmes. There was also a concerted effort to improve the methodological quality of the work that *was* commissioned or mounted in-house.

Sharper focus and better quality are sensible goals, of course, but the RDS approach to driving up quality was a contentious one. RDS managers started to embrace the research philosophy associated with the Cochrane Collaboration (for healthcare) and the Campbell Collaboration (for criminal policy). The basic idea behind these initiatives is that one should be systematic in assembling and reviewing research evidence, admitting only those studies that achieve acceptable methodological standards.[1] The threshold for

---

[1] See http://www.cochrane.org for details of the Cochrane Collaboration, and http://www.aic.gov.au/campbellcj for details of the Campbell Collaboration.

inclusion of studies should be set individually for each review, in the light of available evidence. For example, the Maryland Scale of Scientific Methods is often used as a filtering device.[2] One of the most influential international reviews of effective practice in Criminal Justice, conducted by Sherman and colleagues (1997) adopted systematic review principles, identifying:

(a) what is known to work;

(b) what is promising;

(c) what does not work;

(d) what is not known.

For the purposes of the review, 'known to work' meant 'established as effective by at least two high quality evaluations'.[3]

In fields of study which lend themselves readily to evaluation through randomized controlled trials (RCTs) or to other forms of tightly designed quantitative evaluation, the Campbell/Cochrane approach is clearly appropriate. We can reasonably expect our doctors to base their prescribing decisions on evidence that is filtered to remove all studies of poor quality. This is because pharmaceutical evaluations are *relatively* straightforward: there is usually little implementation failure—in that people in drug trials tend to take their medicine as required—and clearly measurable outcomes. Also important is the fact that pharmaceutical interventions are not usually dependent for their effectiveness on the social meaning that the recipients attach to them. (Though there is obviously the potential for placebo effects in the real world, evaluations can rule out this effect through double blind trials.) Evaluating strategies for reducing crime tends to be more complex.[4]

This shift towards Cochrane/Campbell principles was more marked in some parts of RDS than in others. The pressure on Home Office researchers to embrace these principles derived partly, but not entirely, from the large number of evaluations commissioned for the Crime Reduction Programme that had been unable to provided definitive answers about 'what worked'. There were other factors at work. Throughout the 1990s and into this century, Treasury officials became progressively more bullish in demanding 'hard' evidence to support bids from spending departments for new money. And, as the culture within government departments shifted, along with the balance of power between ministers and officials, the former became increasingly impatient with the latter's equivocation in giving straight answers to apparently straight questions.

This pressure was probably greatest in relation to research on the rehabilitation of offenders, where it seems very reasonable to ask, 'Does this programme work?' However

---

[2] The Maryland Scale assigns evaluative studies into one of five categories, according to the form of experimental control that is used to help to attribute causality. The highest score is reserved for studies that use randomized controlled trial methods. Systematic reviews usually exclude all studies that fall into the lowest two categories, and some include only those that fall into the top, or the top two, categories.

[3] Sherman *et al.* (1997) define programmes that work as follows:

These are programs that we are reasonably certain of preventing crime or reducing risk factors for crime in the kinds of social contexts in which they have been evaluated, and for which the findings should be generalizable to similar settings in other places and times. Programs coded as 'working' by this definition must have at least two level 3 evaluations with statistical significance tests showing effectiveness and the preponderance of all available evidence supporting the same conclusion.

[4] For a fuller discussion of the limits of the Cochrane/Campbell approach in evaluating complex crime reduction programmes, see Hope (2005).

the short answer to the question, 'What works in reducing crime?' is one that civil servants can no longer proffer: 'It depends'. In the past, Sir Humphrey might have indulged himself in explaining to his minister the full complexity of the interactions between characteristics of projects, the quality of staff implementing them, the level of staff morale and the quality of their managers, the organizational settings in which staff and projects operate and the sociodemographic context for which the intervention was planned. Such a response is now regarded as a strategy for securing early retirement.

Our guess—and it is no more than a guess—is that under pressure for 'straight answers to straight questions', RDS officials gave a different, 'can do' answer that was fundamentally misguided: 'We need proper research before we can answer those questions.' As a piece of cultural vandalism, this hardly ranks with the Taliban's destruction of the Bamiyan Buddhas. But it carries the totally unacceptable implication: that the 'good enough' knowledge gleaned from many years of qualitative and quantitative research that failed to meet Campbell experimental standards is no longer good enough for political decision-making, and should be consigned to the bonfire of incompetence.

This is broadly the fate met by much of the research evaluating the Crime Reduction Programme. Some of it went unpublished altogether. Some of it was left unpublished and unpromoted by the Home Office, but with acquiescence to publication elsewhere. Other reports, such as our evaluation of projects mounted under the Burglary Reduction Initiative were published by the Home Office but only after very long delays. Because the body of work had been demoted into the 'methodologically weak' category, the findings that were of real interest in these reports tended to be ignored by RDS and their policy customers.

There are, of course, always two sides to every story. The RDS research managers faced a difficult task of getting a very large amount of evaluative research into the public domain. They had to ensure that the research was of an adequate quality, and that it was presented in a way that would make end-users read it. It has to be said that some of the commissioned research was of poor quality, and some of it was poorly presented. It is hardly surprising that there were *some* delays in publication. The Home Office neither has, nor should have, any obligation to publish every substandard report that contractors submit. But our view is that political interests were well-served—at least in the short term—by the considerable inertia in the system that delayed the publication of negative research findings. We shall return to issues of publication again.[5]

Our own view is that if one examines those pieces of criminological research that have made a really significant contribution to our understanding about crime, many—perhaps the majority—of these actually score low on the Maryland Scale. Theoretical studies and insightful descriptive research have proved of immense value, and generally have a longer shelf-life than many high-quality evaluations. The value of the evidence base is to be found in its *cumulative* nature: individual studies may be tentative, but in combination, we actually know quite a lot about 'what works'. The Cochrane/Campbell approach tends to discount this knowledge, and to admit as knowledge only those findings from studies which individually can be regarded as methodologically 'copper-bottomed'. In the

---

[5] In defence of the Home Office, one might argue that academic publication delays are often even lengthier than those associated with RDS research. However, the delays in academic publication do not come packaged up with *control* over dissemination, and in any case, publicly funded research should be publicly accessible as soon as is reasonably possible.

real world—where political decisions often have to be taken on the basis of less than conclusive evidence, it makes sense to 'lower the bar' evidentially so that one can say *something* of value, albeit with a degree of uncertainty, rather than say *very little* of value but with complete confidence. The promise of the Cochrane/Campbell perspective is that in the fullness of time researchers will be able to say a lot more, with complete confidence. However, this could turn out to be—in a complex world—a vain hope.

We discussed earlier how many academic commentators regard RDS work as theoretically impoverished. We fear that the pressures on RDS to come up with unequivocal answers to complex problems may exacerbate this problem. Invitations to tender for projects now typically require contractors to identify:

i.   *inputs* (the additional human, physical, and financial resources used to undertake the project); the *costs* being the monetary value of the inputs;

ii. *outputs*—the direct products of the implementation process arising during the implementation period;

iii. *impacts*, the initial results of the outputs attributable to the intervention which serve to disrupt the causes of the criminal events;

iv. *outcomes*, the consequences of the intervention both during and subsequent to the implementation, the key outcomes being those that relate to the stated objectives of the intervention and the *benefits* being the monetary value of the outcomes attributed to the intervention (Home Office 1999b: 7).

Outcomes are expected to be assessed through research designs that score at the higher end of the Maryland Scale. The narrowness of the specifications for such evaluations mean that they are even less likely to make a contribution to the process of theory testing and theory building that has actually been of great value to criminal policy over the last three or four decades.

A further narrowing of the range of knowledge that is admitted as policy-relevant results from the short timescales of government research. Governments look always for interventions which have immediate results—'a quick real impact' (Home Office 1999a)—or at least yield benefits that fit within the electoral cycle or the reasonably expected term of a minister's office. Research of this sort is inevitably a long way from the sort of evidence that establishes the impact of growing structural socio-economic inequality, and the sense of social injustice which accompanies it, with which we began this chapter and on which many radical criminologists wish to concentrate their attentions. Admittedly the Crime Reduction Programme aimed to combine short-term interventions with long-term work to tackle the causes of crime and it is true that there are references in the Programme to the need to reduce social exclusion (school exclusions and dealing more effectively with domestic violence, for example). However, the real political concerns, and the associated spending, concerned targeting offenders and managing them more effectively. One does not have to be particularly cynical to see the possibility of this leading to more rather than less social exclusion in the form of custodial penalties—a continuation of a trend which has seen the prison population nearly double over the period from 1991–2001 (Morgan and Carlen 1999; Hough *et al.* 2003).

It is for precisely this reason that the work of the RDS is controversial, and the controversy is, if anything, growing rather than diminishing in intensity. There are two principal reasons for this: first, because there has been some tightening in the manner and degree to which the Home Office exerts control over the delivery of its research programme; second, because the field of academic criminology has itself expanded and because academic criminologists are working in a higher education climate in which there is increased pressure to publish so-called original research and gain externally-funded research contracts. Increased Home Office control over the research agenda is the corollary of the party politicization of 'law and order' policy described above. Because governments now commit themselves prior to election to specific 'law and order' programmes, instead of relying on the recommendations of various 'expert' advisory bodies (Royal Commissions, statutory or ad hoc policy standing committees, and so on—see Downes and Morgan 2007) once they had been elected, the content and outcome of criminological research now has greater party political salience. Home Office-funded contracts have generally become: more specific in their content; of shorter duration; subject to closer supervision; covered by stricter rules of confidentiality; and subject to firmer control regarding the use of data and the content and publication of research results. Furthermore, most contracts are now obtained through a tendering and competitive bidding process that places the external researcher in a more subservient position, constantly second-guessing the will of the Home Office policymakers. This represents a tightening of the reins, not a sea change, however. Research for the Home Office was never a liberal experimental playground, not if one wanted to work for the Home Office again. The reason there is increased, and critical, academic awareness of the Home Office reins is that the Home Office budget now looms so large in the consciousness of university-based criminologists under increasing pressure to secure external research funding.

Competitive tendering has now become a way of life for some 'research-active' criminologists. Tender documents are being published, co-operative research consortia are being put together between universities, contracts jockeyed for, bids submitted, agreements signed and fieldwork begun. It is a frantic process only very loosely linked to an academic agenda. Instead it is a political programme of which different sections of the academic criminological fraternity are simultaneously disdainful and calculatingly and opportunistically respectful. There is an increasing list of academic articles that deplore the narrow, technical, evaluative studies funded by the Home Office and berate the increasingly explicit control over the content of publications. And this critical outpouring emanates from centres of learning whose postgraduate students will nevertheless be familiarized by their tutors with the research initiatives pursued by the government, and who may themselves be involved in contract research.

Which is to say that those who wield the critical pens will mostly be involved, indirectly if not directly, in the controversial research enterprise that sustains, as it has always sustained, criminology in the field of higher education. To the extent that criminology is a discipline prostituted to government it is because criminology is indissolubly a normative discipline. Normative because criminology, uniquely among the branches of social science, has as its subject matter and built into its title a social problem—crime. And crime is a category which is politically and not academically determined. No amount of obscurantist language and arcane conceptual recategorization can evade this fundamental nexus.

This reality means that tensions have always existed between principles of openness in publishing research and the political imperative of having a good story to relate. Hope

(2004) provides a telling case study of an evaluation which he conducted as part of the Crime Reduction Programme. His own analysis had suggested that many of the projects under evaluation failed to reduce burglary. The Home Office published a re-analysis which had the effect of turning failure into success, in part by attributing 'anticipatory benefits' to those projects where falls in burglary predated the formal start date (Kodz and Pease 2003). In this case, RDS staff provided methodological rather than political reasons for preferring the more positive analysis and strenuously deny any political intent.[6] In our experience, the process is usually more oblique, and involves modifications to the contractor's analysis rather than its replacement with a preferred alternative.

Often, small trades with the censor can be justified: it makes sense to soften criticism and to describe failure sympathetically if this means that ministers and officials take the report more seriously. Increasingly, however, and probably as a result of RDS being embedded in policy directorates, policy officials display a sense of entitlement to redraft reports submitted by academic contractors when these conflict with their own judgements.

Publication is rarely blocked totally—though one of us has insisted on the non-publication of research too incompetently supervised and completed to warrant publication. More usually, problematic reports are subject to lengthy delays in publication. It is always hard to judge precisely how purposive the delays are. Certainly, when a 'difficult' report hits the desk of an official, it will require more time to reach a decision, and risks lying at the bottom of the pending tray. It probably also requires more consultation— even before the issues are exposed to ministers. When this happens, officials have to devise plausible ways of presenting unwelcome research findings to ministers who may hold the research managers to account for giving rise to the problem in the first place.

The analysis that one of us conducted of reconviction rates for the pilot Drug Treatment and Testing Orders provides an example of the contorted process. Our original one-year reconviction study, submitted to the Home Office in May 2002, yielded high reconviction rates. The Home Office supplied comments, and we redrafted to take account of these. There were then further comments and discussion around methodological and presentational issues. We redrafted again. As the end of the year approached, it seemed sensible to wait for the two-year results. More time was spent on the analysis; this showed still higher two-year reconviction rates, of course; four in five DTTO offenders were reconvicted. Proofs were agreed in June 2003, so that ministers could decide on publication. It was then suggested that it might make sense to repeat the analysis on a different database, as this might produce more reliable results. This took more time to carry out; identical results were presented to the Home Office in August 2003. The results were eventually published in a low-key way later that year (Hough et al. 2003). Each stage of the delay had its own rationality, and it is impossible to say whether delaying tactics were intended. The RDS research managers may have been concerned simply to ensure that the research was of the highest possible standard. And, it should also be said, some of the

---

[6] Nor are we suggesting that RDS staff set out purposefully to undermine difficult findings. The sincerity and good intentions of the team that mounted the re-analysis is not in question. The team, one of whom was an academic consultant to RDS, had doubts about the methodology employed by Hope. The unavoidable fact remains that the Home Office functions in a way that favours positive results and their early publication. In hindsight, it would have made sense for all those involved in the three burglary evaluations to try to resolve the methodological issues *before* any findings were placed in the public domain.

delays were the responsibility of the research team, who had to fit the extra work around other tasks. But the net result was that the Home Office deferred publication of important but embarrassing findings for well over a year.

Much of our discussion of Home Office research has had a critical edge to it. There is, of course, a more nuanced story to tell. We would emphasize the following points.

1. Even were this or any other government to commit itself to the economic policies that might begin to close the socio-economic gulfs that have opened up over the last twenty years, or promote more inclusive social policies, there would nevertheless continue for the forseeable future to be a major crime problem about which the public would continue to demand from their politicians that something be done.

2. Any good government would, in response to these short-term pressures, adopt an evidence-based substantive approach, rather than purely symbolic measures, to placate the public. This would involve targeting those forms of crime, and those criminals most prolifically responsible for it, that most worry the public.

3. Given that no government, in the short term at least, can greatly change those structural factors which motivate people to commit crime, any sensible government must concentrate on those factors which affect the objective opportunity to commit crime (*objective* opportunities which are *subjectively* interpreted as opportunities) and the likelihood of being apprehended and proceeded against by the authorities. Furthermore, any responsible government must approach these issues from a cost-benefit standpoint.

4. The Home Office programme offers a large number of criminologists, working both in-house and out-house, unrivalled apprenticeship opportunities to engage in research which, however narrowly conceived, is nevertheless methodologically rigorous. Moreover, once the Home Office has given its approval to a research project, it is always open to an imaginative and critically minded researcher to view the data collected within a broader theoretical frame of reference; that is, once the ball has been picked up, there are few real limits to the distance one can run with it. If Home Office-funded research projects are limited in their outputs and outcomes (to use the language deployed above) this typically has more to do with self-censorship or the interpretative failure of academic researchers to realize and seize opportunities than any constraints imposed by the Home Office. The catalogue of criminological books, and articles in scholarly criminological journals, incorporating sophisticated theoretical contributions for which funding originally came from the RDS is substantial (it would be invidious to cite particular examples).

5. It can never be stressed too often that those authors who engage in more abstract theorizing about the social construction of crime and the different reactions to it are dependent for most of their insights on the wealth of empirical data that the RDS has largely been responsible for amassing. These data, collected through processes too often derided, are the clay and straw that produce the bricks which both make for an accountable criminal justice system and permit it to be effectively challenged and analysed. Anyone who has spent time engaged in discussions with academic criminologist colleagues from other European jurisdictions—France, Italy, Spain, Greece, for example—will be aware that their critiques are typically theoretically abstract for want of practical

knowledge about how their criminal justice systems operate in practice. That is, their theoretical edifices are often a sign of weakness rather than strength.

We are not suggesting that the Home Office encourages radical critiques: it does not. Or that the Home Office does not attempt to constrain what it regards as unruly or embarrassing prodigies: it does. Ministers, and their civil servant concierges, generally do their best to suppress, temporarily at least, research findings that ruffle policy assumptions or programmes. Most senior criminologists who have undertaken work for the Home Office during their careers, or who have been dependent on the key criminal justice agencies for access to data, have tales to tell of obstruction, attempted suppression, delays in publication, and so on. It is the research equivalent of traffic calming, even if some of the tales have to be taken with a pinch of salt, which is to say that there are often two sides to the stories. Some academic criminology researchers, as the exchanges between researchers in the pages of scholarly journals testify, are not above claiming findings that their data scarcely warrant. However, the truth about most criminological research is that very few pieces of work are either so categorical in their conclusions, or so broad in their implications, that they have the capacity seriously to discomfort ministers and governments. The work of academic research criminologists is for the most part easily swept aside. Furthermore, a good deal of Home Office policymaking is taken in spite of, rather than because of, criminological research findings. In the 1990s the classic case was Mr Howard's claim that 'prison works', with the result of his rhetoric being the substantial rise in prison numbers. More recently, the raft of initiatives for tackling antisocial behaviour have—in contrast to the Crime Reduction Programme—been almost entirely exempted from the requirement to be evidence-based (Morgan 2006).

In conclusion, a few words about the process by which RDS contracts are obtained. Though it is the case that practically all RDS research contracts now have to be bid for by competitive tender, the process by which academic researchers get invited to bid is far from transparent, and there is currently no peer review of, nor academic representation within, the process through which contracts are allocated. Furthermore, the Home Office equivalent of Chinese walls between contractors and contractees invites suspicions rather than confidence. Finally there are issues raised by the emergence of a new set of policy research contractors. Let us take these issues briefly in turn.

First, it seems often to be a matter of chance whether individual academic researchers are informed about a research tender. Speaking from personal experience, we have sometimes heard about a tendering process only after the closing date for bids has passed. On other occasions we have been phoned or emailed by someone within RDS to see if we would be interested in tendering for a particular contract. Under EU regulations, large contracts now have to be advertised. Those that fall below the threshold—which constitute the majority of RDS contracts—are not openly publicized. This seems both unfair and inefficient. One has the impression that to know what research is to take place one must develop an inside track, be in the know, cultivate contacts within RDS.

Second, it is often far from clear why bids are won or lost and how decisions are made. In the past, assessment of proposals was informal and unstructured. The process is now more rigorous, with invitations to tender (ITTs) setting out explicit selection criteria. Each proposal in a tendering competition is scored independently by a panel, and results are fed back to tenderers. The suspicion remains, however, that there is ample room for subjectivity and bias. Practice over pricing is especially problematic. Sometimes the ITT sets out a budgetary range or maximum. Sometimes it gives no guidance at all. Sometimes there are rumours, and sometimes, informal indications of the sum of money in the budget. Thus, when the process is over, one wonders how important the cost of a bid is in the decision to award it. And, sometimes, when one sees the text of a winning bid, one is at a loss to know what it was about the bid that won the day. Unlike the process whereby ESRC grants, and charitable foundation grants, are allocated, there is no independent peer review, unless one judges the researchers employed within the RDS always to be the appropriate peer reviewers, a proposition which stretches credulity. This is less than satisfactory.

Third, as was noted above, there has been a substantial exodus of researchers from RDS to the universities, which peaked in the 1990s. And many of these ex-RDS personnel were among the largest recipients of RDS contracts in the period of the Crime Reduction Programme. The process was—and to some extent remains—not unlike the manner in which senior Treasury and Defence Department civil servants resign their posts only to take up, within a matter of weeks or months, senior banking or defence industry directorships, and begin trading with their former colleagues. Moreover—and we count ourselves among these ranks—if one is well-known to senior RDS personnel, one may be invited to act as a research consultant overseeing the delivery of a contract by a fellow academic, or assessing the quality of competitive bids from the major criminal justice services for initiative development money, and then being invited to bid for the evaluation of those same policy initiatives. This smacks of insider trading and is at odds with the appearance of transparent fairness which the competitive tendering process is designed to convey.

The problem has been largely solved by the passage of time. In part, this is because the exodus of researchers to universities has slowed. And in part several of these researchers have lost their appetite for working with a paymaster that has become increasingly uncongenial. However, the last few years has also seen the emergence of a new breed of policy researcher within the crime field—niche consultancies in the private sector, who have successfully challenged the position of academics as the Home Office's 'contractors of choice' in policy research. The risk here is that the new group of contractors may in time become more dependent on government research money—and thus more biddable—than academics, who can always look to a broader range of funders, such as trusts and funding councils.

Independent research

The Economic and Social Research Council (ESRC)

The ESRC is quantitatively the second most important port of call for the potential criminological researcher and, for those not wishing to engage in policy-related research, by far the most important. Criminology is among the many areas of work that the ESRC covers, though there is no specific allocation of its budget to this topic. Indeed the electronic catalogue of research work it has funded over the years cannot even be interrogated employing this title to see precisely how much criminology research has been funded. The position is roughly as follows.

The ESRC currently has a spending budget of over £140 million, of which approximately one-third is used to fund postgraduate studentships and two-thirds research projects. Though the work of the ESRC is criticized for being increasingly influenced by government policy, with user panels and user interests (industry, the civil service, the principal state services, and major professions) more and more represented in its counsels (Hillyard and Sim 1997), the research themes that the ESRC funds are broad and inclusive:

Economic Performance & Development

Governance and Citizenship

Lifecourse, Lifestyles, and Health

Work and Organization

Environmental and Human Behaviour

Knowledge, Communication, and Learning

Social Stability and Exclusion

(ESRC 2006 and http://www.esrc.ac.uk)

Though it is not clear where *justice* fits in to the ESRC programme—and there is possibly a good case for *Justice* being a theme—it will no doubt be said in the ESRC's defence that justice, like equality and other values, informs, or is capable of informing, several or all of the substantive themes that the Council has set out. Certainly a good deal of criminological work fits within either or both of the Governance and Citizenship and Social Stability and Exclusion themes. What is clear is that over many years a significant number of ESRC studentships and a reasonable part of the research budget has been allocated for work that can broadly be described as criminological. Furthermore, the breadth of this work—both theoretically and empirically—has been far greater than that sponsored by the RDS.

The ESRC disburses money for research through *programmes*—designated and advertised collections of work tied to a dedicated budget for a particular time period—and in *response* to unsolicited applications. Applicants have a statistically better chance of succeeding in getting money by using the response mode than applying through programmes, though it is questionable whether those likelihoods can reasonably be compared. Anyone who has had any involvement in ESRC decision-making—we have acted as peer reviewers on many occasions and one of us has chaired the steering committee for a criminology research programme—knows that solicited applications to programmes and unsolicited applications are *not* of like quality. When the ESRC publicly announces that it invites research applications for a particular programme it is typically inundated with applicants climbing onto the latest bandwagon: a high proportion of applications are from persons with little or no experience in the relevant field advancing poorly thought-out off-the-top-of-the-head plans. By contrast unsolicited applications more typically come from researchers who have thought long and hard about whatever it is they are proposing.

Space precludes a detailed account of projects and programmes currently funded by the ESRC, but below we give some examples of the sort of research, large and small scale, which the Council from time to time supports. ESRC funding decisions indicate the importance the Council attaches to the development of research excellence and methodo-logical rigour as well as the contribution of criminology to contemporary life and policy.

SCoPiC (Social Contexts of Pathways into Crime) is a five-year-long ESRC-funded research network due to be completed in 2007 with a total grant of £2.3 million. At its core are three major empirical projects: the Peterborough Adolescent Development Study directed by Per-Olof Wikström from the Universitiy of Cambridge; a Childhood Study directed by Terri Moffitt from Kings College, London; and the Sheffield Pathways Out of Crime Study directed by Tony Bottoms from the Universities of Cambridge and Sheffield. The SCoPiC network involves other British projects—on Policy and Prevention Analysis (Alex Hirschfield at the University of Huddersfield) and the Cambridge Study of Delinquent Development (David Farrington, University of Cambridge)—plus international collaborations with university-based studies in the USA, Canada, and Switzerland.

Another programme of empirical work, *Pathways into and out of Crime: Risk, Resilience and Diversity*, also approaching some of the issues addressed by SCoPiC but from a different perspective ended in 2006. This programme, with a total grant of £1.4 million is led by Jean Hine of DeMontfort University, Leicester, and involves data collected from 1,000 10–18-year-olds and projects using a variety of approaches:

i.   children who are offending, excluded from school, or who have behaviour problems (Jean Hine, De Montfort and Alan France, Sheffield);

ii. urban Black and Asian culture (Kaye Haw, Nottingham);

iii. family life of children and young people with a parent in prison (Janet Walker, Newcastle);

iv. social capital and its impact on risk, protection and resilience in young people (Hazel Kemshall, De Montfort);

v.   young offenders and substance use (Richard Hammersley, Glasgow Caledonian and Louise Marsland, Essex).

The ESRC has a comprehensive web site from which details about ongoing projects funded by the Council, their organization, data collection methods, and resulting publications are readily obtainable. There is copious advice also on how to apply for grants.

Finally, it is worth emphasizing that criminological research is sometimes co-funded by the ESRC and other funders. For example, the Edinburgh Study of Youth Transitions and Crime, led by David Smith of the University of Edinburgh until 2006, the largest cohort study ever undertaken in Britain from which a wealth of findings is already flow-ing (see www.law.ed.ac.uk/cls/esytc/) was funded by the Scottish Executive, the Nuffield Foundation and the ESRC.

Charitable trusts

Britain is enormously rich in the number of charitable foundations it possesses: many of these foundations fund research and a good many give money for work—either research or initiatives that can be subject to evaluation—on aspects of crime and criminal justice, though most will absolutely *not* fund work which is also being submitted for a postgraduate qualification. Most readers will be familiar with the largest of these foundations—Nuffield, Rowntree, Leverhulme, and so on—but there are a good many others whose names are less familiar but whose identities can be discovered by consulting the *Charities Yearbook*. A relative newcomer is the Big Lottery Fund, previously called the Lotteries Community Fund.

The large independent research funders have become of increasing importance for criminological research, as Home Office research has becoming increasingly tightly tied to Home Office policy. The ESRC operates primarily within an academic framework; if research is of practical value, this is a benefit but by no means a prerequisite. By contrast, the independent funders are typically committed to funding research that will have an impact on policy or practice. The Joseph Rowntree Foundation (JRF) probably exemplifies this most clearly. The research that it commissions is typically published by JRF, and disseminated with energy by JRF communications staff. Funded researchers are also encouraged to present their results to policy officials in government departments, who are also co-opted where possible onto advisory committees. This is in clear contrast to ESRC research. Certainly the ESRC requires researchers to have clear plans for engaging end-users, and for disseminating results, but the onus is on the researcher to make this happen, and there are no resources within the ESRC to support this process. The JRF approach more obviously involves a partnership between funder and researcher in advancing a shared agenda.

Other charitable funders operate in broadly similar ways. For example in 2001 the Esmée Fairbairn Foundation established a large-scale programme, 'Rethinking Crime and Punishment', worth £3 million over three years, which was intended to stimulate innovative alternatives to imprisonment. The funders invested heavily in the coordination of the programme, to make the constituent components cohere as much as possible, and in the dissemination of results (Esmée Fairbairn 2004). The programme director himself played a significant and visible part in promoting the results of the programme. In our experience funding that derives from the National Lottery is managed in a much less interventionist way than the long-established major charities.

The great strength of research funded by charitable trusts is its independence, and the fact that it often covers terrain avoided by government research. Its weaknesses are that funding is usually much more limited than work funded by government or the ESRC, that funding decisions are sometimes idiosyncratic, reflecting the personal interests of trustees, and that the work it supports is necessarily fragmented. Our own experience of funding through the independent sector is, paradoxically, that the impact on policy can sometimes be much greater than work funded by government departments.

Other sources of research funding

Several government departments apart from the Home Office fund research of a criminological or socio-legal character—principally the Department of Health, the Department for Constitutional Affairs, the Youth Justice Board and the Prison Service. There is a growing body of work, admittedly mostly small-scale—funded by regional government and local authorities. At district and county level, many crime and disorder reduction partnerships now fund academics to mount evaluations and crime audits.

Many police forces, most of which have a limited in-house research capacity, also commission pieces of work or actively seek research partners as the corollary of bidding for central government funding for this or that initiative. Needless to say, however, everything said above in relation to the RDS applies also to research undertaken for other branches of the central and local state: if anything more so. This type of research is for the most part narrow and policy-oriented in scope.

European funding is a relatively new and increasingly important source of funding. Securing funds is complex, and usually involves the building of complex multinational partnerships. However, it seems likely that in time it will emerge as being of equal importance to the ESRC as a funder of criminological research. Whilst EU funding will always be designed to be policy-relevant, it is free of the political pressures that characterize government funding.

It is easy to underestimate the potential of non-mainstream sources of funding. Those who have funded us in the past include: the Nuffield Foundation (on several occasions), the Joseph Rowntree Foundation (on several occasions) the Esmée Fairbairn Foundation (on several occasions) the Paul Hamlyn Foundation, the Wates Foundation, the Police Foundation, the Law Society, the Airey Neave Foundation, the Ford Foundation the Mental Health Foundation, the National Lottery; the European Union; the US Department of Justice; the Government Office for London, various local authorities, probation services, and various police forces. It is worth stressing the variety and range of independent funders: if there is to be a healthy criminology in Britain, it is essential that there should be a better balance between government and independent funders.

Conclusion

Direct Home Office spending on criminological research, and increasingly government policy-influenced ESRC research spending, involves several million pounds annually flowing into academic criminology centres. The bulk of this money goes to the major centres that, as a result, are also the principal academic employers of criminological researchers and the major postgraduate training grounds in criminology. There are exceptions to this rule—universities that have substantial postgraduate courses but which attract little or no Home Office money, and *vice versa*—but they are exceptions. The Home Office agenda and budget is the piper that calls many of the dominant tunes played in contemporary criminology.

Given that, directly or indirectly, the state is the principal employer both of criminology and criminologists, it is scarcely surprising that the major expansion of criminology in the 1980s and 1990s has coincided with its partial retreat from the macro issues of social stratification, wealth and income distribution, and social justice to the narrower managerialist concerns of risk assessment (Feeley and Simon 1992), secondary and tertiary crime prevention (Brantingham and Faust 1976), and the cost effectiveness of one form of government intervention compared to another (Jefferson and Shapland 1994). Needless to say—though this is not an issue on which we have focused in this chapter— the power of the state as the provider of funds is even greater when it comes to data access, an issue which is discussed in some detail by other contributors to this volume. The courts, the Crown Prosecution Service, the police, and the Prison Service have always run relatively tight ships when it comes to allowing criminologists permission to set up their anthropologist huts in judges' retiring rooms, prosecutors' filing rooms, custody suites, and prison landings. Furthermore, as we can testify from the inside of Whitehall, the fact that a Government department or agency supports the granting of access to interview sentencers, view files, or observe critical interactions is no guarantee that permission will be forthcoming. The criminal justice system has in recent years become more of a 'system'—more joined up and closely managed—but despite the best efforts of some ministers it is not yet a command economy.

Criminology is called on to assist the processes by which felons might be better identified or individually targeted, risk-assessed, and treated, but there is much less encouragement for projects that consider crime in terms of broader social and economic policy or which examine closely the quality of justice distributed by criminal justice decision-makers. Thus though New Labour appears committed to an evidential approach to 'what works'—a commendable advance on the previous Conservative administration, during the latter years of which a good deal of policy was made in apparent defiance of the research evidence—the question 'what works' is nevertheless asked and required to be answered in individualistic and narrowly conceived terms (see Raynor and Vanstone 2002), if it is asked in criminological terms at all. That is, the question is posed within the parameters of prevailing government policy. This is the research context in which the newly graduating criminologist researcher is likely to undertake his or her first field-work. But there is nothing to inhibit the budding critic or the seasoned campaigner from using the multiplicity of criminological data collected by these means, and attaching them to the broader socio-economic data streams, in order to demonstrate, or suggest, that there is another interpretation or pathway. The great fortune of the British criminologist is that he or she inhabits a domain in which there is more than enough data available for secondary analysis. And there are no access problems to be overcome for this task.

References

BLAIR, T. (2006). Speech made at launch of 'Respect' Programme. http://www. number10.gov.uk/output/Page8898.asp.

BRANTINGHAM, P. J. and FAUST, F. L. (1976). 'A Conceptual Model of Crime Prevention'. *Crime and Delinquency* 22: 130–46.

CARLEN, P. and MORGAN, R. (eds) (1999). *Crime Unlimited? Questions for the New Millennium.* Basingstoke: Macmillan.

CONSERVATIVE PARTY (1979). *The Conservative Manifesto.* London: Conservative Party.

DAVIS, N. (1998). *Dark Heart: The Shocking Truth about Hidden Britain.* London: Vintage.

DORLING, D. (2005). 'Prime Suspect: Murder in Britain' in *Criminal Obsessions: Why Harm Matters More than Crime.* London: Crime and Society Foundation.

DOWNES, D. (1989). 'Only Disconnect: Law and Order, Social Policy and the Community' in M. Bulmer, J. Lewis, and D. Piachaud (eds), *The Goals of Social Policy.* London: Unwin Hyman.

—— and MORGAN. R. (2007). 'No Turning Back: the Politics of Law and Order into the Millennium' in M. Maguire, R. Morgan, and R. Reiner (eds), *The Oxford Handbook of Criminology* (4th edn). Oxford: Oxford University Press.

ESRC (2006). *Summary of Council's Strategic Priorities and Funding Allocations.* Swindon: Economic and Social Research Council.

ESMÉE FAIRBAIRN FOUNDATION (2004). *Rethinking Crime and Punishment: The Report.* London: Esmée Fairbairn Foundation.

FAULKNER, D. (2006). *Crime, State and Citizen: A Field Full of Folk* (2nd edn). Winchester: Waterside.

FEELEY, M. M. and SIMON, J. (1992). 'The New Penology: Notes on the Emerging Strategy of Corrections and its Implications'. *Criminology* 30: 452–74.

GARLAND, D. (2002). 'Of Crimes and Criminals: The Development of Criminology in Britain' in M. Maguire, R. Morgan, and R. Reiner (eds), *The Oxford Handbook of Criminology* (3rd edn). Oxford: Oxford University Press.

GLENNERSTER, H., HILLS, J., PIACHAUD, D., and WEBB, J. (eds) (2005). *One Hundred Years of Poverty and Policy.* York: Joseph Rowntree Foundation.

HILLS, J. (2004). *Inequality and the State.* Oxford: Oxford University Press.

HILLYARD, P. and SIM, J. (1997). 'The Political Economy of Socio-Legal Research' in P. A. Thomas (ed.), *Socio-Legal Studies.* Aldershot: Dartmoth.

HOME OFFICE (*Morgan Report*) (1991). *Safer Communities: The Local Delivery of Crime Prevention through the Partnership Approach.* London: Home Office.

—— (1999a). *Reducing Crime and Tackling its Causes: A Briefing Note on the Crime Reduction Programme.* London: Home Office.

—— (1999b). *Crime Reduction Programme: Analysis of Costs and Benefits—Guidance*

for Evaluators. Research Development and Statistics Directorate. London: Home Office.

—— (2006). RESPECT Action Plan. London: Home Office.

HONDERICH, T. (1990). *Conservatism.* London: Hamish Hamilton.

HOPE, T. (2004). 'Pretend it works: Evidence and Governance in the Evaluation of the Reducing Burglary Initiative'. *Criminal Justice* 4: 287–308.

—— (2005). 'Pretend it Doesn't Work: the "Anti-Social" Bias in the Maryland Scientific Methods Scale'. *European Journal on Criminal Policy and Research* 11: 275–96.

HOUGH, M. (2004). 'Modernisation, Scientific Rationalism and the Crime Reduction Programme'. *Criminal Justice* 4: 239–53.

—— HEDDERMAN, C., and HAMILTON-SMITH, N. (2004). 'The Design and the Development of the Reducing Burglary Initiative' in N. Hamilton-Smith (ed.), *The Reducing Burglary Initiative: Design, Development and Delivery.* Home Office Research Study No 287. London: Home Office.

—— JACOBSON, J., and MILLIE, A. (2003). *The Decision to Imprison: Sentencing & The Prison Population.* London: Prison Reform Trust.

—— CLANCY, A., TURNBULL, P. J., and McSWEENEY, T. (2003). The Impact of Drug Treatment and Testing Orders on Offending: Two-year Reconviction Results. Findings 184. London: Home Office.

HUGHES, G. (1998). *Understanding Crime Prevention: Social Control, Risk and Late Modernity.* Buckingham: Open University Press.

HUTTON, J. (2005). *Public Service Reform: The Key to Social Justice.* London: Social Market Foundation.

HUTTON, W. (1996). *The State We're In.* London: Vintage.

Jefferson, T. and Shapland, J. (1994). 'Criminal Justice and the Production of Order and Control: Criminological Research in the UK in the 1980s'. *British Journal of Criminology* 34: 265–90.

Jones, T. and Newburn, T. (1998). *Private Security and Public Policing*. Oxford: Clarendon.

Kodz, J. and Pease, K. (2003). Reducing Burglary Initiative: Early Findings on Burglary Reduction. Home Office Research Findings 204. London: Home Office.

Labour Party (1997). *New Labour—Because Britain Deserves Better*. London: Labour Party.

—— (2005). *Britain—Forward not Back: the Labour Party Manifesto 2005*. London: Labour Party.

Maguire, M. (2004). 'The Crime Reduction Programme: Reflections on the Vision and the Reality'. *Criminal Justice* 4: 213–38.

—— (2007). 'Criminal Statistics' in M. Maguire, R. Morgan, and R. Reiner (eds), *The Oxford Handbook of Criminology* (4th edn). Oxford: Oxford University Press.

—— Morgan, R., and Reiner, R. (eds) (1994). *The Oxford Handbook of Criminology* (1st edn). Oxford: Oxford University Press.

Morgan, R. (2006). 'With Respect to Order, the Rules of the Game have not Changed: New Labour's Dominance of the "Law and Order" Agenda', in T. Newburn and P. Rock (eds), *The Politics of Crime Control: Essays in Honour of David Downes*. Oxford: Oxford University Press.

—— (2000). 'The Politics of Criminological Research' in R. D. King and E. Wincup (eds), *Doing Research on Crime and Justice*. Oxford: Oxford University Press.

—— and Carlen, P. (1999). 'Regulating Crime Control' in P. Carlen and R. Morgan (eds), *Crime Unlimited? Questions for the 21st Century*. Basingstoke: Macmillan.

Parkin, F. (1967). 'Working Class Conservatives: A Theory of Political Deviance'. *British Journal of Sociology* 18: 278–90.

Raynor, P. and Vanstone, M. (2002). *Understanding Community Penalties: Probation, Policy and Social Change*. Buckingham: Open University Press.

Sherman, L., Gottfredson, D., MacKenzie, D., Eck, J., Reuter, P., and Bushway, S. (1997). *Preventing Crime: What Works, What Doesn't, What's Promising: a Report to the United States Congress*. Available at: http\\www.ncjrs.org.

Walker, A., Kershaw, C., and Nicholas, S. (2006). *Crime in England and Wales 2005/2006*. Home Office Research Bulletin 12/06. London: Home Office.

Young, J. (1998). 'From Inclusive to Exclusive Society: Nightmares in the European Dream' in V. Ruggiero, N. South, and I. Taylor (eds), *The New European Criminology: Crime and Social Order in Europe*. London: Routledge.

PART II

THEORY, DATA, AND TYPES OF CRIMINOLOGICAL RESEARCH

3

The relationship between theory and empirical observations in criminology

Anthony Bottoms

Theory is never completely isolated from problems of empirical research, any more than empirical research is free from theoretical assumptions. The really interesting questions concern the nature of the relations between theory and empirical research and not whether either domain has some divinely given priority (Layder 1994: vi).

Introduction

When I was preparing the equivalent chapter to this one for the first edition of this book, an experienced empirically-oriented criminologist sent me a message of encouragement. He hoped that I could provide a framework that would help and support the next generation of scholars, because:

Far too many of my graduate students over the years have had difficulty in reaching for a theoretical perspective with which they could make sense of what they have done after the event, let alone guide them before or during the research process.

I warm to some of the phraseology of that message. There is the suggestion of theory 'guiding [a person] before or during the research process', or, at worst, of helping that person to 'make sense of what they have done after the event'. The implicit image is that of a *continuing dialogue* between theory and empirical observations. That image of continuing dialogue will become a central theme of this chapter as it develops.

But we should not downplay the darker side of my friend's message. In his comment, there is an undertone of *struggle*. We can almost hear one of his former graduate students saying: 'I know I have to collect data, and I know there are these theoretical perspectives that are relevant, but I'm finding real difficulty in putting theory and data together in a coherent way'. As many former graduate students would attest, that sense of struggle is indeed often a real feature of the research process, and one of the main aims of this chapter is to provide a kind of compass that might help graduate researchers to navigate what can sometimes seem like rough waters.

So let us begin right at the beginning. The object of any kind of empirically-based science (including social science, and therefore including criminology) is to *generate knowledge*. At a philosophical level, the process of generating knowledge requires first, some understanding of the nature of knowledge; and second, some understanding of the methods or processes by which genuine knowledge (as opposed to false knowledge) can be developed. In more technical language, the generation of knowledge therefore ultimately rests on philosophical foundations in the fields of *epistemology* (the philosophy of the nature of knowledge) and *methodology* (the philosophy of scientific method). In the particular case of the human or social sciences, a further complication is that scholars sometimes disagree on the nature of the human condition—on, for example, whether human beings do or do not have 'free will', or on the extent to which human beings can be seen as rational actors. These are disagreements within a third philosophical subfield, that of *ontology* (the philosophy of the nature of being).[1] Alert readers will already have correctly inferred from these initial remarks that the topic of this chapter—'the relationship between theory and empirical observations in criminology' necessarily raises complex, and sometimes strongly contested, issues in epistemology, ontology, and methodology. It is well beyond my brief to delve deeply into these philosophical questions here, but for those who are intrigued, an excellent introduction to the issues—and one that is scrupulously fair to those holding differing perspectives—will be found in the late Martin Hollis's *The Philosophy of Social Science* (2002).

These initial comments already, however, alert us to a potential problem about the word 'theory'. A 'theory' can be a theory of anything. Thus, for example, there are competing theories in the field of epistemology about what constitutes 'truth', and competing ontological theories about the nature of humankind. At a very different level, there are competing theories in criminology about the causes of juvenile delinquency (a substantive rather than an epistemological or ontological issue). When we encounter the word 'theory', we will need to be clear whether the theory in question is, for example, an epistemological, an ontological, a methodological, or a substantive theory, or whether perhaps it contains elements of more than one of these.

After these ground-clearing definitions, I now move to the substance of this chapter by offering two Key Propositions, upon which the remainder of the chapter is founded. Key Proposition I (KPI) holds that, whether one likes it or not (and some do not like it much), some engagement with theory is inevitable if one is to practise social science (including criminology) at all. Neither the natural nor the social worlds can be neutrally observed and reported upon by the research analyst, for we always approach all our empirical observations through some kind of theoretical understandings. (This is known as the 'theory-ladenness' of observations: Honderich 2005: 914). As the philosopher Karl Popper (1968: 107n) famously put it: 'observations ... are always *interpretations* of the facts observed; they are *interpretations in the light of theories*' (emphasis in original). To demonstrate this point, Popper, when teaching, sometimes simply asked his lecture audience to 'Observe'. The students, of course, invariably replied: 'But *what* shall we observe?', thus making Popper's point for him (see Magee 1973: 33). At a slightly more complex level, one can also

---

[1] Ontology covers a much wider field than the particular issues highlighted here—for example, debates about what distinguishes concrete from abstract entities, and whether abstract entities exist. But for the social sciences, the ontology of the human condition is the central issue.

note that the theory that we bring to an observation can significantly affect what we see. As the *Oxford Companion to Philosophy* nicely puts it, 'with the appropriate knowledge base, we see the Old Bailey as a criminal court rather than as a building inhabited by oddly garbed humans engaged in hectoring and wheedling' (Honderich 2005: 914–15).

But while KPI asserts that criminologists cannot avoid theory, Key Proposition II (KPII) asserts that there is indeed a real world, and that criminologists cannot avoid engagement with that world, whether they like it or not (and some do not like it much). The implication of KPI is that we always see the world only through a set of theoretical spectacles which can be called *interpretations* or *constructions*; and this has given rise to a social science approach called 'constructivism' which—up to a point, quite rightly—emphasizes the need to examine carefully the constructions or interpretations that social actors, including social scientists, bring to their observations of the natural and social world. It is not hard to see, however, that if taken to extremes constructivism quickly runs into difficulties. Since all observations are, admittedly, 'constructions', some have argued that *empirical research findings are therefore always simply another 'construction', with no particular claim to validity.* Some constructivists have themselves not flinched from spelling out the implications of this view:

[Data] derived from constructivist inquiry have neither special status nor legitimation; they represent simply another construction to be taken into account (Guba and Lincoln 1989: 45).

A position of this kind is one that constitutes, in epistemological terms, full-blown *relativism*; that is to say, it maintains that 'there is no such thing as objective knowledge of realities independent of the knower' (Flew 1979: 281).[2] By contrast, the main contemporary philosophical competitor to relativism is *realism*, the view that there do indeed exist realities (from stars to kitchen tables to police stations) that exist independently of the knower, even though the knower can only approach these realities in a theory-laden manner.

If one adopts full-blown epistemological relativism, there is ultimately no point in doing social science (or indeed natural science) at all. That is because, from a fully relativist standpoint, we can never say that Theoretical Account A gives a truer picture than Theoretical Account B of (say) how interrogations are conducted in a given police station: all we can say is that Theorist A is offering one account, and Theorist B another.

In contradistinction to relativism, KPII is realist; it holds that there is a real world available for observation, and that we can observe it with greater or less accuracy. Although we can never make observations except through one or another pair of theoretical spectacles ('interpretations') that does not mean that we can never judge which of two interpretations is nearer the truth. To illustrate this point, let us take a famous (if now somewhat dated) example from the British criminological literature. In the early 1980s the county of Nottinghamshire had, according to police-recorded crime data, a very high crime rate, notwithstanding that it is not one of Britain's major metropolitan areas. David Farrington and Elizabeth-Ann Dowds (1985) set out to investigate whether Nottinghamshire was indeed an exceptionally criminal county. To do this, they took two comparison areas (both, like Nottinghamshire, non-metropolitan counties in the Midlands), and then carried out a victimization survey of the general population in all three areas, together

---

[2] I use the phrase 'full-blown relativism' because a variety of different forms of relativism can be delineated: see, further, Hollis (2002: ch. 11).

with careful analyses of the crime-recording practices of the separate police forces for the three areas. The researchers' conclusions were, in a nutshell: *first*, that the incidence of crime in Nottinghamshire was indeed somewhat higher than that in the other two counties, but not so much higher as the officially-recorded crime figures would lead one to believe; and *second*, that various aspects of police recording practices in Nottinghamshire had led to a higher official recording of criminal incidents than was the case in the other two counties. Farrington and Dowds's research methods, in this study, were rigorous enough to persuade criminologists from a variety of different theoretical orientations that the conclusions of the study were, broadly, to be trusted; or, in other words, that the account the researchers had provided of crime levels in Nottinghamshire and the two comparison counties was much nearer to the truth than was the apparent message of the officially-recorded crime figures. That did not mean that Farrington and Dowds's research data were in all respects 100 per cent accurate (survey data, for example, never are because they are estimates of patterns in the general population); and certainly their data were not based on theory-neutral observations. But the research design, and the researchers' subsequent implementation of that design, was sufficiently strong to suggest to all knowledgeable observers that the research results were convincing.

If (as I contend) both KPI and KPII are true, then three things follow. First, anyone attempting empirical research in criminology must inevitably grapple to some degree with the theory/data relationship, because there are no theory-neutral facts, and theory is therefore inextricably involved in the process of data-gathering and data-interpretation. But second, anyone attempting to write theoretical criminology must also grapple with the theory/data relationship (even if their preference is to analyse the relevance for criminology of the so-called 'general social theorists'—Foucault, Habermas, Bourdieu, Giddens, etc.). This is because there is a real world that is available for observation and interpretation, and a very important test (though not the only test) of any theoretical account will be whether it interprets that real world more accurately and convincingly than do other theoretical accounts—for which purpose, the results of empirical research will have to be taken into account by the theorist. Indeed, as Derek Layder (1998: 94) has challengingly argued, 'all theory is connected with the empirical world (although variably in terms of level of abstraction), *otherwise it would not qualify as "social theory" in the first place*' (emphasis added). Third, it is important to realize that acceptance of KPII necessarily entails that there is a genuine possibility of cumulation of knowledge in criminology. I recognize that such a claim is contentious; but if there is a real world that is (to an extent) knowable independently of the knower, then it must be possible through careful empirical research and insightful theorization gradually to understand more about that world. Personally, I have no difficulty whatever in accepting the claim that knowledge can be cumulative, because in the course of my own professional career huge advances have been made in criminological knowledge—for example, in the fields of understanding official crime statistics, criminal careers, repeat victimization, and policing studies. Further advances in knowledge in these and other fields will certainly follow.

The propositions that I have just enunciated might seem rather daunting to the graduate student, because their implication is that all aspiring criminologists need to grapple to some degree with the theory/data relationship. Is this *really* necessary? After all, some people are good at theory, but dislike 'getting their hands dirty' with empirical research; while others feel comfortable with multivariate statistical analyses, or with ethnography, but don't claim to understand theory very well. Shouldn't we allow a pragmatic division of labour?

Whatever might be ideally desirable, a pragmatic division of labour will of course always occur, because life is short and there is simply not time for all scholars to master all aspects of a subject matter as diverse and complex as that covered by criminology. But that necessary pragmatism has its limits. In the interests of science, theorists cannot be allowed to think that accurate data are unimportant, and data analysts cannot be allowed to think that theory is unimportant. And—let us be quite straightforward about this— taking both theory and data seriously is a tough assignment. But there is good news at hand for the new generation of criminologists. In my judgement, substantial progress has been made by social scientists in the last twenty years in conceptualizing the theory/data relationship. There are, therefore, some surer guiding lights available to the present generation of graduate students than existed for their predecessors; and it will, in part, be the task of the remainder of this chapter to draw attention to some of these.

As an encouragement to creative theorization, I would like to add one further introductory point. Once one really grasps that there are no theory-neutral facts, then virtually no issue is so trivial as to be without the potential for fruitful theoretical reflection if one approaches it aright. To take a personal example from the field of prison studies, when I was myself conducting extensive fieldwork in a borstal institution in my first research project (see Bottoms and McClintock 1973) I can recall being bored by some of the minutiae of the institutional regime that were fairly frequently debated in the meetings of borstal staff that I attended as a research observer. Such details, I then thought, were important for the borstal staff, but not for the criminological researcher, who must concentrate on more substantively important things (the treatment programme being offered, how inmates responded to this programme, and so on). Ironically, however, as I shall briefly describe later in this chapter, some of my more recent work in the field of prison studies (Sparks, Bottoms, and Hay 1996) emphasizes the huge importance, for a theoretical understanding of prisons as institutions, of the minutiae of everyday prison routines.

The remainder of this chapter is divided into five main parts. An initial section sketches briefly some of the obstacles faced by any criminologist wanting to treat the theory/data relationship seriously. This is followed, secondly, by a discussion of some of the differing ways that various kinds of criminologists have, historically, conceptualized this relationship. The next two sections focus on aspects of contemporary understandings of some central problems involved in thinking about the theory/data relationship. Finally, I offer a case example that illustrates some of the key topics discussed in the chapter; this example focuses on developments over time in the so-called 'age-graded social control theory' of American criminologists, John Laub and Robert Sampson.

Common obstacles

Since this book is intended to be a user-friendly volume, before I launch into the more strictly academic sections of this chapter it might be helpful to begin with some pragmatic observations. For the truth is that, however much lip-service is paid to the importance of the theory/data relationship, there are also powerful forces working against younger researchers as they try to develop their own understandings of the interconnections between theory and data, and to develop the skills necessary to handle these interconnections. I shall briefly deal with five of these common obstacles in this section.

Disciplinary specialization

The first obstacle is that, naturally enough, younger researchers wish to make their way in the world. And all too often, it seems, successful academic careers are based on narrow specialization—or at any rate, to get one's first permanent academic job one needs to present oneself as a specialist of a particular kind (for example, a theorist, or a quantitative researcher used to handling large datasets). These pressures can certainly militate against the development of a rounded understanding of theory/data relationships.

Discouragement of theory by 'practical people'

The second obstacle is perhaps a particular problem in the sphere of criminology. University colleagues from other academic specialisms are frequently surprised when I tell them that I give more papers to non-academic audiences than I do to specialist academic seminars or conferences; but, in the nature of the case, a whole host of non-academic people are potentially interested in what criminologists have to say (politicians, Home Office officials, judges, magistrates, police, prison staff, probation officers, victims, crime prevention panels, journalists ... the list is endless). And there is undoubtedly, in many instances, an impatience with theory from those wanting simply to 'get on with the job' of reducing crime, or of running the criminal justice system. This impatience can sometimes manifest itself in two rather different ways. The first—not without some justification in the case of some theorists—is exasperation at the complex language sometimes employed by theoreticians, who may seem to the lay person to be spinning complex webs of words that really mean very little.[3] The second form of impatience is that when the theorist tries to 'boil down' what he/she is trying to say in an accessible form, this may be hailed by the lay audience as 'a statement of the obvious'. Faced with such a 'double whammy', it is important not to lose one's nerve. The point is this: if social theory is to illuminate the social world, then it ultimately *has to* 'make sense' to people who inhabit that world (or at any rate, to those who inhabit that world and have their wits about them); for if it does not, then the theory is failing in its task of explanation. But once a theoretical issue is grasped by a lay person, it can indeed seem 'obvious', precisely because it does help to make sense of the lived world as experienced by that person. To avoid charges of 'stating the obvious' (and for other reasons both more and less reputable), theorists have therefore been prone to take refuge in their own special languages. To an extent, that is necessary in order to be precise in one's theorization; but it can certainly also make theory seem inaccessible to the practical person.

There are no easy solutions to these difficulties, though obviously theorists should be encouraged to state their theories as clearly and as parsimoniously as possible. I would,

---

[3] Indeed, scholars sometimes make similar complaints—see, for example, Peter Hedström's (2005: 4) criticism of Bourdieu's definition of *habitus*, which he considers to be a 'mystifying statement'.

however, like to share some optimistic (though admittedly anecdotal) experiences from the recent past. During the last decade, I have been engaged in the advanced academic training of manager-grade officials in the police, prison, and probation services. When I have introduced to such groups topics such as late modernity theory as applied to criminology, or the relevance of theories of legitimacy to an understanding of the work of the police service, there has been widespread interest—and certainly more interest than such topics would normally evoke from, say, Home Office officials. The reason for this contrast, I believe, is that many Home Office officials are apt to understand the world in terms of a set of discrete analytical problems to be solved; hence, a given problem can, to an extent at least, be analysed in isolation from its wider context. By contrast, a senior manager in command of, say, a police division or a prison inevitably realizes that there are many *interconnections* between different parts of the complex world that he/she is supposed to 'manage'. He/she would like to have some fuller understanding of these interconnections, and that is precisely what theoretical frameworks, when adequately understood and internalized, can begin to provide.

Pigeonholing

The third obstacle to sophisticated criminological work embracing both theory and empirical data is what I shall call 'pigeonholing'. There are two versions of this— 'methodological pigeonholing' and 'theoretical pigeonholing'.

By 'methodological pigeonholing', I mean the tendency to assume that certain sorts of research method 'go with' particular kinds of theoretical approach, to the exclusion of other kinds of data. So, for example, ethnographic research studies naturally use research methods of a qualitative kind, such as participant and non-participant observation, extended interviews, and so on. From within this research perspective, it is not too hard to develop the view that quantitative data are at best irrelevant, or at worst potentially misleading because they fail adequately to reflect the real meanings of social life in a given milieu. But this is unhelpful pigeonholing. In fact there is no reason at all why a primarily ethnographic study should not be assisted by quantitative data. For example, two colleagues and I pursued a qualitative sociological study of the nature of social order in two maximum security prisons (Sparks, Bottoms, and Hay 1996). There was reason to suspect, from observational and interview data in one of the prisons (which ran a deliberately 'relaxed' regime for principled reasons), that the degree of freedom afforded to the prisoners, while it had important advantages, also facilitated behaviour such as the easy formation of gangs and cliques, and the possibility of 'hidden' violence to certain inmates, carried out in one of the rather large number of poorly-supervised locations in the prison. Collection of quantitative data about recorded major incidents in the prison, about the frequency of use of alarm bells, and about head injuries treated in the prison hospital all tended to confirm the picture originally derived from qualitative sources (see Sparks, Bottoms, and Hay 1996: ch. 7).[4]

In my view, the mental barriers that some qualitative researchers have set up against the use of quantitative data, and the equivalent barriers set up by some quantitative

---

[4] An example in the reverse direction—qualitative data helpfully complementing quantitative—is given in the final section of this chapter.

researchers against qualitative research data, have been some of the most unhelpful features of the British criminological landscape in the last quarter-century. There are some signs that these barriers are now being overcome; for the future health of the subject, let us hope so, since there is no justifiable reason for them.

I need say less about 'theoretical pigeonholing', by which I mean attitudes of a kind which assert or believe, explicitly or implicitly, that because a particular person adheres to a theoretical standpoint other than one's own, his/her writings necessarily contain little of interest. (We have all heard, in casual conversations with other academics, statements of the kind that since X or Y is a 'positivist'/'cultural criminologist'/etc., he/she has nothing useful to say.) One might have hoped that criminologists knew enough about the unintended effects of labelling to avoid this kind of pigeonholing, but sadly this has not always been the case. I shall have more to say about this in the next subsection, on synthesizing.

Eclecticism and synthesis

A fourth obstacle to a creative and constructive relationship between theory and empirical research comes from a confusion between eclecticism and synthesis. The confusion is usually implicit rather than explicit, but it is nevertheless very important in obstructing progress.

Theories in criminology are often rather partial in their coverage: we cannot, for example, seriously expect 'labelling theory' or 'strain theory' to explain all criminality, even though in certain specific circumstances such theories might have much to offer. This limited coverage of particular theories would not matter in the least if, in criminology, there were a widespread 'culture of openness'—that is, a culture of being open to the insights offered by many theories, and being willing to consider their possible contribution to social-scientific explanation within a particular set of circumstances. Unfortunately, criminologists have not always advocated or upheld such a culture, and at least in the past there have been some unhelpful 'turf wars' between adherents of certain different theories, in which on occasion the participants have seemed more eager to score points off one another than patiently to try to explain the social phenomena under investigation.

The culture of openness advocated here could and should lead to a process of theoretical *synthesis*, that is, 'the composition or combination of parts or elements so as to form a whole' (first definition of 'synthesis' in *Longman's Dictionary of the English Language*). But good synthesis is difficult. What is much easier is a somewhat unthinking *eclecticism*. Flew's (1979) *Dictionary of Philosophy* defines eclecticism as 'the principle or practice of taking one's views from a variety of philosophical and other sources', sometimes in ways 'that make no strenuous effort to create intellectual harmony between discrete elements' (p. 24). So defined, eclecticism is clearly different (and much more pragmatic than) synthesis, and some eclectic approaches are indeed intellectually disreputable because they do not seriously attempt 'to create intellectual harmony between discrete elements'. Sadly, this justified suspicion of eclecticism has too often led to an unthinking rejection of synthezising approaches.

I remain an unrepentant advocate of serious attempts at synthesis, for the reasons that I gave in a 1993 paper (Bottoms 1993: 59):

Scholars from many different intellectual traditions and nationalities have struggled with the explanation of crime; much of what they have written may now be seen as ephemeral or mistaken, but many have left valuable insights of one kind or another. Each of us, as St. Paul put it in another context, tends to 'see through a glass, darkly' (I Corinthians xiii, 12): it would be surprising, therefore, if only one of us (or one particular school) had grasped the whole truth, and it would accordingly seem appropriate to seek to synthesise the valuable findings and insights of various scholars, even those of very different disciplinary backgrounds, or of different political persuasions from our own. As Anthony Giddens (1984: xxii) puts it, if ideas or data seem 'important and illuminating, what matters much more than their origin is to be able to sharpen them so as to demonstrate their usefulness, even if within a framework which might be quite different from that which helped to engender them'.

It is worth noting that in the passage quoted above, Giddens speaks of *ideas or data* that seem important and illuminating. A good synthesis seeks to weld theory and data together in an ongoing cumulative search for the truth. That is a task of a very high order; I shall discuss possible procedures for this task in a later section of this essay.

The problem of conceptual hegemony

Even if methodological and theoretical pigeonholing is avoided, and even if a research worker is in principle happy to work towards synthesis, there remains a further obstacle that may impede the optimum development of the relationship between theory and research. I shall call this obstacle 'the problem of conceptual hegemony'.

I shall illustrate this problem from experience during a research project carried out in the 1990s. Colleagues and I were commissioned by the Home Office to carry out a literature review on whether, and if so in what circumstances, more severe sentences deter crime. As part of our report, we wrote a section that attempted a thorough conceptual analysis of policies of general deterrence, i.e. any intendedly deterrent policy that aims to reduce future offending among the public at large through fear of the possible consequences (von Hirsch *et al.* 1999, s 3). Within that analysis, we emphasized that deterrence, based as it is on individuals' prudential calculation as the motive for avoiding a given action, is a *subjective concept*;[5] and we then set out five conditions that we argued are *stipulative* (i.e. logically necessary) for the successful achievement of marginal general deterrence in an individual case. [To give a flavour, the first of these five conditions was that where an intendedly general deterrent policy has been freshly introduced, 'a potential offender must realise that the probability of conviction or the severity of punishment has changed'].

Some of the most sophisticated recent studies of general deterrence have been conducted by econometricians. Econometricians work with aggregate data, and, as we pointed out in our report:

general deterrence, as a policy aim, is designed to produce an *aggregate* crime-preventive effect . . . Thus a net deterrent effect may be achievable even if only a portion of the intended

---

[5] To be more precise:

Criminal deterrence (being concerned with fear of penal consequences) is subjective in two senses. First, it depends not on what the certainty and severity of punishment actually are but on what potential offenders *believe* that they are . . . Second, criminal deterrence depends not only on what potential offenders believe the sanction risks to be, but on how they evaluate those risks in terms of their subjective disutilities (von Hirsch *et al.* 1999: 6, emphasis in original).

audience alters its behaviour through fear of the consequences—provided that the effect on this group suffices to reduce the offence rate, and provided also that there are no substantial countervailing effects (von Hirsch *et al.* 1999: 6).

We asked an econometrician friend to look at our draft report. He had no difficulty with our emphasis on aggregate effects, but he could see no purpose in the stress on the subjective character of deterrence. His intellectual training was to work in a certain way, using certain models and approaches: to him, therefore, studying deterrence was a question of looking for aggregate effects. Without being in any way hostile to other approaches to the subject, he initially could not see the point of them. He certainly did not expect us to reply, as we did, that in our view the subjective character of general deterrence was ultimately more fundamental for the research analyst than is the fact that general deterrence policies are designed to produce aggregate effects (see, generally, von Hirsch *et al.* 1999).

Our econometrician colleague was not alone. All of us, as researchers, have our preconceptions and preoccupations that can produce conceptual hegemonies, and corresponding blind spots. That is why the early exposure to others of one's preliminary research findings and tentative theorizing, in a non-threatening atmosphere, can often be so very beneficial to the constructive development of research.

Lessons from the past

In this section, I shall attempt—necessarily very briefly and perhaps therefore a little crudely—to sketch how, historically, some kinds of criminologist have dealt with the theory/data relationship. (Necessarily, only a few groups can be included, so this is an incomplete taxonomy). From this rapid survey, some helpful leads for the creative linking of theory and data can, I think, be developed. At appropriate points, I shall also indicate how different kinds of criminologist have made different kinds of epistemological, ontological, or methodological assumptions, thus linking this discussion back to the introduction to this chapter.

Classicism

Classicism is, perhaps, the earliest kind of criminology that is still seriously read as a potential contribution to contemporary debates. The most celebrated classicist authors are Cesare Beccaria and Jeremy Bentham, as between whom there are many similarities, but also important differences (see Hart 1982). Classicists were essentially political theorists, writing about the principles that should govern how crime is to be dealt with by the State (on classicism, see, for example, Radzinowicz 1966: ch.1). There is thus, within classicism, an important reminder that 'crime', as a concept, is not simply descriptive of a certain kind of human behaviour (as is, for example, the concept of 'running'). Rather, by defining a given behaviour as a 'crime', a society attaches to that behaviour an important element of *societal censure* (see Sumner 1990); and the acts that are censured in this way can and do vary from society to society, and in any one society over time. Thus, crime is ultimately a *normative category*, and significant debates can be, and need to be, generated in any given society not only about what kinds of conduct ought to be defined as 'criminal' (the content of the criminal law); but also about the processes by which alleged crimes ought to be investigated and proved (criminal procedure) and, if proved, punished (penology). Classicists excelled at this kind of normative theorization, but they also sometimes made empirical assertions, some (though by no means all) of which were later shown to be false. These empirical assertions were not based on any kind of systematic research, but rather upon common-sense observations and armchair reflections. Thus, classicists' understanding of the relationship between theory and data was by modern standards seriously deficient, because they carried out no empirical research. But their emphasis upon normative theorization is something to which contemporary criminology could very usefully return (see further below).

Natural-science-based positivism

In the second half of the nineteenth century, the successes of natural science and engineering were everywhere apparent (from Darwin to the railway network, audacious bridge-building, and advances in medical science). Not surprisingly, bold pioneers in psychology, psychiatry, and sociology sought to apply the natural-scientific approach to the study of human behaviour. At that date, 'the natural-scientific approach' was defined as including a strong emphasis on *observations*; the assumption that observations could be made directly (i.e. facts were regarded as *theory-neutral*); a *neutral* and *dispassionate* approach on the part of the scientist; and an assumption that *causal laws* of behaviour could be discovered (in short, *positivism*). In what was to become a very famous aphorism, contrasting the positivists with their classicist predecessors, it was declared that 'the classical school bade men study justice, but the positivists bade justice study men' (see Radzinowicz 1999: 19). In other words, the positivists insisted that the classicists' armchair theorization would no longer serve. Criminologists must get out into the world, and study criminals, criminal areas, and criminal justice scientifically; and policy-makers must then take serious account of what the criminologists had found.

When I began to study criminology in the early 1960s, the specific theories of Cesare Lombroso (the first major criminological positivist) were long since discredited, but Lombroso was still widely revered as the founder of criminological positivism, described as the 'scientific approach' to criminology, and then the dominant paradigm in the field. Many of the approaches to the study of criminology that have developed since the late 1960s have been a reaction of one sort or another to positivism; and, since that is the case, it is worth spelling out in some detail here the main assumptions of the positivist approach. These can be characterized as follows:

1. It was assumed that the methods of natural science could and should be unproblematically applied to the social world (while making allowance, of course, for the fact that the context was empirically different). Since such methods were taken to include assumptions of determinist causation, it was assumed that human behaviour should be studied within a determinist framework.

2. It was assumed that the foundation of all science, natural and social, was 'sense-data', i.e. facts that could be observed with our senses. Such sense-data were assumed to be

directly accessible to the scientific observer, who would report on them dispassionately. Thus, the bedrock of science was theory-neutral facts, carefully collected by the scientist. These foundations to knowledge ('real facts') were seen as much surer than the 'metaphysical speculations' of the classicists.

3. It was assumed that there was a sharp distinction between 'facts' and 'values'. The former were open to scientific observation and verification; the latter were not, but were instead dependent upon 'taste' or personal preferences. Indeed, in philosophical circles influenced by scientific positivism it was in the 1950s and early 1960s quite a commonly held view that rational discussion about substantive normative principles was impossible.[6] Together with the emphasis on empirical observation (see above), all this represented a complete break with the assumptions of the classicists (whose work was therefore sometimes characterised, in derogatory tone, as 'pre-scientific').

4. Positivism had an admitted difficulty with the concept of 'crime', given that what was 'criminal' in a given society was defined by those in power, and that societies differed, sometimes markedly, in what kinds of behaviour they defined as 'crimes'. All this seemed to be very far from the stable and 'natural' *explanandum* (phenomenon to be explained) apparently required for a fully 'natural-scientific' criminology. This important difficulty was usually evaded by positivists through an intellectual fudge to the effect that only some kinds of crimes (murder, theft, etc.) constituted the core subject-matter of criminology, and that these were the 'natural crimes', in contradistinction to other kinds of 'administrative' crimes.

5. Because of its desire to follow as closely as possible the methods of the natural sciences, positivist criminology that focused on the explanation of criminal behaviour was and is primarily concerned 'with how accurate facts can be obtained and how theory can thereby be more rigorously tested' (Glaser and Strauss 1967: 1). That is to say, the ideal research method was seen as an initial collection of facts, the formulation—by logical processes—of a theory in the shape of a formal hypothesis, and then the rigorous testing of that hypothesis, to verify or falsify it. If a modified hypothesis then seemed necessary in the light of the results of the first testing, then that hypothesis (Hypothesis B) was formulated and formally tested—and so on. This is a process that has been aptly described as the *hypothetico-deductive* method, and I shall have more to say about it in the next main section of this chapter.

6. Not all criminological research, of course, is concerned with the explanation of criminal behaviour; for example, quite a lot of it is concerned with evaluating the success or otherwise of various criminal justice interventions such as community policing or intendedly rehabilitative programmes for convicted offenders. True to their core beliefs, positivist criminologists turned once again to natural science to provide a model for their evaluative work, and this was found especially in the 'clinical trial' experimental method widely used in scientific medicine. So positivists advocated, for example, the random assignment of research subjects as between two 'treatments' (e.g. intensive probation and

---

[6] This view was expressed in a strong form by the English philosopher A. J. Ayer in 1936: 'sentences which simply express moral judgements do not say anything. They are pure expressions of feeling ... They are unverifiable for the same reason as a cry of pain or a word of command is unverifiable—because they do not express genuine propositions' (Ayer 1936/1971: 144).

ordinary probation), in an endeavour to eliminate spurious outcomes resulting from pre-treatment differences between the experimental and the control groups.[7]

7. The positivists' preference for methods akin to the natural sciences, for the hypo-thetico-deductive approach to explanatory research, and for the experimental method in evaluative research, all combined to produce a powerful preference for quantitative over qualitative data.

Every one of the above assumptions has been questioned, often heavily, in post-1970 criminology. Space precludes any detailed treatment, but let a few things be said quickly. Many now argue that social science is not the same as natural science, essentially because its subjects are human beings who can attribute meaning to the situations in which they are placed, and may therefore react to and possibly alter those situations (see, e.g., Giddens 1984). Theory-neutral sense-data are now seen as impossible to obtain (see the introduction to this chapter). There has been a major revival in normative theorization about the political and moral worlds since 1970, beginning with the work of Rawls on the concept of justice (see, e.g., Rawls 1972, Skinner 1990). On any objective view, 'crime' has to be seen as a non-natural category of behaviour, crucially definitionally dependent on the censuring processes of a given society. The hypothetico-deductive approach to explanation, and the positivists' preference for quantitative data, were both frontally challenged by Glaser and Strauss as long ago as 1967 (see further below).

None of the above remarks should be taken to mean that the positivist paradigm in criminology is dead, for it manifestly is not. But the paradigm is unquestionably much more severely open to question than it was in, say, 1965. We thus now need to sketch briefly some of the alternative theoretical approaches that have been developed, with spe-cial reference to their differences from positivism, and also to their understanding of the theory/data relationship. Before opening up this discussion, however, we also need to note that in contemporary criminology there is an important group of scholars—who for convenience I shall call 'post-positivist naturalists'[8]—who have jettisoned the clearly unsustainable tenets of positivism (such as 'facts are theory-neutral' and the fudge relat-ing to the definition of crime), but who have sought to maintain, so far as possible, one of the other principal characteristics of positivism, namely the unity of the natural scientific method and the social scientific method. Such scholars tend particularly to emphasize the concepts of *cause* and *explanation*, which lie at the heart of the endeavour of the nat-ural sciences. (On the analysis of *causes*, see further the next chapter in this volume by Per-Olof Wikström.)

A final word about positivism needs to be added. In some criminological circles, the term 'positivism' is now never used without strongly pejorative connotations. This is descriptively unhelpful, but more importantly it can serve to deflect attention from the

---

[7] Random assignment remains very actively promoted in contemporary evaluation-oriented criminology. For example, the 'Maryland Scientific Methods Scale' has been developed (Sherman *et al.* 2006: ch. 2) in order to provide a measure of the internal validity of evaluation research designs on a 5-point scale; in this Scale, ran-dom assignment is the sole qualifier for a score of 5. Similarly, a recent Home Office research report states that: 'the only sure way to increase the quality and validity of knowledge is to use the right research design to answer the research question, and for outcome evaluations this generally means using randomised control trials' (Harper and Chitty 2005: 81).

[8] The term 'naturalist' is used because of the group's preference (*ceteris paribus*) for the methods of the natural sciences.

very real strengths of the so-called 'scientific approach' in criminology. Whatever the defects of old-style positivism (and it had many), it has bequeathed to contemporary criminologists a fine tradition of careful observation of the natural and social worlds; of the scientist's duty to report his/her research data dispassionately, even if he/she finds them personally unwelcome; and of the careful search for causes and explanations. All these traditions are now being maintained by the post-positivist naturalists. For those of us who argue that there is an external world which is in principle capable of being described and explained (albeit not without difficulties), these are vitally important legacies, which—if we are truly interested in advancing knowledge—we should maintain and sustain.

Active-subject socially oriented criminologies

Stuart Henry and Dragen Milovanovic (1996: 17–18) have suggested a very useful way of classifying mainstream criminological theories, along two dimensions. In the first dimension, theories are characterized according to the extent that they view human beings as *active subjects* (that is, do they have the capacity to create and shape their own world, or are they constrained and determined in their behaviour by their individual biology and upbringing and/or by the social world that surrounds them?). In the second dimension, theories are characterized according to whether they see human behaviour as primarily *individual* or primarily *social*. Each of these dimensions is perhaps best understood as a continuous distribution, but for heuristic purposes both can be usefully treated as dichotomies. When this is done, mainstream criminological theories are seen as divided into four principal types, namely: (i) active-subject individually oriented theories; (ii) active-subject socially oriented theories; (iii) passive subject individually oriented theories; and (iv) passive-subject socially oriented theories. The positivist tradition, in its various manifestations, is of course the main—although not the only—exemplar of the third and fourth ('passive subject') types.[9] The first and second types, however, require further discussion. I will start with the second type (active-subject socially oriented criminologies), since it is from this tradition that some of the sharpest challenges to positivism have been articulated. Within this kind of criminology, I shall focus especially upon the contributions of the ethnographic approach, and of social constructivism.

There is a long and distinguished tradition of ethnographic work of a criminological kind; for example, in the inter-war period the Chicago School of Sociology famously championed the ethnographic tradition, and their work included some criminological research, especially by Clifford Shaw. This earlier tradition was drawn upon in the revival of ethnographic work in criminology that took place as the hegemony of positivist criminology was increasingly threatened after the mid-1960s (for a seminal text, see Matza 1969; for examples of subsequent British criminological work of an ethnographic kind, see, for example, Foster 1990, Rock 1993, Hobbs *et al.* 2003).

By comparison with positivism (or post-positivist naturalism), ethnography has very different emphases in three particular respects. First and most obviously, its preference is

---

[9] Positivism is often understood to be associated particularly with an individually-oriented approach. It is therefore important to emphasize that, in the history of criminology, there have been a number of socially oriented positivist approaches, including, for example, many of the subcultural theories of the 1960s.

for carefully-nuanced in-depth reportage, based on the researcher's immersion in the life-worlds of the subjects being studied; hence ethnography has a preference (usually a strong preference) for qualitative rather than quantitative data. Secondly and relatedly, ethnography places much more emphasis than does positivism on the meaning of social actions to actors, and on their detailed understandings of particular social contexts. Thirdly, therefore, the ethnographic approach emphatically rejects the view that social science can be studied in the same way as natural science, for the phenomena studied in natural science do not attribute meaning to their life-worlds as human beings do. These three attributes of the ethnographic approach lead, collectively, to a particular strength of the ethnographic tradition, rarely found in other kinds of criminology; namely, its ability to uncover some of the deep cultural meanings and normative bonds which are often so important in everyday social life.

The contrast between positivism (and post-positivist naturalism) on the one hand, and the ethnographic approach on the other, can be represented as a difference between a primary focus on *causal explanation* and a primary focus on *interpretative understanding*[10] as Martin Hollis helpfully explains:

Naturalistic thinkers [believe] that, since human beings and societies belong to the natural order, a single method, broadly defined, will serve for all sciences. There is a rival tradition, however, which has a profoundly different view of society, human life and social action ... The rival tradition aims at an 'interpretative' or 'hermeneutic' social science (from the Greek work *hermeneus*, an interpreter). *Its central proposition is that the social world must be understood from within, rather than explained from without. Instead of seeking the causes of behaviour, we are to seek for the meaning of action.* Actions derive their meaning from the shared ideas and rules of social life, and are performed by actors who mean something by them. Meanings ... range from what is consciously and individually intended to what is communally and often unintendedly significant (Hollis 2002: 16–17, emphasis added).

So the *explanation/causes* approach and the *interpretative understanding* approach start from very different places. But some social scientists (and I certainly count myself among this group) can see real merit in both approaches. Hence the question naturally arises, is it possible to bridge this apparent divide? Max Weber certainly thought that it was, as is evident from his definition of 'sociology' very early in his *magnum opus*, *Economy and Society* (Weber 1978: 4):

Sociology ... is a science concerning itself with the interpretive understanding of social action and thereby with a causal explanation of its course and consequences.

However, and despite Weber, it would I think be true to say that most criminological writers in the 'interpretative understanding' tradition (including most ethnographers) have been rather suspicious of theoretical generalizations, and of the language of 'causes'. For them, what is all-important is the study of particular actions with particular meanings, occurring in particular social contexts; and they therefore tend sometimes to have difficulty in generalizing from these particulars. In so far as they do generalize, they have a strong preference for the *inductive* rather than the *deductive* approach to

---

[10] 'Interpretative understanding' is an attempt to capture in English what Max Weber (1978) meant when he spoke of the *verstehen* approach to sociology.

theory-construction: that is to say, they prefer to build theory 'upwards' from an under-standing of specific social situations, rather than formally testing hypotheses (the 'inductive versus deductive' debate is more fully considered in the next section).

The social constructivist approach is often in practice closely linked to ethnography. However, for analytical purposes at least, it is worth separating the two. Ethnography dif-fers from positivism especially in emphasizing the *meaning content of actions to actors*. Social constructivism shares that view, but takes it further, pointing out that each of us has frames of understanding within which we view the natural and social worlds, and emphasizing the need to 'unpack' carefully each actor's framework of understanding. Everyone has had the experience of watching a particular social event or action, and then realizing that the event has been understood completely differently by a different observer. (This is perhaps most familiar in situations where a child and an adult together watch a situation developing). The social constructivist stresses the need to understand ('deconstruct') carefully the 'social constructions' which each of us uses in observing and participating in social life. 'By being witness to the day-to-day reasoning of their research subjects, by engaging in their life-world, by participating in their decision-making' (Pawson and Tilley 1997: 21), as well as by careful interviewing of the research subjects about their understandings of the world, a detailed picture of actors' 'social construc-tions' can be assembled. Thus, social constructivism differs from positivism especially in *denying the existence of theory-neutral facts*, and then in *seeking to deconstruct the world-views through which different social actors view particular events and activities.*

We noted in the introduction to this chapter that social constructivism could some-times develop into an unhelpful position of epistemological relativism. While such views must be vigorously contested, there is much to be gained from milder versions of ethnog-raphy and social constructivism. The challenge, which I shall discuss more fully later in this essay, is to try to incorporate such insights into a non-relativistic intellectual frame-work within which the cumulative generation of knowledge remains possible. Such an approach ultimately entails the difficult task of following Weber's intention[11] in seeking to synthesize the *explanation/causes* approach and the *interpretative understanding* approach (on this quest and some of its problems, see Hollis 2002, *passim*).

Active-subject individually oriented criminologies

In the 1980s and 1990s, a number of versions of active-subject individually oriented criminology came to the fore. These criminologies are similar to the ethnographic approach in emphasizing that human beings make real choices, rather than being seen (as in the positivist—though, importantly, not usually in the 'post-positivist naturalist'—tradition) as simply the end-product of various biological, familial, and social forces and influences working upon them. But this kind of criminology nevertheless differs markedly from ethnography in emphasizing primarily the reasoning/rational dimen-sions of human decision-making, rather than normative bonds and cultural contexts; in short, it is markedly more *individualistic* and *rationalistic*. In this respect, active-subject individually oriented criminologies in some ways resemble the classical tradition of

---

[11] I use the phrase 'Weber's intention' in recognition of the fact that there are some acknowledged difficul-ties with his proposed ways of realizing the intention: see, e.g., Runciman 1972, Hollis 2002.

Beccaria and Bentham, and it is because of this that they are sometimes referred to as 'neo-classical' approaches.[12]

Two main strands within this kind of criminology can usefully be distinguished. The first and most important is rational choice theory, which in criminology has been developed especially in connection with the now extensive body of work on 'situational crime prevention' (see, generally, Clarke 1995, Cornish and Clarke 1986), but which has been immensely influential in recent decades in social science more generally (for a very useful collection of essays, presenting contrasting views, see Coleman and Fararo 1992). The second strand is 'routine activities theory', which has many similarities with, but also some important differences from rational choice theory (see Felson 2002, Clarke and Felson 1993).

Criminological work in this tradition has demonstrated quite clearly that subjects' choices can sometimes be read as containing elements of prudential rationality. (This can often be seen most clearly using aggregate data, from which prudential rationality can be inferred—for example, in an early study which showed that vandalism by bus passengers occurred much more frequently on the (unsupervised) upper decks). The rational choice and routine activities approaches have also brought firmly to criminologists' attention the role of opportunity in the aetiology of crime; and, conversely, that if opportunities are restricted, then reductions in criminality will often take place (see the discussion in Clarke 1995). These advances, however, have been made at the cost of a somewhat decontextualized view of the human subject, as, for example, the ethnographic work of Wright and Decker (1994) on active burglars has clearly demonstrated. Similarly, the routine activities approach has strongly emphasized choices made at the site (or potential site) of a criminal act, but it has to a very large extent ignored the biographical histories and social understandings of the potential offenders who might actually be faced with such choices.

There is thus a paradox within much of this kind of criminology, and it is one that is perhaps of special importance to the subject matter of this chapter. These criminologies stress the importance of the active subject, but—with some honourable exceptions—they often show a real reluctance to investigate in detail the actual choices made by the active subject within specific social contexts. The explanation of this paradox is not hard to uncover: for if one incorporates into one's theoretical approach a presupposition of rationality, then it can very easily be assumed that that presupposition does not itself require empirical investigation. That is especially likely to be the case when some empirical research (notably aggregate research) fairly clearly suggests that this presupposition of rationality contains at least some validity.[13] The justified stress on the reasoning subject within this kind of criminology (an emphasis not shared in many other criminological traditions) thus may have an unfortunate tendency to inhibit empirical research on the ways in which subjects' more prudential reasoning processes may interact with other features of their lives, such as the structural and cultural contexts which they inhabit, and emotional reactions to specific situations.

---

[12] It is, however, important to distinguish these kinds of neo-classical explanatory approaches from neo-classical normative theorising in criminology, such as desert theory.

[13] This, of course, is why the discipline of economics has built its analyses primarily upon rational choice models. The oversimplicity of such models has, however, led to criticisms within the field of economics itself: see, for example, the work of Paul Ormerod (1998).

Political-activist criminologies

Anyone acquainted with the development of criminology in Britain since 1970 will be aware that many proffered analyses have been quite explicitly politically activist in their approach to their subject matter. This is most obviously true, perhaps, of various kinds of 'critical criminology' and feminist criminology.

This category of criminology overlaps with Henry and Milovanovic's fourfold typology of mainstream criminologies, because—as these authors make clear—political-activist criminologies can be (i) active-subject socially oriented (perhaps the most common orientation for political-activist criminologies), (ii) active-subject individually oriented (e.g. liberal feminism), and even (iii) passive-subject socially oriented (e.g. some versions of Marxism). From the point of view of the present chapter, there are, however, some distinct points to be made by drawing specific attention to political-activist criminologies, since the explicit element of political activism within such theories obviously raises some rather special issues about the relationship between theory and empirical observations in criminology.

Part of the strong legacy of positivism to British (and other) criminology has been a deep suspicion, in many 'mainstream' criminological circles, about any kind of political or moral engagement on the part of criminologists. (Within the positivist tradition, such an engagement was, as we have seen, denigrated as 'unscientific'). That view must, however, now be regarded as unsustainable; for the concept of 'crime' itself, and the kind of criminal justice system that a given society develops, must necessarily be the product of political and moral choices. Moreover, even the most careful, dispassionate, and rigorous criminological research can have political consequences. As Henry and Milovanovic (1996: 7) point out, the often suggested dualism between 'theory' and 'practice' is in certain respects intrinsically false, since as Paulo Freire (1972: 77) put it: 'there is no true word that is not at the same time a praxis. Thus, to speak a true word is to transform the world'. (Or perhaps we should more modestly say: 'to speak a true word is *potentially* to transform the world'.)

Political-activist criminology thus has the major merit of reminding us that doing research and theory in criminology is itself inevitably linked to the political landscape, whether the criminologist likes this or not (see, further, **Chapter 2** by Rod Morgan and Mike Hough in this volume). In that sense, political-activist criminology returns criminology to its roots in classicism, where the normative dimensions of the subject were explicitly emphasized. Doing criminology, in short, necessarily entails some engagement with normative issues, and it is for that reason that a brief discussion of normative theory is included later in this chapter.

The above comments, however, do not mean that all political-activist criminology is to be celebrated. For, as Key Proposition II claims (see the Introduction to this chapter), there is a real world available for observation, and we can observe it with greater or less accuracy. Very often, political-activist criminologies make *empirical assertions* in support of their chosen cause (they are indeed more or less obliged to do so, since in the modern world many people will be unconvinced by a given moral/political case unless it is supported by empirical data as well as moral/political argument). Those empirical assertions then need to be rigorously tested, in exactly the same way as other empirical assertions—as do the counter-assertions of an empirical kind offered by moral/political opponents of the original activists. Any criminologist with any length of experience will have seen examples of political advocacy (perhaps by a criminal justice pressure group) where inconvenient empirical data are temporarily 'forgotten', or even where strong empirical assertions are made in an attempt to forward the political cause, notwithstanding a distinctly weak empirical base to the argument. Even professional criminologists have been known to engage in this kind of tactic. But to move in this direction is dangerous, for it can, at worst, subordinate scholarship to political goals; and to do this is to move decisively and disastrously away from the search for truth. Many will remember John Rawls's (1972: 3) argument on the opening page of his classic book on justice:

Justice is the first virtue of social institutions, as truth is of systems of thought. A theory however elegant and economical must be rejected or revised if it is untrue; likewise laws and institutions no matter how efficient and well-arranged must be reformed or abolished if they are unjust.

Table 3.1 Summary of some positive and negative features of five approaches to criminology

		Positive Features	Negative Features
1.	Classicism	Emphasis on the normative dimension within criminology.	No empirical research.
2.	Natural Science-based positivism	Careful and precise observations.	Assumption of theory-neutral facts.
		Scientific detachment.	Weak ability to handle the normative dimension within criminology.
		Search for causes and explanations.	Assumption of equivalence of Natural and Social Science.
3.	Active-subject socially-oriented criminologies	No assumption of theory neutral facts.	Often shies away from theoretical generalisations and search for causes.
		Careful observations based on immersion in the social world.	Can relapse into relativism.
		Emphasis on meaning of social actions to actors and on cultural/normative social bonds.	
		Emphasis on need to deconstruct actors' frames of reference.	
4.	Active-subject individually-oriented criminologies	Emphasis on reasoning powers of subjects, and of constraints on individual action.	Over-emphasis on individual-rational choice; decontextualization of human subjects.
5.	Political-activist criminologies	Emphasis that research and knowledge is itself part of a political process.	Political goals can override search for truth.

This passage is most often cited for its emphasis on the primacy of justice within normative debates; but in every way as important is Rawls's emphasis on the primacy of truth as a criterion when one is seeking knowledge about the natural and social worlds. 'Truth' is, of course, not at all easy either to define (see Honderich 2005: 926–7) or to discover; but it remains always the goal and the touchstone of both natural and social science.

An overview

Table 3.1 attempts to summarize much of the argument of this section, by giving an overview of my own assessment of some of the principal features—positive and negative—of the five kinds of criminology that the section has examined. If the arguments so far presented have merit, then obviously in thinking about the relationship between theory and data in criminology, we will wish particularly to make use of, and perhaps to develop, the various items listed in the column headed 'Positive Features'. At this point in the argument, however, we need to remember the previously made distinction between eclecticism and synthesis. Simply selecting items from the 'Positive Features' column, and jamming them together in a random fashion, will not constitute a synthesis; rather, we need some principled and defensible procedures for synthesis. The toughest challenge, in this respect, will be to integrate in a coherent fashion what the 'Positive Features' column of Table 3.1 calls the 'Search for causes and explanation' and the 'Emphasis on the meaning of social actions to actors and on cultural/normative social bonds'; in other words, to integrate the *explanatory* and the *interpretative understanding* approaches (see above).

Doing empirical research: deductive and inductive approaches

I turn now from historical discussion of the development of criminology to the task of actually undertaking empirical research. Here, the key issues are common to all the social sciences, and therefore not specific to criminology.

Traditionally, there have been two main (and very distinct) approaches to the empirical research process, which are usually called the 'hypothetico-deductive method' (or 'theory') and 'grounded theory'. More recently, the term 'adaptive theory' has been coined to describe an approach that attempts to synthesize some features from each of the two older approaches, while also being fully aware of the theoretical dissonance between these approaches in their originally stated forms. In this section, I shall briefly consider all three of these ways of approaching the conduct of empirical research.

By way of preliminary clarification, it is worth emphasizing that the word 'theory' in these formulations ('grounded theory', 'adaptive theory', etc.) is used in the sense of a *methodological theory* rather than, for example, an ontological or a substantive theory (see the introduction to this chapter). Given this, the approaches discussed in this section differ from, and complement, those that were considered in the preceding section.

The hypothetico-deductive method

The *Oxford Companion to Philosophy* (Honderich 2005: 411), in discussing the hypothetico-deductive method, takes as an example the hypothesis: 'All planets have elliptical orbits.' If the hypothesis is valid, and if Mars is a planet, we can obviously then *deduce* from the hypothesis that Mars will have an elliptical orbit;[14] and we can then make observations of Mars's orbit to confirm or falsify the hypothesis in that particular instance.

In the natural sciences in the twentieth century, under the influence (in particular) of Karl Popper, the hypothetico-deductive method came to be seen as the paradigmatic procedure for generating valid knowledge, and this view may still be found in some social science textbooks that favour—so far as possible—the assimilation of social scientific method to the methods of the natural sciences.[15] A classic formulation of the hypothetico-deductive method in the social sciences was put forward in the 1960s by Robert Merton (1967), and Layder (1998: 16) usefully summarizes Merton's approach:

[Merton] argued that although we develop our initial ideas about a research problem through empirical observations of some social phenomenon (like rates of suicide in different societies), we then construct a possible theoretical explanation for the phenomenon through a logical, deductive process, which is consistent with the known facts. Research then proceeds on the basis of finding more facts and information about the topic, area or problem in question in order to 'test-out' the original hypothesis. The unearthing of evidence through empirical research either confirms the initial theoretical ideas or disconfirms them, leading to their refor- mulation or abandonment. [It is argued that] the more theory is tested-out in this manner, the more likely it is that supportive evidence will be found and this can lead to a relatively stabilized body of theory which can help to illuminate other research in the area.

The underlying procedural logic of the approach is intendedly *deductive* throughout. Merton's own account of his proposed methodological approach emphasizes especially the generation of 'middle-range theory' in social scientific explanation, and it is easy to see why.[16] For in hypothetico-deductive theory we start with some limited factual observations, and then we try to formulate a careful hypothesis that will explain these observations; subsequently, we test and revise this hypothesis. Almost inevitably, this process results in theories about particular social institutions (marriage, bureaucracy, prisons, etc.), particular kinds of action (e.g. committing suicide, taking illegal drugs), or particular kinds of social aggregate (e.g. cities versus rural areas). Such theories are

---

[14] However, we cannot of course validly deduce from the hypothesis that, if a heavenly body has an elliptical orbit, it is therefore a planet. That would be to make the same logical mistake as to say that 'all cars have wheels, therefore all conveyances with wheels are cars'.

[15] See, for example, Hoover and Donovan (2004). On p. 33 this text introduces students to '*the* scientific method' (emphasis added), which, it states, is 'quite commonsensical'. The scientific method, it explains, pro- ceeds by a series of five steps, of which the first two are (i) the identification of the variables to be studied, and (ii) the construction of a hypothesis. However, the text goes on to add that 'the actual procedure of research does not always start directly with hypothesis formation', and that social scientists frequently begin by exploring data in an unstructured way, a process that sometimes 'triggers an interesting thought, a chance insight, or a new idea'. How students are supposed to interpret this information about the real-life behaviour of competent researchers, which is apparently often at variance with 'the scientific method', remains obscure.

[16] 'Middle-range theory' is a term originally coined by Merton himself. It refers to substantive theories that are midway between 'minor working hypotheses' and 'master conceptual schemes'.

significantly different from (and obviously more restricted in scope than) the theories of 'general social theorists' such as Foucault or Habermas (discussed in the next section).

The hypothetico-deductive theory has some important strengths. First, it emphasizes, rightly, that theory is involved from a very early stage in the research process. Secondly, it encourages researchers to develop careful and precise formulations of theoretical ideas, in the shape of hypotheses to be tested (neophyte researchers often discover that the process of formulating a hypothesis forces them to think much more carefully than heretofore about exactly what it is they are interested in 'testing out' in the field). Thirdly, it requires the rigorous testing of theoretical ideas against relevant observations where this is appropriate and feasible. These are all very positive attributes that need to be nurtured in the development of empirical research.

However, the hypothetico-deductive approach also has some potential difficulties. First, from a theoretical point of view 'testing a theory is in practice more complex than the ... model suggests' (Honderich 2005: 411). In Karl Popper's writings, for example, although the 'theory-ladenness' of data is in principle fully recognized, the assumption tends to be made that hypotheses can be tested directly and unproblematically against the 'real world'.[17] But actually, of course, matters are more complex than this:

[Theory] is involved in defining the test situation *and* in identifying what is observed in it. When refutation is deemed to occur, the tester must, in effect, be weighing the merits of the theory which yielded the prediction against the merits of the theory which yielded the description of what experience showed. Experiments are a complex business, and there is always scope for contending that they are somehow defective or do not show exactly what is supposed. Interpretation, in short, is never absent (Hollis 2002: 76, emphasis added).

This does not mean that testing a hypothesis necessarily leads to endless argumentation, as the example of the Farrington-Dowds (1985) research on Nottinghamshire's high crime rate has already shown (see above). It does, however, mean that tests of hypotheses always require careful interpretation and assessment.

A second potential difficulty with the hypothetico-deductive method is that, once the 'hypothesis-formulation' stage has begun, the approach taken might unwittingly restrict the researcher's focus. This is because, at that stage, the emphasis is all upon refining the hypothesis, hence fresh data that might make one want to think again about the theoretical framework underpinning the original hypothesis might not be actively sought out by the researcher (this is one version of the 'problem of conceptual hegemony' discussed earlier). For example, I recall attending a research presentation on 'explaining the location of offences' in the early 1980s, i.e. the early days of so-called 'environmental criminology' (see Brantingham and Brantingham 1981). The presenter, strongly influenced by the fruitful and then-recent renaissance of scholarly interest in the detailed study of *offences* (rather than offenders), focused exclusively on offence data and data about the local physical environmental context (road networks, value of local housing, schools, shops, etc.), and he formulated and tested an interesting series of hypotheses within this framework. The strict focus on offences, however, meant that the research (as then

---

[17] Popper argues that hypotheses can be refuted or falsified by a single observation (e.g. sighting a black swan falsifies the hypothesis that 'all swans are white'); however, conclusive verification of a hypothesis is never possible, because future falsifications remain in principle possible.

presented) excluded any data relating to the proximity or otherwise of the various stud-ied locations to the housing areas that were lived in by known offenders—notwithstand-ing that there was already at that date research literature on the potential importance of this topic.[18] When, subsequently, data of this kind were included in the presenter's ongoing research, it proved to be a strong predictor of offence location. The moral obviously is—in using the hypothetico-deductive method, always be very sure to cast a wide conceptual and theoretical net before starting to formulate hypotheses, or you might exclude something important.

A third potential difficulty is that, because the hypothetico-deductive approach places particular emphasis on 'confirming' or 'falsifying' a hypothesis, there has been a tendency for researchers of this kind strongly to favour quantitative as opposed to qualitative data sources, to the point where the latter are quite often accorded only a very secondary status by researchers following hypothetico-deductive procedures. This is not an inevitable draw-back of the hypothetico-deductive method, but it is a point that requires careful watching.[19]

Grounded theory

So-called 'grounded theory' is an approach originally formulated by Barney Glaser and Anselm Strauss (1967) in conscious opposition to the hypothetico-deductive method.[20] Whereas hypothetico-deductive theory emphasizes a deductive approach and quantitative data, grounded theory prefers an inductive approach and the prioritizing of qualitative data.

In the first paragraph of their original book, Glaser and Strauss tell their readers that they wish to further 'the discovery of theory from data—systematically obtained and analyzed in social research'. Two pages later, they elaborate this statement:

Theory in sociology is a strategy for handling data in research, providing modes of conceptu-alization for describing and explaining. The theory should provide clear enough categories and hypotheses so that crucial ones can be verified in present and future research; they must be clear enough to be readily operationalized in quantitative studies when these are appropriate. The theory must also be readily understandable to sociologists of any viewpoint, to students and to significant laymen. Theory that can meet these requirements must fit the situation being researched, and work when put into use. By 'fit' we mean that the categories must be readily (not forcibly) applicable to and indicated by the data under study; by 'work' we mean that they must be meaningfully relevant to and be able to explain the behavior under study . . .

To generate theory that fills this large order, we suggest as the best approach an initial, sys-tematic discovery of the theory from the data of social research. Then one can be relatively sure that the theory will fit and work. And since the categories are discovered by examination of the

---

[18] This literature shows that, other things being equal, areas close to the residences of many known offend-ers usually have higher victimization rates, because these areas are already known to the offenders (who there-fore feel more comfortable operating in them), and there is less effort involved in seeking a target close to home than many miles away.

[19] A fourth important criticism of a more technical nature is that, despite the apparently rationalist founda-tions of hypothetico-deductive theory, some of the most important formulations of this approach, such as Merton's (1967), have in fact been heavily dependent on empiricist criteria of knowledge at certain key points: see Layder (1998: 137–8).

[20] For more recent discussions, see, for example, Strauss (1987) and Strauss and Corbin (1997).

data, laymen involved in the area to which the theory applies will usually be able to understand it, while sociologists who work on other areas will recognise an understandable theory linked with the data of a given area (Glaser and Strauss 1967: 3–4).

The principal method advocated by Glaser and Strauss to further the discovery of grounded theory is that of 'comparative analysis', an approach that they say places 'a high emphasis on *theory as process*; that is, theory as an ever-developing entity, not as a perfected product' (p. 32). Thus, for example, beginning perhaps with a small area of inquiry, the researcher aims constantly to work outwards from the data, in an endeavour to *generalize* from one kind of situation to another, or to *delineate differences*, and thus gradually to generate and to refine theoretical statements. To be maximally effective, this approach requires one *first*, to be comprehensive in the coverage of relevant data features encountered at the first research site, and subsequently in each fresh empirical context, and *secondly*, to be extremely rigorous in the sequential selection of various examples, so as constantly to try to achieve a progressive and systematic elaboration or refinement of the theory (a process described as the 'theoretical sampling' of fresh contexts). In this way, Glaser and Strauss hope, one can generate both 'substantive theory' ('theory developed for a substantive, or empirical, area of sociological inquiry', such as 'order in prisons') and 'formal theory' ('theory developed for a formal or conceptual area of sociological inquiry', e.g. 'bureaucracy'). Overall, it is argued, 'the design involves a progressive building up from facts, through substantive to grounded formal theory' (p. 35).

Glaser and Strauss are clear about what they see as the advantages of this approach, as compared with the hypothetico-deductive approach:

Verifying a [hypothetico-deductive theory] generally leaves us with at best a reformulated hypothesis or two and an unconfirmed set of speculations; and at worst a theory that does not seem to fit or work ... [grounded theory] gives us a theory that 'fits or works' in a substantive or formal area (though further testing, clarification or reformulation is still necessary) since the theory has been derived from data, not deduced from logical assumptions (pp. 29–30).

Additionally, they argue, the use of a hypothetico-deductive approach unduly *restricts* subsequent empirical work to confirmatory or falsificatory processes, and blunts the researcher's sensitivity to the full range of theoretical possibilities in the patterns of data (see the environmental criminology example above).

There is no doubt that some of these ideas have considerable merit. There are, however, at least two significant difficulties with grounded theory, as formulated by Glaser and Strauss. The first is that, by speaking of 'the discovery of theory from data', these authors unjustifiably assume the existence of theory neutral facts. Hence, a key element of their whole approach is, from the outset, theoretically flawed. Secondly, Glaser and Strauss's prioritization of qualitative data seems as unjustified as does the hypothetico-deductive theorists' prioritization of quantitative data.

If we now stand back and consider this brief discussion of the hypothetico-deductive method and grounded theory, it would seem that what is needed is an approach to the theory/research relationship that can incorporate at least the following features:

i.   a firm acceptance that there are no theory neutral facts, and that the process of empirical research is therefore inextricably involved with theoretical issues from

the outset of the inquiry. (Because of the date at which they were originally formulated, some of the classic statements of both hypothetico-deductive theory and
grounded theory fail to grasp the full implications of this crucial point.)

ii.   a willingness to test and to refine hypotheses rigorously where appropriate, but not
     in such a way that one becomes blind to the implications of fresh data that do not
     readily 'mesh' with the pre-existing line of inquiry.

iii. a willingness to employ to the full the benefits of the wide search for relevant data,
     as well as the 'comparative analysis' method, advocated by grounded theory, while
     nevertheless accepting the two key points listed above.

iv.   an unwillingness to foreclose inquiry too quickly, recognizing with Glaser and
     Strauss that theory is indeed always a 'process . . . an ever-developing entity'.

v.   a genuine willingness to utilize appropriately both quantitative and qualitative
     data-sources.

While many empirical researchers have, in real-world research contexts, developed
personal methodological approaches that do indeed fully incorporate all or most of the
above points, we have until fairly recently lacked any formal theoretical statement of such
a methodological approach. Hence the importance, in my judgement, of Derek Layder's
(1998) book on *Sociological Practice*, in which he put forward what he called the 'adaptive
theory' approach to the theory/data relationship, which seeks to draw on the strengths of
both the hypothetico-deductive method and of grounded theory. I would not wish to
defend every proposition that Layder offers in this volume, but Layder's text does offer us,
in my judgement, a definite advance in the formal development of a more fruitful
approach to the traditional 'inductive versus deductive' debate.

Adaptive theory

I shall devote relatively little space here to any formal summary of Layder's proposed
'adaptive theory' approach. That is partly because the main outlines of Layder's approach
will already be apparent from the discussion in the preceding subsection; and partly also
because in the final section of this chapter I shall discuss an example from criminological
research that has adopted, implicitly, an 'adaptive theory' procedure. To give a flavour of
Layder's approach, however, it is worth quoting the core of his answer to the question:
'what is adaptive about adaptive theory?'. This runs as follows:

So the adaptive part of the term is meant to convey that the theory simultaneously contains
two fundamental properties. First, that there is an existing theoretical scaffold which has a relatively durable form since it adapts reflexively rather than automatically in relation to empirical
data. Secondly, this scaffold should never be regarded as immutable since it is capable of
accommodating new information and interpretations by reconfiguring itself. Thus, although
the extant 'theoretical elements' are never simple empiricist 'reflections' of data, they are
intrinsically capable of reformulating ('adapting' or 'adjusting') themselves in response to the
discovery of new information and/or interpretations of data which seriously challenge their
basic assumptions. Such reformulations may involve only minor modifications . . . but they may
also require fundamental reorganization, such as either abandoning an existing category,

model or explanation, or creating new ones, depending on the circumstances (Layder 1998: 150–1).

Thus, adaptive theory recommends that researchers should be aware from the outset of the 'theory-ladenness' of all data, and should preferably construct explicitly an initial 'theoretical scaffold'. This can then be modified, either by inductive processes or by the formal testing of hypotheses. Moreover, the modifications can be either relatively slight, or fundamental.

Three additional comments may be made at this stage, linking 'adaptive theory' procedures to some of the preceding discussions in this chapter. The first of these comments is formal/analytical; the second and third are criminological.

The formal/analytical comment relates to the issue of inductive versus deductive research procedures. Layder (1998: 135) fully recognizes that his 'insistence that adaptive theory employs both deductive and inductive procedures' might be read by some as an attempt to combine what might well be regarded, methodologically, 'as "incompatible" premises or underlying assumptions'. Layder's important response to this objection is worth quoting extensively:

My usage of [the terms induction and deduction] does not invoke the idea that *in the final analysis* theory has *either* to be produced exclusively in a deductive manner *or* solely within an inductive frame of reference . . . In terms of adaptive theory both forms of theory-generation, construction or elaboration are permissible within the same frame of reference and particularly within the same research project and time frame . . . I regard induction and deduction as frameworks of ideas—discourse and the practices they embody—which are potentially open to each other's influence. Thus it is not only a matter of allowing their dual influence on theory-construction, but also of allowing their mutual influence on each other. Moderate (rather than extreme) definitions of these terms will allow for this. As epistemological anchorages neither induction nor deduction can be understood as prior or privileged in terms of their influence—neither must have a fixed starting point as the most basic premise of knowledge production. Induction and deduction must be conceived as equally important and mutually influential approaches to knowledge, according to different empirical and theoretical circumstances. These latter will reflect the ongoing nature of particular research projects (Layder 1998: 136, emphasis in original).

My second—and explicitly criminological—comment on adaptive theory takes us back to the preceding main section in this chapter (on 'Lessons from the Past'), and in particular to Table 3.1. In discussing Table 3.1, I suggested that we needed methodological procedures that would allow us to make full use of the 'positive features' identified in column 1 of the figure, but that this needed to be achieved not eclectically, but within some 'principled and defensible procedures for synthesis'. My argument would now be that the adaptive theory framework potentially provides exactly such 'principled and defensible procedures'. But it does not automatically do so—much depends on the individual researcher's understanding and skills as a research project unfolds. Hence, it should now be clear why this chapter began with a comment endorsing the image of a 'continuing dialogue' between theory and data in empirical criminological research.

My final comment on adaptive theory concerns the role of what might be called 'general social theory' (i.e. the work of theorists such as Bourdieu or Giddens) in relation to the empirical research process. It would, I think, be fair to say that, in their original form, neither the hypothetico-deductive method nor grounded theory found it at all easy to incorporate aspects of general social theories into their approaches.[21] Although, in this brief account, I have not previously drawn attention to this point, an important feature of 'adaptive theory' is that it deliberately seeks to overcome this difficulty. Since general social theories can on occasion be of considerable value to the empirical researcher, this is an important development, as will hopefully become clearer in the next section.

Two special issues

In this section, I shall deal with two important but specialized issues connected to the theory/data relationship: they are general social theories, and the use of empirical data in connection with normative theorization in criminology.

General social theories

'General social theory' (or GST)[22] is the kind of theory that usually most interests and excites theoretical criminologists, but unfortunately, at least until recently, it has often seemed remote and baffling to empirical researchers, with the result that they have not mined the resources of this kind of theory as fully as might have been hoped.

A 'general social theory' has been usefully described as a theoretical approach that 'has a very broad explanatory remit and concerns itself *either* with whole societies and the processes involved in their development, *or* with very general aspects of social reality such as the relationship between agency and structure or macro and micro levels of analysis' (Layder 1998: 14, emphasis added). A good example of general social theory that is well known to criminologists can be found in the work of Michel Foucault. Although he sometimes wrote on directly criminological issues (most famously the prison, in *Discipline and Punish* (Foucault 1979), it is clear both from his major writings themselves, and from interviews, that Foucault was less concerned with crime and punishment per se than he was with broad issues of power, the diffusion of disciplinary mechanisms throughout social systems, and so forth; and these matters are themselves understood within some unorthodox epistemological frameworks. Like most general social theorists, Foucault adopts a number of terms that have a special meaning within the totality of his theoretical scheme: these include, for example, the concept of 'discipline' itself, the concept of 'the examination' (see Foucault 1979: 184–94), and, in his later works, the concept of 'governmentality' (see Burchell, Gordon, and Miller 1991; Garland 1997).

Of course, many other GST approaches have been of interest to criminologists. David Garland's (1990) *Punishment and Modern Society*, for example, in setting out 'to

---

[21] As regards the hypothetico-deductive method, this is not simply a question of neglect by hypothetico-deductive theorists, but arises from a logical difficulty in the way that the approach has been conceptualized: see Layder (1998: 138). As regards grounded theory, Glaser and Strauss's recommended procedures virtually by definition preclude an empirical researcher from including elements of general social theory into his/her analysis.

[22] There is no agreed terminology for this kind of theory. The term 'grand theory' is sometimes used, but (in English anyway) this has unhelpfully pejorative undertones. 'Macrolevel theory' is another possibility, but this misleadingly suggests that GST has nothing to say about microsocial phenomena. 'General social theory' is an adaptation of Layder's (1998) 'general theory'.

provide a rounded sociological account of punishment in modern society', explored the Durkheimian, Weberian, and Marxist traditions in social theory, as well as the work of Foucault and other more modern writers. In recent years, the GST approaches that have been most drawn upon in criminological work are perhaps feminism (of various types), critical theory, psychoanalytic theory (from Freud to Lacan), Giddens's 'structuration theory', poststructural theories (including Foucault), and various theories of 'late modernity'.

GST approaches have sometimes been dismissed as being too ethereal, and too far removed from everyday realities, to be of any serious practical value to the empirical researcher (see, e.g., Gregson 1989). But, in my judgement, to take this view is a serious mistake. For example, some general social theories (such as theorization about late modernity) are particularly concerned with what Layder (see above) called 'whole societies and the processes involved in their development', and it must obviously be the case that any GST with useful insights into the nature of a given 'whole society' might contain ideas that can be fruitfully employed (or adapted) to analyse particular structures or processes within that society.[23] Other GSTs, as Layder noted, are concerned to analyse 'very general aspects of social reality such as the relationship between agency and structure', and again it is likely that such theories, if they contain true insights, could indeed have considerable potential for enriching many research projects, even those that at first glance appear to be severely practical and policy oriented.

By way of a concrete example of some ways in which general social theory can enrich empirical research, let me briefly describe the use that colleagues and I made of Giddens' (1984) 'structuration theory' in a Home Office-funded research project on issues of control and order in two long-term maximum-security prisons. The central requirement of our research, as stated by the Home Office, was 'to describe accurately and to explain the nature of control problems [in long-term prisons] and the conditions leading to their emergence' (Sparks, Bottoms, and Hay 1996: 98). To tackle this problem, we decided to focus on the issue of *how day-to-day order is maintained* in a maximum-security prison, reasoning that this would give us a better theoretical base from which to understand how specific 'control problems' (in the Home Office's language) might emerge. Although we wrote our technical report for the Home Office with virtually no mention of structuration theory, we had from an early point in the research been intrigued by at least two matters which increasingly seemed to us to link up with Giddens's GST approach. These were *first*, an awareness that 'the complexity and refinement of what prison officers do often goes unremarked because there seems to be no vocabulary for talking about it' (Sparks, Bottoms, and Hay 1996: 73); and *secondly*, that in the prison *everyday routines* seemed to play a key part in the maintenance of order, notwithstanding that they had been largely neglected by many (though not all) earlier prison sociologists. These two issues, it seemed to us, linked respectively to Giddens's concept of 'practical consciousness' (which 'consists of all the things that actors know tacitly about how to "go on" in the contexts of social life without being able to give them direct discursive expression': Giddens 1984: xxiii); and to Giddens' emphasis on routine activity 'as crucial both to the reproduction of social life, and to the fending away of personal anxiety and insecurity'

---

[23] See, for example, Alison Liebling's (2004) major volume on the internal social dynamics of prisons. In this volume, two of the chapter headings (for chs 1 and 8) refer explicitly to the concept of late modernity.

(Bottoms, Hay, and Sparks (1990: 86)). From these beginnings, we then attempted a more wide-ranging and systematic assessment as to how structuration theory might play a part in the explanation of the maintenance of order in prisons (Sparks, Bottoms, and Hay 1996: esp. 69–84). Structuration theory, however, was never our only theoretical resource in this quest,[24] and indeed our book is now better-known for its application of the theory of legitimacy to life in a maximum security prison.

Yet despite these kinds of constructive possibility, there are some real potential difficulties which the empirical researcher might encounter when considering the relevance of any given GST for his/her research problem. One possible strategy for such a researcher might be described as that of 'wholesale adoption', that is, a decision 'to employ the whole package of concepts and underlying assumptions [of a given GST] to provide a ready-made "explanation" of the [research] findings' (Layder 1998: 23). But a researcher who chooses a 'wholesale adoption' approach potentially faces a double set of problems. The first is that, when she comes to present her research findings, she may find herself being forced to become a last-ditch defender of every detailed feature of the chosen GST—a position in which she is unlikely to feel comfortable. (She adopted the theory, after all, simply in order to make better sense of some of her empirical research findings; and, not being a general social theorist herself, she very likely did not at that point think through every analytical detail, and potential criticism, of the GST in question). The second potential problem with the 'wholesale adoption' approach is that it might blind the researcher to some aspects of the emerging research findings themselves. Obviously, *some* of the research findings will fit well with the chosen GST (or the researcher would not have been attracted to that theory in the first place); but other findings might be much harder to link sensibly to the GST in question. It is clearly important that the researcher remains alive to the disjunctions between any given GST and the emerging research results, as much as to the congruences between them; but this may be very hard to achieve if there has been a wholesale adoption of a given GST.

An alternative to 'wholesale adoption' is of course the 'selective adoption' of concepts from one or more GSTs as a way of seeking to enrich the theoretical explanation of the topic being studied. Such a strategy would avoid the problems outlined above; but it can bring other problems in its wake. In particular, as Layder (1998: 23) points out, there exists the unfortunate possibility 'of wrenching concepts out of their wider theoretical context [in the work of a general social theorist] and thus inadvertently disfiguring their meaning'. A further, and related, potential problem is that, in this search for synthesis, one might pluck one or two key concepts from several different GST sources, without adequate awareness of the theoretical incongruities that might thus be set up. If this occurs, one will finish up with a poorly-thought-through eclectic approach, rather than an adequate synthesis.

Yet despite these dangers, the 'selective adoption' approach potentially has several advantages. In the first place, given appropriate theoretical awareness, it becomes possible to draw fruitfully upon different concepts from various GSTs (and not just one). This is

---

[24] For non-sociologists, I should add that structuration theory is contested within sociology. The point of the example, in the context of the present chapter, is, however, not to re-enter the controversies about this theory, but to illustrate the point that selective use of a GST approach can indeed enrich empirical research. Other examples using other GST approaches could as well have been selected.

likely to be seen by many empirical researchers as the most useful way of utilizing GST, given such researchers' quite reasonable focus upon specific problems of explanation in their chosen empirical field. Moreover, a 'selective adoption' approach does not necessarily entail any large-scale importation into the research analysis of an extensive 'apparatus of abstract concepts' (Giddens 1991: 213); rather, it allows the researcher, if she wishes, to use GST concepts in 'a sparing and critical fashion' (ibid.) that, hopefully, really can illuminate the social phenomena being studied. Equally, however, a researcher who considers that a given GST (say, feminist or late modernity theory) offers the truest account of 'very general aspects of social reality' may, in a 'selective adoption' approach, use that GST extensively, but not exclusively or uncritically.

It follows from the preceding paragraphs of this subsection that the best way for empirical researchers to use concepts from general social theories is *selectively, but with appropriate sensitivity to the overall theoretical contexts* within which the concept(s) were first generated. Yet this suggestion, though attractive, is nevertheless quite daunting for the beginner, because it places upon the researcher a requirement that he/she should ideally be sufficiently familiar with the GST(s) in question to be able to use concepts derived from them selectively and confidently, yet in an accurate and appropriate way. Hence it is important for the neophyte researcher to check out—maybe with a supervisor, or perhaps with someone who is an expert on general social theory—whether or not the proposed use of a given general social theorist's concept is indeed appropriate in the relevant research context. The neophyte researcher will also find helpful, in this regard, the increasing number of introductory texts on individual general theorists and on certain general GST approaches (such as late modernity theory).

Implicit in the foregoing discussion is one important point which requires emphasis. When we speak of 'the relationship between theory and empirical observation'—the central topic of this chapter—we most naturally think of how theory and data can best be brought together in the service of true explanation. But we need also to recognize that any serious treatment of the theory/research relationship has to take account of the fact that *there is normally a range of competing theories* (including competing GSTs) available to the researcher in developing an explanation. Part of the researcher's choice of theory must depend on the fit between data and theory, *but part of it must also depend upon the analytical coherence of the different theoretical concepts deployed in the overall explanation.* Hence, it is necessary for the researcher to pay close attention to the precise content of the theoretical concepts deployed, and to ensure that these can be utilized in conjunction with one another without analytical discordance.

Is the theory/data linkage relevant to normative analysis in criminology?

Earlier in this chapter, it was claimed that 'doing criminology . . . necessarily entails some engagement with normative issues'. Given such a claim, at least some brief attention to normative theorization in criminology seems appropriate in this chapter.

Normative theory seeks principled answers to 'ought' questions, and, as a leading text (co-authored by three scholars, each committed to a different tradition in normative ethics) has put it, one of the central assumptions in most contemporary normative theory is that 'substantive ethics should proceed analytically: by argument, example, and distinction-making' (Baron, Pettit, and Slote 1997: 2).[25] For example, the question 'ought possessing cannabis to be a crime?' is known to be controversial. The serious normative theorist, in trying to answer such a question, will among other things seek to consider what justifies societies in deeming any given act to be criminal; she would then consider whether the possession of cannabis seems to meet the criteria for appropriate criminal-ization that have been specified. This second stage might well involve the use of empir-ical information, for example about any harmful effects that cannabis might have on health.

This kind of theorization is thus significantly different from explanatory research, where both theory and data are used conjointly in a search for true explanations of social phenomena (see earlier discussions). Normative analysis is not engaged in a search for scientific truth, but rather for 'a general criterion or criteria for distinguishing between right and wrong and between good and evil' (Baron, Pettit, and Slote 1997: 1), and then an application of such criteria to specific social situations. These intellectual procedures can, unquestionably, involve profound and difficult intellectual analysis—as can be seen, for example, by asking the apparently simple question 'what role should mercy have in sentencing decisions?', and then seeing where the analysis takes us. (On this question, see, among others, Murphy and Hampton 1988, Harrison 1992, Walker 1995). And, sometimes, empirical research can certainly help to clarify these normative discussions (in the case of mercy, the debate was enriched by Walker's empirical investigation of how the Court of Appeal in England had used this concept in decided cases). Hence, there can be an important element of theory/data linkage in normative research, but because of the different nature of the intellectual quest, this is not the same kind of linkage as in explanatory research.

A good illustration of these points can be found in a Ph.D. project completed at Cambridge University a few years ago. The 1991 Criminal Justice Act, itself clearly influ-enced by the normative theory known as 'desert theory' (see, e.g., von Hirsch 1986), among other things imposed on courts in England and Wales the requirement that, when passing a sentence including one or more 'community orders' (i.e. probation orders, unpaid work, curfew orders, etc.),

the restrictions on liberty imposed by the order or orders shall be such as in the opinion of the court are commensurable with the seriousness of the offence, or the combination of one or more offences associated with it (s. 6(2)(b) Criminal Justice Act 1991).

Susan Rex (1997) carried out a qualitative Ph.D. research project that sought to explore the on-the-ground reality of what was then called the probation order, in the context of the above legislative provision, with its emphasis on 'restrictions on liberty'. Her main conclusion was that, in the probation order, a mechanical counting of 'contact hours' as 'restrictions on liberty' missed the point. There were indeed restrictions and burdens placed on probationers, but these were not simply the 'contact hours' when they met their probation officers; rather, they arose from the *demands for change* in the offender's behav-iour that both probation officers and probationers understood as the central purpose of

---

[25] Note how radically this approach differs from that put forward by A. J. Ayer and others half a century or more ago (see above, n 6). Criminology is thus not the only subject to have undergone radical self-searching in the twentieth century.

the probation order (and that sometimes required considerable effort from the probationer). It seemed clear that this was significantly different from orders involving offenders doing unpaid work (although Rex herself did not empirically investigate the latter). Unpaid work orders usually involved more contact hours between the offender and the probation service, but were typically completed within a smaller number of months (and the length of the probation order was itself sometimes seen by probationers as restrictive, notwithstanding low contact hours per month). Moreover, and crucially, 'the supervision which is the whole point of probation is entirely different from the supervision involved in community service, where it is the offender's performance of a task (rather than the offender him or herself) which is being supervised' (Rex 1997: 116).

In a subsequent essay, I sought to provide a constructively critical assessment of several aspects of Andrew von Hirsch's version of desert theory (Bottoms 1998). The article was, therefore, primarily intended as a contribution to normative analysis. In one section of the paper, I used Susan Rex's empirical research results extensively, and I concluded as follows:

on the basis of Rex's research, it seems fairly clear that section 6(2(b)) of the Criminal Justice Act 1991, with its attempt to provide a unified desert-based 'penalty-scale' for community sentences based on 'the restrictions on liberty imposed by the order or orders' makes sense only if the phrase 'restrictions on liberty' is interpreted in a very different way for different community orders (Bottoms 1998: 74–5).

In short, normative analysis in criminology is emphatically not the unintellectual pursuit that positivism made it out to be. It can involve extremely intricate philosophical analysis, and this analysis can intersect with, and be illuminated by, empirical research at many points. Hence, the theory/data linkage is important in normative analysis, just as it is in doing explanatory work in criminology, though given the different purposes of normative and explanatory analyses, the theory/data dialogue necessarily manifests itself in different ways. Normative analysis has not often been included in previous discussions of the theory/research relationship in criminology; in the future it needs to be more centrally located in such discussions.

The theory/data relationship: a case example

In this final section, I aim to try to bring to life some aspects of the preceding discussion by means of a case example. The selected example is longitudinal, which means that one can trace shifts in the emphasis of the research over time. And, as will be seen towards the end of the example, it particularly highlights the possibility—flagged earlier in the chapter—of developing analyses that combine the *causal explanation* tradition of scholarship with the *interpretative understanding* tradition.

Among the leading US criminological researchers of the 1950s and 1960s were the Harvard-based husband-and-wife team, Sheldon and Eleanor Glueck. In 1950, they published *Unraveling Juvenile Delinquency* (Glueck and Glueck 1950), which was a comparative empirical study of 500 white male institutionalized juvenile delinquents (aged 10 < 17) and 500 male 'nondelinquents', the two samples being matched on an individualized case-by-case basis on four variables: age, type of home neighbourhood, measured IQ, and 'national origin' (based on parental and grandparental birthplace). In studying these samples, the researchers used interviews with research subjects, parents and teachers, as well as official records. Later, they also followed up the two samples to age 32, with a good re-contact rate (Glueck and Glueck 1968). In consequence, for these samples 'extensive data are available for analysis relating to criminal career histories, criminal justice interventions, family life, and recreational activities . . . in childhood, adolescence and young adulthood' (Sampson and Laub 1993: 29).

The Gluecks' analyses of these data can reasonably be described as 'multidisciplinary' and 'multifactoral' (i.e. aiming to give weight to a somewhat eclectic mixture of different causative factors); as based on 'empiricism' (i.e. based on the view that data can be apprehended directly); and as atheoretical or even anti-theoretical (Sampson and Laub 1993: 41–5). For these reasons, and despite the admirable dataset, the Gluecks' research initially had a mixed reception. Reservations were expressed especially by sociologists, who considered that the Gluecks had 'downplayed or ignored traditional sociological variables like stratification, peer group, culture and community characteristics' (Sampson and Laub 1993: 43). However, these justified sociological criticisms were also fairly often mixed with an opposition that was clearly ideological, being based on a political rather than scientific aversion to the Gluecks' view that some of the causes of crime are biological (Sampson and Laub 1993: 41–2; see also above on the potential dangers of ideological and 'political activist' criminologies).

In the mid-1980s, after the deaths of both Eleanor and Sheldon Glueck, Robert Sampson and John Laub discovered—in the sub-basement store of the Harvard Law School Library—more than fifty unsorted cartons containing the Gluecks' data for the *Unraveling* study, and its subsequent follow-up. They recoded and computerized this information, and set out to understand more fully what these rich data could tell a fresh generation of criminologists about criminal career patterns from childhood through adolescence and up to age 32. Part of this task was straightforwardly empirical—for example, the Gluecks had carried out few multivariate (as opposed to bivariate) analyses, and they had not paid sufficient attention to the temporal order of events in their subjects' lives, a matter that is, of course, potentially crucial to the causal interpretation of the data. But as well as tackling these technical issues, Sampson and Laub (1993) also deliberately located their reanalysis of the Gluecks' data within the theoretical context of the criminology of the 1980s. In that decade, there took place a fierce debate between two opposing camps in developmental criminology. One of these (led by Gottfredson and Hirschi 1990) argued that the central key to understanding criminal propensity and criminal careers is 'low self-control', a trait that was postulated as fixed in individuals by about age 10, and thereafter stable throughout the life course. Given these views, Gottfredson and Hirschi naturally considered the detailed longitudinal study of offenders' lives to be unnecessary (Sampson and Laub 1993: 2). In the other camp, however, researchers such as David Farrington (see, e.g., Farrington 1994) argued that longitudinal research studies on criminal careers revealed more complex empirical patterns than Gottfredson and Hirschi were willing to concede. It can, however, reasonably be argued that the strength of the position of this second group lay very largely in empirical rather than theoretical arguments.

Sampson and Laub (1993: 2) were to an extent attracted by Gottfredson and Hirschi's approach, particularly 'because of its emphasis on the importance of families in explaining the origins of juvenile delinquency', and because it highlighted continuities in behaviour at different stages in the life-course. On the other hand, they were 'troubled' by some features of the 'stability' thesis, and they doubted whether it took sufficient account of matters such as 'individual change and salient life events in adulthood'. Thus, Sampson and Laub set out the initial theoretical starting-point of their reanalysis of the Gluecks' data in the following manner:

By using longitudinal data properly (that is, longitudinally) and in a theoretically informed fashion, we believed new insights could be gained into the causes of crime. In our view, the theoretical puzzle provided by the two sides in the [1980s] debate in essence can be reduced to the following challenge: can we develop and test a theoretical model that accounts for the unfolding of childhood antisocial behavior, adolescent delinquency, and adult crime in longitudinal perspective? In other words, can we unravel crime and deviance over the full life course? (Sampson and Laub 1993: 2).

The term 'life course', at the end of the above quotation, is not used casually by the authors. Rather, it refers explicitly to Glen Elder's (1985) theorization of the 'life-course perspective' in social science, underlying which are two core concepts, namely 'trajectories' and 'transitions', which in certain circumstances can interlock to create a 'turning point':

Trajectories may be described as pathways or lines of development throughout life. These long-term patterns of behavior may include work life, marriage, parenthood, or criminal behavior. *Transitions*, on the other hand, are short-term events embedded in trajectories which may include starting a new job, getting married, having a child, or being sentenced to prison ... Transitional events may lead to *turning points*, or changes in an individual's life-course trajectory. For example, getting married may have a significant influence on a person's life and behavior, from changing where a person lives or works to changing the number and type of friends with whom one associates. Turning points may modify trajectories in ways that cannot be predicted from earlier events (Laub, Sampson, and Sweeten 2006: 314).

To use the language of Layder's 'adaptive theory', what Sampson and Laub are engaged in here is creating an initial 'theoretical scaffold' (the 'life course perspective', with its accompanying theoretical core concepts), which is intended to have a 'relatively durable form since it adapts reflexively rather than automatically in relation to empirical data', although it should be 'capable of accommodating new information and interpretations by reconfiguring itself' (Layder 1998: 150). In practice, what has happened since 1993 is that Sampson and Laub's use of the framework of Elder's 'life-course perspective' has remained fully durable, but within this framework the content of their initial substantive theorisation has—as we shall now see—undergone some significant modifications.

As noted above, Sampson and Laub intended their theory (developed in interaction with the Gluecks' data) to be able to embrace both continuity and change in criminal careers; or, more specifically, to be able to explain (i) the development of childhood and adolescent delinquency; (ii) continuity between adolescent delinquency and adult offending; and (iii) changes in behaviour in the post-adolescent years. To meet this challenge, the initial formulation of the theory linked the life-course perspective (see above) to one other theoretical tradition, namely a developed and modified version of Hirschi's (1969) *control theory*. As Laub, Sampson, and Sweeten (2006: 315) subsequently put it, the organizing principle of the initial theory was that:

delinquency or crime is more likely to occur when an individual's bond to society is attenuated ... Social ties also provide social and psychological resources that individuals may draw on as they move through life transitions. The concept of social bond echoes Toby's (1957) "stake in conformity", suggesting that the stronger an individual's social bonds, the more that person risks by engaging in criminal behavior. From this general theoretical framework Sampson and Laub (1993) propose three major themes. First, structural context is mediated in fundamental respects by informal family and school social controls, which, in turn, explain delinquency in childhood and adolescence. Second, there is strong continuity in antisocial behavior running from childhood through adulthood across a variety of life domains. Finally, informal social control in adulthood explains changes in criminal behavior over the life span, independent of prior individual differences in criminal propensity.

In the present context, in order to keep the discussion within bounds, I shall restrict attention to the third of the above points, namely changes in adult criminal behaviour. Sampson and Laub's (1993) original reanalysis of the Gluecks' data on criminal careers up to age 32 led them to conclude that two fresh control factors in particular had the capacity to alter the criminal trajectories that might seem to have been established during adolescence, and thus to become 'turning points'.[26] These factors were described by Sampson and Laub as weak or strong 'labour force attachment' and weak or strong 'marital attachment',[27] and—it is worth restating—they were found in the empirical analysis to be important '*independent of* prior [adolescent] individual differences in criminal propensity' (Laub, Sampson, and Sweeten 2006: 315, emphasis added).

If we now review the story to this point, we can initially note that Sampson and Laub's re-analysis of the Gluecks' data was set firmly in the context of their theoretical reflections on the developmental criminology debates of the 1980s, and the use of Elder's 'life-course perspective'. Thus, they showed a clear awareness from the outset of the need to bring a coherent initial theoretical focus to data analysis, there being no theory neutral facts. Thereafter, however, their work was essentially inductive in approach, but this led in due course to the creation of a rather ambitious *hypothesis* embracing 'crime, deviance and informal social control over the life-course' (Sampson and Laub 1993: 244). This hypothesis then became available for others to test, and some scholars have indeed done just that. A recent overview of much relevant research, mostly supportive of the theory, will be found in Laub, Sampson, and Sweeten (2006).[28] A further and perhaps particularly interesting study (not discussed in Laub *et al.*'s 2006 article) is by Michael Ezell and Lawrence Cohen (2005), which was based on longitudinal analysis (using official data) of three independent samples of wards of the California Youth Authority (at different

[26] Other but more minor 'turning points' were also identified for men in the sample, for example military service in the Second World War.

[27] 'Attachment to spouse' was a composite variable derived from interview data. 'Weak attachment' was indicated by 'signs of incompatibility'; subjects with 'strong attachment' generally displayed 'close, warm feelings towards their wives, or were compatible in a generally constructive relationship' (Sampson and Laub 1993: 144). Thus, the variable does not simply measure marriage/non-marriage, but also the quality of conjugal relationships.

[28] Of course, not all research testing the hypothesis is supportive. For example, although the empirical research base on the point remains slight, it seems that 'romantic partner attachment' might have different meanings and effects among female offenders than among males (Leverentz 2006).

dates). The authors indicated that their data did not allow them 'to test the specific causal structures of a particular theory or set of theories'; but they were nevertheless able to 'evaluate the empirical validity of the longitudinal implications of three leading criminological theoretical perspectives' (Ezell and Cohen 2005: 258). Of these three, the one that was the most consistent with the California data was that of Sampson and Laub (Ezell and Cohen 2005: 259).[29]

However, Sampson and Laub's theory has not remained unmodified since 1993. Naturally, their book was extensively reviewed, and some of these reviews posed constructively critical challenges to the authors. Laub and Sampson (2003: 7–8) later reported that they considered the 'most important' of these challenges to have been raised by John Modell (1994) in a book review in the *American Journal of Sociology*. Modell noted the authors' claims to have integrated a person-based and a variable-based analysis in *Crime in the Making* (Sampson and Laub 1993: 204), the former focused upon a qualitative analysis of the life history records of a subset of cases from the Gluecks' study, randomly selected from the cells of a typology. According to Modell, however, this qualitative analysis was 'not entirely satisfying', because the authors:

cannot divorce themselves from a variables focus, and they virtually treat this small intensive sample as a microscopic quantitative test of their hypotheses. Nor are they adept at discerning (or portraying) the inner logic of lives as revealed in data such as these.[30]

Very bravely, Laub and Sampson (2003: 8) later said that, having reflected on Modell's critique, they felt 'compelled by the evidence to agree'. For this and other reasons, they therefore embarked upon the difficult task of tracing and interviewing a sub-sample of the Gluecks' original 500 delinquents, in a quest to understand retrospectively 'the inner logic of [their] lives'—or, in other words, to add an 'interpretative understanding' dimension to their earlier work.[31] At the same time, the opportunity was taken to update the quantitative (official records) follow-up of the originally delinquent sample up to the age of *c.*65. To the relief of the authors, the results from these further quantitative data analyses and the fresh interview data were congruent.

In the light of this further research, Laub and Sampson (2003) modified the original formulation of their theory. As regards desistance from or persistence in crime during adulthood, there were two main modifications, namely the addition of 'structured routine activities' and 'purposeful human agency' to the original key variable of social bonds/social control. The 'routine activities' addition is essentially an empirical modification of the original hypothesis:

Structured routine activities modify the array of behavioral choices available to an individual ... The modified theory contends that structured routine activities condition the effect of social controls on offending. Persistent offenders are notable in their lack of structured routine activities across the life course. On the other hand, increased structure surrounding routine

---

[29] The other theoretical perspectives considered were Gottfredson and Hirschi's (1990) self-control theory and Terrie Moffitt's 'dual taxonomy' theory (on which see, now, Moffitt 2006).

[30] Modell (1994: 1391) noted, however, that Sampson and Laub were working with secondary data only, and that the original 'interviews and notes may well lack insight'.

[31] The interviewed subsample consisted of 52 of the original 500 delinquents, including 'persisters', 'desisters', and those with 'zigzag criminal careers'.

activities facilitates desistance from crime regardless of prior offending trajectories (Laub, Sampson, and Sweeten 2006: 323).

The addition of 'human agency' to the theory is, however, rather more radical. Although the authors do not state the matter in this way, this amendment seems to amount to no less than a modification of some of the ontological assumptions of the original theory. As Laub, Sampson, and Sweeten (2006: 323) put the matter:

the concept of human agency might seem inconsistent with the social control perspective, since a key distinction of control theories is their assumption of universal motivation to offend. That is, in the absence of constraints (social controls), individuals will offend ... However, in the revised age-graded theory a less stringent version of control theory is offered, assuming that human nature is malleable across the life course. In addition, the concept of human agency cannot be understood simply as a proxy for motivation. Rather, the concept of agency has the element of projective or transformative action within structural constraints. This goes beyond selection effects; that is, structures are in part determined by individual choices, and in turn structures constrain individual choices. Thus, the bi-directional interaction of choice and structure produces behavior that cannot be predicted from a focus on one to the other. The modified theory refers to agentic moves within structural context as 'situated choice' (Laub, Sampson, and Sweeten 2006: 323).

Perhaps curiously, however, although the authors introduced human agency into their theory in this way, they stopped short of any detailed exploration of what, in detail, the exercise of 'agency' might mean in a human subject, and how exactly this concept could bring further illumination to the task of explaining adult desistance or persistence. Impressed by Laub and Sampson's theoretical approach, but noting also this relative silence about agency, in a recent essay I attempted to advance the discussion by offering further theoretical suggestions about the potential role of human agency in desistance, drawing upon four different theoretical treatments of the concept of 'agency' from mainstream sociology and philosophy (Bottoms 2006).

   In the light of the earlier discussions in this chapter, how can we best describe the addition of 'human agency' to the Laub/Sampson theorization? Essentially, I think, this has to be seen, in the language of Layder's adaptive theory, as a significant modification of the original 'theoretical scaffold'. It will be recalled that, for Layder (1998: 150) a researcher's initially/constructed theoretical scaffold 'should never be regarded as immutable since it is capable of accommodating new information and interpretations by reconfiguring itself'. The incorporation of agency in the Sampson/Laub theorization is clearly more than just an attempt to add 'new information'; it is, instead, very much a 'new interpretation' which requires some definite ontological reconfiguration of the original scaffold. It is because this change is so potentially significant that Laub and Sampson are arguably open to criticism for not discussing more fully the implications of the modification.[32]

   From the point of view of this chapter, one matter of special interest that arises from the introduction of agency into the Laub/Sampson theorization concerns the compatibility of

---

[32] It should perhaps also be noted that Laub and Sampson were not the first to include a specific discussion of agency in considering the topic of desistance: see Giordano *et al.* (2002), published shortly before Laub and Sampson's revised theory. There remains, however, a theoretical disagreement between Laub and Sampson and Giordano *et al.*: see Laub, Sampson, and Sweeten (2006: 326).

the *explanation/causation* and *interpretative understanding* traditions. John Modell's (1994) review judged *Crime in the Making* to be deficient in understanding 'the inner logic of lives'; or, otherwise stated, to be lacking in interpretative understanding. Laub and Sampson's second book seeks to overcome this difficulty, and in doing so it explicitly rejects determinism (Laub and Sampson 2003: 34), so embracing a version of free will,[33] while also being wary of rational choice theory.[34] Yet clearly, Laub and Sampson also remain committed to the explanatory/causal enterprise of explaining criminal careers. Can there truly be a co-existence of (i) explanation/cause and (ii) free agentic choice, viewed in terms of the meaning of the act to the actor, within his/her social context(s)?

We are in very deep waters here, but briefly, my contention would be that coherent co-existence is possible, but only if we develop a concept of *explanation* which does not make *prediction* its central characteristic.[35] As I explained the matter in a recent essay, referring explicitly to the context of desistance:

Let us assume that P, an ex-prisoner, has decided to try to desist for the sake of the future of his newborn child, but one day some of his former criminal associates offer him the opportunity to join in the planning for what looks to be a promising factory break-in, potentially yielding large rewards. Let us further (and, undoubtedly, with more philosophical difficulty) assume that P is truly free to accept or reject this offer; that is, that whichever option he chooses he will afterwards be able to genuinely to say, 'I could have acted otherwise'. In *explanatory* terms, it is actually not at all difficult for us to explain whichever choice he makes. We know why P has decided to try to desist, so if he says 'no' to his criminal associates, we can explain that decision as a natural consequence of the prior desistance decision. But we also know that the lure of the money, a desire for his friends' esteem, and so on, might indeed constitute a real temptation to join their enterprise; so if P does say 'yes' to his friends, we can explain that decision as well ... What is difficult for the social scientist, in circumstances such as these, is in fact not explanation, but the *prediction* of which choice P will make. It is, however, perfectly possible to envisage a version of social science that says it *cannot* effectively predict such decisions, though *ex post facto* it can explain (Bottoms 2006: 281–2).

Let me make one final observation. At the end of their 2003 book, Laub and Sampson reflected upon the key methodological difference between their initial and subsequent research on the Gluecks' sample, namely the addition of qualitative retrospective interviews in the second phase. They noted that the change in research method was linked to the modification to the substantive theory:

as much as our earlier theory was linked to our methodological and analytical approach (for example, regression models focusing on holding individual differences constant to see the

[33] Note that it is normally considered analytical to the concept of human agency that, if it exists, one can truly say, in any normal situation, that 'he/she could have acted otherwise': see, e.g., Giddens (1993: 81); Bhaskar (1979: 146).

[34] On rational choice theory see Laub and Sampson (2003: 30–2). Note also the complex contextual (i.e., not simply rational choice) underpinnings of the authors' summary statement that: 'Offenders desist as a result of a combination of individual actions (choice) in conjunction with situational contexts and structural influences linked to important institutions that help sustain desistance. This fundamental theme underscores the need to examine both individual motivation and the social context in which individuals are embedded' (Laub and Sampson 2003: 145).

[35] This raises important questions about explanation in the social sciences, on which see more fully Hedström (2005).

effects of turning points), our revised theory here is also linked to our method and analytical strategy (for example, life-history narratives derived from the men themselves integrated with quantitative longitudinal data reconstructed from the Glueck archive supplemented by our own follow-up study at age 70). This merging of quantitative and qualitative data allowed us to gain insight into the life course of crime that would not [otherwise] have been possible (Laub and Sampson 2003: 293).

The use, in appropriate contexts, of both qualitative and quantitative research methods has been advocated throughout this chapter. So, too, has another prominent feature of the Laub-Sampson *oeuvre*, namely the obvious presence, throughout their research, of a continuing dialogue between theoretical reflection and empirical data-gathering and data analysis. As Derek Layder put it in the quotation at the head of this chapter, in many ways 'the really interesting questions' for researchers 'concern the nature of the relations between theory and empirical research'; moreover, as we have also seen, there is a continual need to return to those questions throughout the research process. As indicated at the beginning of this chapter, all this can be very challenging; but, as I hope the remainder of the chapter has demonstrated, it can also be exciting.

References

AYER, A. J. (1936/1971). *Language, Truth and Logic*. Harmondsworth: Penguin Books.

BARON, M. W., PETTIT, P., and SLOTE, M. (1997). *Three Methods of Ethics: A Debate*. Oxford: Blackwell.

BHASKAR, R. (1979). *The Possibility of Naturalism*. Brighton: Harvester.

BOTTOMS, A. E. (1993). 'Recent Criminological and Social Theory: The Problem of Integrating Knowledge about Individual Criminal Acts and Careers and Areal Dimensions of Crime' in D. P. Farrington, R. J. Sampson, and P-O. H. Wikström (eds), *Integrating Individual and Ecological Aspects of Crime*. Stockholm: National Council for Crime Prevention.

—— (1998). 'Five Puzzles in von Hirsch's Theory of Punishment' in A. Ashworth and M. Wasik (eds) *Fundamentals of Sentencing Theory*. Oxford: Clarendon Press.

—— (2006). 'Desistance, Social Bonds and Human Agency: A Theoretical Exploration' in P-O. Wikström and R. J. Sampson (eds),

The Explanation of Crime: Context, Mechanisms and Development. Cambridge: Cambridge University Press.

——, HAY, W., and SPARKS, J. R. (1990). 'Situational and Social Approaches to the Prevention of Disorder in Long-Term Prisons'. *The Prison Journal* 70: 83–95.

—— and McCLINTOCK, F. H. (1973). *Criminals Coming of Age*. London: Heinemann.

BRANTINGHAM, P. J. and BRANTINGHAM, P. L. (eds) (1981). *Environmental Criminology*. Beverly Hills, CA: Sage Publications.

BURCHELL, G., GORDON, C., and MILLER, P. (eds) (1991). *The Foucault Effect: Studies in Governmentality*. London: Harvester Wheatsheaf.

CLARKE, R. V. G. (1995). 'Situational Crime Prevention' in M. Tonry and D. P. Farrington (eds), *Building a Safer Society*. Chicago, Ill.: University of Chicago Press.

—— and FELSON, M. (eds) (1993). *Routine Activity and Rational Choice*. New Brunswick: Transaction Publishers.

COLEMAN, J. S. and FARRARO, T. J. (eds) (1992). *Rational Choice Theory: Advocacy and Critique*. London: Sage.

CORNISH, D. B., and CLARKE, R. V. G. (eds) (1986). *The Reasoning Criminal*. New York: Springer.

ELDER, G. H. Jr (1985). 'Perspectives on the Life Course', in G. H. Elder (ed.), *Life Course Dynamics*. Ithaca, NY: Cornell University Press.

EZELL, M. E. and COHEN, L. E. (2005). *Desisting from Crime: Continuity and Change in Long-Term Crime Patterns of Serious Chronic Offenders*. Oxford: Oxford University Press.

FARRINGTON, D. P. (1994). 'Human Development and Criminal Careers' in M. Maguire, R. Morgan, and R. Reiner (eds), *The Oxford Handbook of Criminology*. Oxford: Clarendon Press.

—— and DOWDS, E. A. (1985). 'Disentangling Criminal Behaviour and Police Reaction' in D. P. Farrington and J. Gunn (eds), *Reactions to Crime*. Chichester: John Wiley.

FELSON, M. (2002). *Crime and Everyday Life: Insights and Implications for Society* (3rd edn). Thousand Oaks, Calif.: Pine Forge Press.

FLEW, A. (ed.) (1979). *A Dictionary of Philosophy*. New York: St Martin's Press.

FOSTER, J. (1990). *Villains: Crime and Community in the Inner City*. London: Routledge.

FOUCAULT, M. (1979). *Discipline and Punish: The Birth of the Prison*. Harmondsworth: Penguin Books.

FREIRE, P. (1972). *Pedagogy of the Oppressed*. Harmondsworth: Penguin Books.

GARLAND, D. (1990). *Punishment and Modern Society*. Oxford: Clarendon Press.

—— (1997). ' "Governmentality" and the Problem of Crime: Foucault, Criminology, Sociology'. *Theoretical Criminology* 1: 173–214.

GIDDENS, A. (1984). *The Constitution of Society*. Cambridge: Polity Press.

—— (1991). 'Structuration Theory: Past, Present and Future' in C. Bryant and D. Jary (eds), *Giddens' Theory of Structuration: A Critical Appreciation*. London: Routledge.

—— (1993). *New Rules of Sociological Method* (2nd edn). Cambridge: Polity Press.

GIORDANO, P. C., CERNOVICH, S. A., and RUDOLPH, J. L. (2002). 'Gender, Crime and Desistance: Towards a Theory of Cognitive Transformation'. *American Journal of Sociology* 107: 990–1064.

GLASER, A. and STRAUSS, A. (1967). *The Discovery of Grounded Theory*. Chicago, Ill.: Aldine.

GLUECK, S. and GLUECK, E. (1950). *Unraveling Juvenile Delinquency*. Cambridge, Mass: Harvard University Press.

—— (1968). *Delinquents and Nondelinquents in Perspective*. Cambridge, Mass: Harvard University Press.

GOTTFREDSON, M. R. and HIRSCHI, T. (1990). *A General Theory of Crime*. Stanford, CA: Stanford University Press.

GREGSON, N. (1989). 'On the (Ir)relevance of Structuration Theory to Empirical Research' in D. Held and J. B. Thompson (eds), *Social Theory of Modern Societies: Anthony Giddens and His Critics*. Cambridge: Cambridge University Press.

GUBA, Y. and LINCOLN, E. (1989). *Fourth Generation Evaluation*. London: Sage Publications.

HARPER, G. and CHITTY, C. (eds) (2005). *The Impact of Corrections on Reoffending: A Review of 'What Works'* (3rd edn). Home Office Research Study 291. London: Home Office.

HARRISON, R. (1992). 'The Equality of Mercy' in H. Gross and R. Harrison (eds), *Jurisprudence: Cambridge Essays*. Cambridge: Cambridge University Press.

HART, H. L. A. (1982). *Essays on Bentham.* Oxford: Clarendon Press.

HEDSTRÖM, P. (2005). *Dissecting the Social: On the Principles of Analytical Sociology.* Cambridge: Cambridge University Press.

HENRY, S. and MILOVANOVIC, D. (1996). *Constitutive Criminology.* London: Sage Publications.

HIRSCHI, T. (1969). *Causes of Delinquency.* Berkeley: University of California Press.

HOBBS, D., HADFIELD, P., LISTER, S., and WINLOW, S. (2003). *Bouncers: Violence and Governance in the Night-Time Economy.* Oxford: Oxford University Press.

HOLLIS, M. (2002). *The Philosophy of Social Science: An Introduction* (revised edn). Cambridge: Cambridge University Press.

HONDERICH, T. (ed.) (2005). *The Oxford Companion to Philosophy* (2nd edn). Oxford: Oxford University Press.

HOOVER, K. and DONOVAN, T. (2004). *The Elements of Social Scientific Thinking* (8th edn). Belmont, CA: Wadsworth/Thomson.

LAUB, J. H. and SAMPSON, R. J. (2003). *Shared Beginnings, Divergent Lives: Delinquent Boys to Age 70.* Cambridge, Mass: Harvard University Press.

——, ——, and SWEETEN, G. A. (2006). 'Assessing Sampson and Laub's Life-Course Theory of Crime', in F. T. Cullen, J. P. Wright, and K. R. Blevins (eds), *Taking Stock: The Status of Criminological Theory.* New Brunswick: Transaction Publishers.

LAYDER, D. (1994). *Understanding Social Theory.* London: Sage Publications.

—— (1998). *Sociological Practice: Linking Theory and Social Research.* London: Sage Publications.

LEVERENTZ, A. M. (2006). 'The Love of a Good Man?: Romantic Relationships as a Source of Support or Hindrance for Female Ex-Offenders'. *Journal of Research in Crime and Delinquency* 43: 459–88.

LIEBLING, A. with ARNOLD, H. (2004). *Prisons and Their Moral Performance: A Study of Values, Quality and Prison Life.* Oxford: Oxford University Press.

MAGEE, B. (1973). *Popper.* Glasgow: Fontana/Collins.

MATZA, D. (1969). *Becoming Deviant.* Englewood Cliffs, NJ: Prentice-Hall.

MERTON, R. K. (1967). *On Theoretical Sociology.* New York: Free Press.

MODELL, J. (1994). Book Review of *Crime in the Making. American Journal of Sociology* 99: 1389–91.

MOFFITT, T. E. (2006). 'A Review of Research on the Taxonomy of Life-Course Persistent versus Adolescence—Limited Antisocial Behavior', in F. T. Cullen, J. P. Wright, and K. R. Blevins (eds), *Taking Stock: The Status of Criminological Theory.* New Brunswick: Transaction Publishers.

MURPHY, J. G. and HAMPTON, J. (1988). *Forgiveness and Mercy.* Cambridge: Cambridge University Press.

ORMEROD, P. (1998). *Butterfly Economics.* London: Faber.

PAWSON, R. and TILLEY, N. (1997). *Realistic Evaluation.* London: Sage Publications.

POPPER, K. (1968). *The Logic of Scientific Discovery.* London: Hutchinson.

RADZINOWICZ, L. (1966). *Ideology and Crime.* London: Heinemann.

—— (1999). *Adventures in Criminology.* London: Routledge.

RAWLS, J. (1972). *A Theory of Justice.* London: Oxford University Press.

REX, S. (1997). 'Perceptions of Probation in a Context of "Just Deserts"'. Unpublished Ph.D. thesis, University of Cambridge.

ROCK, P. (1993). *The Social World of an English Crown Court.* Oxford: Clarendon Press.

RUNCIMAN, W. G. (1972). *A Critique of Max Weber's Philosophy of Social Science.* Cambridge: Cambridge University Press.

SAMPSON, R. J. and LAUB, J. H. (1993). *Crime in the Making: Pathways and Turning Points through Life.* Cambridge, Mass: Harvard University Press.

SHERMAN, L. W., FARRINGTON, D. P., WELSH, B. C., and MACKENZIE, D. L. (eds) (2006). *Evidence-Based Crime Prevention* (rev. edn). London: Routledge.

SKINNER, Q. (ed.) (1990). *The Return of Grand Theory in the Human Sciences.* Cambridge: Cambridge University Press.

SPARKS, R., BOTTOMS, A. E., and HAY, W. (1996). *Prisons and the Problem of Order.* Oxford: Clarendon Press.

STRAUSS, A. (1987). *Qualitative Analysis for Social Scientists.* New York: Cambridge University Press.

—— and CORBIN, J. (eds) (1997). *Grounded Theory in Practice.* Thousand Oaks, CA: Sage Publications.

SUMNER, C. (ed.) (1990). *Censure, Politics and Criminal Justice.* Milton Keynes: Open University Press.

TOBY, J. (1957). 'Social Disorganization and Stake in Conformity: Complementary Factors in the Predatory Behavior of Hoodlums'. *Journal of Criminal Law, Criminology and Police Science* 48: 12–17.

VON HIRSCH, A. (1986). *Past or Future Crimes.* Manchester: Manchester University Press.

—— BOTTOMS, A. E., BURNEY, E., and WIKSTRÖM, P-O. (1999). *Criminal Deterrence and Sentence Severity.* Oxford: Hart Publishing.

WALKER, N. D. (1995). 'The Quiddity of Mercy'. *Philosophy* 70: 27–37.

WEBER, M. (1978). *Economy and Society: An Outline of Interpretive Sociology.* Berkeley: University of California Press.

WRIGHT, R. T. and DECKER, S. H. (1994). *Burglars on the Job.* Boston, Mass.: Northeastern University Press.

4

In search of causes and explanations of crime

Per-Olof Wikström

Introduction

The problems of causation and explanation are fundamental to criminology and crime prevention. Explaining and preventing acts of crime requires that there are causes of crime and that we can learn (through reasoning and experience) what these causes are. *If there are no causes, there is nothing to explain, and prevention is not possible.*[1]

When scholars, or politicians and practitioners, argue about such things as whether deterrence prevents crime or whether being brought up in a deprived social environment turns people into criminals, they fundamentally raise questions about causation and explanation. When a local crime prevention partnership devises a strategy and programme of crime prevention they (should)[2] presume that the measures they take will help prevent crime and thus assume (at least implicitly) that they address some factor/s that cause/s individuals to get involved in acts of crime.

The problem of causation and explanation is not always dealt with very well; in fact, it is often ignored within criminology and crime prevention. I have previously argued that criminology suffers from a poor understanding of causal mechanisms and a lack of integration of levels of explanation and suggested that to achieve a better understanding of the causes of crime, we need a clear definition of the concept of crime (what to explain) and a developed theory of action through which levels of explanation can be integrated and (individual and environmental) factors status as potential causes can be assessed (Wikström 2004, 2005, 2006a).

One main consequence of the current state of affairs is that we, so to speak, have *too many* (biological, psychological, and social) correlates (factors) that we struggle to make sense of, a fact which has led some observers to question if 'everything matters' and others whether 'anything matters' (see Wikström 2004).

---

[1] I use the concept of explanation here in reference to attempts to make intelligible *how* a putative cause brings about an effect. Prevention can either be achieved by (a) removing a cause/s or (b) intervening in a causal process.

[2] The reason I stress 'should' is that sometimes crime prevention actors appear to be more concerned with showing that they act and that they spend the funds allocated to them than being concerned with whether their measures are actually capable of preventing crime by addressing some of its causes (see Wikström 2006b).

The common neglect of properly addressing the problem of causation in criminological research frequently makes it unclear whether identified correlates represent causes or constitute only symptoms or markers and often leads to the confusion of prediction and causation. This is a situation that is not only unhelpful for the development of criminological knowledge but also unhelpful to policy makers and practitioners who wish to develop effective crime prevention policies (e.g. it doesn't help them to target the right (causal) factors in their efforts to prevent crime).

In this chapter I shall discuss the problem of causation and explanation and argue that a more in-depth consideration of these topics in our theorizing and empirical research may help us better to understand crime and its prevention. I will start with briefly outlining a scientific realism perspective on the study of crime, then move on to discuss the concept of crime (what is to be explained by theories of crime causation), deal with the concepts of causation and explanation, and thereafter address some specific topics relating to the problem of causation and explanation that, in my view, are particularly important to consider when conducting criminological research and interpreting its findings. I will conclude with some observations on the problem of causation in relation to crime prevention.

A scientific realism perspective on the explanation of crime

Realism is the idea that the world exists independent of us, and our theorizing about it (e.g. Bunge 2001). The aim of science is to find out how the world works (causes, explanations) through theorizing and empirical study (reasoning and experience). According to a realist perspective we do not invent causes and explanations, we *discover* them.

If there is no reality independent of us (e.g. if everything is a social construction), science would have no point since it would be impossible to learn anything about the world and how it works (i.e. about causes and explanations). There would be nothing real outside us to theorize about and nothing to study empirically. All arguments would be equally valid because there would be no objective truth (independent reality) to judge our views against.

A realist perspective should not be confused with classic 'positivism' or 'empiricism', although it shares some of its general approaches to science. Phillips (2000: 157, italics in original) points out that 'the term *positivist* is widely used as a generalized term of abuse' and goes on to say that

the general fantasy is that anyone who is impressed by the sciences as a pinnacle for achievement of human knowledge, anyone who uses statistics or numerical data, anyone who believes that hypotheses need to be substantially warranted, anyone who is a realist (another unanalysed but clearly derogatory word) is thereby a positivist.

On a similar note Bunge (1999: 185) states that 'positivism-bashing has become fashionable' and goes on to say that

'there are two kinds of antipositivist: enlightened and obscurantist. Enlightened antipositivism attacks the narrowness of positivism and seeks to overcome its limitations, in particular its attachment to empiricism, its phenomenalist metaphysics, and its slighting of theory. By contrast the obscurantist antipositivism criticizes what is best in positivism: its (unrequited) love of science and mathematics, its conceptual clarity and use of formal methods, its demands for tests, and its criticism of obscurantism.

Broadly speaking, the hallmark of 'positivism' and 'empiricism' is that these approaches to science do not allow for the inclusion of unobservable mechanisms (processes) as part of scientific study and that science is restricted to collecting and analysing observable data and making empirical generalizations based on relationships between observable data. In contrast, the aim to discover *mechanisms and processes* is an essential feature of the realist approach to science. Gasper (1990: 292, my emphasis) states that

on a realist view, scientific theories *do more* than tell us about observable regularities. They provide us with an inventory of what sorts of entities, mechanisms, processes, etc. (observable and unobservable) exist, and tell us something about the relations between them.

A realist perspective does not deny that *different people may view the same reality differently* and that this is an important insight, but it proposes that such differences can be explained (have causes). They may, for example, be due to differences in previous experiences and knowledge (i.e. the fact that perceptions of reality may differ can be rationally explained). As Bunge puts it, 'acknowledging the truth of the Thomas "theorem" involves no concession to subjectivism: it only adds subjective experience to the domain of facts to be studied objectively' (Bunge 1999: 9)[3].

Scientific progress in a realist view is gaining ever more adequate knowledge about reality (or some aspect of reality) and how it works (mechanisms, processes) through better theorizing and improved empirical study. This knowledge is likely never to be complete. Popper (2000: 13) claims that 'scientific knowledge' is 'guesswork [hypotheses] controlled by criticism and experiment'. To advance science we need good theory and to put our theories to the test by exposing them to and learning from rational criticism and empirical tests so they can be changed or refined the better to approximate reality. Judging if a given theory is better than another theory is fundamentally a question of assessing (based on reason and experience) which theory is nearer the truth (ibid. pp. 22–5).

Social and behavioural science may be viewed as an attempt to gain knowledge about social reality and how it works through theorizing and empirical study. Social reality consists of humans and their actions and their relationships to and interactions with each other and with animals and material things. Understanding and explaining social reality is to understand humans and to explain their actions and interactions.

Criminology[4] may be viewed as a branch of the social and behavioural sciences that aims at a scientific study of, in a narrow sense, acts of crime or, in a broader sense, moral actions (see further below). It is thus a branch of the social and behavioural sciences that attempts to gain knowledge about moral action (crime) through theorizing and empirical study with the goal of understanding and explaining why humans follow and breach moral rules (laws).

---

[3] The Thomas theorem roughly states that what is perceived as real will be treated as real and therefore real in its consequences.

[4] I reserve the term *criminal justice studies* for all research that deals with the operations and administration of the criminal justice system and its organizations.

The concept of crime (what to explain)

The concept of crime is often not very well defined, or sometimes not defined at all, in criminological studies. Without a clear understanding of *what* crime is, it is difficult to build an adequate theory of *its* causes, and therefore also difficult to assess empirically the value of *its* proposed explanations. The first task to address in an analysis of crime causation should therefore be the definition of the concept of crime (what to explain).

There is little doubt that crimes are *acts* (sequences of bodily movements—or withheld bodily movements—under the guidance of an individual) and hence have to be explained as such. However, crimes are not particular types of act. Any act can, in principle, be defined as an act of crime and what acts constitute crime can vary by place and over time[5]. This fact has made some observers despair about the possibility of a general theory of crime (and the possibility of identifying fundamental causes of crime) because (so it is argued) the acts labelled as crimes are too heterogeneous to fit a common explanation, for example, includes everything from shop-lifting to plane hijackings, or because what is labelled crime one day can be legal the next day just by a political decision; in fact, all crimes can be abolished by a political decision (see, further, Wikström 2006a).

However, the fact that crimes are acts is not their distinguishing feature but rather the fact that they are acts (any types of act) that violate a rule stipulated by the law. An act of crime is thus defined by the fact that carrying out the act (or refraining from carrying out the act[6]) violates a rule stipulated by the law, stating what is the right or wrong thing to do (or not to do) in a particular circumstance. Rules that state what is the right or wrong thing to do (or not to do) may be referred to as moral rules. Laws are one kind of moral rules. *Crime* may thus be defined as *acts that breach a moral rule defined in the law*.

Defining crime this way has the great advantage of allowing the concept of crime to encompass what all acts of crime, in all places at all times, have in common, namely, the breaking of a moral rule (defined in law). Explaining crime is not explaining why people hit each other, why they drive at 110 mph or why they smoke, but why they do so when it is illegal to do so. For example, I submit that it is a very different task to explain why someone drives a car at 110 mph on a race track where it is legal to do so from why someone drives a car at 110 mph on a public road where it is illegal to do so; or why someone hits another person in a boxing match which it is legal to do from why someone hits another person in a pub brawl which it is illegal to do.

Viewed in this way, crimes are best analysed as moral actions (actions guided by moral rules) and acts of crimes are best treated as a subcategory of the wider category of moral rule-breakings[7]. In other words, 'the foundation of a general theory of crime is not the law but the

---

[5] However, I do not wish to argue for any position of relativism as regarding what kind of moral rules and laws we have. In fact, I think a good case can be made that most moral rules and laws emerge out of (more or less successful) attempts to deal with the problem of social order, and some may even have grounding in human nature. However, determining the origins of moral rules and laws is not a problem that needs to be specifically addressed when attempting to explain why people follow or breach moral rules (laws), interesting as it may be.

[6] For example, in the UK, refraining from the act of reporting a plot of terrorism of which one is aware is a violation of a law.

[7] The fact that we have certain moral rules and laws does not imply that everyone subscribes to particular moral rules or laws, or finds them legitimate according to higher order moral principles. On the contrary, one important reason why people breach a certain moral rule (law) may be that they disagree with the particular rule.

existence of moral rules (of which laws are a special case)' (Wikström 2006a: 65–6). To explain crime is fundamentally a question of explaining why people follow and break moral rules. It is not the fact that a rule is stated in law that is of importance but that it is a moral rule (a rule stating what is the right or wrong thing to do or not to do). What differentiates crime from other moral rule-breakings is simply that the former is defined in law by political bodies (and enforced and punished by the authority of the state through its agencies)[8].

The key question in any study of crime causation is, in the narrow sense, *what causes individuals to breach moral rules defined in law?* and, in the broader sense, *what causes individuals to breach moral rules?* When we look for causes of crime we should fundamentally look for factors that move people to breach moral rules (defined in law).

A theory of crime causation is a special case of a theory of moral rule-breaking, or more generally, of moral action. I would even go so far as to claim that a theory of moral action is at the core of a theory of human action since rules that regulate conduct (what we ought or ought not to do) is a key element (perhaps *the* key element) in the understanding and explanation of human behaviour more generally.

The concepts of causation and explanation

In our daily life we generally operate under the belief that there are causes, that things which happen have causes (e.g. illnesses or accidents) and that through our actions we can cause some things to happen (e.g. we can light a cigarette by the use of matches) or avoid causing other things to happen (e.g. we can avoid getting killed or seriously hurt by not stepping out in front of moving cars). I submit that our everyday experiences of causation are probably the best intuitive evidence there is of the existence of causation (even if we may often be mistaken about the real cause of a particular event).

The fact that through science we have been able to understand, manage, and control many aspects of nature, and some aspects of human behaviour, is perhaps even more powerful evidence that causation exists. Just imagine if there were no causation (if earthquakes happened for no reason, planes crashed for no reason, people got diseases for no reason, and people killed each other for no reason), nothing we or others could do to influence our own lives and what is happening in the world. Politics would then be meaningless because politics are based on the idea that we can influence things (to be the way we want them to be) and that, in turn, is based on the idea that things have causes which (in principle) can be manipulated.

The fundamental questions about causation

Two fundamental questions about causation are:

i.   What is causation?

ii. How can it be established?

---

[8] The State is, of course, generally a comparatively powerful promoter and enforcer of the moral rules it (through its bodies and agencies) decides to endorse and enforce and this is a relevant consideration in the explanation of why people follow or break the rules of the law.

Addressing these questions is not an easy task as the vast philosophical literature and debate on this topic clearly demonstrates (e.g. von Wright 1971; Bunge 1979; Salmon 1998; Psillos 2002). What follows in the rest of this chapter is (i) my take on the problem of causation (and explanation) based on my reading and assessment of some of the key arguments and debates in the literature on causation and explanation, and (ii) my view on how a more in-depth consideration of these problems may help us to achieve a better understanding of why people commit acts of crime (breach moral rules).

Causation as a regular association

The basic idea of causation appears to be 'if this happens that will happen'; that is, 'if C (the cause), then E (the effect)'. Causation is often understood to refer to a *regularly occurring association* that will hold universally (or, at least, in a specific context or under certain circumstances); that is, 'if C, then always E' or 'if C in this context (circumstance), then always E'. Further, it is often stated that *the effect must succeed the cause in time* (even if we are only talking milliseconds) and that the cause and effect are *spatio-temporally linked* (contiguous in time and space). The view that causation is fundamentally a regular association between events (conditions) is often called Humean Causation or the Regularity View of Causation (e.g. Psillos 2002: 19).

In this view the idea of causation is closely linked to the ability to make *predictions*. The requirement for the possibility of making successful predictions is that we know (from experience) that there is a regular association between C and E and hence when C occurs, we can predict that E also will occur (e.g. we can predict based on previous experiences of what happens when people step out in front of a moving car that if someone steps out in front of a moving car, they will be seriously hurt or killed). In other words, knowledge about regular associations makes it possible to make accurate predictions.

Causation as the production of effects

However, the idea of causation is not only the idea of a regular association (and the possibility of prediction) but also the idea that the cause in some way is *responsible* for the effect. If that was not the case all things that are regularly associated with an outcome would qualify as its cause (for example, barometer readings would be the cause of weather conditions)[9]. Bunge (1979: 44, italics in original) argues that a regular association (correlation) is not enough to establish a cause, 'because it does not state that a given entity (or a change in it) is *produced* by another entity (or by a change in it), but just that the two are regularly associated', and he goes on to claim that 'the reduction of causation to regular association , as propounded by Humeans, amounts to mistaking causation for *one of its tests*' (ibid. p. 46, my emphasis). According to this view, causation is not about regular association but about production of effects, that is, about the *process* (*mechanism*) that (i) connects the cause and the effect *and* (ii) brings about the effect. The question of whether a regular association is also a case of causation is thus a question of whether or not there is a process (mechanism) that connects the cause and effect *and* that brings about the effect (the latter condition ['brings about'] is what makes the process causal as opposed to just a process).

---

[9] The philosophical literature on causation is full of examples like this where it is shown that a particular regular association cannot in any meaningful way be treated as a case of causation (see, e.g., Salmon 1998; Psillos 2002).

Differentiating between correlation and causation

The problem of being able to distinguish between mere correlation and causation is crucial for advancing our knowledge about crime causation (and crime prevention, for that matter). As we have seen, viewing causation as regular association does not help us to solve this problem. For example, the fact that an individual characteristic or an environmental feature is highly (or even perfectly) correlated with individuals' crime involvement is not enough to establish causation.

However, the view that causation is fundamentally about the process (mechanism) that connects the cause and the effect and brings about the effect helps us distinguish between correlation and causation because in cases of mere correlation (such as the association between barometer readings and weather conditions) there is no process (mechanism) by which one produces the other. When there is no connecting process (mechanism) that brings about the effect, the 'cause' at best represents a *symptom*[10] or a *marker* (e.g. the 'cause' and the 'effect' are both effects of a common cause) or is purely accidental. One main implication of what has been said is that *predictions do not necessarily imply causation*. We may very well be able to predict accurately one event (condition) from another without there being a causal dependency between the two.

The concepts of cause and effect

We have already defined causation as the operation of 'a process (mechanism) that connects the cause and the effect and brings about the effect'. Von Wright (1971: 70) defines '*cause*' and '*effect*' in the following way: '*p* is a cause relative to *q*, and *q* an effect relative to *p*, if and only if by doing *p* we would bring about *q* or by suppressing *p* we would remove *q* or prevent it from happening'.

This implies that the concept of cause refers to an entity (event, condition) that when triggered has some kind of intrinsic *powers* (*agency*)[11] to initiate a process (mechanism) that brings about a particular effect. If we make the cause happen, this will initiate the process (mechanism) that brings about the effect; to cause something to happen is thus to initiate a process (mechanism) that brings about that particular something (effect). The main implication of this is that only things (conditions, events) that have some kind of intrinsic powers (agency) to initiate a causal process that brings about a particular effect can be regarded as causes and this is thus what distinguishes them from mere correlates. For example, *attributes*, such as sex and age, cannot be causes (e.g. Holland 1986). If this reasoning is correct, it means that for anything (event, condition) to qualify as a putative cause of crime it has to have some kind of power (agency) to initiate a process (mechanism) that brings about an act of crime (a moral rule-breaking defined in law).

A cause cannot be defined independently of its effect (a cause has to be a cause of something), while an effect can be defined independently of its cause/s. For example, we can define acts of crime without involving any reference to their putative causes, but we cannot (at least should not) define putative causes of crime without referring to what crime is. This implies that the starting point for the search for causes (and explanations)

---

10 Salmon (1998: 45) gives the following example: 'Both fever and characteristic types of spots are symptoms of measles. The fever does not cause the spots and the spots do not cause the fever, yet there is a remarkable statistical relevance [correlation] of the one to the other.'

11 Harré and Madden (1975: 87) state that 'to ascribe a power to a thing asserts only that it can do what it does in virtue of its nature'.

is the identification of a particular effect (problem) whose causes we would like better to understand. This, in turn, highlights the importance of clearly defining the effect (problem) we are interested in explaining because this will guide (and set limits for) our search for possible causes and explanations. For example, the possible causes (and explanations) of 'crime' may very well be different if we define crime as 'acts of force and fraud undertaken in the pursuit of self-interest' (Gottfredson and Hirschi 1990: 15) or if we (as I have done) define acts of crime as 'acts that breach a moral rule defined in the law' (see Wikström and Treiber 2007).

Necessary and sufficient causes

Causes can be necessary or sufficient. The difference between a necessary and a sufficient cause is that in the case of a *necessary cause* the effect will not appear if the cause does not appear (because there are no other causes of the particular effect), whilst in the case of a *sufficient cause* the only claim is that the effect will appear when the cause appears because there may be many other causes of the particular effect (for example, there may be many causes of why a fire starts or why people die). When we are dealing with acts of crime (as the effect concerned) we are likely to deal with sufficient rather than necessary causes. There are most likely many potential causes of why an individual may commit an act of crime (a moral rule-breaking).

Causes and causal processes

The fact that there may be many sufficient *causes* that can produce a particular effect does not rule out the fact that there may be a smaller number of *causal processes* (mechanisms) that connect (many different) causes with a particular effect. Recall that a cause is a factor (event, condition) that triggers the process (mechanism) that brings about the effect, and it is possible that many different factors (events, conditions) can bring about a particular process that result in a particular effect. For example, a person may be fatally injured in many ways (e.g. by being hit by a car or falling off a rooftop) but the process that causes him to die may be the same, even if there are many different ways to receive a fatal injury.

Whilst there may be many sufficient causes that will produce acts of crime, it is plausible that there are a smaller number of causal processes that connect the many different causes with the commission of acts of crime. I have suggested elsewhere that there are basically two processes involved in the explanation of human action (and acts of crime); one habitual and one deliberative process (see, further, Wikström 2006a). One great advantage of (successfully) identifying basic causal processes that produce acts of crime is that they can be used to assess whether suggested causes are, in fact, causes or mere correlates. For example, if I am right that moral habits and moral judgements are the basic causal processes involved in the commission of acts of crime, putative causes of crime are those factors that can trigger the kind of moral habits or moral judgements that will lead to the breaking of moral rules defined in law.

Causal interactions

A *causal interaction* may be conceptualized as 'when the intersection of two or more factors (or processes) set in motion a causal process producing a particular effect'. The concept of causal interaction is one of the more interesting when studying human behaviour.

It is plausible to argue that human acts, like acts of crime, are always an outcome of a particular individual's encounter with a particular setting and hence that the cause of action is always a question of a causal interaction. That is, it is the interaction between (some) individual characteristics and experiences and (some) features of the setting in which the individual takes part that initiates a habitual or deliberative process that in the end makes him or her act in a particular way. For example, only for some adolescents (depending on their individual characteristics and experiences) may the exposure to an opportunity to steal a CD trigger a habitual or deliberative process that results in an act of theft. I submit that human actions, like acts of crime, are best analysed as outcomes of causal interactions that initiate a causal process that brings about the particular effect (e.g. an act of crime). In other words, when we talk about causes of human actions, we are likely to talk about causal interactions.

Establishing causation

Although a regular association (and the ability to predict the occurrence of E from the occurrence of C) might be indicative of causation, there is (as we have discussed above) far from any guarantee that this is the case. The best way empirically to establish causation is through *manipulation*, that is, by demonstrating that *if C is manipulated in certain ways, E will always change in predicted ways*. If it is a question of mere correlation, manipulating C will not produce changes in E because there is no causal process linking (the putative) 'cause' and 'the effect' that can be affected by our manipulations. For example, if we destroy or manipulate a barometer (or all barometers in the entire world) this will have no effect on the weather conditions because the barometer readings do not cause weather conditions (they are merely correlated with them)[12].

To establish causation is thus not to demonstrate that we can predict the occurrence of E from the occurrence of C but to demonstrate that we can predict that the introduction or suppression of C, or particular changes of C, will result in the occurrence or disappearance of E, or particular changes in E.

In principle, the more times and ways in which we can manipulate C and demonstrate that E changes in predicted ways, the more sure we can be that we are dealing with a causal process (i.e. that we have established that there is a causal dependency between C and E).

Establishing causal interactions

I have already argued that human actions, like acts of crime, are best analysed as an outcome of the (causal) interaction between (some) individual characteristics or experiences and (some) environmental features of the settings[13] in which the individual takes part. The basic idea of causal interaction in the explanation of human behaviour may thus be described in the following way: change the individual or change the setting and a different action will follow.

If this assumption is correct (which I believe it is), it implies that a change of the individual (in his or her relevant characteristics and experiences) or a change in the settings in which he or she takes part (in its relevant features) would cause a change in behaviour. We can thus

---

[12] If we manipulate the barometer readings this may only result in there no longer being any correlation between the two.

[13] With a *setting* I mean the part of the environment to which an individual is exposed (can access with his or her senses). The configuration of all settings an individual is exposed to during a specific period of time may be referred to as his or her *activity field*.

Table 4.1 Acts of crime as an outcome of a causal interaction between (some) individual characteristics and (some) setting features

Individual characteristics	Setting features	
	A	B
A	Crime (1)	No crime (2)
B	No crime (3)	No crime (4)

test a theory of a causal interaction between particular individual characteristics and experiences and particular environmental features by either manipulating the relevant individual characteristics and experiences or by manipulating the relevant features of the setting. Lets assume that we have two individual characteristics (A and B) and two features of a setting (A and B) and that our theory states that only individuals with characteristics A when exposed to setting A would act in a particular way, e.g. commit an act of crime (see Table 4.1).

Let us further assume that we can manipulate an individual's characteristics (from A to B or from B to A) or a settings feature (from A to B or from B to A). The predicted outcomes of our manipulations (if the theory is correct) would be the following: for cell (1) in Table 4.1 changing the individual's characteristics or the features of the setting would change the outcome in both cases from crime to no-crime; for cell (2) a change in the features of the setting would result in an act of crime but not a change in the characteristics of the individual; for cell (3) a change in the individual's characteristics would result in an act of crime but not a change in the features of the setting; and for cell (4) neither a change in the individual's characteristics nor a change in the features of the setting would change the outcome.

In practice it is, of course, often difficult (at times virtually impossible) to manipulate many of an individual's characteristics (at least in the short term) so our best option for testing causal interactions through manipulation (even if that too is often difficult) is to expose individuals with different relevant characteristics to a particular setting (or change in setting) and observe whether they respond differently, as predicted, to the exposure to the setting (or change of setting).

The scientific experiment

Arguably the best method for addressing the problem of establishing causation is the *scientific experiment*. The scientific experiment has been described by von Wright (1971: 82) as 'one of the most ingenious and consequential devices of the human mind'. The core idea of the scientific experiment may be described as one of *intervention*. By *manipulating* a regular association and *observing* what happens we can assess whether or not there is a case of causal dependency between C and E (or if it is a case of mere correlation). If there is a causal dependency between C and E, the latter (E) should change as a result of the intervention.

The idea of *counterfactuals* is important in experimentation (von Wright 1971) although controversial among philosophers (e.g. Bunge 2006; Salmon 1998)[14]. For

---

[14] Bunge (2006: 238) points out that 'counterfactuals are neither true nor false, since they cannot be put to the test. However, some counterfactual questions, such as those involved in thought-experiment, do have a heuristic power'.

example, in a clinical trial the logic of the test is that if person A receives 'the treatment' and person B does not receive 'the treatment' one would expect (if the hypothesis is correct) that person A would display the anticipated effect (e.g. 'get cured') whilst person B would not. This implies that if person A had not received the treatment he would not have been cured and that if person B had received the treatment he would have been cured (and these are the counterfactual arguments—that is, arguments about what would have happened if things were otherwise than they are).

The essence of the experiment is that we can produce the effect (or withhold the effect) through manipulation of the cause; the effect will happen *if* we introduce the cause but will not happen *if* we do not introduce the cause (the key word here is *if*). To establish causation through the scientific experiment is thus to establish that the effect appears when the cause appears and that the effect does not appear when the cause does not appear, thereby establishing a causal dependency between the two by manipulating the cause and observing the effects.

This approach to establishing causation is unproblematic when we deal with necessary causes (since there is only one cause) but not when we deal with sufficient causes (where there may be many causes) or causal interactions. When there are other sufficient causes, or causal interactions, the outcomes of the experiment may not only be a consequence of who has received the treatment but also other factors may come into play. For example, if we are dealing with causal interactions, only some people (e.g. due to their genetic make-up) may react favourably to the treatment (e.g. a particular drug), and hence if more people of this kind are in one of the two compared groups (i.e. in the treatment or in the control group) this will distort the estimate of the effect of the treatment.

A common way to try to overcome this potential problem is to do *randomized experiments* in which those who take part in the study are randomly selected from the relevant population, and randomly selected to be in the treatment or the control group. The idea is that the prevalence of other sufficient causes and causal interactions influencing the outcome should not be (significantly) different between those in the control and treatment group (because they are randomized) and thus should not affect the outcome of the trial (the comparison between the groups). In other words, by randomization one aims to 'control for' other influencing factors (i.e. other sufficient causes and causal interactions).

However, if we want to establish a *causal interaction*, rather than to isolate the effect of 'a treatment' (other things being equal), randomized comparison groups may not always be the best way forward. Instead we may want to have comparison groups selected by the criteria we believe (on theoretical grounds) interact with a particular 'treatment' and expose the groups to the same 'treatment'; for example, if we want to test whether exposure to a particular setting causes certain behaviour in one group of individuals but not in another (the first column in Table 4.1). In a full-blown design to test causal interactions, we may even want to vary both the comparison groups and the 'treatment' they receive and observe whether the outcomes for the different group-treatment combinations are as predicted (the full Table 4.1). The main point here is that purposive allocation of subjects to comparison groups rather than random allocation may be more effective when the aim is to test a theory of causal interaction through manipulation.

A major problem with manipulation as a test of causation is that *it is not always (in some cases rarely) possible to manipulate a putative cause* (and sometimes, even if, *in principle*, it is possible to manipulate a putative cause, it may not be legal or ethical to do so).

As Psillos (2002: 103) highlights, 'there is causation even where there is no possibility of human intervention'. In cases were manipulation is not possible (or legal or ethical), we are left with the option of trying to make causation probable by studying patterns of association and analytically developing plausible mechanisms (processes) that can differentiate putative causes from mere correlation.

Causal modelling with nonexperimental data

Most social science (and criminological) empirical research is of a nonexperimental nature. Saris and Stronkhorst (1984: 3) state that 'the major characteristic of nonexperimental research is that none of the relevant variables can be manipulated by the investigator'. If we cannot manipulate the putative cause/s and observe the effect/s we are stuck with analysing patterns of association (correlation) between our hypothesized causes and effects. The question is then whether we can establish causation (causal dependencies) by analysing patterns of association with statistical methods.

The simple answer to this question is most likely to be a disappointing 'no'. As Psillos (2002: 255) points out, 'relations of statistical relevance do not imply the existence of causal relations'. However, this does not mean that analysing patterns of association based upon *causal modelling*[15] (e.g. Blalock 1964; Kenny 1979; Saris and Stronkhorst 1984; Kline 1998) is a useless tool in advancing knowledge about causation. Even if causal modelling cannot be used to demonstrate causation, it can be used to *falsify* models of causal dependencies. Correlation does not prove causation, but causation requires correlation. Blalock (1964: 62) states that, 'it is quite correct that we can never demonstrate causality from correlation data', but he goes on to say 'that we can proceed by eliminating inadequate models that make predictions that are not consistent with the data'.

A major advantage of causal modelling (making causal diagrams) is that it encourages the investigator to think analytically in terms of causes and effects and causal dependencies amongst included factors. All too often in criminological research there is a lack of rationale behind *why* included explanatory factors are considered causes and any specification as to *how* they cause their purported implied effects.

Experiment-like approaches

The fact that it is fundamentally problematic to establish causation through statistical methods using nonexperimental data has not prevented important advances in this area (e.g. Winship and Morgan 1999). For example, efforts have been made to develop statistical approaches that help more closely to approximate the scientific experiment such as *propensity score matching*. Somewhat simplified, the basic idea behind propensity score matching is to create a single measure (propensity score) that summarizes the subjects on as many (pre-treatment) characteristics as possible (according to the maxim 'the more the better') and then match according to their propensity score, case by case, as closely as possible subjects who did receive 'a treatment'[16] with subjects who did not. On this basis

---

[15] Causal modelling is often in the form of specifying *causal chains* in which it is customary to talk about direct and indirect (distant) effects on the outcome. For example, A affects B that, in turn, affects C, where the effect of A on C is seen as indirect (mediated through B).

[16] A 'treatment' can be anything the investigator assumes has a causal influence on the effect considered. For example, one might compare future crime involvement to whether or not a person received a prison sentence for a current crime.

groups of subjects with similar propensity scores can be created, each group including those who have and have not received a treatment.[17] The difference in the outcome between those with similar propensity scores who received 'a treatment' and those who did not can then be compared, taking into consideration ('controlling for') the factors that may have been responsible for them being allocated to treatment or not (i.e. approximating randomization). To be effective this method, however, requires that all important confounding factors have been included in the propensity score, as Rubin (1997: 763), points out, 'it always must be remembered that propensity scores only adjust for the observed covariates that went into their estimation'.

When experimentation is not possible (or feasible), it seems advisable to try to create, as much as possible, experiment-like conditions when trying to establish causation, bearing in mind that manipulation is probably the best method to establish causation with some degree of certainty.

The concept of explanation

Establishing causation (causal dependency) through experimentation does not necessarily provide explanation. We can, for example, establish that if we manipulate C, then E will always change in predicted ways, without really knowing how this happens. To provide an *explanation* is to identify a plausible process (mechanism) that tells us *how* the cause produces the effect (i.e. making plausible that A causes B *because* [specification of mechanism]). To provide a (causal)[18] explanation is thus to be able to propose a credible process (mechanism) that connects the cause and the effect and brings about the effect. This is primarily an analytical (theoretical) question, although in some cases parts of the hypothesized process may be possible to observe. Bunge (2004: 203) states that 'to explain is to exhibit or assume a (lawful) mechanism', and he further claims that 'in the natural sciences no event or process is regarded as having been satisfactorily understood unless its actual or possible mechanism has been unveiled' (1999: 63); there is no reason that it should be otherwise in the social sciences.

Ideally, we should both demonstrate causation through experimentation and provide a plausible causal mechanism that explains how the initiation of a putative cause (or causal interaction) produces the effect. However, when, as is often the case, experimentation is not possible (or feasible), our ability to make a probable case for causation depends strongly on the extent to which we can identify analytically credible causal mechanisms (processes) that can explain observed associations we believe are causal in nature.

Three main types of mechanism in the study of crime

I submit that it may be useful to think in terms of three basic types of mechanism in the study of human behaviour and crime: situational, developmental, and social mechanisms. *Situational mechanisms* help explain what moves an individual in a particular setting to

[17]   The method requires that there are enough subjects in each propensity score group who have and have not received treatment to make valid comparisons of the 'treatment effect'. If this is not the case, the method is not feasible.

[18]   A lawful mechanism does not need to be a causal mechanism and hence we can have explanation without causation (see, further, Bunge 1979, 2004), a topic not treated in this chapter, which is concerned with causal explanations.

commit an act of crime (see, further, Wikström 2004, 2006a). *Social mechanisms* help to explain how broader social conditions (such as patterns of inequality and segregation) influence the occurrence of the kinds of social setting that are present in a society and how different groups of individuals tend to be differentially exposed to particular configurations of settings in which they develop and act (see, further, Wikström and Sampson 2003). *Developmental mechanisms* help explain why an individual, at a given point in time, depending on his or her previous development and life-history in a given society, (i) comes to exhibit certain characteristics and experiences, and why he or she (ii) comes to be exposed to a particular range of social settings (see, further, Wikström 2005).

The situational mechanisms are the most fundamental in the explanation of crime (because they explain what moves an individual to commit an act of crime), whilst the social and developmental mechanisms, so to speak, target 'the causes of the causes' by helping to explain (i) why an individual has certain characteristics and experiences that may influence his or her propensity to engage in acts of crime, and (ii) why he or she operates in environments (settings) that may be more or less conducive to crime involvement. Properly understood, the situational mechanisms help to identify what aspects of society (what social mechanisms) and what aspects of an individual's development and life-history (what developmental mechanisms) are relevant as 'causes of the causes' in the broader explanation of crime.

I have elsewhere suggested that acts of crime are best explained as an outcome of an individual's moral engagement with the moral context of a setting (Wikström 2006a) and therefore that crime causation in the broader sense (the causes of the causes) is fundamentally a question of understanding how societal and developmental factors influence the development of individuals' morality and their exposure to different moral contexts in a society.

Key concepts in thinking about causality

The discussion so far has stressed the value of (i) *experimentation*; and, in cases, where manipulation is not possible, the value of recreating as much as possible experiment-like conditions in testing for causation, and (ii) *theory development* (identifying likely causes and plausible causal mechanisms), to advance our knowledge about crime causation. Table 4.2 offers a summary of some of the terminology discussed so far.

Advancing knowledge about crime causation

After having laid out some of the fundamentals of the problems of establishing causation and providing explanation, I shall now turn to the question of how we can advance knowledge about crime causation in criminological research. I shall do this by first briefly discussing and criticizing the risk factor approach (which is by no means exclusive to criminological study)[19] and thereafter make a number of short notes on some particular problems and practices I feel need highlighting in this context.

---

[19] For example, the newspapers are full of reports of all kinds of different risk factors suggested as contributing to ill health.

Table 4.2 Summary of some key concepts

Effect	The outcome (e.g. act of crime); what we wish to explain (the definition of the effect sets boundaries for potential causes and causal mechanisms to be discovered).
Cause	An entity (condition, event) that has the power (agency) to initiate a causal process that produces the effect concerned.
Attribute	A characteristic that lacks the power to initiate a causal process (but may be correlated with the outcome).
Correlation	An association between entities (conditions, events) (a regular association between entities is not necessarily indicative of causation).
Causal interaction	The intersection of two or more factors (or processes) that set in motion a causal process producing a particular effect.
Causal mechanism	A process that connects the cause and effect and that brings about the effect (tells us how the cause/causal interaction produces the effect).
Causation	A causal mechanism in operation.
Explanation	The specification of a causal mechanism that connects a cause (causal interaction) and effect and produces the particular effect.
Experimentation	Interventions in regular associations to test hypotheses of causation through manipulation.
Manipulation	The main method of testing causation by the introduction, removal, or changing of a putative cause (or causal interaction) and observing whether predicted effects occur.
Causal modelling	Creating diagrams of hypothesized causal relationships between factors (testing whether causal models correspond to observed associations can help us eliminate false causal models).

Beyond the risk factor approach

I think it is fair to say that empirically oriented criminological research is dominated by a risk factor approach. In fact, as Moffitt and Caspi (2006: 109) recently pointed out, 'influential reviewers have concluded that the study of antisocial behaviour is stuck in the "risk-factor stage"'.

The concept of *risk factor* is rarely well defined in criminological research (e.g. a risk factor being defined as a factor that increases risk) and, in practice, it generally refers to a stable correlate that predicts crime involvement (or some aspect of crime involvement). In principle, the risk-factor approach, as commonly applied, can be described as a research orientation without much theory guidance, in which the main activity has been to map out non-random correlates with crime involvement (or some aspect of crime involvement).

The main problem with the risk factor approach is thus its general lack of consideration of *the problem of establishing causation* (differentiating between causes and correlates), and *the problem of identifying plausible causal mechanisms* (providing explanation).

The many problems with the prevalent risk-factor approach in criminology has been well summarized by David Farrington:

While a good deal is known about the correlates of delinquency and crime, there is surprisingly little agreement about the causes (Farrington 1988: 75).

There is no shortage of factors that are significantly correlated with offending and antisocial behavior; indeed, literally thousands of variables differentiate significantly between official offenders and nonoffenders or correlate significantly with self-reported offending (Farrington 1992: 256).

A major problem with the risk factor paradigm is to determine which risks factors are causes and which are merely markers or correlated with causes (Farrington 2000: 7).

Little is known about the causal processes that intervene between risk factors and offending' (Farrington 2003: 207).

Farrington has also highlighted the problem that arises from of our lack of understanding of causal interactions (i.e. the individual and environment interaction in crime causation):

existing research tells us more about criminal potential than about how that potential becomes actuality of offending in any given situation (Farrington 2002: 690).

In a situation such as that described by Farrington, it is easy to argue that we need to move on from a risk factor approach (focused on mapping out non-random correlations) to a more explanatory approach (focused on establishing causes and identifying causal mechanisms) to advance criminological knowledge and its usefulness to policy and practice.

I have previously argued that to achieve this we need (i) *empirically* to conduct more experimentation (or experiment-like research) with the aim of better establishing causal dependencies, and (ii) *theoretically*, to carry out more advanced analytical work with the aim of identifying potential causes (causal interactions) and credible causal mechanisms (Wikström 2006a). We need more advanced theory and more rigorous testing of theory; without such changes of general direction, criminology risks being caught up in a 'mindless search for data and statistical correlations among them' (Bunge 2006: 119).[20]

A note on attributes as causes

It is not uncommon in criminological research for attributes such as sex and race to be included as predictors. In the case of sex, some researchers even (wrongly) claim that it is the best predictor of crime involvement. The problem with the common practice of including attributes as predictors is that they may confuse our search for causes and explanation of crime, and even more worryingly, they may make people think that the fact, for example, that someone is male or black could be a cause of their crime involvement.

We have already established that prediction does not equal causation, and that for a factor to qualify as a cause, we need to make a case that it has some kind of powers to initiate a causal process that produces the effect (e.g. an act of crime). It is difficult to see, for example, how being male or black could constitute a cause of crime (i.e. be a factor that initiates a causal process resulting in an act of crime). 'The philosopher will be surprised to see that . . . investigators take properties ("variables") such as age and sex to be possible causes' (Bunge 2001: 70).

This does not mean that characteristics or experiences that are relevant in crime causation might not be more prevalent, for example, amongst males (such as, for example,

---

[20] There are, of course, individual scholars within criminology who take the problem of causation and explanation seriously, but what I am referring to here is a general tendency of the field.

poor ability to exercise self-control) but the point is that it is these characteristics or experiences on which we should focus on as causal factors in our explanations rather than the fact that the person is male. In principle, if we can measure the real causative factors (e.g. the ability to exercise self-control), there is no need to include attributes (e.g. sex) that at best are 'markers' of the real causative factors among the predictors in our studies.

However, it may not be uninteresting to explain why, for example, males are more likely to have characteristics and experiences that contribute to crime involvement (let us say, as an outcome of particular socialization practices that promote the development of a poor capability to exercise self-control and are more common in the socialization of males), but this is a very different question from what causes their acts of crime. In the former case, differences in crime involvement by attribute is the *outcome* (what is to be explained) while in the latter case, attributes are (mistakenly) treated as potential causes of an individual's acts of crime (what explains). The main point is that while the correlation between attributes and crime involvement can be explained, attributes cannot explain why people commit acts of crime.

This very important insight has significant implications for how research should be conducted (e.g. what research questions should be posed) and what conclusions for policy and practice can be drawn from research findings about correlations between attributes and crime involvement. The fact that a person's sex or race to some degree may *predict*[21] his or her crime involvement does not mean that his or her sex or race *causes* his or her crime involvement. At best it can be a *marker* of causes associated with a particular attribute. We should therefore avoid including attributes as (potential) causes in models which aim to explain what *causes* people's crime involvement and pathways in crime (although we may very well include them if the goal is solely to *predict* people's risk of crime involvement).

A note on past behaviour as a cause of present behaviour

The claim that past behaviour is the best *predictor* of future behaviour does not mean that past behaviour *causes* future behaviour. Thus, while past behaviour may be a very useful predictor for assessing future risk of offending, it should not be part of a causal model to explain crime involvement. The strong correlation between past and future behaviour may reflect an underlying process of *habituation* and/or a stable *exposure* to criminogenic behavioural contexts, and thus behavioural consistency may be a *symptom*, for example, of stable moral values and habits promoting law-breaking and/or a stable exposure to criminogenic behavioural contexts (Wikström 2005).

A note on causes and 'the causes of the causes'

While attributes (and past behaviour) cannot cause acts of crime (or any action for that matter), other commonly suggested causes, such as poor parental monitoring or head

---

[21] The predictive power of sex and ethnicity is in fact much less than is often perceived. For example, an individual's sex generally only explains 1 per cent or 2 per cent of the variance in crime involvement; hence knowing that a person is male or female does not help us very much in knowing whether or not they are likely to commit a crime (e.g. Wikström and Butterworth 2006).

injuries, are (potentially) 'causes of the causes' (or distant causes) rather than direct causes of an act of crime. That is, they are (potentially) part of a causal chain leading up to an act of crime. For example, childhood head injuries may affect the subsequent development of an individual's cognitive capabilities that, in turn, may influence how they respond to environmental features (e.g. whether or not they will engage in an act of crime).

Direct causes are the immediate factors that *move* an individual to carry out an act of crime, while distant causes (or the causes of the causes) are the factors that influence the immediate causes, or are further back in the causal chain, influencing the factors that influence the factors that influence the immediate causes (and so on).

Mixing direct and distant causes in the explanation of crime involvement (without a proper modelling of their different roles in the causal process) may risk 'mixing apples and pears' and obscure our understanding of the causes of crime (and the causal processes in operation), clouding our understanding of how best to address these factors in policy and practice.

Let us develop this point a bit further. An act of crime may be seen as an individual's *response* to the particularities of the setting in which he or she is taking part (i.e. the process of choice of action founded upon his or her perception of action alternatives), which is caused by the interaction of the individual's relevant characteristics and experiences and the relevant features of the setting (see, further, Wikström 2006a). The *causal interaction* between an individual's relevant characteristics and experiences and relevant environmental features may be seen as the *direct cause* of his or her acts (and acts of crime).

Individual differences and experiences are important in that they *predispose* an individual to see certain action alternatives and make certain choices among the perceived action alternatives. An individual's morality and executive capabilities (ability to exercise self-control) are likely to be key predisposing factors influencing his or her propensity to engage in acts of crime (Wikström 2006a).

However, what kinds of action alternatives an individual perceives, and what choices he or she makes, depends not only on his or her predisposing characteristics and experiences but also on the criminogenic features of the setting in which he or she takes part (what he or she reacts to). The key important criminogenic features of a setting that may help *instigate* acts of crime are the opportunities and frictions it provides and, crucially, the moral context in which these opportunities and frictions occur (that is, the monitoring of law abidance and its associated risk of intervention and sanction). An act of crime is thus an outcome of the (causal) *interaction* between an individual's characteristics and experiences (which influences how an individual reacts) and the features of the setting (which influence what an individual reacts to).

Virtually no research has explored the role of the interaction of individual differences and behavioural contexts in an individual's perception of action alternatives and the process of choice of relevance to their engagement in acts of crime. This is a fundamental knowledge gap and a necessary area to research if we want empirically to advance our knowledge about how these interactions work and better understand how the direct causes of acts of crime relate to 'the causes of the causes' of acts of crime.

While the direct causes of an individual's actions is the causal interaction between his or her morality and ability to exercise self-control and the criminogenic features of a setting that moves him or her to act in particular ways, the *first layer* of 'the causes of the causes' is comprised of the factors (and processes) that directly influence *the development* of an individual's morality and executive capabilities (e.g. moral education and cognitive nurturing), and the factors (and processes) that directly influence an individual's *exposure to and features of* the behavioural contexts in which he or she takes part (e.g. exposure may be influenced by parental monitoring and the features of local settings may be influenced by localized processes of informal social control and strategies of policing).

The *second layer* of 'the causes of the causes' (which, in fact, should be read as 'the causes of the causes of the causes') concerns the influence of broader social processes (e.g. processes of inequality and segregation) and their changes on the creation and changes of the different environments (social settings) in which individuals in a particular society develop and act. One could probably explore even further layers, but my aim here is only to illustrate the problem of analysing the role of direct causes and 'the causes of the causes' in crime causation.

To advance knowledge about 'the causes of the causes', we first need to have solid knowledge about the fundamental causes of crime (i.e. what moves people to engage in acts of crime), because on that basis we can then assess the potential candidates for 'the causes of the causes'. It should be obvious that if we do not know the direct causes of acts of crime, we cannot really know the causes of the causes (because we do not know what the causes are). The first step in advancing knowledge about crime causation should be to develop our understanding of the situational mechanisms that move people to engage in acts of crime, and only when we are satisfied that we have a good grasp of these mechanisms will we be in a strong position to address the potentially important social and developmental mechanisms that play a part in crime causation (as the causes of the causes).

A note on longitudinal and cross-sectional studies in relation to the study of causation

A common misunderstanding is that longitudinal studies are *always* better at assessing potential causation than cross-sectional studies. We have already concluded that association and time-ordering is not enough to establish causation. We have also concluded that the best method to demonstrate causation with some certainty is through manipulation (experimentation). When we are dealing with the *direct causes* of crime, we generally deal with processes that can be counted in minutes and seconds (or at times even milliseconds) rather than in months and years (annual or biannual data collection is the most common in longitudinal studies). Therefore, there is no need to have data over long periods of time (e.g. annual or biannual data) to test for direct causation.

Experimentation (and experiment-like research) can be conducted both as part of cross-sectional and a longitudinal research designs. In fact, most tests for causation (direct causation) only require cross-sectional data (e.g. time-ordered data collected the same day), while it is predominantly in the study of developmental processes (as causes of the causes) that longitudinal designs may have a major advantage in addressing the problem of causation (e.g. manipulating early childhood experiences and studying how this affects individuals' subsequent development of predisposing characteristics and experiences).

Prevention and causation

To prevent something is to make that something not happen. If we believe we have prevented an act of crime, we have to believe that if we hadn't done what we did, the crime would have happened (and this is a counterfactual argument). This implies that the idea of causation is at the heart of the idea of prevention. If there is no causation, there can be no prevention. In other words, to believe in the possibility of prevention, one has to believe in causation.

In the field of crime prevention the ability to make accurate *predictions* about people's (primarily children and young people's) future risk of sustained and serious criminality is often essential, since it helps target interventions and resources where they are most needed. We have already established that making accurate predictions and establishing causation are two different things, because what predicts is not necessarily what causes. This seems to be a particularly relevant problem in so-called *risk-focused prevention*, since it appears that policy-makers and practitioners (and sometimes also researchers) often assume that what predicts an individual's crime involvement is also what causes his or her crime involvement and therefore, that interventions to prevent crime should aim to reduce as many of the factors which predict crime involvement as possible. This may be regarded as a fundamental flaw of this approach and highlights the need to separate clearly what predicts from what causes. The factors included in prediction instruments that identify 'people at risk' may not necessarily be the (causative) factors that should be targeted in prevention. These are two separate problems and need to be addressed as such. To advance crime prevention, we need better to distinguish between causes and correlates, and focus our efforts to develop effective interventions that target the main (direct or indirect) causes of crime.

Another important problem regarding causation and prevention is *asymmetric causation* (Lieberson 1985). This is particularly relevant when our prevention efforts concern 'the causes of the causes' (e.g. the development of predisposing factors). The basic idea of asymmetric causation is that *some causal processes may be irreversible* (or in some cases difficult to reverse) so that when an effect has appeared, it cannot be reversed (or in some cases only reversed by great difficulty) by manipulating what caused it to appear in the first place. For example, it seems likely that many developmental processes may have the characteristic of asymmetric causation. One main prevention implication of this (in support of the idea of the importance of early life prevention) is that to affect such developmental processes, one has to intervene early in the process to be successful in preventing the outcome (e.g. the development of a particular predisposition).

Conclusion

Although there is a need to know more about non-random patterns of people's crime involvement and its correlates, I submit that *the overall biggest knowledge gap and need is to advance our understanding of what processes cause people's crime involvement*. To achieve this requires a clear understanding of the differences between *correlation and prediction* on the one hand, and *causation and explanation* on the other. To advance knowledge about crime causation is not primarily a question of demonstrating (more) correlations and making (better) predictions (although this may give us more *clues* about where to look for causation and explanation) but, crucially, one of (better) theorizing established empirical relationships (identifying credible causal mechanisms) and testing causal hypotheses through experimentation (or experiment-like research).

Why is an improved understanding of crime causation important? To be able to prevent something it must have causes (prevention involves removing causes or successfully intervening in a causal process), and the better we understand the causes of a phenomenon such as crime, the more likely we are to develop effective crime prevention measures.

UK public opinion polls, as well as recent political debate, show that the problem of crime and its prevention is regarded as one of the UK's most pressing social problems. Numerous UK cities have areas which are plagued by crime and disorder, dramatically reducing the quality of life for their inhabitants. The high rate of crime involvement amongst young people in these areas makes the life prospects for many of them bleak. At the same time, the UK is facing a crisis in the number of offenders demanding the limited resources of its strained criminal justice system. There appears to be a lack of new knowledge-based insights into understanding and effectively tackling the problem of crime. One of the least-understood factors is the role of the social environment and its interaction with people's individual characteristics and experiences.

A famous slogan of the current Labour government was 'to be tough on crime, and to be tough on the causes of crime'. While we all know the implications of being 'tough on crime', there appears to be less agreement on the implications of being 'tough on the causes of crime'. For the government (and its agencies) to claim to be 'tough on the causes of crime' requires, first, that it knows what the main causes of crime are (which is questionable), and secondly, that it knows how to manipulate these causes in a way that can effectively reduce acts of crime (which is also questionable).

If the government really took crime prevention seriously, one would expect them to provide substantial resources for serious research to advance knowledge about the causes of crime. In many areas (e.g. health or economy), a typical response to a key social problem (such as cancer or unemployment) is to invest in long-term fundamental research to further our understanding of the nature and causes of the problem as a basis for the development of effective policies and interventions. Policy-makers do not expect fast and easy solutions to these difficult problems. However, when it comes to the problem of crime, the typical approach is to respond to the problems of the day by applying quick fixes based on little or no solid knowledge about the causes of crime (Wikström 2006b).

To change this situation fundamentally, we need to prioritize the study of the causes and explanations of crime and to put the problem of crime causation at the top of the crime prevention agenda. If we are to reduce significantly the problem of crime in society, we need advances in criminological theory and more sophisticated theory-testing to provide a stronger foundation for the development of effective crime prevention policies and interventions.

Suggestions for further reading

For an excellent recent general treatment of the problem of causation and explanation see Psillos, S. (2002) *Causation & Explanation* (Montreal: McGill-Queen's University Press); for an enlightened discussion of these problems in relation to the social sciences see

Bunge, M. (1999) *The Sociology–Philosophy Connection* (New Brunswick: Transaction Publishers); for an up-to-date discussion of problems of this kind applied to criminology, see Wikström, P-O and Sampson, R. J. (2006) *The Explanation of Crime: Contexts, Mechanisms and Development* (Cambridge: Cambridge University Press).

References

BLALOCK JR., H. M. (1964). *Causal Inferences in Nonexperimental Research.* Chapel Hill: The University of North Carolina Press.

BUNGE, M. (1979). *Causality and Modern Science* (3rd edn). New York. Dover Publications.

—— (1999). *The Sociology–Philosophy Connection.* New Brunswick: Transaction Publishers.

—— (2001). 'Scientific Realism' in M. Mahner, *Selected Essays by Mario Bunge.* Amherst (NY): Prometheus Books.

—— (2004). 'How Does it Work? The Search for Explanatory Mechanisms'. *Philosophy of the Social Sciences* 34: 182–210.

—— (2006) *Chasing Reality. Strife over Realism.* Toronto: University of Toronto Press.

FARRINGTON, D. P. (1988). Studying Changes within Individuals: the Causes of Offending, in M. Rutter (ed.), *Studies of Psychosocial Risk.* Cambridge: Cambridge University Press.

—— (1992). 'Explaining the Beginning, Progress and Ending of Antisocial Behavior from Birth to Adulthood', in J. McCord (ed.), *Facts, Frameworks, and Forecasts: Advances in Criminological Theory,* Vol. 3. New Brunswick: Transaction.

—— (2000). 'Explaining and Preventing Crime: the Globalization of Knowledge—The American Society of Criminology 1999 Presidential Address'. *Criminology* 38(1): 1–24.

—— (2002). 'Human Development and Criminal Careers', in M. McGuire,

R. Morgan, and R. Rainer (eds), *The Oxford Handbook of Criminology.* Oxford: Clarendon Press.

—— (2003). Developmental and Life-Course Criminology: Key Theoretical and Empirical Issues. *Criminology* 41: 201–35.

GASPER, P. (1990). 'Explanation and Scientific Realism', in D. Knowles (ed.), *Explanation and its Limits.* Cambridge: Cambridge University Press.

GOTTFREDSON, M. and HIRSCHI, T. (1990). *A General Theory of Crime.* Stanford, CA: Stanford University Press.

HARRÉ, R. and MADDEN, E. H. (1975). *Causal Powers.* Oxford: Basil Blackwell.

HOLLAND, P. W. (1986). 'Statistics and Causal Inference', *Journal of American Statistical Association* 81: 945–60.

KENNY, D. A. (1979). *Correlation and Causation.* New York: John Wiley & Sons.

KLINE, R. B. (1998). *Structural Equation Modeling.* New York: The Guilford Press.

LIEBERSON, S. (1985). *Making it Count. The Improvement of Social Research and Theory.* Berkeley: University of California Press.

MOFFITT, T. and CASPI, A. (2006). 'Evidence from Behavioral Genetics for Environmental Contributions to Antisocial Conduct' in P-O. Wikström and R. J. Sampson (eds), *The Explanation of Crime: Contexts, Mechanisms and Development.* Cambridge: Cambridge University Press.

PHILLIPS, D. C. (2000). *The Expanded Social Scientist's Bestiary. A Guide to Fabled*

Threats to, and Defences of, Naturalistic Social Science. Lanham: Rowman & Littlefield Publishers.

POPPER, K. (2000). *Realism and the Aim of Science.* London: Routledge.

PSILLOS, S. (2002). *Causation & Explanation.* Montreal: McGill-Queen's University Press.

RUBIN, D. B. (1997). 'Estimating Causal Effects from Large Data Sets Using Propensity Scores'. *Annals of Internal Medicine* 127: 757–63.

SALMON, W. C. (1998). *Causality and Explanation.* Oxford: Oxford University Press.

SARIS, W. and STRONKHORST, H. (1984). *Causal Modelling in Nonexperimental Research. An introduction to the LISREL approach.* Sociometric Research Foundation: Amsterdam, The Netherlands.

VON WRIGHT, G. H. (1971). *Explanation and Understanding.* London: Routledge & Kegan Paul.

WIKSTRÖM, P-O. (2004). 'Crime as Alternative. Towards a Cross-Level Situational Action Theory of Crime Causation' in J. McCord (ed.), 'Beyond Empiricism: Institutions and Intentions in the Study of Crime'. *Advances in Criminological Theory* 13: 1–37. New Brunswick: Transaction.

—— (2005). 'The Social Origins of Pathways in Crime. Towards a Developmental Ecological Action Theory of Crime Involvement and Its Changes' in D. P. Farrington (ed.), Integrated Developmental and Life Course Theories of Offending. *Advances in Criminological Theory* 14. New Brunswick: Transaction.

—— (2006a). 'Individuals, Settings and Acts of Crime. Situational Mechanisms and the Explanation of Crime' in P-O. Wikström and R. J. Sampson (eds), *The Explanation of Crime: Contexts, Mechanisms and Development.* Cambridge: Cambridge University Press

—— (2006b). 'Doing Without Knowing. Common Pitfalls in Crime Prevention' in G. Farrell, K. Bowers, S. Johnson, and M. Townsley (eds), *Imagination for Crime Prevention.* Crime Prevention Studies Series. Monsey. New York: Criminal Justice Press.

—— (2007). 'Deterrence and Deterrence Experiences. Preventing Crime Through the Fear of Consequences' in S. G. Shoham (ed.), *International Comparative Handbook of Penology and Criminal Justice.* London: Taylor & Francis (in press).

—— and SAMPSON, R. J. (2003). 'Social Mechanisms of Community Influences on Crime and Pathways in Criminality' in B. B. Lahey, T. E. Moffitt, and A. Caspi (eds), *The Causes of Conduct Disorder and Serious Juvenile Delinquency* 118–48. New York: Guilford Press.

—— and BUTTERWORTH D. (2006). *Adolescent Crime. Individual Differences and Lifestyles.* Collumpton: Willan Publishing.

—— and TREIBER K. (2007). 'The Role of Self-Control in Crime Causation. Beyond Gottfredson and Hirschi's General Theory of Crime'. *European Journal of Criminology* 4: 237–64.

WINSHIP, C. and MORGAN, S. L. (1999). 'The Estimation of Causal Effects from Observational Data'. *Annual Review of Sociology* 25: 659–707.

5

Doing evaluation research in criminology: balancing scientific and practical demands

Friedrich Lösel

Introduction

Over many years I have been involved in evaluation studies on the prevention and treatment of criminal behaviour. During this work, I acquired methodological and practical skills that made it easier to carry out an evaluation project. However, I also felt how complicated it was to do sound empirical evaluations. Trying to answer the question whether a specific programme works often resulted in more specific questions, such as: working for whom, in which setting, under what conditions, in which outcomes? Positive findings in one study were questioned when there were less favourable results in another and, in particular, when a programme was implemented during routine practice. Of course, the circle of problem-solving and the rise of new problems is typical for any scientific process and may remind us of Socrates' insight, 'I know that I don't know'. However, in the field of programme evaluation, researchers are not working in an 'ivory tower'. They are confronted with demands from policy makers, practitioners, and the general public who often expect clear, quick, and simple answers. Consequently, more complicated, inconclusive, and time-consuming scientific answers can lead to discontent on both sides. If researchers want to be involved in the challenging world of evaluation and want to contribute to evidence-based crime policy, they need to develop something akin to a 'survival kit'. This kit would contain a methodologically sound and flexible use of research tools that will be described in this chapter.

In addition, it is essential to develop realistic expectations and coping skills regarding the role of evaluation in policy making and practice. For example, current trends in the penal policy of many western countries may discourage researchers who aim for rational policy making. Although the impact of incapacitation on local crime rates is unclear and its effect on individual recidivism seems to be zero or even negative (e.g. Gendreau *et al.* 2000; Lloyd, Mair, and Hough 1994; Webster, Doob, and Zimring 2006), most countries face a strong increase in the rates of imprisonment. Western European countries still have four to eight times lower rates of incarceration than the United States and Russia; however, some seem to follow the paths of the two former cold-war rivals more strongly than others. Great Britain, with its long and admirable tradition of a liberal democracy, even took the lead in Western Europe. With nearly 150 incarcerations per 100,000 inhabitants, this country now has a much higher rate of people in custody than comparable countries such as Germany, France, and, in particular, the Scandinavian countries. Prison over-crowding and emergency reactions (e.g. container cells or prison ships) became a key topic with near daily reports in the British mass media (for the many other prison problems, see King and McDermott 1989; Liebling and Maruna 2005).

Against this background, criminologists may take a pessimistic view on the practical impact of their evaluation research. This is understandable; however, it may partially result from a rather short-term and narrow understanding of the role of research in crime policy. As in other areas of social intervention, criminological evaluators must be aware that their studies are one contribution among many to policy formation (e.g. Cronbach *et al.* 1980; Leviton and Hughes 1981). The problem of an unsatisfactory use of research can be due to several reasons. On the one hand, we find factors on the side of research such as unclear empirical outcomes, weaknesses of methodology, inconsistency between different studies, time delays in the research process, lack of consumer orienta-tion of reports, basic controversies about the appropriate evaluation methodology, or a one-sided influence of personal political opinions on the evaluation of evidence. On the other hand, there are factors on the policy side such as political values that differ funda-mentally from the research conclusions, a change of the social climate in the society, or new political priorities. There are also factors such as the impact of sensational reports in the mass media, financial or organizational obstacles, less engaged personnel in key pos-itions for decision making, resistance from practice, or an abuse of research as a 'fig leaf' from the beginning of the contract (Lösel and Nowack 1987; Weiss 1982).

Evaluators should develop a realistic view of such influences in order to conserve and develop the potentials of science on rational policy making. A closer look also indicates that one must differentiate between the more direct and immediate 'instrumental use' of evaluation projects and the more long-term and indirect 'conceptual use' (Leviton and Hughes 1981). The latter refers to a change in thinking about a problem that can be observed even when there was no direct transformation of research into policy. Patience and sensitivity to the many political influences are essentials in the evaluator's 'survival kit'. What does not receive political attention at a given time can become a key topic a few years later. For example, in the middle of the 1980s we carried out a first meta-analysis on the treatment of adult offenders in therapeutic prisons (Lösel, Köferl, and Weber 1987; see also Lösel and Köferl 1989). In contrast to the 'nothing-works' doctrine prevailing at the time, we found a small but relatively consistent positive effect. In the foreword of our book we stated that this research addressed a topic that ranked low on the political agenda. However, we expected that in the longer run, there would be no sound alterna-tive to improving our knowledge on how to change the behaviour of serious and repeat offenders. A few years later, perhaps promoted by similar systematic research syntheses (e.g. Andrews *et al.* 1990; Lipsey 1992a), and through media reports on sexual and other violent offending, there was an international revival of correctional treatment (Lösel 1993; Palmer 1992). This led to a strong expansion of a 'what works' policy in western countries (McGuire 1995, 2002).

Although some current trends in penal policy may go against evidence-based approaches in the criminal justice system, the latter has in fact not been replaced. In the last 15 years, empirical evaluations on crime and justice substantially increased and led to numerous practical applications (e.g. MacKenzie 2006; McGuire 2002; Morgan 2000; Sherman *et al.* 2002; Towl 2006). Crime policy in modern societies is by no means a homogeneous and one-dimensional system. For example, both punitive and rehabilitative approaches run alongside each other. From time to time, the pendulum swings to one side or the other and leads to changes or 'fashion trends' in crime policy. However, in the long run, there seems to be a trend towards rationality and humanity in criminal justice, at least in the modern western societies.

Regardless of how much policy temporarily follows or ignores empirical evaluations, they must constantly aim for scientific rigour. Only on this basis can evaluation research make substantial contributions to policy and practice. Otherwise, there is an abuse of weak data to justify mere opinions. This is the case when, for example, the decrease in official crime rates is simply attributed to punishment and incapacitation without regarding multiple factors such as aging of the population, decrease in unemployment, declining drug use, or social policies (Farrington, Langan, and Tonry 2004).

Against this background, this chapter will address some basic issues of methodologically sound and practically relevant evaluations in criminology. In particular, I shall address issues of methodological quality, the role of randomized controlled trials, the importance of sound descriptions, the controversy between qualitative and quantitative approaches, issues of offender assessment, participant motivation and dropout, problems of outcome measurement, and the need for systematic research syntheses. I will take most of my examples from evaluations on correctional treatment and crime prevention in which I have my main expertise. My understanding of 'evaluation' follows the comprehensive concept of Rossi and Freeman (1982), which ranges from the assessment of a problem over the design, implementation, and monitoring of a programme to the analysis of its effects and cost-effectiveness. However, for reasons of space I will mainly concentrate on process and outcome evaluation.

Methodological quality

The main aim of any outcome evaluation is to answer the question 'Does the respective intervention have a causal effect?' Although there are various concepts of causality (e.g. Bunge 1959), the classical position of John Stuart Mill is a useful basis for programme evaluation (Cook and Campbell 1979). It is based on an active, experimental manipulation of variables. According to this, we can assume a causal relation between a variable X (independent) and a variable Y (dependent) if (a) the assumed cause X and the effect Y correlate; (b) there is a clear temporal sequence between cause and effect; and (c) one cannot find alternative explanations why a variation in X leads to a change in Y. There are many reasons why an intervention programme may seem to have an effect but in reality does not. Cook and Campbell (1979; see also Shadish, Cook, and Campbell 2002) have subsumed such threats to validity under four categories:

1. *Statistical conclusion validity* refers to the question whether two variables are truly correlated.

2. *Internal validity* refers to the question whether it is justified to assume a causal effect.

3. *Construct validity* refers to the question for the theoretical foundation or interpretation of a causal relationship.

4. *External validity* refers to the question whether a causal relationship can be generalized across treatments, persons, settings, and outcomes (one may also add time
periods).

In each category, there are various threats to validity. Based on Cook and Campbell
(1979), Lösel *et al.* (1987); Lösel & Köferl (1989) gave an overview with examples for the
field of offender treatment in prisons (Table 5.1).

Table 5.1 Judgement scheme of Cook and Campbell's threats to validity with examples
from criminological evaluations

A. Statistical conclusion validity

1. Low statistical power (small sample size)
2. Violated assumptions of statistical tests (parametric tests for rank data)
3. Fishing and the error rate problem (random significances in multiple tests)
4. Unreliability of measures (quality problems in archival data)
5. Unreliability of treatment implementation (unstructured programmes)
6. Irrelevances in the experimental setting (random factors in addition to treatment)
7. Random heterogeneity of groups (no specification of offence types)

B. Internal validity

1. History (improvements in probation when evaluating prison programmes)
2. Maturation (natural desistance with age)
3. Testing (memory effects in repeated staff ratings)
4. Instrumentation (a changing measure becomes confounded with the treatment)
5. Statistical regression (tendency to the mean in cases of frequent offending)
6. Selection (inclusion of the most positive cases in a programme)
7. Attrition (selective dropout of the most difficult individuals)
8. Interaction with selection (selection of spontaneously improving individuals)
9. Ambiguity about the direction of causal influence (in correlation studies)
10. Diffusion or imitation of treatment (transfer of programme information to control group)
11. Compensatory equalization of treatment (introduction of day passes in normal prisons)
12. Compensatory rivalry (changes in parenting in control families of a prevention study)
13. Resentful demoralization (disappointment and disengagement in control group)

C. Construct validity

1. Inadequate preoperational explication of constructs (no theoretical basis for a variable)
2. Mono-operation bias (only self-reported data)
3. Mono-method bias (only questionnaires)
4. Hypothesis guessing within experimental conditions (acting as expected by the investigator)
5. Evaluation apprehension (positive self-presentation in a questionnaire on aggression)
6. Experimenter expectancies (positive ratings of participants when involved in a programme)
7. Confounding constructs with level of constructs (no range of data on re-offending)
8. Interaction of different treatments (offenders receive several correctional programmes)

Table 5.1 *(Contd)*

---

9. Interaction of testing and treatment (pre-test effects on parents in a prevention programme)

10. Restricted generalizability across constructs (no correlation of personal and reconviction data)

D. External validity

1. Interaction of selection and treatment (treatment for cooperative offenders only)

2. Interaction of setting and treatment (correctional programme in a prison with good regime)

3. Interaction of history and treatment (enthusiastic staff in the early stage of a programme)

4. Temporal stability of treatment effects (natural fluctuation of effects)

E. Descriptive validity

1. Description of treatment concept (no programme manual)

2. Assessment of treatment concept (lack of information on programme implementation)

3. Assessment of treatment goals (no assessment of intermediate outcomes)

4. Data on temporal stability of treatment/goals (no information on programme adaptation)

5. Data on statistical parameters (no standard deviations or effect sizes reported)

(Lösel *et al.* 1987; translated and modified)

We introduced *descriptive validity* as a fifth category. This refers to the quality of the information on the programme goals, concept, implementation, and statistical data. Although a study can be valid with respect to the four other categories, only its sound description allows us to interpret it properly and to compare its findings with other research. Deficits in descriptive validity may be due, for example, to low standards of authors, the wish to produce a user-friendly report, space limits in journals, or blind spots of reviewers.

Table 5.1 shows that there are numerous threats to validity (for extended and partially restructured categories, see Shadish *et al.* 2002). Although criminological evaluators can easily apply such a validity rating system after some training, it is rather complex. This is why criminologists often use a simpler, one-dimensional rating (see Farrington 2003a for a good overview). The most popular example is the Maryland Scale of Methodological Rigour (Sherman *et al.* 1997). This 5-point scale integrates features that primarily refer to the equivalence of programme and control groups. In addition, sample size and adequacy of statistical testing are taken into account. The highest level (5) is reserved for non-compromised randomized designs. Level 4 covers studies applying procedures to ensure group equivalence (e.g. individual matching, statistical control) or slightly compromised random designs. Designs based on incidental assignment are on Level 3 if group equivalence can be assumed (e.g. demonstrated equivalence on relevant variables). Studies incorporating a non-equivalent control group correspond to Level 2. Level 1 is reserved for studies without any control group (e.g. one group pre-post design).

The Maryland Scale is particularly useful for systematic research syntheses in which numerous studies on a similar topic need to be compared (e.g. Lösel and Schmucker 2005; MacKenzie 2006; Sherman *et al.* 1997). However, one must also be aware that any one-dimensional scale of methodological quality is a pragmatic solution that neglects other important issues of validity. For example, if two experiments on a correctional treatment programme use very different outcome indicators (e.g. official recidivism versus personality scales) and points of assessment (e.g. at the end of imprisonment versus long-term follow-up) issues of measurement validity become more important than randomization only.

Cook and Campbell (1979) have been criticized for overemphasizing internal/experimental validity and giving insufficient weight to theory and generalization to real-life contexts (e.g. Gadenne 1976; Pawson and Tilley 1997). However, both issues have been clearly addressed by these authors under the concepts of construct and external validity (see also Shadish *et al.* 2002). As a consequence, criminological evaluations that aim at generalization need to take all categories of validity into account. As Lösel and Köferl (1989) have shown, they may correlate differently with effect size.

Criminological evaluations based on such a comprehensive concept of methodological quality follow the demand for searching for theoretical explanations and causes of crime (e.g. Bottoms 2000; Wikström, this volume). However, sound theories on causes of crime are not sufficient for guiding successful measures of intervention. In addition, one needs valid theories of programming and of the change process itself (Chen 1989). For example, the evidence-based hypothesis that attachment to the workforce contributes to resilience and desistance (Lösel and Bender 2003; Sampson and Laub 1993) does not tell us how this concept can be effectively transformed into an intervention programme. The same aim can be addressed by different measures: e.g. by vocational education programmes, supportive through- and after-care, programmes to enhance motivation and social skills, incentives for potential employers, or general improvements on the local labour market.

Evaluations that take all four categories of validity into account are far more than 'inductive' or merely 'technical' studies. If threats to validity are low, such studies are the strongest empirical tests of our criminological theories. However, although all aspects of validity are highly important, internal validity is hierarchically superior: if a design is too weak to justify a causal relationship between the independent and dependent variable, one cannot make any theoretical interpretations or generalizations.

Randomized experiments and quasi-experiments

Randomized experiments are standard in the natural sciences and in the life sciences. Although their application in criminology has increased since the 1980s, they are still rare in our field (Farrington 2003b, c; Farrington and Welsh 2006). This is why recent initiatives aim to promote high-quality experimental research for an evidence-based crime policy (e.g. the Campbell Collaboration Group on Crime and Justice, the Academy of Experimental Criminology, and the new *Journal of Experimental Criminology*). Experts in the Home Office also became sensitive to the need of controlled experimentation in evaluations (e.g. Harper and Chitty 2005). However, many criminologists argue against experimental designs and, in particular, against their use as the one and only 'gold standard' for evaluation (e.g. Pawson and Tilley 1994; and more moderately: Bottoms 2000; Gelsthorpe 2006).

Randomized controlled trials (RCTs) have the unique advantage that the units (e.g. persons or locations) in the programme and control condition are on the average equivalent in all relevant characteristics (if sample sizes are large and there is no selective dropout). Consequently, most threats to internal validity can be ruled out. In principle,

RCTs on crime and justice programmes are as useful as in other fields of social intervention. It is not true that random assignment of participants to a specific programme or to a control condition is unfair. On the contrary, randomization is the fairest procedure if a programme is a limited resource, which is not available to everybody who would need it. For example, if there are only a few free places in therapeutic prisons, random allocation among those who are assessed to be in need and are qualified for this programme is the fairest procedure. Individual preferences of decision makers, financial issues, or other selection criteria would have no impact. Legal regulations are also not in principle an obstacle to RCTs in criminology. For example, if the justice system has various legal options such as community work or day fines, random allocation among a defined category of offenders can be justified for reasons of knowledge enhancement.

RCTs require a clear evaluation plan *before* the intervention under consideration is implemented. If this is the case, RCTs can be applied to measures of policing and situational crime prevention. Typical examples are experiments on the intensity of police patrol and hot spots policing (Braga 2001; Sherman and Weisburd 1993) or on crime prevention through closed-circuit television surveillance (CCTV; Welsh and Farrington 2006a) and improved street lighting (Farrington and Welsh 2006). Similarly, target hardening in public places, security equipment in shops and private housing, measures of defensible space, or screening strategies at airports are suitable for investigation by RCTs (for an overview, see Sherman *et al.* 2002). However, most studies on policing and situational crime prevention are not randomized. One may argue that even sound experiments need to go beyond a simple pre-post-comparison of programme and control areas. For example, they must address crime displacement (e.g. in location, time, victims, and offence type) and positive treatment diffusion (Barr and Pease 1990; Cornish and Clarke 1989). They also require a sufficient number of randomly allocated areas, control for preprogramme crime rates, assessment of additional interventions, non-reactive outcome measures, and a longer follow-up. However, such more complicated issues are relevant for all evaluation designs and can best be investigated by RCTs and differentiated statistical analyses.

RCTs are also appropriate for many individual-oriented approaches in crime prevention and control. For example, they were applied to the evaluation of family- and child-oriented programmes of delinquency prevention (Farrington and Welsh 2003; Lösel and Beelmann 2003a; Farrington and Welsh 2007). A substantial number of RCTs addressed offender–victim mediation in restorative justice (Sherman and Strang 2007). Large multisite community experiments were carried out on the effects of intensive supervision in probation and parole (Petersilia and Turner 1993) and drug testing (Britt, Gottfredson, and Goldkamp 1992). In the field of correctional treatment and rehabilitation, RCTs were used to evaluate cognitive-behavioural programmes (Lipsey and Landenberger 2006), sexual offender treatment (Lösel and Schmucker 2005), multisystemic therapy (MST; Henggeler *et al.* 1998), boot camps (MacKenzie, Wilson, and Kider 2001) and therapeutic prisons (Ortmann 2002). Randomized experiments can also be used in evaluations of training programmes for prison officers (Lösel and Wittmann 1989), studies on biases in sentencing (Schünemann and Bandilla 1989), and other areas of crime and justice (Farrington and Welsh 2006). In my view, one should strive toward RCTs in criminology as far as possible. Evaluators should always ask themselves why an experiment should *not* be carried out in a given situation (Weisburd 2003). However, they should also develop methodologically sound solutions when RCTs are very difficult or even impossible to carry out.

For example, criminologists are frequently asked to evaluate a programme that has already been implemented over years without any research. In this case, it is only possible to recruit a post-hoc comparison group and apply matching procedures and/or statistical controls. Random allocation of individuals is also difficult when evaluating a complete institution or a combination of measures rather than a clearly delimited programme. This is the case in complex programmes such as therapeutic communities or forensic clinics. Here, placement follows specific criteria, and randomization is sometimes impossible for legal and therapeutic reasons. For, example, seriously violent or mentally disordered offenders need specific interventions for their management in the institution. The situation is similar to that for acutely depressive or suicidal patients who cannot be left untreated in a control group over a long period of time. In health care, so-called waiting-list control groups sometimes address such problems. This is less appropriate in criminal justice interventions. On the one hand, intensive programmes may already take up a relatively long time of a prison sentence. On the other hand, and even more important, recidivism as a core measure of outcome requires several years of follow-up. Therefore, a few weeks or months difference between programme implementation in the treatment and waiting-list control group would not make a difference in outcome evaluation.

Small-scale RCTs are useful to evaluate specific treatment modules within a prison (e.g. Crighton 2006); however, such studies often lack sample size and statistical power. Multicentre comparisons may be a solution here, but they have to cope with organizational, financial, or psychological obstacles. In addition, prison climate varies greatly between institutions (Liebling and Arnold 2002). Consequently, a randomized experiment that draws on groups from different prisons may not evaluate the outcome of a specific intervention but rather the impact of the setting.

If an RCT is not feasible, one should be aware that some (not all!) quasi-experimental designs can also deliver valuable information. We must further bear in mind that RCTs are not invulnerable to threats to validity. Randomization is only a guarantee for equivalent programme and control groups if sample sizes are large. In smaller studies both groups can show substantial differences due to chance. For example, in one of the best studies on the treatment of sexual offenders, Marques *et al.* (2005) used a strong randomized design. Although the overall sample was substantial, there were pretreatment group differences that could have been relevant for the outcome. Shadish *et al.* (2002) discuss various approaches as to how one can cope with the problem of non-equivalent randomized groups. The internal validity of RCTs may also suffer from selective drop-outs and the construct validity from diffusion of treatment, experimental rivalry, demoralization of untreated controls, and other threats. Already Campbell and Stanley (1963) emphasized that every experiment is imperfect. In accordance with these pioneers, evaluators must carefully weigh what is the best design under given circumstances.

Let me illustrate this view by our Erlangen-Nuremberg Development and Prevention Study. This project combines a longitudinal analysis of the development of antisocial behaviour in childhood and a controlled evaluation of two prevention programmes (Lösel and Beelmann 2003b; Lösel *et al.* 2006). In the core sample, 675 children and their families were contacted in 61 representative kindergartens. The study design contained four groups: developmental study only, child social skills training programme, parent training programme, and child- plus parent-programme. In the first project phase there were three assessments using a broad range of data sources (child, parent, preschool teacher, direct observation, archival data): Year 1 (pre-test), Year 2 (circa 3 months after training), and Year 3 (circa one year after training). In a further follow-up, we also analysed the teacher report cards in elementary school. Our experience in pilot studies revealed that an individualized randomization of children and parents would increase threats to validity. For example, in spite of detailed information on methodological requirements, control group families from the same kindergarten may be disappointed for not receiving a programme (demoralization), may more frequently drop out before follow-up measurements (experimental mortality), may get information on training contents from the programme group (diffusion of treatment), or may reactively reflect and change their behaviour (experimental rivalry). Therefore, we decided not to randomize on the individual but on the kindergarten level. However, we also could not include all kindergartens for programme allocation because there were large variations in training resources and group sizes. Therefore, we had to make a compromise between methodological and practical requirements and assigned the groups in a stepwise procedure: First, we used organizational criteria to select appropriate kindergartens for the training. Second, we assigned the respective training kindergartens randomly. Third, we recruited matched pairs from the developmental study to form the control groups (taking age, gender, socio-economic background, and pre-training behaviour problem scores of the children as control variables). Although this randomized block design with stratification techniques is not optimal and requires statistical analyses that take within-kindergarten variation into account (e.g. Steyer *et al.* 2000), it enabled relatively sound comparisons between programme and control groups.

Criminologists should implement randomized field trials wherever appropriate; however, they should also not forget that evaluation can benefit from more than one type of information (Cronbach *et al.* 1980). In his classical article on 'reforms as experiments', Campbell (1969) did not only recommend RCTs but also various relatively sound quasi-experimental designs. Such designs are more useful when we know more about 'typical' base rates and outcomes in a field. Instead of endless controversies about experiments as the 'gold standard', criminologists should both promote RCTs and make the best use of available data. For example, evaluators should establish common structured data files on offender risk and recidivism. When such a system is applied uniformly across institutions, relatively equivalent comparison groups can be formed. An example is the evaluation of intensive regimes for young adult offenders (Farrington *et al.* 2002). It is also possible to derive typical base rates of recidivism in specific offender populations. When treated offenders reveal a failure rate that is clearly below the typical range, whereas selection, attrition, and other serious threats to validity are absent, even a post-hoc comparison may become a useful piece of information. A systematic documentation also permits more statistical controls that may be used to rule out alternative explanations. Therefore, the Offender Assessment System (OASYS) in England and Wales is an important step in the right direction (although it seems to be a little overloaded with psychometric data).

In spite of problems of coordination, integrity, or rivalry, we should design multi-centre comparisons more often. A further approach is to separate complex programmes into distinct modules that can be subjected to RCTs within an institution. In addition, attempts should be made to gain information on the efficacy of programmes through a systematic grading of their intensity or 'dosage' (e.g. number of contacts, hours of sessions). If there is a consistent dose–effect relationship, even an otherwise non-interpretable single group pre-test/post-test design may sometimes reveal usable information. As Carlson and Schmidt (1999) have shown, the latter designs can be more valuable than assumed. That they frequently yield larger mean effects than control group designs seems to be due not to methodological weakness but to differences in calculating effect sizes. Whether weaker designs reveal larger effects than RCTs needs further investigation. Weisburd, Lum, and Petrosino (2001) found such a relation; however, their study integrates very heterogeneous types of criminal justice programme. In the more homogeneous domain of offender treatment, for example, outcome differences between RCTs and quasi-experiments are less consistent (e.g. Lipsey and Wilson 1998; Lösel and Schmucker 2005).

Depending on the topic, sound quasi-experiments such as regression-discontinuity, interrupted time series, and cohort designs can be of high value for criminological evaluations. Surprisingly, such designs are rarely used in our field. Cohort studies, for example, can reduce the problems with one-shot evaluations of new programmes. Programmes need time to ripen along with practical experiences and scientific progress. This can be tested by recurring analyses of institutional cohorts. Descriptive data on the offenders can be used to correct population changes over time (e.g. Cuppleditch and Evans 2005). Quasi-experimental, aggregated case study approaches (Howard Orlinsky and Lueger 1994) may also have some use; for example, in forensic hospitals for small groups of offenders with a specific mental disorder. On all levels of methodological rigour, sound theories make interpretations of outcomes more robust.

Description of programmes and control conditions

When we talk about programme evaluation in the criminal justice system, we refer to an extremely wide range of interventions. At one end, we find programmes with a fixed number of structured teaching sessions that are based on detailed manuals (e.g. Antonowicz 2005; McGuire 2005). Most of the accredited offending behaviour programmes in England and Wales belong to this category (Correctional Services Accreditation Panel 2007). The other end is formed by complex packages of basic education and work programmes, psychosocial treatment, supervision, release preparation, and through-care in therapeutic prisons (e.g. Cullen, Jones, and Woodward 1997; Genders and Player 1995). Even more comprehensive is the integrated end-to-end management of the National Offender Management Services (NOMS) that comprises manifold programmes in prison and probation. There is widespread agreement on the advantages of a multimodal approach that addresses a broad range of the offender's needs and social contexts (e.g. Henggeler et al. 1998). However, if a programme is rather complex and heterogeneous in its content, the reliability (integrity) of its implementation becomes questionable (Lösel and Wittmann 1989; Weisburd, Petrosino, and Mason 1993). In contrast, more narrow and standardized programmes normally lead to higher integrity. The implementation of such a programme is more homogeneous because of detailed manuals on the theory, programme, assessment, and management. This can provide us with information on reasons for success or failure of a programme. In cases of very complex interventions or packages of programmes, it is much more difficult to detect such factors. On the level of the overall crime policy, it is nearly impossible to disentangle influences on national crime statistics.

Sherman *et al.* (1997) made the suitable analogy, that in medicine one would only evaluate the effect of aspirin and not a whole hospital or pharmacy in general. This is, however, not totally true as medical reviews, indeed, compare the mortality rates or infection rates in hospitals with similar specializations and patient populations. Nevertheless, when there are substantial variations, narrower evaluations are necessary to detect potential origins of such differences in overall achievement. The pharmacological analogy of evaluating aspirin can also be used for evaluations on correctional treatment. For example, some personality disordered violent offenders get serotonin re-uptake inhibitors (e.g. fluoxetine, sertraline; Kavoussi, Liu, and Coccaro 1994), and a subgroup of sexual offenders receives pharmacological treatment (e.g. cyproteronacetate or medroxy-progesteronacetate) to lower their testosterone to a subnormal level (Rösler and Witztum 2000). However, in most of these cases the drugs are rarely applied without psychosocial interventions as well (Lösel and Schmucker 2005). Thus, the question of efficacy in offender rehabilitation is often similar to multiple medications. In medicine, clinical pharmacology has been established as its own discipline to investigate the complex main and side effects of such combinations that are not simply linear and additive. In a similar way, criminology should run RCTs on various combinations of specified programmes or programme modules. As Lösel and Schmucker (2005) have shown, one can also weigh the relative impact of different modules by multiple regression techniques.

Evaluation on crime and justice is complicated by the fact that we often only know the concept or manual of a programme and not what was really delivered (Lösel 2001; Lösel and Wittmann 1989). Programme labels may over-exaggerate differences and underscore practical similarities. Even within the same type of programme, there can be large differences in outcome (Schmucker and Lösel 2006). Various indicators of programme delivery (e.g. number of sessions, total duration or contact hours per week) show independent and sometimes contradictory relations with effect size (Lipsey and Wilson 1998). Research on psychotherapy demonstrates that process variables such as cooperation, therapeutic bond, and mutual affirmation are more important for the effectiveness than specific techniques or therapeutic models (Orlinsky, Grawe, and Parks 1994). Similarly, criminological meta-analyses show that the type of programme is only one source of outcome variance among others. Characteristics of the offenders, the context and—in particular—the research methods may even account for a larger proportion of the variation (e.g. Lipsey and Wilson 1998; Lösel and Schmucker 2005; Redondo, Sanchez-Meca, and Garrido 1999). Institutional factors such as training and supervision of qualified staff; attitudes and involvement of the personnel; cooperation, support, and other characteristics of the organizational climate are important framing conditions for effective interventions (e.g. Antonowicz and Ross, 1994; Andrews and Dowden 1999; Gendreau, Goggin, and Smith 1999; Lipsey and Wilson 1998). However, they are rarely integrated in evaluations of specific offending behaviour programmes.

Consequently, we need more detailed descriptions and process analyses of programme delivery in practice. Studies should not only assess a specific programme but also the context in which it is embedded. Moos (1975) has already shown that institutional climate variables such as cohesion, openness, and norm orientation are highly important in corrections. More recently, Liebling and Arnold (2002) investigated various relationship dimensions (respect, humanity, support, relationships, and trust) and regime dimensions (fairness, order, safety, well-being, development in the prison, development regarding the family, and decency). Although the impact of such features on re-offending needs further research, Liebling and her colleagues have convincingly demonstrated their relevance for a humane prison life. Similarly, Lösel and Bliesener (1989) analysed time budgets of prison psychologists and found that organizational differences were associated with different types of prison (e.g. regular versus therapeutic prisons). Ortmann (2002) described simple indicators of programme delivery, release preparation, and organizational features in regular and therapeutic prisons. He demonstrated differences in favour of the therapeutic institutions as well as correlations between these factors and the outcome in recidivism. Results on schools (Lösel and Bliesener 2003; Rutter *et al.* 1979) and residential care institutions (Lösel and Bliesener 1994) also underline the importance of psychosocial climate factors.

These and other findings suggest that the future evaluation should go beyond programmes in the narrow sense. This does not at all mean that we should not increase sound experiments on clearly circumscribed measures; however, we need to address the broader framing conditions and specifications under which they do or do not work. Such assessments may contain the above-mentioned dimensions and other theory-based descriptions.

The descriptive data should be gathered for both the programme *and* the control conditions. This is important because control groups do not spend their time in a vacuum or receive 'nothing'. When we evaluate measures such as restorative justice, education, community work, or cognitive-behavioural programmes, it is not only important what happens in the programme but also what 'control condition', 'non-treatment', or 'sentence as usual' means. In evaluations of custodial programmes, for example, basic conditions for control groups from regular prisons are similar to those of the treatment groups. The offenders are also exposed to the effects of loss of freedom and a prison subculture; they participate in work programmes; they can take advantage of schooling and other training provisions; sometimes they receive counselling or crisis intervention through social services; they may obtain day passes, holidays, or work outside; and they may be prepared for release and monitored in the community in a similar way. Depending on which influences arise from these conditions, comparison with the programme group will involve only gradual differences rather than a treatment-versus-nothing dichotomy. In fact, differences between programme and control conditions may be small and difficult to explain. In a review of boot camps, for example, MacKenzie *et al.* (2001) found a mean zero effect but large outcome variations between different regimes. MacKenzie (2006) assumed that the combination of a strict regime with offending behaviour programmes has led to more positive effects. However, this could not be proved because it was unknown how many control sites applied similar programmes.

That the effect of a programme depends on outcomes in the control group just as much as on the programme itself is seen in evaluations of two therapeutic prisons in Germany (Dünkel and Geng 1994; Egg 1990). Both studies produced highly similar recidivism rates using various criteria (e.g. Lösel and Egg 1997). In the study at Berlin, however, outcomes in the comparison groups from regular prisons were worse than in the study at Erlangen. As a consequence, only the Berlin study had a significant 'treatment' effect. Hall's (1995) meta-analysis of sexual offender treatment reveals a similar tendency toward larger effects in studies with relatively negative outcomes in the control group. It is ironic, but the more positive elements we implement in regular prisons or other justice measures, the harder it becomes to confirm effects of a new programme. Vice versa, programme effects are easiest to confirm when the 'normal' reaction of the criminal justice system is particularly ineffective. Perhaps, some international differences in outcome evaluations may result from such differences in the control conditions. Within a country, this issue may also lead to a decrease of effect sizes regardless of an improvement of programmes over time (e.g. Lösel and Schmucker 2005).

Qualitative and quantitative methods of evaluation

The need for sound descriptive analyses has reinforced arguments for more qualitative instead of quantitative methods of evaluation. Critiques of an experimental and quantitative approach noted that such evaluations are often not consistent in outcome, not in accordance with practical experience, and not very helpful for policy making. Careful case studies, participant observation, narrative interviews with clients, and other explorative methods would reveal more valid information on the process, outcome, and problems of interventions than the experimental or quasi-experimental isolation of independent variables and the quantitative analysis of their impact on dependent variables (e.g. Filstead 1979).

Controversies between advocates of qualitative versus quantitative approaches to evaluation have existed over decades and are still prevailing in criminology. They derive from the old dichotomy between the empirical Galilean orientation in the natural sciences and the hermeneutic Aristotelian orientation in the arts. The qualitative paradigm is described as phenomenological, grounded, naturalistic in its observations, subjective, taking an insider-perspective, exploratory, inductive, process-oriented, deep, holistic, and valid. In contrast, the quantitative paradigm is characterized as logical-positivistic, controlled in measurement, objective, taking an outsider-perspective, confirmatory, outcome-oriented, generalizable, particularistic, and reliable.

Such typologies have some value to describe different scientific orientations or subcultures of researchers (Kimble 1984). However, they simplify the manifold transitions, combinations, and moderating positions between both approaches in the concrete process of research (Cook and Reichardt 1979; Lösel 1985). It is not rare that a study fulfils some criteria of the quantitative paradigm and, simultaneously, others of the qualitative approach. Using an experimental design, for example, does not necessarily imply a quantitative statistical data analysis (Shadish *et al.* 2002). Classical experiments on the brutalization of behaviour in a simulated prison (Haney, Banks, and Zimbardo 1973) or on the broken windows effect on further vandalism (Zimbardo 1973) only required controlled observation of events. As the previous section has shown, naturalistic descriptions can be of high value within an experimental paradigm. Even the pioneer of evaluation recommended the combination of qualitative-ethnographic methods with rigorous experimental criteria (Campbell 1979). Because of the numerous influences and interactions of the programmes, individuals, contexts, times, and other factors, the evaluator is in its core a historian (Cronbach *et al.* 1980). On the one hand, practical experience is important for an appropriate evaluation and integration of (quasi-) experimental findings (Campbell 1979). And on the other, qualitative research methods can meet the same criteria of reliability and validity as emphasized in the quantitative approach.

Although a theoretically and analytically sound case study may even serve to make causal inferences (Scriven 1976), qualitative methods are particularly relevant in the following situations: when the aims, research questions, and programmes are in an early stage of development; when legal, anthropological, ethical, and economic issues have to be assessed; and when potential outcome criteria are not yet clear. These are typical tasks of a formative evaluation. In contrast, quantitative and experimental methods are most appropriate when programmes are already elaborated, relatively stable, and carried out under circumstances that allow for a controlled evaluation. This view corresponds to a distribution of labour in which qualitative approaches focus on the hermeneutic, prescientific part of explanation, whereas quantitative approaches address the systematic test of causal hypotheses. However, the concept of a linear sequence of both approaches is too simple. In evaluation practice we often see a more circular or spiral sequence because qualitative methods are also of high value for monitoring programmes, for generating hypotheses on the reasons for success and failure in controlled evaluations, and for illuminating findings for stakeholders.

Let me illustrate this by one of my own research examples (Lösel and Pomplun 1998). We were asked by the Bavarian Ministry of Justice to evaluate an alternative to pretrial remand imprisonment for young offenders. This was a semiclosed residential education institution that had been established years before without any research design. We used various age cohorts of inmates as programme group and court files to select a comparison group of remand prisoners who could be matched according to offence type, previous convictions, age, and other demographic variables. This quasi-experimental design would have evaluated a 'black box' programme only. Therefore, we applied qualitative methods such as intensive interviews, site visits, and analyses of offender files to assess the contents and process of the intervention. These data suggested, for example, that the vocational training played an important role for the moderate success of the programme and that temporary escapes were less important for failure than expected. The next steps in a meaningful sequence of evaluations would have been: (a) use the recommendations of the evaluation report for the future design of the intervention (which partially happened), and (b) implement a better controlled RCT to test its current effectiveness (which did not happen because of financial problems).

Characteristics of programme participants

Person-oriented criminal justice interventions are often designed as if one size fits all. However, evaluations regularly reveal that different offenders react rather differently to the same type of programme. Meta-analyses on treatment programmes suggest that offender characteristics may account for as much of the outcome variance as the type of programme (e.g. Lipsey and Wilson 1998; Lösel and Schmucker 2005; Redondo *et al.* 1999). However, evaluations often contain rather limited information on the participants. Normally, there are brief reports on categories such as age, gender, ethnic group, type of offence, and offence history. Even such data are sometimes not reported. For example, in their review of programmes for serious and violent juvenile offenders, Lipsey and Wilson (1998) found that data on age were missing in 9 per cent of studies, data on previous violence in 16 per cent, and those on ethnic background in 24 per cent.

Evaluations that are sensitive for differential programme indication require detailed assessments of offender profiles or subtypes (e.g. Andrews and Bonta 1998; Friendship *et al.* 2005; Bonta *et al.* 2001). Such assessments may contain valid actuarial instruments and clinical data on offence characteristics, criminal history, general development, social functioning, interpersonal relationships, personality traits, and mental disorders. Although structured risk assessment has made substantial progress in the last decade (e.g. Hanson and Morton-Bourgon 2007; Quinsey *et al.* 1998; Palmer 2001), these data are only partially integrated into studies on correctional programme evaluation. This may be due to small sample sizes that do not allow for differentiating various groups that are more homogeneous. However, a lack of differentiation can also be found in relatively large studies.

Meaningful evaluations must apply structured risk assessment instruments that contain information on static risk factors (e.g. previous offending) and dynamic risk factors (e.g. deviant attitudes). Differences in the offenders' risk are not only relevant for programme assignment but also for outcome evaluation. As a general trend, correctional treatment programmes reveal smaller effect sizes in low-risk groups than in high-risk groups (e.g. Dowden and Andrews 1999; Lipsey and Wilson 1998; Lipsey and Landenberger 2006). Similar results have been found in child and family-oriented developmental prevention programmes. Universal programmes that address unselected groups from the general population had smaller effect sizes than indicated programmes for groups who already had some problems and were treated in clinical contexts (e.g. Farrington and Welsh 2003; Lösel and Beelmann 2003a). At first glance, such findings seem to be counter-intuitive because one would expect that it is easier to change low-risk groups. From a methodological point of view, this finding is plausible: in samples of low risk, a majority of individuals in both the programme and control group would not need an intervention. Natural protective factors are already sufficient to counteract reoffending and lead to desistance (e.g. Lösel and Bender 2003; Sampson and Laub 1993). Therefore, the positive impact of a correctional or preventive programme is more visible if many group members show an enhanced risk for a negative development. However, one should not overgeneralize this message, because it depends on the range of risks that are included in the respective data. As Lösel (1996) proposed, an approximation to an inverted U-shaped relationship between risk level and treatment efficacy is most plausible. It takes into account that in cases of very high risk (e.g. psychopathic offenders) it may be difficult to reach any change at all.

Assessments on the risk of reoffending should not only address differences in degree but also functional issues. For example, the category 'sexual offender' applies to a very heterogeneous group of offenders with different risks, needs, and responsiveness to interventions (Hall 1995; Hanson and Morton-Bourgon 2005). In spite of these differences, there are not many controlled evaluations on subgroups that go beyond the type of the last sexual offence (Lösel and Schmucker 2005). Subtypes of sexual offenders may indicate different motivations and degrees of disorder. For example, in child molesters, the risk of recidivism is lower when victims are female and not strangers, and offenders show no sexual disorder/paraphilia (Hanson and Bussière 1998).

Differences in underlying causal processes are also relevant for other offender categories. For example, persistent property offenders (who may exhibit crime as a routine activity) seem to gain less from correctional treatment than violent offenders (who may have a stronger influence of personality); Lipsey and Wilson (1998). The importance of functional issues is also obvious for psychopathic offenders. Whereas the second factor (impulsive-antisocial lifestyle) of the Psychopathy Checklist-Revised (Hare 2002) is a good predictor of re-offending, the relational and emotional characteristics of the first factor are particularly relevant for the offender management in criminal justice contexts (Lösel 1998). Another example for a functional assessment is the frequent problem of comorbidity between various personality disorders, alcohol and drug dependence, depression, or other mental health problems in offenders (e.g. Dolan, Evans, and Norton 1995; Loeber *et al.* 1998). Although it is not clear how much comorbidities reflect a lack of discriminant validity or an overlap in etiologically different syndromes (Lilienfeld 1994; Rutter 1997), they show the need for differentiated causal explanations, programme planning and evaluation. Functional offender issues are even relevant when we evaluate justice programmes in more or less 'normal' offender populations. For example, Sherman and Strang (2007) found overall positive effects for programmes on restorative justice. However, such programmes were less effective in minority/aboriginal groups. Perhaps, in these groups reconciliation with victims from the white majority may be counteracted by the perception of their own stigmatization and historical injustice.

Differentiated outcomes of criminological interventions are more the rule than the exception. If evaluations do not investigate various homogeneous subgroups of participants the 'one size fits all' design may inappropriately hide significant successes and failures in outcomes. Therefore, studies need to incorporate sufficiently detailed data on the target groups and sufficient sample sizes. In addition, evaluations should use comparable assessment instruments that enable comparisons and integrations across various studies.

Participant motivation and drop-out

The above-mentioned issue of a functional assessment relates to the motivation of programme participants. Motivation to participate and stay in a specific programme is not only a characteristic of the individual but the outcome of a complex interaction between programme content, communication with the staff, and the social context (McMurran 2002). The offender's motivation to change is not a yes-or-no category but has many different facets such as willingness, readiness, and ability. It is also not a stable state but a non-linear process as described in the cycle of change (Prochaska and Levesque 2002): precontemplation—contemplation—preparation/decision—action/change—maintenance—and perhaps lapse and relapse. Therefore, motivational modules such as motivational interviewing are key elements in correctional programmes (e.g. Miller and Rollnick 2002). Similarly, they play an important role in process and outcome evaluation. As described above, various threats to validity relate to motivational factors. Some of them such as reactance or demoralization of control subjects cannot even be ruled out by RCTs. Therefore, careful analyses of motivational issues are key in a valid evaluation study.

Most important is the question of whether those who participate and particularly those who complete a programme are a positive selection of highly motivated individuals. Almost all evaluations on correctional programmes are confronted with substantial drop-out rates. In custodial programmes with specific offender groups, they can be rather low (5–10 per cent) whereas in less specified community programmes they are sometimes much larger (up to 40–50 per cent). Some of these offenders may leave voluntarily because they had had other expectations, found the programme too stressful, or no longer believed that participation would lead to advantages such as early release. Others may have been requested to leave because of lack of engagement, non-cooperation, violence, drug use, or other misconduct. Some long-term programmes such as therapeutic communities include trial phases with a more-or-less regular drop-out. A further decrease in participants may occur between the end of a programme and a follow-up measurement. However, this is more relevant for self-reported than for archival outcome data which can be assessed without contacting the offender. Developmental prevention programmes contain similar problems of selective participation and drop-out. For example, families with a high-risk background or from specific minority populations are more difficult to reach and to keep in programmes (see Eisner, this volume; Lösel 2002).

Programme completers normally represent a positive selection of clients, whereas drop-outs often have higher recidivism rates than both the programme and the control group (e.g. Harper and Chitti 2005; Lösel *et al.* 1987; Lösel and Schmucker 2005; Raynor and Vanstone 2001). If the number and type of drop-outs are not the same in the programme and control group, an originally randomized design or a well-controlled quasi-experiment may fall apart. A conservative estimate of the programme outcome requires an intention-to-treat analysis. This includes all individuals in those groups to which they were (randomly) assigned, regardless of their adherence with the entry criteria, the treatment they actually received, the subsequent withdrawal from programme or deviation from the study protocol. Although intention-to-treat analyses avoid selection effects, they may lead to an underestimation of programme effects, because non-completers were not exposed to the whole programme. Therefore, it is appropriate to present results separately for programme completers, drop-outs, and controls and then perform various conservative or optimistic estimates of effect sizes (if enough information on dropouts is available).

Frequently, drop-outs exhibit even higher failure rates than untreated offenders. This may be due to both individual deficits and negative social reactions. Therefore, evaluations should contain assessments of dropout risks that derive from the programme, the staff, or the social context. For example, intake criteria may be too non-specific, or insufficient information and motivation is provided on the programme. In addition to motivational modules, switching between a group and individual format, opportunities to make up for omissions or absences, or temporary transfers within the institution are just some of the provisions that may relate to low dropping out. However, even with a relatively valid intake assessment and motivational programme modules, it is impossible to prevent all dropouts. Therefore, evaluations should also address individual and organizational processes after an early termination. Of particular interest for evaluation are those drop-outs who did not reoffend more often than the group of regular completers. Such cases may indicate processes of flexible handling, constructive reassignment, and non-stigmatization in the respective institutions. There is a need for more evaluations to understand how benefits can be gained from non-completed treatments through the flexible management of failures.

Outcome measurement

A key issue for any evaluation is the choice of outcome criteria. In evaluations on crime and justice, official data on reoffending and reconviction are particularly important.

However, for good reasons, evaluations also include criteria such as self-reports of delin-quency; measures of personality and attitudes; social skills; behaviour within an institu-tion; or other indicators of adaptation (e.g. at school, at work, in the community). Although the choice of outcome criteria is a central issue, the reliability, validity, and sen-sitivity of the measures used is not always demonstrated (Lipsey 1992b). In addition, although a multisetting-multiinformant approach is most desirable, many evaluations limit themselves to one criterion and data source (e.g. official reconviction).

These are serious problems. For example, undetected crimes and selection processes limit the validity of official reconviction data (Palmer 1992; Lloyd *et al.* 1994). Outcome criteria also vary in their sensitivity (Barbaree 1997). Lipsey and Wilson (1998) found that studies using arrest showed larger effects than those that measured recidivism through court contact, parole violation, or institutionalization. Such discrepancies can even appear within one single study. For example, in our study on an alternative pro-gramme to remand imprisonment for serious young offenders, we observed inconsistent outcomes in different indicators of official reconviction (Lösel and Pomplun 1998). There was no programme effect when we regarded any new entry in the German Federal Central Register (including registrations for petty offences). However, when we com-pared the programme and control group on new entries with an unconditional prison sentence (that indicated the most serious type of recidivism) there was a significant dif-ference in favour of the programme group. Similarly, Farrington *et al.* (2002) did not observe a long-term effect of an intensive regime for young offenders in the rate of recid-ivism but in its frequency. Developmental prevention programmes also did not show effects on all levels of antisocial behaviour but mainly on more intensive and multiple problems (e.g. Conduct Problems Prevention Research Group 2002; Lösel *et al.* 2006).

Another key issue is the length of follow-up. As a general trend, there are larger effects in studies with shorter follow-up periods (Lösel 1995a). Frequently, recidivism in pro-gramme groups is delayed in the first year after intervention but comes closer to the con-trol group when the survival curves typically stabilize after 3–4 years. In sexual offenders, the risk of recidivism is even more expanded over time (Beier 1995). The consequences of such results for evaluation practice are not as simple as they might seem at first glance. Obviously, one should not only use very short periods of follow-up. However, the longer the follow-up period, the less we may measure the specific impact of the programme under evaluation. Its effect becomes more and more confounded with natural develop-mental factors in the community or other interventions. Furthermore, expanded follow-up periods often lead to high attrition rates. And finally, prospective designs with long follow-up periods are not only costly but may evaluate relatively old programmes that have already been improved in the meantime. For these and other reasons, relatively short follow-up times are adequate, but if possible, they should be used as a starting point in a more valid assessment of outcome data over a longer period.

Difficulties with outcome measures become more obvious when evaluations assess different types of criterion. In offender treatment, for example, both recidivism and intermediate criteria such as attitudes, personality measures, or institutional adaptation are of interest. Normally, the latter show larger effect sizes than measures of criminal behaviour with a longer follow-up period (e.g. Feldman 1989; Lösel 1995b). For example, recent evaluations of offending behaviour programmes in England and Wales revealed more positive findings in psychometric measures than in recidivism (Harper and Chitti

2005). This could be due to positive self-presentations and social desirability effects in questionnaire data. On the other hand, stronger changes in attitudes and other psychological data may also reflect that such constructs are closer to the content of the respective programmes.

In principle, larger effects can be anticipated the more an outcome variable is proximal to the programme content (Lipsey 1992b; Lösel and Wittmann 1989). For example, we found that a structured training of prison officers led to changes in knowledge tests and verbalized attitudes toward prisoners; however, they were less visible as indicators of everyday behaviour. Similarly, child social skills training showed larger effects in test assessments of such skills than in ratings of the concrete behaviour (Lösel & Beelmann 2003a). However, in evaluation practice, we are also confronted with inconsistencies between different types of outcome data. For example, in Lipsey's (1992b) meta-analysis on offender treatment, effect sizes in psychological measures and academic performance did not correlate with those in delinquency. Ortmann (2002) found no systematic relationship between intermediate personality measures and recidivism. Hanson and Wallace-Capretta (2000) demonstrated that some factors often believed to inhibit domestic violence showed no relationship with recidivism. On the one hand, such discrepancies may be due to using inadequate intermediate variables. On the other hand, intermediate measures can be so restricted to the specific programme contents that transfer becomes questionable.

In general, effect criteria should reflect symmetry between treatment and outcome (Lösel and Wittmann 1989; Wittmann 1985): The success of a rather specific intervention is not tested adequately with very broad outcome measures and vice versa. In a comprehensive evaluation, assessments should form a systematic chain of proximal to distal outcome. For example, this may include measures of performance in the programme, institutional adaptation, crime-related attitudes, social skills, substance use, self-control in risk situations, and criminal behaviour (e.g. Bettman 2000; Hanson and Harris 2000). However, even within a well-developed chain of outcome measures, we may obtain inconsistent results because of low predictive validity of single risk factors (e.g. Hawkins *et al.* 1998; Lösel 2002). Evaluators should also bear in mind that systematic chains of outcome measures vary in different offender groups. For example, whereas institutional misbehaviour is a predictor of recidivism in general (e.g. Bonta and Motiuk 1992), it is not indicative for sexual reoffending in child molesters.

The need for systematic research syntheses and meta-analyses

Because of the many factors that have an impact on the outcome of one single study, evaluations of a programme or type of intervention may reveal inconsistent results. For example, two of the most long-term evaluations on early developmental prevention of delinquency came to very different conclusions: the High/Scope Perry Preschool Project targeted 3- to 5-year-old children from high-risk areas (Schweinhart *et al.* 2005). It combined cognitive stimulation of the children with parent training and weekly home visits to the mother and child over two years. Randomized long-term evaluations showed positive effects on intellectual competencies, income, lifetime number of arrests, and other indicators of positive development up to middle adulthood. The Cambridge-Somerville Youth Study (McCord 2003) addressed boys younger than age 10 and their families in a congested urban area. The programme lasted for five years and contained academic tutoring, family counselling, medical assistance, sports activities, and summer camps. The long-term evaluation up to age 40 revealed more delinquency, alcohol abuse, family problems, and mental illnesses in the treatment group than in the control group.

Such discrepancies were also observed on rather similar programmes. For example, situational crime prevention through CCTV was repeatedly found to be effective; however, some studies drew a less positive picture (Farrington and Welsh 2003). Several well-controlled studies on early home visiting programmes revealed long-term effects on the child's antisocial behaviour; others could not replicate this finding (Bilukha *et al.* 2005). Cognitive-behavioural treatment of sexual offenders showed positive results in some evaluations, but no effect in other studies on the same level of methodological quality (Schmucker and Lösel 2006). Multisystemic therapy for young offenders worked rather well in various evaluations but not in all (Littell 2005).

Because of such variations, systematic reviews and meta-analyses became a very important branch of evaluation research. They avoid shortcomings of traditional narrative literature reviews such as selective retrieval and presentation of studies, subjective weighting of their quality and importance, and focus on significant findings. To establish an evidence base that is as transparent, objective, reliable, and valid as possible, meta-analyses should contain a clear definition of the field under consideration, explicit criteria for studies included and a comprehensive literature search (also for unpublished studies). It should also include a systematic coding of study characteristics (e.g. design, programme, subjects, outcome measures), a computation of effect sizes that are comparable across studies, and systematic analyses of general and moderator effects.

Meta-analyses on crime and justice evaluations have shown that even small and non-significant effects on the level of single studies may reveal a practically relevant and statistically significant effect when aggregated over many studies. They also demonstrated differential findings for various types of programme, setting, offender group, and methodological characteristic. And finally, yet importantly, they revealed blind spots in the available studies and research activities. However, a chapter that aims to bridge gaps between scientific standards and practical demands would be incomplete if I did not mention some experiences and problems in doing meta-analyses since the 1980s.

For example, there is the question of whether one should define the field under evaluation relatively broadly (e.g. sexual offender treatment) or narrowly (e.g. hormonal treatment for adult child molesters). The advantage of the first choice is a broader database that enables more differentiated analyses. The second type of approach is more focused but often lacks a substantial number of comparable studies. Criteria for study inclusion may also become a difficult issue. A focus on RCTs would be desirable; however, one may end up with too few studies to derive any useful information for practice. Therefore, it is preferable to include studies on a lower but not too low level of methodological rigour. However, differences due to design quality need to be analysed. A further practical problem refers to study retrieval. Most North-American meta-analyses on crime and justice programmes concentrate on English-language reports only. The search for unpublished literature and web-site information also contains selective decisions. The same is the case when primary studies are categorized. Although coder training normally leads to sufficient reliability, the respective categories (e.g. programme types) are often not the same in various meta-analyses on the same topic.

The integration of various outcome measures, treatment of extreme findings, selection of appropriate statistical models (e.g. random or fixed effects), the level of differentiation and techniques for analysing moderator effects and other procedures, are further steps on which various meta-analyses on the same topic may differ. Of course, excellent textbooks on the methods of meta-analysis (Lipsey and Wilson 2001) and methodological guidelines of the Cochrane and Campbell Collaborations help to make objective and transparent decisions on such issues. However, one should be aware that even a very thorough meta-analysis does not provide the one and only 'truth' on the evidence for a specific type of intervention. Therefore, it is meaningful to conduct and compare various research syntheses on the same types of programme (e.g. Lösel 1995a). Such evaluations should also be carried out by independent researchers who are not motivated to promote their own programme.

Conclusions

This chapter has shown that criminological evaluation research has to cope with many scientific and practical demands and problems. However, there are flexible tools and strategies to meet standards and requirements in both areas. This essay focused on process and outcome evaluation and addressed basic issues of methodological quality, the implementation of randomized experiments, the importance of sound descriptions of both programme and control conditions. It also examined the relation between quantitative and qualitative approaches, the impact and assessment of offender characteristics, problems of participant motivation and drop-out, the measurement of outcome, and the need for replications and systematic research integrations. In all these fields, it becomes apparent that there is not the one and only standard solution. The researcher must have a solid methods basis but also needs to adapt flexibly to the practical context of the evaluation. For reasons of space, the chapter could not address other important issues of criminological evaluations, for example: information and communication with stakeholders, potential resistance from institutions or opinion leaders in the field, problems of data access and protection, or ethical and practical questions of informed consent (e.g. King 2000). There are also important topics such as resource allocation into one big or several smaller studies, conflicts of interests when evaluating own programmes, cost-effectiveness and cost-benefit analyses, appropriate report-writing, and promoting the use of findings in policy and practice. The interested reader can refer to general textbooks on evaluation (e.g. Rossi, Lipsey, and Freeman 2004) or criminological volumes on some of these issues (e.g. Bernfeld, Farrington, and Leschied 2001; Welsh, Farrington, and Sherman 2001). As with the problems addressed in this chapter, evaluators need to cope with them in a flexible but methodologically grounded way. Doing evaluations is not a one-shot activity but a process in which a system learns about itself (Cronbach *et al.* 1980).

Suggestions for further reading

Because the topic of this chapter is very broad, one has to cope with a huge amount of literature. For the basics on evaluation methodology, I recommend Rossi, Lipsey, and Freeman (2004) and Shadish, Cook, and Campbell (2002). The classical article from

Campbell (1969) is still inspiring and Cronbach *et al.* (1980) give a refreshing view on the practice of programme evaluation. Many examples of evaluations on crime and justice topics can be found in Sherman *et al.* (2002), Welsh and Farrington (2006) and MacKenzie (2006). The volume from Bernfeld, Farrington, and Leschied (2001) addresses practical issues of programme implementation and evaluation. However, as in real life, no reading can fully replace one's own experience in evaluation (including learning from mistakes).

References

ANDREWS, D. A. and BONTA, J. (1998). *The Psychology of Criminal Conduct* (2nd edn). Cincinatti, OH: Anderson.

—— and DOWDEN, C. (1999). 'A Meta-analytic Investigation into Effective Correctional Intervention for Female Offenders'. *Forum on Corrections Research* 11(3): 18–21.

—— ZINGER, I., HOGE, R. D., BONTA, J., GENDREAU, P., and CULLEN, F. T. (1990). 'Does Correctional Treatment Work? A Clinically Relevant and Psychologically Informed Meta-analysis'. *Criminology* 28: 369–404.

ANTONOWICZ, D. H. (2005). 'The Reasoning and Rehabilitation Program: Outcome Evaluations with Offenders' in M. McMurran and J. McGuire (eds), *Social Problem Solving and Offending*. Chichester: Wiley.

—— and ROSS, R. R. (1994). 'Essential Components of Successful Rehabilitation Programs for Offenders'. *International Journal of Offender Therapy and Comparative Criminology* 38: 97–104.

BARBAREE, H. E. (1997). 'Evaluating Treatment Efficacy with Sexual Offenders: The Insensitivity of Recidivism Studies to Treatment Effects'. *Sexual Abuse: A Journal of Research and Treatment* 9: 111–28.

BARR, R. and PEASE, K. (1990). 'Crime Placement, Displacement, and Deflection' in M. Tonry and N. Morris (eds), *Crime and Justice: A Review of Research*, Vol. 12. Chicago, IL: University of Chicago Press.

BEIER, K. M. (1995). *Dissexualität im Lebenslängsschnitt [Antisocial Sexual Behaviour in the Life Course]*. Berlin: Springer.

BERNFELD, G. A., FARRINGTON, D. P., and LESCHIED, A. W. (eds) (2001). *Offender Rehabilitation in Practice*. Chichester: Wiley.

BETTMAN, M. (2000). *Violence Prevention Program: Accreditation Case File*. Ottawa: Correctional Service Canada.

BILUKHA, O., HAHN, R. A., CROSBY, A., FULLILOVE, M. T., LIBERMAN, A., MOSCICKI, E., SNYDER, S., TUMA, F., CORSO, P., SCHOLFIELD, A., and BRISS, P. A. (2005). 'The Effectiveness of Early Childhood Home Visitation in Preventing Violence: a Systematic Review'. *American Journal of Preventive Medicine* 28: 11–39.

BOTTOMS, A. (2000). 'The Relationship between Theory and Research in Criminology' in R. D. King and E. Wincup (eds), *Doing Research on Crime and Justice*. Oxford: Oxford University Press.

BONTA, J. and MOTIUK, L. (1992). 'Inmate Classification'. *Journal of Criminal Justice* 20: 343–53.

——, BOGUE, B., CROWLEY, M., and MOTIUK, L. (2001). 'Implementing Offender Classification Systems: Lessons Learned' in G. A. Bernfeld, D. P. Farrington, and A. W. Leschied (eds), *Offender Rehabilitation in Practice*. Chichester: Wiley.

BRAGA, A. A. (2001). 'The Effects of Hot Spots Policing on crime'. *The Annals of the American Academy of Political and Social Science* 578: 104–25.

BRITT, C. L., GOTTFREDSON, M. R., and GOLDKAMP, J. S. (1992). 'Drug Testing and Pretrial Misconduct: An Experiment on the Specific Deterrent Effects of Drug Monitoring Defendants on Pretrial Release'. *Journal of Research on Crime and Delinquency* 29: 62–78.

BUNGE, M. (1959). *Causality*. Cambridge, MA: Harvard University Press.

CAMPBELL, D. T. (1969). 'Reforms as Experiments'. *American Psychologist* 24: 409–29.

—— (1979). 'Degrees of Freedom and the Case Study' in T. D. Cook and C. S. Reichardt (eds), *Qualitative and Quantitative Methods in Evaluation Research* 49–67. Beverly Hills, CA: Sage.

—— and STANLEY, J. C. (1963). *Experimental and Quasi-experimental Designs for Research*. Chicago: Rand McNally.

CARLSON, K. D. and SCHMIDT, F. L. (1999). 'Impact of Experimental Design on Effect Size: Findings from the Research Literature'. *Journal of Applied Psychology* 84: 851–62.

CHEN, H. T. (1989). *Theory-driven Evaluation*. Newbury Park, CA: Sage.

CONDUCT PROBLEMS PREVENTION RESEARCH GROUP (2002). 'Evaluation of the First 3 Years of the Fast Track Prevention Trial with Children at High Risk for Adolescent Conduct Problems'. *Journal of Abnormal Child Psychology* 19: 553–67.

COOK, T. D. and CAMPBELL, D. T. (1979). *Quasi-experimentation. Design and Analysis Issues for Field Settings*. Chicago: Rand McNally.

—— and REICHARDT, C. S. (eds)(1979). *Qualitative and Quantitative Methods in Evaluation Research*. Beverly Hills, CA: Sage.

CORNISH, D. B. and CLARKE, R. V. (1989). 'Crime Specialisation, Crime Displacement and Rational Choice Theory' in H. Wegener, F. Lösel, and J. Haisch (eds), *Criminal Behavior and the Justice System*. New York: Springer.

CORRECTIONAL SERVICES ACCREDITATION PANEL (2007). *The Correctional Services Accreditation Panel Report 2005–06*. London: NOMS/Home Office.

CRIGHTON, D. A. (2006). 'Methodological Issues in Psychological Research in Prisons' in G. J. Towl (ed.), *Psychological Research in Prisons*. Oxford: BPS Blackwell.

CRONBACH, L. J., AMBRON, S. R., DORNBUSCH, S. M., HESS, R. D., HORNIK, R. C., PHILIPS, D. C., WALKER, D. F. and WEINER, S. S. (1980). *Toward Reform of Program Evaluation*. San Francisco: Jossey Bass.

CULLEN, E., JONES, L., and WOODWARD, R. (eds) (1997). *Therapeutic Communities for Offenders*. Chichester: Wiley.

CUPPLEDITCH, L. and EVANS, W. (2005). *Re-offending of Adults: Results from the 2002 Cohort*. Home Office Statistical Bulletin 25/05. London: Home Office.

DOLAN, B., EVANS, C., and NORTON, K. (1995). 'The Multiple axis-II Diagnosis of Personality Disorders'. *British Journal of Psychiatry* 166: 107–12.

DOWDEN, C. and ANDREWS, D. A. (1999). 'What Works for Female Offenders: A Meta-analytic Review'. *Crime & Delinquency* 45: 438–52.

DÜNKEL, F. and GENG, B. (1994). 'Rückfall und Bewährung von Karrieretätern nach Entlassung aus dem sozialtherapeutischen Behandlungsvollzug und aus dem Regelvollzug (Recidivism and Desistance of Career Criminals after Release from Social-therapeutic Prisons)' in M. Steller, K.-P. Dahle, and M. Basqué (eds), *Straftäterbehandlung (Offender Treatment)*. Pfaffenweiler: Centaurus.

EGG, R. (1990). 'Sozialtherapeutische Behandlung und Rückfälligkeit im länger-fristigen Vergleich (Social therapy and Recidivism in a Long-term Comparison)'. *Monatsschrift für Kriminologie und Strafrechtsreform* 73: 358–68.

FARRINGTON, D. P. (2003a). 'Methodological Quality Standards for Evaluation Research'. *The Annals of the American Academy of Political and Social Science* 587: 49–68.

—— (2003b). 'A Short History of Randomised Experiments in Criminology: A Meager Feast'. *Evaluation Review* 27: 218–27.

—— (2003c). 'British Randomized Experiments on Crime and Justice'. *Annals of the American Academy of Political and Social Science* 589: 150–67.

—— and PETROSINO, A. (2000). 'The Campbell Collaboration Crime and Justice Group'. *The Annals of the Academy of Political and Social Science* 578: 35–49.

—— and WELSH, B.C. (2003). 'Family-based Prevention of Offending: A Meta-analysis'. *Australian and New Zealand Journal of Criminology* 36: 127–51.

—— and —— (2006). 'A Half Century of Randomised Experiments on Crime and Justice'. *Crime and Justice* 34: 55–132.

—— and —— (2007). *Saving Children from a Life of Crime*. Oxford: Oxford University Press.

——, LANGAN, P. A., and TONRY, M. (2004). *Cross-national Studies in Crime and Justice*. Washington, DC: US Department of Justice.

——, DITCHFIELD, J., HANCOCK, G., HOWARD, P., JOLLIFFE, D., LIVINGSTON, M. S., and PAINTER, K. (2002). *Evaluation of Two Intensive Regimes for Young Offenders*. Home Office Research Study 239. London: Home Office.

FELDMAN, P. (1989). 'Applying Psychology to the Reduction of Juvenile Offending and Offences: Methods and Results'. *Issues in Criminological and Legal Psychology* 14: 3–32.

FILSTEAD, W. J. (1979). 'Qualitative Methods: a Needed Perspective in Evaluation Research' in T. D. Cook and C. S. Reichardt (eds), *Qualitative and Quantitative Methods in Evaluation Research*. Beverly Hills, CA: Sage.

FRIENDSHIP, C., STREET, R., CANN, J., and HARPER, G. (2005). 'Introduction: the Policy Context and Assessing the Evidence' in G. Harper and C. Chitty (eds), *The Impact of Corrections on Re-offending: a Review of 'What Works'*. Home Office Research Study 291. London: Home Office.

GADENNE, V. (1976). *Die Gültigkeit psychologischer Untersuchungen (The Validity of Psychological Research)*. Stuttgart: Kohlhammer.

GELSTHORPE, L. (2006). 'What is Criminology for?: Looking Within and Beyond'. *Plenary Paper at the British Society of Criminology Conference*, July 2006, Glasgow, Scotland.

GENDERS, E. and PLAYER, E. (1995). *Grendon: A Study of a Therapeutic Prison*. Oxford: Clarendon Press.

GENDREAU, P., GOGGIN, C., and SMITH, P. (1999). 'The Forgotten Issue in Effective Correctional Treatment: Program Implementation'. *International Journal of Offender Therapy and Comparative Criminology* 43: 180–87.

——, ——, CULLEN, F. T., and ANDREWS, D. A. (2000). 'Does "Getting Tough" with Offenders Work? The Effects of Community Sanctions and Incarceration'. *Forum on Corrections Research* 12: 10–13.

HALL, G. C. N. (1995). 'Sexual Offender Recidivism Revisited: A Meta-analysis of Recent Treatment Studies'. *Journal of Consulting and Clinical Psychology* 63: 802–9.

HANEY, C., BANKS, C., and ZIMBARDO, P. G. (1973). 'Interpersonal Dynamics in a Simulated Prison'. *International Journal of Criminology and Penology* 1: 69–97.

HANSON, R. K. and BUSSIÈRE, M. T. (1998). 'Predicting Relapse: A Meta-analysis of Sexual Offender Recidivism Studies'. *Journal of Consulting and Clinical Psychology* 66: 348–62.

—— and HARRIS, A. J. R. (2000). *The Sex Offender Need Assessment Rating (SONAR): A Method for Measuring Change in Risk Levels.* User report. Ottawa: Department of the Solicitor General of Canada.

—— and MORTON-BOURGON, K. E. (2005). 'The Characteristics of Persistent Sexual Offenders: A Meta-analysis of Recidivism Studies'. *Journal of Consulting and Clinical Psychology* 73: 1154–63.

—— and —— (2007). *The Accuracy of Recidivism Risk Assessments for Sexual Offenders: A Meta-analysis.* Corrections research user report 2007–01. Ottawa: Department of Justice Canada.

—— and WALLACE-CAPRETTA, S. (2000). *Predicting Recidivism among Male Batterers.* User report. Ottawa: Solicitor General Canada.

HARE, R. D. (2002). *The Hare Psychopathy Checklist-Revised* (2nd edn). Toronto: Multi-Health Systems.

HARPER, G. and CHITTY, C. (eds) (2005). *The Impact of Corrections on Re-offending: a Review of 'What Works'.* Home Office Research Study 291. London: Home Office.

HAWKINS, J. D., HERRENKOHL, T., FARRINGTON, D. P., BREWER, D., CATALANO, R. F., and HARACHI, T. W. (1998). 'A Review of Predictors of Youth Violence' in R. Loeber and D. P. Farrington (eds), *Serious & violent juvenile offenders* 106–46. Thousand Oaks: Sage.

HENGGELER, S. W., SCHOENWALD, S. K., BORDUIN, C. M., ROWLAND, M. D. and CUNNINGHAM, P. B. (1998). *Multisystemic Treatment of Antisocial Behavior in Children and Adolescents.* New York: Guilford.

HOWARD, K. I., ORLINSKY, D. E., and LUEGER, R. J. (1994). 'Clinically Relevant Outcome Research in Individual Psychotherapy: New Models Guide the Researcher and Clinician'. *British Journal of Psychiatry* 165: 4–8.

KAVOUSSI, R. J., LIU, L., and COCCARO, E. F. (1994). 'An Open Trial of Sertraline in Personality Disordered Patients with Impulsive Aggression'. *Journal of Clinical Psychiatry* 55: 137–41.

KIMBLE, G. A. (1984). 'Psychology's Two Cultures'. *American Psychologist* 39: 833–9.

KING, R. D. (2000). 'Doing Research in Prisons' in R. D. King and E. Wincup (eds), *Doing Research on Crime and Justice.* Oxford: Oxford University Press.

—— and McDERMOTT, K. (1989). 'British prisons 1970–1987: The Ever-deepening Crisis'. *British Journal of Criminology* 29: 107–28.

LEVITON, L. C. and HUGHES, E. F. (1981). 'Research on the Utilization of Evaluations: A Review and Synthesis'. *Evaluation Review* 5: 525–48.

LIEBLING, A. and ARNOLD, H. (2002). 'Measuring the Quality of Prison Life'. *Research Findings 174.* London: Home Office.

—— and MARUNA, S. (eds) (2005). *The Effects of Imprisonment.* Cullompton, UK: Willan.

LILIENFELD, S. O. (1994). 'Conceptual Problems in the Assessment of Psychopathy'. *Clinical Psychology Review* 14: 17–38.

LIPSEY, M. W. (1992a). 'Juvenile Delinquency Treatment: A Meta-analytic Inquiry into Variability of Effects' in T. D. Cook, H. Cooper, D. S. Cordray, H. Hartmann, L. V. Hedges, R. L. Light, T. A. Louis, and F. Mosteller (eds), *Meta-analysis for Explanation.* New York: Russell Sage Foundation.

LIPSEY, M. W. (1992b). 'The Effect of Treatment on Juvenile Delinquents: Results from Meta-analysis' in F. Lösel, D. Bender, and T. Bliesener (eds), *Psychology and Law: International perspectives*. Berlin: de Gruyter.

—— and LANDENBERGER, N. A. (2006). 'Cognitive-behavioral Interventions' in B. C. Welsh and D. P. Farrington (eds), *Preventing Crime: What Works for Children, Offenders, Victims, and Places*. Dordrecht, NL: Springer.

—— and WILSON, D. B. (1998). 'Effective Intervention for Serious Juvenile Offenders' in R. Loeber and D. P. Farrington (eds), *Serious & Violent Juvenile Offenders*. Thousand Oaks, CA: Sage.

—— and —— (2001). *Practical Meta-analysis*. Thousand Oaks, CA: Sage.

LITTELL, J. H. (2005). 'A Systematic Review of Effects of Multisystemic Therapy'. *Paper presented at the 14th World Congress of Criminology*, August 2005. Philadelphia.

LLOYD, C., MAIR, G., and HOUGH, M. (1994). *Explaining Reconviction Rates: A Critical Analysis*. London: Home Office.

LOEBER, R., FARRINGTON, D. P., STOUTHAMER-LOEBER, M., and VAN KAMMEN, W. B. (1998). *Antisocial Behavior and Mental Health Problems*. Mahwah, NJ: Lawrence Earlbaum.

LÖSEL, F. (1985). 'Zur Kontroverse um eine gegenstandsangemessene psychologische Forschung: Bemerkungen aus der Sicht der Forschungspraxis (The Controversy on Psychological Research Paradigms: Remarks from the Perspective of Research Practice)' in W. F. Kugemann, S. Preiser, and K. A. Schneewind (eds), *Psychologie und komplexe Lebenswirklichkeit (Psychology and the Complexity of Real Life)*. Göttingen, Germany: Hogrefe.

—— (1993). 'The Effectiveness of Treatment in Institutional and Community Settings'. *Criminal Behaviour and Mental Health* 3: 416–37.

—— (1995a). 'The Efficacy of Correctional Treatment: A Review and Synthesis of Meta-evaluations' in J. McGuire (ed.), *What Works: Reducing Reoffending*. Chichester: Wiley.

—— (1995b). 'Increasing Consensus in the Evaluation of Offender Rehabilitation? Lessons from Research Syntheses'. *Psychology, Crime and Law* 2: 19–39.

—— (1996). 'Changing Patterns in the Use of Prisons: An Evidence-based Perspective'. *European Journal on Criminal Policy and Research* 4: 108–27.

—— (1998). 'Treatment and Management of Psychopaths' in D. J. Cooke, A. E. Forth, and R. D. Hare (eds), *Psychopathy: Theory, Research and Implications for Society*. NL: Kluwer.

—— (2001). 'Evaluating the Effectiveness of Correctional Programs: Bridging the Gap between Research and Practice' in G. A. Bernfeld, D. P. Farrington, and A. W. Leschied (eds), *Offender Rehabilitation in Practice*. Chichester: Wiley.

—— (2002). 'Risk/need Assessment and Prevention of Antisocial Development in Young People: Basic Issues from a Perspective of Cautionary Optimism' in R. Corrado, R. Roesch, S. D. Hart, and J. Gierowski (eds), *Multiproblem Violent Youth*. Amsterdam: IOS/NATO Book Series.

—— and BEELMANN, A. (2003a). 'Effects of Child Skills Training in Preventing Antisocial Behavior: A Systematic Review of Randomized Experiments'. *The Annals of the American Academy of Political and Social Science* 587: 84–109.

—— and —— (2003b). 'Early Developmental Prevention of Aggression and Delinquency' in F. Dünkel and K. Drenkhahn (eds), *Youth violence: New Patterns and Local Responses*. Mönchengladbach: Forum Verlag.

——, ——, STEMMLER, M., and JAURSCH, S. (2006). 'Prävention von Problemen des

Sozialverhaltens im Vorschulalter: Evaluation des Eltern- und Kindertrainings EFFEKT. (Prevention of Conduct Problems in Preschool Age: Evaluation of the Parent- and Child-oriented program EFFEKT). *Zeitschrift für Klinische Psychologie und Psychotherapie* 35: 127–39.

—— and BENDER, D. (2003). 'Protective Factors and Resilience' in D. P. Farrington and J. Coid (eds), *Prevention of Adult Antisocial Behaviour.* Cambridge: Cambridge University Press.

—— and BLIESENER (1989). 'Psychology in Prison: Role Assessment and Testing of an Organizational Model' in H. Wegener, F. Lösel and J. Haisch (eds), *Criminal Behavior and the Justice System.* New York: Springer.

—— and —— (1994). 'Some High-risk Adolescents do not Develop Conduct Problems: A Study of Protective Factors'. *International Journal of Behavioral Development* 17: 753–77.

—— and —— (2003). *Aggression und Delinquenz unter Jugendlichen: Untersuchungen von kognitiven und sozialen Bedingungen (Aggression and Delinquency in Adolescence: A Study on Cognitive and Social Origins).* Neuwied, Germany: Luchterhand.

—— and EGG, R. (1997). 'Social-therapeutic Institutions in Germany: Description and Evaluation' in E. Cullen, L. Jones, and R. Woodward (eds), *Therapeutic Communities in Prisons.* Chichester: Wiley.

—— and KÖFERL, P. (1989). 'Evaluation Research on Correctional Treatment in West Germany: A Meta-analysis' in H. Wegener, F. Lösel, and J. Haisch (eds), *Criminal Behavior and the Justice System.* New York: Springer.

——, ——, and WEBER, F. (1987). *Meta-Evaluation der Sozialtherapie (Meta-evaluation of Social-therapeutic Prisons).* Stuttgart: Enke.

—— and NOWACK, W. (1987). 'Evaluationsforschung (Evaluation research)' in J. Schulz-Gambard (ed.), *Angewandte Sozialpsychologie (Applied social psychology).* München: Psychologie Verlags Union.

—— and POMPLUN, O. (1998). *Jugendhilfe statt Untersuchungshaft: Eine Evaluationsstudie zur Heimunterbringung (Residential Education instead of Pretrial Detention for Young Offenders: An Evaluation Study).* Pfaffenweiler: Centaurus.

—— and SCHMUCKER, M. (2005). 'The Effectiveness of Treatment for Sexual Offenders: A Comprehensive Meta-analysis'. *Journal of Experimental Criminology* 1: 117–46.

—— and WITTMANN, W. W. (1989) 'The Relationship of Treatment Integrity and Intensity to Outcome Criteria'. *New Directions for Program Evaluation* 42: 97–108.

MACKENZIE, D. L. (2006). *What Works in Corrections.* Cambridge: Cambridge University Press.

——, WILSON, D. B., and KIDER, S. B. (2001). 'Effects of Correctional Boot Camps on Offending'. *The Annals of the American Academy of Political and Social Science* 578: 126–43.

MARQUES, J. K., WIEDERANDERS, W., DAY, D. M., NELSON, C., and VON OMMEREN, A. (2005). 'Effects of a Relapse Prevention Program on Sexual Recidivism: Final Results from California's Sex Offender Treatement and Evaluation Project (SOTEP)'. *Sexual Abuse* 17: 79–110.

MCCORD, J. (2003). 'Cures that Harm: Unanticipated Outcomes of Crime Prevention Programs'. *The Annals of the American Academy of Political and Social Science* 587: 16–30.

MCGUIRE, J. (2005). 'The Think First programme' in M. McMurran and J. McGuire (eds), *Social Problem Solving and Offending.* Chichester: Wiley.

McGuire, J. (ed.) (1995). *What Works: Reducing Reoffending—Guidelines for Research and Practice*. Chichester: Wiley.

—— (ed.) (2002). *Offender Rehabilitation and Treatment: Effective Programmes and Policies to Reduce Re-offending*. Chichester: Wiley.

McMurran, M. (2002). 'Motivation to Change: Selection Criterion or Treatment Need?' in M. McMurran (ed.), *Motivating Offenders to Change*. Chichester: Wiley.

Miller, W. R. and Rollnick, S. (2002). *Motivational Interviewing: Preparing People to Change* (2nd edn). New York: Guilford Press.

Morgan, R. (2000). 'The Politics of Criminological Research' in R. D. King and E. Wincup (eds), *Doing Research on Crime and Justice*. Oxford: Oxford University Press.

Moos, R. (1975). *Evaluating Correctional and Community Settings*. New York: Wiley.

Orlinsky, D. E., Grawe, K., and Parks, B. K. (1994). 'Process and Outcome in Psychotherapy' in A. E. Bergin and S. L. Garfield (eds), *Handbook of Psychotherapy and Behavior Change* (4th edn). New York: Wiley.

Ortmann, R. (2002). *Sozialtherapie im Strafvollzug (Social Therapy in Prisons)*. Freiburg i. Br.: Max-Planck-Institut für ausländisches und internationales Strafrecht.

Palmer, E. J. (2001). 'Risk Assessment: Review of Psychometric Measures' in D. P. Farrington, C. R. Hollin, and M. McMurran (eds), *Sex and Violence:The Psychology of Crime and Risk Assessment* 7–22. London: Routledge.

Palmer, T. (1992). *The Re-emergence of Correctional Intervention*. Newbury Park, CA: Sage.

Pawson, R. and Tilley, N. (1994). 'What Works in Evaluation Research'. *British Journal of Crimonology* 34: 291–306.

—— and —— (1997). *Realistic Evaluation*. London: Sage.

Petersilia, J. and Turner, S. (1993). *Evaluating Intensive Supervision Probation/parole: Results of a Nationwide Experiment*. Washington, DC: US Department of Justice, National Institute of Justice.

Prochaska, J. O. and Levesque, D. A. (2002). 'Enhancing Motivation of Offenders at each Stage of Change and Phase of Therapy' in M. Mc Murran (ed.), *Motivating Offenders to Change*. Chichester: Wiley.

Quinsey, V. L., Harris, G. T., Rice, M. E., and Cormier, C. A. (1998). *Violent Offenders: Appraising and Managing Risk*. Washington, DC: American Psychological Association.

Raynor, P. and Vanstone, M. (2001). 'Straight Thinking on Probation: Evidence-based Practice and Culture of Curiosity' in G. A. Bernfeld, D. P. Farrington, and A. W. Leschied (eds), *Offender Rehabilitation in Practice*. Chichester: Wiley.

Redondo, S., Sánchez-Meca, J., and Garrido, V. (1999). 'The Influence of Treatment Programmes on the Recidivism of Juvenile and Adult Offenders: A European Meta-analytic Review'. *Psychology, Crime and Law* 5: 251–78.

Rösler, A. and Witzum, E. (2000). 'Pharmacotherapy of Paraphilias in the Next Millennium'. *Behavioral Sciences and the Law* 18: 43–56.

Rossi, P. H., Lipsey, M. W., and Freeman, H. E. (2004). *Evaluation: A Systematic Approach* (7th edn). Thousand Oaks, CA: Sage.

Rossi, R. R. and Freeman, H. E. (1982). *Evaluation: A Systematic Approach*. Beverly Hills, CA: Sage.

Rutter, M. (1997). 'Comorbidity: Concepts, Claims, and Choices'. *Criminal Behaviour and Mental Health* 7: 265–85.

——, MAUGHAN, B., MORTIMORE, P., and OUSTON, J. (1979). *Fifteen Thousand Hours: Secondary Schools and their Effects on Children.* Cambridge, MA: Harvard University Press.

SAMPSON, R. J. and LAUB, J. H. (1993). *Crime in the Making: Pathways and Turning Points through Life.* Cambridge, MA: Harvard University Press.

SCHMUCKER, M. and LÖSEL, F. (2006). 'Beyond Programs: Outcome Differences between Cognitive-behavioral Programs of Sex Offender Treatment'. *Paper presented at the Annual Meeting of the American Society of Criminology*, November 2005, Los Angeles.

SCHÜNEMANN, B. and BANDILLA, W. (1989). 'Perseverance in Courtroom Decisions' in H. Wegener, F. Lösel, and J. Haisch (eds), *Criminal Behavior and the Justice System.* New York: Springer.

SCHWEINHART, L. J., MONTIE, J., XIANG, Z., BARNETT, W. S., BELFIELD, C. R., and NORES, M. (2005). *Lifetime Effects: The High/Scope Perry Preschool Study through age 40.* Ypsilanti: High/Scope Press.

SCRIVEN, M. (1976). 'Maximizing the Power of Causal Investigation: The Modus Operandi Method' in G. V. Glass (ed.), *Evaluation Studies Review Annual* 1: 101–18. Newbury Park, CA: Sage.

SHADISH, W. R., COOK, T. D., and CAMPBELL, D. T. (2002). *Experimental and Quasi-experimental Designs for Generalized Causal Inference.* Boston, MA: Houghton Mifflin.

SHERMAN, L. W. and STRANG, H. (2007). *Restorative Justice: The Evidence.* London: The Smith Institute.

—— and WEISBURD, D. (1993). 'General Deterrent Effects of Police Patrol in Crime 'Hot Spots': A Randomized Controlled Trial'. *Justice Quarterly* 12: 625–48.

——, FARRINGTON, D. P., WELSH, B. C., and MacKENZIE, D. L. (eds) (2002).

Evidence-based Crime Prevention. New York: Routledge.

——, GOTTFREDSON, D. C., MacKENZIE, D. L., ECK, J. E., REUTER, P., and BUSHWAY, S. D. (1997). *Preventing Crime: What Works, What Doesn't, What's Promising.* Washington, DC: US Department of Justice, National Institute of Justice.

STEYER, R., GABLER, S., von DAVIER, A., NACHTIGALL, C., and BUHL, T. (2000). 'Causal Regression Model I: Individual and Average Causal Effects'. *Methods of Psychological Research-Online* 5: 39–71.

TOWL, G. J. (ed.) (2006). *Psychological Research in Prisons.* Oxford: BPS Blackwell.

WEBSTER, C. M., DOOB, A. N., and ZIMRING, F. E. (2006). 'Proposition 8 and Crime Rates in California; The Case of the Disappearing Deterrent'. *Criminology & Public Policy* 5: 417–48.

WEISBURD, D. (2003). 'Ethical Practice and Evaluation of Interventions in Crime and Justice: The Moral Imperative for Randomised Trials'. *Evaluation Review* 27: 336–54.

——, LUM, C. M., and PETROSINO, A. (2001). 'Does Research Design Affect Study Outcomes in Criminal Justice?' *The Annals of the American Academy of Political and Social Science* 578: 50–70.

——, PETROSINO, A., and MASON, G. (1993). 'Design Sensitivity in Criminal Justice Experiments: Reassessing the Relationship between Sample Size and Statistical Power' in M. Tonry and N. Morris (eds), *Crime and Justice* vol. 17. Chicago: University of Chicago Press.

WEISS, C. H. (1982). 'Measuring the Use of Evaluation'. *Evaluation Studies* 2: 129–46.

WELSH, B. C. and FARRINGTON, D. P. (2006a). 'Closed-circuit Television Surveillance' in B. C. Welsh and D. P. Farrington (eds), *Preventing Crime.* Dordrecht: Springer.

WELSH, B. C. and FARRINGTON, (eds) (2006b). *Preventing Crime: What Works for Children, Offenders, Victims, and Places.* Dordrecht: Springer.

——, ——, and SHERMAN, L.W. (eds) (2001). *Costs and Benefits of Preventing Crime.* Oxford: Westview Press.

WITTMANN, W. W. (1985). *Evaluationsforschung (Evaluation Research).* Berlin: Springer.

ZIMBARDO, P. G. (1973). 'A Field Experiment in Auto Shaping' in C. Ward (ed.), *Vandalism.* London: Architectrual Press.

6

Doing criminological research in ethnically and culturally diverse contexts

Manuel Eisner and Alpa Parmar

Introduction

Ethnic diversity is a feature of many criminological study populations and research questions in criminology often bear on the ethnic dimension of modern society. This raises theoretical and methodological questions that are not easily resolved. By way of introduction, we illustrate some of these challenges by looking at a well-funded and sophisticated recent study. In 2004, the Home Office published a report on 'Domestic violence, sexual assault and stalking: Findings from the British Crime Survey' (Walby and Allen 2004). Amongst other things, the report compares rates of victimization due to interpersonal violence amongst ethnic groups. It concludes that there is little variation in levels of violent victimization between Whites, Blacks, and Asians, noting that this 'is an interesting finding because, since ethnicity is associated with variations in economic resources, it might have been expected to show parallel variations' (Walby and Allen 2004: 29). In other words, members of ethnic minorities appear to have a less-than expected risk of victimization if compared to Whites in similar conditions of social disadvantage.

The British Crime Survey (BCS) is based on a sophisticated methodology and includes a large ethnic minority booster sample (Mayhew 2000 and this volume). There may therefore be some truth in the reported findings. However, this requires that several assumptions are met, each of which may be amenable to debate. First, one must assume that White, Black, and Asian are theoretically and empirically defensible classifications of ethnicity. Yet they may conceal rather than illuminate the complex ethnic and social boundaries relevant in the UK (similarly, see, e.g., Garland *et al.* 2006).

A second assumption is that victims of interpersonal crime were equally likely to participate in the BCS within each ethnic group, i.e. that there are no significant differences in response rates. Yet while the overall response rate to the BCS was 74 per cent it dropped to 50 per cent in the minority booster sample (Bolling *et al.* 2003). Thus no information is available for half of the targeted minority respondents, meaning that true victimization rates may be significantly different from those found amongst study participants. Thirdly, the findings imply that members of various sociocultural groups attribute the same meanings to the questions, that they are equally confident in using a computer-aided self-completion questionnaire, and that they are equally likely to remember and report their experiences. However, only about 80 per cent of the BCS respondents completed the self-completion module without interviewer interference (Walby and Allen 2004: 116). Amongst those, the less educated, less literate, and less integrated respondents were probably again considerably under-represented, meaning that the most vulnerable minority members become even less visible. Also—despite the undoubted merits of using a drop-down questionnaire—it is probably optimistic to assume that members of different cultural backgrounds were equally likely to report domestic or sexual abuse.

Across the western world, the challenge of ethnic diversity to criminological research has become more important to the extent that societies have become increasingly culturally diverse over the past fifty years, that disadvantaged minority groups account for a disproportionate share of victims of crime, and that they tend to be over-represented amongst police arrests, convictions, and prisoners (e.g. Tonry 1997; Phillips and Bowling 2002; Peterson *et al.* 2006; Smith 2005a). However, ethnically diverse contexts require far-reaching study adaptations at each stage of a research process, including the development of theoretically based conceptual frameworks, the organization of access to the field, the development of research instruments, the planning of research settings, and the analysis of data.

In the first section of this chapter we examine some of these general issues, highlighting the need for making the ethnic dimension a core element of planning and conducting research. In the second part we illustrate strategies of criminological research in ethnically diverse contexts by discussing methodological challenges each of us encountered in our respective research projects.

Major themes in conducting research in an ethnically diverse context

If present, ethnic diversity potentially affects all stages and aspects of conducting a criminological research project. The concepts and identity-forming processes associated with ethnicity, ethnic identity, race, and racism have occupied much scholarly writing well beyond the criminological canon and its research base. In addition to a vast literature on the subject within both sociological and psychological thought, important insights have been gained from scholarly work drawing from and upon cultural studies, anthropology, history, critical race studies, and sociolegal studies, to name but a few. Indeed, some of the best academic thought on ethnicity and race has emerged from work that has crossed disciplinary lines and pushed the boundaries and peripheries of traditional academic disciplines. The following discussion integrates research from a range of disciplines and subdisciplines well beyond the remit of criminology. We would suggest that any inquiry into aspects of ethnicity, race, and their related diverse concepts should look to extant research across wide disciplinary boundaries. In this section we briefly examine five questions that are likely to be relevant in any research conducted in an ethnically diverse context, namely: how should ethnic diversity be conceptualized? How does diversity affect the development of theory? How does ethnic diversity affect the research design of a project? How can researchers gain access to an ethnically diverse field? And lastly: how does sociocultural and ethnic diversity affect the development of research instruments?

Conceptualizing ethnic and sociocultural diversity

Arguably the first concern that should occupy criminologists doing research in an ethnically diverse context is to address two questions: how should ethnicity be conceptualized theoretically? And how can it be measured empirically?

This is not the place to review the many recent discussions of ethnicity and its complexities (see Rutter 2005, Hall 1991, Gilroy 2000, 2004, Back 1999, Bowling and Phillips 2002, Bulmer and Solomos 2004), but we offer a working definition for the remainder of this paper. It follows the *Oxford English Dictionary*, which defines ethnicity as a social group 'that shares a distinctive cultural and historical tradition' (for a detailed discussion, see Rutter 2005). This definition is similar to the one offered by the sociologist, Max Weber. According to him, ethnicity is constituted by the subjective belief in a shared ancestry, which facilitates processes of group formation. Also, Weber emphasized that group formation based on ancestry as its main building block is facilitated if people share economic positions, migration experiences, or exposure to discrimination (Weber 1968: 387). Importantly, both definitions see ethnicity essentially as a cultural phenomenon and highlight the importance of beliefs in a shared collective history as its cornerstone. In contrast, neither includes 'race' as a defining element. Rather, commonalities in phenotype are a possible but not a necessary dimension that may be used by societies to impose, and by minority groups to maintain, ethnic boundaries.

There is, of course, no such thing as the correct definition of ethnicity. However, it is possible to identify a series of conceptual tools that may help researchers empirically to explore ethnicity.

In most research contexts the first encounter with ethnicity is likely to consist of statistical information that classifies data by ethnicity as officially defined. In the United Kingdom, for example, the 2001 census introduced a standard classification that distinguishes sixteen 'ethnic groups' and is now compulsory for official publications. It is based on so-called self-declared ethnicity, which means that respondents are asked to choose amongst a given list of options. The classification system has been repeatedly criticized (Spencer 2006; Bowling and Phillips 2002; Ahmad and Sheldon 1993; Aspinall 2002). Its main categories are a strange mixture of classification by 'race', colour, and by colonial heritage (White, Mixed, Asian or Asian British, Black or Black British, Chinese, or other ethnic group). Additionally, the system includes a series of somewhat odd options such as 'Mixed—White and Black African' or 'Chinese or other ethnic group—other ethnic group'. We have doubts about the academic wisdom and the theoretical value of such classifications. Indeed, although many publications in highly regarded criminological journals uncritically throw a Black/White/Asian/Hispanic variable into sophisticated statistical models, we doubt whether anything but prejudice can be gained from such vague applications of ethnic categories.

A more flexible approach is to ask respondents for self-classification by means of open questions. However, the self-descriptions one is likely to collect with such an approach highly depend on what respondents are asked to understand by 'ethnicity'. If, for example, one accepts a shared cultural and historical tradition as a possible definition, then one has to accept that respondents may classify themselves as Cornish, Irish-Catholic, Gujarati, British-Jewish, etc. Also, research on self-declared ethnicity amongst adolescents suggests that self-descriptions are highly fluid over the life-course (Modood *et al.* 1997, Modood 2005; Jacobson 1997). Furthermore, it is important to consider that the salience of any ethnic identity may vary greatly between individuals and between groups. It is likely, for example, that collective ethnic identity is more salient if discrimination is experienced systematically, if armed conflict renders plausibility to ethnic cleavages, or if media amplify specific ethnic classifications. If one assigns ethnicity on the basis of self-identification, therefore, it is important to get an understanding of its salience both in its own right, but also in relation to other sources of identity (e.g. sex, age, youth culture, class).

Researchers planning to study ethnically diverse contexts are always well advised to get a sound prior understanding of the cultural and historical backgrounds represented by the ethnic minorities. Also, if possible, researchers should use official statistics to assemble statistical profiles of their target populations. This includes, where available, statistical data on criteria such as countries of origin, religious affiliations, mother tongue languages, and social class composition including education and occupation. Even if such information needs refinement at later stages and should not be seen as a replacement for specific efforts to understand ethnic diversity, it will help to plan subsequent project stages and to sensitize researchers to potentially important issues.

However, any study in which ethnicity plays a potentially substantive role should carefully consider how the concept is to be operationalized. Too often, researchers are content with administering some closed-category self-identification questionnaire of ethnicity. Yet if researchers want to get an understanding of the multiple facets of ethnicity and its potential criminological relevance, a more sophisticated approach is needed. In particular, whether a study is qualitative or quantitative, we advocate that researchers should strive to capture the various dimensions that pertain to the experiences of ethnic diversity. More particularly, if one accepts the *Oxford Dictionary* definition of ethnicity as a group sharing a cultural and historical tradition, then any of the following four dimensions are likely to be highly relevant: mother tongue, because shared language is a major force that creates group identity; individual and collective migration history, because they are pivotal for a sense of shared origin; religion, which has turned out to remain a highly powerful source of collective identity and shared values; and national origin, because the nation state has been such a power source of shaping identities over the past 200 years. It is desirable to collect information about the salience of various dimensions of ethnic identity, since their importance may vary between individuals and between groups. Furthermore, one might consider to include assessments of non-ethnic identity such as youth-subcultures, professional identities, or class, etc. (Rutter and Tienda 2005). Finally, ethnic identities are part of lived patterns of interaction and it can be most relevant empirically to assess their importance by examining, for example, the strength of intra-ethnic and inter-ethnic networks or people's involvement within ethnically specific associations.

Theorizing ethnic diversity

Research in ethnically diverse contexts must confront the question of how diversity bears on criminological theory. Certainly the answer partly depends on the specific subject matter of a study, its methodological premises and the wider substantive theoretical approach taken. While we can't discuss these issues in more detail we briefly examine three interrelated general questions that each study undertaken in a multicultural context should address: does ethnicity matter? Why should it? And how does the distal factor of ethnicity relate to more proximal processes and mechanisms?

It is likely that many researchers who start doing research on a criminological topic related to ethnicity initially assume that ethnicity is 'somehow' relevant to their research question. However, it is crucial to recognize the importance of initial theoretical reflection on why and in what sense ethnicity is expected to be relevant. To illustrate our case we briefly consider theories of crime causation. With good reasons, most of these theories (e.g. learning theory, social control theory, differential association theory, strain theory) do not assume that ethnicity is a major explanatory factor that would help to understand crime. Rather, they assume that universal mechanisms cause crime across societies and over time. Probably the most explicit statement to this effect comes from Gottfredson and Hirschi (1990: 174–5), who argue that 'cultural variability is *not* important in the causation of crime'. Rather, differences in child socialization during early childhood are universally associated with the development of self-control, which in turn is the major cause of crime. Hence they expect that cross-cultural differences in crime rates can be fully accounted for by differences in parenting practices (and differences in opportunity structures). Similar arguments can be derived from other theories. Strain and anomie theories, for example, have often been used to argue that socio-economic disadvantage and neighbourhood disorganization rather than ethnicity is what really matters in explaining groups-differences in crime (see, e.g., Hawkins 1995; Short 1997).

Universal theories are intellectually attractive because they offer the most parsimonious models of crime causation. They can be empirically validated by demonstrating that theoretically more fundamental variables can account for all variation between ethnic groups (see, e.g., Junger-Tas 2001; Farrington *et al.* 2003). This does not necessarily mean that sociocultural diversity is irrelevant; but it implies that ethnicity has a mediated and distal effect, meaning that it affects those proximal mechanisms that are more directly relevant (Rutter 2005). For example, cultures differ in the extent to which they positively value wider kin networks of trust and solidarity, which in turn may operate as protective mechanisms against youth problem behaviour (e.g. Mawby *et al.* 1979 in reference to Asian peoples' levels of offending). Also, it entails that solid theoretical thinking requires integration of arguments at the group level with arguments that account for variation within groups.

However, it is currently not clear whether universalist theories stand up to empirical scrutiny. For example, some risk factors may only be experienced by minorities to a significant degree. Such mechanisms could be related to the migration process itself including, for example, exposure to trauma resulting from violent conflict. But they could also result from the tensions between the value system and resources of the first generation of immigrants and their children, a hypothesis found to explain sometimes the phenomenon of elevated delinquency amongst second-generation immigrants (Sellin 1938; Killias 1989; Smith 2005a). In this case one assumes that ethnicity is relevant in that it mediates specific experiences conducive to delinquency that are not usually experienced as such by members of the dominant majority. Finally, an increasing number of studies suggest that sociocultural environments may have an impact on the importance of certain causal mechanisms. For example, a recent study by Le *et al.* (2005) found that the effects of peer delinquency on crime were only about half as strong amongst Chinese juveniles as compared to other minorities. This kind of finding presents a serious challenge to universal theories. It ultimately suggests that crime may be caused by (at least partly) different mechanisms in different cultures.

As mentioned above: in each piece of research the relevant theoretical alternatives will be different. But in all studies clarity about what they are will help to clarify whether and why ethnicity is expected to be theoretically relevant.

Ethnic diversity and research design

It is important to think creatively and systematically about how a study can be designed in such a way that it allows for answering research questions related to ethnicity. For example, if a study wants to analyse data for specific ethnic subgroups, careful reflection on sampling strategies is needed, for approaches that randomly sample the target population usually result in small numbers for any specific group, meaning that the possibilities for comparative empirical analysis are severely limited.

The strategy usually recommended in standard textbooks is to use a stratified sampling procedure whereby minority groups of particular interest are oversampled, or to define target sample sizes for specific groups. However, one should be aware that this is more than a mere technicality. In particular, it requires consideration of two substantive questions, namely: what are the group designations and the inclusion criteria for membership in any specific ethnic group? And on what grounds does one decide which groups are to be chosen for inclusion in a criminological research project? Often, availability and convenience are the main drivers behind the answers to both questions. However, they should ultimately depend on theoretical reasoning and can have complex empirical implications. Thus, ethnic minority communities often superficially may appear to have clear and stable boundaries; however, a closer look may reveal several interlocking circles of identity that may be relevant for research. Also, the mere fact that an ethnic group is a minority constitutes a weak reason for conducting specific criminological research. Rather, we advocate that criminological studies with an ethnic/cultural comparative dimension should select groups on conceptual and theoretical grounds (see Johnson and Malgady 1999). For example, it is of little criminological value to conduct comparative analyses of victimization rates between ethnic groups that differ widely along several dimensions such as place of residence, socio-economic status, life-style, etc., because the groups will differ along many potential explanatory factors, meaning that no decision is possible about which factor is empirically relevant. In contrast, a similar study that carefully matches groups on various structural dimensions has a much greater chance to identify group-specific mechanisms that may contribute to different victimization rates.

There is wide scope for innovative studies along the lines of such an approach. For example, there is evidence suggesting that minorities with precisely the same origin and identical cultural and sociostructural background sometimes have widely differing delinquency rates depending on the country and city in which they live (see, e.g., the observations on Turkish youth in Junger-Tas 1997). This suggests that wider institutional arrangements and dynamics of social integration are important in understanding group differences. Yet there is hardly any research that systematically compares experiences with crime amongst members of one minority group living in different cities, neighbourhoods, or countries. Also, evidence suggests that crime prevention programmes (e.g. parenting programmes) or criminal justice interventions (e.g. restorative justice programmes) do not reach different minorities equally well and are not equally effective across groups (see, for example, Strang and Braithwaite 2002). However, there is a glaring gap in well-designed experimental studies that investigate whether and how prevention programmes need to be adapted to the needs of sociocultural minorities (but see Harachi *et al.* 1997).

Gaining access to the field

Any research that generalizes beyond the immediate subjects of a study assumes that the available observations are in some way representative of a wider population (King *et al.* 1994). If this not the case and observations are systematically biased, then research conclusions may lack validity and can be seriously misleading (Couper and Leeuw 2003; Grovew *et al.* 2002). One important cause of such lack of validity is non-participation of significant proportions of a targeted study population (Stoop 2005).

Across Europe, ethnic minorities have been found to be more difficult to contact and more likely to refuse participation in most types of social-science research (Couper and Leeuw 2003; van Goor *et al.* 2005). Amongst others, this is true for many victim surveys. The 1998 Dutch national victim survey, for example, had a response rate of only 40 per cent for 'Non-Western Foreigners' in comparison to 60 per cent in the main sample (Feskens *et al.* 2004). The 2003/3 British Crime Survey achieved a response rate of 48 per cent in the minority booster sample and of 73 per cent in the main sample (Bolling *et al.* 2004: 12).

In ethnically diverse contexts criminologists therefore need to pay close attention to how minority groups can be included in a study. Importantly, researchers should allocate plenty of time to identifying possible problems and developing appropriate research strategies at an early stage of a research project. In particular, this includes gathering information about possible barriers to contacting and participation for each targeted ethnic group (e.g. availability of addresses or telephone numbers, literacy rates, spoken language, working hours) well ahead of the actual field phase, consulting intercultural experts, and to adapt the research plan in such a way that the obstacles can be overcome. This may entail considerable adaptations in the study design.

Consider barriers connected to language and reading skills, for example. According to a study by Carr-Hill *et al.* (1996) about 23 per cent of ethnic minorities born in China, Bangladesh, India, and Pakistan had no English language skills and 70 per cent could not function fully in an English-speaking social environment in the mid-1990s. Also, the Skills for Life survey (Williams *et al.* 2003) showed that 27 per cent of adults living in the most disadvantaged neighbourhoods in England had literacy levels at entry level or below, and that those whose first language was not English had considerably lower average literacy skills. In such research contexts careful planning is needed to overcome barriers, which in turn means that specialized methodological knowledge must be acquired. For example, with the issue of translating questionnaires and surveys, researchers need to understand the various methodological principles necessary for high-quality translations—specifically, to ensure that the questions achieve an exact as possible cross-language parity of meaning (Harkness 2003) (this issue is addressed further later). Or one may conclude that posted information about a study is unlikely to be read by some target groups and that one needs to develop alternative ways of disseminating information.

Also, members of sociocultural minorities are often in particularly vulnerable positions. For example, refugees may have suffered persecution in their home countries, the residency status of asylum seekers may be undecided, or immigrants may have had adverse experiences with authorities (also see Garland *et al.* 2006). Any such experience is likely to lead to greater distrust of academic research and doubts about the effectiveness of data protection, especially if a study touches upon such sensitive issues as crime and victimization (Johnson *et al.* 2002: 66). Building up trust in such communities is likely to require careful consideration and potentially extended efforts before the study itself can start. One approach to consider is to mobilize community stakeholders, gate-keepers, and other community resources for support. Such strategies have been found to be highly successful in recruiting minority groups, amongst others, in criminological studies that involve prevention trials (Harachi *et al.* 1997). However, great care is needed when the support of community leaders is sought, as there is the possibility that they represent partisan views within a wider community and thus introduce unintended bias in the recruitment efforts (Fisher and Masty 2006).

Ethnic matching of interviewers needs careful consideration. However, findings from research on the effects of ethnic matching are quite ambiguous, especially as regards the quality of the collected data. While some studies suggest that ethnic matching is desirable because a shared understanding of the cultural background may result in more honest responses (Anderson *et al.* 1988), others find the opposite. A recent study in the Netherlands, for example, examined the effects of interviewer ethnicity on the reporting of alcohol use in face-to-face interviews with respondents of Turkish and Moroccan origin (Dotinga *et al.* 2005). It did not find that minority interviewers were more successful in recruiting respondents in comparison to Dutch interviewers. However, it found that significantly less alcohol use was reported to interviewers of the same ethnicity than to Dutch interviewers. As alcohol use is stigmatized in both communities, ethnic matching was hence found to lead to less valid results in this case. However, it seems that there is no simple rule on whether matching is necessary or desirable.

Sometimes it is worthwhile considering 'ethnic tailoring' of recruitment strategies. A qualitative study on health and social capital in a multi-ethnic neighbourhood in South England found, for example, that local advertisements and media contact worked best for recruiting members of the white English community, interpersonal contacts were crucial in recruiting Pakistani-Kashmiri informants, and institutional contacts were the most useful way of accessing African-Caribbean individuals (McLean and Campbell 2003).

Developing culturally adequate research instruments

Good research instruments provide unbiased and reliable information on the construct that one wishes to measure. In ethnically diverse contexts, the development of good research instruments is a particularly complex task. The most critical challenge here is *cross-cultural equivalence*. Cross-cultural equivalence broadly means that a given concept is measured (or captured in a qualitative context) equally well and on the same scale across all sociocultural groups. The notion of cross-cultural equivalence has been developed in the context of cross-cultural survey research. But at least some aspects are equally relevant in qualitative research.

Criminologists doing research in ethnically diverse contexts need to gain a good understanding of the complexities of developing culturally adequate instruments. Extensive recent literature in the field such as the volume on Cross-Cultural Survey

Methods edited by Harkness *et al.* (2003) greatly helps to approach this complex area of methodological expertise. In particular, it is important to understand different causes of bias in cross-cultural research, how they can be avoided, and how equivalence can be assessed once data have been collected (see Johnson 1998 for a more detailed discussion).

Consider the notion of conceptual (or interpretive) equivalence. It refers to the extent to which a research instrument captures the full meaning of a theoretical concept equally well in various cultures (Buss and Royce 1975; Lam *et al.* 1998; Straus 1969). An instrument can be said to be conceptually biased, then, if manifestations of a concept that occur in culture A are represented well while manifestations in culture B are not included. A highly relevant criminological aspect of this problem is the cross-culturally valid measurement of personality and the diagnosis of mental-health problems (for a comprehensive discussion, see Dana 2000). In this area it is now widely recognized that some instruments cannot be assumed to be conceptually equivalent across cultures. For example, Spencer *et al.* (2005) recently examined the factorial equivalence of the widely used Behavior Problem Index. They found that neither the full instrument nor its subscales can be assumed to be equivalent across three US ethnic groups. This means that different combinations of items account for an overall score in each sociocultural group and that therefore the instrument measures somewhat different things for different groups of people.

Developing new survey instruments for use in an ethnically diverse context can be a daunting exercise, especially if the instrument touches on culturally sensitive issues. It may mean extensive exploration, sometimes with the help of focus groups, of the ways in which a phenomenon manifests itself in different cultures. It is therefore often preferable to use instruments that have already been validated in minority settings. Also, criteria developed by Brislin (1986) provide guidance about whether questionnaire items may be suitable for equivalent translation into other languages.

The most demanding level of equivalence is *scalar equivalence*. It means that a construct is measured on the same metric across groups. Scalar equivalence is always presupposed when levels of problem behaviour or victimization rates are compared across groups. However, it is effectively very difficult to achieve. In particular it can be jeopardized if differential social desirability bias—the tendency to respond in line with the assumed expectations of the interviewer—affects the response behaviour amongst ethnic minorities (van de Vijver 1998: 50). To this effect, self-report questionnaires pose an interesting example. In many countries studies suggest large differences in official arrest rates between majority and minority youth and much smaller differences according to self-report studies (see, e.g., Smith 2005b). While this may in part be due to ethnically biased policing, reverse record check studies pioneered by Hindelang *et al.* (1981) suggest that minority youth are considerably less likely to report police-recorded offences than their majority peers. In this vein, Junger (1989) found that Moroccan und Turkish juveniles were much less likely to admit delinquent acts than Dutch or Surinamese youngsters (for a critical discussion, see Bowling 1990). One of the underlying mechanisms is group differences in social desirability bias—the tendency of respondents to project favourable images of themselves and to avoid anticipated possible negative evaluations (Johnson and van de Vijver 2003: 200).

One way to assess scalar equivalence is external validation against independent measures (see, e.g., Lau et al. 2004). For example, 'blinded' observational measures of child problem behaviour at home may serve as a benchmark to assess differential parent response styles to interview-based child behaviour items. Also, social desirability scales may be used in ethnically diverse contexts in order to get a better understanding of possible systematic bias in the data (Johnson and van de Vijver 2003).

Research strategies in ethnically diverse contexts: two case studies

In the second part of the chapter we present two case studies and highlight how each of these studies has tackled the practical, conceptual, and methodological challenges of doing criminological research in ethnically diverse contexts. The studies differ in respect of size, methodology, and substantive research topic and have been written by each author separately. The accounts demonstrate the highly engaging (and at times personal) nature of conducting research in an ethnically diverse context, especially as such studies introduce various nuances that other research projects simply may not recognize. The first case study by Manuel Eisner is a large longitudinal project that uses standardized interviews better to understand the determinants of behaviour problems amongst 1,300 children at primary-school age in Zurich, Switzerland. The second case study discusses an ongoing Ph.D. project by Alpa Parmar, part of which involved conducting qualitative interviews better to understand the perception of crime amongst members of a Pakistani-British urban community.

Case Study 1: The Zurich Project on the Social Development of Children

The Zurich Project on the Social Development of Children, *z-proso*, is a prospective longitudinal study of a cohort of about 1,300 children that started primary school in 2004 (i.e. average age 7) in Zurich, the largest city of Switzerland with a population of about 360,000. It includes a randomized experimental component that entails universal preventive interventions at school and family level and aims to understand the early developmental prevention of violent behaviour and delinquency. The study currently comprises three waves of interviews at annual intervals. At each wave a computer-aided face-to-face interview is conducted with the primary caregiver (at home) and the child (individually at school). Also, teachers complete standardized written child assessments at 6-month intervals (for a more detailed overview, see Eisner and Ribeaud 2005).

Like most other European cities, Zurich has experienced a significant increase in socio-cultural minorities over the past decades. According to the 2000 census, about 23 per cent of the total population are foreign born and approximately 22 per cent speak a language other than German as their main language. However, the proportion of immigrant minorities varies significantly between neighbourhoods and age-groups. Amongst the target population of this study (i.e. all children entering year 1 of primary school in 2004 and their parents) 50 per cent had learned a language other than German as their first language. Furthermore, because of a combination of low-average occupational qualifications, discrimination, institutional racism, and the effects of the housing market, minority families are concentrated in disadvantaged neighbourhoods. Thus, the proportion of children with minority backgrounds is above 80 per cent in some primary schools in disadvantaged neighbourhoods.

A voluminous literature reveals that the combination of parental immigrant and low socioeconomic status is correlated with a series of negative youth outcomes, including low scholastic performance and reduced chances on the labour market. Not least, they tend to be considerably over-represented in the criminal justice system. For these reasons the practical and scientific significance of this study critically depended on whether minority parents could be motivated to participate in the study, whether trajectories of child antisocial behaviour can be measured validly and reliably across groups, whether the study could help to better understand the causal mechanisms, associated with minority status, that contribute to a higher likelihood of negative outcomes, and whether the preventive interventions could be demonstrated to be equally effective across groups.

This being an ongoing study, answers to the substantive side of these questions are simply not yet available. In the following paragraphs I will therefore discuss two issues related to research development, namely our approach to reducing under-representation of disadvantaged minorities and our strategy for measuring sociocultural diversity within the context of a criminological study.

Avoiding 'Hidden Minorities'—achieving good response rates

In a longitudinal study, the first wave of interviews defines the maximum number of available respondents. Afterwards, it can only go down. Giving every possible attention to planning the initial contact with parents is therefore key to any possible later usefulness of the study. In a culturally diverse context this means paying particular attention to group-specific barriers to participation and building up trust and communicating effectively within minority communities.

In this study statistical data and expert information suggested that language would be the most significant objective barrier to study participation, as a significant fraction of minority mothers would not be able to understand a German questionnaire. Supported by a grant from the Swiss Commission of Foreigners, we therefore opted for a comprehensive multilanguage strategy. In particular, all written and oral contact with the parents including the interviews themselves were to be offered in all eight languages spoken by at least 4 per cent of the target sample, i.e. in descending order of frequency: Albanian (9 per cent), Portuguese (7 per cent), Serbian (5 per cent), Tamil (5 per cent), Spanish (5 per cent), Turkish (5 per cent), Italian (4 per cent) and Croatian (4 per cent). Additionally, interviews could also be conducted in English as the most likely generic foreign language amongst those who speak one of the roughly fifty remaining languages in the target sample.

Developing a translation strategy that would be adequate for scientific purposes was a major task in itself. But the decision to offer the interview in ten languages had repercussions on practically all aspects of preparing the field phase: it changed the way we thought about developing the initial questionnaire, it required a technical solution to conducting computer-aided interviews in a multi-language environment, it necessitated the recruitment of motivated interviewers in ten languages, and it could only bear fruits if the whole process of initial written and oral contact with parents was carefully adapted to a multicultural environment.

We initially had little idea of what it meant practically to translate a full questionnaire into ten languages simultaneously, let alone what methodologies should be chosen to achieve a good translation quality. Initial reading of some of the relevant literature ultimately brought us in contact with Janet Harkness at the Centre for Survey Research and

Methodology in Mannheim (Germany), the foremost expert in the theory and practice of translating social-science questionnaires in Europe. She made numerous valuable suggestions, but two stood out as particularly consequential. The first was her insisting that creating a questionnaire suitable for use in a culturally diverse context was more than simply producing good translations. In particular, she emphasized that the goal of achieving cross-cultural conceptual validity affects the whole process of questionnaire development. Secondly, she emphasized that the standard strategy of forward and backward translation, recommended in many standard references, is not necessarily optimal.

Harkness and Schoua-Glusberg (1998) and Harkness (2003) discuss various ways of designing questionnaires for cross-cultural comparative research. As the optimal strategy they recommend the simultaneous development of instruments in all target languages in order to maximize equivalence and minimize bias in favour of a source language. Yet, developing and validating a whole set of new instruments across ten languages was neither financially nor organizationally feasible. Also, developmental research on child problem behaviour is an established field where many instruments have been thoroughly tested and validated. The risks involved in replacing these instruments, by new and self-created instruments, therefore seemed to be significantly larger than the potential benefits.

Therefore, the strategy in this study was first to scrutinize alternative instruments available for measuring core concepts (e.g. parenting style, child problem behaviour). We then chose the instrument where conceptual equivalence was more likely to be achieved. In particular, instruments were rejected if they seemed inadequate for cross-cultural use according to criteria developed by Brislin (1986). For example, previous Triple P evaluations (e.g. Sanders *et al.* 2000) had administered the *Parenting Sense of Competence (PSOC)* questionnaire (Johnson and Mash 1989). However, the PSOC comprises several long and grammatically complicated items. Consider, for example: 'I would make a fine model for a new mother/father to follow in order to learn what she/he would need to know in order to be a good parent.' This is a very complicated sentence in English. But translating it into ten different languages and achieving conceptual equivalence is probably impossible. Further, as a tool to measure child problem behaviour we favoured the Social Behaviour Questionnaire (SBQ) by Tremblay *et al.* (1991) over the Achenbach Child Behaviour Check List (Achenbach and Edelbrock 1981). One reason is that the Social Behaviour Questionnaire comprises both negative (e.g. aggressive behaviour) and positive items (various prosocial behaviours). We hypothesized that this mix of items might reduce the risk of culturally specific acquiescence bias and possibly of social desirability bias.

The translations were based on an *expert team approach* (Harkness 2003: 37) which involved three steps. For each language, the English and the German source versions were sent to a formally qualified translator for initial translation. Criteria for the selection of the *translators* were excellent knowledge of both German and English, the target language as their respective mother language, familiarity in both cultures, and—ideally—some social-science background (Hambleton and Kanjee 1993). The translators received written guidelines about the translation process (e.g. general criteria for questionnaire item translation, need to document potentially ambiguous wordings, etc.). Furthermore, brief descriptions explained the purpose of each scale. Translators were asked to treat the German and the English version as equally relevant—and take written notes if the German or the English source would result in different translations.

The initial translation was then sent to an independent *translation reviewer*. If possible, translation reviewers had a social-science background and at least some experience in working with psychometric instruments. Their main task was to examine the entire translation with a view to adequacy for standardized interviews, and to suggest changes wherever believed to be necessary.

In a third step, the translator, the translation reviewer, and the translation coordinator met to discuss all arising issues and agree the final version. At this stage, we also involved the future foreign-language interviewers in the adjudication process. They proved to be a highly valuable additional resource. Many of them were psychology, sociology, or education students with a migration background and a research methods training—an excellent profile for assisting in questionnaire translation. Importantly, too, interviewers had an interest in scrutinizing the translation as regards their adequacy for the spoken word.

Interviewer recruitment and training

Interviewers are the face of any survey that involves direct contact with respondents. They are the decisive actors in the process of contacting parents, setting up interviews, receiving informed consent, and conducting the interviews. This study therefore invested a lot of energy into recruiting, training, and supervising 20–30 interviewers for each wave. There was a series of specific challenges as regards interviewers for sociocultural minorities. First, recruiting cross-culturally competent, bi-lingual, motivated, and reliable interviewers in all minority languages was a major exercise that extended over several weeks. In our experience, second-generation social-science university students were generally the best bet. Importantly, many of them had an understanding of, and an interest in, the overall goals of the study, the measurement issues involved in the translation process, and the problems of contacting minority parents. While language competency was important, ethnic matching per se was not a selection criterion and in our experience the general social competency and conscientiousness of the interviewer was more important than the precise fit of sociocultural background.

A significant part of the interviewer training for the initial contact was devoted to explaining the purpose of the study and reacting to potential concerns. Because it was important that interviewers provided correct information and complied with ethical standards, they were asked to simulate initial telephone contacts and provide us with lists of possible concerns, to which we gave written guidelines regarding the appropriate responses. Also, we collected information about culturally specific rules of conduct such as religious holidays that were to be avoided for contacting. Finally, interviewers had strict instructions not to allow the presence of any other adult person during the interview and not to accept invitations for drinks, coffee, or biscuits.

Parent contact and recruitment strategy

Gaining access to the field and recruiting participants included a series of steps that extended over several months. The process started with presenting the project at the parent information evenings, held before the summer break, about their child's entry into primary school. Two weeks after the start all presumed primary caregivers in the sampling frame received an information pack that consisted of four elements: namely a personalized letter, a short description of the project, a response slip asking the parent to indicate preferred dates for the interview, and a reply envelope. Amongst others, the information pack explained that information would only be collected after a written consent had been received and that parents could withdraw their consent at any time. It also explained that interview partners would receive a thank you for participating and that one could choose between a shopping voucher worth about 13 Euros and a voucher for sports courses and activities worth 20 Euros. Although culturally unspecific, incentives are probably especially effective in recruiting low-income and minority respondents, groups that would otherwise be underrepresented (Singer 2002).

All 1,675 addresses were screened to identify the presumed mother language of the primary caregiver, a process greatly facilitated by information provided by the school authorities. All non-German speaking caregivers received the information pack bilingually. Where necessary, interviewers helped to identify the correct language on the basis of surnames (e.g. to distinguish Indian and Tamil respondents). During the first weeks of the interviewing period a total of 47 per cent of the parents actively consented to participate by returning a response slip.

Interviewers actively contacted all remaining parents in their allocated language group. There was no upper limit to the number of required trials and in some cases more than twenty telephone calls were necessary before an initial contact could be made. Detailed interviewer instructions explained, amongst other things, how alternative contact numbers could be searched if no landline number was available and what kind of messages could be left on answer machines. About four weeks after the sending of the initial information pack and co-ordinated with interviewer schedules, reminders were sent out to the remaining parents, again bi-lingually and with a significantly shorter explanatory text. We allowed interviewers to tailor ethnically the reminder letter as long as the contents adequately reflected the goal of the study.

After three months we began to use door-knocking as an alternative strategy amongst those minority groups where all prior contacts had been unsuccessful. Here a male and a female interviewer visited parents during early evening hours to explain the goals of the study. It was found to be an effective, if expensive approach.

If successful contact had been made, interviewers had written instructions about how to present the study and explain the study goals. They were also instructed how to react to possible concerns. Furthermore, dates had to be arranged directly with the primary caregiver, usually the mother, and not with the father or some other person in the household. If appointments were broken, interviewers were instructed to recontact the person and arrange another date until the interview could be conducted. A 24-hour support structure also ensured that we always tried to provide replacement if an interviewer unexpectedly could not conduct the interview. Importantly, too, all interviewers were closely supervised during the interview periods and were required to report on their progress and the difficulties they encountered. This was helpful in that slow progress of specific interviewers or amongst some language groups could be identified early and adequate measures be taken.

The first wave of child interviews started after all parent interviews had been completed. In consultation with the school authorities a final attempt to win participants was made immediately before the start of the child interviews. In particular, non-participating parents received a letter where we acknowledged their wish not to participate themselves but asked whether they would agree in their child's participation and the completion of the teacher assessments. Of course, this final contact was again accompanied by parent information and we accepted only active written consent as permission for conducting the child interviews.

Having completed waves 1 and 2 of the parent interviews at the time of writing this paper we are in a position to assess the extent to which one of the main goals of the study, namely to include parents and children of disadvantaged minority background in a longitudinal study, could be achieved. Table 6.1 provides an overview of participation rates for the decisive first wave. Data are broken down by the initial contact language with the primary caregiver, which was usually based on the information provided by the primary caregiver to the school authorities. They show that overall, 74 per cent of the parents in the target sample agreed to participate. Moreover, a further 9 per cent of the parents agreed to their child's participation (including teacher assessments) while not wishing to be interviewed themselves. As regards the children, the initial participation rate therefore is 83 per cent. This is a highly satisfactory result for a culturally diverse urban context.

Table 6.1 Parent and child participation rates by parent contact language

Parent contact language (Target sample N)	(1) % female PC completed compulsory school or less	(2) % female PC not fluent in German	(3) % interviews conducted in respective mother tongue	(4) % total parent response rate	(5) % additional child interviews	(6) % total child participation rate
German (N = 789)	4	–	–	88	4	92
Spanish (N = 83)	32	56	71	75	10	84
Italian (N = 74)	19	20	23	70	10	80
Portuguese (N = 118)	66	74	94	66	6	72
Croatian (N = 66)				65	5	70
Other languages (N = 127) (English as contact language)				62	19	81
Turkish (N = 80)	55	62	84	60	4	64
Serbian (N = 92)		33	84	58	12	70
Albanian (N = 151)	62	62	96	53	18	71
Tamil (N = 88)	66	83	98	53	23	76
Full Sample				74	9	83
N				1234	144	1378

Note: Data sorted by total participation rate.

However, the data also show remarkable differences between sociocultural groups. They document, first, that significant proportions of immigrant minority caregivers have low levels of formal education and very limited levels of competency in German. Indeed, data based on the first interview suggest that significantly more than 50 per cent of the interviews with minority caregivers could not have been conducted without translation. Overall, results thus suggest that offering translated versions played an important role in accessing immigrant populations. Moreover, there may have been additional non-quantifiable 'soft' effects of translation on participation. Thus, some migrant parents may have been motivated to participate because communication in their native language was understood as an accommodation toward their needs. Secondly, the data show that significant proportions of non-participating minority parents were willing to give informed consent to the participation of their children, which significantly reduced the gap in participation rates between all language groups.

In conclusion, in relation to the first issue then, this study demonstrates that it is possible to start a major longitudinal study in a highly culturally diverse urban context with a very satisfactory initial participation rate. It should also be emphasized, though, that this requires very substantial time, money, and energy.

Measuring sociocultural background and child problem behaviour

In tackling the second issue we opted for a research strategy that did not endorse any pre-existing classification but rather one that conceptualized sociocultural 'Otherness' as a multidimensional phenomenon throughout the research. Also, we believe that classifications by ethnic, cultural, religious, or linguistic criteria, used in academic research, ultim-ately need some theoretical justification if one wants to progress beyond using markers rooted in the vagaries of everyday ideologies. Hence, our approach to capturing the multidimensional nature of sociocultural diversity includes four dimensions, each of which may serve to examine mechanisms that may have an impact on the life-course of children and adolescents.

One dimension refers to ethnicity in the sense of *shared history, values, and norms*. This dimension is partly represented by markers of shared origin such as religious affiliation, country of birth, or mother tongue. But we also included, for example, a questionnaire of parenting values that tap into the extent to which parents may have socioculturally transmitted beliefs in what is good parenting. This allows us to examine whether specific parenting values, embedded in a minority culture, serve as protective factors. Secondly, it seemed conceptually relevant to get a better understanding of the *migration history* of the families included in the study. For example, trauma research suggests that experiences of war, torture, and prosecution may have lasting effects on adults, which, in turn, may have an impact on children. Also, efforts were made to understand the socio-economic background of the parents before they moved to Switzerland. Thirdly, it seemed important to understand the extent of *sociocultural integration and assimilation* of minority families. For example, we asked primary caregivers about the ethnic closure of their social networks, their ability to communicate in German, and their use of various mass media (e.g. TV channels). This may be relevant, amongst other reasons, because externalizing problem behaviour during childhood has consistently been found to be associated with poor school performance, which, in turn, may be affected by the extent to which parents can effectively support their children. Finally, it seems theoretically relevant to capture empirically the extent of *discrimination*, a factor associated with a higher likelihood for adolescent crime and problem behaviour across the world. We also administered a scale that measured experiences of discrimination in daily life and in interactions with state institutions.

Case Study 2: Community perceptions of crime: qualitative interviews in a British-Pakistani urban context

Introduction: the research context

Recent scholarship has suggested that over the past two decades, perceptions of young Muslim males have shifted from them being regarded as inherently law-abiding to them perceived by the public (and portrayed by the media) as increasingly deviant, criminal, and violent (Webster 1997, Desai 1999, Alexander 2000). This perception has inevitably magnified recently because of the associations between Muslim men and global concerns about terrorist activity. Although academic research has highlighted important ways in which information about such youth is represented and constructed by the media, less consideration has been given to the community level perceptions. One of the aims of my research was to focus on understanding the community level perceptions of British-Pakistani-Muslim youth around the pivotal issue of criminality. Alongside this, I was interested in how youth in the area, who had been involved in offending, explained and expressed their involvement in crime and how they located themselves within the community. The following discussion outlines a selection of issues that were encountered whilst conducting the research including non-uniform access strategies and the ethnic categorization of 'Asian' groups, the complexity of ethnic matching and how one might more broadly conceptualize ethnic minority experiences and histories.

The chosen community was characterized by a majority of residents from Pakistani backgrounds who had migrated to the UK during the late 1950s and early 1960s because of the displacement of peoples as a result of the building of the Mangla Dam in Mirpur (Pakistani Kashmir). The establishment of the community in Britain over a number of years resulted in a significant proportion of second generation Pakistanis born in the UK as well as a certain level of internal cohesion (amongst the older members especially) because of the shared regional, religious, and migration experiences. The small geographical context of the area enhanced the development of tight social networks based on family and friendship. Other resident groups in the area included a small number of White-British, British-Indian, Portuguese, and Polish families and recent refugees from Iraq and Bosnia. Characterized by some of the oldest housing in the city, the community was located within a 10-minute walking distance to the city centre and suffered from high levels of socio-economic deprivation[1] and unemployment. Those who were employed tended to work in

---

[1] The 2004 Index of Multiple Deprivation found that the community where the research was conducted, ranked 1,880 out of a total of 32,482 super output areas, where rank number 1 was the most deprived.

the service sector or through self-employment (e.g. taxi drivers, take-away businesses) or were typically employed in working-class occupations (e.g. factory work, cleaning). The majority of mothers who were interviewed were housewives or unemployed.

Ninety-four semi-structured interviews were conducted with various community members including local community and religious leaders, young British-Pakistani and British-Indian males and parents. Key agency representatives were also interviewed, the majority of which came from White-British and British-Pakistani ethnic backgrounds. All of the key agencies were situated within a 15-minute radius (walking distance), of the community, and included the police, the youth-offending team, the local media, the local commission for racial equality, the local council, a women's group, and local schools. Working against the traditional mould of trying to obtain a high response rate from one section of the community, my research scope was intentionally panoramic to include the voices of a broad range of members and representatives. Discussions with both individuals and institutional representatives within the community allowed for a dual understanding of micro and macrolevel perceptions and the relationships between the two.

Access to this community and its members was gained and maintained by a mixture of formal and informal methods, sometimes organized and at other times serendipitous. Letters were sent, local meetings were attended, and community members advised me of other people I should approach. I spent a significant amount of time physically in the community, walking around, going to local events, volunteering at a youth club, and so on. Gaining access was an ongoing process, and the development of relationships with people had the effect of making 'my face known' in a community where I was not a member. Consequently, people mentioned that they had heard of me when I contacted or asked to conduct an interview with them. My presence in the area had fostered a certain level of tacit trust and familiarity between myself and many of the community members which enabled my access into the community.

This process was also facilitated by the fact that the community was geographically small and characterized by tight community networks, which relied heavily on 'word of mouth' for the conveyance of information and assurance. This was especially pertinent, given the levels of mistrust and apprehension towards those regarded as external to the 'Muslim community'[2] since 9/11 and the ensuing media and governmental attention surrounding Muslim people. An access strategy that was organic rather than episodic was important because many of the respondents (both individually and as a community) felt marginalized from wider society and expressed resentment towards research and media projects that only gained a superficial and short-term understanding of Muslim communities but nevertheless went on to make broad generalizations[3]. Hence in this context, an access strategy that was reassuring and sustained facilitated the trust of participants and developed a reputation of integrity around myself and the research I was conducting. Prior to engaging in fieldwork (and due to the sociopolitical context) I had anticipated that my interest in criminality, would be met with a certain level of suspicion and reticence.

---

[2] It is acknowledged that the concept of 'the Muslim community' requires further deconstruction and is by no means homogeneous. For reasons of space only, this discussion is not expanded upon here; however, understanding the facets, differences, similarities, and conceptions of 'community' was an important part of the research.

[3] This was expressed to me early on in the project by a parent and this view was subsequently supported by further comments made by others in the community.

Despite my concerns, I decided that clarity about my specific interest was important in terms of establishing trust as well as regular assurances of confidentiality. I also emphasized that criminality was not the sole aspect of the community in which I was interested, especially because crime was inextricably linked to wider social factors. A minority of community members were indeed questioning and resistant to discussing youth criminality with me—in the telling words of one parent: 'there is enough of a spotlight on the Muslim community'. Alongside this, however, the majority of participants were welcoming of the opportunity to express their views on local issues and found it amenable to talk to someone outside of the area about racism, crime, youth, and local services. Young people in particular felt empowered in being able to express their views about crime as it was regarded as an issue for which they were regularly blamed but rarely asked about.

Ticking the right boxes?

Clarity about which Asian groups or specific communities criminological research is exploring and reporting findings about is essential to conveying accurate information. Indeed, disaggregation of crime statistics reveals that generic categories such as 'Asian' can mask the differences between Indians and Pakistanis, for example (Fitzgerald 1993, Gelsthorpe 1993, Phillips and Bowling 2003, Garland *et al.* 2006).

The research dangers of ambiguous ethnic classification were shown in my research, which exposed the gulf between the ways in which key agencies employed the term 'Asian' and how the young people chose to define themselves. The majority of agencies in the community labelled the ethnic population as 'Asian' whereas the young Pakistani-Muslims were critical of this categorization and argued that they did not feel represented by the broad term 'Asian'. In their view, it highlighted that the agencies did not want to recognize the differences between the groups within the category Asian and in their view this was reflective of the institutionally racist practices of the area's local services. Clearly, although the category 'Asian' was not inaccurate, it lacked the level of specificity required by some residents and highlights the political connotations and consequences of the utilization of broad classification schemes at the expense of more precise ones. The issue of ethnic classification is not easy to resolve, as inevitably some people will feel excluded or misrepresented, whatever terminology is used, given that ethnic identity and its description is at once a political choice, context-specific, and a semiotic struggle (Spencer 2006). Within my research the importance of understanding and expressing both inter-and intra-ethnic group diversity yet also appreciating the unities between groups was incorporated into the initial conception of the project, which resulted in both a more nuanced understanding of the issues I was researching as well as respect from the community respondents.

In addition, I found that there were intergenerational preferences for different ethnic labels. For the parents and community leaders, the hyphenated option of 'British-Pakistani' (as offered by the census scale and reflected in much criminological research) was regarded as representative of their ethnic identity. However, for the young males, the census scale was regarded to be misrepresentative and the overwhelming majority preferred the identifier 'British-Muslim' (an option not offered by the census scale and would need to be inserted as 'Other'). Shifts in the ways in which ethnic identities are constructed and negotiated by people may provide valuable insights for the types of question that criminological research would seek to address. Wider trends that bear directly on the phenomenon being studied may be elicited, as in the above example, where the self-identification preference of younger people as 'British-Muslim', versus the older generation's preference for 'British-Pakistani', has very different connotations in a post 7/7 sociopolitical climate. Such links are sensitive and require careful understanding and unravelling. Indeed, ethnic identities and experiences have been raised as salient features in criminological questions about gang membership, political crimes including terrorism, and the ways in which issues such as domestic violence, honour and guilt are conceptualized and understood, to name a few examples.

The intergenerational differences revealed in my research also highlight the need to appreciate the stratifying processes of age, gender, and class within ethnic minority communities and the need to integrate these factors into analysis, rather than assuming homogeneity on the basis of ethnicity within such groups. The intersections of age, gender, and class are central to most criminological questions and conundrums and so the fact that demographic factors stratify ethnic minority communities as sharply as they do wider society is an essential factor to recognize. Researcher awareness of the sensibilities and intricacies surrounding ethnic group labelling and classification as well as avoiding essentialist frameworks are clearly important components to ensure the veracity of criminological research.

From the inside looking in?: ethnicity, generation, and gender

Within my research, I occupied a position whereby I was assumed to have 'insider status'[4] by academic colleagues and those external to the research because (in accordance with broad ethnic categorization), I was Asian, and the community I was researching also came under the broad umbrella category Asian. However, as an Indian female of Hindu background, interviewing a predominantly Pakistani-Muslim male population, my status, as an assumed insider was also at times that of an outsider. The unities that I shared with the community members in terms of class background, being from the same ethnic group, and sharing some broad cultural similarities were side by side with differences including my religious, cultural, historical, and migratory background. A range of scholarship has questioned the possibility of a researcher, including an ethnic minority researcher ever being exactly matched with their respondents (Stanfield and Dennis 1993, Song and Parker 1995, Bhavani 1993, Alexander 2004, Gunaratnam 2003, Reinharz 1997). The liminal status (of being somewhere in-between an insider and an outsider) was enabling in a research sense, as it ensured that I was able to gain access to the community, but also meant that there were certain issues from which I was considered to be distanced and hence about which I was able to ask clear and sometimes fairly naive questions.

The format of some of the exchanges between myself and the respondents appeared to be linked to my position as an Asian person, and also related to my being an Asian female. Some might argue that this may have biased my findings and lessened my objectivity; however, I drew upon the experiences as informative and illuminating of the process of conducting research in an ethnically diverse community whilst belonging to an ethnic minority group myself. First, there was the issue of my religion, which was an implicit factor that was raised with the majority of my interviews with community leaders and parents. The respondents were keen to confirm whether or not I was Muslim (though most would have intuitively known that I was not from my name and the way I greeted them).

---

[4] The 'insider'–'outsider' debate is also known as the ethnic-matching/non-matching debate.

A second interesting process subverted the archetypal researcher–respondent encounter as I was often asked a range of questions before the interviews began, by community leaders in particular. These questions included where I was from and where I was really from (the latter of which was usually a question about my post-colonial history and where my parents had migrated from). Alongside this I was often asked my age, marital status, my education history, religiosity, and so on. All of these questions seemed to stem from the curious intersections of ethnicity, gender, generation, and culture melding together to produce a situation whereby I was strongly expected to answer the questions that I was asked. Within qualitative research in particular, it is of course often the case that dialogue and interaction with respondents is a two-way process (Noaks and Wincup 2004, Oakley 1981), regardless of whether ethnicity is a factor being explored. Within my research I felt under pressure to answer the leaders' questions primarily because of my gender and age and because it seemed polite to do so—given that I would be asking them questions too. Although deference towards older males is a structural-cultural feature of many sections of society, arguably this practice is particularly enshrined within Asian communities and in this particular situation it seemed an implicit prerequisite for the exchange between researcher and respondent to continue.

My specific questions to the community respondents varied according to which section of the community I was interviewing. The broad theme of questions tended to focus on perceptions of crime, the interactions with and perceptions of youth, views on policing and the characteristics of the community context. Often, the responses did not make any direct reference to ethnicity or racism. At other times, however, there was an apprehension from community members about raising certain issues because of the fact that they were from ethnic minority backgrounds. In some of these situations it seemed that my ethnic minority status did come into play in terms of generating and maintaining implicit understandings; for example, one community leader stated:

there are youth crime gang problems in this area, and its our youth that are the cause and making things worse. I wouldn't ever say that officially though, as you don't want to look as though you are causing problems when we have come to this country to live. It doesn't look good does it?—you know what I mean—all Asian communities have a responsibility.

Clearly, the issue of ethnic matching is complex and we can see how it can be concurrently enabling and restrictive. The addition of the inherently sensitive topics of crime and deviance serve to add a further dimension to the insider–outsider debate. Arguably, researcher reflexivity about their own positioning and an understanding of the recurrent political connections that are made between ethnicity and crime are vital factors to ensuring that criminological research is truly reflective of the inner dynamics of diverse societies.

Roots, routes, and contexts

Much previous criminological research has aimed to capture the ethnic background of respondents; however, the methods used to acquire this information are questionable for their lack of sensitivity and specificity regarding ethnic categorization, as discussed earlier. The understanding of ethnicity and the influences on ethnic identity were central components of my project, hence I was interested in gaining as nuanced an understanding as pos-sible of the respondents' views and experiences of belonging to an ethnic minority group. In conjunction with asking about people's ethnic background I also asked respondents about the contexts under which they had migrated (their routes[5]) to the UK. The understanding of postcolonial migration trajectories, the contexts and impacts of migration are rarely asked about in criminological research, although arguably, this can reveal important intricacies about the previous and current diasporic experiences of those who have migrated to countries such as the UK (Brah 1996, Smith 2005a). In my interviews, both pre-and post-migration experiences were discussed vividly by respondents, some of whom highlighted the fact that they were twice migrants. Some mentioned that the apparent rise in crime rates amongst British-Pakistani youth in their community was an issue with which they had not contended with, despite their various displacements and settlements across the world, and this had resulted in heightened levels of concern about crime and deviance amongst the younger members of the community.

The methodological technique of speaking with individual members of the community, understanding how the dense social networks interacted to shape the community, and embedding these processes within the broader historical-migratory context of the area allowed for a kaleidoscopic vision that is likely to be overlooked by research that only focuses on one section of a community. This approach also enabled an understanding of how global events had different local consequences for different sections of the community, despite the ethnic homogeneity of the area. For example, young people's responses to 9/11 and subsequent anti-terror criminal justice practices were highly differentiated from the responses of parents in the community. One of the main findings in my study suggested that there was a consensus amongst many parents and community leaders about the notion that levels of offending in the area were spiralling out of control. Both parents and community leaders reasoned that many local second-generation Pakistanis were engaged in offending because of a lack of social control in the area and because they were experiencing a 'culture clash' which resulted in them feeling confused and frustrated and therefore drawn towards crime. In the words of one community leader: 'if the youngsters had recently migrated to the UK they would be too busy keeping their heads down and concentrating on getting a job, like I did when I first came here'. In contrast to the community elders' perceptions of crime in the area, youth-offending team statistics suggested that levels of offending were either lower than or in parity with the expected rate, given the local demographic profile. Young people in the area who had engaged in offending did not express or explain their criminality by referring to cultural or ethnic frameworks of reasoning and rather referred to more structural problems in the community such as a lack of resources or racism. Considering this issue in terms of social relationships (between community leaders, parents, and the young people) illuminated the fact that the young people were acutely aware of the community perceptions and labelling of them as criminal. This resulted in them feeling distanced from as well as external to the local community to which they were automatically expected to belong (by wider society). Such a finding has important implications in terms of revealing the facets of social perception and variant normative frameworks that may be in operation with regard to crime, and endorses the contemporary need to understand the 'lived experiences'[6] relationships and nuances of diverse urban communities.

---

[5] This play on words is borrowed from Gilroy (1993) and Brah (1996) who discusses the importance of understanding the collective histories of ethnic minority groups in the UK as well as their personal subjective experiences.

[6] The need to understand more fully the 'lived experiences' of ethnic minorities is advocated by Phillips and Bowling (2003) and Shallice and Gordon (1990) who discuss the difference between the suggestions made by empirical criminological data and the personal and collective experiences of ethnic minorities.

Conclusion and recommendations

The extent to which cultural diversity affects criminological research certainly varies across countries, according to specific research questions, and the type of crime being investigated. Equally, and certainly in most large cities, it is hard to imagine a criminological research question that does not require close attention to the ways in which ethnic and cultural diversity affects the research design at various stages of a research project. In this paper we have discussed the approach adopted by the Zurich Project on the Social Development of Children, Z-Proso, and the issues encountered in a doctoral research project that aimed to understand both the perceptions and reality of young British-Pakistani people's criminality. We would like to conclude the chapter by drawing on a couple of overarching themes that we regard as integral to research and which have emerged from our ongoing research projects.

Most fundamentally, we believe that criminological research in culturally diverse contexts should no longer be planned and conducted as though methods developed for monocultural (western) contexts will automatically yield valid results. Developing research questions that reflect experiences of ethnic minorities, gaining access to the research field, developing and using cross-culturally valid research instruments and ways of assessing potential cultural bias in the collected data should become issues that are embedded at every stage of the process of conducting research. This may indeed have implications in terms of adding significant additional amounts of time and money at each stage of a research project; however, these are undoubtedly sound investments and should be factored in during the planning phase.

Secondly and even more importantly, research of this kind requires various (and at times specific) forms of knowledge that is not easily found within criminology. For example, researchers working in culturally diverse fields may need knowledge about cross-cultural measurement, translation theory, culturally specific mechanisms leading to crime, or ways in which to recruit cross-culturally competent interviewers. A wealth of relevant methodological knowledge is available in related academic disciplines such as cross-cultural psychology, social anthropology, and ethnic and cultural studies-areas which have yet to be recognized by much criminological research (Harkness *et al.* 2003; Hui and Triandis 1985; van de Vijver and Leung 1997). The use and integration of such broader insights are indeed essential to achieving research findings that truly reflect and understand the ethnic and cultural diversity of the society that is being researched.

Suggestions for further reading

There is no introductory text available which covers all the issues discussed in this chapter. A comprehensive recent discussion of conceptual and theoretical issues may be found in *Ethnicity and Causal Mechanisms* by Rutter and Tienda (2005). The collection of reviews in *Ethnicity, Crime and Immigration: Comparative and Cross-National Perspectives* edited by Tonry (1997) is still important and includes various contributions on European and North American countries. The volume *The Many Colors of Crime: Inequalities of Race, Ethnicity and Crime in America* edited by Peterson *et al.* (2006) includes some excellent papers but is limited to the situation in the USA. Although very much to be desired, there is no good up-to-date overview of research in Europe. The chapter by Smith (2005) 'Ethnic Differences in Intergenerational Crime Patterns', in *Crime and Justice,* and the textbook by Bowling and Phillips (2002) *Race, Crime and Justice* provide good entry points to the theoretical and empirical discussion in the UK. Students planning to conduct survey research in ethnically diverse contexts will find the methodo-logical discussions in *Cross Cultural Survey Methods* by Harkness *et al.* (2003) is very useful. To students planning qualitative research we would recommend *Researching 'Race' and Ethnicity: Methods, Knowledge and Power* by Gunaratnam (2003) and Bulmer and Solomos' (2004) *Researching Race and Racism,* both of which address conceptual and theoretical issues.

References

ACHENBACH, T. M. and EDELBROCK, C. S. (1981). 'Behavioral Problems and Competencies Reported by Parents of Normal and Disturbed Children aged Four through Sixteen'. *Monographs of the Society for Research in Child Development* 46; 1–82.

AHMAD, W. I. U. and SHELDON, T. (1993). ' "Race" and Statistics' in M. Hammersley (ed.) *Social Research: Philosophy, Politics and Practice.* London: Sage.

ALEXANDER, C. (2000). *The Asian Gang: Ethnicity, Identity, Masculinity.* Oxford: Berg.

—— (2004). 'Writing Race: Ethnography and the Imagination of The Asian Gang' in M. Bulmer, and J. Solomos (eds), *Researching Race and Racism.* London: Routledge.

ANDERSON, B. A., SILVER, B. D., and ABRAMSON, P. R. (1988). 'The Effects of the Race of the Interviewer on Race-Related Attitudes of Black Respondents in SRC/CPS National Election Studies'. *Public Opinion Quarterly* 52(3): 289–324.

ASPINALL, P. (2002). 'Collective Terminology to Describe the Minority Ethnic Population: The Persistence of Confusion and Ambiguity in Usage'. *British Journal of Sociology* 36(4): 803–16.

BACK, L. (1999). *New Ethnicities and Urban Culture: Racisms and Multiculture in Young Lives.* London: UCL Press Limited.

BHAVANI, K.-K. (1993). 'Tracing the Contours of Feminist Research and Feminist Objectivity'. *Women's Studies International Forum* 6(2): 95–104.

BOLLING, K., CLEMENS, S., GRANT, C., and SMITH, P. (2003). 2002–3 British Crime Survey (England and Wales), Technical Report, Vol. 1. London: Home Office, Development and Statistics Directorate.

——, GRANT, C., SMITH, P., and BROWN, M. (2004). 2003–4 British Crime Survey (England and Wales); Technical Report, Vol. 1. London: Home Office.

BOWLING, B. (1990). 'Conceptual and Methodological Problems in Measuring "Race" Differences in Delinquency: A Reply to Marianne Junger'. *British Journal of Criminology* 30(3): 483–92.

—— and PHILLIPS, C. (2002). *Racism, Crime and Justice.* Essex: Pearson Education Limited.

BRAH, A. (1996). *Cartographies of Diaspora: Contesting Identities.* London: Routledge.

BRISLIN, R. W. (1986). 'The Wording and Translation of Research Instruments' in W. J. Lonner and J. W. Berry (eds), *Field Methods in Cross-cultural Research.* Newbury Park: Sage.

BULMER, M. and SOLOMOS, J. (eds) (2004). *Researching Race and Racism.* London: Routledge.

Buss, A. R. and Royce, J. R. (1975). 'Detecting Cross-Cultural Commonalities and Differences: Intergroup Factor Analysis'. *Psychological Bulletin* 82: 128–36.

Carr-Hill, R., Passingham, S., Wolf, A., and Kent, N. (1996). *Lost Opportunities: the Language Skills of Linguistic Minorities in England and Wales*. London: Basic Skills Agency.

Couper, M. P. and Leeuw, E. D. d. (2003). 'Nonresponse in Cross-Cultural and Cross-National Surveys' in J. A. Harkness, F. J. R. van de Vijver, and P. P. Mohler (eds), *Cross-Cultural Survey Methods*. New York: Wiley.

Dana, R. H. (ed.) (2000). *Handbook of Cross-Cultural and Multicultural Personality Assessment*. Mahway: Lawrence Erlbaum Associates.

Desai, P. (1999). *Spaces of Identity, Cultures of Conflict: The Development of New British Asian Masculinities*. Unpublished Doctoral Thesis, Goldsmiths, London.

Dotinga, A., van de Eijnden, R. J. J. M., Bosveld, W., and Garretsen, H. F. L. (2005). 'The Effect of Data Collection Mode and Ethnicity of Interviewer on Response Rates and Self-Reported Alcohol use among Turks and Moroccans in the Netherlands: An Experimental Study'. *Alcohol and Alcoholism* 40(3): 242–8.

Eisner, M. and Ribeaud, D. (2005). 'A Randomised Field Experiment to Prevent Violence: The Zurich Intervention and Prevention Project at Schools, ZIPPS'. *European Journal of Crime, Criminal Law and Criminal Justice* 13: 27–43.

Farrington, D. P., Loeber, R., and Stouthamer-Loeber, M. (2003). 'How can the Relationship between Race and Violence be Explained?' in D. J. Hawkins (ed.), *Violent Crimes: Assessing Race and Ethnic Differences*. New York: Cambridge University Press.

Feskens, R., Hox, J., Lensvelt-Mulders, G., and Schmeets, H. (2004). 'A Multivariate Analysis of Nonresponse among Ethnic Minorities' in Statistics Canada (ed.), *Statistics Canada International Symposium Series—Proceedings*.

Fisher, C. and Masty, J. (2006). 'Through the Community Looking Glass: Participant Consultation for Adolescent Risk Research' in B. Leadbeater, L. Banister, C. Benoit, M. Jansson, A. Marshall, and T. Riecken (eds), *Ethical Issues in Community-Based Research with Children and Youth*. Toronto: University of Toronto Press.

FitzGerald, M. (1993). ' "Racism": Establishing the Phenomenon' in D. Cook and B. Hudson (eds), *Racism and Criminology*. London: Sage.

Garland, J., Spalek, B., and Chakraborti, N. (2006). 'Hearing Lost Voices: Issues in Researching 'Hidden' Ethnic Communities'. *British Journal of Criminology* 46(2): 423–37.

Gelsthorpe, L. R. (1993). 'Approaching the Topic of Racism: Transferable Research Strategies?' in D. Cook and B. Hudson (eds), *Racism and Criminology*. London: Sage.

Gilroy, P. (1993). *The Black Atlantic: Modernity and Double Consciousness*. London: Verso.

—— (2000). *Nations, Culture and the Allure of Race: Between Camps*. London: Allen Lane.

—— (2004). *After Empire: Melancholia or Convival Culture?* London: Routledge.

Gottfredson, M. T. and Hirschi, T. (1990). *A General Theory of Crime*. Stanford: Stanford University Press.

Grovew, R. M., Dillman, D. A., Eltinge, J. L., and Little, R. J. A. (eds) (2002). *Survey Nonresponse*. New York: Wiley.

Gunaratnam, Y. (2003). *Researching 'Race' and Ethnicity: Methods, Knowledge and Power*. London: Sage.

Hall, S. (1991). 'Old and New Identities, Old and New Ethnicities' in A. D. King (ed.), *Culture, Globalisation and the World System*. Basingstoke: Macmillan.

HAMBLETON, R. and KANJEE, A. (1993). 'Enhancing the Validity of Cross-cultural Studies: Improvements in Instrument Translation Methods (Paper presented at the annual American Educational Research Association Conference, Atlanta, Georgia).

HARACHI, T. W., CATALANO, R. F., and HAWKINS, J. D. (1997). 'Effective Recruitment for Parenting Programs Within Ethnic Minority Communities'. *Child and Adolescent Social Work Journal* 14: 23–39.

HARKNESS, J. A. (2003). 'Questionnaire Translation' in J. A. Harkness, F. J. R. V. d. Vijver, and P. P. Mohler (eds), *Cross-Cultural Survey Methods*. New York: John Wiley.

—— and SCHOUA-GLUSBERG, A. (1998). 'Questionnaires in Translation'. *ZUMA-Nachrichten Spezial* 3: 87–127.

——, VAN DE VIJVER, F. J. R., and MOHLER, P. P. (eds) (2003). *Cross-Cultural Survey Methods*. New York: John Wiley.

HAWKINS, D. F. (ed.) (1995). *Ethnicity, Race and Crime: Perspectives Across Time and Place*. Albany: State University of New York Press.

HINDELANG, M. J., HIRSCHI, T., and WEIS, J. G. (1981). *Measuring Delinquency*. Beverly Hills: Sage.

HUI, C. H. and TRIANDIS, H. C. (1985). 'Measurement in Cross-cultural Psychology—A Review and Comparison of Strategies'. *Journal of Cross-Cultural Psychology* 16: 131–52.

JACOBSON, J. (1997). 'Religion and Ethnicity: Dual and Alternative Source of Identity among Young British Pakistanis. *Ethnic and Racial Studies* 20: 238–56.

JOHNSON, C. and MASH, E. J. (1989). 'A Measure of Parenting Satisfaction and Efficacy'. *Journal of Clinical Child Psychology* 18: 167–75.

JOHNSON, P. B. and MALGADY, R. (1999) 'Cultural/Ethnic Comparisons: A Research

Agenda'. *Journal of Gender, Culture and Health* 4: 171–85.

JOHNSON, T. P. (1998). 'Approaches to Equivalence in Cross-Cultural and Cross-National Research'. *ZUMA-Nachrichten Spezial* 3: 1–32.

——, O'ROURKE, D., BURRIS, J., and OWENS, L. (2002). 'Culture and Survey Nonresponse' in R. M. Groves, D. A. Dillman, J. L. Eltinge, and R. J. A. Little (eds), *Survey Nonresponse*. New York: Wiley.

—— and VAN DE VIJVER, F. J. R. (2003). 'Social Desirability in Cross-Cultural Research' in J. A. Harkness, F. J. R. van de Vijver, and P. P. Mohler (eds), *Cross-Cultural Survey Methods*. Hoboken: Wiley.

JUNGER, M. (1989). 'Discrepancies between Police and Self-report Data for Dutch Racial Minorities'. *British Journal of Criminology* 29: 273–84.

JUNGER-TAS, J. (1997). 'Ethnic Minorities and Criminal Justice in the Netherlands' in M. Tonry, *Ethnicity, Crime and Immigration: Comparative and Cross-national Perspectives* (Vol. 28 of *Crime and Justice: A Review of Research*), Chicago: University of Chicago Press.

—— (2001). 'Ethnic Minorities, Social Integration and Crime'. *European Journal on Criminal Policy and Research* 9: 5–29.

KILLIAS, M. (1989). 'Criminality among Second-Generation Immigrants in Western Europe: A Review of the Evidence'. *Criminal Justice Review* 14: 13–42.

KING, G., KEOHANE, R. O., and VERBA, S. (1994). *Designing Social Inquiry: Scientific Inference in Qualitative Research*. Princeton: Princeton University Press.

LAM, C. L. K., GANDEK, B., REN, X. S., and CHAN, M. S. (1998). 'Tests of Scaling Assumptions and Construct Validity of the Chinese (HK) Version of the SF-36 Health Survey—How to Score the SF-12 Physical and mental Health Summary Scales'. *Journal of Clinical Epidemiology* 51: 1139–47.

LAU, A. S., GARLAND, A. F., YEH, M., McCABE, K. M., WOOD, P. A., and HOUGH, R. L. (2004). 'Race/Ethnicity and Inter-Informant Agreement in Assessing Adolescent Psychopathology'. *Journal of Emotional and Behavioral Disorders* 12: 145–56.

LE, T. N., MONFARED, G., and STOCKDALE, G. D. (2005). 'The Relationship of School, Parent, and Peer Contextual Factors with Self-Reported Delinquency for Chinese, Cambodian, Laotian or Mien, and Vietnamese Youth'. *Crime and Delinquency* 51(2): 192–219.

MAWBY, R., McCULLOCH, J., and BATTA, I. (1979). 'Crime Amongst Asian Juveniles in Bradford'. *International Journal of the Sociology of Law* 7: 297–306.

MAYHEW, P. (2000). 'Researching the State of Crime: Local, National, and International Victim Surveys' in R. D. King and E. Wincup (eds), *Doing Research on Crime and Justice*. Oxford: Oxford University Press.

McLEAN, C. A. and CAMPBELL, C. M. (2003). 'Locating Research Informants in a Multi-ethnic Community: Ethnic Identities, Social Networks and Recruitment Methods'. *Ethnicity and Health* 8: 41–61.

MODOOD, T. (2005). 'Ethnicity and Inter-generational Identities and Adaptations in Britain: The Socio-Political Context' in M. Rutter and M. Tienda (eds), *Ethnicity and Causal Mechanisms*. Cambridge: Cambridge University Press.

——, BERTHOUD, R., LAKEY, J., NAZROO, J., SMITH, P., VIRDEE, S., and BEISHON, S. (1997). *Ethnic Minorities in Britain: Diversity and Disadvantage*. London: Policy Studies Institute.

NOAKS, L. and WINCUP, E. (2004). *Criminological Research: Understanding Qualitative Methods*. London: Sage.

OAKLEY, A. (1981). 'Interviewing Women: a Contradiction in Terms' in H. Roberts (ed.), *Doing Feminist Research*. London: Routledge.

PETERSON, R., KRIVO, L., and HAGAN, J. (2006). *The Many Colors of Crime: Inequalities of Race, Ethnicity and Crime in America*. New York and London: New York University Press.

PHILLIPS, C. and BOWLING, B. (2002). 'Racism, Ethnicity, Crime, and Criminal Justice' in M. Maguire, R. Morgan, and R. Reiner (eds), *The Oxford Handbook of Criminology* (3rd edn). Oxford: Oxford University Press.

—— and —— (2003). 'Racism, Ethnicity and Criminology: Developing Minority Perspectives'. *British Journal of Criminology* 43: 269–90.

REINHARZ, S. (1997). 'Who am I? The need for a Variety of Selves in the Field' in *Reflexivity and Voice*. Thousand Oaks, CA: Sage.

RUTTER, M. (2005). 'Natural Experiments, Causal Influences, and Policy Development' in M. Rutter and M. Tienda (eds), *Ethnicity and Causal Mechanisms*. Cambridge: Cambridge University Press.

—— and TIENDA, M. (2005). 'The Multiple Facets of Ethnicity' in M. Rutter and M. Tienda (eds), *Ethnicity and Causal Mechanisms*. Cambridge: Cambridge University Press.

SANDERS, M. R., MARKIE-DADDS, C., TULLY, L. A., and BOR, W. (2000). 'The Triple P-Positive Parenting Program: A Comparison of Enhanced, Standard, and Self-Directed Behavioral Family Intervention for Parents of Children with Early Onset Conduct Problems'. *Journal of Consulting and Clinical Psychology* 68: 624–40.

SELLIN, T. (1938). 'Culture Conflict and Crime'. *American Journal of Sociology* 44: 97–103.

SHALLICE, A. and GORDON, P. (1990). *Black People, White Justice? Race and the Criminal Justice System*. Runnymede Trust: London.

SHORT, J. F. Jr (1997). *Poverty, Ethnicity and Violent Crime*. Boulder, Colorado: Westview Press.

SINGER, E. (2002). 'The Use of Incentives to Reduce Nonresponse in Household Surveys' in R. M. Grovew, D. A. Dillman, J. L. Eltinge, and R. J. A. Little (eds), *Survey Nonresponse*. New York: Wiley.

SMITH, D. (2005a). 'Ethnic Differences in Intergenerational Crime Patterns'. *Crime and Justice: A Review of Research* 32: 1–58.

—— (2005b). 'Explaining Ethnic Variations in Crime and Antisocial Behavior in the United Kingdom' in M. Rutter and M. Tienda (eds), *Ethnicity and Causal Mechanisms*. Cambridge: Cambridge University Press.

SONG, M. and PARKER, D. (1995). 'Commonality, Difference and the Dynamics of Disclosure in In-depth Interviewing'. *Sociology* 29: 241–56.

SPENCER, M. S., FITCH, D., GROGAN-KAYLOR, A., and MCBEATH, B. (2005). 'The Equivalence of the Problem Behavior Index across U.S. Ethnic Groups'. *Journal of Cross-Cultural Psychology* 36: 573–89.

SPENCER, S. (2006). *Race and Ethnicity: Culture, Identity and Representation*. Oxford: Routledge.

STANFIELD, J. and DENNIS, R. (1993). *Race and Ethnicity in Research Methods*. London: Sage.

STRANG, H. and J. BRAITHWAITE (eds) (2002). *Restorative Justice and Family Violence*. Cambridge: Cambridge University Press.

STRAUS, M. A. (1969). 'Phenomenal Identity and Conceptual Equivalence of Measurement in Cross-National Comparative Research'. *Journal of Marriage and Family* 31: 233–9

STOOP, I. A. L. (2005). *The Hunt for the Last Respondent: Nonresponse in Sample Surveys*. The Hague: Social and Cultural Planning Office of the Netherlands.

TONRY, M. (ed.) (1997). 'Ethnicity, Crime, and Immigration; Comparative and Cross-National Perspectives'. *Crime and Justice—A Review of Research*, Vol. 21. Chicago: Chicago University Press.

TREMBLAY, R. E., LOEBER, R., GAGNON, C., CHARLEBOIS, P., LARIVÉE, S., and LEBLANC, M. (1991). 'Disruptive Boys with Stable and Unstable High Fighting Behavior Patterns during Junior Elementary School'. *Journal of Abnormal Child Psychology* 19: 285–300.

TWINE, F. W. (2000). 'Racial Ideologies and Racial Methodologies' in F. W. Twine and Warren, J. (eds), *Racing Research, Researching Race*. New York: New York University Press.

VAN GOOR, H., JAMSMA, F., and VEENSTRA, R. (2005). 'Differences in Undercoverage and Nonresponse between City Neighbourhoods in a Telephone Survey'. *Psychological Reports* 96: 867–78.

VIJVER, F. J. R. v. d. (1998). 'Towards a Theory of Bias and Equivalence'. *ZUMA-Nachrichten Spezial* 3: 41–65.

—— and LEUNG, K. (1997). *Methods and Data Analysis for Cross-Cultural Research*. Beverly Hills: Sage.

WALBY, S. and ALLEN, J. (2004). 'Domestic Violence, Sexual assault and Stalking: Findings from the British Crime Survey.' *Home Office Research Study 276*. London: Home Office, Development and Statistics Directorate.

WEBER, M. (1968). *Economy and Society* (ed. by Guenther Roth and Claus Wittich). New York: Bedminister Press.

WEBSTER, C. (1997). 'The Construction of "Asian" Criminality'. *International Journal of the Sociology of Law* 25: 65–86.

WILLIAMS, J., CELEMENS, S., OLEINIKOVA, K., and TARVIN, K. (2003). 'The Skills for Life Survey; A National Needs and Impact Survey of Literacy, Numeracy, and ICT Skills' (DfES Research Brief RB490). London: Department for Education and Skills.

7

International comparative research in criminology

Frances Heidensohn

Introduction

In one sense, all criminology can, or should, be comparative in nature. Any observed trends such as rising or falling rates of recorded crime in one country need to be checked against those in other nations. As long ago as the 1830s Adolphe Quetelet used 'statistical material, drawn from French and Belgian sources' to show the constancy of crime rates in certain countries over time—his 'penchant au crime' (Mannheim 1965: 96–7). Quetelet also proposed a 'thermic law' of the incidence of crime in warmer or cooler climates, a theme later taken up by Lombroso and others.

Many theories of crime, while originally based on research within one country, have been exported or tested out in another. Morris (1957) applied the ecological concepts of the Chicago School in his work on Croydon, and Downes took subcultural theory, also an American import, as his framework in his study of delinquent youth in the East End of London (Downes 1966). Neither found that these ideas fitted their British case studies very precisely. As well as providing a test bed for theory and speculation: 'in the absence of a comparative frame of reference, it is not possible to distinguish speculative from actual causes of crime' (Neapolitan 1997: xi), such approaches have also proved vital to criminal justice policy making. One obvious advantage of what is called 'policy transfer' is to borrow success from another system, or to learn from its mistakes (Newburn 2000: 28).

With such clear benefits from undertaking comparative research in criminology and criminal justice, it might be assumed that it would hold a central, established place in the field. As the editors of a recently published collection assert:

Any criminology worthy of the name should contain a comparative dimension. The contents of cultural meanings that are loaded into the subject of criminology are too variable for it to be otherwise. It is fair to say that *most of the important points made by leading scholars of criminology are comparative in nature* (Hardie-Bick et al. 2005: 1, emphasis added).

The same authors nevertheless go on to assert that 'although criminologists are comparative by nature, they are also very often rather ethnocentric and quite parochial' (2005: 1). They briefly sum up the situation as follows: 'there has long been a significant vein in academic criminology that has aimed to be fully comparative' (2005: 1). Their account gives Mannheim's (1965) work as the pace-setter and 'the only significant landmark' until the late 1990s (2005: 1). In fact, these are contended statements. While some other authors agree with the designation of Mannheim as the founding father of this field (e.g. Winterdyk and Cao 2004: 2), others note the long tradition of 'travelling' criminal justice policies and travellers, such as Voltaire, who compared, and especially, contrasted different systems (Karstedt 2004: 16–19). Further, far from seeing the featureless comparative landscape depicted by Hardie-Bick and colleagues in the twentieth century, others reflected that 'comparative criminology has recently become a growth area' (Vagg 1993: 541) while even earlier, I had noted the range of key developments in the field in relation to Europe (Heidensohn 1991: 10–11).

Not only are there different historical accounts of the field, writers also vary in the terminology they select to describe it. Many authors use 'comparative' and 'international' criminology interchangeably or in combination, as do the editors of the text from which many of the quotations above were taken (Sheptycki and Wardak 2005). The editors of another recent collection also employ the two terms in their title, divided only by a forward slash (Winterdyk and Cao 2004); in their introduction to this set of essays, they distinguish 'international' as a less normative approach than 'comparative' which they argue is not a methodological but a geopolitical approach (2004: 2). Yet they go on to employ the two words 'interchangeably'.

Other criminologists frown on this elision. Barak has devoted a notable essay to clarifying these points and acknowledging that 'there are still alternative views, definitions, and theories of, as well as approaches to comparative crime and crime control' (Barak 2000a: 1). He defines 'comparative criminology or ... cross-national study' as 'the systematic and theoretically informed comparison of crime and crime control in two or more cultural states' (Barak 2000a: 1). Note that he has already introduced a *third* name for the object of our attention here with 'cross-national study'. Despite his claim that 'as the number of comparative studies have grown some clarity of purpose has been established in the field' he acknowledges that 'transnationalists' would argue that 'the nation-state is in demise ... and contend that before comparative criminology gets its act together, that we will have moved on to doing international and transnational criminology' (2000a: 2). He goes on to illustrate his approach to this subject with the example of his own study, with fellow contributors, of the institutional relationships of crime and crime control in fifteen nation-states. These were selected to give global coverage and fitted into three groups: developed nations—e.g. the USA; post-traditional nations—e.g. Ghana; and developing nations—e.g. China (Barak 2000b). The researchers agreed to present material focused on political and economic contexts and reviews of qualitative and quantitative data. This impressive undertaking did not generate particularly surprising or challenging results. As have others before them (see, e.g., Heidensohn 1991) they found that 'expressions of crime and criminality were more uniform between the three types of nation than were the responses to crime or the expressions of crime control' (Barak 2000a: 3).

This study is a significant example of what I later call 'multistudies' for the purposes of this chapter. This is an important genre, largely originating in the late twentieth century and of growing importance in the field. Yet the adjectives 'comparative' and 'international' remain contested by some authors, even as others consolidate their claims to the territory. Yacoubian (2003: 223–4) declares that comparative criminology involves cross-cultural study while international criminology is the study of violations of international law. There is a further specialist sub-branch of our topic, namely the study of organized crime, which has almost always been placed in a global perspective and over whose definitions, boundaries, and forms of analysis, much debate flourishes (see Hobbs in the first edition of this volume and Rawlinson in this one).

In short, the concept of international comparative criminology is still somewhat contended and confused. This undoubtedly reflects the state of the discipline in general; 'globally, criminology does not have a single coherent, integrated body of knowledge or practice, *nor should it*', insist Hardie-Bick and his colleagues (2005: 13). Yet they also conclude that as 'there is no established paradigm for transnational and comparative criminology it is necessary to invent one' (2005: 3). They cite the importance of different types of comparative work in an era of globalization, a phenomenon which they and their contributors emphasize, has had profound impact on criminology and criminal justice (2005, and see also Chan 2005).

So far, the possibilities of international research may seem daunting: no clear territorial boundaries and haphazard signposting. Yet there are very many positive aspects to be weighed against these problems. This is, just about everyone agrees, a burgeoning field: Newburn and Sparks (2004: 7), Heidensohn (2006: 236), Cavadino and Dignan (2006: 3). Serious, thoughtful research from a wide range of points of view is increasingly being published (Garland 2001; Winterdyk and Cao 2004). International research is made easier than ever before by many of the widely noted effects of globalization: ease and relative cheapness of travel, instant communication through electronic means, near-universal access to data and to scholarly material such as journals and expert reports.

The contexts, both local and global, of comparative study have shifted markedly in the past few decades. When Downes produced his analysis of the Dutch penal system, it was with the aim of answering questions about the British penal crises of the time and to learn from experience in the Netherlands (Downes 1988: 4–5). In the twenty-first century, however, massive social and political changes have produced a much more punitive, less tolerant situation there (Pakes 2004: 284). Developments in transnational arrangements, especially in Europe, have had considerable effect, leading to the setting up of Europol and of the 'third pillar' of the Maastricht Treaty on crime and security (see Heidensohn 1997 for a history). Wood and Kempa, bringing their account up to date, notes the seismic impact of 11 September 2001 on EU policing strategies (Wood and Kempa 2005), an impact which, together with subsequent acts of terror and aggression, has altered the setting for global study forever.

In the rest of this chapter I shall outline some of the most important research studies in the field and cover their more interesting findings as well as the methodologies by which they were achieved. As a heuristic device, I have grouped this work under two main headings: *multistudies* and *case studies*. This distinction reflects, in part, that referred to above made by Beirne and Nelken (1997) and Barak (2000b) to accept as a cross-national study only those which include 'systematic and theoretically informed comparison of crime and crime control in two or more cultural states' (Barak 2000a 2). This, as I have already noted, has been a productive field since the latter part of the twentieth century; for novice researchers and those whose funding is modest, these may seem models which are exacting to emulate. Nevertheless, there are many lessons to be learnt from them. More replicable as models for those starting out on the comparative trail may be *case studies* of one or perhaps two topics or issues studied cross-culturally as well as in depth. This is not to prescribe in any way the course a criminological career should take.

Looking at the autobiographical accounts of fourteen established scholars in the field contained in Winterdyk and Cao (2004) it is clear that they arrived at their comparative destinations by many different routes. Some did serve apprenticeships in what I have called the multifield (e.g. Joutsen 2004) but most describe histories of accident, serendipity or, if this is not too disrespectful to my eminent colleagues, of *drift* (Albrecht 2004).

The growth of comparative study, in the context, in the UK especially, of expansion in all criminological research and teaching, as well as the changes in society, politics, and the economy, all suggest that future careers will be different. Indeed, they already show signs of this. Multistudies, such as the International Crime Victims Surveys, are labour-intensive, as indeed are alternatives, such as the customized approach adopted in Tonry and Farrington's project, where they conclude that '(L)aborious work by many people underlies this volume' (Tonry and Farrington 2005: 33). This adds to the costs and complexities of such work, but of course, also provides scope and opportunities for researchers.

In the first two sections of this chapter I shall review case studies and multistudies and I shall include my own experiences of conducting each type. The third section will discuss methodological and theoretical issues related to comparative study and focus particularly on the role of the researcher her-/himself, an issue which I think is one of the most distinctive and significant in this field (Heidensohn 2006). Finally, I shall consider possible future areas of research.

It is a testament to the growth of this field of study, and of its topics' rise in political significance, that it is not possible to provide comprehensive cover within one chapter of this volume. Nevertheless, readers should find the key texts in the English language here and be able to trace their routes to related studies and I shall give some guide to further reading at the end. The reader should perhaps be warned that the division I am making here between case studies and multistudies is essentially an arbitrary one, designed to simplify the subject, and also to ensure the inclusion of pivotal studies omitted by some definitions of this field. As we shall see, some projects do not fit readily on one or other side of this divide; indeed, it can be argued that case studies are the building blocks or the cases for some multistudies. As I have suggested above I will go on to show, that several types of multistudy are expensive to conduct, complex to manage and analyse and many of them are run with the support of governments or of international agencies. For those starting off in this field, it should, I trust, be encouraging to see the links as well as the distinctions in ways of conducting comparative research.

Case studies

David Downes' *Contrasts in Tolerance* (1988) 'is widely regarded as a key contribution to comparative work' (Heidensohn 2006: 173). Vagg (1993: 541) cites it as the first contribution to a trend in which 'comparative criminology has recently become a growth area'. In his introduction to *Contrasts*, Downes explains how he came to study the Dutch penal system of the post-World War Two era. He began with concern about the penal crisis in Britain in the 1980s: rising crime rates, prison expansion, penal squalor, variation in regimes, and fears about 'loss of control within the jails'. This led him to 'the question "Does it have to be so?" ' which 'entails comparative study' (1988: 4). In short, he sought in the Netherlands of that period, a 'negative example' of a nation which imprisoned fewer offenders, did so more humanely and yet did not suffer consequent higher crime rates. Evidently, while Downes begins *Contrasts* with some discussion of comparative methods and their importance in sociology and anthropology (op. cit. 2–3) and thus has intellectual curiosity as an aim for this project, it is the *policy* concerns which most motivated him.

Downes' account of his methods is brief, in contrast to the tasks he reports on '12 research visits ... for a total of some 150 days, some hundred interviews ... 25 judges' (1988: 8). Later on in the research he interviewed thirteen English-speaking prisoners in Dutch jails and Dutch prisoners in English ones (1988: 163). He discusses striking differences in the ways he gained *access* to these prisoners and their consent to inspect their files. In England, this was centrally controlled and directed, with strict time limits on the length of the interviews. 'In the Netherlands (he) was allowed to contact *any* prison at which British prisoners were held' (1988: 164) and he wrote directly to them to ask permission, although the letters were not received! Whereas he needed inmates' consent in the Dutch system, 'no such constraint applied in England' (1988: 165).

Contrasts also includes an outline of the main legal and other differences between the two criminal justice systems, emphasizing the distinctive features of the Dutch. He concludes that 'comparing serious crime rates is not, therefore, fraught with too much difficulty, providing that certain adjustments are made to ensure that like is being compared with like' (1988: 10). The text that follows includes numerous tables, most of them setting out such data as serious crime trends, sentencing patterns, and drug use. Downes makes clear that, for the most part, he relied on the 'fluency in English of people interviewed (which) approached near-mastery of the language' relying on a translator for summaries of documents and reports (1988: 8).

Contrasts is a central, canonical text in case-study comparisons. It provides a thoughtful and penetrating analysis of another system at a time of change. Downes' conclusions about how the Dutch criminal justice system achieved its more humane, balanced approach are partly sociological—the effects on social control of the 'pillars' of Dutch society—but also institutional—the coordinated ways in which the judiciary and prosecution service worked together to achieve strategic goals (1988: ch. 7).

In a somewhat similar category is King's (1991) comparative study of the riot-prone English dispersal prison at Gartree with the 'new generation' prison at Oak Park Heights in Minnesota, which showed that it was possible to run a maximum security prison in humane ways, with rich regimes, and still keep both prisoners and staff safe. This was very different from what he subsequently found (King 1999) in most of the American supermax prisons he studied where questions of humanity and prisoner programmes had been more or less abandoned in favour of isolation and coercive power.

As Downes himself noted, he was by no means the first person to travel in search of better solutions in criminal justice policies (1988: 5). In the eighteenth century, John Howard famously presented his review of the state of the prisons in England and Wales together with his *Preliminary Observations and an Account of Some Foreign Prisons and Hospitals* (Howard 1784). Elizabeth Fry, the pioneer of prison reform for women, also became an inveterate traveller in her later years, seeking and promoting better regimes for female inmates (Rose 1980). In the early part of the twentieth century there were many such reformers who travelled in order to collect material to promote change at home.

Policing was a major focus of such activities. Raymond Fosdick (1915), a New York City Police Department administrative officer, interviewed senior officers across Europe before World War One; not only did he provide comparative data, he also produced 'a classification of police systems . . . superficial . . . but unrivalled for over 40 years' (Mawby 1999: 14).

Chloe Owings, one of the pioneers of the police women's movement, also undertook such a tour on which she reported (Owings 1925). I have recounted elsewhere how much her counterparts in Britain made use of their own experiences abroad, working for instance with the International Bureau for the Suppression of the White Slave Trade, and their knowledge of the introduction of women into law enforcement elsewhere, to try and persuade reluctant Home Secretaries, civil servants, and chief constables of the justice of their cause (Heidensohn 2000: ch. 4).

Nevertheless, Garland has insisted that these reformers were not criminologists in any meaningful sense and places the origins of the subject at a more recent date. In the case of Britain, the first and undoubtedly most significant role was played by three refugees from the Third Reich who arrived in Britain in the 1930s: Radzinowicz, Mannheim, and Grünhut. Radzinowicz, as the youngest of the three and the only one to come initially as a volunteer, played the most vital role in setting up criminology as a research field in Britain (Hood 2002) and especially at Cambridge, while the latter two made foundational contributions in London and Oxford (Hood 2004). All three wrote case studies, largely on topics in England and Wales, yet very much from comparative standpoints of a very particular kind: they were foreigners, only Radzinowicz had a good command of English on arrival, and the other two came penniless and depressed (Hood 2004).

While these authors came from Europe and referred to continental scholars in their writings, they did not succeed in breaking the 'American hegemony' in British criminology (Hood 2004). Indeed, it is Downes' *Contrasts* which arguably signposts the arrival of 'Europe' as an area of interest for comparative criminology.

Its publication was quickly followed by a series of selections of case studies which focused on crime and criminal justice in Europe, in particular what was then the European Community: Hood (1989), Cain (1989), Heidensohn and Farrell (1991). This trend has continued (Ruggiero *et al.* 1998); in 1996 South reviewed twenty-five books on crime or criminal justice 'which prioritize a *European* perspective over parochial, national preoccupations or familiar transatlantic (i.e. Euro-USA) orientations' (South 1996: 13). All of the cited texts were based on conferences and each contains a mixture of case studies and commentaries on European topics. It is notable that the range of topics and the geographical spread covered had grown considerably. Some chapters report on multistudies (e.g. Mawby 1998) but many are based upon the Downes template of a combination of statistical material, the use of records such as official reports and sources such as interviews with participants. We can find accounts of conflict resolution between victims and offenders in Austria and in Germany (Pelikan 1991) and of prison discipline systems (Vagg 1991), comparisons of the relationship between crime and the welfare state in the UK and Sweden (Tham 1998) and an observational study of youth cultures in Athens (Vidali 1998). In sum, within a decade of *Contrasts* appearing, comparative criminology had become a crowded arena where every kind of methodology was represented. The remarkable new feature was that this very diverse material was presented for international comparison, raising many questions about equivalence of data, definitions of crime, and the appropriateness of different paradigms and theories. This development paralleled and followed changes first in the constitution of Europe itself, through the Single European Act, which came into force in 1992, and also the related changes in criminal justice in Europe through the TREVI and Schengen groupings (Heidensohn 1997: 84–6).

As a spur to conferences and research, these were key developments and I want to refer briefly to my own experiences at this time to illuminate some of the issues involved. In 1988, the Institute for the Study and Treatment of Delinquency (now the Centre for Crime and Justice Studies) set up and ran the first major Europe-wide congress on crime and criminal justice. In one sense, this was a return to ISTD's roots, since Mannheim, among others, had been a vital figure in its earlier days. Together with ISTD's then Director, I set out to find comparative research in and about Europe and aimed to publish it to stimulate interest and debate, which we considered to be missing.

The conference (and the subsequent book we eventually produced) was successful, but what I want to stress here are the conclusions about comparative study in Europe which I drew from work on this project. First, definitional issues gained an added dimension: what and where was 'Europe' and could we talk of 'crime in Europe' in any meaningful sense? As it turned out, we became part of a self-fulfilling prophecy: by holding the conference, which gained considerable media interest, and then publishing some of the key papers, we stimulated discussion and raised the profile of this topic. The coming into force of the Single European Act, the setting up of Europol and the third pillar of the Maastricht Treaty all formed part of the formal political landscape in Europe which also accounted for new interest in crime in Europe. There were other historic shifts too: between the publication of the first and the revised edition of *Crime in Europe* the Berlin wall fell, an event which presaged the eventual fall of communism in Europe and the reunification of Germany and the break-up of the old Soviet Union (Heidensohn and Farrell 1993: xi). In other words, several of the states whose crime and criminal justice processes had been the subjects of our volume had already been altered within a few years. Secondly, it reinforced the three key methodological messages which I had begun to gather from my own studies in the field. They merit repeating since their validity has been borne out in the course of nearly two more decades of comparative work:

In order to study crime comparatively three conditions need to be met. There must be sources of material and data with which to make comparisons: crime statistics, victim surveys, research studies. Second, translatable concepts have to be available to make possible the collecting, ordering and analysis of such data. Finally, some kind of framework, part universe of discourse, part set of common concerns, must exist (Heidensohn 1991: 10).

The scarcely hidden agenda item in *Crime in Europe* and in most of the succeeding work on these topics is, of course, the American dimension. All of us involved in this enterprise were aware that British-based criminologists usually made their comparisons with the USA. The reasons for this are fairly clear: we all speak English, have values based on the same broad principles, and there has long been a transatlantic trade in criminal justice policies. Early forms of US law enforcement, for instance, owe much to the early modern English 'watch' while the introduction of the 'New Police' in London, was with modifications, deliberately emulated in US cities such as New York (Miller 1977). To this day, American police officers usually wear blue uniforms, as do the British, a styling introduced by Robert Peel to distinguish them from the military 'redcoats' of the early nineteenth century. More serious parallels can be found in the later twentieth century trends where British police appear to be following US directions (McKenzie and Gallagher 1989: 175). Most comparative classifying systems developed to analyse policing globally place Britain and the USA under a single heading; indeed they are often labelled as 'Anglo-American policing' or even, by Bayley 'Anglo-Saxon' policing (Bayley 1982). When I undertook an international study of policing of my own, I chose to look at these two nations because

(I)n their institutions of law enforcement Britain and the USA provide an invaluable example of a ready-made comparative research situation and a device for exploring the considerable range of possibilities which can stem from one plant grown in different climates and conditions (Heidensohn 1992: 41).

In undertaking this project, I was very much aware of the formidable army of scholars who had made comparative studies of policing into a significant sub-branch of studies of criminal justice. There was already such a range that by 1990, Mawby could classify them into

three main areas of work which we can label as international comparative analysis: overall comparisons of two or more countries; a focus of policing in one specific country; and a comparison of particular issues related to policing in two or more countries (Mawby 1990: 6).

Scholars such as Bayley (1985) had produced magisterial accounts, taking the USA as a measuring stick, of policing across the world. My own book fell into the third of Mawby's categories and I was interested in carrying out a study of women's role in law enforcement in the two nations, a form of enquiry never previously undertaken. It was an ambitious project. Some of the requirements listed above were in place—I used the 'translatable' concepts of policing and social control to introduce my study. The integration of women into mainstream policing had been enforced in both systems in the previous decade, following equality legislation, and this had resulted in evaluative studies of their new role, extensive in the USA, more limited in Britain, but at least meeting the basic need for some data and research findings (Heidensohn 1992: ch. 3). Nevertheless, during the USA-based part of the project, I had to collect data and reports locally from police departments since this was not published nationally (Heidensohn 1989). The study also involved interviews with fifty female serving (or recently retired) officers and gaining access to these subjects involved a 'snowball' sampling technique of personal contact (a much more difficult procedure in an era before the arrival of email). All the interviews in the USA were arranged before I arrived there and I relied greatly on the support and co-operation of my interviewees (Heidensohn 1992: 250–6). It is worth noting here some of the ways in which the participants themselves influenced this study. While I interviewed each one separately and taped each interview, they themselves set up group discussions in several of the cities I visited so that many of the topics of the project became the themes of focus groups: harassment by male officers, training and deployment, and the formidable issues of race and ethnicity were all debated and these debates shaped my awareness and thinking. These officers arranged for me to go on patrol with them and to observe other law enforcement situations. Above all, as I have noted elsewhere, they knew themselves to be 'interesting' and were interested in themselves (Heidensohn 1994). Moreover, they too made comparisons about their British counterparts—their being unarmed, wearing uniforms which were not the same as their male colleagues'. What I endeavoured to do in this project was to achieve a double case study—to examine British and US experience equally and to this end, developing a set of concepts which I used to frame the analysis of both (Heidensohn 1992: 118) and was to use in another international study a decade later.

There are many comparisons which make use of the possibilities of the Anglophone model. A notable twenty-first-century one is Garland's (2001) *Culture of Control* in which he employs a range of evidence from research and from documentation to put forward a complex argument about the ways transformations in society in the USA and Britain have led to a punitive turn in criminal justice policies. Such a formidably scholarly work does not fit easily into a comparative paradigm and indeed Garland has been criticized for exaggerating the resemblances between the two nations and minimizing American exceptionalism—its use of the death penalty, for instance. As Young puts it 'the use of the comparative method in ways which highlight similarities and repress differences fails to pick up on the very particular structural and criminogenic attributes of the United States when compared to the majority of advanced industrial countries' (Young 2003: 240). Ironically, however, Pakes points out that the Netherlands, once a beacon of humane policies in Downes *Contrasts*, has become in the twenty-first century a punitive, far less tolerant society and one that does now fit Garland's 'crime complex' model (Pakes 2004a: 284). Indeed, as King and Resodihardjo (2007) argue, the process of Americanization has in some respects gone further in the Netherlands where a supermax model has been adopted than in Britain where it has been rejected.

Transatlantic trade in this area has come to mean more than merely case study comparison. Another new genre of study, known as 'policy transfer', has been developed which largely examines the global spread of American crime control policies. In presenting a series of case studies which cover the USA, Australia, South Africa, Canada, and Europe, Newburn and Sparks seek to step away from the 'shared experience' model of Garland (Newburn and Sparks 2004: 11). Yet they assert that their book is concerned 'with the apparent influence that the culture of control that has emerged in the USA has exercised in other parts of the world ... [that] has made the States ... the penal workshop of the world' (2004: 9). Elsewhere, Newburn has put forward seven elements that he sees as underpinning policy transfers from the USA to Britain, most of them either political or cultural (Newburn 2000: 12–23).

Case studies are a powerful form of comparison. They can attract the politician and the policymaker as well as the researcher. Some of the most interesting are based on archival studies and historical analysis. Whitman, for instance, uses French and German sources to argue, from a historical sociological perspective, that harsh punishment in America (and Britain) is related to a 'levelling down' of the treatment of offenders in America, in contrast to a generalizing of high-status treatment to all in continental Europe (Whitman 2003: 10–11). Whitman's arguments are pitted firmly against those of the theorists of late modernity and underline the importance, also stressed by Newburn and Sparks (2004) and especially by Nelken (2002), of the importance of studying local histories and cultures very specifically in comparative work.

Most of these examples are taken from studies by established scholars. It is vital to stress, however, that notable projects have also been achieved by postgraduate researchers and I want to highlight a few of these before summing up the advantages of this type of comparative work.

Lisa Maher's award-winning book (1997) about her research on crack cocaine users in Brooklyn is a remarkable piece in a number of ways. First, she was a female, Australian student undertaking participant observation of a volatile, dangerous situation on the streets of Brooklyn. In addition, for part of the period of the study, she was pregnant with twins. Notwithstanding the risks and problems she encountered, she produced a nuanced study of gender, race, and resistance in this drug market. Her perspective as an Australian outsider clearly added a special dimension to this intense and intensive study. Another Australian, Sharon Pickering, also explored a difficult and hard-to-reach group: that of women on both sides of the sectarian divide in Northern Ireland who had experienced policing during the troubles. Again, an outsider's perspective enabled her to make connections within a divided community and to produce a study which contributes to the comparative literature (Pickering 2000).

More recently, two British-based researchers have looked at innovative prison regimes for women in other jurisdictions (Hayman 2006; Mason 2006). Where the two Australians had concepts about gender and agency, and women's relationship to social control to apply to their findings, Hayman and Mason explore theirs within another gendered framework. They examine prisons for women in Canada and Ireland respectively in the light of much past research which suggests that, however well-intentioned, experimental penal programmes for females always fare badly: they lead to net-widening and they fail to meet the aims of the regime. Whereas Hayman finds that the Canadian experience did more than fulfil such pessimistic expectations, Mason's conclusions about the Duchas Centre in Dublin contradict them. She found that it did meet its founders' aims and was not more oppressive. Both of these projects involved a series of research visits, rather than the participant observation, community basis of the first two. Two further studies by British students were based on participant observation. Piacentini (2004) conducted her prize-winning work in Russian corrective labour colonies and McGunigall-Smith (2005) carried out her case study on Death Row in Utah. All of these show what can be achieved by comparative researchers at a postgraduate level.

Case studies, as I have outlined them here, have many merits. They allow for in-depth coverage of issues such as imprisonment or policing. They can uncover multiple layers of meaning and subtlety, although Nelken, a proponent of such approaches, seems to advocate living in the country to be studied in order to tease these out properly (Nelken 2002).

Lacey and Zedner (1995, 1998) have very effectively shown how their participation in an Anglo-German comparative study revealed how very different was the meaning of 'community' in crime prevention discourse in the two countries. Cain illustrates the same problem in a study of the sociology of crime in the Caribbean, where assumptions about 'the sameness of key cultural categories … [lead to] a constant misdiagnosis of problems' such as domestic violence' (Cain 2000: 239).

Sometimes, the work of the comparative researcher highlights or refocuses problems in a more positive way. Downes found that the Dutch had not perceived themselves as quite such a powerful model when he studied their penal system; nor had they developed their own explanations of their system and its success at the time. Pakes (2004a: 284) notes that Downes' work led to the beacon status for the enlightened treatment of wrongdoers which the Dutch later acquired (and have more recently lost). Rock (1986) reports on the striking difference between the rise of the victim support movement in

England —from the penal reform grassroots, and based on research and welfare concerns, in contrast with Canada where a top-down model was introduced from the centre.

Case studies can provide the answers to a range of policy questions, although where they have a small empirical basis there may be questions about their generalizability. They can be used to explore institutional and historical issues in ways which multistudies cannot. While some demand considerable resources, others can be achieved by sole researchers with modest support. Most case studies use a mixed repertoire of methods—observation and participation, interviews as well as archives and media sources. They also rely on at least some forms of 'hard' data from criminal statistics, surveys, and other information systems. This balance of qualitative and quantitative methods can provide triangulation and validation and, of course, enables the apprentice researcher to develop and hone his/her range of methodological skills.

Multi-studies

When van Dijk and his colleagues introduced their report on the first International Crime Survey (now known as the International Crime Victims Survey) their excitement and confidence in their achievement was palpable:

There has long been a need for comparable information about levels of crime and patterns of criminal victimisation in different countries. Researchers have principally wanted to test theories about the social causes of crime by means of cross-national comparisons. Policymakers have principally wanted to understand better their national crime problems by putting these into international perspective (van Dijk *et al.* 1990: 3).

They were announcing what they felt was a major breakthrough for their field. The ICVS was, and is, a sample survey of countries, asking questions about the respondents' experiences of crime. Fourteen countries took part in the first survey, by the time of the fourth in 2000, this had been extended to twenty-four industrial nations and forty-six cities in developing countries and countries in transition (Mayhew 2004: 60 and see also Mayhew in the first edition and this volume for health warnings about international surveys) with a 2004–5 survey in the European Union. There are several significant points to be made about the ICVS and its relationship to comparative work. First, the authors clearly hail it as a breakthrough because

it used tightly standardised methods . . . (thus) . . . the survey provides a measure of the level of crime in different countries that is independent of the conventional one of offences recorded by the police. The police measure has well-known limitations for comparative purposes as it is based only on those crimes . . . reported to the police by victims, and which are recorded by police (van Dijk *et al.* 1990: 1).

In other words, although the term 'victimization' was in its title, this particular instrument extended to the international stage the use of the victim survey already in established use in the USA, the UK, and elsewhere. As the originators of such studies have always made clear, their aim was the improvement of measurement and of accuracy in the recording of crime. Serendipitously, the concepts of the fear of crime, and the sociology of victimhood have also been derived from the first findings of the early surveys.

While nothing quite like the ICVS, and especially not its subsequent sweeps, which can provide time series, had ever been achieved before, there had, as Mayhew, one of the founders of the survey and joint author of the report makes clear, been several previous attempts at administering standardized questionnaires using various samples (Mayhew 2004: 59). Although the questionnaire was standardized, it was then translated into the relevant languages and then administered via a computer-assisted telephone interview, except in one or two countries, such as Northern Ireland, where this was done face to face. With samples of about 2,000 for each country, response rates were 'rather low', an average of 41 per cent, though reaching 60 per cent in places. This can mean that such a small sample size is 'too small for adequate coverage of serious crimes' (the British Crime Survey, in contrast, now has a sample size of 50,000). Mayhew (2004) argues firmly that there is not a serious problem of definitions of crime in this instrument that may hamper the accuracy of the study. Certainly, the data are widely used, though largely by what I have called elsewhere (Heidensohn 2006a) the 'comparative bureaucrats'. By this term I mean the growing army of those who administer international organizations and make their policies; it is from them that the pressure for collecting and compiling these data comes. It is largely they who have denounced the other types of available international data such as the *European Sourcebook of Crime and Criminal Justice Statistics*, and Interpol.

In 1992, UNICRI (the UN Interregional Criminal Justice Research Institute) became involved with the survey, and it was then expanded to non-western nations. Ironically, the European Commission, which had no interest in, nor capacity to fund, anything to do with crime and criminal justice in the 1980s, is providing funds for another sweep of the EU nations.

Despite the confidence and bright tones of the authors of the report on the first ICVS round, there are critics who have sought to get more comparable and more robust data. Tonry and Farrington (2005) did just this with what they describe as their 'template' sent to the contributors to their volume on crime and punishment in western countries between 1980 and 1999. They set out their requirements in great detail, down to the formula respondents should use to 'estimate the probability of police recording a reported offence' (Tonry and Farrington 2005: 35). The template is complex, demanding, and somewhat unwieldy. It was administered in eight selected countries. Where it has clear advantages over the ICVS or other measures is in its in-depth coverage of criminal justice matters which lie beyond the scope of victim surveys—in conviction rates, police recording, or sentence lengths, for example. As the authors observe, 'the individual country analyses address the . . . key questions that any theory of crime or criminal justice should be able to explain'. Nevertheless there were still 'problems of comparability. The most important concern crime definitions victim surveys, and time served' (Tonry and Farrington 2005: 9).

These studies seem sometimes to be pursuing a holy grail that we were all taught long ago to be sceptical of: the perfect, accurate measure of crime, and in the case of cross-cultural comparisons, the precise measure which can be applied across the board to crimes around the world. But there are surely serious problems of positivistic oversimplification going on here? A further issue is that the standardized measure may not catch the interesting, complex facets of the crime problem.

Mayhew is correct in noting that global surveys of crime were patchy and infrequent, but still around, at least as an idea and for an experiment in the 1970s and 1980s. In fact, enquiries involving one or two researchers, whom I refer to as *explorers*, looking at a problem in several countries yet using the same measures, have a long pedigree. At the very beginning of the twentieth century, a Dutch Ph.D. student undertook a systematic survey, commissioned by the National Women's Council of the Netherlands, on the role of women in the police at that time. She designed a proper questionnaire, sent it to all the cities in the German-speaking world where she knew female officers were employed. Later she visited ten of these cities to collect more data. Her findings were presented in a spreadsheet format and she derived 'general principles' from her work and eventually had it published in German (Beaujon 1911).

On a related topic, the League of Nations formed many committees and subcommittees during its short lifespan. One of its most prominent was concerned with trafficking in women and children. They regularly sent out questionnaires to police authorities on these topics, but in 1930, several members actually embarked on a fact-finding voyage around the cities of the Far East (see Heidensohn 2000 for an account).

Not all those who seek data or information for comparative purposes through what I have called a multi-study, are engaged in pursuing ever more rigorous measures of trends. For some, a questionnaire or other technique may be a helpful way of collecting information. I have been involved in two such, very different projects and will outline how they developed and what their outcomes were.

In the first, *International Perspectives*, Nicky Rafter and I wanted to explore what impact, if any, feminism had had on criminology in a range of countries. We had met at the first international congress on women, law, and social control held in Canada in 1991. This event had shown us that there was a considerable network of female scholars around the globe, involved in some way with criminology. We were interested in their experiences as feminists and we asked them to tell us what these meant to them. We described it 'as an act of documentation, an effort to show where, after twenty-five years, feminism has carried the criminological enterprise' (Hahn Rafter and Heidensohn 1995: 1) It was not difficult to elicit these replies, since we knew our contributors already and knew them to have stories to tell and analyses to offer. However, we failed utterly to persuade anyone from Africa or Asia to contribute (1995: 11) and I will say more about the 'colonial' problem below. We set out some clear and direct questions for everyone and sometimes pressed for further information.

We were looking at the impact of feminism on academic criminology, but some respondents suggested that, while they understood the question, one or other had not had much of an existence in their country at the time. Thus Platek (1995) described Poland, a society in transition from communism, where everyone, including herself, was too busy with revolution to think about women. The issues in the research for *International Perspectives* revolved mainly around translation in its broader sense, especially as our approach left our respondents free to answer in ways of their own choice. It was not difficult, however, to check some of the stories and compare them with other information.

My second encounter with the single template multi-study was very different. In the late 1990s, Jennifer Brown and I carried out a study of gender and policing in comparative perspective. We were very concerned to achieve as wide a sample of officers to study as we could, and given my previous experience of not finding non-westerners to take part, doing so this time was very important. We devised two instruments. First was a questionnaire (available in English and French) which asked for routine demographic and career data, but also material on harassment and discrimination. We distributed it to serving officers via various routes and achieved 800 + responses. The second instrument was an interview schedule which probed more fully and in greater depth the women's careers and experiences. Both instruments were piloted at international policing conferences. An important aside to note about this experience was how extensively we used a series of such conferences, in settings around the world, to develop and administer these research protocols. This was an enormously valuable and cost-effective technique. We then made use of an international police conference to gain access to more officers in order to add depth to our sample. This yielded forty-seven respondents from nineteen countries (Brown and Heidensohn 2000: 172). One of the vital aspects of this was, by using the conference as our basis, we obtained interviews with officers from several African countries. I have written elsewhere about using a conference as a site for gaining access to elusive groups (Heidensohn 2000).

One of the most complex and sophisticated recent multistudies is by Cavadino and Dignan (2006). With a very different orientation from Tonry and Farrington, they too seem to have sent a kind of template to fellow authors in twelve nations—i.e. six questionnaires with queries about the penal system. They then wrote the chapters themselves, although they did allow their 'associates' to comment on what they had written. *Penal Systems* is also very different since it is heavily informed by Marxist theories.

Although multistudies are not well adapted to deal with institutional and historical contexts, they can do most of the same things that case studies can. They also are able to provide what is perceived as 'hard' data, and thus especially pleasing to policymakers who still ask for 'facts' or evidence. They may be able, as Tonry and Farrington suggest, to refine problems and measures with the rigour they bring to the process of gathering material. All of these measures are costly and time-consuming, although the ones with which I was involved were much less so.

As I observed above, what I have termed the 'colonial' problem is not easily solved here. Neither Tonry and Farrington nor Cavadino and Dignan had respondents from any non-western country, unless one counts South Africa. It is not just these studies that fail in this matter; case studies can also leave these gaps. This can be through acts of omission—no one from Africa was asked—but sometimes citizens from nations with a colonial past simply do not see the point of criminological research, let alone its comparative variant, or else they wish to make a statement about how badly they believe their ancestors were treated by the old regime. Some writers in the comparative field are now challenging the dominant perspective and arguing that criminology is 'a social science that served colonialism more directly than many other social sciences' (Agozino 2003: 18).

The problems associated with large-scale, international studies are broadly the same as those found in single-country studies—of definitions, legislative changes, dark figures, and the like. Attempts such as those outlined above, to standardize as many aspects of measurement as possible, have strong advocates and have received growing political and financial support. But there are also significant criticisms of these approaches. The ICVS is, generally, a telephone-based interview survey, with all the limitations involved in interviewee/interviewer interaction; the response rates vary, though some are quite low and clearly some of the groups most highly vulnerable to victimization (such as the homeless) do not have telephones.

Even their firmest supporters acknowledge the complexities in setting up and running such surveys and of owning and managing their results. As Mayhew points out, international league tables of crime rates are highly political matters.

More fundamental criticisms come from those who are sceptical about all attempts to compare crime and criminal justice in this way. Beirne (1983: 7: 371–91), for instance, argues that it is reasonable to compare *trends* in different countries: is crime falling everywhere?, but not actual figures. Nelken (1994) has repeatedly put forward the notion that proper comparison is only possible between two, or possibly three, different countries. His is one of many voices which challenge the positivism of such projects. He sees crime data as socially constructed materials which are not 'facts' in any true sense, but rather reflect administrative, political, and other choices. Juvenile crime, he points out, is a major public policy issue in Britain, but hardly at all in Italy. Such critics advocate that the *social control* and *law enforcement* processes should be the focus of research. Indeed, such studies have become another subgenre of the field in the late twentieth century. For instance, Hebenton and Thomas' (1995) *Policing Europe* is an account of developments at the European level, while Deflem's *Policing World Society* (2002) analyses the history of international police cooperation. Strictly speaking, these texts, and the numerous works on cross-border policing, etc., are not *comparative* as such, but rather international in the sense that they are looking at crime and criminal justice at a supranational level. Nonetheless, comparisons are sometimes included and Deflem looks at the USA and Germany in particular in his book.

One of the major advantages of multi-studies is that they generate material in considerable quantities which can provide a basis or background for other researchers. The ICVS as well as national victim and other surveys are available to researchers who can thus learn both from their design as well as their results. In addition to surveys with global reach, many other bodies now collect data and compile it in forms which researchers can use easily. The Council of Europe collects figures on prosecutions, convictions, and prisons and publishes them in sourcebooks (Council of Europe 1999, 2003). They use advisors in each of the forty nations to select their material; hence, as in so many cases, an international source is a summing of the national figures and reports and will, inevitably, replicate any flaws or problems with these. The United Nations has produced regular surveys on crime trends and criminal justice for over three decades. Mayhew notes that 'health warnings' on these surveys 'are still substantial ... As with the Sourcebook the UN survey figures on prosecutions, convictions and sentencing are especially problematic for comparative analyses because system differences mean like is usually far from like' (Mayhew 2004: 66). Despite these caveats, Mayhew encourages newcomers to the field and proposes that they use the many existing sources for secondary analysis.

Methodological and theoretical issues in comparative work

Almost all the methodological issues encountered in comparative criminological work can also be found in other kinds of criminological enquiry, or have long been listed in the guides to comparative method in other fields. Problems of definition and ensuring equivalence are common to any study of crime within, as well as between, countries. International studies, however, increase one of the commonest queries in such endeavours: how do we define and measure crime? Indeed, since they are for the most part based on looking at sets of national figures, or on data aggregated from such sources, this must be so (Westfelt and Estrada 2005). The exceptions to this generalization are sources such as the International Crime Victim Surveys discussed above, which use a single instrument, modified and translated for each state or city, to produce their data.

All these approaches invite the challenge that they are part of a project of criminological construction, which may well be questioned by those who would highlight environmental, rather than personal crime, as the ICVS does, or introduce cultural variance (see Sheptycki 2005 for an extensive discussion on this). As we have seen, some of the scholars whose work was described above seek to refine templates and instruments still further in order to achieve greater rigour and achieve standardized 'crime and punishment data' (Tonry and Farrington 2005: 3).

Yet in every sense, such attempts are likely to be both taxing and still produce flawed results and, almost literally, to be 'lost in translation'.

Indeed, where the nation, system or issue to be studied is in another language, this raises a range of distinctive issues. There is the simple matter of translating documents, or interpreting interviews or observations. More profound and more subtle are all the questions to do with deeper and hidden meanings, which only a native speaker can understand. Melossi has argued that

in the field of the sociology of punishment ... the problem of comparison is first and foremost a problem of translation. 'Translation', however, strictly speaking is impossible. Conversation between different cultures is possible, but not translation from one to another ... (Melossi 2004: 80).

He does not here elaborate on such a stark statement, which itself is ironic since he is an Italian-speaking academic writing in English. Translation, at least of a kind, is nevertheless possible; it is interpretation which is the more fraught business. Downes' view of Dutch tolerance, for instance, was challenged as a partial version by Franke (1990). King (2004) abandoned his attempt to research the Russian prison system, either directly (King 1994) or with Russian colleagues (King and Mikhlin 2000) because of the difficulty of working through interpreters. He did, however, persuade his research student Laura Piacentini to learn Russian before arranging for her to have initial access to the gulag and to continue the enterprise (King and Piacentini 2005.) Piacentini's reporting and analysis of prison conditions in Russia (Piacentini 2004) is a tour de force both as a triumph of access, but also of the acquisition and application of language skills by a young scholar.

I would not be either as cautious or pessimistic as Melossi, or his colleague Nelken. Melossi in any case goes on to cite Schutz's description of the stranger's experience when

not only the picture which the stranger has brought along of the cultural pattern of the approached group but the whole hitherto unquestioned scheme of interpretation current within the home group becomes invalidated. It cannot be used as a scheme of orientation within the new social group.

Melossi interprets Schutz's essay as representing 'a radical critique of social scientists' imperialism vis-à-vis the rights of the standpoint of society's ordinary members'

(Melossi 2004: 81). But this is only one interpretation of Schutz. Downes, for instance, takes a much more positive and encouraging message from Schutz which he sees as

a directive for sociological travel. The stranger may be vouchsafed confidences withheld from fellow-members of the hoist community ... to be a foreigner may confer certain privileges, in particular a licence to naïveté. In short, there is an affinity between the role of stranger and comparative sociology (Downes 1988: 2–3).

Schutz himself was also less extreme, seeing the stranger's need is 'to acquire full knowledge of the elements of the approached cultural pattern and to examine what seems self-explanatory to the group' (Schutz 1966: II, 104).

Schutz was an extraordinary example of someone who, in his own life and career, overcame the problems of translation. He left Austria with his family after the *Anschluss* and went into exile in the USA. There in New York he pursued both a career as a successful banker and held a post as a part-time researcher at the New School of Social Research. (The problem of translation and interpretation is not just confined to explicitly comparative work—see Eisner and Parmar, **Chapter 6** of this volume on researching crime in situations of cultural diversity.)

Which role will you take?

In another essay on the development of comparative methodology, I have proposed a taxonomy of nine different categories of comparative criminologist as a device to simplify the study of the subject by starting with those who do this work and the positions they take. There I argued that 'in some senses, all comparative scholars are strangers when they embark on the study of other cultures or systems' (Heidensohn 2006a: 184). The role of refugees such as Schutz, and the other three Europeans discussed above, is very significant and symbolic. All, except Radzinowicz, arrived in their new countries unwillingly and all as middle-aged men, yet they did learn English, researched and wrote in it, and made major contributions in their fields. An adapted version of the taxonomy is reproduced in Table 7.1.

Nelken has argued that 'most texts on comparative criminology say very little about the actual process of doing cross-cultural research'. He then presents three kinds of

Table 7.1 A taxonomy of comparative criminologists

Strangers	Armchair travellers
* refugees	* bureaucrats
* rendezvous-ers	* global theorists
* travellers	
* explorers	
* reformers	

(adapted from Heidensohn 2006a)

possible research strategy to be adopted: 'virtually there, researching there or living there' (Nelken 2002: 181). It is manifest that he practises and preaches the last of these, although he is not himself an Italian. For those embarking on comparative work, the model set out in Figure 7.1 (devised to provide a heuristic device to distinguish and categorize different types of approach to cross-national work and their pluses and minuses) suggests that there are two main options to take: the role of 'stranger' or of 'armchair traveller', each with its own subcategories, and, of course, with the possibilities of further development. In this taxonomy, I propose five main groups of 'strangers', that is, those who visit the country or countries they have chosen to study. They are refugees, rendezvous-ers, travellers, explorers, or reformers. Refugees are clearly like those mentioned above, who came from the Third Reich and whose impact on our subject was profound. They can appear at any time and their status may, as the examples of Mannheim or Radzinowicz illustrate, bring exceptional insight to their research, but it is not a position which one can select and, as was true for some of these scholars, it can bring huge problems.

Rendezvous-ers is a name invented by David Downes, for those who only make a brief sojourn in the world of criminology, even if by doing so they enhance it. The term has a particular resonance for comparative research, since some scholars have made occasional ventures abroad to pursue their enquiries, but this is, and arguably should be, a declining trend. As Zimring and Johnson point out, 'American criminology has been provincial' (2005: 794); they urge their compatriots to undertake much more cross-national research because '(i)t is an essential device for understanding what is distinctive (and problematic) about domestic arrangements ... it may be a special necessity to promote and illustrate *the domestic values of comparative methods* in the United States' (2005: 794 emphasis added). These authors are pleading for a serious international dimension to all major projects. The rendezvous category is a reminder of what may happen when a comparative study is treated by locals as showing too limited a knowledge or understanding of their country or its culture, as Killias (1991) did with Clinard's view of Switzerland. It is a charge which can easily be made and beginners in the field need to address how to refute it.

Reformers are another specific and restricted category, whose role has been noted above. It is again, not the primary role which a researcher should aim to undertake. To quote a personal example, when I studied the careers and experiences of women in law enforcement in the USA in 1988, I received some funding for the project from the Police Foundation. It was assumed by the Foundation that the position of female officers in the States would be very much more advanced than in the UK and that there would be important lessons to be learned. In fact, while there was enormous confidence in their superiority among US police deptartments, and some did have reasonably good records of recruitment and of equality policies, Britain compared favourably on a number of measures (Heidensohn 1989 and 1992), a difference which has continued until the present (Heidensohn 2003).

These categories are all variations on the stranger model, but the two most important variants of this are travellers and explorers determined by how long they spend in their place(s) of comparative study, how deeply they engage with the local languages and cultures, and so on. Reformers, too, such as Howard and Fry mentioned above, were strangers whose commitment to comparison arose from their moral perspectives. Each category involves varied levels of reliance on local experts and interpreters (Heidensohn

2006: 186–7). Travellers are likely to cover more countries, as in King's range of studies of penal policy in various contrasting settings(see above) while explorers look in depth at one place, perhaps contrasted with their home country, as with Downes' work. Common to them all is an assumption that the translation problem, whether of language or of culture or legal system, can be solved, with local help, interpreters, and translators. The arguments have been put very clearly in a recent introduction to a set of comparative case studies on the history of crime:

Underpinning all categories of comparative approach is the belief that researchers can disaggregate, interrogate and theorise a culture that is not their own. No social scientific research would be possible if we could not understand 'the other' to some extent ... but this issue is a more explicit one for comparative researchers. It reduces to a set of interlinking beliefs in effect:

- That the cultural world in which the researcher was socialised is not a straitjacket which forever inhibits comprehension of other cultures ...

- That universal phenomena exist but are conditioned by specific contextual and local factors

- That cultural shifts can create new realities

With these beliefs in mind, it seems clear that comparability is possible, indeed desirable, and that by adopting appropriate methodologies, we can begin to understand 'the other' (Godfrey *et al.* 2003: 2–4).

These categories can be applied in many other ways to those in which comparative scholars achieve their tasks. For instance, we can ask why the particular study is being done, to what theoretical development will its findings contribute? (Morrison 2003: 202). Most strangers in all groups will want to send or take some kind of message 'home', but the refugees considered above could not do so. Their homes, and often families and friends too, had gone forever; hence maybe their determination to adjust and engage with their new cultures.

The stranger role enacted by researchers involved in cross-cultural work has its parallels in other kinds of social enquiry. W. F. Whyte (1943), for example, in his classic account of how he studied the Italian neighbourhood of Boston depicted in his *Street Corner Society*, is very honest about his distance and strangeness as an upper-class WASP from the working-class community in which he sought to integrate and understand. There are some distinctive features, nevertheless. *All* comparative work will involve a conscious choice of a stranger role, or certainly all which require empirical work and travel to another country, although we are increasingly approaching the era of 'virtual' research.

As I suggested above, most commentators agree that the problems and issues encountered in this realm of research resemble those of criminology in general: definition, measurement, dark figures, and icebergs. Other problems, such as access, an especial problem for criminal justice organizations, are the same; indeed, Downes gained access to Dutch prisons, as did King, more easily to Russian and American prisons than either did to English ones. In my study of female police officers, I found American women both more willing to be interviewed and less constrained by their departments than their British counterparts. Sometimes strangers are less visible, or less threatening. It is perhaps worth noting that, notwithstanding their greater openness, the USA officers were more puzzled by me and how to make sense of what I was doing there and why. Their British colleagues on the other hand were easily able to 'place' me as a middle-class academic and not think that I might be a serving or former police officer, a common misperception in the USA (Heidensohn 1992: 252). But of course, criminologists always need a study to explain why they are there. One of the notable features of the modern global research village is that it is very easy to find the organizations, library resources, activists, or policymakers who are involved with or even guard the institution or population you wish to study. When I prepared a paper for the Tenth UN Congress on Crime and Crime Prevention in 2000, I carried out almost all the research for it (it was on gender, justice, and trans-national crime) via web sites (Heidensohn 2001). There are some older sources which stress that comparative work requires major reshaping of disciplines and theories (e.g. Beirne 1983), but many more agree that 'cross-cultural analyses do not merit the creation of new methodologies nor require any special methodological consideration' (Morrison 2003: 202).

If criminology remained 'strikingly incomparative' (Downes 1988: 2) for many years, that was not true, as Downes himself observed, of the other social sciences, especially anthropology. Anyone embarking on a comparative study should give some attention to the very long and well-developed traditions of comparisons in the other social sciences and the debates related to them. Reviewing this history, which reaches right back to the origins of the disciplines, can be salutary. It reminds us of how central comparative method has been seen to be to social enquiry. Auguste Comte himself, the founding father of sociology, insisted 'that all living things must be studied using the comparative method; the higher the organism in the hierarchy of living things, the more important comparative method becomes' (Restivo 1991: 27). Philosophers, too, emphasized its importance; Evans-Pritchard, a distinguished anthropologist, credits Comte and Hume as the progenitors of comparative method and supports their belief in its value 'we must be satisfied with collecting the facts and circumstances as they may be gathered from the laws of different countries: and these put together (may) make a regular system of causes and effects (Evans-Pritchard 1963: 24).

John Stuart Mill also contributed to the debate with his essay on the logic of compari-sons and the criteria by which case studies should be selected (Mill 1888), themes taken up nearly a century later by Smelser (1976). No one is more confident in their advocacy of the method, even when it had been relatively neglected in favour of intensive field studies, than social anthropologists. More than fifty years ago, Radcliffe Brown asserted that 'in comparative sociology or social anthropology the purpose of comparison is . . . to explore the varieties of forms of social life as a basis for the theoretical study of human social phenomena' (1951: 15). He goes on to name this method as that 'of those who have been called "armchair anthropologists" since they work in libraries' (1951: 15) and to insist that such an approach, which will lead to theoretical conjecture, must be combined 'with intensive studies of particular primitive societies' (sic).

The other main group of my types of comparative researcher is 'armchair travellers' and is intended to match this group and reflect an established tradition. 'Since at least the time of Durkheim, armchair travellers have studied problems of crime and deviance cross-culturally without ever leaving their studies or their libraries' (Heidensohn 2006: 189–90). Such approaches can make some commentators shudder at their superficiality and failure to give the full depth and richness of a culture (Nelken 1994: 225). Yet the same author also deplores attempts to build a culture-free theory of crime (1994: 224).

We have already seen above that a number of international victim studies were carried out in the later twentieth century and that their origins lay in the desire of the bureaucrats of both national governments and international organizations, such as the United Nations and the Council of Europe, to improve the standards of crime figures and to ensure the possibilities of comparisons. As I suggested above, such activities require serious funding resources, but some novice comparativists do start their careers with such work, and their scope will inevitably grow with the blossoming of so many transnational and international initiatives, from the Channel Tunnel to the monitoring of trafficking and of terrorism. Globalization, the growth of transnational crime, and the rise of numerous bodies whose tasks are to confront such developments, all ensure that more and more researchers will desert their armchairs. Nevertheless, while international travel by academics is increasing, there is another subgroup, whom I christened 'global theorists', who have written extensively about what they see as worldwide trends towards penal punitiveness and the regulatory state (see, e.g., most of the articles in the *British Journal of Criminology* 40(2) (2000). Most of these theorists are clearly seeking to demonstrate their theories rather than starting from any local cultural or empirical basis. Indeed, their descriptions of regulation are often hauntingly anomic: no stroppy citizens or ingenious delinquents populate these dystopias: regulation and repression always work and are never opposed or resisted.

Comparative method has a long history in social research in other fields and is seen as critical to every type of enquiry from the most positivistic search for 'equivalence' in social facts to much more speculative endeavours. The puzzle is why criminology remained so aloof from such endeavours for so long and why, when there has been a relative explosion of interest in the field, criminologists can still lack awareness of its place in the comparative tradition.

There are, nevertheless, amongst some of the studies cited in this chapter, real signs of interest in much greater rigour in comparative analysis. Of particular note are those which address some of the classic themes of cross-cultural work and acknowledge its philosophical roots, but then move into newer dimensions and methods. A telling example comes from the work of the European Governance of Public Safety Research Network (EUGPSRN), which published five papers in *Theoretical Criminology* in 2005 (9(3) 2005). In the last of these, Edwards and Hughes consider the predominant traditions of comparative criminology, which they typify as seeking either universality or uniqueness and contrast these with their preferred method of what they term 'critical realism' (Edwards and Hughes 2005).

That all social research must be informed with a theory of some kind is the most basic of truisms. In practice, much comparative work on crime and criminal justice has drawn on concepts of convergence and divergence. In *Crime in Europe*, for example, I discussed the observed 'congruence between recorded crime rates in the major west European nations' and the reasons for the additional similarity in 'definitions of what constitutes crime problems and issues between nation-states in Europe' and suggested three possible reasons for this: 'the *internationalising* of certain crimes ... terrorism, drug offences. Second *common social influences* ... (the) "global village". Finally ... the *diffusion of new discovery*, especially of a new crime agenda' (Heidensohn 1991: 7–8). Responses to crime were, however, much more diverse (1991: 9). Concepts of convergence between western nation states are, of course, derived from the vast literature which has analysed welfare systems in cross-national perspectives, including arguments about how common and convergent their forms are (e.g. Wilensky 1975 and see Kennett 2001 ch. 3 for a summary). More recent studies suggest that convergence in criminal justice systems is now more likely, given the globalizing tendencies of today. A further argument is put forward by Fairchild and Dammer (2001), who suggest that modern criminal justice systems may be altered by a combination of pressures both to converge and to diverge.

Students of comparative criminal justice policy have, on the whole, been far less willing to employ models to analyse different types of regime and to theorize the ways in which they have developed than their colleagues in social policy. This is particularly remarkable as, in a classic study published before the Second World War, Rusche and Kirchheimer (1939) did develop a theory of the relationship between criminal justice and penal systems on the one hand and political economy on the other. Cavadino and Dignan's formidable analysis of the penal systems of twelve nations mentioned above follows on in some ways from Rusche and Kirchheimer, but they employ a series of four types of state and of approaches to punishment as well as theories about the relationship between these and the political and economic systems of the twelve nations they study (Cavadino and Dignan 2006: ch. 1). They acknowledge the origins of some of their frameworks and concepts in the social policy literature. They also engage with debates about modernization and its impact on penality, in which they follow Garland's lead (2001: 8). Garland's conceptualization of the punitive turn, and the decline of the ideal of rehabilitation is another key theoretical perspective which has had recent resonance in the field.

One sub-branch of the subject where paradigms and classificatory models are popular and widely used is police and policing. The literature on comparative studies of police and policing is crowded with examples. Thus Bayley has suggested a threefold typology, of 'authoritarian, oriental and Anglo-Saxon' cited in (Brewer *et al.* 1996: 227) and these were later used by Mawby in his research (1990) and see Brown and Heidensohn (2000: 28–34) for a discussion of the value and application of comparative taxonomies. In fact, later in our international study of gender and policing, Jennifer Brown and I developed our own framework for analysing women's experience of policing across the world. We found four types: cops, colonial histories, transitionals, and gendarmes (2000: 159). These models were derived from our empirical data and related to some of the frameworks used to analyse law enforcement systems more generally. Our model, however, suggested some important differences: US and UK officers had much more in common than either did with their Australian or Canadian counterparts.

Research on crime and criminal justice generally draws its theoretical inspiration from other disciplines. In this section I have tried to show how some of these ideas have been applied to the study of the criminal justice system. There could be many other examples, what is important is that concepts are proposed and used so that comparisons are made.

Earlier in this chapter, I set out the three basic requirements for best achieving the goals of comparative criminology, which I had proposed originally in one of my own earliest contributions to the comparative debates. To return to these and to match them to the categories of criminologists in the field will sum up some of the central themes of this chapter. Each requirement seems best fulfilled by a different type of researcher.

Data can certainly be generated by *bureaucrats*, although *explorers* produce the deepest and richest material. Concepts come most fruitfully from *strangers*, whose insights into their new societies and their old, will be the most telling. Frameworks are most productively produced by *travellers* of both types who gain overviews from their real or virtual journeys (Heidensohn 2004: 190).

Futures

Writing towards the end of his eventful and distinguished career, Hermann Mannheim suggested that

criminology, unhampered by the limits of any national legislation, can afford to tackle its problems in a worldwide spirit. Actually the opportunity has not always been taken, in part because of language difficulties, in part because of the varying nature of the problems concerned and the existing contrasts in approach and outlook (Mannheim 1965: 21).

He stressed the 'international' character of criminology and so clearly confident about the subject's comparative prospects was he that *Comparative Criminology* was the title he gave his two-volume text. Yet this is not a book about comparative research and methods in the sense understood in this chapter. It is international in covering an immense amount of scholarship from the American literature on gangs and subcultures to the most esoteric European forensic studies (Mannheim often leaves quotations in their original French or German and cites many works not translated into English). It is unlikely that any contemporary researcher could achieve either Mannheim's mastery of languages or his wide disciplinary knowledge. Even a polyglot, or someone using technical translation software, could not possibly cover in one career the range of material now available.

Mannheim's confidence that the era had arrived for comparative, international criminology turned out to be misplaced. Several decades were to pass before the current burgeoning began. That we are now in that era cannot be doubted. There are, as I have tried to show above, many texts, monographs, and collections which show this. Governments and international bodies fund it, courses are offered to students at all levels (Pakes 2004). The Division of International Criminology is now the largest section of the American Society of Criminology; a European Society of Criminology was founded in 2001 and now holds annual conferences. Not only do international journals abound, but there is strong emphasis in many others on including comparative content (see, for instance, the recently founded *Feminist Criminology*). So anyone entering this area nowadays is joining an expanding and promising endeavour.

There are still gaps; a very obvious one is that the coverage of many comparative studies is not global; not merely countries, but continents scarcely figure on comparative charts. Africa is all but uncharted territory (Kalunta-Crompton and Agozino 2004), as are Latin America and large parts of Asia. As one critic puts it—in 2006: 'Criminology remains a resolutely Eurocentric discipline. Much of what passes for comparative criminology is limited in its perspective to the societies of ... Europe, North America and New Zealand' (Dixon 2006: 521). These gaps are, if anything, made wider by some types of research (e.g. Tonry and Farrington 2005) which use selection criteria for their comparative subjects that exclude countries with no past histories of baseline studies. Moreover, it is neither possible nor appropriate simply to add in new nations without very careful consideration. The wider the range of cultures, the greater the complexities of collection of material, interpretation, and analysis.

There are also, as I suggested above, major issues of what, for short, may be called 'colonialism'. For most observers, this will mean the impact of European colonial powers, mainly Britain, France, and Spain and to a lesser extent the Netherlands, Belgium, Italy, and Germany, on either the 'settled' former colonies of Australia, Canada, New Zealand, and Latin America or the 'pacified' ones of Africa and Southeast Asia, and the Pacific. These histories mean that, on the one hand, criminology may be rejected as an imperialist social science, irrelevant to the realities of life in Third World countries. On the other, the colonial links may have already been addressed in research which begins from the perspective of, say, the history of policing. Thus in tracing this strand in the development of law enforcement in Britain and her 'New Commonwealth', many commentators have stressed that the consensual model of the 'New Police' of London was not the one exported to Nigeria, and other former colonies. Instead, it was the more militaristic system which had its prototype in Dublin, and later in the Royal Irish Constabulary (Brogden 1987, Emsley 1997, Ahire 1991). In our analysis of female officers' experiences, Jenny Brown and I found that an ex-'colonial' aspect featured in the framework which we developed (Brown and Heidensohn 2000). It is interesting to note that these colonial legacies have been traced for those once ruled by Britain, but much less work has been done on those once under the sway of France, Germany, Spain, and Portugal. Shelley (1999) has argued that states which were once part of the Soviet Union should also be viewed as ex-colonies of a kind, as a single Soviet model was imported and then imposed upon them.

As well as the flourishing nature of the comparative field itself, (and gaps are only unfilled research opportunities), there is a major series of changes in the background of all comparative work which has significant impact. Globalization is discussed elsewhere in this volume, as are the particular aspects of transnational, cross-border, and organized crime (see Rawlinson, **Chapter 10**). New kinds of crime—cybercrime (see Williams, **Chapter 16**), trafficking of people for illegal work or sexual purposes, terrorism in new forms—tend to be frontierless. These changes mean that more questions will be asked and more issues discussed within an international context.

There are many other missing parts to our international, comparative picture. Aside from the colourful memoirs of retired villains (not the most reliable sources), we do not hear the voices of offenders themselves very much in the international context. When we do, as with women who act as drug couriers, they relate tragic and brutal stories. The apparatus of international social control and judicial processes has had relatively little attention so far from social scientists. In short, there is a long agenda on which many points can be listed.

In a smaller world, the global can become local. After 11 September 2001 and 7 July 2005, no one can doubt that. What criminologists can do, in their modest way, is to contribute to greater understanding of both that world and the trends in crime and criminal justice which its citizens experience.

Suggestions for further reading

The following all provide useful materials for the novitiate comparative researcher: Newburn, T. and Sparks, R. (eds) (2004) *Criminal Justice and Political Cultures*, Cullompton: Willan; Winterdyk, J. and Cao, L. (eds) (2004) *Lessons From International/Comparative Criminology/Criminal Justice*, Toronto: de Sitter Publications; and Sheptycki, J. and Wardak, A. (eds) (2005) *Transnational and Comparative Criminology*, London: GlassHouse Press.

References

AGOZINO, B. (2003). *Counter-Colonial Criminology: A Critique of Imperialist Reason.* London: Pluto Press.

AHIRE, P. (1991). *Imperial Policing.* Buckingham: Open University Press.

ALBRECHT, H-J. (2004). 'From Legal Doctrine to Criminology' in Winterdyk and Cao (eds), *Lessons From International/Comparative Criminology/Criminal Justice.* Toronto: de Sitter Publications.

BARAK, G. (2000a). 'Comparative Criminology: A Global View'. *The Critical Criminologist* 10: 2.

—— (ed.) (2000b). *Crime and Crime Control: A Global View.* London: Greenwood Press.

BAYLEY, D. (1982). 'A World Perspective on the Role of the Police in Social Control' in R. Donelan (ed.), *The Maintenance of Order in Society.* Ottawa: RCMP.

—— (1985). *The Future of Policing.* Oxford: Oxford University Press.

BEAUJON, C. M. (1911). *Die Mitarbeit der Frau bei der Polizei.* The Hague: University of Utrecht.

BEIRNE, P. (1983). 'Cultural Relativism and Comparative Criminology'. *Contemporary Crises* 7: 371–91.

—— and NELKEN, D. (eds) (1977). *Issues in Comparative Criminology.* Aldershot: Ashgate.

BREWER, J., GUELKE, A., HUME, I., MOXON-BROWNE, E., and WILFORD, R. (1996). *The Police, Public Order and the State* (2nd edn). Basingstoke: Macmillan.

BROGDEN, M. (1987) 'The Emergence of the Police: the Colonial Dimension'. *British Journal of Criminology* 27(1): 4–15.

BROWN, J. and HEIDENSOHN, F. (2000). *Gender and Policing: Comparative Perspectives.* Basingstoke: Palgrave/Macmillan.

CAIN, M. (2000). 'Orientalism, Occidentalism and the Sociology of Crime'. *British Journal of Criminology* 40: 239–60.

—— (ed.) (1989). *Growing Up Good.* London: Sage.

CAVADINO, M. and DIGNAN, J. (2006). *Penal Systems: A Comparative Analysis.* London: Sage.

CHAN, J. (2005). 'Globalisation, Reflexivity and the Practice of Criminology' in J. Sheptycki and A. Wardak (eds), *Transnational and Comparative Criminology.* London: GlassHouse.

COUNCIL OF EUROPE (1999) and (2003). *European Sourcebook of Crime and Criminal Justice Statistics.* Strasbourg.

DEFLEM, M. (2002). *Policing World Society.* Oxford: Clarendon.

DIXON, B. (2006). Review of Kalunta-Crompton and Agozino (eds), *British Journal of Criminology* 46(3): 521–4.

DOWNES, D. (1966). *The Delinquent Solution.* London: RKP.

—— (1988). *Contrasts in Tolerance.* Oxford: Clarendon Press.

DURKHEIM, E. (1952). *Suicide.* London: Routledge.

EDWARDS, A. and HUGHES, G. (2005). 'Comparing the Governance of Safety in Europe: A Geohistorical Approach'. *Theoretical Criminology* 9(3).

EMSLEY, C. (1997). 'The History of Crime and Control Institutions' in Maguire *et al.* (eds), *The Oxford Handbook of Criminology.* Oxford: Oxford University Press.

EVANS-PRITCHARD, E. E. (1963). *Social Anthropology.* London: Athlone Press.

FAIRCHILD, E. and DAMMER, R. (2001). *Comparative Criminal Justice Systems.* California: Wadsworth.

FOSDICK, R. (1915). *European Police Systems* (Reprint 1969). Montclair NJ: Patterson Smith.

FRANKE, H. (1990). 'Dutch Tolerance: Facts and Fables'. *British Journal of Criminology* 30: 81–93.

GARLAND, D. (2001). *The Culture of Control.* Oxford: Oxford University Press.

GODFREY, B., EMSLEY, C., and DUNSTALL, G. (eds) (2003). *Comparative Histories of Crime.* Cullompton: Willan.

——, ——, —— (2003). 'Introduction: Do You Have Plane-Spotters in New Zealand? Issues in Comparative Crime Histories at the Turn of Modernity' in B. Godfrey, C. Emsley, and G. Dunstall (eds), *Comparative Histories of Crime.* Cullompton: Willan.

HAHN RAFTER, N. and HEIDENSOHN, F. (eds) (1995). *International Perspectives in Feminist Criminology.* Buckingham: Open University Press.

HARDIE-BICK, J., SHEPTYCKI, J., and WARDAK, A. (2005). 'Transnational and Comparative Criminology in a Global Perspective' in J. Sheptycki, and A. Wardak (eds), *Transnational and Comparative Criminology.* London: GlassHouse Press.

HAYMAN, S. (2006). 'The Reforming Prison: A Canadian Tale' in F. Heidensohn (ed.), *Gender and Justice: New Concepts and Approaches.* Cullompton: Willan.

HEBENTON, B. and THOMAS, T. (1995). *Policing Europe-cooperation, Conflict and Control.* Basingstoke: Macmillan.

HEIDENSOHN, F. (1989). *Women in Policing in the USA.* London: The Police Foundation.

—— (1991). 'Introduction: Convergence, Diversity and Change' in F. Heidensohn and M. Farrell (eds), *Crime in Europe.* London: Routledge.

—— (1992). *Women in Control? The Role of Women in Law Enforcement.* Oxford: Clarendon Press.

—— (1994). 'From Being to Knowing: Some Issues in the Study of Gender in Contemporary Society'. *Women and Criminal Justice* 6(1): 13–37.

—— (1997). 'Crime and Policing' in V. Symes, C. Levy, and J. Littlewood (eds), *The Future of Europe.* Basingstoke: Macmillan.

—— (2000). *Sexual Politics and Social Control.* Buckingham: Open University Press.

—— (2001). 'Research on Women in the Criminal Justice System and Transnational Crime', in N. Ollus and S. Nevala (eds), *Women in the Criminal Justice System: International Examples and National Responses.* Helsinki: European Institute for Crime Prevention and Control.

—— (2003). 'Gender and Policing' in T. Newburn (ed.), *A Handbook of Policing.* Cullompton: Willan.

—— (2004). 'Finding New Frontiers to Cross in Criminology' in J. Winterdyk and L. Cao (eds), *Lessons From International/ Comparative Criminology/Criminal Justice.* Toronto: de Sitter Publications.

—— (2006). 'Contrasts and Concepts: Considering the Development of

Comparative Criminology' in T. Newburn (ed.), *The Politics of Crime Control*. Oxford: Oxford University Press.

—— and FARRELL, M. (eds) (1991). *Crime in Europe*. London: Routledge.

—— and —— (eds) (1993, rev. edn) *Crime in Europe*. London: Routledge.

HOOD, R. (2002). 'Recollections of Sir Leon Radzinowicz' in A. Bottoms and M. Tonry (eds), *Ideology, Crime and Criminal Justice*. Cullompton: Willan.

—— (2004). 'Hermann Mannheim and Max Grünhut: Criminological Pioneers in London and Oxford'. *British Journal of Criminology* 44: 469–95.

—— (ed.) (1989). *Crime and Criminal Policy in Europe*. Oxford: Centre for Criminological Research.

HOWARD, J. (1784). *Preliminary Observations and an Account of Some Foreign Prisons and Hospitals*. Warrington: W. Eyres.

JOUTSEN, M. (2004). 'From Criminology to Applied Comparative Criminology: Life as a Peripatetic Comparativist' in J. Winterdyk and L. Cao (eds), *Lessons From International/ComparativeCriminology/ Criminal/Justice*. Toronto: de Sitter Publications.

KALUNTA-CROMPTON, A. and AGOZINO, B. (eds) (2004). *Pan-African Issues in Crime and Justice*. Aldershot: Ashgate.

KARSTEDT, S. (2004). 'Durkheim, Tarde and Beyond: The Global Travel of Crime Policies' in T. Newburn and R. Sparks (eds), *Criminal Justice and Political Cultures*. Cullompton: Willan.

KENNETT, P. (2001). *Comparative Social Policy*. Buckingham: Open University Press.

KILLIAS, M. (1991). 'Crime and Crime Control in Switzerland' in E. Hilowitz (ed.), *Switzerland in Perspective*. Westport, Ct: Greenwood.

KING, R. D. (1991). 'Maximum Security in Britain and the USA: a Study of Gartree

and Oak Park Heights'. *British Journal of Criminology* 31: 126–52.

—— (1994). 'Russian Prisons after Perestroika: End of the GULag?'. *British Journal of Criminology* 34, special issue.

—— (1999). 'The Rise and Rise of Supermax: an American Solution in Search of a Problem?' *Punishment and Society* 1: 163–86.

—— (2004). 'On being a comparative criminologist' in J. Winterdyk and L. Cao (eds), *Lessons From International/Comparative Criminology/Criminal/Justice*. Toronto: de Sitter Publications.

—— and MIKHLIN, A. S. (2000). 'The Russian Prison System: Past, Present and Future' in R. Matthews and P. Francis (eds), *Prisons 2000: An International Perspective on the Current State and Future of Imprisonment*. Basingstoke: Macmillan.

—— and PIACENTINI (2005). 'The Russian correctional system during the transition' in W. Pridemore (ed.), *Ruling Russia: Law, Crime and Justice in a Changing Society*. Lanham MD: Rowman & Littlefield.

—— and RESODIHARDJO, S. (2007 forthcoming). 'To Max or not to Max: Dealing with Difficult and Dangerous Prisoners in England and Wales and The Netherlands'.

LACEY, N. and ZEDNER, L. (1995). 'Discourses of Community in Criminal Justice'. *Journal of Law and Society* 22: 301–20.

—— and —— (1998). 'Community in German Criminal Justice: A Significant Absence?'. *Social and Legal Studies* 7–25.

MAGUIRE, M., MORGAN, R., and REINER, R. (eds) (2002). *The Oxford Handbook of Criminology* (3rd edn). Oxford: Oxford University Press.

MAHER, L. (1997). *Sexed Work*. Oxford: Oxford University Press.

MANNHEIM, H. (1965). *Comparative Criminology*. II vols. London: Routledge.

MASON, B. (2006). 'A Gendered Irish Experiment—Grounds for Optimism?' in F. Heidensohn (ed.), *Gender and Justice: New Concepts and Approaches*. Cullompton: Willan.

MAWBY, R. (1990). *Comparative Policing Issues: The British and American Experience in International Perspective*. London: Routledge.

—— (1998). 'Victims' Perceptions of Police Services in East and West Europe' in V. Ruggiero, N. South, and I. Taylor (eds), *The New European Criminology*. London: Routledge.

—— (ed.) (1999). *Policing Across the World*. London: UCL Press.

MAYHEW, P. (2004). 'Comparative Research in A Government Environment' in J. Winterdyk and L. Cao (eds), *Lessons From International/Comparative Criminology/Criminal Justice*, Toronto: de Sitter Publications.

McGUNNIGAL-SMITH, S. (2005). 'Men of a Thousand Days: a Study of Death Row'. Unpublished Ph.D. thesis. University of Wales, Bangor.

McKENZIE, I. and GALLAGHER, G. (1989). *Behind the Uniform: Policing in Britain and America*. Hemel Hempstead: Harvester Wheatsheaf.

MELOSSI, D. (2004). 'The Cultural Embeddedness of Social Control' in T. Newburn and R. Sparks (eds), *Criminal Justice and Political Cultures*. Cullompton: Willan.

MILL, J. S. (1888). *A System of Logic*. London: John Murray.

MILLER, W. (1977). *Cops and Bobbies*. Chicago: University of Chicago Press.

MORRIS, T. (1957). *The Criminal Area*. London: RKP.

MORRISON, B. (2003). 'Practical and Philosophical Dilemmas in Cross-Cultural Research: The Future of Comparative Crime History?' in B. Godfrey, C. Emsley, and G. Dunstall (eds), *Comparative Histories of Crime*. Cullompton: Willan.

NEAPOLITAN, J. (1997). *Cross-National Crime A Research Review and Source Book*. Westport Ct: Greenwood.

NELKEN, D. (2002). 'Comparing Criminal Justice' in M. Maguire, R. Morgan, and R. Reiner (eds), *The Oxford Handbook of Criminology* (3rd edn). Oxford: Oxford University Press.

—— (ed.) (1994). *The Futures of Criminology*. London: Sage.

NEWBURN, T. (2000). 'Atlantic Crossings: Contemporary Crime Control in America and Britain'. Inaugural Lecture. Goldsmiths College, London.

—— and SPARKS, R. (2004). 'Criminal Justice and Political Culture' in T. Newburn and R. Sparks (eds), *Criminal Justice and Political Cultures*. Cullompton: Willan.

—— and —— (eds) (2004). *Criminal Justice and Political Cultures*. Cullompton: Willan.

OWINGS, C. (1925). *Women Police: a Study of the Development and Status of the Women Police Movement*. New York: Bureau of Social Hygiene.

PAKES, F. (2004). 'The Politics of Discontent: The Emergence of a New Criminal Justice Discourse in the Netherlands'. *Howard Journal* 43: 284–98.

PELIKAN, C. (1991). 'Conflict Resolution between Victims and Offenders in Austria and in the Federal Republic of Germany' in F. Heidensohn and M. Farrell, (eds), *Crime in Europe*. London: Routledge.

PIACENTINI, L. (2004). *Surviving Russian Prisons: Punishment, Economy and Politics in Transition*. Cullompton: Willan.

PICKERING, S. (2000). 'Women, the Home and Resistance in Nothern Ireland'. *Women and Criminal Justice* 11: 49–82.

PLATEK, M. (1995) 'What it's Like for Women: Criminology in Poland and Eastern Europe' in N. Hahn Rafter and

F. Heidensohn (eds) (2005), *International Perspectives in Feminist Criminology*. Buckingham: Open University Press.

RADCLIFFE-BROWN, A. R. (1951). 'The Comparative Method in Social Anthropology'. *Journal of the Royal Anthropological Institute* 81(1/2): 15–22.

RESTIVO, S. (1991). *The Sociological Worldview*. Oxford: Blackwell.

ROCK, P. E. (1986). *A View from the Shadows: The Ministry of the Solicitor General of Canada and the Making of the Justice for Victims of Crime Initiative*. Oxford: Clarendon.

ROSE, J. (1980). *Elizabeth Fry :A Biography*. London: Macmillan.

ROSE, N. (2000). 'Government and Control'. *British Journal of Criminology* 40: 321–339.

RUGGEIRO, V., SOUTH, N., and TAYLOR, I. (eds) (1998). *The New European Criminology*. London: Routledge.

RUSCHE, G. and KIRCHHEIMER, O. (1939) *Punishment and Social Structure*. New York: Columbia University Press.

SCHUTZ, A. (1966). 'The Stranger' in G. Schutz (ed.), *Alfred Schutz: Collected Papers Vol. II, Studies in Social Theory*. The Hague: Martinus Nijhoff.

SHELLEY, L. (1999). 'Post-Soviet Policing: Limitations on Institutional Change' in Mawby, R. (ed.), *Policing Across the World*, London: UCL Press.

SHEPTYCKI, J. (2005). 'Relativism, Transnationalism and Comparative Criminology' in J. Sheptycki and A. Wardak (eds), *Transnational and Comparative Criminology*. London: GlassHouse.

—— and WARDAK, A. (eds) (2005). *Transnational and Comparative Criminology*. London: GlassHouse.

SMELSER, N. J. (1976). *Comparative Methods in the Social Sciences*. Princeton: Prentice Hall.

SOUTH, N. (1996). 'Eurovisions: Some Recent Europe-Focussed Contributions on Criminology, Crime and Control'. *Crime and Social Order in Europe* ESRC 4–5.

THAM, H. (1998). 'Crime and the Welfare State: the Case of the UK and Sweden' in V. Ruggeiro, N. South, and I. Taylor (eds), *The New European Criminology*. London: Routledge.

TONRY, M. and FARRINGTON, D. (eds) (2005). 'Crime and Punishment in Western Countries 1980–1999'. *Crime and Justice: A Review of Research*, vol. 33. Chicago: University of Chicago Press.

VAGG, J. (1993). 'Contest and Linkage: Reflections on Comparative Research and Internationalism'. *British Journal of Criminology* 33: 541–54.

—— (1991). 'A Touch of Discipline: Accountability and Discipline in Prison Systems in Western Europe' in F. Heidensohn, and M. Farrell (eds), *Crime in Europe*. London: Routledge.

VAN DIJK, J. (2004). 'On the Victims' Side' in J. Winterdyk and L. Cao (eds), *Lessons From International/Comparative Criminology/ Criminal Justice*. Toronto: De Sitter Publications.

—— MAYHEW, P., and KILLIAS, M. (1990). *Experiences of Crime across the World*. Kluwer Deventer.

VAN SWAANINGEN, R. (2005). 'Public Safety and the Management of Fear'. *Theoretical Criminology* 9: 289–305.

VIDALI, S. (1998). 'Youth deviance and social exclusion in Greece' in V. Ruggeiro, N. South, and I. Taylor (eds), *The New European Criminology*. London: Routledge.

WESTFELT, L. and ESTRADA, F. (2005). 'International Crime Trends: Sources of Comparative Crime Data and Post-War Trends in Western Europe' in J. Sheptycki and A. Wardak (eds) *Transnational and Comparative Criminology*. London: Glass House.

WHITMAN, J. (2003). *Harsh Justice*. Oxford: Oxford University Press.

WHYTE, W. F. (1943). *Street Corner Society*. Chicago, Ill.: University of Chicago Press.

WILENSKY, H. (1975). *The Welfare State and Equality: Structural and Ideological Roots of Public Expenditure*. University of California Press.

WINTERDYK, J. and CAO, L. (eds) (2004). *Lessons From International/Comparative Criminology/Criminal Justice*. Toronto: de Sitter Publications.

WOOD, J. and KEMPA, M. (2005). 'Understanding Global Trends in Policing: Explanatory and Normative Dimensions'

in J. Sheptycki and A. Wardak (eds), *Transnational and Comparative Criminology*. London: GlassHouse.

YACOUBIAN, G. S. (2003). 'Disentangling the Definitional Confusion between Comparative and International Criminology'. *International Journal of Comparative Criminology* 3: 223–6.

YOUNG, J. (2003). 'Searching for a New Criminology of Everyday Life: A Review of Garland's Culture of Control'. *British Journal of Criminology* 42: 228–61.

ZIMRING, F. and JOHNSON, D. (2005). 'On the Comparative Study of Corruption'. *British Journal of Criminology* 45: 793–809.

PART III

RESEARCH ON CRIME, CRIMINALS, AND VICTIMS

8

Researching the state of crime: national, international, and local victim surveys

Pat Mayhew

Introduction

Advances in survey methodology and improved facilities for computer analysis opened the way for the development of victim surveys (or crime surveys as they are sometimes called). In the scale of things, they are a comparatively new form of criminological research, but have developed substantially over the past two decades or so. Victim surveys ask people directly about their experience of victimization, whether or not they reported what happened to the police. Most surveys take samples of householders, but not always. In any event, they offer a measure of crime a distance apart from police records, of which more below.

This chapter looks at the rationale for different types of victim survey and discusses some of the main differences between them. The emphasis throughout is more on methodological issues than substantive results (though see *Further Reading* for those who want a broad overview). I concentrate mainly on UK surveys, in particular the British Crime Survey (BCS) as an example of a national survey. This is because I was once closely involved with it, and because it has in large part contoured what is known about victimization in the UK. It has also been important in setting standards for other national surveys on a more economical scale than set by the USA. The BCS is also important in using innovative computer technology that has sometimes been adapted elsewhere. Mention is also made of the International Crime Victim Survey (ICVS) and the International Violence against Women Survey (IVAWS), with which I have also been involved. The latter is one of many surveys of violence against women. Some surveys have looked at non-household targets and some reference is made to these. There is also coverage of surveys of young people, and ethnic minorities. Local surveys share many features of national survey, but as the name implies look only at local areas. I have not personally been involved in local surveys, but have reviewed many.

The development of victim surveys

National surveys

National surveys took hold in the main first. The earliest major survey was carried out in the United States for the President's Crime Commission in the 1960s. This was followed in 1972 by the first round of a very large survey, now called the National Crime Victimization Survey (NCVS), which has been conducted continuously since—see Catalano (2005) for the latest results. It is by far the largest of any of the national surveys with nearly 150,000 people aged 12 or more interviewed in 84,000 households a year.

In Europe, the first large-scale survey was in Finland in 1970. The first BCS ran in 1982 in England and Wales (Hough and Mayhew 1983), and Scotland (Chambers and Tombs 1984). The BCS in England and Wales then ran seven more times until 2001 after which it has run on a continuous basis with a bigger sample (see below)[1]. After the 1982 sweep in Scotland, there were five more Scottish surveys (see Campbell *et al.* 2004 for latest results).[2] A new and larger Scottish Crime and Victim Survey was re-launched in June 2004, after a review of the previous design. At the time of writing, there appear to be no results from this. Developments in the design of national surveys are discussed later.

There is no full list of the main national victim surveys, although the United Nations Economic Commission for Europe (UNECE) has recently attempted an inventory of them in the UNECE region. Thirty-two countries reported that they had undertaken national surveys, many more than once (Lamon 2006). Probably the best known (or at least those about which most have been written in English) are those from England and Wales, Scotland, Switzerland, the Netherlands, Germany, Finland, the USA, Canada, Australia and New Zealand. (At the time of writing, I am co-co-ordinating the third (2006) round of the New Zealand survey.)

While the victim surveys above were 'bespoke' ones, in some countries victimization questions have been included in surveys with other main perspectives. In the UK, perhaps the earliest use of victimization questions was in a 1966 OPCS survey about moral attitudes (Durant *et al.* 1972). The General Household Survey also carried questions on burglary for some time. Victimization questions sometimes appear in polls conducted by MORI, Gallup, etc., as well as in polls by magazines and newspapers. They often give only crude measures, and the form of the questions varies widely.

The International Crime Victimization Survey (ICVS)

The ICVS came on the scene later than the first main national victim surveys. It was set up because international comparisons of police statistics, though much in demand, are problematic because of differences in the way the police define, record, and count crime. Moreover, since most crimes the police know about are reported by victims, police figures can differ simply because of differences in victims' reporting rates. Comparisons using independently organized surveys were of little help because differences in survey

---

[1] After the 1982 sweep, it was repeated in 1984, 1988, 1992, 1994, 1996, 1998, and 2000.
[2] These were in 1988, 1992, 2000, and 2003.

methodology made for substantial differences in the count of victimization. The ICVS uses the same questionnaire and analysis methods to produce more equivalent results.

Standardized ICVS household surveys were conducted in about twenty western indus- trialized countries over four rounds in 1989, 1992, 1996, and 2000 (see van Kesteren *et al.* 2001 for latest results). Some countries participated more than once. Samples are fairly small—about 2,000 in each sweep in each country—although a few countries have increased sample size to allow a more robust national measure. Surveys have also been carried out in over fifty countries in transition and developing countries, usually at city level, through a programme directed by the United National Interregional Criminal Justice Research Institute (UNICRI) in Italy (see Gruszczyńska 2004, Zvekic 1998, and Alvazzi del Frate 1998 for results).

A fifth round of ICVS surveys took place in about eighteen European Union countries in 2004–5, though there are no results at the time of writing. Unlike the earlier surveys, where countries met their own costs, the European Commission funded the 2004–5 sur- veys. They have used a slightly revised questionnaire. It is difficult to say yet whether this will alter the count available from the worldwide ICVS and the data series already exist- ing. It will be unfortunate if it does.

Under the ICVS programme, there have also been a number of commercial victim sur- veys, as well as an International Violence against Women Survey (IVAWS). These are touched on below.

International surveys are logistically difficult and not to be recommended without good financial backing, guaranteed interest in host countries, and willingness on the part of organizers to get involved in tedious technical oversight to ensure consistency. International surveys have other special problems, too, regarding the ownership of results, and how and when results are released (crime 'league tables' can be sensitive).

Violence against women (VAW) surveys

Most 'general purpose' adult victim surveys cover experience of sensitive victimization— notably, that of a sexual nature or that perpetrated by someone well known to the victim. In addition, there has been a formidable raft of 'bespoke' surveys of violence against women, including umpteen studies of sexual victimization among students (a rather overconvenient population for university-based researchers). Note that VAW surveys is something of a misnomer, as some include male respondents—principally I would say to try and illustrate lower victimization rates.

The UNECE also collected information on VAW surveys. It identified twelve national surveys, but there are clear gaps.[3] For instance, there is no mention of a multi-country World Health Organization survey that collected data from 24,000 women aged 18–49 in twelve countries between 2000 and 2003 (Garcia-Moreno *et al.* 2005).[4] The UNECE inven- tory included three countries that had taken part in the IVAWS, developed within the

---

[3] The national surveys were in Australia (IVAWS), Canada, Denmark, Finland, France, Italy, Mexico, Poland (IVAWS), Rep. Moldova, Spain, Sweden, and Switzerland (IVAWS). They seem to focus only on women, but it is not clear.

[4] The countries were Bangladesh, Brazil, Ethiopia, Japan, Namibia, Peru, Samoa, Serbia and Montenegro, Thailand, Tanzania, and two areas of New Zealand. Only women were interviewed.

ICVS programme; but there are eight others.[5] No comparative results have yet been published from IVAWS, but an Australia report has appeared (Mouzos and Makkai 2004).

With the exception of the IVAWS, which uses a standardized questionnaire and methodology, the main feature of surveys to date has been their differences in approach, both as regards the sorts of questions asked, and the samples taken. (Age range and 'partnered' status are two issues here.) I reviewed several surveys of sexual victimization, for instance, and explained many of the reasons for the disparity in estimates in terms of simple methodological differences (Percy and Mayhew 1997). Most VAW surveys, too, have resulted in such different estimates of the extent of victimization that, in my view, comparisons between them are largely fruitless. Many measures include minor forms of interpersonal conflict, frequently building on the first or second version of the Conflict Tactic Scale (CTS), devised to capture the escalation of tactics used to deal with family problems (Straus 1979; Straus and Gelles 1992). A problem for researchers is saying where the 'violence' line should be drawn. In practice, researchers usually avoid drawing the line at all, in the absence of sufficient information about the context, frequency, severity, and intention of behaviour. This means that many types of low-level conflict are classified as violence.

In the USA, estimates of VAW have come from the NCVS as well as the National Violence against Women Survey (NVAWS). Figures from the former changed considerably after the NCVS redesign in 1992 (see below), testament to the influence of what sorts of question are asked (see Bachman and Saltzman 1995). On the face of it, NCVS estimates are lower than those from the 1995–6 NVAWS, although careful reanalysis by Rand and Rennison (2005) bringing samples and counting methods more in line largely eliminates the difference. This again is testament to the influence of design and counting protocols.

In the UK, there were a number of VAW surveys which are now rather dated (e.g. Dobash and Dobash 1980; Stanko 1988; Painter 1992), although Painter and Farrington (1998) surveyed 1,000 married women more recently. The BCS's conventional measure of violence allows a categorization of domestic violence (as opposed to acquaintance or stranger violence). However, the BCS has run special self-completion modules on domestic violence (1996 survey), sexual victimization (1998 and 2000) and domestic violence and sexual assault (2001). (The mode of administration is discussed more later.) A feature of these modules has been that they have tried different approaches to questioning, in tacit recognition of the fact that there is no clear best one.

There is little doubt that an academic industry will continue to thrive on surveys of VAW, especially as it is poorly covered in police statistics because of low reporting rates. 'Bespoke' surveys are likely to be more favoured, as it is recognized that a weak point of 'general purpose' victim surveys is poor measurement of crimes between offenders and victims known to each other. These need to provide clear 'health warnings' about the estimates produced.

Commercial victim surveys

Some victim surveys have looked at non-household targets. These have taken less firm hold, but are growing (see Hopkins (2002) for a good review.) For convenience here, they

---

5 In addition to Australia, Poland and Switzerland, IVAWS surveys (women only) were planned in Costa Rica, the Czech Republic, Denmark, Mozambique, Greece, China (Hong Kong), Italy, and the Philippines. I also know of a VAW survey in New Zealand, which covered women only (Morris 1997), and the list leaves out the US NVAWS covering men and women.

are called commercial victim surveys, although this fudges their coverage somewhat. An elementary point is that they fill a gap in police statistics, which do not usually allow types of target to be singled out within legal offence categories. (Theft from shops is an exception in England and Wales.)

In the USA, there was a set of commercial surveys in the early NCVS programme covering burglary and robbery in businesses and selected non-governmental organizations (US Department of Justice 1976). However, although large, they were discontinued when it was found that most incidents were reported to the police.

There was work on a comparative international commercial victim survey that took place in 1994 within the ICVS programme of work. Nine countries took part, but problems of different sector coverage and small sample sizes meant that little became of it (though see van Dijk and Terlouw 1996).[6] Another International Crime Business Survey was conducted in nine Central-Eastern European capital cities in 2000 with extended sections on fraud, corruption, extortion and intimidation (Alvazzi del Frate 2004).

While many surveys have taken samples of businesses, the 2001 and 2004 surveys by the British Chambers of Commerce canvassed all members, albeit with far from complete response (British Chambers of Commerce 2004). Some studies have also used administrative or 'head office' records, such as the annual survey of retailers by the British Retail Consortium (BRC), now in its twelfth year (BRC 2005). These are useful for gathering information held centrally and can cover a large number of outlets. At the same time, they omit crimes not reported to the head office, and do not usually look at factors that put some premises at greater risk, such as location, size, and opening hours.

The main national commercial victim surveys in England and Wales have been done by the Home Office. The first was in 1993, covering 3,000 retailing and 3,000 manufacturing premises (Mirrlees-Black and Ross 1995). This was repeated in 2002 with 4,000 retailing premises and 2,500 manufacturing premises with 250 employees or less (Shury *et al.* 2005). Gill (1998) covered about 2,600 premises with a questionnaire to the Forum of Private Businesses, straying beyond the retail and manufacturing sectors. Scotland has also made inroads into commercial victimization (Hopkins and Ingram 2001), while Australia has done some work on risks for retailers (Taylor and Mayhew 2002) and farms (Anderson and McCall 2005). I was involved in the latter work while I worked for a time at the Australian Institute of Criminology. Sheep-rustling provided a refreshing change.

Commercial surveys have often been done to illustrate the nature of the crime problem in a particular sector, or its extent in a local area—for example Mawby's (2003) study in Cornwall, and in Leicester by Tilley and Hopkins (1998). Many other studies are now rather dated, although they have covered the crime problems of building societies and banks (Austin 1988; Gill and Matthews 1994), post offices (Ekblom 1987), small shops (Hibberd and Shapland 1993), chemists' shops (Laycock 1984), a large shopping centre (Phillips and Cochrane 1988), and industrial estates (Johnson *et al.* 1994). Gill (1993) looked at risks for nearly 350 small holiday accommodation businesses, using a postal questionnaire. Levi (1988) used the same methodology to study fraud against businesses. Outside the commercial sector, Smith (1987) did an exploratory study of victimization among hospital staff in a large general hospital.

---

[6] England and Wales was one of the countries. Results were written up independently (see Mirrlees-Black and Ross 1995).

Few commercial victim surveys have examined trends over time, although the BRC Survey does so with their 'head office' figures, as well as the two British Chambers of Commerce surveys, and the two from the Home Office. The last estimated the number of total crimes against retailers and manufacturers in England and Wales, by grossing up survey estimates. The BRC also gives grossed-up totals of the volume of crime and financial losses for retailers.

There are signs of new activity in surveying business crime. For instance, the USA has recently announced a new national survey to measure the impact of cybercrime on businesses. The survey, by Bureau of Justice Statistics and the Department of Homeland Security, is to estimate the number of cyber attacks, frauds, thefts of information, and resulting losses during 2005. This development echoes the expansion of questions in household surveys on identity and Internet fraud, as will be seen.

One focus of recent research has been on crimes against ethnic businesses, especially robbery and extortion against Chinese and Vietnamese businesses in the USA (e.g. Kelly *et al.* 2000). These surveys face particular difficulties—for instance the need to interview respondents in their own language, and get them to divulge business matters they might well want to keep to themselves. The early study in the UK of crime and racial harassment in Asian-run small shops still seems to be the only one with a focus on ethnic businesses (Ekblom and Simon 1988).

Youth populations

Most household surveys take samples of adults, usually those aged 16 or more. Younger respondents are generally omitted because of the need to negotiate parental permission, and because youngsters are not necessarily seen as good respondents for reporting household crime, or general matters such as income levels. Conventional victimization questions also need to be adapted to reflect the day-to-day experiences of the young and to bring into scope behaviour which some may not appreciate is 'criminal'.

This said, victimization among young people in the USA has been well covered, as the NCVS sample goes down to age 12, and it has run periodic School Crime Supplements to examine crime and safety issues among those aged 12–18 years old. There are also a number of other school surveys, which are combined with NCVS results to produce *Indicators of School Crime and Safety* (see DeVoe *et al.* 2005).

The 1992 BCS also carried a sample of 1,350 12- to 15-year-olds selected from homes where an adult was interviewed for the main BCS. Using a self-completion paper questionnaire, they were asked about victimization and harassment away from home. Briefly, results showed that the young teens experienced high levels of incidents covered by the survey, although many were not seen as serious. Few incidents came to the attention of the police, and many were not reported to parents or teachers either (see Aye Maung 1995a).

In the UK, there have been a number of surveys of young people where the focus has been on offending (and often drug use), but which have also asked about victimization, including being bullied. One was the *On Track Youth Lifestyles Survey* undertaken in 2001 by Sheffield University as part of the evaluation of the On Track component of the Crime Reduction Programme. Some 30,000 primary and secondary school pupils in high-deprivation areas in England and Wales completed a paper-based questionnaire (see

Armstrong *et al.* 2005). An earlier survey was the Home Office *Youth Lifestyles Survey* (YLS), conducted in 1992–3 (Graham and Bowling 1995) and again in 1998–9 (Flood-Page *et al.* 2000). MORI has run an annual survey since 1999 for the Youth Justice Board of about 5,000 11- to 16-year old pupils, again using a paper questionnaire (see Phillips and Chamberlain (2006) for latest results). In a slightly different vein, victimization and offending have been investigated in the *Edinburgh Study of Youth Transitions and Crime*, a longitudinal study (to age 30) of around 4,300 young people who started their first year of secondary school in Edinburgh in 1998, when most of them were aged 11 or 12 (see Smith *et al.* 2001).

The Offending, Crime and Justice Survey (OCJS) is a new Home Office national household survey first carried out in 2003, with annual repeats until 2006. It focuses on the extent of offending, antisocial behaviour, and drug use, particularly among young people aged from 10 to 25, but includes victimization questions (see Wood (2005) for victimization results). There is a 'panel' element with repeat interviews with the younger respondents.

These youth surveys have focused mainly on property victimization and violence outside the home. Asking children about abusive behaviour within the home raises obvious difficulties. Leaving aside cohort studies, the most common approach has been to ask adults in household surveys about their early experiences. The IVAWS has done this for instance, as has the New Zealand national survey, and the NVAWS in the USA. A principal feature of results on childhood victimization is their variability. Differing methodologies and, above all, differing questions explain this in the main.

Ethnic minorities

There is clear interest in the experience of ethnic minorities as regards victimization. There was one bespoke survey by the Policy Studies Institute of ethnic minorities in Britain that covered victimization (Modood *et al.* 1997). Some local surveys have also covered ethnic minority populations—notably, the Moss-Side study (Tuck and Southgate 1981), that by the London Borough of Newham 1987, and the first and second Islington crime surveys (respectively, Jones *et al.*1986; Crawford *et al.* 1990). The BCS has regularly carried an ethnic minority 'booster sample' in an attempt more adequately to tap victimization and harassment (see, e.g., Percy 1998; Clancy *et al.* 2001). Victimization levels are generally higher than for whites, although to a large degree this can be explained by demographic, social, and residential factors which increases risks. These factors need to be adequately taken into account in analysis.

Local surveys

Local surveys aim for a better picture of risks at a local level. Sample sizes in national household victim surveys (at least in the early days) precluded even much interregional analysis, though some surveys have now grown sufficiently to allow this. Even the very large NCVS in the USA only presents results by size of locality, stopping short of estimates for given cities. The lowest level of analysis in the BCS was for some time the eleven Government Office Regions in England and Wales, although it is now big enough to give headline police force results (discussed later).

The number of local surveys can only be guessed at, but some of the early UK ones remain well known. The first was the London study by Sparks *et al.* (1977), which pre-dated the first BCS. Two other local surveys also predated it: that in Sheffield (Bottoms *et al.* 1987) and in Moss-Side, comparing black and white residents (Tuck and Southgate 1981). After this, there was a crop of local victim surveys concerned to highlight the scale of crime in particular high-crime areas—e.g. in Merseyside (Kinsey 1985; Kinsey *et al.* 1986), in Islington (Jones *et al.* 1986; Crawford *et al.* 1990), and Newham (London Borough of Newham 1987). These were often part of a political bid for more locally accountable policing. Rural areas were largely left out, though Koffman (1996) reports a survey in Wales.

Local community surveys are now big business in the USA, especially since the Bureau of Justice Statistics and the Office of Community Oriented Policing Services (COPS) developed software for localities to conduct their own telephone surveys of residents to collect data on crime victimization, attitudes toward policing, and other community-related issues. In Australia, too, some state surveys have been set in place to augment the rather broad figures from the national survey run by the Australian Bureau of Statistics.

Local surveys for evaluation purposes

Some local surveys have been conducted to evaluate crime prevention programmes, looking at 'before and after' risks and perceptions of risk. They are often intended to complement the picture from police figures which could potentially change simply because crime prevention programmes often encourage reporting to the police. A large-scale example in the UK was the surveys to evaluate Phase 1 of the *Safer Cities* burglary programme (Ekblom *et al.* 1996). They covered areas targeted for action, and 'control' areas in other cities. They looked at victimization experience before and after *Safer Cities* action, fear of crime, changes in security behaviour, and whether people were aware of the burglary action taken (they were surprisingly unaware as it happened). The effectiveness of improved street lighting has also been tested with local victim surveys, to assess both changes in risks and feelings of security (see Farrington and Welsh (2002) for a review).

Police surveys

In the UK, police forces were for some time required by the Audit Commission to measure the quality of policing, and by the Police Act 1996 to assess what people felt about objectives set for local policing. There was much variation in what was done, but some forces used local sample survey to canvass views, and a few included measures of victimization (see Chatterton *et al.* 1997). Few results are widely available.

The introduction of Best Value Performance Indicators (PI) for the police in the UK in 2000 replaced other demands. Three survey-based indicators, consistent across forces, were proposed on the level of crime, fear of crime, and feelings of public safety. This was the first time the BCS was asked to deliver police PI results. At the same time, though, police forces were being encouraged to do their own standardized local surveys and guidance was given for a 'model survey' using heavily stripped down BCS questions (Ashworth *et al.* 2000; Kershaw and Myhill 2001). I do not know whether this was taken up. Later on, though, the police seem to have ventured into local survey of those contacting the police to supply data for part of a suite of indicators within the Police Performance Assessment Framework (Home Office 2005).

UK Crime Prevention Partnership crime audits

After the 1998 Crime and Disorder Act, local victim surveys looked likely to become a significant growth industry because of the statutory duty for crime audits to be carried out every three years by local Crime and Disorder Partnerships of the police, local authority, and other agencies. Local problems of crime and disorder were meant to be identified and monitored based on sound information. Surveys were one obvious way of collecting this—although there were others (see Hough and Tilley 1998).

In the first edition of this book (Mayhew 2000), I anticipated a number of features of these auditing surveys. In the event, I rather the missed the mark, at least in so far as it is difficult to compare my predictions with what was actually done. Thus, Newburn and Jones (2002) surveyed just over 260 Partnerships after the first audits should have been completed. Ninety per cent said they had used 'surveys', but these seemed eclectic, and not often in the business of estimating local victimization risks. More often, they simply sought views on attitudes to crime, fear of crime, and the priorities set by the Partnerships for reducing crime and disorder.

There are probably several reasons why local victim surveys for the crime audits did not take much hold. Costs would have been one, since robust samples would have been needed to allow analysis of sub-groups, or changes in risks over time.[7] (Assessing attitude change is less demanding in sample size terms.) Lack of requisite survey knowledge among local practitioners would also have been a factor although a number of guides were provided— for instance those by the Audit Commission (1999), and Hough and Tilley (1998). There was also the sheer burden placed on local agencies at the time to deliver a New Labour agenda across wide social policy fronts. One aspect of this was trying to dovetail numerous public 'consultation tasks' (Newburn and Jones 2002). Another factor may have been the increasing popularity of geographical 'mapping' of police data; it may just have been simpler to map the police recorded crime for local analysis.

The partnership provisions of the Crime and Disorder Act 1998 have recently been reviewed (Home Office 2006a), removing the requirement for three-yearly audits which were acknowledged to be resource intensive. (Six-monthly 'strategic intelligence assessments' replace them.)

What household victim surveys are about

Victim surveys of householders have served five main purposes. They are to:

i.   provide an alternative measure of crime to offences recorded by the police;

ii. look at levels of reporting to the police and why crimes are not reported;

iii. give information on crime risks in a way police figures allow much less well;

iv. flesh out the nature of victimization from crime; and

v.   take up other crime-related issues.

---

[7] On a sample of 1,000, for instance, the change in the overall burglary risk in an area would need to be about a full 50 per cent up or down before it could be said to be statistically significant.)

Each of these is explored a little below. After that, I turn to the question of how well surveys measure what they set out to.

Victim surveys as an alternative measure of crime

Comparing police and survey figures

Victim surveys essentially try to measure the 'real' extent of victimization by asking people about crimes they have not reported to the police. Many surveys do this to emphasize the widespread nature of victimization, simply noting the extent of unreported crime along the way. Relatively few try to estimate the 'real' number of household burglaries, say, compared to the number recorded by the police. The ICVS, for instance, makes no attempt at this. Nor do most national surveys in other countries. Results from the NCVS in the USA, for instance, are not set alongside the police Uniform Crime Reports in any precise way.

There are a few exceptions in the early UK surveys. Sparks *et al.* (1997) attempted a match in survey and police figures for London, while the first Islington survey also made some comparisons (Jones *et al.* 1986). Farrington and Dowds (1985) assessed whether victimization risks in Nottinghamshire supported the picture from police statistics, in which Nottinghamshire topped the force league. (It showed that levels of victimization in Nottinghamshire were only slightly higher than in two adjacent counties, with other data suggesting that high police figures in Nottinghamshire were largely attributable to distinctive recording practices.) The early surveys in different parts of Sheffield also acted as a check on the picture gained from police figures (Bottoms *et al.* 1987).

The BCS attempts a fairly tight comparison between police figures and its own risk estimates. Offences are classified according to police rules, based on detailed information in a 'Victim Form' rather than through affirmative answers to 'screener' questions (discussed more below). The process of matching BCS offences with the police count allows for comparisons of trends in crime according to the two sources, with the BCS risk estimates grossed up to provide national England and Wales totals, and with some adjustment made to police figures to maximize comparability.[8] At least this is done for a sub-set of 'matchable' offences.[9] The matching process allows an estimate of an evident 'recording shortfall' between the number of offences estimated to have been reported to the police and the actual number recorded—this being part of the 'dark figure' of crime, additional to offences not reported at all. The 2004–5 BCS, for instance, showed that whereas just over 40 per cent of 'matchable' survey crimes were said to have been known to the police, the number of recorded crimes was only three-quarters of the estimated number reported. The latter figure is suggestive rather than precise, and it has been higher over the last three years largely because of the introduction of the National Crime Recording Standard (NCRS).[10] The considerable extra work involved in linking police

---

[8] For instance, crimes against those under 16 are excluded, as they are not covered by the survey; and recorded vehicle thefts are adjusted to exclude commercial vehicles.

[9] Some offences cannot be matched as they are recorded by the police in broad categories spanning offences against both institutional victims and private individuals.

[10] The figure is imprecise because there is sampling error on the survey estimates of 'experienced' and 'reported' crime. Some of the apparent shortfall will also reflect inevitable differences in the way offences are

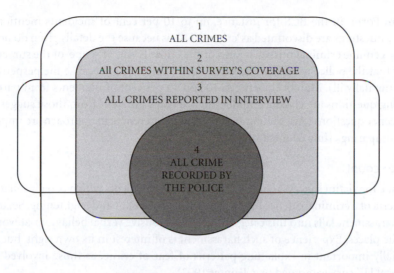

Figure 8.1 Comparing survey data and police counts

and survey figures has undoubtedly increased the value of BCS information, but the more parsimonious approach of letting survey results speak for themselves is probably the best way forward for most victim surveys.

Figure 8.1 illustrates the points above by showing the overlap between survey and police counts. While not suggesting that the relative size of the counts is accurate, it shows how some types of crime will be captured by both counts, some by only one, and some by neither. Within the coverage they take, victim surveys capture incidents respondents are *prepared to talk about* . These exclude some incidents that the survey wants to capture, if some victimizations are withheld. At the same time, they can be more inclusive than what the survey wants to cover, if incidents are reported which actually fall out of the scope of the survey. In contrast, the police record incidents that come to their attention, and they chose to record. For many incidents, the public and the police will agree about what is 'crime'. Agreement will be poorest for less serious incidents, and where there is most discretion for taking legal action.

The BCS procedures highlight a distinction worth noting as regards what incidents are counted in victim surveys. Many surveys essentially leave the task of defining crime to the respondent. They use quasi-legal terms in 'screener' questions to determine whether a respondent had been 'burgled' for instance; and they apply no checks on respondents' definitions. They give a count of crime, therefore, as defined by the sampled population. (Examples here are the Australian surveys, the ICVS, and virtually all of the local UK surveys.) In contrast, the BCS (and the NCVS and the New Zealand survey for example) trawl for possible crimes incidents through screener questions, but surveyors post hoc define these as crimes (or not) using more detailed information in what is usually called

classified in the BCS and by the police, although in principle the same rules are followed. Police figures have changed recently because (i) common assaults are now included; and (ii) there are new rules for the police to record crimes on a prima facie rather than evidential basis. Both these changes have substantially increased the count of crime that can be 'matched' with BCS crimes (see *http://www.homeoffice.gsi.gov.uk/rds/ countrules.html*).

a Victim Form. In the BCS for instance, up to 10 per cent of incidents mentioned in screener questions are discounted as 'crimes'. This is because the details given do not suggest any genuine criminal misbehaviour; or the crime is 'out of scope' of the survey; or it is clear that the police would not have recorded a crime (e.g. because the perpetrator is clearly mentally ill). Moreover, between 10 and 30 per cent of incidents from particular screening questions are classified under offence types different from those suggested by the screener questions (Aye Maung 1995b). These differences in approach are important when comparing crime counts from different surveys.

What to count

One issue for victim surveys is how far to encompass incidents which usually fail to meet the criteria of a criminal offence but which can be unpleasant and frightening. Sexual and racial harassment falls into this category, as well as abusive verbal behaviour at work and in public places. Experience of such harassment is of interest in its own right, but is also potentially important in explaining patterns of fear of crime, as those involved in the early local UK surveys argued (e.g. Painter 1992).

Local surveys were often considered to have done more on this measurement front than the BCS. The criticism holds less strongly now since various types of harassment have now been covered. This includes racial harassment (e.g. Aye Maung and Mirrlees-Black 1994; Salisbury and Upson 2004), sexual harassment (e.g. Hough 1995), verbal abuse at work (Aye Maung and Mirrlees-Black 1994), obscene telephone calls (e.g. Buck *et al.* 1995), and 'road rage' (Marshall and Thomas 2000). Antisocial behaviour, particularly topical now, has also come into the frame (Budd and Sims 2001; Wood 2004).

There are no special problems in designing questions to cover disorderly conduct and 'lower level' harassment, and it is appropriate to analyse it in much the same way as 'conventional' victimization. There are two caveats, however. First, harassment may be a continuing process rather than a discrete one-off event (cf. Bowling 1993). Trying to tally the number of incidents, then, is less appropriate than assessing different levels of exposure, bearing in mind that few people avoid being subject to uncivil behaviour at some time or other. Secondly, and related to this, is the issue of what stands as relevant victimization. This is a matter of choice, of course, but too broad a coverage of everyday petty harassment can lead to overinclusivity if simply added to more unequivocally 'criminal' victimization.

Reporting crime to the police

A feature of most victim surveys is to ask victims what went unreported to the police, and why. This has been primarily to show that many incidents of a criminal nature never come to police attention. As to why the police are not informed, the evidence consistently shows that this is mainly because victims feel that what happened was too trivial or not amenable to police action. But this is not the whole story. Skogan's (1994) analysis of BCS results remains one of the best assessments of influences on reporting. He showed that harm, level of loss, and insurance cover are most influential, but that related-party incidents go unreported more often. Who the victims are is also relevant. Older people and homeowners are more likely to report and council tenants more likely than private renters. People in urban areas and Afro-Caribbeans report less often, controlling for other factors. An implication of this for local surveys is that they may uncover a greater disparity in risk between areas of different types than indicated by police figures. This said, other victim characteristics do not have much influence once offence-related factors are taken into account: e.g. gender, having been a victim in the past, or attitudes to the police.

Victimization risks

A principal focus of victim surveys has been to show how risks of crime vary for different types of victim. In this respect, they have stolen a considerable march on police data, which provide very little about victims even in terms of gender and age, let alone variables such as social class and household composition. One of the aims of the early local surveys was to highlight disparities in risk, discrediting the focus of the early BCS on national average figures. The conclusions drawn by these 'left realist' victim surveyors was that crime has a severe impact on those in inner cities, and an even greater one on the disadvantaged. The charge laid against the BCS was that it glossed over extensive pocketing of crime (and portrayed fear of crime as irrational along the way). As it happens, the criticisms largely ignored the content of BCS publications, but achieved currency simply through repetition (see, e.g. Zedner 2002).

The considerable literature on risks of victimization shows five things, in brief summary.

i.   First, risks vary for different people. Men are much more vulnerable than women are to assaults and robbery, although the gender difference reverses for domestic violence. Higher risks are also evident among younger people, single people, households with children, and younger household heads. (Some of these overlap, of course.)

ii. There is a concentration of risk among the less economically and socially well placed, who tend to live in higher-crime areas. A third of recent BCS crime took place in the 10 per cent 'highest-risk' Crime and Disorder Reduction Partnerships, with the number of victimizations 70 per cent higher per capita than elsewhere (Nicholas *et al.* 2005). The conflation of area and household type is captured in the BCS by the use of the ACORN classification of neighbourhood types.[11]

iii. Variations in risk across area differ somewhat according to offence type, with robbery, for instance, being very much an 'inner-city' crime.

iv. The probability of repeated (or multiple) victimization is even more unevenly spread than the probability of being victimized at all. This is now one of the best-known products of victim surveys, the BCS and others besides. Explanations have focused partly on the inherent 'attractiveness' of targets that are repeatedly victimized, and partly on the fact that the same offenders—or their associates—sometimes return to the scene of the crime to exploit knowledge gained 'first time round'. Pease (1998) has a good overview of findings about repeat victimization, as well as the strengths and limitations of survey data on it.[12] Identifying repeat victimization, in any event, has implications for the design of crime-counting questions.

[11] ACORN stands for 'A Classification of Residential Neighbourhoods' (CACI Ltd). This assigns each home in the country to one of seventeen neighbourhood groups or fifty-four neighbourhood types according to the social and housing characteristics of its immediate area as measured by the 1991 Census. There are a few other so-called commercial 'geo-demographic profile' classifications available based on the same principles as ACORN-for instance, Mosaic and Pinpoint.

[12] For instance, the usual twelve-month 'recall period' in which respondents report their experiences places an artificial boundary on the number of repeat incidents that can be counted.

v.   There is an overlap between victimization and offending, best evidenced in the UK
     by the youth studies referred to above (e.g. Smith *et al.* 2001; Hayward and Sharp
     2005; Wood 2005; Budd *et al.* 2005). The OCJS, for instance, found that just over a
     half of those who admitted offending in the last year had also been victims, com-
     pared with less than a quarter of non-offenders (Budd *et al.* 2005). The strongest
     predictors of higher risks of personal crime victimization among 10-to 15 year-
     olds included criminal or antisocial offending, as well as drug use, being male, hav-
     ing negative parenting experiences, living in households in financial difficulty, and
     having friends in trouble with police (Wood 2005)

The nature of victimization

The police, of course, have a lot of information on the nature of crimes they know about.
Little of it is routinely reported, although it can be accessed by criminologists for special
studies. In principle, victim surveys are an additional way of charting the nature of victimization. The BCS currently reports, for instance, on levels of injury in assaultive crime,
whether offenders were under the influence of drink or drugs, whether there was believed
to be a racial element, where and when offences occurred, how burglars got into a house,
and the financial costs of victimization.

   How well victim surveys can unpick the nature of crime depends on their size. Larger
national surveys produce more crime incidents from which to generalize. It also depends
on the number of questions asked, and the number of incidents that are followed up.
Some surveys extrapolate from details of the 'last' incident of a particular type (the ICVS
and the IVAWS do so, for instance). This is efficient in reducing interviewing time, but
risks bias in so far as respondents choose a 'last' incident which is most salient to them, or
about which they have more to say.

   Asking a large number of questions about the nature of victimization in smaller surveys is of questionable value since they will produce too few incidents for reliable analysis. The costs of crime, for instance, are made up of damage and theft losses, and
account should be taken of compensation through insurance. Several questions are
needed to untangle the extent of real net loss. Sound conclusions about when and how
different crimes happen are also difficult to draw from small samples, and it is probably
better to try to access local police information. Insufficient incidents are also a problem
for looking at what was stolen (which requires a long code list), and where property was
stolen from.

   Probably the most useful question for smaller surveys is the victim's relationship to the
offender(s), since this highlights the extent of related-party crimes, and usefully explains
patterns of reporting to the police. The emotional and practical effects of crime are also
worth documenting since police information is poor. Another useful question to victims
is their perception of the seriousness of what happened, which can show that while many
'seriously-judged' crimes are reported to the police, many are not. Questions about how
far victims feel they contributed to what happened (through lax security or provocation,
for instance) can be illuminating, but are more often than not avoided for fear of 'victim
blaming'. I return later to a question on whether or not victims felt what happened was
'a crime'.

Other crime-related issues

It is expensive to arrange interviews with respondents to discuss their experience of crime. Having paid the price, nearly all larger-scale, repeated victim surveys delve into other crime-related issues not strictly relevant to victimization. The NCVS, for instance, has an intermittent supplement on police–public contact. The BCS also routinely looks at fear of crime (e.g. Hough 1995), interactions with the police (e.g., Skogan 1994); and attitudes towards the criminal justice system (e.g. Mirrlees-Black 2001; Allen *et al.* 2006). It has also covered knowledge and use of illicit drugs since 1992 (see Chivite-Matthews *et al.* 2005 for latest results).

In local surveys, probably the two most popular topics have been fear of crime and attitudes to the police, although I know of no good synthesis of their findings. The approaches taken to measuring fear have been diverse, mindful of the fact that fear questions have been subject to particular academic scrutiny. One focus was on the effects of fear on 'quality of life'—though this was more implicit than ever rigorously measured. It would have been difficult anyway, needing imaginative questions, and benchmarking against other local stressors. It is difficult in practice, too, to assess how far people's lifestyles are negatively affected by crime when the choices they make (e.g. about whether or not to go out at night) reflect several domestic considerations, as well sometimes as rational good sense rather than dysfunctional fear.

The value of questions on what the public want from prevention programmes and the police is also somewhat debatable in my view. People may be poorly informed about what is best, or may not have thought much about it (*cf.* Hough and Tilley 1998). Nor are respondents necessarily aware of competing demands on the police; or likely to give answers that take account of opportunity costs—e.g. that more patrolling (a consistent favourite) might mean fewer resources available to tackle drunken driving. Focus groups are possibly better for unpicking public expectations of policing (Bradley (1998) reported a useful study on these lines).

How well do victim surveys count?

The victim survey count

Victim surveys have a number of methodological limitations that affect the reliability of their counts. The main ones are below.

i. Household victim surveys—the main genre—come nowhere close to measuring all 'crime'. They leave aside victimization of children, as we have seen. Crimes against commercial and public sector targets are omitted, as well as 'victimless' crimes such as drug possession. Homicide is obviously not counted, since no victim is available. And it is difficult to cover fraud, since many people will not be aware they have been victimized.

ii. No sample survey represents the population adequately. Household sampling frames exclude those in communal establishments (They form about 2 per cent of the UK population, so bear in mind that they would not make much difference to national estimates.) They also exclude groups such as the homeless, who may have higher victimization rates than others.

iii.   In addition, surveys do not achieve complete response rates. Some respondents are not at home when interviewers call, and others refuse to be interviewed because of lack of time, interest, or concerns about the validity of the survey. It is widely thought that low response rates undermine the reliability of survey estimates on the premise that victimization rates for non-respondents are likely to be higher than for those who do respond. In fact, methodological results on this are less conclusive than might be thought—see, for example, Groves *et al.* 2001; van Kesteren *et al.* 2001 (for the ICVS); Hope 2005 (for the results of Scottish methodological work discussed below); Lynn 1997 and Aye Maung 1995b for the BCS). Differential response across groups is sometimes taken into account in weighting in any event.

iv.   As only a sample of the population is questioned, findings are subject to sampling error. The BCS is large by the standards of most surveys, but even so many of its estimates are imprecise, in particular for rare crimes such as robbery and serious assault. The error range on victimization figures from smaller local surveys will be considerable, and will greatly limit respectable analysis of changes over time or between groups.

v.   Victim surveys are prone to undercount 'offences' which are either on the borderline of what people actually regard as criminal (e.g. pub fights), or which they might be reluctant to talk about because the offender is known to them. Sexual and domestic offences are the most obvious examples, with the added problem that we cannot be sure whether different groups respond to survey questions in the same way. One problem area here is whether men are as prepared to report incidents of a sexual or domestic nature as women.

vi.   There is a set of specific limitations in asking people to remember victimization incidents and locate them accurately in time. One concern is whether victimization that is repetitive in nature can be readily located in time as discrete and definitionally tidy events. This bears in particular on domestic and sexual violence, as well as on many forms of harassment—if these are a focus. Genn's (1988) essay on crime on a London housing estate still remains the best illustration of how conventional victim survey counting methods fail to do justice to the chaotic lives of victimized (and victimizing) women. Related to this is that most victim surveys either ask people to recall victimizations over the last 12 months, or from the beginning of the calendar year before interviewing takes place (with incidents in the 'counting year' selected out). Methodological work done in the USA shows that a six-month 'recall period' (which the NCVS adopts) produces many more incidents than a 12-month period.

Most work done on how accurately people remember incidents of victimization has been in relation to the NCVS. Skogan (1986) and Sparks (1981) reviewed the evidence some time ago, but both their essays are still outstanding. The overall conclusion is that response biases work, on balance, to undercount survey defined offences, but with differential losses across crime categories. Thus, proportionately fewer trivial offences are reported with a twelve-month recall period than a six-month one. And in checks where people have been asked about offences *known* to have been reported to the police, more trivial crimes (e.g. minor thefts, vandalism, and some assaults) are less likely to be recalled in interview.

On the other hand, incidents that are more serious are more likely to be recalled in interview, and indeed may be overcounted, as events that are more salient tend to be pulled forward in time. The count of crime from victim surveys, then, is both incomplete and biased.

Memory prompts

An elementary but little-regarded point about how accurately surveys measure victimization bears simply on the number of screener 'prompts' that are offered. For instance, respondents can be reminded about thefts by someone with a right to be in the home; whether someone might have *tried* to get in; or whether someone might have got in but not stolen anything. Essentially, the more prompts, the more criminal victimization will be counted—since different screeners will jog the respondent's memory in different ways. There is a case for saying 'more is better' as far as screener questions are concerned. (For example, separate screeners about attempted and completed burglaries produce a higher count than a single screener covering both.) Using more restricted screener questions, moreover, runs the risk of respondents 'forcing' incidents into inappropriate screeners, thereby contaminating what the screener is meant to be measuring. The main danger of using an expansive array of screeners is that respondents can report on the same incident in response to different screener questions (despite being instructed not to do so). This is difficult to detect unless screener questions are followed through with additional questions on the event being recalled, which allows double counting to be identified.

Current research methodology

This section starts with remarks about how some of the main national surveys have changed over time. It then looks at various methodological issues, including sampling, and mode of interview. There is no exhaustive review here of the technical pros and cons of different approaches. Rather, I simply signal some more important technical considerations. There is an element of 'horses for courses' in choosing how to do a survey, with timescales and available funds being constraining factors.

Recent developments

As national surveys have become established, there have been developments to them to improve accuracy and extend the range of questions they ask. Here, though, the designers of large-scale victim surveys are caught in a bind. While inclined to make improvements, they also need to retain comparability of measurement in order not to jeopardize trend data, which is the main justification for the large financial outlay involved in repeated surveys.

The NCVS has undergone a series of changes since it started in 1972, including more telephone interviews (to contain costs), and new questions to victims on the characteristics and consequences of crime victimization. However, there was a substantial redesign in 1992, recognized to change the amount or types of crime measured by the survey. The main changes related to the screener questions. A 'short-cue' design was introduced to increase the effectiveness of screeners to prod respondents' memories. There were also new screeners on sexual assault and vandalism; and additional ones for rape, and crimes by relatives and intimate partners. 'New' and 'old' versions of the questionnaire were run alongside for 18 months. The main effect of the new screeners was to increase estimates of difficult-to-measure offences. The violent crime rate rose by about 50 per cent overall, with the greatest impact on rape, the rate for which more than doubled and incidents involving non-strangers, which almost doubled (Kindermann *et al.* 1997).

The main change to the BCS was a substantial hike in sample size in 2001 and a move to continuous, rolling fieldwork to facilitate this, since no survey company could undertake to conduct 40,000 interviews in a limited period at reasonable cost.[13] (There have been no results on the effect of the change reported.) The bigger sample was to provide a more reliable measure of violent crime, and to supply 'performance indicators' data for the forty-three police forces in England and Wales on confidence in the police, and the level of BCS-measured household and personal crime at force level. (The possibility of developments of this sort had never occurred to us in the early days of the BCS, when we promoted the survey largely as a research tool, and in no sense as a means of performance management.) The 2004 survey in Scotland also moved to continuous fieldwork, with interviews by telephone, the only way to deliver the greatly increased sample size of 27,000 annually.

One way in which many national surveys have changed has been to take up issues of emerging interest, or improve those that the 'conventional' questionnaire did not handle particularly well. Thus, the BCS has now covered various types of harassment. In the NCVS, there is now a regular count of 'hate crime'—i.e. crimes committed because of a victim's race, ethnicity, religion or disability, gender or sexual orientation (see Harlow 2005). A NCVS supplement on extent of stalking will run in 2006, as well as one on risks in the work environments. The Canadians have already asked questions about stalking, as has the BCS (see Budd and Mattinson 2000; Walby and Allen 2004). Questions were recently added to NCVS to measure identity theft, encompassing credit-card thefts, thefts from existing accounts, and misuse of personal information (Baum 2006). The BCS has strayed into the same territory, looking at credit and debit card fraud, Internet fraud, computer viruses, computer hacking, and receiving harassing or offensive email or mobile-phone messages (see Wilson *et al.* 2006 for latest results). The count of these offences is not added to the conventional BCS crime count.

Many new areas of questioning are run only periodically, since there is not space (or even need) to keep them on the books all the time. In Canada, for instance, the five-yearly General Social Survey on Victimization run by Statistics Canada has run components on

---

[13] Until 2001, the survey was mounted in the first three months of the year, with respondents asked to report on their experiences of crime in the previous calendar year. They are now asked about their experiences in the past twelve months. Thus, for instance, the latest published BCS figures are based on the interviews between April 2004 and March 2005 (the BCS year ending March 2005) and incidents experienced by survey respondents in the previous 12 months, with estimates centering on March 2004. Averaging over the moving recall period, the BCS generated estimates most closely comparable with police recorded crime figures for the 12 months up to the end of September 2004. The police recorded crime figures related to crimes recorded in the financial year 2004/05.

victim services, elder abuse, public perceptions of alternatives to imprisonment—amongst other things. In the NCVS, there is a periodic Police–Public Contact supplement to obtain information on interactions the public has with police. The BCS has looked at security behaviour (Budd 1999), neighbourhood watch schemes (e.g. Sims 2001); knowledge of Victim Support (e.g. Ringham and Salisbury 2004), and handling stolen goods (Finney and Wilson 2005).

Sampling

Most victim surveys want to document the experience of 'ordinary' people. For some time, Electoral Registers (ERs) provided the most obvious household sampling frame in the UK. They were readily accessible, and allowed a sample of named individuals to be picked beforehand (at least from those aged 18 or older). However, it is now well established that ERs under-represent some groups (e.g. the unemployed and ethnic minorities). The other sampling frame is the Small Users Postcode Address File (PAF). This lists all postal delivery points, and represents the fullest register of household addresses since almost all households have a delivery point, or letterbox. The main disadvantage of PAF is the lack of a list of named occupants, which means that any introductory letter can only be sent to the 'Occupant', who may or may not be the household member one is really after. (Note that most surveys pick one randomly selected householder, mainly to reduce interview burden. The NCVS is an exception, questioning all household members aged 12 or more about personal crime.)

Different sampling decisions apply if the focus is to be on particular groups (e.g. children or ethnic minorities). Some can be picked up from representative sampling frames, although will usually need to be augmented—by oversampling residential homes to get an elderly population, for instance. A large initial sample will produce enough numbers for some special groups. The 1998 BCS, for instance, identified about 1,400 people with a limiting disability out of a sample of 15,000 (nearly 10 per cent). However, without an initially large sample, one would need to resort to other sources (disability payment records, perhaps, to get a sampled of disabled people).

The experience of ethnic minorities with regard to victimization and harassment is likely to remain of interest. Normal samples produce insufficient numbers for reliable analysis so special sampling techniques need to be employed. The usual one goes under the term 'focused enumeration' (see Brown and Ritchie 1981).

Mode of interview

There are three main possibilities as regards the way in which victimization can be measured: mail questionnaire, telephone interviews, and face-to-face personal interviews. Web-based surveys may come into fashion, but their use now is small, and they are not dealt with here.

Mail surveys

The advantage of mail (or postal) surveys is that they are relatively cheap. However, they restrict what sorts of question can be asked because they have to accommodate the 'lowest common denominator' in literacy level. They also rarely achieve high response rates, although the three-yearly Australian National Crime and Safety Survey which uses a mail questionnaire is an exception—perhaps because the customer is the Australian Bureau of Statistics. Low response would not necessarily be a problem if those who do respond are representative, but there is reason to doubt this. Those with 'something to say', particularly the more literate, may be more likely to take the trouble to complete a mail questionnaire.

Telephone surveys

The use of telephone interviews in victim surveys has been growing. The usual mode now is Computer Assisted Telephone Interviewing (CATI) where the questionnaire is a computer program that specifies the questions, the structure of permissible answers, and the routing instructions that determine which questions are asked, and in what order. Samples are typically drawn using a form of random digit dialling (RDD), where one digit of a listed number is changed to circumvent the problem of ex-directory numbers (about half of telephone households in the UK have ex-directory numbers).[14]

The NCVS now uses telephone interviews in large part; most countries in the ICVS and IVAWS do so; and the Scottish crime survey changed to telephone mode in 2004. The two Home Office Commercial Crime Surveys chose telephone interviews as more acceptable to busy managers—though early pilot work showed the need to send an introductory letter to identify the person best placed to answer the questions and to allow them to collate information before the interview.

The merits of CATI surveys are obvious. They are cheaper, take choices away from interviewers, and allow centralized supervision. They also enable more standardization of questionnaire administration, which was a key advantage in the ICVS, for instance. What people are prepared to divulge over the telephone is a moot point, but tests in advance of the Canadian Violence against Women Survey suggested that telephone interviews might provide more confidentiality and minimize interviewer effects (Smith 1989). This was one reason for their use in the IVAWS. The US NVAWS also used telephone interviews.

As against this, telephone interviews are less suitable for long interviews and obviously do not allow self-completion modules. (The new 2004 Scottish survey, for instance, had to cut questions and drop the self-completion modules on drug use and domestic abuse.) In earlier years, a concern was the representativeness of telephone owners, as penetration varied by socio-economic group. Today, penetration is virtually complete, and bigger problems now are unlisted numbers, call-screening devices, and the use of mobile phones instead of a main landline. Mobile-only households are particularly important given that they are distinctive in a ways that possibly relate to victimization levels: they are younger, lower-income, more often unemployed, renters, single-adult households, and in deprived areas (Hope 2005). The growth of mobile-only households will pose an increasing problem of bias and instability in time series data from telephone surveys. In 2005, 9 per cent of households in the UK were mobile-only (Ofcom 2005).

Telephone interviews also tend to draw lower response rates than face-to-face interviews. This is not because contact rates are lower (they are not), but because it is easier to refuse over the phone. For instance, in a test of the effects of changing to telephone surveys

---

[14] Mobile phones are excluded from most RDD samples because there is no link between mobile numbers and terrestrial geography.

in the 2004 Scottish Crime survey, face-to-face and telephone interviews were run in tandem: the response rate was 67 per cent in the former, but 49 per cent in the latter, the difference accounted for by refusals (Hope 2005). Whether higher rates of refusal, then, lead to unreliability in victimization estimates becomes critical. In the Scottish test, the results went against prevailing wisdom: victimization estimates were *higher* in the telephone surveys on a large number of measures, suggesting that those who respond are the ones with 'something to say'.[15]

Telephone interviews can sometimes be a platform for follow-up interviews with those who have initially taken part in a face-to-face interview. This could be useful for tracking changes in attitudes over time, for instance, or for assessing how long the effects of victimization last. Conversely, face-to-face interviews could follow telephone surveys. This happened in the 2002 Commercial Victim Survey when forty establishments were visited personally, with quotes from them providing context to findings from the much larger telephone survey.

Face-to-face interviews

Many victim surveys use face-to-face interviews nonetheless. This is partly because of response rates, and partly because of residual suspicion about the 'respectability' of telephone surveys. They also allow scope for interviewer ratings, though outside the BCS they seem less used than they might be. For instance, the physical condition of a respondent's home or immediate neighbourhood can be noted, or whether a burglar alarm or other obvious security devices are visible. These can provide useful analysis variables.

The high costs of face-to-face interviews are more competitive where interviews are only within a local area. Even so, some local surveys have tried to contain costs by using student interviewers, special constables, or even police officers. It would be over-pious to disparage these, but clearly, proper training is needed. There is also the problem that police personnel cannot conceal their identity, and when a survey is about crime, it is hard to think that this does not introduce bias.

Computer administration in face-to-face surveys

The use of Computer Assisted Personal Interviewing (CAPI) in large surveys of all kinds has rapidly replaced paper-and-pen interviewing (PAPI)—where the interviewer carries a large bundle of interview schedules and enters answers onto them. (The BCS has used CAPI since 1994.) CAPI can be cheaper than PAPI if the initial hardware is in place and interviewers already trained. For small local sponsors—and university researchers—costs can be considerable. It is likely to be in their interests to subcontract data collection to larger 'CAPI-ready' organizations.

The consensus is that CAPI improves data quality, mainly through automating routing, in-built range and consistency checks, and minimizing missing data (see, e.g., Martin and Manners 1995; de Leeuw and Nicholls 1996). CAPI also facilitates more complex questionnaire design, and allows for randomization of question order and response categories to avoid 'order effects'. It also increases the speed of results once interviews are completed,

---

[15] Another test was to compare a subset of 10 per cent of those who initially refused in the telephone survey but had their refusals 'converted', with others who remained refusers. Victimization levels were lower for the latter group than the 'converted', again suggesting that non-victims are less likely to participate.

though this is offset by longer questionnaire development time. Most pertinently, too, evidence suggests that respondents may well answer more frankly in CAPI than in PAPI mode. This may be because computers enhance the appearance of interviewer's professionalism, or make them seem more neutral to respondents.

Self-completion in CAPI interviews

One by-product of CAPI in victim surveys is the potential for respondents to use the computer themselves to answer questions of a sensitive nature. This technique is known as Computer Assisted Self Interviewing (CASI). It has been used since 1994 in the BCS with respondents aged 16–59 to cover self-reported drug-taking, domestic violence, sexual victimization, stalking, and being offered and buying goods known to be stolen. Results have been encouraging. Few respondents need help from interviewers and few refuse (indeed many positively enjoy self-keying). More pertinently, much higher rates of admission have emerged with CASI for topics covered by existing BCS questions. (Results are reported by Mirrlees-Black (1999) for domestic violence results; Percy and Mayhew (1997) for sexual victimization; and Ramsay and Spiller (1997) for drug-taking.) One explanation is that respondents may feel that answering a 'black box' affords more privacy than showcards or a self-completion paper-based questionnaire. It could also be that the technical formality of a computer screen prompts more thoughtful and honest answers. In any event, self-keying techniques are clearly a major breakthrough as regards getting a more complete count of sensitive topics.

The Home Office OCJS includes CAPI, CASI, and (for offending questions) the offer of Audio-CASI whereby respondents could listen to questions through headphones. This helps cope with literacy problems, but is not common. Questions and response sets must be kept short, and it increases questionnaire completion time.

Some other issues

Survey sponsors

Who sponsors a victim survey can be important. The BCS is introduced as a Home Office survey. The fairly high response rate it achieves (75 per cent on the most recent figures) may reflect the 'status' of the sponsor, but it may be that some people feel participation is required—even though advance letters and 'doorstep' introductions stress that it is voluntary. As a generalization, it is likely that response will be higher in surveys sponsored by agencies that respondents see as in a position to influence change. Surveys presented as serving the interests of university researchers may do less well.

Crime prevention questions

One problematic area of questioning is about household crime prevention. Being asked by unknown interviewers whether you have high-quality locks, a burglar alarm, or the number of hours (and even which hours) the house is left empty provokes a wary reaction from many respondents. Asking these questions in telephone interviews is particularly problematic. A careful introduction to the questions is needed, and respondents should be given the choice to miss them out altogether. Not covering the questions at all is probably less of a loss than might be supposed. Some respondents may exaggerate security 'just in case' the information is passed on. More important is that assessing the effectiveness of security (usually the purpose) is complicated. One needs to compare security levels of (i) non-victims, (ii) victims at the time they were victimized, and (iii) victims currently. This is because many people will upgrade security after victimization, so that simple comparisons of non-victims and victims will show victims to be better protected. Moreover, security coverage is highly related to income, itself related to risk. Assessing security patterns, therefore, needs to take account of income.

Question order

Questionnaire designers are probably less aware than they should be of the implications of where particular questions are placed. It is usually recognized that surveys should start with some not overly important 'warm-up' questions, and that high-priority questions should not be at the end, because some respondents will have drawn a halt before then. Question position, however, can influence observed frequencies. This is important for both comparing results over time, and those from independently organized surveys.

One example from the BCS relates to attitudes to the police. Virtually all sweeps have included a general question: 'taking everything into account, would you say the police in this area do a good job or a poor job?' In 1988, the question was included twice—a simple mistake. The question was first asked early on, and for half the sample it was asked again, late in the interview, set among a set of questions on contacts with the police. The results are interesting. Among those asked the question twice, 66 per cent gave the same rating, but 22 per cent were more positive the second time of asking (a smaller 13 per cent gave a less favourable rating). There is little obvious explanation, except perhaps that having become more sensitized to crime issues as the questionnaire proceeded, respondents became more sympathetic to the demands on the police.

Another example is from the 1994 BCS in relation to a question on women's fear of rape. In previous sweeps, the 'worry about rape' question was in a battery of fear questions near the beginning of the questionnaire. In 1994, the 'worry' questions were split into two, and some—including the rape question—were put much later in the questionnaire, along with new questions of fear of non-criminal misfortunes. In the 1992 BCS, 30 per cent of women said they were very worried about rape, whereas 22 per cent said this in 1994. (When there was no question order change, the percentage reporting that they were worried about crime increased.) Tentatively, one might suppose that greater worry is registered in a more 'off-the-cuff' answer early in the questionnaire before women have gone through questions that remind them of the mundanity of most criminal victimization. In any event, though, it is clear that measurement can be sensitive to question position.

Future developments

Victims as a policy focus

The BCS started when victims were taking centre stage in policy terms. Victim issues have waxed and waned somewhat over the last 25 years, but are now again high on the policy agenda—for instance, with the formalization of a *Code of Practice for Victims of Crime*

(Home Office 2006b). This adds some impetus to the BCS, but in truth it is now well established in its own right. Also, it already provides a number of measures pertinent to people's experiences as actual or potential victims, including public satisfaction with the police, and victim satisfaction on reporting crime. It cannot do much in the way of measuring what victims feel about how they are treated by the criminal justice system as a whole—as most victims of the 'ordinary' crimes the survey predominantly uncovers only get engaged with the police (if them).

The BCS, though, has cemented the practice of using surveys to track how those who have contact with the criminal justice system feel about it. For instance, there have been two surveys of witness satisfaction in Crown and Magistrates courts (see Angle *et al.* 2003), as well as surveys of vulnerable and intimated witnesses (Hamlyn *et al.* 2004). (Note that many 'witnesses' are victims.) Moreover, results from surveys of those contacting the police are now part of the suite of indicators within the Police Performance Assessment Framework (Home Office 2005).

The BCS

There are no doubt improvements that could be made to the BCS. For one, the survey itself has shown fallibility in measurement, with the self-completion modules eliciting much higher rates of interpersonal crime than the interviewer-administered questions do. The difficulty is that the BCS count of crime is one of its major strengths, and changing or using different techniques is highly likely to alter this.

As stated earlier, the survey also now pays its way by providing a raft of 'performance indicators' for the Home Office. The questions have now become routinized to provide consistent trends over time. They also use up a lot of questionnaire space. Indeed, a fair challenge is that the questionnaire has fallen foul of 'administrative criminology'. Thus, while new topics still appear, these have responded more to concerns of the moment (e.g. antisocial behaviour) than to theoretical matters. An important issue here is the overlap between victimization and offending. While this has been covered well in the youth surveys mentioned earlier, the BCS has only dabbled so far (e.g. Mayhew and Elliott 1990). Another topic that could do with more attention is victims' response to 'victimizations' in terms of the need for official action (see below), and their impact relative to other 'misfortunes'.

Extending the scope of victims surveys

I would dispel the notion that victim surveys can realistically reveal the full extent of the 'dark figure' of crime by covering all relevant populations. For instance, children are difficult to interview, and some residents (e.g. in old people's homes) may not answer relevant questions very well anyway. Although it seems likely that business or commercial victim surveys will play a bigger part in future research, it is hard to envisage that adequate samples can be taken from the plethora of different types of institution that exist: hospitals, hotels, schools, banks, car parks, shipyards, transport firms, government offices, etc. Even for businesses, the best available sampling mechanism—Yell Data (formerly British Telecom's Business Database)—is poorer than that available for households and gives a weaker base for grossing up survey estimates for particular commercial sectors.

Some crimes against businesses will also be resistant to measurement through surveys: companies could be particularly resistant to saying much about fraud for instance.

Probably, the best way forward is to improve current victimization surveys so that they provide more reliable and valid information on victimization risks, which is their main concern. At both national and local level, this requires financial investment so that sample sizes are adequate to the task. While household surveys have by now laid good foundations for understanding how and why risks vary, there is probably more that could be done on this front with commercial victim surveys. Hopkins (2002) for instance argues for better measures of 'customer contact', location, business 'rewards and risks', and likely sources of offenders.

Understanding the meaning of victimization

There is also more scope for exploring the victims' subjective interpretation of what happened to them. In this regard, it is worth underlining that many survey figures simply count as 'victims' those who answer affirmatively to 'screener' questions, or complete a Victim Form that indicates an 'in scope' offence. This takes little account of the victim's own assessment of the wrongfulness of the behaviour involved. A question now often asked in victimization surveys is how the victim judged the incident (asked in the BCS, the ICVS, and the New Zealand surveys for instance). Results from the interpersonal violence module in the 2001 BCS, for instance, showed that only 36 per cent of women and 6 per cent of men subject to domestic violence (as measured) in the last year thought that what happened was 'a crime'; the rest thought it was it 'wrong but not a crime'; or 'just something that happens'. The 'was it a crime' question, of course, is relatively crude for assessing whether or not the incident should be within scope of official attention. Nor do the answers necessarily signify the degree of distress incurred—something that 'just happens' may have been frightening, even so. Nonetheless, the tendency for many victims not to label as such what surveyors count as 'crimes' gives pause for thought.

Suggestions for further reading

There are several 'victimology' overviews. Useful ones are Karmen (1990), *Crime Victims: an Introduction to Victimology*, and Fattah (1991), *Understanding Criminal Victimisation*. A more 'left realist' perspective is Mawby and Walklate (1994), *Critical Victimology*. The first part of Zedner's (2002) essay on 'Victims' in *The Oxford Handbook of Criminology* covers some of the same ground as in this chapter, with more emphasis on the results of the UK surveys rather than the methodology. Koffman (1996) and Maguire (2002) also give a good overview of the UK victim surveys.

There are numerous textbooks on how to design and conduct surveys and the lessons are applicable to victim surveys. A fairly recent one in the UK is *Survey Research* by Sapsford (1999). The book by Groves *et al.* (2004) on *Survey Methodology* is also useful. Hough and Tilley's (1998) guidance on *Auditing Crime and Disorder* (ch. 2) covers many of the same issues about policing and victim surveys as here and provides some illustrative costings for different types of survey. Nicholas Fyfe's (1997) report for the Scottish Office on *Designing Police User Surveys* is also useful. Tourangeau and McNeeley (2003) cover measurement issues in relation to crime victimization.

Richard Sparks' (1981) early but elegant and long essay on the methodological problems of victim surveys remains unrivalled. There is shorter coverage in Coleman and Moynihan (1996).

References

ALLEN, J., EDMONDS, S., PATTERSON, A., and SMITH, D. (2006). *Policing and the Criminal Justice System—Public Confidence and Perceptions: Findings from the 2004/05 British Crime Survey.* Home Office Online Report No. 07/06. London: Home Office.

ALVAZZI DEL FRATE, A. (1998). *Victims of Crime in the Developing World.* Publication 57, Rome, UNICRI.

—— (2004). 'The International Crime Business Survey: Findings from Nine Central-Eastern European Cities'. *European Journal on Criminal Policy and Research* 10: 137–61.

ANDERSON, K. and McCALL, M. (2005). *Farm Crime in Australia.* Canberra: Australian Government Attorney-General's Department.

ANGLE, H., MALAM, S., and CAREY, C. (2003). *Witness Satisfaction: Findings from the Witness Satisfaction Survey 2002.* Home Office Online Report No. 19/03. London: Home Office.

ARMSTRONG, D., HINE, J., HACKING, S., ARMAOS, R., JONES, R., KLASSINGER, N., and FRANCE, A. (2005). *Children, Risk and Crime: the On Track Youth Lifestyles Surveys.* Home Office Research Study No. 278. London: Home Office.

ASHWORTH, J., WANDS, S., TURTLE, J., and LLOYD, R. (2000). *Police Public Consultation: Developing a Model Survey.* BMRB Social Research Report for the Home Office. London: BMRB.

AUDIT COMMISSION (1999). *A Measure of Success: Setting and Monitoring Local Performance Targets.* London: Audit Commission.

AUSTIN, C. (1988). *The Prevention of Robbery at Building Society Branches,* Crime Prevention Unit Paper No. 14. London: Home Office.

AYE MAUNG, N. (1995a). *Young People, Victimisation and the Police: British Crime Survey findings on experiences and attitudes of 12 to 15 year olds.* Home Office Research Study 140. London: Home Office.

—— (1995b). 'Survey Design and Interpretation of the British Crime Survey' in M. Walker (ed.), *Interpreting Crime Statistics.* Oxford: Oxford University Press.

—— and MIRRLEES-BLACK, C. (1994). *Racially Motivated Crime: a British Crime Survey Analysis.* Home Office Research and Planning Unit Paper No. 82. London: Home Office.

BACHMAN, R. and SALTZMAN, L. E. (1995). *Violence against Women: Estimates from the Redesigned Survey.* Washington DC: Bureau of Justice Statistics.

BAUM, K. (2006). *Identify Theft: First Estimates from the National Crime Victimization Survey.* NCJ 212213. Washington DC: Bureau of Justice Statistics.

BOTTOMS, A. E., MAWBY, R. I., and WALKER, M. (1987). 'A Localised Crime Survey in Contrasting Areas of a City'. *British Journal of Criminology* 27: 125–54.

BOWLING, B. (1993). 'Racial Harassment and the Process of Victimisation: Conceptual and Methodological Implications for the Local Crime Survey'. *British Journal of Criminology* 33: 231–50.

Bradley, R. (1998). *Public Expectations and Perceptions of the Police.* Police Research Series Paper No. 96. London: Home Office.

British Chambers of Commerce (2004). *Setting Business Free from Crime.* London: British Chambers of Commerce.

British Retail Consortium (2005). *12th Annual Retail Crime Survey 2004–2005.* London: British Retail Consortium.

Brown, C. and Ritchie, J. (1981). *Focussed Enumeration: the Development of a Method of Sampling Ethnic Minorities.* London: Social and Community Planning Research.

Buck, W., Chatterton, M., and Pease, K. (1995). *Obscene, Threatening and other Troublesome Calls to Women in England and Wales: 1982–1992.* Research and Planning Unit Paper No. 92. London: Home Office.

Budd, T. (1999). *Burglary of Domestic Dwellings: Findings from the British Crime Survey.* Home Office Statistical Bulletin No. 4/99. London: Home Office.

—— and Mattinson, J. (2000). *The Extent and Nature of Stalking: Findings from the 1998 British Crime Survey.* Home Office Research Study No. 210. London: Home Office.

—— and Sims, L. (2001). *Antisocial Behaviour and Disorder: Findings from the 2000 British Crime Survey.* Findings No. 145. London: Home Office.

—— Sharp, C., Weir, G., Wilson, D., and Owen, N. (2005). *Young People and Crime: Findings from the 2004 Offending, Crime and Justice Survey.* Home Office Statistical Bulletin No. 20/55. London: Home Office.

Campbell, S., McVie, S., and Lebov, K. (2004). *Scottish Crime Survey 2003.* Edinburgh: Scottish Executive Social Research.

Catalano, S. M. (2005). *Criminal Victimization 2004.* NCJ 210674. Washington DC: US Department of Justice.

Chambers, G. and Tombs, J. (eds) (1984). *The British Crime Survey: Scotland.* Edinburgh: HMSO.

Chatterton, M. R., Langmead-Jones, P., and Radcliffe, J. (1997). *Using Quality of Service Surveys.* Police Research Series Paper 23. London: Home Office.

Chivite-Matthews, N., Richardson, N., O'shea, J., Becker, J., Owen, N., Roe, S., and Condon, J. (2005). *Drug Misuse Declared: Findings from the 2003/04 British Crime Survey.* Home Office Statistical Bulletin No. 04/05. London: Home Office

Clancy, A., Hough, M., Aust, R., and Kershaw, C. (2001). *Crime, Policing and Justice: the Experience of Ethnic Minorities. Findings from the 2000 British Crime Survey.* Home Office Research Study No. 223. London: Home Office.

Coleman, C. and Moynihan, J. (1996). *Understanding Crime Data: Haunted by the Dark Figure.* Milton Keynes: Open University Press.

Crawford, A., Jones, T., Woodhouse, T., and Young, J. (1990). *The Second Islington Crime Survey.* London: Centre for Criminology, Middlesex Polytechnic.

De Leeuw, E. and Nicholls, W. (1996). 'Technological Innovations in Data Collection'. *Sociological Research Online* 4. http://www.socresonline.org.uk/ socresonline/ 1/4/leeuw.html

De Voe, J. F., Peter, K., Noonan, M., Snyder, T., and Baum, K. (2005). *Indicators of School Crime and Safety: 2005.* Washington DC: National Center for Education Statistics and Bureau of Justice Statistics.

Dobash, R. P. and Dobash, R. E. (1980). 'Women's violence to men in intimate relationships: working on a puzzle'. *British Journal of Criminology* 44: 324–49.

Durant, M., Thomas, M., and Willcock, H. D. (1972). *Crime, Criminals and the Law.* London: HMSO.

Ekblom, P. (1987). *Preventing Robberies at Sub-Post Office.* Crime Prevention Unit Paper No. 9. London: Home Office.

—— and Simon, F. (1988). *Crime and Racial Harassment in Asian-run Small Shops.* Crime Prevention Unit Paper No. 15. London: Home Office.

—— Law, H., and Sutton, M. (1996). *Safer Cities and Domestic Burglary.* Home Office Research Study No. 164. London: Home Office.

Farrington, D. P. and Dowds, E. A. (1985). 'Disentangling Criminal Behaviour and Police Reaction' in D. P. Farrington and J. Gunn (eds), *Reaction to Crime: The Public, the Police, Courts, and Prisons.* Chichester: John Wiley.

—— and Welsh, B. C. (2002). *Effects of Improved Street Lighting on Crime: a Systematic Review.* Home Office Research Study No. 251. London: Home Office.

Fattah, E. A. (1991). *Understanding Criminal Victimisation.* Scarborough, Ontario: Prentice Hall Canada Inc.

Finney, A. and Wilson, A. (2005). *Handling Stolen Goods: findings from the 2002/03 British Crime Survey and the 2003 Offending, Crime and Justice Survey.* Home Office Online Report No. 38/05. London: Home Office.

Flood-Page, C., Campbell, S., Harrington, V., and Miller, J. (2000). *Youth Crime: Findings from the 1998/99 Youth Lifestyles Survey.* Home Office Research Study No. 209. London: Home Office.

Fyfe, N. (1997). *Designing Police User Surveys.* Edinburgh: Scottish Office.

Garcia-Moreno, C., Jansen, H. A., Ellsberg, M., Heise, L., and Watts, C. (2005). *World Health Organisation Multi-country Study on Women's Health and Domestic Violence against Women: Iinitial Results on Prevalence, Health Outcomes and Women's Responses.* Geneva: World Health Organisation.

Genn, H. (1988). 'Multiple victimisation' in M. Maguire and J. Pointing (eds), *Victims of Crime: A New Deal?.* Milton Keynes: Open University Press.

Gill, M. (1993). *Crime on Holiday: Abuse, Damage and Theft in Small Holiday Accommodation Units.* Studies in Crime, Order and Policing: Research Paper No. 1. Leicester: Centre for the Study of Public Order, University of Leicester.

—— (1998). 'The victimisation of business: indicators of risk and the direction of future research'. *International Review of Victimology* 6: 17–28.

—— and Matthews, R. (1994). 'Robbers on robbery: offenders' perspectives' in M. Gill (eds), *Crime at Work: Studies in Security and Crime Prevention.* Leicester: Perpetuity Press.

Graham, J. and Bowlin, G, B. (1995). *Young People and Crime.* Home Office Research Study No. 145. London: Home Office.

Groves, R., Dillman, D., Eltinge, J., and Little, R. (eds) (2001). *Survey Nonresponse.* New York: Wiley.

——, Fowler, J. F., Couper, M., Lepkowski, J., Singer, E., and Tourangeau, R. (2004). *Survey Methodology.* New York: Wiley-IEEE.

Gruszczyńska, B. (2004). 'Crime in Central and Eastern European countries in the enlarged Europe'. *European Journal on Criminal Policy and Research* 10: 123–36.

Hamlyn, B., Phelps, A., and Sattar, G. (2004). *Key findings from the Surveys of Vulnerable and Intimidated Witnesses 2000/01 and 2003.* Home Office Findings No. 240. London: Home Office.

Harlow, C. W. (2005). *Hate Crime Reported by Victims and Police.* Bureau of Justice Statistics Special Report, NCJ 209911. Washington DC: US Government Printing Office.

HAYWARD, R. and SHARP, C. (2005). *Yong People, Crime and Anti-social Behaviour: findings from the 2003 Crime and Justice Survey*. Home Office Findings No. 245. London: Home Office.

HIBBERD, M. and SHAPLAND, J. (1993). *Violent Crime in Small Shops*. London: Police Foundation.

HOME OFFICE (2005). *Police Performance Assessment Framework*, http://www. homeoffice.gov.uk/about-us/news/police-performance-assessments

—— (2006a). *Review of the Partnership Provisions of the Crime & Disorder Act 1998—Report of Findings*. London: Home Office.

—— (2006b). *The Code of Practice for Victims of Crime*. London, http://www.cjsonline. gov.uk/downloads/application/pdf/Victims %20Code%20of%20Practice.pdf

HOPE, S. (2005). *Scottish Crime and Victimisation Survey Calibration Exercise: a Comparison of Survey Methodologies*. Edinburgh: Scottish Executive.

HOPKINS, M. (2002). 'Crimes against business: the Way for Future Research'. *British Journal of Criminology* 42: 782–97.

—— and INGRAM, M. (2001). 'Crimes against Business: the First Scottish Business Crime Survey'. *Security Journal* 14: 43–59.

HOUGH, M. (1995). *Anxiety about Crime: Findings from the 1994 British Crime Survey*. Home Office Research Study No. 147. London: Home Office.

—— and MAYHEW, P. (1983). *The British Crime Survey: First Report*. Home Office Research Study No. 76. London: HMSO.

—— and TILLEY, N. (1998). *Auditing Crime and Disorder: Guidance for Local Partnerships*. Crime Detection and Prevention Series Paper No. 91. London: Home Office.

JOHNSON, V., LEITNER, M., SHAPLAND, J., and WILES, P. (1994). *Crime on Industrial Estates*. Home Office Crime Prevention Unit Series Paper No. 54. London: Home Office.

JONES, T., MACLEAN, B., and YOUNG, J. (1986). *The Islington Crime Survey*. London: Gower.

KARMEN, A. (1990). *Crime Victims: an Introduction to Victimology*. Pacific Groves, Cal.: Brooks Cole.

KELLY, R. J., CHIN, K., and FAGAN, J. (2000). 'Lucky Money for Little Brother: the Prevalence and Seriousness of Chinese Gang Extortion'. *International Journal of Comparative and Applied Criminal Justice* 24: 61–90.

KERSHAW, C. and MYHILL, A. (2001). *Conducting Community Surveys: Results of a Feasibility Study*. Policing and Reducing Crime Unit Briefing Note No. 8/01. London: Home Office.

KINDERMANN, C., LYNCH, J., and CANTOR, D. (1997). *Effects of the Redesign on Victimization Estimates*. BJS Technical Report, NCJ 164381. Washington DC: US Department of Justice.

KINSEY, R. (1985). *Merseyside Crime and Policing Survey: Final Report*, Liverpool: Liverpool Police Committee Support Unit.

—— LEA, J., and YOUNG, J. (1986). *Losing the Fight against Crime*. Oxford: Blackwell.

KOFFMAN, L. (1996). *Crime Surveys and Victims of Crime*. Cardiff: University of Wales Press.

LAMON, P. (2006). *General Results of the UNECE-UNODC Questionnaire on Victim Surveys* UNECE-UNODC Meeting on Crime Statistics, 25–7 January 2006, http://www.unece.org/stats/documents/ ece/ces/ge.14/2006/2.e.ppt

LAYCOCK, G. (1984). *Reducing Burglary: a Study of Chemists' Shops*. Crime Prevention Unit Paper No. 1. London: Home Office.

LEVI, M. (1988). *The Prevention of Fraud.* Crime Prevention Unit Paper No. 17. London: Home Office.

LONDON BOROUGH OF NEWHAM (1987). *A Report of a Survey of Crime and Racial Harassment in Newham.* London: London: Borough of Newham.

LYNN, P. (1997). *Collecting Data about Non-respondents to the British Crime Survey.* London: Social and Community Planning Research.

MAGUIRE, M. (2002). 'Crime statistics: the "data explosion" and its implications' in M. Maguire, R. Morgan, and R. Reiner (eds), *The Oxford Handbook of Criminology* (3rd edn). Oxford: Oxford University Press.

MARSHALL, E. and THOMAS, N. (2000). *Traffic Calming: the Reality of 'Road Rage'.* Briefing Note No. 12/00. London: Home Office.

MARTIN, J. and MANNERS, T. (1995). 'Computer Assisted Personal Interviewing in Social Research' in R. M. Lee (ed.), *Information Technology for the Social Scientist.* London: UCL Press.

MAWBY, R. I. (2003). 'Crime and the Business Community: Experiences of Businesses in Cornwall, England'. *Security Journal* 16: 45–61.

—— and WALKLATE, M. (1994). *Critical Victimology.* London: Sage.

MAYHEW, P. (2000). 'Researching the State of Crime: Local, National and International Victims Surveys' in R. D. King and E. Wincup (eds), *Doing Research on Crime and Justice* (1st edn). Oxford: Oxford University Press.

—— and ELLIOTT, D. (1990). 'Self-reported Offending, Victimization, and the British Crime Survey'. *Victims and Violence* 5: 83–96.

MIRRLEES-BLACK, C. (1999). *Domestic Violence: Findings from a New British Crime Survey Self Completion Questionnaire.* Home Office Research Study No. 191. London: Home Office.

—— (2001). *Confidence in the Criminal Justice System: Findings from the 2000 British Crime Survey.* Home Office Research Findings No. 137. London: Home Office.

—— and ROSS, A. (1995). *Crime against Retail and Manufacturing Premises: Findings from the 1994 Commercial Victimisation Survey.* Home Office Research Study No. 146. London: Home Office.

MODOOD, T., BERTHOUD, R., LAKEY, J., SMITH, P., VIRDEE, S., and BEISHON, S. (1997). *Ethnic Minorities in Britain: Diversity and Disadvantage.* London: Policy Studies Institute.

MORRIS, A. (1997). *Women's Safety Survey.* Wellington NZ: Ministry of Justice.

MOUZOS, J. and MAKKAI, T. (2004). *Women's Experience of Male Violence: Findings from the Australian component of the International Violence against Women Survey.* Research and Public Policy Series No. 56. Canberra: Australian Institute of Criminology.

NACRO (2001). *The NACRO Guide to Crime.* London: NACRO.

NEWBURN, T. and JONES, T. (2002). *Consultation by Crime and Disorder Partnerships.* London: Home Office.

NICHOLAS, S., POVEY, D., WALKER, A., and KERSHAW, K. (2005). *Crime in England and Wales 2004/2005.* Home Office Statistical Bulletin No. 11/05. London: Home Office.

OFFICE OF COMMUNICATIONS (2005). *The Communications Market 2005.* London: Ofcom.

PAINTER, K. (1992). 'Different Worlds: the Spatial, Temporal and Social Dimensions of Female Victimisation' in D. J. Evans, N. R. Fyte, and D. T. Herbert (eds), *Crime Policy and Place.* London: Routledge.

—— and FARRINGTON, D. F. (1998). 'Marital Violence in Great Britain and its Relationship to Marital and Non-marital Rape'. *International Review of Victimology* 5: 257–76.

PEASE, K. (1998). *Repeat Victimisation: Taking Stock.* Crime Detection and Prevention Series Paper No. 90. London: Home Office.

PERCY, A. (1998). *Ethnicity and Victimisation: Findings from the 1996 British Crime Survey.* Home Office Statistical Bulletin No. 6/98. London: Home Office.

—— and MAYHEW, P. (1997). 'Estimating Sexual Victimisation in a National Survey: a New Approach'. *Studies in Crime and Crime Prevention* 6: 125–50.

PHILLIPS, A. and CHAMBERLAIN, V. (2006). *MORI Five-Year Report: an Analysis of Youth Survey Data.* London: Youth Justice Board.

PHILLIPS, S. and COCHRANE, R. (1988). *Crime and Nuisance in the Shopping Centre: a Case Study in Crime Prevention.* Crime Prevention Unit Paper No. 16. London: Home Office.

RAMSEY, M. and SPILLER, J. (1997). *Drug Misuse Declared in 1996: Latest Results from the British Crime Survey.* Home Office Research Study No 172. London: Home Office.

RAND, M. R. and RENNISON, C. M. (2005). 'Bigger is not Necessarily Better: an Analysis of Violence against Women Estimates from the National Crime Victimisation Survey and the National Violence against Women Survey'. *Journal of Quantitative Criminology* 21: 267–91.

RINGHAM, L. and SALISBURY, H. (2004). *Support for Victims of Crime: Findings from the 2002/2003 British Crime Survey.* Home Office Online Report No. 31/04. London: Home Office.

SALISBURY, H. and UPSON, A. (2004). *Ethnicity, Victimisation and Worry about Crime: Findings from the 2001/02 and 2002/03 British Crime Surveys.* London: Home Office.

SAPSFORD, R. J. (1999). *Survey Research.* London: Sage.

SHURY, J., SPEED, M., VIVIAN, D., KUECHEL, A., and NICHOLAS, S. (2005). *Crime against Retail and Manufacturing Premises: Findings from the 2002 Commercial Victimisation Survey.* Home Office Online Report No. 37/05. London: Home Office.

SIMS, L. (2001). *Neighbourhood Watch: Findings from the 2000 British Crime Survey.* Home Office Research Findings No. 150. London: Home Office.

SKOGAN, W. G. (1986). 'Methodological Issues in the Study of Victimisation' in E. Fattah (ed.), *From Crime Policy to Victim Policy.* London: Macmillan.

—— (1994). *Contacts between Police and Public: Findings from the 1992 British Crime Survey.* Home Office Research Study No. 133. London: HMSO.

SMITH, D. J., McVIE, S., WOODWARD, R., SHUTE, J., FLINT, J., and McARA, L. (2001). *The Edinburgh Study of Youth Transitions and Crime: Key Findings at Ages 12 and 13.* Online report, *http://www.law.ed.ac.uk/cls/esytc/findingsreport.htm*

SMITH, L. J. F. (1987). *Crime in Hospitals: Diagnosis and Prevention,* Crime Prevention Unit Paper No. 7. London: Home Office.

SMITH, M. D. (1989). 'Women Abuse: the Case for Surveys by Telephone'. *Journal of Interpersonal Violence* 4: 308–24.

SPARKS, R. (1981). 'Surveys of Victimisation: an Optimistic Assessment' in M. Tonry and N. Morris (eds), *Crime and Justice: An Annual Review of Research* Vol. 3. London: University of Chicago Press.

—— GENN, H., and DODD, D. J. (1977). *Surveying Victims.* London: John Wiley.

STANKO, E. A. (1988). 'Hidden Violence against Women' in M. Maguire and J. Pointing (eds), *Victims of Crime: a New Deal?.* Milton Keynes: Open University Press.

STRAUS, M. A. (1979). 'Measuring Family Conflict and Violence: the Conflict Tactics Scale'. *Journal of Marriage and the Family* 41: 75–88.

STRAUS, M. A. and GELLES, R. (1992). *Physical Violence in American Families: Risk Factors and Adaptions to Violence in 8,145 Families.* New Brunswick, NJ: Transaction Publishers.

TAYLOR, N. and MAYHEW, P. (2002). *Patterns of Victimisation among Small Retail Businesses.* Trends and Issues in Crime and Criminal Justice No. 221. Canberra: Australian Institute of Criminology.

TILLEY, N. and HOPKINS, M. (1998). *Business as Usual: an Evaluation of the Small Business and Crime Initiative.* Policy Research Series, Paper No. 95. London: Home Office.

TOURANGEAU, R. and McNEELEY, M. E. (2003). 'Measuring Crime and Crime Victimization' in J. V. Pepper and C. V. Petrie (eds), *Measurement Issues in Criminal Justice Research: Workshop Summary.* Washington DC: The National Academic Press.

TUCK, M. and SOUTHGATE, P. (1981). *Ethnic Minorities, Crime and Policing.* Home Office Research Study 70. London: HMSO.

US DEPARTMENT OF JUSTICE (1976). *Criminal Victimization in the United States, 1976. A National Crime Survey Report.* Washington DC: US Government Printing Office.

VAN DIJK, J. J. M. and TERLOUW, G. J. (1996). 'An International Perspective of the Business Community as Victims of Fraud and Crime'. *Security Journal* 7: 157–67.

VAN KESTEREN, J., MAYHEW, P., and NIEUWBEERTA, P. (2001). *Criminal Victimisation in Seventeen Industrialised Countries: Key Findings from the 2000 International Crime Victims Survey.* The Hague: Ministry of Justice.

WALBY, S. and ALLEN, J. (2004). *Domestic Violence, Sexual Assault and Stalking: Findings from the British Crime Survey.* Home Office Research Study No. 276. London: Home Office.

WILSON, D., PATTERSON, A., POWELL, G., and HEMBURY, R. (2006). *Fraud and Technology Crimes: Findings from the 2003/04 British Crime Survey, the 2004 Offending, Crime and Justice Survey and Administrative Sources.* Home Office Online Report 09/06. London: Home Office.

WOOD, M. (2004). *Perceptions and Experience of Antisocial Behaviour: Findings from the 2003/2004 British Crime Survey.* Home Office Research Findings No. 246. London: Home Office.

—— (2005). *The Victimisation of Young People: Findings from the Crime and Justice Survey 2003.* Home Office Online Report No. 49/04. London: Home Office.

ZEDNER, L. (2002). 'Victims', in M. Maguire, R. Morgan, and R. Reiner (eds), *The Oxford Handbook of Criminology* (3rd edn). Oxford: Oxford University Press.

ZVEKIC, U. (1998). *Criminal Victimisation in Countries in Transition.* Publication No. 61. Rome: UNICRI.

9

Researching 'street criminals' in the field: a neglected art?

Mike Maguire

Introduction

I began my contribution to the first edition of this volume in 2000 by stating that 'criminologists nowadays spend surprisingly little of their time talking to "criminals"'. As will be discussed later, in the intervening years there have been some welcome signs of change. Nevertheless, research based on interactions with offenders still remains the exception rather than the rule. Previous generations of criminologists probably spoke to offenders more often, but the majority of encounters were formal interviews with samples of convicted offenders in prisons or probation offices, usually to apply psychological tests or to elicit quantifiable data about their backgrounds. It has thus always been relatively unusual for researchers to get to know their subjects well, to meet them in less artificial settings, and to allow them to talk about crime and criminality at length in their own terms. It has been even rarer—for readily understandable reasons—for researchers to get close enough to criminal groups to learn in detail about (still less to observe) how they plan and commit illegal acts.

Criminologists as a body probably deserve criticism for this situation, which has left some important gaps in knowledge at the heart of the subject. Over the last thirty years, the scope, depth, and funding of crime-related research have grown enormously, benefiting from new computerized data sources in police and criminal justice agencies, as well as (since 1982) from the regular 'sweeps' of the British Crime Survey. However, this growth has been unbalanced, with some significant shifts in focus. We now know far more about spatial and temporal patterns of offences and about their physical circumstances (for overviews, see Maguire 2007; Bottoms 2007), but this has not been matched by comparable advances in our understanding of the people responsible for most of these offences. For example, we still know relatively little about how they make decisions on where and when to commit (or not to commit) particular kinds of crime, or how they perceive the risks involved: such knowledge is not only of academic interest, but is potentially valuable for the development of crime reduction strategies. Equally, penal policy has seen a broad shift away from interest in 'rehabilitating' individual offenders, towards methods of categorizing them according to their level of 'risk' and the development of strategies—including surveillance, curfews, and preventive prison sentences—to 'manage' that risk (Feeley and Simon 1992; O'Malley 1998; Garland 2001; Robinson

2002): advocates of these new approaches tend to pay little attention to what offenders think or why they commit crime.

Importantly, too, these shifts in focus have been accompanied by declining attention among criminologists to some of the central theoretical questions (for example, about 'explaining crime' or the 'transmission of criminal values') which preoccupied their predecessors. Despite the overall expansion of research, many basic theories of crime remain largely untested empirically, thus inhibiting their refinement and development—and, ultimately, the progress of criminology as an academic discipline. To counteract this, more direct and detailed knowledge about criminal groups and the relationships between their members could stimulate re-thinking about, for example, subcultural or social learning theories, which have been largely neglected for years. And even those more recent theories which stress the importance of situation, environment, or opportunity—such as rational choice theory (Cornish and Clarke 1986) and routine activities theory (Felson 1994)—would benefit from more studies of the actual decision-making behaviour of offenders.

In sum, there is a strong case for 'righting the balance' in current patterns of criminological work, by encouraging—and allocating more funding to—research with offenders. In particular, it will be argued here—with due recognition of the practical, ethical, and personal safety limitations—there is a need for more qualitative research using ethnographic, field interview, or participant observation methods. The use of such methods has a long, if precarious, tradition within the discipline, which has been kept alive through several generations by small numbers of highly skilled—and in some cases very brave—individual researchers. Most of these have been passionate advocates of the value to criminology of ethnographic fieldwork with offenders, sometimes in the face of hostility from 'mainstream' criminologists who have attacked it, variously, as 'unscientific', 'too risky', 'too difficult', or 'immoral' (for a selection of arguments on both sides, see, for example, Sutherland and Cressey 1960; Polsky 1971; Hobbs 1998; Wright and Bennett 1990; Hobbs and May 1993; Wright *et al.* 1992; Cromwell 2006).

The main focus of this chapter will be upon the perpetrators of so-called 'volume crime': the generally small-time thefts, burglaries, assaults, vehicle crimes, and acts of vandalism which make up the bulk of offences recorded annually by the police. Research on those involved in more serious and 'organized' crime is discussed by Patricia Rawlinson in the next chapter (and by Dick Hobbs in the previous edition). This distinction is somewhat arbitrary, and some overlaps are inevitable. Indeed, as Hobbs (2000) points out, individuals can oscillate between quite different modes of offending, which leads Hobbs to question the validity of dividing them into separate categories at all. Even so, most commentators would agree that, while the boundaries are certainly fuzzy, there are different levels of criminal organization (distinguished, for example, by their complexity, resources, or capacity to enforce discipline or subvert criminal justice processes) and that relatively few offenders ever take part in criminal enterprises at the 'higher' levels.

Our main interest here, then, is in what writers have variously called 'ordinary', 'run of the mill', or 'street' criminals, or (emphasizing the frequency of both their criminal activities and their court convictions) 'persistent' or 'recidivist' offenders. The police—and many offenders themselves—tend either to use general slang terms such as 'villains' or to refer to categories based on criminal specialisms ('burglars', 'car thieves', 'fighters', 'street dealers', etc.). None of these labels is entirely satisfactory (for a discussion of their relative merits, see Maguire and Bennett 1982: 63–6), but it is difficult to find one suitable term for what is in reality a very broad category with unclear boundaries and diverse membership. It is also important to stress that—despite their lack of precision—social classifications of this kind are often more useful to researchers than classifications created on the apparently more 'objective' basis of official criminal records: the latter only reflect people's interactions with the criminal justice system, which may be merely one factor among many in the construction of their social identity as 'criminals'.

The basic shape of the chapter is as follows. It begins with a brief historical overview of the main kinds of research which have been carried out with offenders, relating these to broad shifts in criminological theory and penal policy, and to consequent changes in the kinds of research question which have been asked. This is followed by discussion of some illustrative examples of studies (of 'criminal networks', 'burglars', 'street kids', and 'gangs') which have relied heavily on field research and have used a range of qualitative methodologies, from semi-structured interviewing to 'participant observation'. As will quickly become clear, I am not a specialist in qualitative methodology, let alone an expert ethnographer, and I do not intend to venture into the sophisticated theoretical debates which have developed among sociologists in these areas over the last twenty or so years (see, for example, Atkinson 1990; Morse 1994; Glaser and Barney 1998; Denzin and Lincoln 2000). Rather, the focus here will be firmly upon my own (limited) and other researchers' experiences of practical issues which arise in the course of fieldwork with offenders. The first two studies discussed are research projects in which I was involved as a young fieldworker in the 1970s. It is interesting (if a little painful) to look back on one's own early fumbling attempts, and I have highlighted my mistakes as well as lessons I learned from them. These two studies also provide striking evidence of how much the policies and practices of funding bodies have changed since the 1970s. The remainder are chosen to illustrate some of the most creative and resourceful approaches which have been adopted in qualitative research on offenders, all of them showing that it is possible to achieve a great deal more in this direction than pessimists perennially suggest.

Research on offenders: an historical perspective

In criminology, as in any other area of social research, it is important to place any discussion of research methods within the context of the kinds of question to which answers are sought. Very different kinds of research question tend to be asked at different periods, depending upon fashions and developments in theory, current policy concerns, the priorities of funding bodies, and so on. Research on offenders has been particularly affected by broad shifts of these kinds, and it is instructive to consider it briefly from a historical perspective.

Before the 1930s in the USA—and for much longer in Britain—criminology was dominated by psychiatrists and psychologists, whose main interest was in explaining why some people become 'criminal' and why others do not. This was generally combined with a belief that the only appropriate methodology was one based on 'scientific' principles: chiefly, that samples of 'criminals' should be compared in a systematic way with equivalent samples of 'non-criminals', in order to identify any significant differences between them. Broadly known as a 'positivist' approach to the study of crime, this led to the adoption of quasi-laboratory methods of research based mainly on detailed explorations of the backgrounds and mental and physical characteristics of convicted offenders, usually in prisons. However, from the 1920s onwards, the study of crime began to strike out in new directions, in which sociologists were increasingly prominent. The causes of crime came to be sought less in individual pathology than in social and structural factors such as the rapid growth of cities, social inequality, or blocked opportunities. Interactions between offenders—particularly in the shape of 'gangs' or criminal 'sub-cultures'—also came to be seen as a major factor in the facilitation of crime, perpetuation of criminal attitudes, and transmission of criminal skills.

The consequences of these kinds of theoretical interest for research methodology were that, instead of studying samples of captive offenders, American criminologists began to look for ways of studying the lives, attitudes, and behaviour of criminal groups 'on the streets'. The key pioneering group in this respect was the so-called 'Chicago School'. Although associated with some significant theoretical developments—particularly 'social disorganization theory' and the (now largely discredited) 'ecological' model of the development of cities and their crime patterns (Park *et al.* 1925; Shaw 1931)—the work of the Chicago-based criminologists was arguably more important in its encouragement of experimentation with a variety of more adventurous and imaginative research methodologies. Several had previously worked as journalists, and their first instinct in conducting research was simply to get out into the streets and find out for themselves what was happening, using whatever sources of information they could acquire.

A classic example was Frederic Thrasher's (1927) study, *The Gang*, which used a combination of observation, interviews, life histories, casual discussions, newspaper reports, personal documents, census data, and court records to draw a comprehensive picture of youth gangs in Chicago. Although some of the reported findings were dubious—especially the claim to have identified precisely 1,313 separate gangs!—the methodology had a hugely liberating effect on criminology. Other well-known innovative studies of offenders from this era, both based primarily upon constructing life histories from lengthy interviews, include Clifford Shaw's *The Jack-Roller* (1930) and Edwin Sutherland's *The Professional Thief* (1937).

Although the Chicago school withered after the 1930s, and most of the major American criminologists devoted their energies to theoretical debates, a number of individuals continued the Chicagoan tradition by producing high-quality empirical studies of 'street criminals'. In some cases, they went further than their predecessors, spending long periods in the company of groups of offenders and using methods which might be called 'participant observation'—though the researchers did not actually participate in crime (further comments will be made later about what kinds of research activity are covered by this and alternative terms). The majority involved work with youth gangs (e.g. Whyte 1943; Yablonsky 1962; Liebow 1967), but one of the most interesting and original was Ned Polsky's (1971) first-hand account of the lives of adult pool-room hustlers and of the Greenwich Village 'beat scene'. His book contains an excellent discussion of 'dos and don'ts' in this kind of research, as well as a polemical defence of field research with adult criminals, repudiating criticisms from other American criminologists.

Meanwhile, studies of this kind remained very rare in Britain. However, just as the Chicago school had earlier 'liberated' American criminology, a number of young sociologists began in the late 1960s to attack the positivist tradition in British criminology, producing at the same time some excellent new kinds of studies of offenders—or, as they preferred to call them, 'deviant' groups. Building on the insights of the American labelling theorists (e.g. Becker 1964), these 'deviancy theorists' emphasized the point that 'criminals' do not constitute a 'natural' category, but are people labelled as such as a result of complex social and legal processes. One consequence of this viewpoint was that researchers set out to explore the 'social construction' of crime and deviancy in the everyday world, including the reactions of the people who become labelled as deviant. A good example is Jock Young's (1971) study of drug-takers, which charts a process of 'deviancy amplification' as the subjects, who regard drug-taking as a relatively harmless recreational pursuit, are demonized by more powerful social groups and react in turn by escalating their deviant behaviour. A similar process was demonstrated in Stan Cohen's (1972) classic study of 'mods and rockers' on seaside beaches. The methodology for such studies was eclectic and qualitative, using anything from observation of, and lengthy discussions with, members of the groups in question, to cuttings from popular newspapers—the central aim being to analyse how different social groups understood and defined the situation in question.

The general term most commonly used today to describe this kind of research is 'ethnographic', although I still particularly like David Matza's (1964) concept of 'appreciative' research. This does not imply that the criminologist is an admirer of those he or she studies, but simply that a key feature of the approach is (at least temporarily) to suspend judgement and observe and listen to offenders—in a sense, to allow them to 'tell their own story'. The data obtained may be used—as with the deviancy theorists—to develop or support criminological theories, but the researcher often set outs without a clear hypothesis to test: rather, in the mode of many social anthropologists, he or she may aim to develop theoretical insights as they emerge out of the fieldwork (another term often used in this context is 'grounded theory', a concept originally applied by Glaser and Strauss 1967). Equally, if interviews are conducted, they are likely to be relatively unstructured, allowing the offender to give as free an account as possible. It would be wrong to think of this as a haphazard process, with no testing of the ideas or the data obtained. On the contrary, methodologists have developed quite sophisticated sets of principles and techniques, such as 'reflexivity' and 'progressive focussing', to ensure that ethnographers approach their research in as rigorous a manner as possible (see Hammersley and Atkinson 1995; Atkinson 1990; Hobbs and May 1993; Fielding 1993). However, at the end of the day, the success of this kind of research hinges on the personal qualities of the researcher, whose key tool is his or her imaginative insight.

Rather like the Chicago school some forty years earlier, the 'deviancy school' produced a number of excellent research monographs within a short period, the supply then drying up as the sense of unity dissolved and its members struck out in a variety of directions. Many, in fact, moved away quickly from 'hands on' research with offenders, towards study of the institutions which 'create' criminals and which influence the ways we think about crime and criminality: the government, the law, the police, the courts, and the media. This institutional focus soon extended to interest in, for example, the 'occupational cultures' of criminal justice agencies and to debates about their accountability. By the mid-1970s, studies in which offenders (or deviant groups) were a central focus of the research, had become quite a rarity in Britain.

Meanwhile, as criminologists were turning away from both positivist methodologies and fieldwork-based studies of deviant groups, the key funding agency for policy-related research, the Home Office Research Unit, was also beginning to lose interest in offenders as an object of study and it, too, soon struck out in a number of new directions. First, under the leadership of Ronald Clarke in the late 1970s and early 1980s, the Unit directed its attention and its research funds away from seeking ways to 'rehabilitate' offenders, towards finding ways of manipulating the environment (e.g. through target hardening or design) to reduce opportunities for the commission of crime (see, e.g., Mayhew *et al.* 1976; Clarke and Mayhew 1980). The central research question thus became whether or not a particular prevention practice 'worked': how it affected offenders' thoughts or attitudes was of only secondary interest. Secondly, with the Conservative governments of the 1980s insisting strongly upon 'value for money' in the public sector, the Home Office began to commission more research on the effectiveness and accountability of criminal justice institutions. And thirdly, from 1982 onwards, the investment of a large proportion of the Home Office research budget in the British Crime Survey stimulated greater attention both to patterns of victimization and to the views and experiences of crime victims—at the same time boosting the profile and status of quantitative research methods (especially the statistical manipulation of large datasets) at the expense of more qualitative methods. While some theoreticians and radical criminologists initially wished to steer clear of the policy-oriented research funded by the Home Office, the huge amounts of new knowledge it generated about crime patterns, victims, and the performance of criminal justice institutions could not be ignored and, together with similar developments in the United States, eventually propelled these topics into centre stage of academic debates (for further discussion, see Maguire 2007).

These shifts of focus in the then main funding body for criminology further accelerated the already declining interest among university-based researchers in conducting studies of offenders. Over the late 1970s and the 1980s, most criminologists came to see their standard sources of data, not as interviews with samples of offenders, but as published documents and statistics, public surveys, agency records, or interviews with policymakers, managers, and practitioners. An increasing number (myself included), also turned their attention to crime victims, getting involved with the British Crime Survey or local victim surveys, or conducting interviews in victims' homes. When offenders were interviewed, it was often simply to provide some form of 'consumer feedback' on the performance of a particular agency: for example, to obtain prisoners' views of complaints procedures (Maguire and Vagg 1984), or suspects' experiences of the safeguards introduced by the Police and Criminal Evidence Act 1984 (Brown *et al.* 1992).

Despite the rapid growth of criminology as an academic subject throughout the 1990s, there were for several years relatively few signs of a revival of interest in ethnography. Most of these were to be found in North America, where a small number of scholars produced field-based studies of burglars and persistent thieves (among the best being Wright and Decker 1994 and Shover 1996) and a more substantial number kept alive a long American tradition of research on young people in street gangs (see Klein 1998, Huff 2002). Ethnographic work in the USA has also been boosted since the mid-1990s by a growing number of sociocultural studies, particularly work exploring violence and drug-dealing among socially excluded ethnic minority communities, much of which has emphasized the importance of gender and drawn on the concept of 'masculinities' (see, for example Messerschmidt 2000; Bourgeois 1996; Topalli *et al.* 2002; Miller 2000; Jacobs *et al.* 2003; Mullins 2006; for overviews, see Bowker 2000; Levi *et al.* 2007).

In Britain, by contrast, such work was conspicuous by its absence throughout much of the 1980s and 1990s, and ethnographic writers such as Hobbs (1993, 1998) were very much the exception. However, partly stimulated by concerns about increases in robberies, recent years have seen a number of interview-based studies of street crime (Fitzgerald *et al.* 2003; Hallsworth 2005; Wright *et al.* 2006), while studies based on in-depth ethnographic fieldwork have also begun to emerge in greater numbers. Examples of the latter include Sanders' (2004) research on sex workers, and forthcoming books by Silverstone on night-clubbing and drugs, and by O'Brien on neighbourhood drug markets. The latter two studies are part of a new series of ethnographic monographs of which Hobbs is the series editor, and which may encourage more young academics to consider undertaking this kind of research. In addition, the growth of theoretical interest in 'cultural criminology' and its associated focus on the 'lived realities', emotions, and subjective meanings of criminal lifestyles (Ferrell *et al.* 2004; Hayward and Young 2007) is likely to lead more in the direction of ethnography .

To sum up, it can be seen from the above review that throughout the history of their discipline, most criminologists' personal contact with offenders in the course of research has been much less direct and less frequent than outsiders might expect. In Britain, the history of such contacts can be broadly divided into a long period of interviewing 'captive' offenders in order to collect personal and psychological data about them and, after a brief flurry of innovative, 'appreciative' studies of 'deviant' groups based on a variety of fieldwork-based methods, a 30-year period in which (with a few notable exceptions) contact was minimal. It is only very recently that signs have emerged of a rekindling of interest in ethnographic fieldwork, and as yet little of this has focused on older offenders who engage in more serious forms of property crime. Moreover, although there is a stronger and longer tradition of qualitative studies of offenders in the United States, and although recent interest in sociocultural approaches to the study of crime has encouraged more work in this tradition, the amount of ethnographic work conducted remains very small in relation to the overall numbers of criminologists working in the country. In other words, in the remainder of this chapter, which looks in more detail at studies which focus in some depth on offenders' activities, lifestyles, and attitudes, it should be kept in mind that we are describing a minority tradition in criminology, the exception rather than the rule.

Research with offenders: some concrete examples

It is now time to look in a more concrete fashion at some of the practical issues which arise in conducting research with offenders. I am going to concentrate here on the 'appreciative' styles of research referred to above, in which the main objective is to find out (and develop explanations of) how offenders think and behave outside custody, rather than on aims and methodologies associated with 'positivist' approaches to criminology.

A study of 'criminal networks'

I shall begin with some comments about my own experiences of this kind of research, with burglars and with other persistent property offenders, in fieldwork conducted during the 1970s. Although I have often subsequently interviewed offenders for other purposes (such as to canvass their opinions about complaints systems or the parole system) it was only in the two studies described that the focus of the research was on their lifestyles and criminal activity: since then, like many other criminologists, I have been drawn increasingly into studies of the agencies which respond to crime, rather than of the perpetrators. Secondly, I shall refer to some studies in which other academics have engaged in research with offenders which comes closer to 'participant observation' than I was able (or sought) to achieve.

I certainly do not put forward the first study as a shining example: mainly as a result of my inexperience, it became too unfocused and fragmented, and its eventual output was limited to the unpublished official research report, a few working papers, and a conference paper (Webster and Maguire 1973). In the present-day climate in which funding bodies have to demonstrate 'value for money' in the research they commission, this would probablly have been seen as an insufficient return on their investment. Nevertheless, from a purely selfish point of view, it was extremely interesting and educative to work on, generated some original (if only half-formed) ideas which influenced my later writing, and raised some important practical, methodological, and ethical issues. It also—unusually for this kind of research—focused on adult, rather than juvenile, offenders. Hence, while it may serve here partly as a salutary lesson on mistakes to avoid in field research, it had strong redeeming features and I look back on it essentially as a 'good try' at an extremely difficult piece of research.

I was employed on the project as a research assistant to Douglas Webster, of Salford University. Having just completed a postgraduate degree in social anthropology, this was my first 'real job'. It was a substantial study, employing me full-time and two other researchers part-time for nearly four years. The main aim of the research, which was funded by the Social Science Research Council (the predecessor of the ESRC), was to explore the nature of 'criminal networks' in three medium-sized British towns. There was no immediate policy objective and the project was not shaped by any clear theoretical perspective: despite the long timescale, it was essentially exploratory in character, and we were given a great deal of latitude to alter our approach as the study progressed (again, one would be unlikely to be given this degree of freedom by present-day funding bodies).

The rationale for the research was as follows. It was well known that every sizeable town contains a number of persistent property offenders who see the town as their home and who usually return to live there (and often re-offend there) after any prison sentence. It was also clear that many of these are familiar faces to the local police and to each other. However, little was known about how such people relate together: how often and in what contexts they meet, whether they form cohesive groups (or 'subcultures'), how much they help or support each other, how they gain reputations as (un)reliable or (in)competent criminals, how they handle disputes, and so on. A starting assumption of the study (based on Douglas Webster's previous experience) was that the best broad description of their inter-relations was of loose 'networks' rather than 'groups': rather like an 'old boy network' of ex-public school pupils, individuals would be able to call upon others for collaboration, help, or services when they needed them, and would be able to verify their '*bona fides*' to those they did not know by means of a verbal 'reference' from mutual acquaintances. Our main task was to explore the nature and parameters of such networks and to develop insights into how they 'worked'.

I was made responsible for most of the work in one of the three towns ('Southtown'), about thirty miles from where I lived. As I was employed full-time, I was expected to work in a more intensive, field-oriented style than my two part-time colleagues, who were based in towns in Scotland and the north of England, and it was planned that eventually their findings would be used to support or complement mine in an integrated document. In the event, the research took rather different directions in each of the three towns and we failed to produce any coherent conclusions from the study as a whole. Consequently, I shall concentrate here only on my own research in Southtown.

The first important decision to be made was how, and to what extent, to involve the local criminal justice agencies, and especially the police, in the study: clearly, they had a great deal of information about offenders which would be valuable to us, but if I developed close relations with them, there was a danger that local offenders would doubt my independence (or even regard me as a police informer) and hence not give me the necessary trust and co-operation to achieve the aims of the study. Vice versa, of course, there was a risk that local police officers or members of other criminal justice agencies would not trust someone who was 'associating with criminals' and would not willingly assist the research. Such problems have been seen as quite acute by some researchers: for example, Richard Wright and Scott Decker, in their study of burglars 'in the wild', decided 'not to use contacts provided by the police or probation officers, fearing that this would arouse the suspicions of offenders that the research was the cover for a sting operation' (Wright *et al.* 1992; Wright and Decker 1994). As it turned out, however, my own concerns on these scores were allayed more easily than expected, and I managed to maintain good relationships with both 'sides', without hiding from either the fact that I was talking to the other. Early on, I was introduced to the governors of two local prisons and to local court administrators, probation managers, and senior police officers, all of whom promised assistance and access when it was needed for research purposes. It was also agreed with the police that I would not be asked or expected to pass on any information I might gather about any of the individuals I spoke to. The importance of this to my credibility with offenders was fully understood, and the agreement was respected throughout. (Of course, if I had ever picked up any information about a very serious crime—which, thankfully, I did not—the situation might have had to be reviewed.) Equally, I made it clear to offenders that the study had official co-operation, but that anything they told me would remain confidential. On the whole, they seemed to accept my assurances, and I can recall very little open suspicion about my motives or truthfulness (further comment on these issues will be made later).

The main research strategy adopted was a dual one: on the one hand, to use court and police records to identify and interview an initial sample of male offenders with a substantial number of previous convictions in the town and, on the other, to use a 'snowball' method, following up any recommendations to speak to particular people. The 'interviews' that resulted were very varied in duration, frequency, style, subject-matter, and location. In some cases, they led on to research which was closer to 'participant observation'. I interviewed some people in prisons, some in probation offices, some in their homes, and others in pubs, clubs, or cafes. Some interviews lasted only a few minutes, others for hours. Some were relatively formal, others were wide-ranging conversations. Some offenders I saw only once, others I got to know well and met several times. I was also sometimes invited to go for a drink with small groups in pubs and, on two or three occasions, in people's homes. While these were chiefly social gatherings, I also managed to use them partly as informal 'focus groups'. At other times, I went on my own to pubs or cafes where I knew that offenders frequently 'hung out', hoping to meet someone I knew and be introduced to others. Although this happened occasionally, in most cases the visits were unproductive and I sometimes felt very uncomfortable, knowing nobody and not knowing what to do (do you walk up and introduce yourself to a group of strangers who you think may be 'criminals'?).

I should confess at this point that, although I had studied social anthropology and had some vague knowledge of the standard anthropological technique of recording 'field notes' when staying with remote tribes, I (like most of my contemporaries) had had absolutely no formal training in social research methods. I therefore had to learn everything through a combination of 'apprenticeship' and experimentation. I began by accompanying Douglas Webster, who was an experienced fieldworker with exceptional interviewing skills, on four or five visits to probation offices and pubs to meet offenders whom he knew from previous research in the town; from then on, I was on my own. In retrospect, this had both advantages and disadvantages. On the one hand, it gave me confidence in my own abilities, and I think also it made me less inhibited and more creative in my approach to tackling difficult research questions than I would have been if I had first studied methods in an abstract fashion from textbooks. On the other hand, I made a number of mistakes, especially in insufficient awareness of the need to tailor data collection and recording in the field to the process of analysis and writing. Where interviewing was concerned, I soon developed my own style, which—while not necessarily a model I would urge others to follow—has always worked for me in terms of putting people at their ease and 'getting them to talk'. Although sometimes advised otherwise, I decided early on never to use a tape-recorder, even in prison interviews, as it could damage the crucial trust I had to build up with those I spoke to. I generally took notes in my own version of shorthand or speed-writing (more accurately described as 'scribble'), although I did not try to write down everything. My basic aim was to record any points that appeared to me to be important, or any statements that would make useful quotations. Even then, I quickly acquired the habit of writing only at times which would not interrupt the 'flow' of important parts of the conversation: this entailed remembering points or sentences for some minutes and writing one thing while speaking about something else. I also made it a general rule that if people gave me sensitive information about, for example, recent offences they had committed (and it was surprising how many openly volunteered information about such matters), I would make no written record of this. Indeed, as far as possible, I tried to discourage them from giving me this kind of information at all.

Perhaps the key lesson I learned, quite early on, was that the best way of establishing a good relationship with interviewees was to be completely honest about who I was, what I was doing, and why, and—importantly—not to hide the fact that I had access to information about them from the local police, prison records, and so on. I also answered honestly any general questions they had about the research (though I refused to tell them what other individuals had told me). Despite some uninformed portrayals of them, most offenders are anything but naive, and can quickly sense any attempt to dissimulate. Moreover, I was sometimes seen going into the local police station, and if I had pretended not to have any contact with the police, the attempted deception would soon have become common knowledge. Of course, whether they believed my assurances of confidentiality is a different matter, but my impression was that, despite occasional initial suspicion, most appeared to trust me to a considerable extent by the end of the interview. The establishment of trust was helped by one or two other factors. One was that, as I got to know some offenders quite well, they let it be known that I was 'alright', and as time went on, many of those I came to interview had already heard about the study and that I could be trusted. A second factor was that I discouraged people from telling me about recent offences for which they had not been caught. I was aware that, if they happened to be arrested for such offences shortly after speaking to me, it could be thought that I had passed on information to the police. I explained this to several interviewees, and they understood the point.

It might seem strange that offenders would volunteer such information, but this was not an uncommon experience. Of course, some of their accounts may have been inventions, some may have been 'planted' to test whether I would pass them on, and some offenders may simply have calculated that, even if I turned out to be a 'police spy' and informed on them, the police were unlikely to have enough evidence to prove a case against them. However, the important general point to emerge from this experience is that, provided that one follows some basic rules on confidentiality, this somewhat 'hybrid' form of research—a mix of semi-formal interviewing and (something approaching) participant observation, in which frequent contact is maintained with both offenders and the police—is not only feasible, but can produce some very rich data. Quite contrary to my initial expectations, I found that most offenders were open, friendly, and interested in the study, and were often anxious to tell me a great deal more than I required for the research. Indeed, several tried hard to persuade me to write their 'life story'.

This is not to say that there were no risks involved. Personal safety was certainly an issue, and I was always conscious that, despite all my assurances, somebody in the 'criminal world' might take serious exception to the research. Fortunately it never happened, but I was clear in my own mind that if I received any threats or warnings, I would modify what I was doing, or even give up the research entirely. Perhaps one reason that I was tolerated is that I did not get close to offenders at the more 'professional' end of the spectrum, nor asked in any detail about connections with criminals in London or other large cities. Our focus was very much upon local networks and what one might call 'run-of-the-mill' offenders. Although many of those I spoke to were prolific offenders and had committed some serious crimes, I never had any sense that I was dealing with groups which were 'organized' to the extent of having mechanisms in place to protect their secrets from outsiders—nor, indeed, that they felt any overriding need to do so. I am well aware, however, that anyone attempting to repeat this kind of study today might face a much more risky situation. In the intervening years, criminals have become more mobile, they are arguably more likely to be violent, and, as Hobbs (2000 in the first edition of this book) points out, drug-dealing has permeated the crime world at all levels: those asking a lot of questions about local criminal networks might soon inadvertently find themselves defined as a threat to some major interests.

A second risk which deserves attention is that of the researcher getting too close to the offenders being studied. There was one occasion on which, following an evening spent with two offenders in a pub, I was invited to watch them do a 'job', in order, as they put it, to see what it was 'really like'. Like the classic tabloid journalist, I 'made my excuses and left', but the experience made me very aware of the risk of being swept along by the natural curiosity which every researcher possesses and crossing one of the ethical boundaries which it is vital to maintain strictly in this kind of research. Some of the offenders I saw several times were very likeable, but—especially after this experience—I was always careful to maintain a clear 'distance' in our relationship. This was helped, it is worth noting, by my need to drive 30 miles home each evening, rather than spend the night in the town (the driving could also be used as a legitimate excuse for not drinking heavily). But more generally, I became more aware of the need for conscious setting of limits, or 'line-drawing'. This is an extremely important principle in research with criminals. While they have drawn the line at different points, field researchers have been almost unanimous that it is vital to define that line clearly both to oneself and to the offenders. Ned Polsky went a great deal further than most, admitting openly that he was prepared, in the cause of 'science', consciously to break the law by witnessing illegal acts. The researcher, he wrote:

must make the moral decision that in some ways he [*sic*] will break the law himself. He need not be a 'participant' observer and commit the criminal acts under study, yet he has to witness such acts or be taken into confidence about them and not blow the whistle. That is, the investigator has to decide that when necessary he will 'obstruct justice' or have 'guilty knowledge' or be an 'accessory' before or after the fact, in the full legal sense of those terms (Polsky 1971: 138).

Even so, he stressed as heavily as anyone the need to be absolutely clear about the limits to which one is prepared to go:

You must draw the line, to yourself and to the criminal. Precisely where to draw it is a moral decision that each researcher must make for himself in each research situation . . . You need to decide beforehand, as much as possible, where you wish to draw the line, because it is wise to make your position on this known to informants rather early in the game. For example, although I am willing to be told about anything and everything, and to witness many kinds of illegal acts, when necessary I make it clear that there are some such acts I prefer not to witness . . .

Letting criminals know where you draw the line, of course, depends on knowing this yourself. If you aren't sure, the criminal may capitalize on the fact to manoeuvre you into an accomplice role . . . I have heard of one social worker with violent gangs who was so insecure, so unable to 'draw the line' for fear of being put down, that he got flattered into holding and hiding guns that had been used in murders (Polsky 1971: 130–1).

Others have taken a different view of the acceptable limits. Yablonsky (1965), for example, argued that one should not conduct field research with adult criminals at all, as it was both immoral and amounted to 'romantic encouragement of the criminal'. Moreover, while he undertook some important field studies of juvenile offenders, where he saw fewer ethical problems, he argued that in this context the researcher should act as a 'social worker' at the same time as an ethnographer, adopting what he called the 'dual role of practitioner-researcher' (Yablonsky 1965: 56). At the other extreme, one of the most interesting approaches has been that of Adler (1993), who undertook a 'participant observer' study of some fairly high-level drug dealers, in which she witnessed numerous illegal deals, often without letting some of those involved know that she was a researcher (she was taken in tow by a drug-dealer friend, and many of those she met assumed that she, too, was a dealer).

Before leaving the 'networks' study, it is worth making one or two more comments about techniques of data collection and analysis. First of all, while the interviews were deliberately wide-ranging, allowing a full exploration of each offender's perceptions of the size and nature of 'criminal networks' in the town, they also included some tightly structured elements. One such was a chart on which each interviewee was asked to represent graphically his relationships with significant others (the initial sample was all male, and I cannot recall interviewing any female offenders through the 'snowball'). This chart consisted of a series of concentric circles with the interviewee located at the centre spot. The latter was then asked to draw a number of lines from the centre point outwards, each one representing a relationship, friendship, or acquaintanceship with one or more people: the shorter the line, the more significant that person or group of people was perceived to be in the interviewee's life. (No pressure was put upon them to attach names to the lines, although some did.) The nature of these relationships was also explored in discussions. It is worth noting in passing that the exercise was often helpful in terms of 'breaking the ice' and engaging interviewees' interest: as a general rule, interviews are improved by using some devices which allow 'hands on' participation and visual representation of concepts. More importantly, though, analysis of a large number of these charts helped the research team to gain a sense of, for example, the relative closeness of offenders to family members and to 'criminal' or 'straight' friends; or to calculate the average number of other persistent offenders whom each interviewee regarded as close to them. This provided some evidence on the question of whether criminal networks are primarily about the facilitation of crime, or whether they are also important as a form of social support (the findings might also have been used to explore aspects of 'differential association' theory, although we never pursued this).

Of course, techniques of this kind are very crude, and the results could only be used as broad indicators, but they provided at least some systematic support for (or challenges to) other conclusions emerging from interviews and conversations with offenders. This is a general lesson I have subsequently carried into many other studies: bringing as many different sources of evidence as possible to bear on any particular question—i.e. what is usually called 'triangulation'—is one of the most valuable of all basic approaches to research in the criminological field. One is almost always dealing with topics on which there is no absolutely reliable information, but if findings from a number of different methods (however weak they may be individually) all point clearly in the same direction, one can have a great deal more confidence in making general statements (see Bryman 2004).

A second comment concerns sampling. This was essentially a qualitative study, and the main purpose of constructing an initial 'sample' of offenders for interview—the selection criteria being a minimum number of previous convictions in the town for property offences—was simply to make contact with a substantial number of local persistent offenders in a rapid and efficient fashion. While, based on their answers to a number of questions which were always asked in interviews, some quantitative statements could be made about this group, it became clear that they could not be regarded as a representative sample of members of 'criminal networks' in the town. Some were very much 'loners', others (despite their records) spent very little time in the town, and so on. By the same token, others I met through the 'snowball' method, or was told about, were well-known figures in the town and clearly part of local 'criminal networks', but had very light criminal records or most of their convictions were elsewhere. It was also interesting sometimes to find that a person said to have a reputation as a 'good villain' had numerous convictions for very petty offences: in such cases, it was not always easy to decide whether it was the reputation or the record that was misleading. In other words, although they are a good starting-point, it is important to recognize that criminal records are not always a good guide to people's actual behaviour. This kind of mismatch between social and official categorizations of people is an issue which confronts criminologists on many occasions, and is one that should always be borne in mind when constructing samples or interpreting quantitative data based on samples drawn from criminal justice records. (A striking illustration of the point is the finding of Wright *et al.* (1992) that, among a sample of 'active burglars' outside custody which they constructed through a snowball method, only around 25 per cent actually turned out to have any convictions for burglary!)

My final comment here concerns the nature of the data we collected and the problem of analysis. Although, as noted above, a certain amount of the interview data could be quantified (percentages of interviewees answering particular questions in particular ways, average numbers of 'criminal' and 'straight' acquaintances drawn on the chart, and so on), this provided only indicative findings. The study was essentially a qualitative one, and relied primarily upon the strength of the interview material and the insights of the researchers. Perhaps the most successful outcome was the production of what we referred to as 'concerted criminal activities' (Webster and Maguire 1973). These were careful reconstructions of how particular groups of offenders had come together for a period of time and successfully committed a series of offences, before eventually the 'bubble burst' when someone made an error and arrests followed. In these cases, I managed to interview all or most of those involved, went into considerable detail, and developed good insights into the nature of criminal collaboration. Apart from this, however, the interviews turned out to be less productive in terms of final output than I had hoped or expected when conducting them. On reflection, principally through lack of training in qualitative research techniques, many were too unfocused, and I did not record the conversations carefully enough. Hence, although the interviews generated a swathe of ideas, when it came to writing sections of papers on a particular theme or idea I often had available only large numbers of brief notes on the topic from different interviews, together with a few 'pithy quotations', rather than a full record of some in-depth discussions about it.

I took two general lessons from this experience. First, rather than trying to 'cover everything', I should have been more mindful of focusing the interviews upon themes which would be central to the papers which would be the product of the research—including, that is, new themes which emerged in the course of fieldwork. As one experienced researcher once told me in relation to data collection for commissioned research (a piece of advice I have often followed since), 'the best tip is to imagine the final report and work backwards'. Secondly, even if it was difficult to write things down during the interview, I should have been much more diligent in writing up full notes immediately afterwards (I could also perhaps have experimented with tape recording in suitable cases, although I still remain instinctively resistant to this). These points are even more pertinent to present-day qualitative research, where computer packages such as Nudist or The Ethnograph are available to assist the systematic analysis of conversation.

It can be seen from the above account that I was very 'spoiled' in my first introduction to criminological research. Our research team was given a great deal of freedom to explore the topic, a long period of time, considerable resources, and wide-ranging access to institutions and their records. Times have since changed, and such luxuries are rare in a research-funding context which has become dominated by short-term projects and risk-averse decision-makers striving to obtain 'value for money'. It might be argued, of course, that the relative unproductivity of the networks project is a good illustration of why 'gambles' should not be taken with unfocused exploratory studies, but even if we did not make the best use of opportunities we were given, I would still argue that some gambles of this kind are necessary if creativity is to be maintained in research. Sadly, there are few posts for young researchers today which offer the time or the flexibility to explore issues through genuine ethnographic fieldwork with offenders: perhaps their best chance of doing so now lies in study for a doctorate, though of course this is likely to be handicapped by limited resources. The other way in which I was 'spoiled' is less defensible, but is anyway much less likely to occur today, when research has to be approved by ethics committees: namely, that a largely untrained researcher was let loose, with minimal supervision, on a difficult and risky type of fieldwork. From my own point of view, being 'thrown in at the deep end' and allowed to learn by my mistakes was an invaluable experience for my future career, but at the same time it undoubtedly contributed to the relative failure of the project in terms of its focus and output.

Studies of burglars

The second of my own projects I shall describe—much more briefly—is a three-year study of burglars and burglary, funded by the Home Office and conducted together with Trevor Bennett between 1976 and 1979 at the Centre for Criminological Research in Oxford University. I shall also comment on an innovative piece of research undertaken later by Trevor Bennett with Richard Wright (1984) which took the study of burglars forward in a new direction.

While Home Office research funding practice is nowadays characterized by the tendering of short-term contracts to conduct pre-designed studies on topics relevant to immediate policy concerns (see Morgan and Hough this volume), in the mid-1970s the Home Office Research Unit was still prepared to invest in longer term and more fundamental research in response to proposals from academics. The Unit was very supportive of the idea of a broad look at the subject of residential burglary—until then a surprisingly neglected topic—although, as always, it was keen to see significant use made of quantitative methods, as well as to receive specific policy recommendations based on the findings. The ultimate value of the proposal, from the funder's viewpoint, was the collection of information to inform the design of more effective policies to prevent residential burglary. The fieldwork was designed principally to find out more about how burglars chose their targets and committed their offences, to identify any common patterns of burglary through the analysis of police data, and to canvass the views and experiences of victims. We are concerned here only with the offender element of the project, but it is worth mentioning that when the resulting book was published (Maguire and Bennett 1982), the findings from the interviews with victims attracted far more attention than the chapters on offenders—in itself an interesting comment on the priorities of criminology in the 1980s.

As the study of burglars comprised only one element of what was a large and complex study, we adopted a less ambitious methodology than in my previous work with offenders. We simply went into a local prison and, with the Governor's permission, went on to the landings and let it be known, first to staff and subsequently to prisoners, that we wished to 'talk to house burglars'. As inmates were recommended to us, we asked them if they were prepared to be interviewed in confidence, and most agreed. They were, in turn, asked to recommend others, and by a 'snowball' process—which became more effective as the 'grapevine' spread the news that we were harmless—gradually extended our list of interviewees. Some, indeed, approached us and volunteered their assistance. This selection strategy seemed to 'work', in that over a period of about four months we eventually conducted forty lengthy interviews with people who clearly had considerable experience of burgling residential property (we rejected a few other interviews with 'time wasters', particularly from the early stages of the process, but the great majority of interviews turned out to be productive). All forty admitted having broken into at least twenty homes, and the majority over 100. Most, too, described themselves first and foremost as 'burglars', although they also had other forms of crime on their records. The interviews generally lasted for at least an hour, and some prisoners were seen more than once.

For these interviews we used a semi-structured schedule, divided into a number of clear themes. Although still allowing a great deal of freedom for discussion under each theme, this ensured that our interviews were generally more focused than those I had conducted in the previous study, with a specific set of topics to explore. For one thing, we were interested in shedding more light on questions raised by our other interviews with victims and by our analysis of geographical patterns of burglary from police records: for example, how persistent burglars reacted to crime prevention measures (such as alarms, window locks, dogs in the house, and so on) or why disproportionate numbers of burglaries seemed to occur just off main roads or close to junctions. Such questions had both theoretical and practical implications. We also explored more systematically some of the themes which had begun to emerge from the 'networks' study, such as the nature of relationships between burglars (focusing, for example, on questions such as how long they tended to 'work' with the same 'partners', or how strong were professed principles such as 'not stealing from your own kind' or 'never grassing').

At the conclusion of this study, following the submission of the report to the Home Office, Trevor Bennett left to take up a post in Cambridge, but I obtained an extension to my contract to expand the 'burglars' element of the study, and in particular to follow up one particular man we had found, who had been unusually successful as a burglar, stealing large amounts of antiques and jewellery over several years before being apprehended, and who was willing to describe his experiences to me in detail. (I also took the opportunity over this period to begin incorporating the text of our report into a more general book on burglary.) This man, 'Peter Hudson', was serving a long prison sentence, and was eventually transferred to a distant training prison, but I continued to visit and interview him at length. We went through his life together in a systematic way, concentrating on a different period each time. Although I still did not use a tape recorder (though I now partly regret not having done so, so rich was his account), I wrote lengthy notes, asking him to pause if I could not keep up. He was also an excellent writer himself, and prepared for my visits by writing accounts of particular incidents. In the end, I built up a great deal of material which not only gave me insights into the practice of professional burglary, but an excellent chronological account of how my informant—who did not have a 'criminal' family background—had moved through various stages of criminal behaviour to acquire the exceptional level of skill and the 'connections' he needed to become a specialist country house burglar. His 'story' was eventually incorporated into the book as a complete chapter (Maguire and Bennett 1982: ch. 4).

This intensive method of studying criminal lifestyles—usually known as the 'life-history' method—has been used to excellent effect by a number of writers, some of whom have based whole books around one person's account, rather than merely one chapter (as mentioned earlier, two of the best examples are Shaw's (1930) study of an adolescent 'jack-roller' and the story of 'Chic Conwell', Sutherland's (1937) 'professional thief'; more recent examples include the study by Klockars (1975) of the life of a receiver). It has the advantage of introducing a strong dynamic element into one's understanding of offenders, enabling one to explore changes in attitudes and behaviour (and the reasons for those changes) over time. It also allows one to develop a relationship with the offender in which he or she may allow the researcher to probe much more deeply than is possible in 'one-off' interviews into issues and incidents that are discussed. There remains, of course, the perennial criticism made of qualitative research, but above all of research based on single case studies, that the person is not 'typical', and that therefore one cannot generalize from the findings. The simplest response to this is that the aim is to understand a particular case in full, with a proper appreciation of its context, ideally in order to develop new theoretical insights and ideas: other kinds of study can be used to test how frequently what is identified occurs (for a useful discussion of the main arguments for and against the method, see Faraday and Plummer 1979; most methods textbooks also have sections on case studies and life histories: see, for example, Burns 2000; De Vaus 2001; Silverman 2004; Bryman 1988, 2004). It is, however, the case that the success of the life history method depends heavily, not only upon the skills of the interviewer, but—especially when seeking to understand criminal behaviour—upon finding the 'right person' to study. It is important that the person studied is reasonably articulate, and can recall and describe incidents in detail. It is also important to avoid people who are 'plausible liars' and who exaggerate or invent accounts in order to boost their ego. It is wise for this reason to seek independent corroboration of at least some of what the subject says. In the above case, I had the benefit of reading evidence given at 'Peter Hudson's' trial which made it clear that the offences he had committed were exceptional in both scale and skill. I also spoke to his wife (to whom I gave a lift to the prison to visit him) at some length, which gave me another perspective on his life. Beyond that, I could only use my own judgement of his character, together with tests of 'internal consistency', to decide whether what he was telling me was true. Over our several meetings, I felt that I got to know him quite well, and on occasion he revealed a vulnerable side to his outwardly stoical and good-humoured character: this, again, gave me more confidence in the accounts he was giving me.

Before leaving my own work and moving on to comment on Trevor Bennett's later study, I shall digress briefly to round off the story of my own involvement in research on offenders. In broad terms, the burglary study marked the beginnings of my transition from an enthusiastic, if somewhat disorganized, young fieldworker, keen to follow up new ideas in all directions, to a much more pragmatic and 'hard-nosed' career researcher, aware of the need to tailor research proposals and fieldwork to match the policies and requirements of funding bodies and to deliver a timely and professional 'product'. Anyone contemplating a career in criminology will come face-to-face with these kinds of reality, but the path I chose brought me up against them more sharply and more quickly than colleagues who moved into lectureships at an early age. In my case, the burglary project was the last study in which I pursued my original interest in the lifestyles and behaviour of 'street criminals' to any significant degree. Subsequently, my decision to continue for some years as a 'contract researcher' at the Oxford Centre, rather than to seek a lecturing post (where I might at least have continued such research on a small scale in my spare time), dictated that I move away from offender studies entirely.

Following the burglary study, I spent another ten years at the Centre, where the principal source of funding was Home Office grants and all researchers were 'only as good as their last research report' in the competition to land a new grant and hence a new fixed-term contract of employment. On reflection, although I was quite successful and often enjoyed the very different kinds of research that I learned to conduct, I perhaps stayed too long. Over that period, the Home Office Research Unit not only virtually ceased to fund studies of offenders, but moved towards a position where funding decisions were almost exclusively driven by narrow short-term policy concerns, and where the objectives, substance, methods, and (ever shorter) time-frames of research projects were increasingly rigidly determined in advance by civil servants. Having earlier been self-critical about the lack of rigour and focus in the networks study, I should also admit here that, by the time I left Oxford, I had the quite different concern that so much time spent in policy-driven research was limiting my opportunities and capacity to engage in broader academic debates. It was not until I moved in 1989 to a lectureship post that I was able to regain a significant sense of academic freedom and, relieved of the need to apply for one grant after another, found more time and greater stimulus to write in a reflective style. This is not at all to say that I have repudiated policy-oriented research, which—despite the above mentioned trends—can sometimes be innovative and intellectually challenging, as well as influential and important. My experience at Oxford gave me the skills to deliver a 'professional product' in the form that government funders require, and I have continued at intervals to bid for research money from the Home Office as well as from other sources. The difference is that this is by choice rather than necessity, and with a view to integration with broader academic interests. In conducting such research, the basic aim should be to deliver two quite different types of product, both to the highest possible standards: first, to produce a succinct, publishable report in straightforward language to answer the funder's original research questions; and subsequently, to incorporate elements of the acquired knowledge and material into publications aimed at an academic audience.

Returning now to burglars, I shall finish this section with a few comments to draw the reader's attention to what I consider to be one of the best British studies of offenders to emerge in the last 20 years, Bennett and Wright's (1984) neatly titled book *Burglars on Burglary*, as well as to one of the best American studies of burglars, Wright and Decker's (1994) *Burglars on the Job* (although they have an author in common, the two studies are very different). The first of these—one of the last major offender-centred studies to be funded by the Home Office—was not 'ethnographic' in the normal sense of the term, but used a number of innovative and cleverly designed research techniques to tackle the central questions which the authors had set themselves. Their main interest was in burglars' decision-making processes, and in the implications of these processes both for theories of deterrence and for the (then highly fashionable) policies of situational crime prevention which were being developed in the Home Office.

The authors constructed an interview sample of male convicted burglars over the age of 16, drawn from both prison and probation service records, the principal criterion being that they must be currently serving a prison sentence, or be on probation for, an offence of burglary. (As noted earlier, this does not mean that the sample can be regarded as representative of 'burglars' as a whole, but we shall not dwell on the point here.) The innovation in the study lay in the use of a number of techniques to explore systematically with the burglars how they decided when and where to offend. For example, in order to identify 'situational cues' used by offenders in their choice of targets, they showed the interviewees video recordings of a variety of streets and buildings, filmed at walking pace to simulate someone going along each street on foot. The offenders were asked to rate each building in terms of its potential as a target, at the same time 'thinking aloud' to explain their reasoning. The researchers also used still photographs and lengthy semistructured interviews (each lasting 2–4 hours) to explore other aspects of decision-making. These methods allowed both quantitative and qualitative analysis, and contributed significantly to thinking about both deterrence and crime prevention.

Wright and Decker's (1994) study was also aimed at exploring the factors which burglars take into account when contemplating an offence, but the authors used rather different methods for selecting their subjects and obtaining data. They employed a 'snowball' method right from the start, avoiding all contact with criminal justice agencies. They began by hiring an ex-offender who was now attending university, but who still had many contacts from his 'previous life' (a similar approach was used successfully by Laurie Taylor (1985) in researching his book on London criminals, *In the Underworld*). With his help, the researchers contacted a number of offenders on the streets of St Louis, Missouri, interviewing them and asking them to refer them on to others. They provided a 'sweetener' in the shape of a $25 fee for being interviewed, which they concluded to have been an excellent investment, although by no means the only reason why they received good co-operation: normally, they point out, offenders have to keep much of what they do secret, and they can find it enjoyable and even 'therapeutic' to talk freely to an independent person who poses no risk to them (from my own experience, I concur with this fully). They did not pay for 'referrals', but found that some offenders were taking 'cuts' from the interview fees of those they referred! In terms of their main research objectives, one of the most successful aspects of their methodology was to take Bennett and Wright's idea further and, rather than relying on videotapes, actually to walk the streets with their burglar interviewees, asking them to assess the potential of properties as targets. Finally, as noted earlier, another important outcome of this study was the finding that the majority of the self-confessed 'burglars' they contacted by means of the above method had no convictions for burglary.

Participant observation: studies of young offenders on the streets

I finish this chapter with necessarily very brief accounts of two of the British studies of offenders which have come closest to what has traditionally been referred to as 'participant observation'. It is worth noting in passing that this term is not an entirely satisfactory description of what is done in the course of field research, and that various writers have suggested alternative terms or sub-classifications. For example, Gold (1969) distinguishes between 'observer-as-participant', 'participant-as-observer', and 'complete participant' techniques (the last being the rarest and most controversial, raising ethical and legal issues as well as carrying greater personal risks), while Collins (1984) challenges these distinctions as misconceived, preferring the general term 'participant comprehension' (see Cromwell 2006 for further discussion of such distinctions). However, our purpose here is to look at what was done in the studies in question, rather than label it. Both concerned young offenders, rather than adults, which perhaps made the researchers' tasks a little easier, but both are nevertheless impressive examples of what can be achieved by good ethnographers with the necessary time, resourcefulness, and discretion to conduct research of this kind. Both were conducted in the late 1960s.

The first is the study by Howard Parker (1974) of a loosely structured group of male 'street kids' in a deprived area of Liverpool, who were frequently involved in offences such as theft from cars, shop and warehouse burglary, and low-level dealing in marijuana. As implied in the title, *View from the Boys*, the main aim was to present their delinquent activities, and other aspects of their lives, through the eyes of the young people themselves. Parker sums up his methodology as 'knocking around with a group of adolescents', on the streets and in the local pubs. He first got to know several of the group—who were mainly around 16–17 years old—when employed as a community youth worker in a holiday centre for disadvantaged city children, continuing to see them afterwards in the city. Subsequently, having taken up a university research post, he decided to make a systematic study of the group. The role he adopted came closer than that of most other field researchers to what Gold (1969) called 'complete participant'. To a considerable extent, he set out to present himself to his subjects as being 'one of them' and, indeed, claims that his relationship with them was primarily one of 'friendship':

By the time I came down town I was established as OK—that is, amongst other things, boozy, suitably dressed and ungroomed, playing football well enough to survive and badly enough to be funny, 'knowing the score' about theft behaviour and sexual exploits . . .

I am still a regular at the Roundhouse [the area where the boys gathered] and hope to continue to be, for I enjoy the friendship I like to think I have there. Such friendship has been the basis of the whole study . . . Perhaps to those who have attempted a depth-participant observation study such sentiments will seem less irrelevant. All I can say is that this study would not have survived without such reciprocity (Parker 1974: 16).

Moreover, he conducted the research in a fairly 'covert' manner, letting it be known only that he was 'at the university', and pretending that he was studying (in a critical manner) 'the police and the courts', rather than the behaviour of the boys on the streets. He also tried to demonstrate to the boys that his loyalties lay entirely with them, and passed various 'tests' to prove this. More controversially, going even further than Polsky, he admits in the book to participation in property offences by acting as a lookout or receiving part of the proceeds, although he drew the line at actually stealing himself. In a passage that many ethnographers would interpret as an admission to having 'gone native', he attempts to justify this position by claiming that many others in the area behaved similarly:

My position in relation to theft was well established. I would receive 'knock off' and 'say nothing'. If necessary I would 'keep dixy' [keep watch], but I would not actually get my hands dirty. This stance was regarded as normal and surprised nobody; it coincided with the view of most adults in the neighbourhood (Parker 1974: 219).

In terms of data collection and recording, he admits (as I did earlier in relation to the 'networks' study) to mistakes in choosing what to write down in what form:

In retrospect, I was too selective in recording data. I did not take enough time in keeping my fieldwork diary, especially in recording what I considered mundane events. Quite often I would be obsessed with a small conversation piece to the exclusion of other events. Had I been more concerned with detailed writing earlier on I would have probably hit upon ongoing social processes more rapidly than I did. My general conclusion here therefore is that keeping a detailed and accurate diary may be of great significance (Parker 1974: 223).

However, this clearly proved to be less of a handicap to Parker than it was in my case, almost certainly because, by being so deeply immersed in the street life of the boys, he was able to recall and draw on a great many more experiences than I could. He also had the advantage of a fairly small and clearly defined group of subjects, who spent most of their time in a small geographical area, helping him to create a tight focus for his written product. The resulting book is rich in material, ideas, and insights, and is valuable not only for its description of 'life on the streets', but for his efforts to relate his observations to previous theoretical explanations of 'juvenile delinquency' and crime-oriented 'subcultures' (none of which he found entirely satisfactory).

The final study I shall mention is James Patrick's *A Glasgow Gang Observed* (Patrick 1973). In contrast to the Liverpool 'street kids', whom Parker (1974: 64) describes as 'a network, a loose-knit social group', Patrick was in no doubt that his subjects constituted a 'gang' (or, as its members referred to it, a 'team'): one of many named gangs in the slum areas of Glasgow in the late 1960s. In locating his study within a wider literature, then, we should look less towards the well-known sociological theories of delinquency, subcultures, and so on, than towards the sizeable body of work—most of it American, and much of it based on field research—which has grown up on the specific phenomenon of street gangs. A recurrent theme in this literature—and one which is central to Patrick's study— is the violence of gang members, which receives considerably more attention than other forms of crime in which they may engage (see, e.g., Bloch and Niederhoffer 1958; Yablonsky 1962; Liebow 1967; Keiser 1969; Miller 1975; for more recent general overviews of gang literature, see Spergel 1990, 1995; Maguire 1996; Klein 1998; Huff 2002).

Generally speaking, British criminologists have paid little attention to street gangs, and many have claimed either that they do not exist in this country in anything like the American form, or that they are a rare and fleeting phenomenon. Indeed, Gibbens and Ahrenfeldt (1966) once reported that a research project on gangs had to be abandoned because none could be found! However, Patrick argued that Glasgow was a major exception, possessing a combination of structural conditions—notably, 'long traditions of slum housing and violence'—which were, as he put it, 'conducive to ganging' (Patrick 1973: 169). (It should be noted that in recent years, some observers have claimed that 'US-style' gang cultures are emerging in several British cities, though, as yet, there is little direct research evidence to support this: see Bennett and Holloway 2004.)

What is almost unique about Patrick's field research with the 'Young Team' is that it was totally covert. Patrick, a college lecturer, spent his summers as a teacher in an Approved School. One day, he was invited by one of the pupils, a gang member, to come with him during a home leave to see 'how it really is'. Between them, they devised a plan to conceal his identity from the rest of the gang, presenting him as an older boy from the Approved School who had no family. They returned together to the gang's area at intervals over a period of four months, during which Patrick joined the gang and got to know many of its members, in the process witnessing a considerable amount of serious violence. He eventually described his experiences in detail in the book, albeit having to leave out many incidents and disguising all names and places, including his own (James Patrick is a pseudonym). Moreover, he never revealed what he had been doing to the Approved School, nor to other authorities. Unfortunately from our point of view, he declines 'for legal reasons' to describe his methodology in any detail, or to discuss the many ethical and other issues arising from it. However, much can be inferred from reading his accounts of meetings and incidents: quite clearly, although he did not commit violent acts himself, he got very close to the 'action', and felt concerned enough about his own safety on the one hand, and police interest on the other, to want to wait a considerable time (and to take legal advice) before publishing a truncated account.

The bulk of the book is descriptive, written in a style accessible to ordinary readers, albeit infused with Glasgow dialect and slang, but it ends with an academic discussion of its implications for theories of gang delinquency and violence. Interestingly, he leans towards the unfashionable view, held by Yablonsky but by few other sociologists at the time, that the core members of gangs tend to be pathologiocally disturbed, the gang providing a vehicle through which they can express their violent feelings.

Concluding remarks

It is hoped that this chapter has provided at least a flavour of what it is like to conduct fieldwork with persistent offenders, particularly outside the safety of prisons or probation offices, as well as illustrating the range and variety of methods which have been used to try to obtain a closer and more realistic picture of how they think and behave when contemplating or committing crimes. These range from the relatively unproblematic method of in-depth interviews (including frequent re-interviewing to build up life histories) to the other extreme of 'participant observation' in its various guises. The latter is relatively unusual, and even then has been confined principally to studies of young offenders rather than adults (with very few exceptions, too—one being Anne Campbell's (1991) excellent work on girl gangs—studies of female offenders are sadly lacking). It has to be recognized that it is both difficult and time-consuming, carries a variety of tangible risks (including physical harm and being drawn into criminal activity oneself), and is by no means always successful. Even so, if carried out with forethought and preparation, and with full awareness of the risks, it can be rewarding and productive in terms of both description and the development and testing of theory.

A number of themes and issues have emerged in the course of the discussions of individual studies. On some of them, there seems to be no strong consensus: for example, there are successful examples of both 'covert' and 'overt' fieldwork; some researchers (such as Parker) have tried consciously to become 'one of the boys' by dressing similarly or drinking heavily, while others have maintained some social distance in such matters; and some have avoided any relations at all with 'authority' while others have kept in touch with local agencies. On other issues, however, there is fairly clear agreement, and some important lessons can be drawn. For example, while they may disagree on where it is appropriate to draw it, most researchers underline the need to 'draw a line' in terms of one's willingness to observe or play a part in illegal activities. Again, promising and maintaining confidentiality are generally seen as essential. Where research techniques are concerned, most agree on the value of the 'snowball' method of creating interview samples or expanding contacts—a popular approach being to secure one or two strong 'allies' at the outset (whether friends such as Parker's companions from the holiday centre, or a hired 'guide' such as the man employed in the 1992 study by Wright and colleagues). They also agree on the need for comprehensive field notes; and (the hardest lesson I learned in the 'networks' study) the need to maintain a clear focus to the study, rather than trying to achieve too much.

In conclusion, I would support the view that, while the majority of modern criminologists have moved in other directions, largely neglecting the direct study of offenders, it is very important to the health of the discipline that the traditions of field research built up by the Chicago School and kept alive by a relatively small number of individuals, are maintained by new generations of academics. Without this correcting influence, it is all too easy for those studying crime to lose their sense of reality and begin to perceive offenders not as people, but merely as 'problems' or 'numbers' (or, indeed—though much less common now than in the 'left idealist' years of the 1970s—as romanticized figures resisting the injustices of capitalist society). Certainly, from a personal point of view, the few years I spent in research of this kind—albeit not entirely successful, as well as falling far short of the full-blown 'participant observation' of writers such as Parker and Patrick—gave me an excellent introduction to criminology. Perhaps above all, they impressed upon me the heterogeneity and complexity of the 'criminal world' and the variety of people who become involved in it: the consequent realization that there are no simple 'solutions' has undoubtedly influenced my thinking ever since.

Suggestions for further reading

There are a number of good general methodological books on ethnography and participant observation, including Hammersley and Atkinson's *Ethnography: Principles in Practice* (Routledge 1995), Burgess' *In the Field* (Allen & Unwin 1984) and Silverman's *Doing Qualitative Research* (Sage 2004). There are relatively few books specifically on ethnographic methods in criminological research, but Hobbs and May's edited collection *Interpreting the Field: Accounts of Ethnography* (Clarendon 1993) is a valuable exception, while Cromwell's edited 'anthology' *In Their Own Words: Criminals on Crime* (Roxbury, Pennsylvania 2006) has a number of excellent texts on specific pieces of research, including brief discussions by Adler and by Wright *et al.* of studies discussed in this chapter. There are also a couple of useful chapters in Maxfield and Babbie's *Research Methods for Criminal Justice and Criminology* (Thompson/Wadsworth Publishing, Canada 2005). Victor Jupp's textbook, *Methods of Criminological Research* (Unwin Hyman 1989) is also useful in placing this kind of study within a specifically criminological context, but goes into relatively little detail. For discussion of the special issues and problems involved in researching offenders in the field, it is therefore best to go direct to some of the studies mentioned in this chapter, in which the authors include detailed accounts of how they undertook their fieldwork. In particular, I would pick out the Appendix in Parker's *A View from the Boys* (David & Charles 1974), the methodological paper by Wright *et al.* (1992) in the *Journal of Research in Crime and Delinquency* (29: 148–61), and the third chapter of Polsky's *Hustlers, Beats and Others* (Pelican 1971:115–47). Finally, while the rest of the methodology is not described in detail, it is interesting to read the first four sections of Patrick's *A Glasgow Gang Observed* (Eyre Methuen 1973), in which the author describes his initial introductions to the gang and their violent behaviour.

References

ADLER, P. (1993). *Wheeling and Dealing: An Ethnography of an Upper-Level Drug Dealing and Smuggling Community*. New York: Columbia University Press.

ATKINSON, P. (1990). *The Ethnographic Imagination: Textual Constructions of Reality*. London: Routledge.

BECKER, H. (ed.) (1964). *The Other Side: Perspectives on Deviance*. New York: Free Press.

BENNETT, T. and HOLLOWAY, K. (2004). 'Gang Membership, Drugs and Crime in the UK', *British Journal of Criminology* 44: 305–23.

—— and WRIGHT, R. (1984). *Burglars on Burglary: Prevention and the Offender*. Aldershot: Gower.

BLOCH, H. A. and NIEDERHOFFER, A. (1958). *The Gang: A Study in Adolescent Behaviour*. New York: Philosophical Library.

BOTTOMS, A. (2007). 'Place, Space, Crime and Disorder' in M. Maguire, R. Morgan, and R. Reiner (eds), *The Oxford Handbook of Criminology* (4th edn). Oxford: Oxford University Press.

BOURGEOIS, P. (1996). *In Search of Respect: Selling Crack in El Barrio*. Cambridge: Cambridge University Press.

BOWKER, L. H. (ed.) (2000). *Masculinities and Violence*. London: Sage.

BROWN, D., ELLIS, T., and LARCOMBE, K. (1992). *Changing the Code: Police Detention Under the Revised PACE Codes of Practice*. Home Office Research Study No. 129. London: HMSO.

BRYMAN, A. (1988). *Quantity and Quality in Social Research*. London: Unwin Hyman.

—— (2004). *Social Research Methods*. Oxford: Oxford University Press.

BURNS, R. B. (2000). *Introduction to Research Methods*. London: Sage.

BURGESS, R. (1984). *In the Field*. London: Allen & Unwin.

CAMPBELL, A. (1991). *The Girls in the Gang* (2nd edn). Oxford: Blackwell.

CLARKE, R. and MAYHEW, P. (1980). *Designing Out Crime*. London: HMSO.

CLOWARD, R. and OHLIN, L. (1960). *Delinquency and Opportunity: A Theory of Delinquent Gangs*. Chicago, Ill.: Free Press.

COHEN, A. (1955). *Delinquent Boys: The Culture of the Gang*. New York: Free Press.

COHEN, S. (1972). *Folk Devils and Moral Panics*. London: Paladin.

COLLINS, H. (1984). 'Researching Spoon-bending: Concepts and Practice of Participatory Fieldwork' in C. Bell and H. Roberts (eds), *Social Researching*. London: Routledge & Kegan Paul.

CORNISH, D. and CLARKE, R. (eds) (1986). *The Reasoning Criminal: Rational Choice Perspectives on Offending*. New York: Springer.

CROMWELL, P. (ed.) (2006). *In Their Own Words: Criminals on Crime. An Anthology* (4th edn). Pennsylvania: Roxbury.

DE VAUS, D. (2001). *Research Design in Social Research*. London: Sage.

DENZIN, N. K. and LINCOLN, Y. S. (eds) (2000). *Handbook of Qualitative Research* (2nd edn). California: Sage.

FARADAY, A. and PLUMMER, K. (1979). 'Doing Life Histories'. *Sociological Review* 27: 773–98.

FEELEY, M. and SIMON, J. (1992). 'The New Penology: Notes on the Emerging Strategy of Corrections and its Implications'. *Criminology* 30: 449–74.

FELSON, M. (1994). *Crime and Everyday Life*. Thousand Oaks, Cal.: Pine Forge.

FERRELL, J., HAYWARD, K., MORRISON, K., and PRESDEE, M. (eds) (2004). *Cultural Criminology Unleashed*. London: GlassHouse.

FIELDING, N. (1993). 'Ethnography' in N. I. Gilbert (ed.), *Researching Social Life*. London: Sage.

FITZGERALD, M., STOCKDALE, J., and HALE, C. (2003). *Young People and Street Crime*. London: Youth Justice Board. *http://www.youth-justice-board.gov.uk/Publications/Scripts/prodView.asp?idProduct = 75&e P = PP*

GARLAND, D. (2001). *The Culture of Control: Crime and Social Order in Contemporary Society*. Chicago: University of Chicago Press.

GIBBENS, T. and AHRENFELDT, R. (eds) (1966). *Cultural Factors in Delinquency*. London: Tavistock.

GLASER, B. G. and BARNEY, G. (1998). *Doing Grounded Theory. Issues and Discussions*. Mill Valley, Cal.: Sociology Press.

—— and STRAUSS, A. (1967). *The Discovery of Grounded Theory*. Chicago, Ill.: Aldine.

GLUECK, S. and GLUECK, E. (1950). *Unravelling Juvenile Delinquency*. London: Routledge & Kegan Paul.

GOLD, R. (1969). 'Roles in Sociological Field Investigation' in G. McCall and J. Simmons (eds), *Issues in Participant Observation*. Reading, Mass.: Addison-Wesley.

HALLSWORTH, S. (2005). *Street Crime*. Devon: Willan.

HAMMERSLEY, M. and ATKINSON, P. (1995). *Ethnography: Principles in Practice*. London: Routledge.

HAYWARD, K. and YOUNG, J. (2007). 'Cultural Criminology' in M. Maguire, R. Morgan, and R. Reiner (eds), *The Oxford Handbook of Criminology* (4th edn). Oxford: Oxford University Press.

HOBBS, D. (1993). *Doing the Business: Entrepreneurship, The Working Class and Detectives in the East End of London*. Oxford: Oxford University Press.

—— (1998). 'Going down the Glocal: The Local Context of Organized Crime'. *Howard Journal* 37: 407–22.

—— (2000). Researching Serious Crime, in R. D. King and E. Wincup (eds), *Doing Research on Crime and Justice* (1st edn). Oxford: Oxford University Press.

—— HADFIELD, P., LISTER, S., and WINLOW, S. (2005). *Bouncers: Violence and Governance in the Night time Economy*. Oxford: Oxford University Press.

—— and MAY, T. (eds) (1993). *Interpreting the Field: Accounts of Ethnography*. Oxford: Clarendon.

HUFF, C. R. (ed.) (2002). *Gangs in America III*. Thousand Oaks, Cal.: Sage.

JACOBS, B. A., TOPALLI, V., and WRIGHT, W. (2003). 'Carjacking, Streetlife and Offender Motivation'. *British Journal of Criminology* 43: 673–88.

JUPP, V. (1989). *Methods of Criminological Research*. London: Unwin Hyman.

KEISER, R. (1969). *The Vice Lords: Warriors of the Streets*. New York: Holt, Rinehart & Winston.

KLEIN, M. (1998). 'Street Gangs' in M. Tonry (ed.), *The Handbook of Crime and Punishment*. Oxford: Oxford University Press.

KLOCKARS, C. (1975). *The Professional Fence*. New York: Macmillan.

LEVI, M., MAGUIRE, M., and BROOKMAN, F. (2007). 'Violent Crime' in M. Maguire, R. Morgan, and R. Reiner (eds), *The Oxford Handbook of Criminology* (4th edn). Oxford: Oxford University Press.

LIEBOW, E. (1967). *Tally's Corner*. Boston, Mass.: Little, Brown.

MAGUIRE, M. (ed.) (1996). *Street Crime*. Aldershot: Dartmouth.

—— (2007). 'Crime Data and Criminal Statistics' in M. Maguire, R. Morgan, and R. Reiner (eds), *The Oxford Handbook of Criminology* (4th edn). Oxford: Oxford University Press.

—— in collaboration with BENNETT, T. (1982). *Burglary in a Dwelling: The Offence, the Offender and the Victim*. London: Heinemann Education.

—— and VAGG, J. (1984). *The 'Watchdog' Role of Boards of Visitors*. London: Home Office.

MATZA, D. (1964). *Delinquency and Drift*. New York: Wiley.

MAXFIELD, M. and BABBIE, E. (2005). *Research Methods for Criminal Justice and Criminology* (4th edn). Scarborough, Canada: Thomson/Wadsworth Publishing.

MAYHEW, P., CLARKE, R., STURMAN, A., and HOUGH, M. (1976). *Crime as Opportunity*. Home Office Research Study No. 49. London: HMSO.

MERTON, R. (1938). 'Social Structure and Anomie'. *American Sociological Review* 3: 672–82.

MESSERSCHMIDT, J. (2000). *Nine Lives*. Westview Press.

MILLER, J. (2000). *One of the Guys: Girls, Gangs, and Gender*. New York: Oxford University Press:

MILLER, W. (1975). *Violence by Youth Gangs and Youth Groups as a Crime Problem in Major American Cities*. Washington, DC: Department of Justice.

MORSE, J. (ed.) (1994). *Critical Issues in Qualitative Research Methods*. Thousand Oaks, Cal.: Sage.

MULLINS, C. (2006). *Holding your Square: Masculinities, Streetlife and Violence*. Devon: Willan.

O'BRIEN, K. (forthcoming 2007). *Tac: Dealing, Young People, Gender and Neighbourhood Markets*. Cullompton: Willan.

O'MALLEY, P. (ed.) (1998). *Crime and the Risk Society*. Aldershot: Ashgate.

PARK, R., BURGESS, E., and McKENZIE, R. (eds) (1925). *The City*. Chicago, Ill.: University of Chicago Press.

PARKER, H. (1974). *View from the Boys: A Sociology of Down-town Adolescents*. Newton Abbot: David & Charles.

PATRICK, J. (1973). *A Glasgow Gang Observed*. London: Eyre Methuen.

POLSKY, N. (1971). *Hustlers, Beats and Others*. Harmondsworth: Pelican.

ROBINSON, G. (2002). 'Exploring Risk Management in Probation Practice: Contemporary Developments in England and Wales'. *Punishment and Society* 4: 5–25.

SANDERS, T. (2004). *Sex Work: A Risky Business*. Devon: Willan.

SHAW, C. (1930). *The Jack-Roller: A Delinquent Boy's Own Story*. Chicago, Ill.: University of Chicago Press.

—— (1931). *Delinquency Areas*. Chicago, Ill.: University of Chicago Press.

SHOVER, N. (1996). *Great Pretenders: Pursuits and Careers of Persistent Thieves*. Boulder, Colorado: Westview.

SILVERMAN, D. (2004). *Doing Qualitative Research* (2nd edn). London: Sage.

SILVERSTONE, D. (forthcoming 2007). *Night Clubbing: Drugs, Clubs and Regulation*. Cullompton: Willan.

SPERGEL, I. (1995). *The Youth Gang Problem*. New York: Oxford University Press.

—— (1990). 'Youth Gangs: Continuity and Change' in N. Morris and M. Tonry (eds), *Crime and Justice: An Annual Review* 12: 171–267.

SUTHERLAND, E. (1937). *The Professional Thief: By A Professional Thief*. Chicago, Ill.: University of Chicago Press.

—— and CRESSEY, D. (1960). *Principles of Criminology*. Philadelphia, Penn.: Lippincott.

TAYLOR, I., WALTON, I., and YOUNG, J. (1973). *The New Criminology*. London: Routledge & Kegan Paul.

TAYLOR, L. (1985). *In the Underworld*. Oxford: Blackwell.

THRASHER, F. (1927). *The Gang: A Study of 1,313 Gangs in Chicago*. Chicago, Ill.: University of Chicago Press.

TOPALLI, V., WRIGHT, R., and FORNANGO, R. (2002). 'Drug Dealers, Robbery and Retaliation'. *British Journal of Criminology* 42: 337–51.

WEBSTER, D. and MAGUIRE, M. (1973). *Why Can't You Guys Get Organised Like That? Criminal Organisation, Partial Organisation and Disorganisation in Medium-Sized British Towns*. Paper to Fifth National Conference on Teaching and Research in Criminology, Cambridge, 4–6 July 1973.

WHYTE, W. (1943). *Street Corner Society*. Chicago, Ill.: University of Chicago Press.

WRIGHT, R. and BENNETT, T. (1990). 'Exploring the Offender's Perspective: Observing and Interviewing Criminals' in K. Kempf (ed.), *Measurement Issues in Criminology*. New York: Springer.

—— and DECKER, S. (1994). *Burglars on the Job: Streetlife and Residential Break-ins*. Boston Mass.: Northeastern University Press.

——, BROOKMAN, F., and BENNETT, T. (2006). 'The Foreground Dynamics of Street Robbery in Britain'. *British Journal of Criminology*, 46: 1–15.

—— DECKER, S., REDFERN, A., and SMITH, D. (1992). 'A Snowball's Chance in Hell: Doing Fieldwork with Active Offenders'. *Journal of Research in Crime and Delinquency* 29: 148–61.

YABLONSKY, L. (1962). *The Violent Gang*. New York: Macmillan.

—— (1965). 'Experiences with the Criminal Community' in A. Gouldner and S. Miller (eds), *Applied Sociology*. New York: Free Press.

YOUNG, J. (1971). *The Drugtakers*. London: Paladin.

10

Mission impossible? Researching organized crime

Patricia Rawlinson

Introduction

In 1969 Donald Cressey published *Theft of a Nation*, an account of the nature and structure of organized crime in America. Cressey drew on material from the 1967 Task Force on Organized Crime which, together with previous official commissions and conferences, had identified Italian and Sicilian groups as the most powerful criminal organizations in the country. The book described a nationwide confederation of twenty-four crime families, each having a hierarchical structure and a clear division of labour whose activities were centrally overseen by a clandestine organization known as the Commission made up of representatives from the most powerful families (Cressey 1969). *Theft of a Nation* was to become one of the most influential texts on American organized crime. The year of its publication, Mario Puzo's novel, *The Godfather*, hit the bookshelves to be turned into a Hollywood box office success, the first of a trilogy, three years later. Both books, with acutely different readership figures, reinforced the notion of a highly organized syndicate, whose members were bound by arcane rituals and behaviours, a perception that was to become globally entrenched in the minds of law enforcement, governments, and the public for decades.

Cressey's book drew accolades from many members of the academic world, but has not been without its critics (Albini 1997; Block 1978; Smith 1991; Woodiwiss 1990). Much of their criticism was based on the methodology employed, in particular the reliance on official data, and most notably, on the testimony of a single informant, Joseph Valachi. While Cressey was aware of the hazards of informant testimony, going as far as warning one of his colleagues, Joseph Albini, against interviewing Valachi on the grounds that the guy 'was totally unreliable as a witness', his own use of Valachi's testimony was a blatant contradiction of this advice. Albini accounts for this inconsistency as follows:

I cannot help but believe that Cressey, though always attempting to keep a scholarly and objective view in his interpretations of the task force data, was captivated by the phenomenon that Dwight C. Smith, Jr (1975) has so aptly termed *the Mafia mystique* (Albini 1997: 18).

This mystique, the aura of power, the exotic, and the alien, still prevails around the subject of organized crime, prompted by its relative impenetrability, particularly for researchers. As James Finckenhauer and Elin Waring (1998) wrote in relation to his own work on Russian organized crime (ROC) in the United States: 'the typical tools of the criminologist—observation, surveys, interviews, samples and questionnaires—are either exceedingly difficult or impossible to use when studying organized crime' (Finckenauer and Waring 1998: 7). For these reasons, recourse to official data such as police and intelligence statistics by academics is more common than in other areas of criminological research. These data, in the absence of other easily accessible forms of information, are then accepted with a greater level of trust in their reliability than one might normally afford. The ever-present element of danger can also tempt the researcher into methodological laziness, discouraging approaches such as ethnography, a much favoured method for studying hidden communities, because of the potential risks.

A further problem in doing research on organized crime lies with the nature of the subject matter; in other words, what exactly is it? The definition debate has been running for well over half a century, engaging diverse academics with equally diverse interpretations. Some understand it according to the relationships between members (Ianni and Ianni 1972), some according to the motivation and *modus operandi* of their activities (Abadinsky 1994; Maltz 1976) and others in terms of its economic and social relations with licit counterparts (Chambliss 1988; Rawlinson 1997; Ruggiero 1996). Peter Reuter (1983) famously argued against the concept of 'organized' crime, describing its operations as 'disorganized' loose network formations, the antithesis of Cressey's confederation model. Levi understands it as a sociopolitically constructed concept, being 'a set of people whom the police and other agencies of the State, regard or wish us to regard as 'really dangerous' to its essential integrity' (Levi 1998: 335).

Whilst academics slug it out in the intellectual arena they are privileged to inhabit, the criminal justice system is tasked to take a more pragmatic approach. Law enforcement strives for a concise and uniform definition wherever possible, having only one motive in mind, that is to catch, prosecute, and convict those it suspects of this type of activity. As organized crime has gone transnational, the need for a standard multi-jurisdictional definition has become even more pressing. However, attempts at harmonization bring with them their own problems. The 'catch all' definition, such as that adopted by the United Nations as part of the 2000 Convention against Transnational Organized Crime, is by its very nature and intention, relatively ambiguous, allowing different states the flexibility to adapt it to their legal codes. It defines the structure as comprising 'three or more persons, existing for a period of time and acting in concert with the aim of committing one or more serious crimes ...' (United Nations 2000). The European Union's definition of an organized criminal structure, again aiming at standardization, is defined as 'a lasting, structured association of two or more persons ...' (European Union 1998). Two supranational institutions thus provide differing notions of what constitutes a group. As different resources are brought to bear in the fight against organized as opposed to 'normal crime' and given that sentencing is also affected by whether a proscribed act is carried out by a single perpetrator or a group, the differences between definitions are significant. So too will definition influence the type of research carried out, what to include, and what to leave out.

Despite all these challenges and minefields, research into organized crime is an area of increasing interest and activity. The concern over the proliferation of Eastern European and Russian organized crime during the 1990s, and a growing awareness of the numerous groups operating across the world, as issues such as the trafficking of people, drug smuggling, cybercrime, piracy, etc. are brought to our attention through the media and government policies, engender a greater demand for more extensive study into what has been a relatively under-researched area of criminology. As organized crime crosses borders, so too does the research process. The internationalization of higher education is bringing together students and researchers from different backgrounds, facilitating cross-cultural investigation into diverse societies, their crimes and law enforcement responses. Researchers into organized crime will therefore not only have to negotiate the difficulties of investigating such an opaque and covert subject but are increasingly called upon to do this within a comparative context. As criminologists such as Block (1978) and Dolgova and Dyakov (1989) maintain, organized crime is a product of the social and economic histories of its indigenous region or country. Thus an understanding requires that we see it not just as an autonomous phenomenon but against the cultural background from which it sprang and the others in which it operates.

The purpose of this chapter is twofold: first, critically to assess the research methods used in investigating organized crime. A particular emphasis will be laid on ethnographic or fieldwork studies, in part, because of the relatively small number of studies conducted in this way but also because, despite the usefulness of official data, they have had a dominant influence on how we perceive and respond to organized crime. It is now time to turn up the volume of the voices 'in the field'. Secondly, the chapter looks at the challenges and rewards of researching organized crime from a comparative perspective. This will draw on two case studies from my own research, one into Russian organized crime in St Petersburg and the other looking at the same in the context of the Baltic States as part of a team project for the ESRC *One Europe or Several?* Programme.[1] Some of what is included in the first part has already been published in the first edition of this book but in this edition there are a significant number of additions. These are due not just to the word limit previously imposed but because, in the process of teaching qualitative methods over the past five or six years, students' questions and comments have encouraged me to reassess what I regard as 'significant' to the research process. The additions and changes have also been informed by a year spent in Moscow (2003–4) not actively researching anything at all, but instead teaching Russian adolescents and working as a volunteer for a charity which rehabilitates victims of sex trafficking. Nonetheless, it provided a further insight, which only 'being there' can, into the day-to-day realities of living in, and trying to understand Russia and its people. As I wrote in 'Mafia, Methodology and "Alien" Culture' (Rawlinson 2000) the learning process continues, except now, I realize that my learning curve is steeper and longer than previously imagined.

Entry points and exits

In his comparative study of the Wickersham Commission and the 1967 Presidential Commission, both tasked to look at the problem of inter alia organized crime, Dwight Smith (1991) set out 'to show how the entry points in each case affected the conclusions reached about the meaning of organized crime, and to reflect on some reasons why their

[1] 'Crime, Borders and Law Enforcement: a European "Dialogue" for improving security', a project in the ESRC's *One Europe or Several?* programme, Award No. L2132522013.

results were dissimilar'. 'Clearly', he reiterated, 'a different point of entry can lead to important differences in the conclusions drawn' (1991: 135). Extend this concept to the research process, and our preconceptions of the subject we are about to investigate will determine how we go about this investigation. The level of danger, for example, we attach to organized crime will impact on how we research it. The predominance of secondary data usage is not just a consequence of access difficulties but of the perception of risk we attach to more qualitative approaches such as interviews or fieldwork. Most of what we know about organized crime comes from the media, which even in the documentary genre is required to provide some dramatic nuance to what, most of the time, is a mundane topic. Hence, in the interests of keeping the viewers' attention, the link between organized crime and violence is almost routinely amplified. But violence, even when it does occur, has a purpose. Those most likely to get hurt do so because they pose a threat to the aims and/or well- being of organized crime groups as, for example, certain types of investigative journalist. Albini's reassuring words that organized criminals 'couldn't care less about what type of data academics usually collect' (1997: 18) more accurately describes the situation. There are always the exceptions, such as the death of Ken Pryce, a sociologist, found drowned in unexplained circumstances during his research into Jamaican gangs (Hobbs 2000). As neither the details of this alleged 'killing' nor the circumstances leading up to it are clear, there is a tendency to let the imagination run riot and fall into the 'mystique' of organized crime.

Other factors influence the entry point. Cressey's role as consultant to the President's Commission Task Force would have ensured a level of ideological allegiance to the ethos of those with whom he worked and the data they supplied. In contrast, conflict theorists such as Block and Chambliss (1981), begin their work on organized crime from a Marxist stance, looking at the activities of organized crime as part of a criminogenic capitalist framework which makes them naturally suspicious of any official data, seeing them as tools of the powerful, whose function is to strengthen and protect the interests of the elite (Block and Chambliss 1981). No researcher begins his/her investigation free from preconceived notions concerning the identity of their subject. The methodology pursued, even as a combination of different approaches, will reflect these preconceptions and in doing so, can easily reiterate them through the findings. So do we become part of the process of the social construction of organized crime, acting as Berger and Luckmann (1968) explain, creators of social realities which are the product of continuous reciprocities between the researcher and the world under investigation. What we initially put in is what we tend to get out by virtue of on whom and what we focus, and how we respond to the subject of that focus.

Positivist methodologies

The current dominance of positivist methodology in the field of criminology has provided interesting challenges for those studying organized crime. In its myriad forms, criminological positivism takes a scientific perspective on offending, explaining crime according to factors which can be measured and categorized (but see Wikström, this volume). Motivations for crime are not so much down to free will or self-motivation but come from observable facts outside (or within) the criminal. In producing various aetiologies of crime, individual, psychological, and sociological positivism incorporate them into a comprehensive and policy-supportive framework, which relies on statistical evidence as a validation for these policies. However, in official crime statistics in England and Wales, figures on organized crime, as with other generic forms such as corporate and white collar, are not included. Recently, other data-sets have been constructed to try and provide a quantifiable sense of the scale of organized crime in the UK. The Organized Crime Notification Scheme (OCNS) was set up as a way of systematically collecting data from various agencies, including the National Criminal Intelligence Service, Customs and Excise, the Serious Fraud Agency as well the police forces (the newly formed Serious and Organized Crime Agency has now integrated many of the functions of these other agencies) . This was carried out through tick-box questionnaires asking for statistics on numbers of arrests, disruptions, international links, characteristics such as use of violence and activities, etc. (Gregory 2003). There were problems, however, with the methodology used for the OCNS. As Gregory summarized them, data collection was carried out 'against very broad qualifying characteristics ... and a lack of insistence on evidence of adequate quality assurance procedures to back-up claims being made in terms of outcomes' (Gregory 2003: 93). And even if such data were reliable, what do they tell us about the state of organized crime? Clearly, they provide a picture of crime trends, and can act as performance indicators for the agencies concerned, but do little to enhance an understanding of the character of organized crime, its relationship with society, the underlying causes of its apparent proliferation, and so on.

Even in those areas of criminology which do lend themselves more readily to statistical analysis, the real value of data lies in the quality of interpretation. For example, how do we interpret the continuous rise in the number of inmates in the UK over the past decade? For John Reid, the Home Secretary, rising prison figures provide public confidence in the criminal justice system's ability to protect them (Hansard 2006). Consider Nils Christie's take on prison figures, that their increase in the Atlantic states (the USA and the UK) is not an indication of rising crime rates or the efficiency of criminal justice systems, but a slide towards the commodification of 'pain', or, incarceration, an *industry* which requires ever more consumers and consumed (Christie 2000). Each interpreter is driven by a different agenda, one policy oriented, the other sociological. Christie places them within a social, political, and economic context, questioning the very construction of crime itself. Unless, as researchers, we are dealing strictly with policy, positivist methodologies provide a limited or even misleading picture of our subject. Positivist research has been accused of blocking our vision of social life, a blindness which, in Morrison's words, 'has occurred as a result of the translation of social life into the language of the incalculable, the rigorous; [where] the coherence of mathematical formula is produced at the expense of insight into the contexts of action ...' (Morrison 1995: 175). Organized crime, especially, demands insights into its multifarious contexts.

Qualitative research

Most methodologies are not self-contained and researchers often cross the quantitative and qualitative divide in the practice of triangulation, the deliberate use of different approaches to investigate the same topic (Noaks and Wincup 2004).

Qualitative research covers a broad spectrum of methodologies including semi- and open-ended interviewing, case histories, biographies, and ethnography. Indeed, most approaches that do not fall squarely under the scientifically measurable are considered to be qualitative. Because of the breadth of approaches, triangulation can be contained solely within the qualitative framework, combining, for example, ethnography with case histories and interviews.

Research into organized crime lends itself to these different qualitative approaches, in particular, the interview and ethnography, depending, of course, on the nature of one's research inquiry. However, given the difficulty in accessing sources for interview, or gaining entry in the world of crime groups, other methods, some frowned on by 'serious' academics, have helped to add invaluable insights into this elusive subject. The use of biography, autobiography, and non-fiction accounts of criminal careers, helps offset 'the intransigence of a positivism that colludes so closely with administrative analysis [and] ignores narrative accounts at the cost of a considerable loss of detail, tone and depth' (Hobbs 1994: 443). One of the most famous examples is Pileggi's (1987) account of the life of gangster Henry Hill, turned into the successful *Goodfellas* film. *Brigada*, a Russian television serial, traced the life of a young Afghan war veteran on his return to Moscow against the background of social and political change in the 1990s where he became a leading crime boss and entrepreneur (Sidorov 2003). Whilst the character was fictional, the context in which his life was placed resonated with thousands of his generation and provided an informative and graphic example of how an anomic environment can create the conditions for criminality: Durkheim on plasma. In contrast to the Manichean good/evil divide which most orthodox accounts of organized crime offer, both these non-academic narratives provide a banal realism in place of the mafia mystique and in doing so challenge the viewer to assess organized crime not as the 'other' but as an integral part of ordinary lives.

Journalistic accounts too have their place. While much opprobrium has been placed on the media, often justified, the denigration of journalists has also tarred many a sound investigative reporter. Even with the eternal remit of finding the 'good story', and sometimes sacrificing detail for drama, a discerning look at material from investigative journalism can produce useful data. Andrew Jennings' investigation into organized crime and the Olympic games (Jennings and Sambrook 2002) and Duncan Campbell's exposure of the links between British American Tobacco and drug smugglers (Campbell 2004) deserve review not only because they have gone where others fear to tread, but as with most journalism, for legal purposes sources are checked three or four times to ensure the veracity of statements and conclusions, a rigour many academics would not follow. So, too, do we need to bear in mind that investigative journalism in societies with high levels of violence, such as Russia and Brazil, is motivated by that rare ideal (in a world of squalid celebrity gossip and political muck-raking) of uncovering the truth for the betterment of their respective societies, rather than the fulfilment of largely meaningless tables of academic output.

Some of the most interesting qualitative research into organized crime, however, both for the researcher and the reader, comes from ethnography, and indeed it is this 'in the field' approach which marked some of the earliest studies into the subject.

Ethnography

The history of research into organized crime, 'in the field' does not equate with 'in the grave'. Many of the dangers of this type of research are less those perceived to be inherent in the research topic than those brought about by the unpreparedness of the researcher (Lee 1995). And, as mentioned above, the track record for safety is very high.

Early studies of organized crime were conducted by members of the Chicago School, in which getting out into the real world took precedence over secondary data analysis. Landesco's *Organized Crime in Chicago* (1968) and Thrasher's *The Gang* (1927) conducted in the 1920s demonstrated the ability of the researcher to access difficult communities and provide a unique glimpse into criminal organizations at different levels. Subsequent studies such as Whyte's (1993) observation of street gangs in a Boston slum, Ianni and Ianni's (1972) study of family relationships and crime, Chambliss's (1988) foray into Seattle society and its criminal connections and Decker and Van Winkle's (1996) work on street gangs in St Louis have given voice to communities and groups whose narratives are normally drowned out by outsider accounts of their networks, values, and aspirations. Despite the roller-coaster popularity of ethnographic work, American scholars have consistently dominated ethnographic research into organized crime and related fields. The dearth of ethnographic research in Britain might be accounted for by the apparent lack of organized crime activity relative to that in the USA, but even with the recent increase of this type of crime, it remains seriously under-researched both as a topic and 'in the field'. A notable exception is the work of Hobbs (1988, 1995) whose colourful observation of professional criminals in the East End broke with a tradition of intellectual elitism in British criminology and helped reinstate the respectability of ethnography which had enjoyed greater popularity during the 1960s and early 1970s.

The pitfalls of ethnography are obvious. Immersion in a situation alien to our own normal experience challenges the researcher on every level, from how best to record data, the complexities of writing up what can be amorphous and emotive observations and experiences, and the personal impact of doing such research. Ethnography is as much part of a self-educational process as it is the collection of data. As Hammersley and Atkinson point out, 'We act in a social world and yet are able to reflect upon ourselves and our actions as objects in that world' (1995: 21). Hence the researcher brings to the study the skills and limitations peculiar to them, all of which impact on the data collected. In effect, the entry point is that known and unknown self. Being 'replete with the unexpected', any ethnographic study comes with a list of caveats, the greatest risk coming from the researchers themselves. Unreal expectations, assumptions, prejudices, in fact, a whole list of negative human traits, not least a laziness that anticipates just 'slipping into' someone else's world, dog the ethnographer as s/he conducts their experiment from inside the test tube. Nowhere is this more graphically illustrated (or felt) than in comparative ethnographic research.

Compare and contrast . . .

The spread of transnational crime over the past two decades, whether organized crime from former communist states or neo-terrorism from Washington-defined rogue states, has focused increasing attention on comparative research. The need to understand other cultures and the specific contexts that give rise to criminal behaviour which travels beyond indigenous borders into a global arena, has become essential to international crime fighting, intelligence, and security. All the factors present in researching organized crime per se, are compounded when extended to a comparative framework, incorporating as it does, issues such as language, culture, ideology, and so on. Some knowledge of the source country, beyond the superficial, is therefore essential (Hantrais 1996). (See also Heidensohn as well as Eisner and Parmar in this volume.)

Nelken's (1994) observation that doing comparative research 'may have as much to do with understanding one's own country better as it has with understanding anyone else's' rings particularly true in the study of organized crime. For the non-native researcher, these histories and contexts stand in distinction (or in some cases, similarity) to their own experience of history and context and in doing so demand an epistemological consideration of what we 'know' from our experience. Research, whether positivist or interpretive, can only begin from what is familiar. While there are different forms of comparative research (Vagg: 1993) most will lead us to question the familiar and in doing so, remove the comfort zones of tradition and habit. My own research into organized crime in Russia tended to provoke as much deliberation on the nature of western capitalism as it did on crime groups in a former communist state, erasing the boundaries that neatly compartmentalized 'good' and 'bad' business. The annihilation of presupposed realities thus leaves the comparative investigator with the daunting task of trying to reconstruct a new touchstone of reality out of the debris of culturally determined preconceptions.

The need for 'first-hand familiarity with daily life in the societies to be compared' (Nelken 1994: 227) is not just the concern of the researcher. It also has significant implications for policy and cross-cultural co-operation. A good example of how a lack of local knowledge can impact on crime fighting was provided by a postgraduate student of mine from the Middle East, a police officer attached to his country's antiterrorist unit. He wrote of the collaboration on fighting terrorism between his own country and the USA. This partnership produced some sound antiterrorist strategies but one proposal proved awkward. Amongst the new measures proposed for the improvement of airport security, at the behest of the Americans, was the use of sniffer dogs. This was a particularly difficult moment, he explained, as dogs were regarded as unclean in his country and this form of deterrence and detection would be offensive to indigenous airline passengers.

Language is crucial to building an understanding of other cultures. Nor is this only applicable to 'foreign' cultures: Landesco's study of American-Italian organized crime capitalized on the fact that he 'could speak their language as well as the language of the academic' (1968: xv). While the dominance of English as the world business lingua franca has enabled native Anglophones the luxury of communicating in their own language, being a monoglot has its limitations. Speaking the language of the country in which one's research is being conducted is by no means necessary, but not having certain linguistic capabilities can have an impact on the methodological approaches chosen and the data collected. Even in quantitative research, the simplest issues can be exacerbated by language difference. Robertson's (2006) observation of the sociocultural importance of language during her research on community policing in Ukraine, is indicative. She describes the difficulty of translating the term 'neighbourhood watch', where 'the main problem was to produce an equivalent in Ukrainian which did not have connotations of spying on neighbours!' (Robertson 2006: 143). So too, as she points out, did the very process of questionnaire distribution require sensitivity to cultural difference where respondents from an erstwhile totalitarian state were unused to having their opinions solicited. Reaction to a bona fide request for people's views veered from the overly cautious to the welcomingly enthusiastic, a situation replicated even more so in the semi-structured/open-ended interview.

A level of linguistic ability can also provide access to a vast range of literature not available in the English language. It is possible to get material translated, usually at a cost well beyond that of the researcher, particularly at postgraduate and doctoral level. But the researcher is still faced with the problem of selection, of knowing which texts, out of a complex array on offer, will be best suited to their research (Bennett 2004). The presence of a mediator between researcher and source material, whether as a translator or interpreter, can also 'lead to the corruption of all types of data in one way or another' (Robertson 2006: 151). However, language skills are not always an advantage. Respondents often speak very quickly in interviews with researchers who understand their language, or slip into the vernacular, an especially potent part of discourse in the criminal underworld. For the sake of fluency in the interview there is often a hesitancy to ask respondents to repeat what they have said. And unless the researcher is bilingual, linguistic faux pas are inevitable, some of which can inflict life-long scars of embarrassment. My ability to mix up verbs had me once ask the chairman of Leningrad's lawyers, in a public setting with the microphone on, whether he had just had an orgasm, when I meant to ask whether he had finished (his speech). His riposte, 'No, but I would have liked to' defused the situation but did little for an already faltering ego.

Other modalities of ethnographic research, such as considerations of gender, are highlighted in the comparative context. The fact that I got away with such an embarrassing slip up was very much to do with the patronizing (but useful, in this case) attitude to women by Russian men. Laura Piacentini's experiences from conducting research inside Russian prisons were more acutely painful. She describes being expected to 'perform' for the governor of one of the labour 'zones' by reciting poetry, otherwise access would have been problematic. She writes of feeling 'exposed and vulnerable, recalling school days where there was the threat of chastisement and possibly public humiliation had I not "done my homework"' (Piacentini 2004: 19). It seems inconceivable, given the dominance of patriarchy, that a male researcher would have been treated in such a way. Yet in disadvantage lies its polar opposite. Respect, of sorts, afforded the female 'outsider' in contrast to the sometimes appalling behaviour towards Russian women, both in domestic and institutional settings, can allow certain forms of immunity from the travesties of male patriarchy and at the same time, an ability to 'manipulate' cultural differences (Rawlinson 2000; Smith and Wincup 2000). This in turn raises a number of ethical issues for female ethnographers conducting comparative research, including the extent to which they can and should behave in a way that betrays their own values, which may only serve to reaffirm the values of a society they would normally hold up for criticism.

Ethical demands abound in comparative ethnographic research, perhaps more so than for that conducted in indigenous or common cultural settings. The dearth of comparative criminological research through the ethnographic process means that, at the present time, many of the studies being carried out are 'firsts'. Those who enter a field hitherto untrodden leave behind a distinctive research footprint, an impression of the researcher, their academic and cultural world. Piacentini as the first western female to live in Siberian prisons, did achieve a balance between the need to survive and gather data with a general deference to the more unpleasant cultural facets of Russian life without losing her integrity. It was important, she acknowledged, that she assume 'a Russian mindset to reflect an empathy and understanding of Russian culture' (Piacentini 2004: 19). In doing so, as I hope I too have in my research, she has left the door open for other researchers on Russian prisons.

Despite the obvious difficulties with comparative research, there are some positive pay-offs beyond the personal. Any research that engages with cross-cultural issues, that breaks down the barriers of misunderstanding, particularly in the current dichotomized environment where the 'if you're not with us, you're against us' mentality draws simplistic lines of difference and hostility between states and cultures, can only be advantageous. Cross-cultural contact, whether through the construction of datasets through international teamwork, conducting interviews, or living in the midst of the 'other' challenges the myriad assumptions and prejudices each party holds as a consequence of political and ideological agendas and media representations which form much of our knowledge base. The contacts might reaffirm or refute some of these preconceived notions but at least provide a modicum of individual experience from which future pronouncements and perceptions can spring.

Comparative criminological research can also make a significant contribution to the development of theory, broadening debates 'beyond a stress on crime and social structure towards the study of the relationship between crime and culture, ideology and discourse' (Nelken 1994: 223). As the dominant discourse of criminology has been determined by the 'socially powerful' (Morrison 1995: 475), the challenges to this dominance come most forcefully from beyond the perimeters of this discourse. Comparative criminology helps us to reflect on and question not just the most entrenched explanations of crime, but the thinking behind these explanations, shuffling back and forth between realities, trying to fathom cultural idiosyncrasies or embrace similarities. The more that globalization becomes an integral part of local, regional, and national crime issues, such as the illicit, Afghan-sourced opiate-based drugs sold on the streets of western cities, towns, and rural areas, the need to understand the socio-economic 'push–pull' factors of the source and target countries, and the cultural dynamics which facilitate or impede them is crucial. So too is the need for criminology to move beyond the confines of its own discipline, to question the discourse of the 'socially powerful' by engaging with a whole range of other fields such as sociology, politics, and international relations. In doing so, comparative criminology becomes more than the pursuit of knowledge of crime in different societies but a critical reflection of criminology itself, of the role it plays in sustaining or countering the ideologies that help shape and limit its identity.

Case study one: Russia

My research on organized crime in Russia was the subject of a Ph.D. which set out to try and fathom the nature of ROC, its relationship to the changing political and economic structures in a society undergoing draconian change. It was a daunting task, in a world of uncertainty, of ideological chaos and contradictions, underpinned by the semantic ambiguities of the subject area dominated by men and exacerbated even further by the cultural distinctions that separated a British postgraduate's knowledge of the world from that of a Russian's. Zinoviev (1986) warned that one of the biggest mistakes westerners made in their understanding of the Soviet Union was to judge it according to their own benchmarks (Zinoviev 1986: 128). But in those anarchic years there appeared to be no benchmarks against which my own understanding could be compared.

For seven years I had been visiting Russia, and its former incarnation, the Soviet Union, under numerous guises; as an undergraduate student, a television researcher, freelance journalist, informal liaison between the Metropolitan Police and the St Petersburg Higher Police Training Academy and finally, as a doctoral student. In 1994, the year I completed fieldwork for the Ph.D., Russia had became embroiled in its first war with Chechnya, the value of the rouble had plummeted in October leaving people panic-stricken over the loss of their savings, and organized crime, allegedly involved in almost every aspect of Russian society, had been linked to the high-profile assassination of the journalist Dmitri Kholodov during his investigation of supposed links between the army and the criminal underworld. It was a time of huge anxiety. After the 1991 coup, the expectations that democracy and the free market would deliver prosperity and stability to a country historically wracked by political and economic uncertainty, were being cruelly dashed as the benefits of the promised reforms were delivered, in Soviet style, to the usual suspects.

If I have lingered long on the events of those years, it is because they were crucial to the research. Trying to understand organized crime meant making sense of its environment. Unlike Federico Varese (2001), whose research into the Russian mafia was informed by a precise interpretation of a specific area of organized crime—illegal protection—my own was initiated by a vague notion of protean structures and socially constructed labels. The length of time spent engaged with the subject and various approaches from which this engagement sprang both helped and complicated the research process. Access to the police and eventually to the criminal world during the dedicated period of fieldwork in the autumn of 1994 had been greatly facilitated by my liaison and journalist roles of previous years. But this access treasure trove had its downside. Ambiguity of topic was also matched by uncertainty of approach. The journalist goes for the 'good story', the police liaison, no matter how informal, has certain loyalties. Learning to be an 'academic' researcher', and utilize the advantages of the other roles without being directed away from the academic purpose proved to be one of the more difficult tasks. So too was the organization of the research.

Ungrounded research

Every researcher has a plan of how they intend to conduct their study, even if it requires adaptation during the process (Burgess 1993, Hobbs and May 1993). Mine was to base the study in St Petersburg, a city I knew well and where I had some good contacts in the police (*militsia*). There was also planned the odd trip to Moscow, mainly for academic sources of information. Much of the research was to be interview-based, targeting members of the police dealing with organized crime, crime correspondents and, hopefully accessing one or two willing members of organized crime groups through a number of contacts made during the filming of a Channel 4 *Dispatches* documentary on Russian organized crime. Secondary data were to be accessed through the appropriate police and municipal libraries. I had also factored in time to hang around in the bars and restaurants where organized crime members were rumoured to visit—ESRC money well spent. This was Russia, though, where certainty and prediction are in eternal short supply. Experience should have taught the inevitability of unbridled spontaneity in a country whose catch phrases include 'no-one knows what will happen tomorrow', and 'nothing is permitted but everything is possible'. In an initial attempt to emulate best practice research British-style, I worried about the order of interviews, whether to conduct them with the police first and then the underworld, but as the first two weeks went the unassailable truth hit home. What plan I had was scrapped as the research went into precarious ad hoc mode. The following is therefore not a chronological account.

Getting to the Police

Access to Regional Anti-Organized Crime Department (RUOP), the organized crime unit, was relatively easy. The invaluable and ubiquitous practice of *blat*, broadly speaking, the acquisition of favours through mutually beneficial dealings and networks (Ledeneva 1998) had opened a cautious door to the workings of the St Petersburg police. Time spent as an informal liaison and interpreter for a number of reciprocal visits between the St Petersburg and Metropolitan police had put credit in my contact bank. Interviews were granted with a couple of RUOP officers and I was provided with a 'mentor', Alyosha (not his real name), a young and enthusiastic officer who met with me at regular intervals off site for informal discussions on St Petersburg's criminal underworld. If getting to the police was easy, getting any substantive information from them was less so. In order to interview RUOP's second-in-command I had to waive the right to tape the interview, a request which came as little surprise. Russia's totalitarian legacy, as Robertson (2006) implies, has helped to confuse the distinction between interviewing and interrogation, particularly for respondents working in state institutions, such as the police, recorded information being seen as potentially incriminating. It was also obvious that any insight into organized crime gleaned from these formal police interviews would be limited to the less sophisticated forms, the local rackets and so on, which were already covered by the local media. The previous four years of journalistic-based research and the odd bit of fieldwork conducted in my spare time whenever I visited Russia for other work, hinted at more complex and institutional linked criminal networks. Questions concerning political corruption and the underworld were brushed away, not surprisingly given the sensitivity of police interviews per se (Reiner 1991). For someone who professed to know about Soviet culture I realized early on how ignorant and insensitive these questions were, but not early enough to prevent me from asking them. Despite the veneer of democracy and freedom of speech, Russian state buildings were still bugged.

Off-site and off-the-record interviews (more akin to discussions) predictably were more productive. One high-ranking officer spoke of the utilitarian role of organized crime's middle echelons who kept hooliganism to a minimum in some of the troubled suburbs of the city, saving police power for the more serious crimes. Alyosha, when pressed, alluded to links between the underworld and St Petersburg's power elite but, at that point, gave few details. Only in a different context, and almost incidentally was this linkage discussed in more depth.

At no time during academic research was money paid to the police for interviews. The practice of 'cash for questions' to the Russian police (and which occurs regularly in media interviews, including those I was involved with) has only helped exacerbate the problem of corruption. Further, this practice prices subsequent prospective academic researchers out of the interviewing process (Whyte 1984) and, in the case of the Russian police, has commodified information in such a way that the they have now become 'script writers' (this is what you want to hear) and directors (this is what you want to see) in the information market (Rawlinson 1998).

Informal interviews with Alyosha entailed regular meetings in an assortment of cafes and restaurants. I never wrote anything down during our conversations other than names of people mentioned, writing up notes back at the hostel. Aside from the usual constraints of note-taking in this type of situation (Rowe forthcoming) there were specific culturally motivated reasons for desisting. Note-taking drew attention to our table, not such a banal concern as the following illustrates. We once met up, at my insistence, at a decent, cockroach-free café off the Fontanka canal. During our conversation a small group of men came in and sat down behind us. Alyosha slowly got up from his chair having told me quite categorically that I must wait and pay the bill five minutes after he had left and then meet him round the corner. The men behind us were members of the Tambov gang, one of St Petersburg's most powerful groups at that time. They knew Alyosha by sight and he was keen to distance himself from me, for my own personal safety. Secondly, listening in a foreign language and writing in my native language (not advisable), tended to break concentration. The absence of rigorous note-taking did, however, leave me vulnerable to the vagaries of memory and in doing so probably sacrificed detail for gist.

As we established mutual trust, questions became more incisive and what I did elicit from Alyosha, was probably as close as it was possible to get to some clear picture of what was occurring in St Petersburg's underworld. There are times when the gut rather than the intellect provides a more accurate barometer of 'truth'. If there was any doubt about his knowledge of organized crime, this was allayed when he personally arranged an interview with Vladimir, head of one of the city's most notorious protection rackets.

Getting to the criminals

Prior to the ESRC-funded part of the research, there had been the 'grab when you can' approach to information-gathering on criminals. During the filming of '*Moscow's Mafia Millions*' in 1990 there had been a few off-camera meetings with members of the capital's underworld. Our driver, himself closely linked to Moscow's criminal community, introduced us to an array of 'businessmen' who provided, at a substantial price (mea culpa) insights and anecdotes on their profitable life, though the level of veracity remained questionable. When payment is involved there is arguably even less inclination for the delivery of facts, as the very need to purchase at a price leaves the buyer vulnerable to wildly imaginative narratives—caveat emptor! In one off-camera interview in Moscow we were given a spiel about 'red mercury', a putative nuclear material which caught the attention of the western media in the mid-1990s in a near-hysterical bout of 'world takeover' by the Russian mafia. Much of this was the need to impress, particularly during the days when all things from the West were afforded prime and celebrity status, including film crews.

From 1991 to 1994, amidst the toing and froing to Moscow and St Petersburg, I managed to locate some lower-ranking figures, pimps, and smugglers, in one of St Petersburg's hotels, the Moskva, simply by sitting in the bar where the 'rich' westerners hung out. Oleg, one of my 'catches', was more than happy to talk and show me some of the spoils of his business, from carrier bags full of condoms, for the prostitutes he ran, to the sale of a couple of decommissioned tanks, waiting outside the city, he assured me (I resisted his exhortations to buy one, explaining the parking restrictions in London), and any other weaponry I might need. Russia was 'up for sale'.

By 1994, any aspiring criminal/petty businessmen had seen the financial wisdom and personal kudos in referring to himself as a member of the Russian 'mafia', such was the image of power and danger bestowed on the concept. It was the quiet 'respectable' organizations that held the real power. Hence Vladimir.

The fact that the anti-organized crime unit were able to fix an interview with a powerful crime boss in a non-custodial setting provided more insight into the connections between the upper and underworlds of 1990s Russia than any interview itself could. The meeting itself was a fiasco. On my own, surrounded by Vladimir's henchmen and disarmed by his apparent smugness and my unconcealed nervousness I spilled a cup of coffee, lost the thread of the conversation, mumbled some meaningless questions and bowed out, embarrassed at my incompetence and angry that a golden opportunity had been squandered. It was not unpreparedness that threw the interview. I had concise questions and was permitted to write notes freely. Ironically, while intellectually dismissing Cressey's attraction to the mystique of organized crime I had fallen prey to the same attraction and belief in its dangerousness. Though there was never any real risk my own behaviour in a 'real' situation validated that which I had been so keen to criticize.

Just looking

One of the most important aspects of being in an alien culture is the ability to observe not just the subject of study, but the context in which it lies. The St Petersburg of 1994 was (and probably still is) a city of stark contrasts. On the one hand there was the growing opulence of the tourist destinations, new and reconstructed hotels and shops, on the other the hidden squalor of poverty and human misery, the Janus picture of capitalist 'success'. In a society which had once prided itself on welfare provision for the vulnerable, children as young as nine were selling themselves for sex, begging or stealing, abandoned, as many of them were, by financially pressed parents and the state. The old, too, felt the impact of this success story, many forced to sell what meagre surplus they had as a means of supplementing miserable pensions, made more worthless by constant inflation. One sight was especially poignant, that of a head-scarfed babushka selling a single shoe. So, too, was that of the young boy, mouth covered in sores, too tired to beg but with his arm limply stretched out as if wanting to. It was these 'incidentals', the moments when life throws itself into the path of the researcher and can either be sidestepped as irrelevant or refocuses the more formal aspects of data collection into a 'human moment' of enduring significance, that became enduring memories. These are the events or images, sometimes dramatic, more often banal, that impress themselves on the emotions and in doing so, colour our perceptions, consciously or otherwise, of the country or community we seek to understand.

These incidentals revealed much about the nature and impact of organized crime. It was clear that the younger generation could provide a recruiting ground for a next generation of gang members, prostitutes, targets for sex trafficking, and clients for illegal drugs. It was also clear that the real threat to Russia was not from organized crime, certainly in the more traditional sense of hierarchical groups driven by violence and greed in the maximization of illicit profit acquisition. Crime groups exploited what was already there, thriving in the Darwinian realities of the free market, in which the fittest survive and the rest are left breathlessly running further and further behind. The real threat, it seemed, when reflecting on the state of one of Russia's major cities, was the inhumanity of an ideology which clung onto false assumptions, which preached empty promises of a better future for all, through the mechanism of an invisible hand. Parts of the Russian media and much of those in the West, were immersed in the rhetoric of the free-market miracle. What I read, and what I saw were two different worlds. Even the mantra that 'things would get better' became empty when faced with the day-to-day reality of life's rejects, those for whom tomorrow was unconsidered, desperately needing, as they did, to survive today.

Interviews and statistics drew an outline of the problem of organized crime, its multifarious identities and operations in post-communist Russia. 'Just looking' put this contentious subject into a broader social and political context and in doing so brought into focus the nature of its impact on the lives of ordinary citizens. Organized crime per se did not create the conditions, which gave rise to its exploitative activities (although it certainly exacerbated them). Its proliferation was essentially a *response* to the absence of the rule of law, to endemic corruption in political circles and, most significantly, to the ideology of laisser-faire capitalism, the adoption of the American dream of monetary success as the new defining principle of social aspiration. It was the violence of the free market, rather than that of organized crime, which stood out on the streets of St Petersburg.

We do need 'to interpret what we observe with caution' (Whyte 1984: 95) but without the 'just looking' factor to complement the 'hard' data of surveys and interviews, our vocabulary of understanding, particularly of a phenomenon as complex as organized crime, is severely limited. From observation came some of the most important questions for the research and beyond. For clear-cut definitions of crime had been blurred by the realities of human suffering as a consequence of legal activities. Which is worse: to be robbed of one's property or life with a gun, or to suffer such abject poverty that life is barely worth living because of ruthless competition and reckless gambling on the world's stock markets? This was more than 'just looking'.

Case study two: doing the Baltics

In contrast to the chaos of the Ph.D. research, the 'Crime, Borders and Law Enforcement: A European Dialogue for Improving Security' (L213 25 2013) as part of the ESRC's *One Europe or Several* programme was a more ordered affair. Comprising a team of two other academics (Gregory and Brooke) from different universities, the research involved an investigation into the problems of transitional, in particular, Russian organized crime in the Baltic States before their accession to the European Union. My remit was to gather data from the three Baltic countries, spending eight weeks in Latvia, six in Lithuania and a month in Estonia between October 1999 and May 2000. Interviews were to be carried out across a number of parallel institutions, including the newly formed anticorruption and organized crime units, and other relevant sections of the criminal justice systems. Formal and informal meetings were also arranged with European and US liaison officers from the appropriate embassies. When possible, links were created with those university departments in each country, which might be involved in research in organized crime. Once in the field, any other agencies or bodies that might have information, such as NGOs, businesses, and journalists, were also interviewed.

Despite the common use of the generic term 'Baltic States' each country, now freed from almost half a century of communist control, was keen to emphasize its cultural uniqueness (Lieven 1994). This was especially evident in the insistence, or even legal requirement, that public sector employees work in their indigenous language (banned in Estonia and Latvia under Soviet rule), a defiant gesture to the Kremlin and a 'vengeance is sweet' blow to ethnic Russians. As a non-Estonian/Latvian/Lithuanian speaker I now experienced the handicap of being linguistically incapable, though only officially so. Most of those interviewed in the police understood, and indeed spoke, Russian fluently, oftentimes more capably than their native language. These legal incursions into communication produced the absurd scenario in which we could easily have conducted the interviews in Russian, thus saving time and money on interpreters. In moments of heated dialogue, and there were many (below), common sense and common language prevailed so that the barriers of a third party were removed and the interviews took a more relaxed turn. This is not to denigrate the role of the interpreter; quite the opposite. Communication is not just about language, but includes the crucial presence of cultural semantics, semiotics, and social nuance, all of which were willingly provided by my intrepid interpreters.

Not lost in translation

An academic who shall remain nameless once confided that he was appalled at the quality of interpreters allocated to him when visiting Russia on a short-term research project. It was not the capacity for translation that upset him, but what he perceived as their deliberate attempt to misconstrue what he had said, gleaned from answers received to his questions. In our linguistically challenged, Anglophonic world, finding a home-grown interpreter, especially for the more exotic languages such as Russian, Mandarin and, in my case, minority languages, is problematic. The availability of indigenous interpreters, whose grasp of the English language can put many a British and American adult to shame, provides an easy, but not always satisfying, solution to the Babel tower. Historically, in communist states such as the Soviet Union and China (the latter still) the interpreter has been linked to security and intelligence agencies, having the added role of informant and ideologue. It is his/her job to ensure that the 'right' kind of information is given to the visitor, and that the hosts are not unduly irritated by awkward questions from their guests. They act as filters, sentries at the gates of political dialogue, but always manifesting loyalty, naturally, to their paymasters. Hence, choosing one's interpreter (if such a choice is available) is as important, if not more so, as locating appropriate interviewees.

In two of the Baltic States I worked with postgraduates, all having excellent English and an endless enthusiasm for the subject. The younger generation are much more open than their elders, especially those under 25, having had little experience of communism as an inculcated mode of thinking. They also struggle for money, particularly those who shun the overpopulated business studies degrees and opt for social sciences or humanities. In both cases I insisted that they received direct payments (money had a habit of getting diverted into other 'funds', in one of the countries particularly) giving more than the declared amount which was purposely kept to a minimum to stop them being harassed for bribes. I told them they could refuse to attend any interview they might feel uncomfortable with, whether because of the subject matter or the person being interviewed. They were also asked to surreptitiously signal if an interview was going in a difficult direction, as we were asking some delicate questions on a sensitive subject. My prime concern was their safety once I had left the Baltics. A few years previously, I had worked as a consultant for a British current affairs programme on crime in Chechnya. The journalist providing on-site support in Grozny was murdered the day after the TV crew had left the country. While the situation in the Baltics was a far cry from the violent mayhem of Chechnya, the legacy of Soviet authoritarianism was still evident and being thrown off their university courses for 'inappropriate' behaviour was not impossible.

All the interpreters volunteered, unprompted, to provide a cultural analysis of the interviews. This entailed a most pleasant debrief after a day's work in some café or bar when we discussed the way questions were received, answered, or evaded. They would invariably give me a potted history of the institutions or respondents, if they had any background information on them and if it enhanced the quality of the interview material. In a reversal of roles, I became the student to the professorial experts on Latvian and Lithuanian affairs. Most valuable was their instruction on how to 'read' the culture. In one particular instance we were crossing the car park by the Ministry of Justice in one of the Baltic capitals, having just interviewed a high-ranking judge, when the interpreter pointed out a line of expensive imported cars. He drew my attention to a couple of the questions we had put to the judge about corruption and the assurances she had given that this was no longer a problem because recent legislation, in line with the EU requirements for accession, was being successfully implemented. Salaries for members of the judiciary were moderately good, he explained (he was training to be a lawyer) but not enough to afford anything remotely close to the asking price of those imports. Bribery remained a thriving practice. Another time, I was struck by the beautiful flower arrangements in a Central Tax Office reception. These were more or less a compulsory offering to the inspectors for the sought-after rubber stamp which turned the gaze away from unpaid revenue, though hardly equivalent to the hard cash paid for an innocent verdict from the Ministry of Justice.

Colonialism and 'civilized' Europe

It was not just language which erected a barrier to free communication. Six or so months prior to the project, I had visited Latvia and Lithuania as an organized crime 'expert' on a fact-finding mission for the European Commission. This tick box exercise involved making sure that accession states had fulfilled the criteria set out by the Justice and Home Affairs *acquis*, in readiness for full membership of the EU in 2004. To enable their progression, a number of bilateral programmes offering technical assistance had been set up with law enforcement in member states. These involved training programmes and exchanges between the relevant agencies. What became apparent, however, during interview was the insensitivity and arrogance which often emerged from the EU side. As one senior police official grizzled, they were fed up with delegations coming over to show them how to use computers or explain what human rights meant. While some of these programmes had the desired effect, many of them were criticized by those in the accession states for their colonialist attitude and the inability to understand the differing needs and problems faced by accession states, collectively and individually (Rawlinson 2001). While this spurious role of expert helped to acquaint me with the relevant gate-keepers to the police, customs, and intelligence, it also acted as an obstacle to even a limited openness from officialdom. This required constant reassurances that I was no longer in the Baltics in the capacity of EU observer.

While interviewing a group of the anti-organized crime unit in one of the countries, and getting little more than a few monosyllabic responses to my questions, I asked, in as sympathetic a tone as possible, whether they felt they were being patronized by European member states. The atmosphere in the room changed as a vitriolic diatribe against Brussels ensued, in Russian too. From these outpourings, and subsequent interviews conducted along the same lines, came a common narrative. Russian organized crime was not an issue. The real problem, according to every organized crime unit in each country, came from indigenous crime groups, the control of which was constantly stymied by Brussels' focus on the 'Russian mafia' and the insistence that in the interests of 'fortress Europe' resources be prioritized for the protection of supranational over national interests. The irony of these hostilities towards me as colonial 'outsider' (which were, in some cases, mitigated through generosity of spirit on the part of my hosts) is that the recommendations made as a result of the 'expert' visits were largely ignored by the Commission. As some criminologists realize, their expertise is inconsequential when in collision with the agendas of those who pay the piper (Hope 2004). We need always to be aware that those benefits acquired from comparative research by academics are always vulnerable to the tensions created by political elites from the relevant states.

Almost a conclusion

The research projects conducted in Russia and the Baltic States into the problems of organized crime, while producing different conclusions on the characteristics, behaviours, and levels of threat posed, converged in the sense that they both demanded a reappraisal of perceived norms and realities in my own culture. This was not just a re-evaluation of legal definitions of organized crime and 'respectable' business, but a review of how one goes about investigating these phenomena. Doing ethnographic research in alien cultures requires a declaration of our own cultural and personal baggage when passing through (or into) the customs of other realities. Otherwise we become a part of that cultural imperialism which pronounces on the dangers of the Russian Mafia, or Islamic fundamentalist terrorism, out of intellectual ignorance and the arrogant claim that we have nothing to declare other than an unmoveable belief in our own systems and values. It is worth noting that while the flow of academics and researchers from East to West continues apace, particularly in the social sciences, traffic in the opposite direction is scarce and hesitant. Perhaps, as with transnational organized crime, the view is that there are more rich pickings in the civilized West than the struggling East. Perhaps, as with the realization that Russia is sitting on vast resources of mineral wealth, we might just turn our gaze to its hidden intellectual resources and help mine new types of thinking out of new types of research. The rigours of rational thinking are often absent in Russian scholarship, in what can often appear to be a stream of consciousness based on subjective responses to outer phenomena. But as a complement to what often comes across as strait-jacketed positivism, conducting research from both the head *and* the neck downwards opens up new possibilities for developing methodologies which take the best from all worlds. From this perspective, I ask for a concluding word on research.

And finally ...

As academics, aspiring to create tidy, logical thinking, we aim to conduct our research in like manner. We favour smooth edges, typologies, neat conclusions, avoiding the messy and illogical. Now that research methodology has become integral to the university curriculum, this aspired-for precision makes its way into lectures and seminars on how *best* to conduct research. We stand in front of students as success stories in the research process, models of best practice, arriving as professionals through research and publications. Our narratives on research tell mainly of what works. Crises we might have faced are usually related, if at all, as anecdotal asides. We avoid the most essential 'failure' of all, *emotional* engagement with the research process. Anger, frustration, tears, confusion, depression, excitement—a whole gamut of feelings, untidy, messy intrusions are pushed away or repackaged into a catalogue of vague 'don'ts', to be acknowledged by new researchers, but rarely the 'old hands'.

   While writing this chapter I asked a number of colleagues about their emotional experiences during the research process, what they *felt* in certain moments and had not revealed in writing their methods section. They spoke of fear, embarrassment, and disloyalty. To this I can add frustration, inadequacy, guilt—the list could go on. When asked why they had omitted to write about these feelings the response was pretty uniform: perhaps we should have done. These emotions, after all, are very much a part of the research experience, particularly in the field. In writing up the research methods, we are effectively acting as witnesses to what we have been doing, and as with any witness testimony our memory reconstructs, edits out, or simply forgets certain experiences. The difficult part of research—the 'human'—is largely omitted from our witness statements. Instead, we increasingly produce an opaque account of what it means to conduct research 'out there' and reaffirm as best practice the striving for objectivity through the denial, or subjugation of the subject as emotional being.

Prison research, especially that conducted by women, notably breaks this trend. Alison Liebling's (2001) discussion on the effect of sympathy on prison researchers sees as an essential requirement for ethnographic research the '*full use of your self*', being able to work with 'shared feelings and experiences' as part of the research process. Yvonne Jewkes, too, reflects on her empathetic engagement with inmate Harry Roberts, convicted of the murder of a police officer and whose period of incarceration spanned her entire life at the time she interviewed him. She candidly reflects on the various links (location, time, and networks) with Roberts and how this evoked some form of identification with him that impacted on the direction of her research. She challenges the aspiration of disengagement and argues for more critical self-reflection on the human dynamics of prison research urging that 'the relationship between research and emotion should be utilised and celebrated' (Jewkes 2006). So too does Piacentini's description of the physical and psychological trauma of her ethnographic study behind Russian prison walls reiterate the need for a more transparent consideration and prioritizing of the role of emotions in the research process. We must not lose sight of reason, nor throw ourselves into emotion-led research, but harmonize the different aspects of what it means to be a *human* researcher investigating a *human* environment. An offer we can't refuse.

Suggestions for further reading

On organized crime in general, a good introduction to the debates and issues around definition, policy and international perspectives is P. J. Ryan and G. E. Rush (eds) (1997) *Understanding Organized Crime in Global Perspective: A Reader*, Thousand Oaks: Sage Publications. Mike Levi's (2007) 'Organized Crime and Terrorism' in M. Maguire, R. Morgan, and R. Reiner, (eds), *The Oxford Handbook of Criminology*, Oxford: Clarendon Press, complements Dick Hobbs contribution to the second edition of *The Oxford Handbook of Criminology* (see references) both of which make reference to the relatively neglected area of organized crime in the UK and Europe. Two of Hobbs' ethnographic studies on professional crime work (1988, 1995), and his chapter 'Researching Serious Crime' in the first edition (2000) of this book, provide darkly humorous and highly informative accounts of how to survive being 'out in the field', 'out of your depth', and 'out of your tree'. On comparative or cross-national research, see the *International Journal of Social Research Methodology* 2(2) April 1999 and Nelken's chapter 'Whom can you Trust? The Future of Comparative Criminology' (see below). To get a sense of Russia, its people, and culture, see Orlando Figes (2003) *Natasha's Dance: A Cultural History of Russia*, London: Penguin—a wonderfully accessible book best read with a good vodka in hand and Borodin playing in the background. For a more contemporary and controversially insightful account, see Anna Politkovskaya ((2004) *Putin's Russia*, London: The Harvill Press, best not read in a London sushi bar.

References

ABADINSKY, H. (1994). *Organized Crime* (3rd edn). Chicago: Nelson Hall.

ALBINI, J. (1997). 'Donald Cressey's Contribution to the Study of Organized Crime: An Evaluation' in P. J. Ryan and G. E. Rush (eds), *Understanding Organized Crime in Global Perspective: A Reader*. Thousand Oaks: Sage Publications.

BENNET, R. (2004). 'Comparative Criminology and Criminal Justice Research: The State of our Knowledge'. *Justice Quarterly* 21: 1–21.

BERGER, P. and LUCKMANN, T. (1966). *The Social Construction of Reality: A Treatise in the Sociology of Knowledge*. New York: Anchor Books.

BLOCK, A. (1978). 'History and Study of Organized Crime' in *Urban Life* 6: 455–74.

—— and CHAMBLISS, W. (1981). *Organizing Crime*. New York: Elsevier.

BURGESS, R. (1993). *In the Field: An Introduction to Field Research*. London: Routledge.

CAMPBELL, D. (2004). 'Lost in Transit'. *New Internationalist*, July, Issue 369.

CHAMBLISS, W. (1988). *On the Take: From Petty Crooks to Presidents*. Bloomington: Indiana University Press.

CHRISTIE, N. (2000). *Crime Control as Industry: Towards Gulags Western Style*. London: Routledge.

CRESSEY, D. (1969). *Theft of the Nation: the Structure and Operations of Organized Crime in America*. London: Harper & Row.

DECKER, S. H. and VAN WINKLE, B. (1996). *Life in the Gang: Family, Friends and Violence*. New York: Cambridge University Press.

DOLGOVA, A. and DYAKOV, S. (eds) (1989). *Organizovannaia Prestupnost'*. Moscow: Yuridicheskaia Literatura.

EMERSON, R. M., FRETZ, R. I., and SHAW, L. L. (1995). *Writing Ethnographic Fieldnotes*. Chicago: University of Chicago Press.

EUROPEAN UNION (1998). *Article 1 of the Joint Action of the Justice and Home Affairs Council to Create a Criminal Offence to Participate in a Criminal Organisation*. Brussels: European Union, Council of Justice and Home Affairs Ministers.

FINCKENAUER, J. O. and WARING, E. J. (1998). *Russian Mafia in America: Immigration, Culture and Crime*. Boston: Northeastern University Press.

GREGORY, F. (2003). 'Classify, Report and Measure: The UK Organised Crime Notification Scheme' in A. Edwards and P. Gill (eds), *Transnational Organised Crime: Perspectives on Global Security*. London: Routledge.

HAMERSLEY, M. and ATKINSON, P. (1995). *Ethnography: Principles in Practice*. London: Routledge.

HANSARD (2006). 20 July, col 473.

HANTRAIS, L. (1996). *Cross-national Research Methods in the Social Sciences*. London: Pinter Press.

HOBBS, D. (1994). 'Professional and Organized Crime in Britain' in Maguire, M., Morgan, R., and Reiner, R. (eds), *The Oxford Handbook of Criminology*. Oxford: Clarendon Press.

—— (1988). *Doing the Business*. Oxford: Clarendon Press.

—— (1995). *Bad Business*. Oxford: Oxford University Press.

—— (2000). 'Researching Serious Crime' in R. King and E. Wincup (eds), *Doing Research on Crime and Justice*. Oxford: Oxford University Press.

—— and MAY, T. (eds) (1993). *Interpreting the Field*. Oxford: Clarendon Press.

HOPE, T. (2004). 'Pretend it Works: Evidence and Governance in the Evaluation of the Reducing Burglary Initiative'. *Criminology and Criminal Justice* 4: 287–308.

IANNI, F. and IANNI, E. (1972). *A Family Business: Kinship and Social Control in Organized Crime*. London: Routledge & Kegan Paul.

JENNINGS, A. and SAMBROOK, C. (2002). *The Great Olympic Swindle: When the World Wanted its Games Back*. London: Simon & Schuster.

JEWKES, Y. (2006). A Prison Tale: The Role of Empathy and Emotion in the Formulation of Knowledge. Paper presented at Department of Criminology, University of Leicester, 22 March.

LANDESCO, J. (1968). *Organized Crime in Chicago Part III of the Illinois Crime Survey 1929*. Chicago III: University of Chicago Press.

LEDENEVA, A. V. (1998). *Russia's Economy of Favours: Blat, Networking and Informal Exchange*. Cambridge: Cambridge University Press.

LEE. R. (1995). *Dangerous Fieldwork*. Thousand Oaks: Sage.

LEVI, M. (1998). 'Perspectives on "Organised Crime": An Overview'. *Howard Journal of Criminal Justice* 37: 335–45.

LIEBLING, A. (2001). 'Whose Side are We on? Theory, Practice and Allegiances in Prisons Research'. *British Journal of Criminology* 41: 472–84.

LIEVEN, A. (1994). *The Baltic Revolution: Estonia, Latvia, Lithuania and the Path to Independence*. Harvard: Yale University Press.

MALTZ, M. (1976). 'On Defining Organized Crime: The Development of a Definition and a Typology'. *Crime and Delinquency* 22: 338–46.

MORRISON, W. (1995). *Theoretical Criminology From Modernity to Post-modernism*. London: Cavendish Publishing.

NELKEN, D. (1994). 'Whom can you Trust? The Future of Comparative Criminology' in D. Nelken (ed.), *The Future of Criminology*. London: Sage.

NOAKS, L. and WINCUP, E. (2004). *Criminological Research: Understanding Qualitative Methods*. London: Sage.

PIACENTINI, L. (2004). *Surviving Russian Prisons: Punishment, Economy and Politics in Transition*. Cullompton: Willan.

PILEGGI, N. (1987). *Wise Guy*. London: Corgi.

PUZO, M. (1980). *The Godfather*. London: Pan.

RAWLINSON, P. (1997). 'Russian Organized Crime: A Brief History' in P. Williams (ed.), *Russian Organized Crime: The New Threat?* London: Frank Cass.

—— (1998). 'Mafia, Media and Myth—Representations of Russian Organized Crime' in *Howard Journal of Criminal Justice* 37(4).

—— (2000). 'Mafia, Methodology and "Alien" Culture' in R. King and E. Wincup (eds), *Doing Research on Crime and Justice*. Oxford: Oxford University Press.

—— (2001). *Russian Crime and Baltic Borders: Assessing the Real Threat*. Final Report/Translation. ESRC L213252013.

REINER, R. (1991). *Chief Constables*. Oxford: Oxford University Press.

REUTER, P. (1983). *Disorganized Crime: Illegal Markets and the Mafia—The Economics of the Visible Hand*. Cambridge MA: MIT Press.

ROBERTSON, A. (2006). 'The Significance of Language, Culture, and Communication in Researching Post-Soviet Crime and Policing' in *Journal of Contemporary Criminal Justice* 22: 137–56.

ROWE, M. (forthcoming). 'Tripping Over Molehills: Ethics and the Ethnography of Police Work'. *International Journal of Social Research Methodology, Theory and Practice*. 10: 37–48.

RUGGIERO, V. (1996). *Organized and Corporate Crime in Europe: Offers that Can't be Refused.* Aldershot: Dartmouth.

SIDOROV, A. (2003). *Brigada.* RUTV.

SMITH, C. and WINCUP, E. (2000). 'Breaking in: Researching Criminal Justice Institutions for Women' in R. King and E. Wincup (eds), *Doing Research on Crime and Justice.* Oxford: Oxford University Press.

SMITH, D., JR (1975). *The Mafia Mystique.* New York: Basic Books.

SMITH, D. C. (1991). 'Wickersham to Sutherland to Katzenbach: Evolving an "Official" Definition for Organized Crime'. *Crime, Law and Social Change* 16: 135–54.

THRASHER, F. (1927). *The Gang.* Chicago Ill.: University of Chicago Press.

UNITED NATIONS (2000). *Convention Against Transnational Organized Crime.* Palermo, Sicily: United Nations.

VAGG, J. (1993). 'Context and Linkage: Reflections on Comparative Research and "Internationalism" In Criminology'. *British Journal of Criminology* 33: 541–54.

VARESE, F. (2001). *The Russian Mafia: Private Protection in a New Market Economy.* Oxford: Oxford University Press.

WHYTE, W. F. (1993). *Street Corner Society: The Social Structure of an Italian Slum* (4th edn). Chicago: University of Chicago Press.

—— (1984). *Learning from the Field: A Guide from Experience.* Beverley Hills: Sage Publications.

WOODIWISS, M. (1990). 'Organized Crime, USA: Changing Perceptions from Prohibition to the Present Day'. *BAAS Pamphlets in American Studies.*

ZINOVIEV, A. (1986). *Homo Sovieticus.* Paladin: London.

11

Researching victims

Sandra Walklate

Introduction

In approaching the second edition of this chapter I have brought things up to date where necessary but have left the basic structure and much of the text unchanged. In particular I decided to leave the case study as it was in the original—though it is now ten years old the lessons remain pertinent. I have, however, taken the opportunity to develop my argument more fully in the section on feminism and victimology and to add a new section on the prospects for the future which also contains a more extensive review of recent developments.

My first foray into conducting research into victims of crime was in the early 1980s as part of a team which failed to win the contract to conduct the Merseyside Crime Survey. As a part of that process it became known, locally, that someone 'at the poly' was interested in engaging in such research and I was contacted by a then Senior Probation Officer, George Murphy, who was involved in a Liverpool Victim Support Scheme. He wanted someone to get a feel for how the scheme was working and what victims thought of what they were trying to do. All of that was during 1982–4. It was a salutary experience moving from bidding for over £100,000 for a research contract to conducting a piece of work in one's spare time, but it was also a highly rewarding one. That move was certainly a turning point for me both academically and personally. Over the next ten years I forged strong links with Victim Support on Merseyside, ultimately becoming the deputy chairperson of the Liverpool Crown Court Witness Support Scheme. During that time my views about victims, victimization, and the criminal justice response to such experiences changed considerably.

At the beginning of the 1980s academic and political interest in the victim of crime was in its early stages and was fuelled by a view that the impact of crime, though varied, was not to be taken lightly. My own experience of interviewing victims in Liverpool within three weeks of their victimization confirmed that view and added weight to the minimalist argument to take the needs of victims into account and the maximalist argument for victims' rights. Arguably both positions conferred a special status on victims of crime. However, as the decade progressed, culminating in the first Victims' Charter in 1990, I became less convinced that this 'special status' could usefully inform either policy or research. As a consequence, when I was asked to write this chapter on researching victims I was presented with a real dilemma; why accord researching victims of crime such a status from a research point of view or any other? Surely the issues facing researchers of crime victims were the same issues facing anyone attempting to research any substantive criminal justice issue? On reflection, of course, such a view is not entirely an accurate one. For example, the emotional impact of victimization for some victims may present itself as part of what it is necessary to handle in an interview situation with a researcher. Moreover, in some circumstances the researcher may become an important source of information and/or support for the victim (see, for example, comments of this kind made by Shapland, Wilmore, and Duff 1985). However, the impact of factors such as these varies markedly from individual to individual, making it difficult either to generalize or predict when it might be necessary to take such issues into account. This raises some questions not only about the policy possibilities, which may or may not be derivable from victim-centred research, but also the extent to which such issues are the same as or different from research centred in different ways. I have, of course, reached this position over a long period of time. Moreover, since the first edition of this book appeared, the focus of attention that they have received in the context of criminal justice policy has changed significantly. In the contemporary policy arena now, much is made of placing the victim at the centre of criminal justice concerns in an effort to calibrate the workings of the system more towards their interests. The extent to which this process of reorientation has been either influenced or informed by academic research is a moot point (Sebba 2001), however it is a process that increasingly endeavours to improve the status of the victim within the criminal justice system. Such developments notwithstanding, this chapter will provide some clues as to how and why this author would challenge the presumption that victims per se occupy a special status either within criminal justice research or within the criminal justice process.

The aims of this chapter are threefold: first, to explore what methodological questions are raised by engaging in research on victims of crime; secondly, to relate such questions to the broader conceptual problems embedded within the (sub)discipline of victimology; and thirdly, to situate the research, and the research findings on criminal victimization, within a broader political context. In addressing these aims, one of the central concerns of this chapter will be to raise the question whether or not there is anything particular about the experience of criminal victimization which renders researching victims of crime distinctive in any way from other substantive areas of research. This will be approached through a critical reflection on a two-and-a-half-year research project on the 'fear of crime' completed in August 1996. I will then bring the chapter to an end by considering some new directions for victimology and victimological research. But first it will be useful to offer a brief overview of the different theoretical perspectives available to researchers concerned with victims of crime and the connections between those theoretical perspectives and different styles of research.

Theory and practice in victimology

In many ways the emergence and development of the (sub)discipline of victimology parallels that of criminology. Early victimological work was concerned to identify different types of victim in much the same way that early criminological work endeavoured to identify different types of criminal. Original concerns such as these reflect the extent to which victimology was as embedded in the processes of differentiation, determinism, and pathology as was criminology (Roshier 1989). These concerns, and their subsequent development, have led commentators to identify different theoretical strands of criminological thought broadly categorized as positivist, radical, and critical victimology by Mawby and Walklate (1994). It will be of value to say a little about each of these, as well as feminism and victimology, since each leads the research agenda in different directions.

Positivism and victimology

The label 'positivist' victimology was initially assigned to a range of victimological work by Miers (1989). He identified the key characteristics of this kind of work in the following way: '[t]he identification of factors which contribute to a non-random pattern of victimisation, a focus on interpersonal crimes of violence, and a concern to identify victims who may have contributed to their own victimisation' (Miers 1989: 3). In other words this version of victimology is centrally concerned to identify patterns of victimization, the regularities, and precipitative characteristics of victimizing events, and thereby to produce victim typologies. It is a view of the data-gathering process which privileges traditional conceptions of science and scientific objectivity and, as a consequence, has been very influential in setting the victimological research agenda along a particular path. That path has, for the most part, been characterized (though not exclusively) by the use and development of the criminal victimization survey.

Since a more detailed discussion of criminal victimization survey methods and findings is given by Mayhew in this volume, it is sufficient to say here that this kind of victimological work has made an important contribution in identifying and understanding the nature and extent of most conventional forms of criminal victimization; that is, its patterning and regularity. Much of that survey work has been informed by the lifestyle conceptual framework as developed by Hindelang, Gottfredson, and Garofalo (1978) which has also facilitated the analysis of such survey data to explore both the risk from and the impact of crime. The findings that such analyses reveal have been summarized by Mawby and Walklate (1994: 55) and are reproduced in Table 11.1.

Quantitative findings such as these, then, are not without their uses. They can, and do, inform policy and have arguably made their own unique contribution to the movement from crime prevention to victimization prevention (Karmen 1990).

Although there are beneficial qualities which can be identified in positivist victimology, such work reflects a research agenda which is nevertheless conceptually and empirically

Table 11.1 Relationship between risk from crime and impact of crime according to victim survey data

	High risk	High impact
Class	Poor, living in private rented housing	
Gender	Males	Females
Age	Young	Elderly
Ethnicity	Ethnic minority groups	
Marital/family status	Those living in households with no other adults	

impoverished. Such limitations shape the focus and understanding of the 'victim' in very particular ways. This statement requires fuller exploration. Positivist victimology is concerned to identify regularities (Keat and Urry 1975). It reflects a traditional view of science and the scientific knowledge-gathering process which is concerned to separate that which is knowable—the observable, the measurable, and the objective—from that which is not knowable—belief. Hence the methodological focus on the construction of victim typologies and the search for patterns of victimization through the use of the criminal victimization survey. This process, positivist victimology presumes, equips us with objective, measurable information. This does not mean that such information is without its applied uses, in the spheres of either politics or policy. The development of the criminal victimization survey was clearly influential in placing the question of criminal victimization on the political and policy agendas. Moreover, the use to which such information has been put has, on occasions, been quite clear: in one context to downplay the risk of crime (Hough and Mayhew 1983) and in another to emphasize the risk of crime (see, e.g., the President's Task Force on Victims of Crime 1982).

Despite the value to be attached to the empirical findings which positivist victimology has generated, there are important limitations. Such work is limited because, for the most part, it focuses our attention primarily on what has been called 'conventional crime' (Walklate 1989), as illustrated in the definition of positivist victimology offered by Miers (1989). This work also often takes the meaning of the term 'victim' itself to be self-evident, either as a consequence of the identification of individual suffering or as defined by the legal framework. One gets little sense from within this strand of victimological work of how the state (including the law) actively contributes to the victims we see or do not see, or of the ways in which individuals may actively resist, campaign against, or survive the label 'victim'. This is a direct consequence of the methodological restrictions that derive from a positivist position and this results in research that focuses on incidents rather than processes, and on measuring the surface manifestation of regular patterns of behaviour as opposed to their underlying causes. Some would argue that the research agenda emanating from radical victimology addresses some, if not all of these issues.

Radicalism and victimology

Whilst the presence of a radical victimology can be traced back to the discipline's early days this radical strand takes on its most substantial form in the 1960s. Essentially a radical victimology, somewhat paralleling (again) a radical criminology, concerns itself with 'victims of police force, the victims of war, the victims of the correctional system, the victims of state violence, the victims of oppression of any sort' (Quinney 1972: 315). In other words, for Quinney all of these victims could be rendered visible by calling into question the role of the capitalist state in defining the social construction of both the offender and the victim. This broader definition of victimology has been associated by Elias (1986) with the whole question of human rights. Indeed, Elias goes so far as to argue that the standards of human rights can provide victimology not only with its definitional framework but also with 'more objective measures of victimization' (Elias 1985: 17). With the possible exception of the work of Reiman (1979) and Box (1983), this rhetorical brand of victimology has done little to establish an empirical body of knowledge. There has, however, been another version of a radical victimology, the impact of which has been somewhat more substantial.

The emergence of radical left realism within criminology and victimology during the 1980s had an impact in the United Kingdom and elsewhere in its determination to take the victim of crime seriously. Young (1986: 23–4) calls for an 'accurate victimology' which starts with the 'problems as people experience them' and embraces an understanding of the geographically and socially focused distribution of criminal victimization. This position has argued that it has embraced the concerns of feminism (Young 1988); an issue to which we shall return. The research findings emanating from this work, and their policy implications, need to be put into the broader political context in which the Labour Party sought to recapture the high ground in the law and order debate from the Conservative Party. So what kind of research has emanated from this version of radicalism that is relevant to researching victims of crime?

Radical left realism uses the same research tool as positivism: the criminal victimization survey. The use of that tool, however, is informed by different theoretical concerns. Radical left realism is committed to geographically and socially focused surveys. In other words its research agenda endeavours to incorporate that which is already known about the patterning of victimization according to age, sex, class, and race. As a consequence it has been very successful at offering a much more detailed picture and analysis of who are the victims of crime (being particularly more successful, for example, at uncovering incidents of racial and sexual harassment than national victimization surveys). It has also included some efforts to explore an understanding of disproportionate victimization in the area of 'commercial crime' (Pearce 1990). However, the use of the same research instrument as positivist researchers highlights an important tension in radical left realism. That tension emanates from this version of victimology's use of the term 'realism'. What is to be understood by the term realism is an issue to which we shall return; suffice it to say at this juncture that radical left realism's understanding and application of this concept is partial and has the cumulative effect, according to Smart (1990), of a latent slippage into positivism.

In general terms, radicalism within victimology endeavours to shift the conceptual framework of the discipline from one which is primarily concerned with victims of crime as defined by the law to one in which the law, the application of the law, and the state are all considered to be problematic. For the most part this has resulted in a rather simplistic reading of the relationship between the law and social class on the one hand and the role of the state on the other (Sumner 1990). Perhaps as a result, radical victimology has failed to develop a coherent research agenda which can usefully explore these issues. In many ways, from the concerns of Elias (1985) with human rights as a universal standard of objective measurement through to the tensions emanating from the radical left realist use of the criminal victimization survey, the agenda which has been set under the radical umbrella has failed to break away from the hold of positivism. A resolution to some of these tensions has been suggested by the emergence of what has been called critical victimology. However, before considering the relevance of that framework to researching victims of crime it is important to say something about the role of feminism in these debates.

Feminism and victimology

The marginalization of feminism by victimology has been commented on by several writers. Rock (1986), for example, implies that this has occurred to a certain extent in the choices made by feminists themselves who have regarded the concept of 'victim precipitation', so central to much conventional victimological work, as 'victim blaming' not only in its everyday usage but in the way it has been translated in the courts as 'contributory negligence' (Jeffries and Radford 1984). Some aspects of this uneasy relationship between victimologists and feminists are epitomized in their respective use of the term victim and survivor. As Spalek (2006: 43) states,

Although some women are killed by men, and some feel that certain aspects of their lives have been completely ruined by violence, many women nonetheless manage to reconstruct their lives, emotionally, psychologically and physically, and this kind of reconstruction should be acknowledged through the use of the word 'survivor' rather than 'victim', the same might also be said about all kinds of less powerful groups in society.

Spalek makes a good point, however: the genealogy of the term 'victim' connotes the sacrificiant who was frequently, female and the word itself, when gendered as in French, is denoted as female. Feminists, recognizing the power of such a linguistic heritage, regard the term as emphasizing passivity and powerlessness in contrast to what they argue is the active resistance to oppression that most women display in their everyday life in order to survive. Hence the feminist preference for the term 'survivor'. But of course, whilst these terms are often presented as oppositional, experientially speaking they frequently are not, as the quote from Spalek implies. It is as possible to think in terms of an active or passive victim as it is to identify an active or passive survivor. Indeed, an argument can be mounted which presents these concepts as capturing different elements of the same process (Walklate 1993) and moreover are embedded in women's own experiences of their day-to-day lives (Kirkwood 1993; Hoyle 1998). However, the challenge posed by feminism to victimology runs much deeper than this conceptual debate. This tension leads us into to the question of not only how we can know things about the world but also who can have knowledge about the world and what that knowledge might look like. It is the question of the relationship between method and methodology.

Some time ago Stanley and Wise (1987: 110–11) made the following observation;

If we wanted to 'prove' how terribly violent women's lives were, we'd go to women who live in violent places—run-down inner-city areas of large conurbations—who have actually experience male violence and ask them about it . . . However if we called this research a 'survey', then with exemplary motives and using 'scientific' means 'the problem for those women there' could be generalized into 'the problem for all women everywhere'. The consequence would be that we would have over-estimated the amount of overt violence and actual powerlessness in the average woman's life.

We could, of course, insert any structural variable into this quote and the issue would remain the same; what are we actually finding out about, and why are we doing it in the way that we are? In the context of this chapter, given the earlier reference to the concept of lifestyle it will be of use to explore this in a little more detail by offering another way of thinking about this concept. Genn (1988: 92–3) offers one:

Becoming interested in what appeared to be examples of 'victim-proneness' in one geographical area, I visited one particular block on a council estate over a number of months, tape-recorded interviews with several families, their neighbours and friends, and eventually moved in for a short period with the woman who had suffered the greatest number of victimisations in our survey. The views which I formed after this period of intensive observation have a substantial bearing not simply on the experiences of multiple victims but on the limitations of victim surveys as they are currently designed...What also became apparent was the fact that events reported to us in the survey were not regarded as particularly remarkable. They were just part of life.

The quote above particularly relates to one woman's experience of criminal victimization, some of which she probably identified as criminal victimization and others she did not. However, for the purposes of the argument to be developed here the key phrase is: 'They were just part of life'. This encourages us to think about lifestyle not as a series of discrete, measurable incidents, but as a process. Lifestyle as process cannot be captured by survey methodology, as the quote from Genn clearly implies. It demands a different way of thinking about and exploring what 'just part of life' means for people. It is the case, of course, that much feminist inspired work has always been committed to different ways of thinking about the routine nature of women's lives and has always been committed to challenging accepted knowledge(s). However, the impact of the feminist challenge is not only pertinent to the exploration of women's lives. It is also pertinent to the lives of other structurally powerless groups, like children, the elderly or those from ethnic minorities, for whom the routine experience of exploitation and/or harassment, threat or other forms of abuse are not easily separable or separated into discreet events (see for example, Hesse *et al.* 1992 on racial harassment and Moran and Skeggs 2004 on sexuality). Feminist work also encourages ways of thinking critically about how things get done, including criminal victimization research, in arenas that are valuable for understanding the knowledge production process in general. These are the questions to which the phrase 'just part of life' connects us. Inevitably this leads us to think about methodology rather than method, to think about the knowledge production process.

The differences between the different feminisms notwithstanding, the value of feminist work that is built into the arguments presented here is influenced by the work of Harding (1991). That work explicitly adopted a Hegelian stance to the knowledge production process arguing that women, rather like the proletariat, had access to and information about the world both from the perspective of being powerless and from knowing who the powerful are in their lives. This access to knowledge, from both sides of this dichotomous relationship, made the kind of knowledge that women (and the proletariat for Hegel) have, more complete. In this sense the knowledge that women possess is more objective. Thus the feminist concern with women as occupiers of both the public and private domain means that women's knowledge can render visible and name processes that were once invisible and unnamed. In this way the objectivity of the knowledge production process is enhanced, not by detachment (or *qua* Fattah 1991, by the separation of the humanist from the scientist, discussed earlier) but by recognizing that the researcher and the researched operate in the same critical plane. Hence the feminist claim for work by women, with women, for women. The implication of this argument is that the knowledge produced by the powerful is therefore less complete. In this context this points to not only the serious limitations of sole reliance on criminal victimization survey data, at a methodological level, in producing valid knowledge about the nature and extent of people's experiences of criminal victimization, but also to the theoretical paucity of such work. Spalek (2006: 43) goes further and suggests that:

It appears that a 'white perspective' has underpinned research, so that what appears to be 'normal', 'neutral' or 'common-sense', is in fact a particular lens through which the world has been viewed.

So feminist informed work throws into clear relief the world-view of (positivist) victimology in particular as one that takes for granted the white, male, heterosexual as the norm
against which all other forms of knowledge are measured as well as all other forms of victimization. In this sense the possibilities for feminism and (positivist) victimology to talk
to each other look very slim indeed.

It is at this deeper level, at the level of what it is that can be known and whom it is who
can know things, that work emanating from the feminist movement poses a radical challenge to mainstream victimological work. This does not mean that feminist work has not
influenced the academic and policy agenda. As Bottoms (this volume) has demonstrated,
this is clearly not the case. That work has clearly contributed to a contemporary agenda
that has made it possible for not only a wider range of criminally victimizing concerns to
be recognized (like violence behind closed doors) but arguably has also contributed to a
more subtly nuanced understanding of the 'just part of life' experience of other relatively
powerless groups.

In some respects, feminism challenges the very heart of the conventional victimological agenda. That challenge comprises a different understanding of the relationship
between what it is to be researched and how that research process might be put into place.
Such work challenges the implicit acceptance by the social sciences in general, and
victimology in particular, that it is possible to engage in objective value-free research and
consequently raises the major fundamental question of what counts as knowledge.
Moreover, much feminist work has not in and of itself been centrally concerned with
criminal victimization, yet many of the areas and issues with which feminists have concerned themselves, and campaigned against, are very much about criminal victimization.
Rape, domestic violence, child abuse, are all areas in which feminist informed work has
achieved much in documenting both the extent and the impact of such events on
women's lives. Much, though by no means all, of the empirical work which has documented these events has been qualitative rather than quantitative, although Russell's
(1990) seminal work on rape in marriage is a highly notable exception.

The findings associated with this work differ from those of more conventional victimological work in two ways. First, they present the safe haven of the home as a significant
arena in which to understand criminal victimization, and secondly they postulate an
underlying mechanism which produces the surface manifestation of this kind of patterning of criminal victimization, namely patriarchy. Although there is a danger inherent
in feminist work which can leave the impression that women are 'victims' and men are
not (Walklate 2004), this consideration of feminism returns us to the question of what
alternative conception of the knowledge-gathering process might set a different kind of
agenda for research on victims of crime. In this context it returns us to the question
of what can meaningfully be understood by the term realism.

Critical victimology

Efforts have been made to construct an alternative agenda for victimology incorporating
an understanding of both feminism and realism by Mawby and Walklate (1994) through
the proposal of a critical victimology. The term critical has been used in a number of different ways to articulate an agenda for victimology (see, e.g., Miers 1990; Fattah 1991).
However, the version of critical victimology proposed by Mawby and Walklate (1994)

endeavours to address the problematic aspects of both positivist and radical victimology in three ways; by building on the achievements of radical left realism, through an understanding of scientific realism, and in adopting Giddens' (1984) theory of structuration. This view of victimology demands that we move beyond the mere appearance of things towards understanding what generates that appearance and to ask the question: what constitutes the real?

In order to understand the nature and impact of social reality it is necessary to search underneath the 'mere appearances' associated with positivism and to posit mechanisms by which those appearances are produced. Leaning on Giddens' theory of structuration, endeavours to research the 'real' need to take account of a number of different processes which contribute to the construction of everyday reality: people's conscious activity, their 'unconscious' activity, the unobserved and unobservable mechanisms which underpin daily life, and the intended and unintended consequences of people's action. In other words this kind of theoretical starting point privileges process over incidence and argues for duality rather than dualism. As such it is reminiscent of some feminist concerns (Harding 1991) and provides one way of beginning to understand the dynamism between the structural location of women (victimization) and women's negotiation of that structural location (survival). So structuration theory, and the desire to understand the complexity of human interaction through time and space, demands a research agenda which is both longitudinal and comparative, and which breaks down the barriers between quantitative and qualitative techniques (Pawson 1989). In the context of victimology this kind of starting point postulates the importance of understanding the processes which go on behind our backs, which contribute to the victims (and the crimes) which we 'see' as well as those we do not 'see', in order fully to understand the 'lived realities' (Genn 1988) of criminal victimization. Clues to a research agenda informed in this way are offered in Mawby and Walklate (1994). This form of victimology makes no special claims to privilege one form of knowledge over another. Indeed, its only special claim would lie in the requirement to recognize the political nature of the knowledge production process. It is this view of the knowledge production process which underpins the discussion of the research project which is the focus of concern in the next section.

To summarize: these different versions of victimology set the question of researching victims of crime in quite different ways. Positivist approaches focus on criminal victimization as it is conventionally understood and are concerned to map the patterning of such experiences. Much has been learned about the nature and impact of crime generated by this kind of work albeit from within a limited frame of reference. The impact of radical victimology is a little more difficult to assess. Some versions of this kind of work have been impactive in a more polemical than empirical fashion, though the work of the radical left realists has certainly played its part in widening the debate and consideration of who are the victims of crime. Feminist work, though marginalized by victimology, has also played its part in encouraging a much wider understanding of the nature and impact of crime even though criminal victimization was not its main focus of concern. It is clear that without this feminist input understanding the nature and impact of particular crimes, especially violent crimes, would be significantly impoverished. Each of these approaches has also been differently utilized in the political domain to downplay or highlight the plight of the crime victim at different historical moments. What is now without question, however, is that no political voice is likely to talk about the problem of crime without addressing the concerns of the victim. Victimology in all its various guises has played a significant part in that process of recognition.

However, taking these approaches together it is easy to see that the methodological questions associated with researching victims of crime are very similar to those raised by any social scientific research. These are: how to address the all-pervading influence of positivism in the social sciences, how to resolve the resultant perceived tensions between qualitative and quantitative research, and how to come to terms with the interconnections between research and politics. There are ways of resolving some of these tensions and such a resolution is implied in the discussion which follows.

Theory into practice

Community safety, personal safety, and the fear of crime

In this section I shall consider the extent to which the ideas implicit in a critical victimology outlined above can be translated into a meaningful research agenda and how that agenda might be realized. The project under discussion was funded under the ESRC's Crime and Social Order Initiative from February 1994 to August 1996. It must be said that this was not a project necessarily envisaged as being informed by victimology per se though it was situated in two high crime areas, which we came to call Oldtown and Bankhill, and was concerned to address the fear of crime in those areas. However, it has also to be said that the methodological ideas of a critical victimology were implicit, if not explicit, throughout the proposed work. What follows is a resumé of, and commentary on, that work.

When this project was conceived its concerns were centrally located within the 'fear of crime' debate. That debate has moved through a number of phases over the last 25 years; from the fears constructed in relation to the perceived rising phenomenon of 'black crime' in the 1970s, through the questioned rationality and/or irrationality of people's fears characteristic of the debate during the 1980s (a debate in which the criminal victimization survey played a central part), to the more focused attention on community safety in the 1990s. In the context of that changing debate this project sought to situate an understanding of the 'risk from' and 'fear of' crime in a comparative local urban context. We wanted to understand how people who lived, worked, and went to school in these localities constructed their own responses to such 'risks' and 'fears'. There were two key concepts which underpinned this concern; the notion of 'ontological security' and that of 'community'.

Giddens (1991: 44) suggests that:'[a]ll individuals develop a framework of ontological security of some sort based on routines of various forms. People handle dangers and the fear associated with them in terms of emotional and behavioural formulae which have come to be part of their everyday behaviour and thought'. For Giddens, managing our 'ontological security' is a central problem of late modern society. In part, he argues, this is a consequence of the extent to which 'the risk climate of modernity is [thus] unsettling for everyone: no-one escapes' so that as individuals we 'colonise the future' (Giddens

1991: 124–5) in order to manage (though not necessarily reduce) our anxieties. In the particular context of managing crime and its associated fears and anxieties some of those management processes may be articulated in our understandings of how, when, and where we feel safe. This research project was interested in exploring those processes.

This study also centred on the role of the community, and people's relationship to their community, as a mediating factor in the management of their ontological security. Given that these communities under investigation were also high-crime areas, this presumption reflects the historical, sociological, and criminological focus on the inner city (the zone of transition) and its assumed socially disorganized and dangerous nature of that part of the city (Shaw and McKay 1942). Moreover, the communities under investigation appeared, on the basis of local knowledge, to be responding differently to their socio-economic circumstances. This was, therefore, also a comparative study of the validity of the notions of disorganization and dangerousness in these particular settings.

Against this general theoretical framework, the research had five main objectives with regard to these two communities;

  i. to document and analyse lay perceptions of 'risk' and 'safety' in a variety of social contexts: on the street, in the workplace, at school, at home;

 ii. to document and analyse professional perceptions of 'risk' and 'safety';

iii. to document and evaluate the nature of formal policy interventions;

 iv. to document and evaluate the informal policy processes;

  v. to assess the future trajectory of policy processes.

The research used a variety of different research techniques to meet these varied objectives. As we were concerned to explore the 'lived realities' (Genn 1988) of the people in these two locations the research process endeavoured to obtain a feel for and remain sensitive to local issues as local people experienced them. To this end the research, informed by the ideas of methodological pluralism, reflected an empirical strategy which deployed both qualitative and quantitative techniques.

Methodological pluralism, sometimes referred to in the North American literature as triangulation, reflects a view of the research process which privileges neither quantitative nor qualitative research techniques. It is a position which recognizes that different research techniques can uncover different layers of social reality and that the role of the researcher is to look for confirmations and contradictions between those different layers of information. So, for example, for the first stage of our data-gathering process we walked our two research areas with police officers, we frequented the public houses, and we engaged in in-depth interviews with a variety of people working in the localities. Then, on the basis of this information, we produced a criminal victimization survey instrument and conducted a survey in each area, and on the basis of this experience moved into focus group discussions with survey participants. So, as a research process, we were always moving between quantitative and qualitative data looking for ways of making sense of the different layers of social reality in these two areas which were being revealed to us.

It is also important to note at this juncture, that all the members of the research team were female, which, for this kind of work and for the projects funded under this ESRC initiative, was unusual. However, given the nature of some of the issues which came to light during the course of this project, especially the importance attached to the presence of the criminal gang in one of the areas, the fact that we had an all-female research team may arguably have been advantageous. The strong working-class chauvinism of localities like these meant that both men and women talked to us, including those active in criminal activity, perhaps feeling that we posed no threat to them. Moreover, all the members of the research team had pre-existing connections with the locations under investigation; one of us had lived in one of the research areas for three years, another was engaged in voluntary work in one of the locations, and the third had formal links with those charged with the responsibility for implementing community safety strategies in these areas. These links equipped the team with different levels of prior knowledge about the locations under study, some of which certainly facilitated access.

The first six months of the project were spent gaining an in-depth knowledge of the areas by interviewing professional and semi-professional workers in both locations, through ethnographic work (walking around the areas, going to the pubs, going to local meetings), and regular analysis of the local newspapers. Twenty-six interviews were completed with professional and semi-professional workers in each of the areas (fifty-two interviews in total). From this knowledge we were able to build a detailed picture of each of the locations; a knowledge which formed the backcloth against which we conducted our house to house survey of residents. The conduct of that survey built on this knowledge in several ways.

The criminal victimization survey which we conducted comprised tried and tested questions taken from pre-existing criminal victimization surveys amended to take account of our own more localized concerns. It was administered by groups of Salford University students working in pairs, trained by us, to take account of local police advice on such work in these locations and being mindful of the experience of a Home Office sponsored survey conducted a few months earlier. These latter two comments require a fuller explanation.

First, during the time we spent with police officers in each of these locations at the start of this research we learned a good deal, from a policing perspective, about the timing and the placing of criminal activity in these areas. So, for example, we were advised to go out in some streets before 11 a.m. (whilst all the 'baddies' were still in bed) and, certainly as initial strangers to the locations always go out in pairs, and never carry anything which could obviously or easily be snatched. This advice we passed on to our interviewers. (Indeed, one of the research team always acted as supervisor whilst the interviewers were working, noting who went where, for how long, especially if they were invited in to a house.) Secondly, a couple of months prior to the implementation of our survey, the Home Office had chosen one of our locations to do some survey work into witness intimidation. It had used a professional survey company to conduct this work and it very quickly became common knowledge that within four days (some say two) that these interviewers had been 'asked' to leave the estate. It transpired that this was more than rumour as it was commented on in the Home Office's own report from that project (see Maynard 1994). The research on intimidation was intimidated. Both of these sources of information clearly fed the conduct of our own research.

The interviewers we used were not stereotypical university students. They were all mature with northern connections; some were from Salford itself. And although they were going into houses with traditional survey instruments we ensured that the students remained sensitive to the process they were engaging in. We trained the interviewers to pay particular attention to the importance of informality and of asking questions as if they were a part of a conversation. We asked them to be fairly informal in their dress and not to carry clip boards or briefcases but to carry the questionnaires around in plastic bags. This was done as a way of trying to increase their safety on the streets as well as helping the respondents feel more relaxed and confident about the process.

The survey's sampling technique was one which might be called a targeted random sample. Our initial work in these two locations had alerted us to the way in which each of the areas under investigation was differently structured for the people who were living and working there. From the information gathered during our six months of ethnographic work we learned that it was possible to identify nine smaller localities in Oldtown and thirteen in Bankhill. As a result the individuals who actually participated in our survey were chosen at random but in a context in which we had ensured that each separate locality was equally represented. This process generated a total of 596 completed interviews (we had a target of 600 completed interviews) and our sample of respondents closely represented the demographic profile of the areas. We conducted interviews at different times during the day and different days of the week.

One of the purposes of the house-to-house survey was to help decide how focus groups might be constructed and to identify local people who might be willing to participate in them. On the basis of this we held focus group discussions with twenty-one residents of Oldtown and with twenty-nine residents in Bankhill during the next six months. Following on from this work we identified three localities in each ward as 'typical case' studies for further in-depth work. In each of these localities we sent out a postal questionnaire to all the businesses, and other organizations in existence there with a view to capturing a picture of their experiences of working in these areas. A total of 100 community groups and 219 businesses were contacted. These contacts were supplemented with telephone interviews with respondents where there was an expressed willingness on the part of the respondents to do this. In parallel with this activity we collected and analysed police command and control data for our two research areas for the month of January 1995, and conducted in-depth interviews and focus group work with officers patrolling these two wards. This involved a total of eighteen officers of varying ranks. In addition we held eight focus group discussions with 13–15-year-olds in each of the local secondary schools. Ethnographic work continued throughout the course of the study, exemplified by regular attendance at police–community consultative meetings, other local forums as well as continued analysis of the local press. Wherever possible in the last six months of the work we attended local policy group meetings both to disseminate our initial findings and also as a means of establishing some critical feedback on our work.

Commentary

Whilst the preceding discussion offers an overall descriptive outline of what was done, and why, it says little about the process which took place. That process is an important dimension to any research project and is often difficult to capture. However, there are a number of elements to the process of conducting this research project upon which it is important to offer some reflective comment: the kind of comment not often made available in the research methods books.

The interaction between empirical discovery and conceptual development

This research began its life concretely situated within the 'fear of crime' debate, and for the first six months of its life that debate continued to fuel its concerns. However, a significant moment of change occurred during the conduct of the criminal victimization survey. This survey was conducted in parallel in Oldtown and Bankhill, in August and September 1994. During the course of that process the student interviewers, who were debriefed after every session of interviewing, reported to us that the survey questions appeared to be working in Bankhill but not Oldtown. When pressed further as to what was meant by this the students told us that people in Oldtown were saying that the questions we were asking did not make any sense to them because 'you were alright round here if you were local'. The students had been instructed to record any response they received to the questions asked, whether or not they matched a particular category, and it became clear that this sense of being 'alright' was being offered often enough for us to re-think whether or not our conceptual apparatus was appropriate. A return to some of the more qualitative interview and ethnographic work, alongside this response to some of the survey questions, led us to consider the extent to which the concept of trust might be a more useful analytical tool than those we had originally adopted. On further analysis we are happier with what this kind of analytical framework can reveal about how people manage their lives in high-crime areas than that proffered by either the notions of 'fear', 'risk', or 'safety' (see in particular Evans, Fraser, and Walklate 1996). When this concept was applied to the data relevant to Bankhill it was found to be equally illuminating though differently expressed (see Evans and Walklate 1999 for a much fuller exposition of this argument).

The serendipity of empirical information

Again, as the description of the research process offered here implies, this work was primarily conceived in terms of people's experiences of crime and criminal victimization. We had not originally envisaged being concerned with offending behaviour per se nor with offenders. However, a shooting incident in Bankhill during the course of conducting our survey led to a minor local demonstration directed at the police handling of this incident which subsequently established, in a very clear way, the role and importance of one criminal gang in particular. The nature of the local knowledge and the contacts of one of the researchers led to a very useful interview with the spokesperson for this criminal gang and provided a further, and unpredicted, important source of information about the nature of crime and criminal victimization, especially in Oldtown. The importance of that information was subsequently validated by the data we gathered from the businesses in that location. Given that this was not a piece of research concerned centrally with the nature of criminal gang activity the opportunities for exploring this dimension of life in these two areas was not taken further. Arguably, however, without the local acceptability of one of the researchers, the sex of the research team, and the particular incident which occurred, the importance of this aspect of community life in these two areas may not have been grasped.

Exploring conceptual subtleties

When this research was originally conceived, and the research proposal initially put together (in 1993) little attention was paid to the viability or otherwise of the concept of victim or victimization. Broadly put, there existed considerable tension between victimology's use of the term 'victim' and the feminist use of the term 'survivor' discussed earlier in this chapter. These two terms are in some respects also reflected in the conceptual usage of the terms 'fear' and/or 'safety'. During the focus group discussions, which were guided but never led, the subtleties of such terms were explored more fully. The starting point for the group discussion was some photographs of the research locations. We asked what people thought of the photos and of living in the area. We hoped they would talk about crime, victimization, and the fear of crime. They frequently did. In that context we could identify people who were not victims, but felt themselves to be; people who were victims and did not see themselves in those terms; and organizations which were both seen to be and actually were victims rather than victimizers. This aspect of the research process would benefit from further exploration. It is clear, however, that without the use of the focus group technique a good deal of subtle, nuanced understanding would have been lost.

Controlling dissemination

Part of the research process as described above was very much concerned with dissemination. To this end we allocated six months of the research time to this and produced two reports, one for Oldtown, one for Bankhill, which were distributed to all who had participated in the research and which were made freely available to any appropriate local forum. Our research findings were used by a range of local organizations. Despite these efforts, and the goodwill which we felt had been established during this process, a report produced in the local press in the summer of 1996 significantly soured these relationships. Our first article from the research was published in the *Sociological Review* in August of that year and a conscientious local reporter read it and produced a rather more sensational newspaper article on its contents. Needless to say that newspaper reporting paid significantly more attention to the presence and impact of the criminal gang in one of our localities, much to the chagrin of the City Council, than we had. No amount of persuasion would convince the officers of the council that we had played no part in the newspaper report and letters were exchanged between the City Council, the ESRC, and the Director of the Initiative under which this research had been funded. It reminded the researchers of the old adage from Howard Becker that a good piece of research will make someone angry. It was fortuitous that the month of August 1996 also saw the end of the project.

It is important for researchers to keep in mind the sensitivity and the sensitive nature of this kind of research and the sensibilities of those involved as respondents. In particular, one has to be mindful that people who live in high-crime areas can feel victimized by the research whose intention might nevertheless be to work with them and to improve things for them: there are greater, usually economic, interests at stake for the locally powerful trying to bring business and work to an area. To deny the problems which exist, however, is not perhaps the best way of addressing these sensibilities; to look for the possibilities for change might be a more useful option.

Lessons from this research process

What lessons might be learned from this research process in the context of researching victims as a whole? First this research, arguably, highlights very effectively the stranglehold that positivist-oriented work and its commitment to the use and deployment of the criminal victimization survey, has had on both criminology and victimology. That hold has significantly defined the parameters of the fear of crime debate in such a way that it has become almost commonplace to link fear with risk. Yet, as this research illustrated, a subtly nuanced and locally informed use of the same technique, though arguably differently informed at a methodological level, revealed the value of quite a different conceptual apparatus within which to locate an understanding of people's fears. Secondly, aspects of this research are challenging to the concept of victim. It is clear that being identified or identifying oneself as a victim is neither an easy nor a straightforward process; nor is it gendered. In other words it is important not to presume that either femininity or masculinity affords in and of itself management techniques for coping with victimization (for discussion of this last point, see Evans and Walklate 1999, chs 2 and 3). A fuller appreciation of the process of victimization and an understanding of how such processes are or are not attributed and/or embraced would seem to be a valuable area for further investigation. Finally, for the purposes of this discussion, what this case study has hopefully highlighted is a sense of the research process. We started this project concerned with the fear of crime. We finished, we hope, with a better understanding of community dynamics and how these fuel, or do not fuel, people's fears. Such a process can be viewed rather like Sherlock Holmes' 'dog in the night time'; it was the *absence* of the dog's barking which led him to solve the crime in the *Hound of the Baskervilles*. Negative results encouraged us to think again about the data-gathering process and its conceptual validity.

Ten years have elapsed since this project was completed and at this juncture it will be of value to reflect upon the extent to which the victimological agenda and/or the status of the victim of crime has changed or remained the same since the early 1980s, which is where this chapter began.

New directions for victimology and victimological research?

When I was first involved with researching and working with victims of crime, such an area of interest both in academic and policy terms was relatively novel. However, that did not last overlong. As the 1980s unfolded and the 1990s developed, preoccupation with criminal victimization grew apace in both those arenas that gave added value to the increasing politicization of the crime victim (Miers 1978). This politicization has reached new heights under New Labour. A process of politicization that has arguably played its part in fuelling both the increased punitive stance to antisocial behaviour (interestingly part of the present government's 'Respect' agenda) and the increased prominence being offered to victims' voices in the criminal justice system. The latter being exemplified in 2006 with the introduction of an opportunity for families of murder victims to have their views on the impact that the crime has had on them being put before the court by a third party. This marked shift in the position potentially accorded to the victim of crime is reflected in the academic and policy agendas in different ways and it will be worth spending a little time on how those agendas might speak to us contemporarily about the victim of crime.

In some respects the fundamental academic agenda within victimology has changed very little. Kauzlarich, Matthews, and Miller (2001) have made some attempt to develop a theoretical framework for understanding the relationship between victimization and state crime. Rock (2002) and Spalek (2006) have both pointed to the theoretical lacuna of understandings issues relating to victim identity within victimology and Walklate (2005a, and forthcoming) looks to develop an appreciation of theories of the state for the victimological agenda. Others, especially in the collection edited by Hoyle and Young (2002), have proceeded to challenge some of the dichotomous thinking endemic within victimological work (like for example, female equals victim, male equals non-victim). In addition, Goodey (2005) has offered a framework for victimological work that tries to break down the barriers between those working within the field as campaigners, as policymakers or as academics. These developments notwithstanding, the deep structure of the victimological agenda has remained much the same. That deep structure ties victimology to the modernist project; to being intertwined with policy. So whilst Spalek (2006: 157) is very critical of victimology's endeavours fully to embrace an understanding of ethnic minority group experiences and members of other marginal groups experiences in relation to victimization and states;

it seems that differences between victims have rarely been acknowledged or fed into research plans, so that generalised accounts of victimisation have resulted . . . However, social scientists here have rarely questioned the applicability of generalist frameworks of understanding to individual victims who may differ according to their class, race, religion, gender (etc.) subject positions. As a result, diversity issues have been somewhat neglected, amidst the use of rather essentialist categories that overlook significant differences between individual victims.

It should be remembered that victimology has a deeply embedded commitment to the modernist project. Because of this it cannot see the individual and, despite what might appear to be a surface manifestation of an ever more differentiated victim in the literature and an increasingly diverse campaigning voice for the victim, this deep structure stands in the way of a full embrace of such a differentiated victim. This problem is nowhere more self-evident than in the policy agendas that have proceeded apace since the 1980s and which contemporarily make the claims of offering a space for the individual victim of crime. As a way of illustrating this problem it will be useful to say something about the contemporary embrace of restorative justice. This embrace illustrates not only the changing status of the victim of crime within criminal justice policy, it also illustrates the way in which academic research and commentary in this area has become increasingly both the object and subject of politics in ways that are clearly much more subtle than those experienced by the research project discussed in the preceding section.

Miers (2004) observes that in the UK the importance of the victim of crime to the criminal justice system has been variously described as a supplier of information, a beneficiary of compensation, a partner in crime prevention, and a consumer of services. In his words: 'Restorative justice purports to take this relationship and these changes a step further—to one of victim participation in the system' (2004: 24) and 'has at its core the bringing together of victims and offenders' (Hudson 2003: 178). In the light of these efforts to shift criminal justice policy in the direction of such participation, much time and effort has been spent in the UK establishing whether or not this works and who it works for, without, and this is the nub of Miers' analysis, there being any consensus on what the question of what works actually means. So who is the victim in all of these developments, and how, if at all, does this victim mirror or challenge the victim of victimology? In addition, what might the role be of research in responding to such a challenge?

As Dignan (2005) has observed, many practitioners and advocates of restorative justice (RJ) have implicitly worked with the 'ideal type' victim that was identified by Christie in 1986. Moreover, Dignan goes on the comment that questions relating to the concept of the victim rarely appear in the RJ literature, perhaps with the notable exception of the observations made by Young (2002) who also suggests that RJ works with a highly undifferentiated view of the victim; so exploring concepts of the victim within RJ is relatively uncharted territory. Arguably, it is possible to trace three differently constructed images of the victim within RJ in the UK: the structurally neutral individual victim; the image of the socially inclusive community as victim; and the offender as victim. I shall say something about each of these and their relationship with victimology in turn.

From the point of view of most people in the UK their experience of crime is, as Goodey (2005: 229) suggests, home-grown, conventional, and local. In other words, the experience that people are likely to have of criminal victimization is more often than not the result of some petty act of vandalism or more serious burglary that has been committed by someone in their locality who is likely to have access to the same kinds of personal and social resources that they do. If we take these kinds of experience as given, then it is not surprising that the victim of RJ initiatives directed towards these kinds of offence, which for the most part reflect a desire to bring an individual victim face-to-face with their offender, would also take as given a structurally neutral image of the victim. This is the victim of positivist victimology discussed earlier. The victim, who through lifestyle choices, proneness, or their own precipitating behaviour, had a part to play in what happened to them; so, in restoring the harm done and reintegrating the behaviour of the offender, the focus of attention is on bringing the two parties to the event together, in the sense of an equal relationship, to make repairs for what has happened. This depiction captures some of Marshall's (1999) interpretation of RJ's role in dealing with the aftermath of an event that may have much to commend it. However, what if we take another interpretation of people's routine experiences of criminal victimization that may also be characterized as home-grown, conventional, and local? What if we take that experience to be 'domestic' violence, child abuse, or elder abuse? Here the victim imagery is not the structurally neutral victim of positivist victimology but implicated and embedded in the power relationships of a critical victimology and/or radical feminism. There are serious concerns about the efficacy of RJ in this context, some of which have been documented by Stubbs (1997), Gelsthorpe and Morris (2000), and Strang and Braithwaite (2002). These concerns point up the difficulty of how such individuals might be brought together face to face, resolve their 'differences', and in that process assume an equality where none may exist. This view, by implication, raises the importance of these questions more generally. Whose agenda is being met by RJ, whose is being lost, how do RJ initiatives connect with other aspects of people's lives, where do those people fit whose starting point is from a structurally less powerful position? As Goodey (2005) points out, it should not be assumed that the inequalities of the adversarial system cannot, or are not, reproduced in RJ.

The second depiction of the victim of RJ to be discussed here is that of the socially inclusive community. In this depiction of the victim, the offender is required to make amends not to their victim but to a rather more diffuse imagery of their community. As Goodey (2005) observes, community is frequently invoked as the third element that underpins successful RJ. However, as Crawford (2000) has cogently argued, there is a good deal of slippage between the political and policy rhetoric on which some RJ initiatives are built and the lived reality of communities. Parallel work on the role of informal justice in communities (see, for example, the work discussed above and in Evans and Walklate, 1999; Feenan 2002; McEvoy and Newburn 2003) offers quite a different take on what restorative justice might look like in socially included communities whose dynamics are rooted in law-breaking behaviour rather than law-abiding behaviour. Nevertheless, some aspects of the RJ movement reflect a commitment to the idea of reintegrating the offender into their community and look to community based options to facilitate this. Such a socially inclusive view of the relationship between the victim and the offender sees both categories as being 'just like us'. In other words they challenge the either/orism of being either a victim or an offender that can be found in positivist victimology.

In some respects it could be argued that both of the depictions of the victim discussed so far and found in RJ within the criminal justice system in the UK, taken together, contribute to a view that RJ policy contrives to render the offender as victim. This is a view that can be discerned within the use of RJ for young offenders in the UK in particular and returns us to some dimensions of the radical victimology proposed by Quinney (1972). According to Muncie (1999), in giving a prominent position to restorative justice, New Labour have established not only a 'new correctionalism' but also an 'institutionalised intolerance' of the young, that has been exacerbated by the antisocial behaviour legislation. In the space provided by these political processes RJ has developed an unprecedented swagger in the UK;

Far from wilting in the face of controversy and resistance as so many other justice innovations of recent vintage have, restorative justice appears to be trading the temerity of cautious reform for a kind of *swagger*. Whether such self-confidence is justified, time will tell. It will however be very difficult to ignore (McEvoy *et al.* 2002: 475. My emphasis).

This swagger is sustaining this policy for a range of different reasons that need not concern us here (but see Walklate 2005b), few of which connect with the victim of crime, since, as Rock's (2004) study suggests, until the turn of the century RJ was considered to be a dead duck by the Home Office. So why has the change in direction occurred? Arguably this has happened since RJ initiatives explicate and demonstrate the expressive relationship between contemporary penal populism and the inexorable targeting of the young offender, with RJ contributing to a net-widening and mesh-thinning process (Pitts 2001) in which more and more young people appear to be 'punished' for less and less. So it would seem that, some of the above comments notwithstanding, work within the RJ industry seems to have reflected little on how it has imagined the victim of crime, working for the most part with either pre-ordained or implicit assumptions about this. Given this framing of RJ, are different imaginings of the victim in RJ possible and might academic research speak to these?

It is evident that some efforts have been made to extend the use of RJ to those victims of crime that were imagined in the critical victimology of Mawby and Walklate (1994). Young (2002), for example, makes a convincing case for the use of restorative justice between business corporations. Moreover, there are clear implications for the possibilities of RJ to be derived from Goodey's (2005) expansive victimological agenda that includes such activities as Internet crime, environmental crime, sex trafficking, and genocide, some of which takes victimology into the realm of human rights. Moreover, in the same collection of papers in which Young (2002) is to be found, there is clear support for an extended victimological agenda that takes the critical victimology of Miers (1990) a stage further introducing us, as it does, to the male victim of domestic violence (Grady 2002), the male victim of rape (Allen 2002), or indeed the male victim of paramilitary violence (Hamill 2002), all of which share in similar opportunities for RJ intervention including, in the case of the latter, peace and reconciliation work. It would seem, there-fore, that different imaginings of the crime victim are possible and indeed, are being tried. However, despite these imaginings, there are structural, cultural, and political limitations to their realization. Elsewhere I have called this the rhetoric of victimhood as a source of oppression (Walklate 2005a) in which both RJ and victimology are implicated as vehicles for contemporary state policy, alongside the policy claims that may be made or the kind of research questions that might be asked. By implication this suggests that there has not only been an increasing politicization of the victim, there has also been an increasing politicization of the research process and its findings (see Hillyard *et al.* 2004; Hope 2006). This increased commitment to RJ associated with the political commitment of placing the victim at the centre of the policy stage carries important consequences for what kinds of research question are being asked and what kind of finding are being listened to (Walklate 2005b).

Within this process of politicization, it is difficult to deny the increasing importance of victimhood, not just as a cultural process (Furedi 2002) but also as a claim to status. Yet, at the same time, it should be remembered that in that same political and policy setting, there are real divisions of inequality that have a real impact (*qua* Young 2001). As Hutton (2002: 84) has observed:

It is not just a matter of accepting what the state can and should act to build an infrastructure of justice that diminishes inequality, equalises opportunity and tries to enlarge individual's capacity for self-respect. It is as the German philosopher Hannah Arendt argues about needing a public realm to allow the full flowering of our human sensibilities. For taken to its limits, a society peopled only by conservative 'unencumbered selves' jealously guarding their individ-ual liberties and privacy, is a denial of the human urge for association and meaning.

It is within these processes that the real nature of oppression can be found and the possi-bilities for change lie both of which arguably return us to the concept of respect. Treating people with respect, that is as individuals with personal resources, is key for ensuring that, traumatic circumstances notwithstanding, they are enabled to make use of their resources in order to make sense of what has happened in their lives. A number of impli-cations can be derived from this position. But first and importantly, it challenges any pre-sumed 'special' status associated with being a victim of crime. Victims are, after all, complainants in the criminal justice system as offenders are defendants. To use any other terminology prejudges the outcome of a case. Moreover, victims are not necessarily the 'good' in opposition to the offender's 'bad'. Secondly, this position serves to remind us that whilst crime does impact upon people's lives, victims of crime are people too. By implication, in this regard, it makes little sense to talk of people as victims or offenders, or indeed victims or survivors. They are people and people need to feel OK about them-selves and sometimes need some help and support to achieve that. And what makes people feel OK? Respect. Whether male or female, whether a member of an ethnic minority, whether old or young, the maintenance of respect and the avoidance of contempt sustains a sense of well-being and contributes to people feeling OK. This is not the respect of a government policy agenda, it is the respect that is derived from knowing that we can all make choices even if not in circumstances of our own choosing. So as Harre (1979: 405) said: 'The task of the reconstruction of society can be begun by anyone at any time in any face to face encounter'. A statement that is equally applicable to the research process as anywhere else.

Conclusion

This chapter has tried to demonstrate the way in which theory and method are inter-linked within victimology, the way in which the different theoretical frameworks presented define the scope for researching victims of crime in different ways, and the kinds of methodological issues which result. One of the key themes is, by implication, the way in which the conceptual vision of social reality, in this context the nature and extent of criminal victimization, informs how any research agenda proceeds, and consequently both what is included and what is excluded from those research findings. It is probably clear to the reader that this author now favours comparative, longitudinal studies, because of their capacity to capture some aspects of social reality over time and space, and because they permit a process to develop between the researcher, the researched, and the research findings. The project, offered as an empirical illustration of a research agenda focused on high-crime areas, presents some insight into how both structuration theory and realism might be made to work. In that process the project started in one place and finished in another and yet simultaneously met most of its objectives. Recapturing that process now is difficult; as is capturing the process of victimization. However, in researching victims of crime there is arguably much more to be learned from trying to film the whole picture than continuing to take snapshots along the way.

It may now have become clear to the reader why this author no longer thinks there are any special issues raised in the course of researching victims of crime. Yes, some interviews may be more emotionally charged, and sometimes the researcher is an important source of information and support. But are these special questions to be taken account of in the research process? In terms of actual practice there are of course questions to consider when interviewing children (some of which are to do with parental consent) or when interviewing other vulnerable groups such as the elderly. The questions raised, however, are those raised by any piece of empirical work in any substantive area not in relation to researching victims of crime per se. Issues of harm done or discovered in the process of research can arise at any time in any context. In addition some fundamental research issues are also common in the research process; does the methodology fit that which is to be researched; is the researcher listening to the data; is the researcher reflecting upon the interaction between the theory and the data? If the answer to these questions is yes, then it goes almost without saying that one is treating one's research subjects with respect; that is, providing support and information and dealing with people sensitively. In a sense this is all that victims of crime would desire from the criminal justice system and the policy process: not to be made special, but to be treated with respect.

Suggestions for further reading

As far as researching victims of crime is concerned I would recommend Sparks, Genn, and Dodd (1977), *Surveying Victims*. This study paved the way for the development of the criminal victimization survey in England and Wales and discusses all the major methodological pitfalls associated with that technique. As a follow-on from that research, the essay by Genn (1988) on 'Multiple Victimisation' in Maguire and Pointing (eds), *Victims of Crime: a New Deal?* (Milton Keynes: Open University Press) raises some fundamental questions about researching victims of crime. And finally, Russell (1990), *Rape in Marriage* (Bloomington, Ind.: Indiana University Press) offers a sound analysis not only of a feminist informed survey but also of the relationship between conceptual clarity and research technique The more recent collection by Hoyle and Young (eds) (2002) *New Visions of Crime Victims* provides an insightful and more extended view of some of the victimological lacunae discussed here.

References

ALLEN, S. (2002). 'Male Victims of Rape: Responses to Perceived Threat to Masculinity' in C. Hoyle and R. Young (eds), *New Visions of Crime Victims*. Oxford: Hart Publishing.

BOX, S. (1983). *Power, Crime and Mystification*. London: Tavistock.

CHRISTIE, N. (1986). 'The Ideal Victim' in E. A. Fattah (ed.), *From Crime Policy to Victim Policy*. London: Macmillan.

CRAWFORD, A. (2000). 'Salient Themes and the Limitations of Restorative Justice' in A. Crawford and J. Goodey (eds), *Integrating a Victim Perspective within Criminal Justice*. Aldershot: Ashgate.

DIGNAN, J. (2005). *Understanding Victims and Restorative Justice*. Maidenhead: Open University Press.

ELIAS, R. (1985). 'Transcending our Social Reality of Victimization: Towards a New Victimology of Human Rights'. *Victimology* 10: 6–25.

—— (1986). *The Politics of Victimisation*. Oxford: Oxford University Press.

EVANS, K., FRASER, P., and WALKLATE, S. (1996). 'Whom can you trust? The politics of "grassing" on an inner city housing estate'. *Sociological Review* 44: 36–80.

—— and WALKLATE, S. (1999). Zero Tolerance or Community Tolerance? Managing Crime in High Crime Areas. Aldershot: Ashgate.

FATTAH, E. (1991). *Towards a Critical Victimology*. London: St Martins Press.

FEENAN, D. (ed.) (2002). *Informal Justice*. Aldershot: Ashgate.

FUREDI, F. (2002). *The Culture of Fear*. London: Cassell.

GELSTHORPE, L. and MORRIS, A. (2000). 'Re-visioning men's violence against female partners'. *Howard Journal* 39: 412–28.

GENN, H. (1988). 'Multiple victimisation' in M. Maguire and J. Pointing (eds), *Crime Victims: A New Deal?* Milton Keynes: Open University Press.

GIDDENS, A. (1984). *The Constitution of Society*. Oxford: Polity Press.

—— (1991). *Modernity and Self Identity*. Oxford: Polity Press.

GOODEY, J. (2005). *Victims and Victimology*. London: Longmans.

GRADY, A. (2002). 'Female on Male Domestic Violence: Uncommon or Ignored? in C. Hoyle and R. Young (eds), *New Visions of Crime Victims.* Oxford: Hart Publishing.

HAMILL, H. (2002). 'Victims of Paramilitary Punishment Attacks in Belfast' in C. Hoyle and R. Young (eds), *New Visions of Crime Victims.* Oxford: Hart Publishing.

HARDING, S. (1991). *Whose Science? Which Knowledge?* Milton Keynes: Open University Press.

HARRE, R. (1979). *Social Being.* London: Basil Blackwell.

HESSE, B., DHANWANT K. R., BENNETT, C., and MCGILCHRIST, P. (1992). *Beneath the Surface: Racial Harassment.* Aldershot: Avebury.

HILLYARD, P., SIM, J., TOMBS, S., and WHYTE, D. (2004). 'Leaving a Stain upon the Silence: Critical Criminology and the Politics of Dissent. *British Journal of Criminology* 44: 369–90.

HINDELANG, M. J., GOTTFREDSON, M. R., and GAROFALO, J. (1978). *Victims of Personal Crime: an Empirical Foundation for a Theory of Personal Victimisation.* Cambridge, Mass.: Ballinger.

HOPE, T. (2006). 'Things can only get better'. *Criminal Justice Matters* 62 (Winter).

HOYLE, C. (1998). *Negotiating Domestic Violence.* Oxford: Clarendon.

—— and YOUNG, R. (eds) (2002). *New Visions of Crime Victims.* Oxford: Hart Publishing.

HOUGH, M. and MAYHEW, P. (1983). *The British Crime Survey.* HORS, 76. London: HMSO.

HUDSON, B. (2003). *Justice in the Risk Society.* London: Sage.

HUTTON, W. (2002). *The World We're In.* London: Little Brown.

JEFFRIES, S. and RADFORD, J. (1984). 'Contributory Negligence or Being a Woman? The Car Rapist Case' in P. Scraton and P. Gordon (eds), *Causes for Concern.* Harmondsworth: Penguin.

KARMEN, A. (1990). *Crime Victims: An Introduction to Victimology.* Pacific Grove, Cal.: Brooks Cole.

KAUZLARICH, D., Matthews, R., and MILLER, W. (2001). 'Towards a Victimology of State Crime'. *Critical Criminology* 10: 173–94.

KEAT, R. and URRY, J. (1975). *Social Theory as Science.* London: Routledge.

KIRKWOOD, C. (1993). *Leaving Abusive Partners.* London: Sage.

MAWBY, R. and WALKLATE, S. (1994). Critical Victimology: The Victim in International Perspective. London: Sage.

MARSHALL, T. (1999). *Restorative Justice: An Overview.* London: HMSO.

MAYNARD, W. (1994). *Witness Intimidation: Strategies for Prevention.* Police Research Group Paper 55. London: HMSO.

McEVOY, K. and NEWBURN, T. (eds) (2003). *Criminology, Conflict Resolution and Restorative Justice.* London: Macmillan.

—— MIKA, H., and HUDSON, B. (2002). 'Introduction: Practice, Performance and Prospects for Restorative Justice'. *British Journal of Criminology* 42: 469–75.

MIERS, D. (1978). *Responses to Victimisation.* Abingdon: Professional Books.

—— (1989). 'Positivist victimology: a critique'. *International Review of Victimology* 1: 3–22.

—— (1990). 'Positivist Victimology: a Critique Part 2'. *International Review of Victimology* 1: 219–30.

—— (2004). Situating and Researching Restorative Justice in Great Britain. *Punishment and Society* 6: 23–46.

MORAN, L. and SKEGGS, B. (2004). *Sexuality and the Politics of Violence and Safety.* London: Routledge.

MUNCIE, J. (1999). *Youth and Crime.* Buckingham: Open University Press.

PAWSON, R. (1989). *A Measure for Measure: a Manifesto for Empirical Sociology*. London: Routledge.

PEARCE, F. (1990). *Second Islington Crime Survey: Commercial and Conventional Crime in Islington*. Middlesex Polytechnic: Centre for Criminology.

PITTS, J. (2001) 'Youth Justice'. *Research Matters* April–October.

PRESIDENT'S TASK FORCE ON VICTIMS OF CRIME (1982). *Final Report*. Washington, DC: US Government Printing Office.

QUINNEY, R. (1972). 'Who is the Victim?' *Criminology* 10: 309–29.

REIMAN, J. H. (1979). *The Rich Get Rich and the Poor Get Prison*. New York: John Wiley.

ROCK, P. (1986). *A View from the Shadows*. Oxford: Clarendon Press.

—— (2002). 'On becoming a victim', in C. Hoyle and R. Young (eds), *New Visions of Crime Victims*. Oxford: Hart Publishing.

—— (2004). *Constructing Victims' Rights*. Oxford: Clarendon.

ROSHIER, B. (1989). *Controlling Crime*. Milton Keynes: Open University Press.

RUSSELL, D. (1990). *Rape in Marriage*. Bloomington, Ind.: Indiana University Press.

SEBBA, L. (2001). 'On the Relationship between Criminological Research and Policy: the Case of Crime Victims'. *Criminal Justice* 1: 27–58.

SHAPLAND, J., WILMORE, J., and DUFF, P. (1985). *Victims in the Criminal Justice System*. Aldershot: Gower.

SHAW, C. and McKAY, H. (1942). *Juvenile Delinquency and Urban Areas*. Chicago Ill.: University of Chicago Press.

SMART, C. (1990). 'Feminist Approaches to Criminology; or Post-modern Woman Meets Atavistic Man' in L. Gelsthorpe and A. Morris (eds), *Feminist Perspectives in Criminology*. Milton Keynes: Open University Press.

SPALEK, B. (2006). *Crime Victims*. London: Palgrave.

SPARKS, R. F., GENN, H., and DODD, D. (1977). *Surveying Victims*. London: John Wiley.

STANLEY, L. and WISE, S. (1987). 'Geogie, Porgie'. *Sexual Harassment in Everday Life*. London: Macmillan.

STRANG, H. and BRAITHWAITE, J. (2002). *Restorative Justice and Family Violence*. Cambridge: Cambridge University Press.

STUBBS, J. (1997). 'Shame, Defiance and Violence against Women' in S. Cook and J. Besant (eds), *Women's Encounters with Violence: Australian Experiences*. London: Sage.

SUMNER, C. (1990). *Censure, Politics and Criminal Justice*. Milton Keynes: Open University Press.

WALKLATE, S. (1989). *Victimology: The Victim and the Criminal Justice Process*. London: Unwin Hyman.

—— (1993). 'How do we help them? Responding to victims of sexual assault'. Paper presented to the International Congress of Criminology, Budapest, August.

—— (2004). *Gender, Crime and Criminal Justice*. Cullompton, Devon: Willan.

—— (2005a). 'Victimhood as a Source of Oppression' in T. Kearon and R. Lippens (eds), *Social Justice* (Special Edition) 32(1): 88–99.

—— (2005b). 'Researching Restorative Justice: Politics, Policy and Process'. *Critical Criminology* 13: 165–79.

—— (forthcoming). *Imagining the Victim of Crime*. Maidenhead: Open University Press.

YOUNG, J. (1986). 'The Failure of Criminology: the Need for a Radical Realism' in R. Matthews and J. Young (eds), *Confronting Crime*. London: Sage.

—— (1988). 'Risk of Crime and Fear of Crime: a Realist Critique of Survey based Assumption' in M. Maguire and J. Pointing (eds), *Victims of Crime: A New Deal?* Milton Keynes: Open University Press.

—— (2001). 'Identity, Community and Social Exclusion' in R. Matthews and J. Pitts (eds), *Crime, Disorder and Community Safety*. London: Routledge.

YOUNG, R. (2002). 'Testing the Limits of Restorative Justice: the Case of Corporate Victims' in C. Hoyle and R. Young (eds), *New Visions of Crime Victims*. Oxford: Hart Publishing.

PART IV

RESEARCH ON CRIMINAL JUSTICE AGENCIES AND INSTITUTIONS

12

Police research

Robert Reiner and Tim Newburn

Introduction: what is police research?

The police are by far the most visible part of the criminal justice system, and the everyday face of public authority. They are ubiquitous in popular entertainment and the news media (Mawby 2002; Leishman and Mason 2003; Reiner 2003; O'Sullivan 2005). In the middle decades of the twentieth century they achieved totemic status as symbols of national pride (Reiner 2000: ch. 2), and even today, after more than three decades of scandal and politicization they remain social security blankets, more trusted than most other institutions and bastions of public identity (Loader and Mulcahy 2003).

Yet the meaning and ambit of the concept 'police' are problematic in many ways. Because most research on the police has had a practical policy agenda, it has taken for granted the police institution as it exists in contemporary society. Historical studies of the origins of modern police organizations might have been expected to raise the issue of what policing is, but for the most part they have also limited themselves to an account of the emergence and development of specific institutional forms. Since Maureen Cain first drew attention to this failure to make the concept of police problematic (Cain 1979) several studies have attempted to analyse the ideas of police and policing. Indeed the term 'policing' has increasingly replaced 'police' in the titles of publications, as a gesture of recognition that modern police forces are but one historically specific variant of the array of policing processes found in different forms of social order. Nonetheless most research, and certainly public and political discussion, tacitly assume that contemporary forms exhaust the meaning of 'police'.

As in the first edition, this chapter will review and analyse the nature of research on police and policing. But in this second edition the chapter falls into five rather than four parts. As before the first will consider the fundamental concepts of 'police' and 'policing' which bound the field. The second will chart historically the development of research on police and policing, and identify the different strands of research which have emerged. Part three looks at some of the key methods that have been used to study police and policing. In a new fourth section we look at problems of researching areas of current controversy, including private security, racism following the Lawrence inquiry, and terrorism. Finally, in part five we consider critically the future(s) of research on policing and the police.

The concepts of 'police' and 'policing

'Policing' connotes a set of social processes, whilst 'police' has come to refer more specifically to a particular kind of institution, with the primary function of 'policing' (Reiner 2000: 1–7).[1] Policing may be carried out by a variety of social institutions, agents, or mechanisms, not just the police. Specialized police institutions are not found in all societies, but emerge only with high levels of social complexity (Schwartz and Miller 1964; Robinson and Scaglion 1987; Robinson *et al.* 1994). 'Policing' is arguably a universal requirement of any social order, but specific police institutions are not.

Policing is a specific sub-set of control processes[2], directed at preserving and reproducing security and social order by particular means. These are surveillance and investigation to detect potential or actual deviations and initiate sanctions in response, and the gathering and analysis of information about risks to security and order. At the same time policing involves the symbolic representation of social authority through its processes of surveillance and capacity for sanctioning. Policing activities are intended to achieve security and order, but whether they do so is always an open empirical question. Policing may also be evaluated differently by people with varying social interests, positions, and values.

The term 'police' has come to be associated with a historically specific way of performing policing functions (Rawlings 1999). It refers to state organizations employing pro fessionals who are trained and equipped as specialists in policing. Such bodies are characteristic of all modern societies, although they came into being through somewhat different historical trajectories according to variations in culture and political circumstances in different countries. In many places, for example in most of Europe, they originated explicitly as agencies of the state (Mawby 1991). In Great Britain and North America they were represented as having some continuity with earlier forms of communal self-policing, and have had more ambiguous relationships to the central state (Robinson 1979; Emsley 1996; Reiner 2000). In many other countries they originated as instruments of colonial domination (Brogden 1987; Palmer 1988). In earlier societies, however, policing functions were performed by institutions and processes of a diverse kind, albeit not for the most part by specialist professionals. It has always been true in modern societies as well that policing is carried out in many ways by ordinary citizens themselves, apart from the importance of their co-operation for the working of state police organizations (Shapland and Vagg 1988; Jones and Newburn 2002). There continue to be a variety of forms of volunteer policing bodies, with different relationships of harmony or conflict with the professional police themselves, such as the Special Constabulary and neighbourhood watch schemes (Johnston 2000). There are also various 'hybrid' police: state institutions policing in particular places, such as the British Transport Police or the Ministry of Defence Police (Johnston 1992: ch. 6). There has also been a private policing sector throughout the history of modern societies (Spitzer and Scull 1977b; Jones and Newburn 1998; Button 2002).

---

[1] The term 'police' itself used to have a much broader connotation than the contemporary usage. It originally encompassed all the internal aspects of governmentality (Foucault 1979). In 18th-century Europe there flourished a 'science of police' covering the gamut of issues relating to the welfare and happiness of populations (Pasquino 1978; Reiner 1988; ; Neocleous 2000; Dubber 2005; Zedner 2006).

[2] For analysis of the vexed concept of social control, see Cohen 1985; Innes 2003.

Modern societies continue to be policed by social relationships and institutions which do not have any overt policing role, such as families, peer groups, fashion, the mass media. Even the least likely settings have policing embedded in their architecture, routines, symbols, and general staff, as Shearing and Stenning's seminal study of Disney World demonstrates (Shearing and Stenning 1984). The distinctive characteristic of the police is thus not that they have the monopoly of policing in modern societies, or even of policing's ultimate resource, legitimate force (Bittner 1974; Waddington 1999). It is that they are employed by modern states to be specialist professionals organized on a permanent basis for policing, with specific training and capacity for the use of legitimate coercion and force if necessary.

Despite the existence of a plethora of other policing processes and institutions the police had until recently become so dominant symbolically that they monopolized the concept of policing, not only in popular culture but in the research of most academic criminologists. That this is no longer the case is partly because of the work of some pioneering researchers (notably Shearing and Stenning 1983; South 1988; Johnston 1992; Jones and Newburn 1998) but more fundamentally because of changes in policing itself. These are usually characterized as the 'pluralization' of policing, and some analyse this as a fundamental break in the character of policing—the much-debated transformation thesis (Bayley and Shearing 1996; Jones and Newburn 2002; Johnston and Shearing 2003; Crawford 2003; Zedner 2006).

It is beyond dispute that policing has been profoundly affected by the social transformations of the last quarter of the twentieth century. Many perceive a qualitative break in the development of the world order analogous to the rise of industrial capitalism itself, although controversies abound concerning how to characterize and analyse this supposed break, and indeed some question the novelty or profundity of contemporary change. Whether or not we are entering a new postmodern, globalized, risk or liquid society and information age (Beck 1992; Giddens 1994; Bauman 2000; Castells 1996, 1997, 1998; Held 2005), or just a later stage of capitalist modernity (Callinicos 1989; Hirst and Thompson 1999; Panitch and Leys 1999), there are certainly profound shifts in the modalities of social control. Over the last two centuries modernism has involved an optimistic project of gradually increasing incorporation of all sections of society into a common status of citizenship in terms of legal, political, and social rights, although enjoyment of these has never been equal (Marshall 1950; Bulmer and Rees 1996). In the last quarter of the twentieth century this long-term trajectory of gradual inclusion has been set into reverse, as inequalities of all aspects of material and cultural existence have widened rapidly (Wilkinson 2005). An increasing proportion of the population is qualitatively excluded from the way of life of the majority, and economic insecurity is experienced increasingly by most of the population. The consequences for crime and order of this social earthquake are profound (Davies 1998; Currie 1998; Young 1999; Taylor 1999; Reiner 2007).

Policing has become embedded in a plethora of environmental, spatial, architectural, and technological modes of achieving and protecting spatial exclusion of the burgeoning new 'dangerous classes' from the castles of consumerism in which the more privileged strata live, work, and play, the advent of what has aptly been called a 'new feudalism' (Shearing and Stenning 1983). The privileged flit between 'security bubbles' in 'cities of quartz' guarded not so much by police or other specialized security personnel as by more or less subtle forms of physical and social barrier (Davis 1990; Bottoms and Wiles 1997: 349–54). States and populations have to adjust to permanent high crime levels, learning a variety of tactics for minimizing the risks or the harm of victimization (Garland 2001). Although there is much can-do political talk of more effective, knowledge-based crime prevention or reduction, and frequent crackdowns, no prospect is envisaged of returning to earlier levels of security. The police have to compete with an array of rival, mainly private, security organizations within an increasingly competitive 'pick'n'mix' policing industry. At the same time they are subject to increasing managerial and financial forms of accountability from governments seeking to achieve value-for-money 'businesslike' policing (Morgan and Newburn 1997; McLaughlin and Murji 1996, 1997; Long 2003). Effectiveness and cost-benefit research are inscribed increasingly into the routine practices of policing, and police forces become collectors and processors of information about risk and insecurity for an array of public and private organizations (Ericson and Haggerty 1997).

The development of police research

Police research only began in Britain in the early 1960s. The dearth of earlier work is largely a reflection of the smaller extent of social science research of any kind. In Britain empirical work in criminology began to proliferate only after the late 1950s, following the establishment of the Home Office Research Unit and the Cambridge Institute of Criminology.

The impetus for research on the police in Britain came both from the politics of criminal justice and theoretical developments in criminology, sociology, and law. This parallels the pressures generating the contemporaneous growth of police research in the USA (Walker 2004; Sklansky 2005: Part II). The underlying context was rising concern about crime and disorder, and a growing public questioning of authority. The police became increasingly visible, controversial, and politicized in response to these tensions and pressures. Many academics have been motivated primarily by the intellectual project of advancing the analysis of policing as a mode of control and governance. Nonetheless the politicization of law and order in the last thirty years (Downes and Morgan 2002) has shaped the trajectory of police research (Reiner 1989).

Sources of police research

Police research in Britain has emanated from a variety of sources. These include: academic institutions, official government-related bodies, think tanks and pressure groups, and journalists.

Academic research

Until recently most police research was carried out by academics, in a variety of disciplines including criminology, sociology, social policy, law, history, psychology, and economics. Several university centres have been established concentrating on policing studies (such as the Institute of Police and Criminological Studies at Portsmouth). Policing research is also a mainstay of the many centres for criminology and criminal justice which have burgeoned around the country since the late 1970s. Several academic journals have been founded (such as *Policing and Society*). Textbooks and monographs on policing are being published at a pace that is no longer possible for even specialists in the field to keep up with.

Official police research

The greatest volume of police research today no longer emanates from academe. There has been a rapid growth of research by policy-making bodies and by the police themselves (Sherman 2004 traces the same trend in the USA). In the last 25 years the research focus of the Home Office Research, Development, and Statistics Directorate (formerly the Research and Planning Unit) has become increasingly concerned with policing matters. Before 1979 hardly any of its work touched on policing, but during the 1980s police research became a prominent focus of the Unit's research (Reiner 1992*a*: 447). In the 1990s a specialist Police Research Group[3] (all research is now embedded in policy directorates) was set up in the Home Office. Home Office research on policing had a further large boost of funding from the government's £250 million Crime Reduction Programme, although there is much debate about how successful this was in achieving its aims before its premature termination in 2002 (Hough 2004).

Official government police research is not confined to the Home Office. Local government bodies have sponsored police research. During the 1980s several radical Labour local authorities established police-monitoring groups which collected information on a regular basis about police practices and policy (Jefferson *et al.* 1988), and financed outside research projects by academics (e.g. Kinsey 1985; Jones *et al.* 1986; Crawford *et al.* 1990). Following the Crime and Disorder Act 1998 local authorities became involved in police research once more, albeit in a rather different way. The earlier local government police research was primarily of a critical character. The new model of research, conducted in conjunction with the police, is of a more policy oriented, cost-benefit kind, directed at achieving the most effective and efficient crime reduction policies tailored to an audit of local circumstances and problems .

A number of government-established quangos also became important producers of police research in the 1990s. By far the most influential has been the Audit Commission, which produced a stream of highly influential studies of aspects of police performance aimed at enhancing the value for money of police activities (Audit Commission 1990, 1993, 1996).

Perhaps the most significant growth point in official police research is by the police themselves (Brown and Waters 1993; Brown 1996). This takes a variety of forms. During the 1980s there was a large increase in the number of graduates joining the service, as well as a growth in the number of serving officers taking degrees on a seconded or part-time basis. Many officers acquired the skills for conducting research, and often some research experience. Occasionally research projects begun by serving police officers as students have resulted in influential publications (Holdaway 1983; Young 1991, 1993 are early examples). A significant number of former police officers have become academic specialists in police research (e.g. Wright 2002; Williamson 2000).

---

[3] The Police Research Group was an amalgam of parts of the Research and Planning Unit and social science-oriented research carried out by the earlier Police Requirements Support Unit. This had also conducted technological research, which was transferred to the Police Scientific Development Branch (Brown 1996: 182–3).

As recently as the mid-1980s in-house police research departments were mainly one- or two-person operations with little research expertise. Their function was primarily to collate the statistics and information required for such routine publications as the chief constable's annual report and the design of bureaucratic forms. At best their research projects were 'foregone conclusions', evaluations of pet schemes which were designed never to show failure (Weatheritt 1986). However, there is an increasing proportion of force research departments which produce methodologically sophisticated research on many aspects of policy and practice, sometimes coming to critical conclusions (Brown and Waters 1993; Brown 1996). Forces have also on many occasions contracted research from outside agencies.

Think-tanks and independent research organizations

Independent research organizations, notably the Policy Studies Institute (PSI) and the Police Foundation, have made significant contributions to policing research. The Policy Studies Institute had a distinguished record of research on economic and social issues before its influential first venture into the policing field (Smith, Gray, and Small 1983). It subsequently conducted significant work on such topics as developments in police governance (Jones *et al.* 1994; Jones and Newburn 1997); and private policing (Jones and Newburn 1998).

The Police Foundation is a politically independent registered charity with no core government funding. Although it has firm establishment roots (Prince Charles is its president), it has succeeded in maintaining a quality of critical independence and objectivity in its work (Irving and McKenzie 1989; Irving *et al.* 1989; Weatheritt 1986, 1989, 1998). In addition to a variety of in-house research projects the Police Foundation has sponsored research by academics and by police officers (e.g. Blair 1985).

The Police Foundation and the Policy Studies Institute joined forces in 1994 to establish an independent inquiry into *The Role and Responsibilities of the Police*. This was explicitly intended to be an unofficial substitute for the Royal Commission on policing, which many commentators inside and outside the force felt was called for by the increasing controversies surrounding the police and their evident decline in public support. It resulted in a significant research-informed report, and several important publications (Police Foundation/Policy Studies Institute 1996; Saulsbury *et al.* 1996; Morgan and Newburn 1997).

In addition to these independent research organizations, and other more recent additions such as Policy Exchange (Loveday and Reid 2003; Loveday 2006), several pressure-groups and politically aligned think-tanks have generated influential research-based work on the police. They include Liberty (formerly the National Council for Civil Liberties) which, as well as producing regular reviews of new legislation and policy developments, finances work by academics through its research arm, the Civil Liberties Trust (formerly the Cobden Trust,). It also commissioned an independent inquiry chaired by Professor Peter Wallington into the policing of the miners' strike in 1984 (McCabe *et al.* 1988). Other examples of police research by politically oriented think-tanks include studies of police accountability by the New Labour-oriented Institute for Public Policy Research (Reiner and Spencer 1993), and work by Conservative-leaning bodies such as the Institute of Economic Affairs (Dennis 1997) and Civitas (Dennis and Erdos 2005).

Journalists

Since the beginnings of police research in this country in the early 1960s, studies by journalists have made significant contributions to analysis and debate. These include Whitaker 1964; Laurie 1970; Humphry 1972; Cox *et al.* 1977; Graef 1989; Chesshyre 1990; Rose 1992, 1996.[4] The hallmark of much of the best journalistic studies has been the ability to probe aspects of police malpractice with which academics have seldom dealt.

The changing agendas of police research

Several stages can be distinguished in the development of British police research, in terms of the evolving focal concerns of different periods. These seem to be related closely to the changing politics of criminal justice. Earlier surveys of police research in Britain have suggested that four stages could be distinguished: consensus, controversy, conflict, and contradiction (Reiner 1989, 1992a). The contradictory stage now seems to have resolved into a period in which research is dominated by a clear (though not unchallenged) crime-control agenda.

The first empirical research on policing by a British academic was Michael Banton's *The Policeman in the Community* (Banton 1964). Like almost all writing on the police at that time it was framed within a celebratory mode, and assumed a harmonious view of British society. Its premise that 'it can be instructive to analyse institutions that are working well in order to see if anything can be learned from their success' (Banton 1964: vii) exemplifies the *consensus* stage of police research.

During the 1970s and 1980s British police research was increasingly characterized by themes reflecting the growing conflicts in which policing came to be embroiled. During the *controversy* stage of police research in the late 1960s and early 1970s policing was beset by a flurry of problems, ultimately resulting from growing divisions and declining deference in society generally. The main manifestations were the rise of forms of middle-class political protest, such as CND, the anti-Vietnam War movement, and student demonstrations, a rebirth of industrial militancy, and increasing revelations of police malpractice including corruption scandals on an unprecedented scale, racial discrimination, and other abuses of police powers (Reiner 2000: ch. 2).

Reflecting these issues an increasing number of academic researchers began working on the police in the late 1960s and early 1970s. Unlike Banton's pioneering work they did not start from palpably consensus assumptions. The key theoretical influences were symbolic interactionism and the labelling perspective, which saw policing as an important process in shaping (rather than merely reacting to) the pattern of deviance through the exercise of discretion (Lambert 1969, 1970; Cain 1971, 1973; Rock 1973; Chatterton 1976, 1983; Holdaway 1983; Manning 1977, 1979; Punch 1979a, 1979b).

The introduction to Simon Holdaway's 1979 collection of essays on the British police, which includes examples of most of the research then being conducted, sums up accurately the focal concern: 'one of the basic themes running through this book . . . is that the

---

[4] Many of these, notably Roger Graef and David Rose, have also made very significant contributions through the medium of television documentaries on policing. Roger Graef's celebrated series on Thames Valley in particular is usually credited with having been a major influence on the reform of police procedures for dealing with victims of rape or domestic violence (Hoyle 1998; Gregory and Lees 1999).

lower ranks of the service control their own work situation and such control may well shield highly questionable practices' (Holdaway 1979: 12).

Research tended to be critical of police practice, whatever its institutional base. Whilst academics, journalists, and pressure groups were concerned primarily with police deviance, official government research was pointing out the limitations of policing as a means of controlling crime. A body of research by the Home Office Research and Planning Unit in particular was highlighting the limited impact of traditional police tactics on crime, reflecting a more general 'nothing works' mood about penal policy (Clarke and Hough 1980, 1984; Morris and Heal 1981; Heal *et al.* 1985).

The issues examined in the controversy stage linked directly to the key focus of the *conflict* stage of police research: accountability—who controls policing? This indicated the increasing politicization of policing in the late 1970s and early 1980s, embodied most vividly in the major urban riots of the early to mid-1980s, the bitter clashes over the 1984–5 miners' strike, and the acrimonious debates about the extensions of the legal powers of the police proposed by the 1981 Royal Commission on Criminal Procedure and embodied—after a tortuous legislative history—in the 1984 Police and Criminal Evidence Act. It also reflected the growth of Marxist and other forms of radical criminology out of the critical questioning of criminal justice initiated by labelling theory. Many academic studies of the police in this period were explicitly Marxist, and almost all the others (including some Home Office research as well as the work sponsored by radical local authorities) were critical of the police on issues such as racial discrimination.[5] Uniting all the various causes of concern and controversy was a critique of the inadequacy of existing mechanisms for holding the police to account, whether as individuals through the complaints process or the courts, or force policy and operations as a whole through the institutions of police governance (Lustgarten 1986).

By the late 1980s a new stage of debate and research on policing was emerging, in which a number of *contradictory* tendencies seemed to be in competition (Reiner 1989: 14–15). The key theme of this stage was the growth of an avowed 'realism', across the political spectrum. Most marked in this country was the new 'left realism' advocated explicitly by Jock Young and others (Lea and Young 1984; Kinsey, Lea, and Young 1986; Young 1986). This contrasted itself with what it called the 'administrative criminology' of the Home Office and other parts of the criminal justice policy making circle, and the 'new right' realism associated most clearly with James Q. Wilson in the USA (Wilson 1975). Although clearly these different variants embodied vastly different political and theoretical assumptions, they shared a similar direction of development.

Again the espousal of 'realism' reflected wider developments in both criminological theory and criminal justice politics. In criminology this was part of a more general tendency to turn away from grand theory (Jefferson and Shapland 1994). Although some have continued to try and analyse current crime and criminal justice developments theoretically, the momentum was towards research of a policy oriented and managerialist kind. The common premise was that crime was a serious problem, above all for the poorer and weaker sections of society, and research should be directed primarily at developing concrete, immediately practicable tactics for crime control.

---

[5] Examples of academic work from a critical perspective in this period include Hall *et al.* 1978; Cain 1979; McBarnet 1979; Brogden 1982; Reiner 1978b and c; Jefferson and Grimshaw 1984; Grimshaw and Jefferson 1987; Scraton 1985.

Police research came increasingly to focus on the search for effective crime control practice, rather than the issues of police discretion, deviance, and accountability. Increasingly, police research was moving in the direction of monitoring and evaluating the policing initiatives that proliferated in the search for greater effectiveness. 'Community policing' became a fashionable rubric around the world (Skolnick and Bayley 1986, 1988; Fielding 1995, 2005; Tilley 2003; Brogden and Ellison 2005). It offered to unite the earlier concerns with accountability and the new concern with effective policing: accountability was for good, effective policing, which could only be achieved through cultivating community consent (Skogan and Frydl 2004). Its close relative, problem-oriented policing, also became a world-wide movement (Goldstein 1990; Bullock and Tilley 2003). Both were linked to a search for evidence-based and intelligence-led, targeted crime prevention and investigation (Tilley 2003; Cope 2003; Maguire 2003). These innovations have been credited with an important share in crime reduction during the 1990s, especially in the USA but also elsewhere (Sherman 2004). At the harder end of crime control tactics, the much-touted 'zero tolerance' approach, rooted in the idea of 'broken windows' developed by James Q. Wilson and George Kelling (1981), has also been popularly seen as the basis of the New York 'miracle' of rapidly declining violence and crime in the 1990s, although these claims have been questioned (Bowling 1999a; Karmen 2000; Harcourt 2001; Dixon and Maher 2005). In so far as policing changes are responsible for the crime drop, the 'smart' intelligence-led rather than the 'hard' zero-tolerance aspects are more likely to have been significant (Weisburd *et al.* 2003; Burke 2004).

This was paralleled by a new, 'second order', consensus about law and order which was emerging in the political sphere in the 1990s (Downes and Morgan 2002). In the 1970s the political parties had become polarized over law and order. During the 1980s the police basked in a prolonged honeymoon period with the Thatcher government. They were treated as a special case with regard to the drive for 'value for money' and cuts in public expenditure, a loyal police being seen as essential to defeat the 'enemy within' in the shape of militant trade unionism and other expressions of resistance to the economically polarizing consequences of free-market economics. Labour was successfully stigmatized as anti-law and order, because of its social democratic interpretations of crime and disorder as—at least in part—produced by economic inequality and social exclusion, and because of its civil libertarian concerns. In the later 1980s Labour struggled to regain public confidence in its criminal justice policies, and in particular to repair broken bridges with the police. This process began under Neil Kinnock, but only succeeded during Tony Blair's tenure as shadow Home Secretary in 1993, when he promulgated his famous sound-bite, 'tough on crime, tough on the causes of crime'. During the 1990s there clearly emerged a new cross-party consensus on law and order, based on a shared commitment to toughness in the war against crime. There was renewed faith in the efficacy of policing and punishment, epitomized by Michael Howard's 'prison works' mantra. The over-riding priority for the police had to be crime control. This was spearheaded by Kenneth Clarke and Michael Howard, architects of the mid-1990s policy package embodied in the 1993 White Paper on Police Reform, the 1993 Sheehy Report on pay and career structures, and the 1994 Police and Magistrates' Court Act, aimed at creating a 'business-like' police, constrained by market disciplines to achieve efficient and economic delivery of their primary objective, 'catching criminals' (as the White Paper put it). New Labour left this reform package intact, although it gave it a spin in a more sophisticated direction with the 1998

Crime and Disorder Act and its programme for crime reduction through partnership and evidence-led implementation and evaluation. The promise of a research-based strategy was rapidly dashed by the relentless drive for short-term results (Maguire 2004; Hope 2004), and the proliferation of headline-catching initiatives to deal with immediate crises (Tonry 2004, chs 1, 2).

The driving paradigm for police research now is clearly *crime control*. Both in the USA and Britain there is a resuscitated belief amongst policymakers and some researchers that policing is a key element in crime control, not only through broader community strategies but through the deterrent strategy of tougher and more directed patrol and detective work (such as the fashion for 'zero-tolerance' policing: cf. Dennis 1997). There has been explicit rejection of the earlier 'nothing works' pessimism (most explicitly by Sherman 1992, 1993, 2004; but see also Bayley 1998 ; Nuttall *et al.* 1998; Smith and Tilley 2005).

In this new intelligence-driven crime-control paradigm, policing research figures in an integral way. Policy oriented research is no longer just a matter of post hoc evaluation of police initiatives, although the quantity and sophistication of evaluation has (debatably) grown (Bennett 1990, 1991, 1996; Pawson and Tilley 1994; Cohen 1997; Brodeur 1998; Tilley 2002). Detailed crime analysis and the tailoring of specific local policing responses in conjunction with other agencies were at the heart of the problem-oriented and intelligence-led approaches which the new Labour government promoted (Jordan 1998; Tilley 2003; Cope 2003; Maguire 2003; Sherman 2004). These require an ongoing research capacity within police forces, as well as closer collaboration with policy oriented researchers outside. The failure of public confidence in policing to rise as crime rates have fallen in the later 1990s has stimulated a particular policy concern with reducing fear as well as crime itself, focused on the 'reassurance policing' programme (Hough 2003; Millie and Herrington 2005; Innes 2006).

Critical and theoretical work have certainly not disappeared in recent years, in Britain or elsewhere (Sharp 2005).[6] In Britain, for example, the influential and much-debated study by McConville, Sanders, and Leng of the impact of legal change on policing (McConville *et al.* 1991; Sanders and Young 2003) was clearly both theoretical and critical (although it attracted much controversy because of this: cf. Smith 1997, 1998; Travers 1997; McConville *et al.* 1997). There has also been a substantial body of work seeking to analyse the impact of the fundamental social changes of post- or late modernity on policing (Reiner 1992b; Sheptycki 1995, 1997; McLaughlin and Murji 1997; Bayley and Shearing 1996, 2001; O'Malley and Palmer 1996; Morgan and Newburn 1997; Ericson and Haggerty 1997; South 1997; Johnston 2000; Jones and Newburn 2002; Zedner 2006; Jones 2007). There has also been a continuing concern with race and gender discrimination by and in the police (Holdaway 1996; Heidensohn 1992, 2003; Martin 1996; Hoyle 1998; Gregory and Lees 1999; Brown and Heidensohn 2000; Westmarland 2001; Bowling 1999b; Fitzgerald *et al.* 2002; Bowling and Phillips 2003). Accountability remains a vexed issue (Walker 2000; Newburn and Hayman 2001; Smith 2004; McLaughlin 2005; Loveday 2006). Public-order policing still arouses controversy (Waddington 2003).

---

[6] To take some key examples, in Australia there is Chan's work on changing police culture (Chan 1997), and Dixon on legal regulation of policing (Dixon 1997); in Canada the work of Shearing, Ericson, and others on theorizing policing in contemporary post-modern or risk societies (Shearing and Ericson 1991; Shearing 1996; Ericson and Haggerty 1997; Johnston and Shearing 2003).

Nonetheless, critical and theoretical work has been eclipsed by the rapid growth of policy oriented research on crime control by the police. It is noteworthy that the most prominent cause célèbre concerning police malpractice over the last 15 years has been the failed investigation into the murder of Stephen Lawrence in 1993, culminating in the Macpherson Inquiry's Report in 1999, which centred on the issue of inadequate protection of ethnic minorities against victimization by crime. As will be elaborated below, Macpherson has been the stimulus for considerable research on both discrimination and effectiveness in the policing of minority ethnic groups (Fitzgerald 1999; Miller *et al.* 2000; Quinton *et al.* 2000; Marlow and Loveday 2000; Waddington *et al.* 2004; Rowe 2004, 2006; Foster *et al.* 2005; Shiner 2006; Delsol and Shiner 2006).

The methods of police research

Research on policing and the police has been carried out using the full gamut of social science research methods: overt or covert participant and non-participant observation; surveys; interviewing; field diaries; policy evaluation; analysis of organizational data like calls for service or personnel deployment; documentary analysis of historical or contemporary records and files; analysis of official statistics. This section will focus on some of the methodological issues which are peculiar to, or peculiarly acute in, researching the police. These arise partly out of the nature of police work and organization in general, but assume different forms in different social and historical contexts, and according to the characteristics of the researcher vis-à-vis the police. Social research always involves an interaction with people in order to generate or obtain data or texts for analysis and reporting to a wider audience. The peculiarities of research on policing derive from special characteristics of police work, the relationship between the researcher and the police, and the purposes of and audience for the report.

The peculiarities of policing as a research subject

As argued earlier, policing is an aspect of social control, and there is inevitably overt or potential conflict with those who are policed (Fielding 2005). Although the legitimacy of policing will vary in different periods and contexts (Reiner 2000) it is bound up ultimately with coercion and force (Bittner 1974). Much policing is dangerous, 'dirty' work: getting people to do what they do not want to, or making them desist from doing what they do want to do. The tactics used for accomplishing this are almost inevitably going to be controversial even if they are legal, and they are frequently of dubious legality or clearly illegal. This indicates one aspect of the peculiar difficulty of police research. Much research is directed at questions of police deviation from the rule of law, and most addresses issues which are extremely controversial—such as the effects of highly contested legal changes like the 1984 Police and Criminal Evidence Act or the 1986 Public Order Act (Waddington 1994; Brown 1997; Dixon 1997; Reiner 2000: ch. 6; Newburn and Hayman 2001; Sanders and Young 2003). Such work may uncover information which the subjects studied wish to keep secret. The police studied will inevitably be anxious about how they are going to be represented to other audiences, such as the managers or agencies to whom they are accountable. The resulting problems of access and trust are shared with much other social research that has the potential to uncover dangerous knowledge, but the extent of the difficulty is particularly severe in studying policing because of the highly charged nature of its secrets. On some topics the problems of researching the police are virtually insuperable (for example corruption, which has never been observed or discovered directly by researchers, so that studies of it tend to be based on scandals which are already in the public domain: cf. Punch 1985; Newburn 1999).

There are other aspects of policing which make it especially hard to uncover information which the subjects wish to keep hidden. Since the birth of police research in the 1960s researchers have pointed to the 'low visibility' of everyday police work as a major factor hampering the achievement of effective accountability to organizational supervisors, let alone processes of external accountability (Goldstein 1960). The main modes of police work are uniform patrol and plain-clothes investigation. Both take place outside the organization, away from immediate oversight by managers, with officers generally working alone or in pairs. This gives the rank and file considerable scope for making their accounts of incidents the authoritative ones, as there is usually no challenging version other than those of the people who are being policed, who are normally low in 'the politics of discreditability' (Box and Russell 1975). The wish to penetrate this low visibility is why participant observation has been the main technique adopted by researchers wishing to analyse the practices and culture of policing (Noaks and Wincup 2004: ch. 10). All other methods rely on some sort of account offered by the police themselves (whether in interviews or official documents and statistics), the veracity of which is often precisely the question being studied. Many studies have been based on interviewing officers, or the analysis of records and documents. Research projects commonly combine different methodological tools, notably observation, interviewing, and documentary analysis (Noaks and Wincup 2004), though the revival of interest in 'what works' is leading to an increase in the use experimental and quasi-experimental methods (see the work reviewed by Weisburd and Eck 2004; Sherman 2004).

Even with observational work there is the problem of whether the researcher has the trust of the subjects of the research, and how their behaviour may be modified by the presence of a researcher. Trust is unlikely ever to be complete (which is why such extreme deviance as corruption has never been witnessed by observers). In order to maximize trust, observers have to spend extensive periods in the field as a means of becoming accepted. This makes observational work extremely time-consuming and labour-intensive. Thus the price of its arguably greater validity is that it is usually based on only a limited number of sites and times, and the representativeness of these will always be problematic.[7]

In addition to the 'low visibility' problem arising from the scattered and dispersed nature of police work, there is the particular skill officers are likely to have in tactics for covering up what they do not want known. Police researchers are investigating subjects whose job it is to investigate the deviance of others. These are problems which have bedevilled attempts to make officers accountable through such mechanisms as complaints systems (Smith 2004), but they pose similar obstacles for researchers.

---

[7] The only example of an observational study which was sufficiently well funded for it to be able to mount observations on an arguably representative range of sites was the Black and Reiss study for the 1967 Presidential Committee on Law Enforcement (Mastrofski *et al.* 1998). The resources for so large a study are unlikely to be forthcoming again.

Ultimately there is no way of knowing for certain whether what police do in front of observers, or what they say to interviewers, is intended to present an acceptable face to outsiders. Researchers may reassure themselves a little that they have achieved some degree of trust as observers or interviewers if they see or hear things that would cause the subjects embarrassment if they appeared on the front page of the next morning's *Guardian,* or more feasibly if they became known to supervisors or colleagues (Reiner 1978a: 14–15; 1991: 47–9). Occasionally there may be opportunities for triangulation of material from different sources, although which to rely on if they do not confirm each other is problematic. The precise nature of all these difficulties, and the strategies which might help overcome them, vary according to the characteristics and agenda of the researcher, and her relationship to the police.

The relationship between the researcher and the police

Clearly the material researchers can obtain from the police will be affected by who they are, and their relationship to the force. Brown has usefully distinguished four possible permutations: inside insiders; outside insiders; inside outsiders; outside outsiders (Brown 1996), each of which will typically have different access to police data and material.

Inside insiders are police officers conducting police research. In one sense their problems of access to police are eased, especially if the research is officially sanctioned, giving the researcher some power to compel co-operation. However, whilst access problems are different for an inside insider they do not disappear, and indeed may be particularly acute if the researcher represents a higher authority. The inside insider is usually at an advantage in overcoming the first hurdle of formal access to police sites, but this does not overcome problems of access altogether, and in some instances may exacerbate them.

It is important to recognize that access to research sites is not achieved once and for all. There are two clearly different stages which can be distinguished, but the latter in particular is really a matter of continuous negotiation. The first access hurdle is the one usually emphasized in research reports: getting formal permission from the authorities who control any access at all to research sites. A less visible access problem is securing the trust and genuine co-operation of the people in the research site itself, after formal access has been given. This involves continuous negotiation with individuals who may have different interests and perspectives and hence distrust each other, leading to the problem that the achievement of good relationships with some people may itself pose a barrier to achieving this with others. In general the very fact of having official approval for the research can be a difficulty when it comes to being trusted by the research subjects themselves, who may regard the researcher with suspicion as a tool of management. For this reason some researchers avoid the first hurdle of gaining official approval for access, and go straight to the research subjects themselves, cultivating individuals through such methods as snowball sampling. This is problematic if the research wishes to make claims of representativeness, but, as with all research decisions, there are no clear 'right answers'—it all depends on what the researcher is seeking to achieve. With almost all methodological choices there is a tension between getting rich and valid material on the one hand, and the scale and representativeness of the data on the other. This problem may actually be greater for inside insiders than for other researchers.

Apart from the generalized issues of overcoming the inevitable suspiciousness that police may have of anyone outside their immediate work group (and indeed within it), the characteristics and status of researchers will affect their interaction with the research subjects, and influence the results. This is true for inside insiders as much as outside researchers. A black or woman officer doing research on issues of discrimination, for example, will probably generate a different pattern of results from a white male researcher. There is no neutral Archimedean point from which objective data can be collected: the researcher always influences the social interactions that constitute the data. All one can do is seek to be reflexively aware of this and interpret material in the light of probable biases. It is useful to keep a record of all remarks indicating how the researcher is seen, to try and understand how this might affect the pattern of results. This kind of reflexive awareness of how the researcher structures the findings is as important for inside insiders as any other relationship to the field being studied.

Outside insiders are those officers who conduct police research after deciding to leave or actually leaving the force. A few researchers have been serving officers who systematically analyse their experiences as research material, having privately decided to leave and pursue academic careers. In effect they are covert participant observers, which clearly raises acute ethical issues about potential abuse of trust (Norris 1993). Once they have left the force, their previous inside experience still presents unique advantages and problems compared to complete outsiders. Again, however, the precise nature of the opportunities and hurdles varies according to the researcher's characteristics and relationship to the force. Some will have become alienated from the cultural values of most other officers before leaving, and may well have not enjoyed complete trust from their colleagues even whilst in the force (Holdaway 1983: 8). Others may continue to identify with rank-and-file police culture after becoming academics, and act as interpreters of this to outsiders. The role of the outside insider may range all the way from spy to propagandist, with different impacts on the relationship with those studied and hence on the nature of the information discovered.

Inside outsider researchers are non-police officers who have official roles within police forces or governmental organizations with responsibilities for policing such as the Home Office, or have been commissioned by them. As mentioned earlier there is a small but growing number of civilian researchers employed by police forces (Brown 1996; Stanko 2004). There are also many civilians conducting research on policing for a variety of government departments (mainly within the Home Office), for local government and for quangos such as the Independent Police Complaints Commission and the Audit Commission. Some outside research is commissioned by police forces or government. Like inside insiders police- or government-employed civilian researchers may find it easier to overcome the hurdle of getting formal access to forces. However, such researchers may have acute problems of gaining genuine co-operation and trust from police officers precisely because they represent authority, and their findings may have more immediate impact on policy than those of outsiders. It has been suggested that official researchers would tend to be less critical of policing because of lack of distance from and incorporation into the organization (Sheptycki 1994: 130). In fact much inside outsider research has been very critical of both the effectiveness and the justice of police practices (e.g. Clarke and Hough 1980, 1984; Anderson *et al.* 1993; Fitzgerald 1999; Foster *et al.* 2005; Shiner 2006). It is probable, however, that inside outsider research will have a policy focus rather than one concerned with developing a theoretical analysis of policing.

Outside outsider studies have until recently constituted the bulk of police research—work conducted by academics and others who are not employed or commissioned by the police or other governmental bodies with responsibility for policing (although in recent years the various kinds of insider research have grown much more rapidly and may well become predominant soon).

Outside outsiders clearly face the greatest barriers in gaining formal access to police forces for research. They have no official status that mandates formal police co-operation and may (often rightly) be perceived as having critical concerns about police malpractice or failure. Nonetheless, such work has proliferated in the last 40 years, so the barriers are clearly surmountable. The extent of difficulty will vary from time to time according to the political climate amongst the Home Office and police elite. Clearly the potential researcher will have to make a case out in terms of the contribution of the work not only to academic understanding but in policy terms (however indirect). A track record as an established researcher (or the backing of one) may be an asset, although it can also generate suspicion, depending on how earlier work was perceived by the police.

Negotiating access usually involves more than one hurdle. For example, in order to carry out research based on interviews with chief constables in the late 1980s it was necessary to get the agreement and co-operation of the key figures in all the institutions of the police policy elite, including the Home Office, and the Association of Chief Police Officers (Reiner 1991, ch. 3). This actually took nearly ten years from the first abortive attempt, and depended crucially not only on changes in personnel in the police world, but also the development of the researcher's own work which enabled him to forge links with crucially placed individuals. Nor is formal access something which can be taken for granted after it has been given. If the authorities involved discover that the research is leading in directions they are unhappy with, they can of course abort it, as happened in the late 1940s with the first ever sociological study of policing (Westley 1970). Anxiety about the loss of access may be a factor constraining research throughout the study. One of this chapter's authors remembers standing on a station platform in 1987 two days before the General Election, on his way home after an interview with a chief constable who had just told him that during the 1984–5 miners' strike Margaret Thatcher had put pressure on the police to establish an undercover unit to infiltrate trade unions to prove links with Moscow, at a time when there was blanket denial of government intervention in the operational policing of the strike (Reiner 1991: 191). He was sorely tempted to ring a newspaper with the information, but in the end decided that the likely sacrifice of the research, and the career of the chief constable who had confided in him (not to speak of his own!) was too high a price to pay for an act of whistle-blowing that probably would not affect the election outcome.

The researcher is likely to have to give certain undertakings such as protecting the confidentiality of individuals or specific forces by guaranteeing anonymity, which probably do not pose any great limitations for work concerned with general policy or analytical issues. What is more problematic is the question of editorial control of the final report. It is common and reasonable to undertake to show a draft for comment to the bodies that allow access. However, allowing the organization researched to censor all or even substantial parts of a study undermines any value the research might have as a contribution to knowledge about policing. However it would be legitimate to edit out errors of fact pointed out by the organization, or information that may be unequivocally harmful if published, for example because it could endanger or discourage witnesses or make specific detection methods widely known and hence less effective. It is also the case that there may be methodological restrictions placed on the research, such as not permitting tape-recording. Frequently it will be specified that certain information cannot be sought. For example, one of the authors has been prohibited from asking questions about political opinions when interviewing samples of officers of different ranks (Reiner 1978a, 1991). It is a matter of judgement whether the specific restrictions imposed make it worthwhile continuing with the research.

Although outside outsiders face greater problems of official access the difficulties of gaining the trust of the actual people researched are shared with insiders. They vary according to the same characteristics of different researchers. The researcher's relationship with the different individuals being studied requires constant and delicate negotiation, and also the reflexive awareness of how the subjects' perceptions of the researcher can alter the material. Many researchers have described what amount to initiation rituals or rites of passage before they gain a modicum of acceptance (these are paralleled by the trials imposed on new colleagues in the force before they are incorporated into the group). Common examples include holding your own in extended drinking sessions at bars, pubs, or clubs after shifts of research work (Reiner 1991: 46; 1992b: 124, 276–7). Researchers will be perceived in different ways by the police they are studying, depending partly on their own characteristics and presentation of self, but partly on circumstances within the police context over which they have little or no control. For example during his Ph.D. research one of us was often taken to be a student radical who had inexplicably been let loose on the force. However in one division his research period coincided with a Home Office survey and he tended to be mistaken for a 'Home Office spy'. Whether this accounted for the fact that the officers in that division appeared far more conformist than in any other is impossible to say with certainty—it was nicknamed the 'dull' division in the force, and it is hard to disentangle the effects of suspicion of the researcher as a management snoop (Reiner 1978a: 15–16). Although gaining entry is always a problem, and trust needs to be continuously cultivated, many police officers are only too glad to tell you of their views and experiences once initial barriers have been overcome, and exiting may be as problematic as gaining access in some instances. As police research has become increasingly preoccupied with questions of efficiency and effectiveness, issues of access have eased. In many respects, entrée into police forces is now relatively straightforward compared with the situation 20 years ago when there was far greater suspicion of researchers' motives and concern about the likely consequences of criminological research (see Smith *et al.* 1983). That this is at least partly related to the less critical approach taken in much policing research would be hard to deny.

Recording data is always problematic in policing research. Tape-recording of interviews is clearly the most reliable and convenient method, but frequently raises initial alarm among respondents. In our experience this can usually be alleviated by promising to turn off the tape on request from the interviewee if respondents worry about specific replies. This seldom happens because of the momentum generated by the interview once it has begun, but when it does it is of interest in itself to note the points that arouse particular concern. In observational fieldwork tape-recording is almost always impossible. Contemporaneous note-taking is also almost always ruled out by the physical circumstances, and reliance must be placed on memory. Frequent visits to the toilet to jot down very brief reminders for subsequent report writing are helpful—but may raise concerns about the researcher's health.

Researching areas of current controversy

Private security and pluralized policing

As we noted in the introduction it has now become commonplace in much criminological scholarship to refer to *policing* rather than *the police*. In large part, this is in recognition of the array of organizations and agents that engage in such formalized social control activities. However, it is only relatively recently that scholars have come to focus attention on policing bodies beyond the police themselves. The first empirical investigation of private security was conducted in the USA by the Rand Corporation in the early 1970s (Kakalik and Wildhorn 1972), and this was followed a decade later by another major empirical study undertaken by the Hallcrest organization (Cunningham and Taylor 1985). The path-breaking sociological work, also North American, was undertaken initially by Spitzer and Scull (1977a; 1977b) and subsequently and most importantly by Clifford Shearing and Philip Stenning in Canada (e.g. Shearing and Stenning 1981, 1983). In the UK, although the 1971 Cropwood conference at Cambridge considered private security (McClintock and Wiles 1971), the pioneering work remains Nigel South's Ph.D. research (South 1988; though see also Draper 1978). As South describes it, the research began as an observational study of private security 'at work', but later expanded into a much broader exploration of the relationship between public and private sectors in policing and in the problems of governance and accountability. Shearing and Stenning's work in Canada, and South's work in the UK, paved the way for the explosion of scholarship in this area that has occurred since.

With the apparent proliferation of organizations and agents involved in policing activities, together with the growing influence of managerialism and privatization since the mid-1980s, researchers have increasingly explored the nature of private provision, how it may be theorized, and the analytical distinctions that may be drawn between the different sectors. Initial work paralleled much early sociology of policing in its concern with function and powers, though this was subsequently criticized for its rather essentialist and reductionist character (Johnston 1992). The complexity of 'postmodern' (Reiner 1992b) or 'post-Keynesian' (O'Malley and Palmer 1996) policing led authors to move beyond such an approach and to focus on the sectoral, spatial, and geographical boundaries as a further means of analysing this patchwork of provision (Johnston 1992; Jones and Newburn 1998). So profound are the changes affecting contemporary policing—reflecting the broader and deeper political and socio-economic changes associated with late modernity—that it has led some commentators to claim that the system of policing that has dominated the last century and a half is in the process of being replaced by a new and distinctive set of arrangements best described as 'pluralized' or 'multilateralized' (Bayley and Shearing 1996; 2001), or even that the term *policing* be abandoned entirely in favour of the 'governance of security' (Johnston and Shearing 2003). Although the extent of such a transformation has been contested (Jones and Newburn 2002; Zedner

2006) the pluralized nature of policing in most modern liberal democracies is now incontestable (Jones and Newburn 2006). Although recent research in the UK has continued to demonstrate an interest in the nature and activities of private security organizations (Button 2002; Wakefield 2003), particularly in relation to the spread of the new technologies of surveillance (Norris *et al.* 1998; Norris and Armstrong 1999) and the provision of security in the night-time economy (Hobbs *et al.* 2003; Hadfield 2006 and this volume), arguably the largest growth area for research has focused on the emergence of 'new auxiliaries' and the expansion of what has come to be called the 'extended policing family' (Crawford 2003; Crawford and Lister 2004; Crawford *et al.* 2003; 2005). Such developments raise a host of important questions about the future of policing, not least those concerning regulation.

The impact of the Lawrence Inquiry

The relationship between the police and minority communities has been a long-standing theme in policing scholarship (for a summary, see Bowling and Phillips 2002). In the 1970s, work by the Birmingham Centre for Cultural Studies drew attention to the centrality of black youth to the moral panic around 'mugging' that developed in that period (Hall *et al.* 1978). During the 1980s academic research, and official and semi-official inquiries began to explore in some detail the differential treatment accorded black people, and minority communities generally, and were broadly critical of the use of stop and search/SUS powers (Gordon 1983), targeted patrol policies (Keith 1993), the treatment of suspects in custody (Institute of Race Relations 1991) and saturation policing tactics (Scarman 1981; Institute of Race Relations 1987). For much of the period the general approach adopted by the Scarman Inquiry provided the general orienting philosophy for senior police officers (Reiner 1991). The murder of Stephen Lawrence in April 1993, and the Inquiry under Lord Justice Macpherson (1999) established in 1997 following a campaign by the Lawrence family, gave research in this area renewed impetus.

The Stephen Lawrence Inquiry, as it became known, concluded that there had been a series of fundamental flaws in the police investigation and that these had resulted from 'professional incompetence, institutional racism and a failure of leadership by senior officers' (para 45.24). It made seventy recommendations including: a new ministerial priority and associated performance indicators covering the reporting and recording of racist incidents; family and victim liaison; racism awareness training; disciplinary and complaints procedures; the recording of stops and searches; and the recruitment and retention of minority ethnic officers and staff. Although it was far from uncritically received (Miles and Brown 2003; Solomos 1999; Tonry 2004), the Report has effectively set the academic agenda in this area since its publication. The major themes have been racist offending and the policing of racist incidents and hate crimes (Ray and Smith 2001; Hall 2005); police recruitment and race relations training (Tamkin *et al.* 2004); the experiences of minority ethnic officers and their representative organizations (Holdaway and O'Neill 2004; Phillips 2005); public confidence in the police (FitzGerald *et al.* 2002; Allen *et al.* 2006) as well as the impact of the Inquiry on policing and police culture more generally (Foster *et al.* 2005). Police use of stop-and-search powers continues to be the source of greatest controversy and has arguably stimulated more research than any other area.

Despite the criticisms voiced by the Lawrence Inquiry, the requirement imposed on police officers to record stops (Shiner 2006), and the recent research finding that officers now feel under much greater scrutiny when conducting stops and searches (Foster *et al.* 2005), it remains the case that black people continue to be over six times as likely to be stopped and searched as white people (Home Office 2005). Some studies have suggested that demographic factors may explain at least some of this disproportionality (Clancy *et al.* 2001), whereas others have argued that it is a reflection of who is 'available'—i.e. who is on the streets, at the times and in the places where stops are most frequently made (MVA and Miller 2000, Waddington *et al.* 2004). A small study of the use of police strip-search powers in a North London police station, based on an analysis of the experiences of all people in custody over an 18-month period (i.e. the entire 'available population'), found that minority ethnic prisoners were significantly more likely to be strip searched than were white prisoners, controlling for all other factors such as offence type (Newburn *et al.* 2004). Irrespective of any potential explanation, it is clear that those on the receiving end of such police action experience it negatively (Skogan 2006; Smith 2006). This has been a long-standing source of controversy and conflict. However, a new dimension has been added since the London bombings of July 2005 with evidence suggesting that new search powers introduced under the Terrorism Act 2000 have also been found to be have been used disproportionately against black and Asian people, with Muslims in particular feeling targeted.

Terrorism and policing

The attacks on the World Trade Center in New York in 2001, nightclubs in Bali in 2002 and 2005 and the public transport systems of Madrid and London in 2004 and 2005 respectively, have stimulated public debate about national security, and have pushed issues connected with anti-terrorist policing significantly higher up the agenda. Given this prominence, this is an area of study that criminologists have come to belatedly. The end of the Cold War and the rise of international terrorism have led to the emergence of what some observers now refer to as the 'new security agenda'. Concerns about the 'new terrorism' have begun to reshape the governance of domestic security generally and policing more particularly (Shearing 2006), with the consequence that the boundaries between 'high' and 'low' policing (Brodeur 1983) appear increasingly blurred (Bowling and Newburn 2007).

The bulk of terrorist activity in the UK since the Second World War, and the bulk of criminological writing on the subject, has been connected with the Troubles in Northern Ireland (see, for example, Ellison and Smyth 2000; Mulcahy 2006; Weitzer 1995). The Metropolitan Police established its Bomb Squad in 1971, and renamed it the Anti-Terrorist Branch in 1976. Much of the policing of the Troubles involved an uneasy and shifting relationship between the police, the army, and the security services. Many of the paramilitary policing tactics and uses of equipment first developed in Northern Ireland have found their way into everyday policing on the mainland. Arguably, many of the covert approaches first utilized during the Troubles are now 'normalized' as part of the more general push toward 'intelligence-led policing that is now underway. Indeed, anti-terrorist activity is as close as contemporary policing comes to the 'risk society' model outlined by Ericson and Haggerty (1997).

Although terrorist attacks have almost inevitably been swiftly followed by the intro-duction of new and more extensive policing powers, there is evidence that the majority of terrorist arrests in England, Wales, and Northern Ireland could have been made under PACE provisions (Hillyard 1993). Equally, much anti-terrorist activity is merely a more intensive version of routine police work, of a problem-oriented variety. One of the lessons of the Troubles is that emergency powers, usually introduced as temporary meas-ures, tend to become permanent. This inevitably raises questions about police account-ability and how the use of such powers is to be overseen and regulated. Perhaps more importantly, it raises questions about police legitimacy. The last year has seen anti-terrorist operations in Britain result in the fatal shooting of Jean Charles de Menezes at Stockwell Tube Station and more recently in the shooting of another unarmed man dur-ing a police raid as a result of what appears to have been inadequate intelligence. The impact of such operations on public trust in the police is unlikely to be positive. Quite possibly, it is this area—'high policing' and its implications for public trust and confi-dence, and for human rights—which will be the biggest growth area in policing studies over the next decade.

Conclusions: the future of policing research

Policing research has altered fundamentally during its forty or more years of history. In Britain until the mid-1980s most of it was done by outsiders to policing, and it was motivated primarily by critical and theoretical concerns. The methodological prob-lems were primarily those of detectives or spies: how to get information from people who were (often rightly) suspicious of your motives, had much to hide, and much to lose from its discovery. Most researchers came to be more sympathetic to the police as they did their research, but almost always without going native. Understanding the pressures and constraints of police work mellowed all-out hostility or criticism, but researchers' concerns about discrimination and abuses of power remained undiminished.

An interesting study of the impact of police research on researchers demonstrates how these tensions tend to be resolved according to the disciplinary backgrounds of different researchers (Reiss 1968). Dozens of graduate students were recruited as observers for the large-scale study of patrol work conducted for the Presidential Commission on Law Enforcement, and their views on the police were surveyed before and after the fieldwork. At the outset most shared the anti-police consensus then normal amongst students. But after riding along with the 'dreaded pigs' for many hours in the stressful intimacy of patrol cars, the majority became much more positive in their views of police officers. However, their own political views remained as liberal as at the outset. The dissonance between their assessments of the officers as people and the aspects of their practices which the students disapproved of was resolved in a variety of ways characteristic of their disciplinary backgrounds. Law students saw the issue as bad laws enforced by well-meaning police. Management students sympathized with the street cops and saw the problem as bad management. Sociologists attributed undesirable police behaviour to the structural pressures of an unjust social system.

More recently relations between the police and academe have been transformed (Reiner 1994). The police have been seen as useful new sources of students and research funding by increasingly cash-pressured academics, whilst the police have sought to relegitimate themselves through academic credentials and increasing their own capacity to do research on policy implementation. Thus, research is increasingly of a pragmatic kind, governed by the over-riding goal of crime reduction (for the same reasons this is true of criminology in general: Hillyard *et al.* 2004). In the USA, however, the Bush administration's suspicion of social science has slashed funding even for policy oriented policing research: (Sherman 2004). In Britain, by contrast, it was given an enormous impetus by the new Labour government's initial enthusiasm for intelligence-led and problem-oriented approaches to policing and crime control, requiring regular analysis before initiatives and evaluation afterwards, although this too has withered somewhat (Hough 2004). The danger is that the necessarily quicker and more focused assessments of specific problems and attempted solutions may not shed light on the low-visibility practices of everyday policing. Our knowledge of such basic matters as why people join the force, the way day-to-day decisions about the use of powers are made, and other key aspects of cop culture are based on increasingly out-of-date research such as the PSI study conducted in the early 1980s. Replication of the classic observational studies of routine police work is needed.

There are many topics crying out for research of the older kind that sought to understand routine practices without being directed to the immediate solution of practical problems. Ultimately such work can provide a better grounding for policy as well. An example is the construction of criminal statistics. Much research has shown how statistics have frequently been manipulated by the police to provide support for their organizational interests (Young 1991; Taylor 1998, 1999). The pressure to produce results in the new performance indicator-driven culture of police management in the early 1990s led to massaging of crime figures (Davies 1999: 12). Since 1998 there have been profound changes in the rules governing the collation and presentation of crime statistics by the police (Maguire 2002). Although these have clearly had a considerable impact on the measurement of crime trends, there is no detailed evidence about how they shape police-recording practices. It is nearly two decades since any observational work has been conducted on the routine construction of crime data by the police (Chatterton 1976, 1983; McCabe and Sutcliffe 1978; Bottomley and Coleman 1981). Much other work of a fundamental kind is necessary, building on what has gone before. We know little, for example, about the social characteristics of those who call upon the police for help by telephone, although there has been a plethora of work on the content of their demands. Yet this is fundamental for understanding the social role of policing.

At present the thrust of research seems to be away from such fundamental and theoretical questions. However, it is possible that recent events will force a change. The controversies raised by the publication of the inquiry into the disastrous and shameful investigation of Stephen Lawrence's murder in 1993 (Macpherson 1999; Foster *et al.* 2005; Rowe 2006) have brought back to the forefront of political debate racism and other issues of police malpractice which were being sidelined. It seemed that two decades of reform since the 1981 Scarman Report had achieved little if anything. Nor has concern for value for money as exhibited by performance indicators necessarily delivered policing of basic competence, as recent mishaps in the policing of terror suspects indicate. Both police research and police reform of a critical and constructive kind are back on the agenda.

Suggestions for further reading

Few works address the methods of police research as such. However, most research studies include chapters detailing the methods used, why they were chosen, the problems encountered, and how at least some of these were overcome. For examples discussing observational methods, see Skolnick (1966); Reiss (1968); Cain (1973); Manning (1977); Punch (1979*a*); Holdaway (1983); Young (1991, 1993); Waddington (1994); Westmarland (2001). For the special problems of researching private policing, see Jones and Newburn (1998); Wakefield (2003); Noaks and Wincup (2004: ch. 10); Button (2006). On interview-based research, see Reiner (1978, 1991). Weatheritt (1985); Brown and Waters (1993); Sheptycki (1994); and Brown (1996) consider the growth of research by the police themselves, and its relative merits and limitations compared with research on the police by outsiders. Smith (1997, 1998); Travers (1997); and McConville, Sanders, and Leng (1997) represent a recent series of exchanges about the issues of balancing scholarship and political engagement in research. Pawson and Tilley (1994); Bennett (1996); Cohen (1997); and Brodeur (1998) are recent assessments of the methodology of evaluation research. Morgan and Newburn (1997) is a succinct analysis of contemporary policing issues. Waddington (1999) and Reiner (2000) are reviews of the content of police research. Reiner (1989 and 1992b) are historical accounts of the development of British police research. Newburn (2003) provides a definitive collection of original papers on all aspects of modern policing, and Newburn (2005) offers a comprehensive selection of key readings.

References

ALLEN, J., EDMONDS, S., PATTERSON, A., and SMITH, D. (2006). *Policing and the Criminal Justice System—Public Confidence and Perceptions: Findings from the British Crime Survey*. Home Office Online Report 07/06. London: Home Office.

ANDERSON, R., BROWN, J., and CAMPBELL, E. (1993). *Aspects of Discrimination Within the Police Service in England and Wales*. London: Home Office Police Research Group.

AUDIT COMMISSION (1990). *Effective Policing: Performance Review in Police Forces*. London: HMSO.

—— (1993). *Helping With Enquiries*. London: HMSO.

—— (1996). *Streetwise: Effective Police Patrol*. London: HMSO.

BANTON, M. (1964). *The Policeman in the Community*. London: Tavistock.

BAUMAN, Z. (2000). *Liquid Modernity*. Cambridge: Polity Press.

BAYLEY, D. (1998). *What Works in Policing*. New York: Oxford University Press.

—— and SHEARING, C. (1996). 'The Future of Policing'. *Law and Society Review* 30: 585–606.

—— and SHEARING, C. (2001). *The New Structure of Policing*. Washington DC: National Institute of Justice.

BECK, U. (1992). *Risk Society*. London: Sage.

BENNETT, T. (1990). *Evaluating Neighbourhood Watch*. Aldershot: Gower.

—— (1991). 'The Effectiveness of a Police-initiated Fear-reducing Strategy'. *British Journal of Criminology* 31: 1–14.

—— (1996). 'What's New in Evaluation Research?' *British Journal of Criminology* 36: 567–73.

BITTNER, E. (1974). 'Florence Nightingale in Pursuit of Willie Sutton: A Theory of the Police' in H. Jacob (ed.), *The Potential For Reform of Criminal Justice*. Beverly Hills, Cal.: Sage.

BLAIR, I. (1985). *Investigating Rape: A New Approach For Police*. London: Croom Helm.

BOTTOMLEY, A. K. and COLEMAN, C. (1981). *Understanding Crime Rates*. Farnborough: Gower.

BOTTOMS, A. and WILES, P. (1996). 'Crime and Policing in a Changing Social Context' in W. Saulsbury, J. Mott, and T. Newburn (eds), *Themes In Contemporary Policing*. London: Police Foundation/Policy Studies Institute.

—— and —— (1997). 'Environmental Criminology' in M. Maguire, R. Morgan, and R. Reiner (eds), *Oxford Handbook of Criminology* (2nd edn). Oxford: Oxford University Press.

BOWLING, B. (1999a). 'The Rise and Fall of New York Murder'. *British Journal of Criminology* 39: 531–54.

—— (1999b). *Violent Racism*. Oxford: Oxford University Press.

—— and NEWBURN, T. (2007). 'Policing and National Security' in B. Bowling and J. Fagan (eds), *Police, Community and the Rule of Law*. Oxford: Hart.

—— and PHILLIPS, C. (2002). *Racism, Crime and Justice*. Harlow: Longman.

—— and PHILLIPS, C. (2003). 'Policing Ethnic Minority Communities' in T. Newburn (ed.), *Handbook of Policing*. Cullompton: Willan.

BOX, S. and RUSSELL, K. (1975). 'The Politics of Discreditability'. *Sociological Review* 23: 315–46.

BRODEUR, J. P. (1983). 'High Policing and Low Policing: Remarks about the Policing of Political Activities'. *Social Problems* 30: 507–20.

—— (ed.) (1998). *How to Recognise Good Policing*. Thousand Oaks, Cal.: Sage.

BROGDEN, M. (1982). *The Police: Autonomy and Consent*. London: Academic Press.

—— (1987). 'The Emergence of the Police: The Colonial Dimension'. *British Journal of Criminology* 27: 4–14.

—— and ELLISON, G. (2005). *Community Policing: International Concepts and Practice*. Cullompton: Willan.

BROWN, D. (1997). *PACE Ten Years On: A Review of the Research*. Home Office Research Study 155, London: HMSO.

BROWN, J. (1996). 'Police Research: Some Critical Issues' in F. Leishman, B. Loveday, and S. Savage (eds), *Core Issues in Policing*. London: Longman.

—— and HEIDENSOHN, F. (2000). *Gender and Policing: Comparative Perspectives*. London: Macmillan.

—— and WATERS, I. (1993). 'Professional Police Research'. *Policing* 9: 323–34.

BULLOCK, K. and TILLEY, N. (2003). *Crime Reduction and Problem-Oriented Policing*. Cullompton: Willan.

BULMER, M. and REES, A. M. (eds) (1996). *Citizenship Today: The Contemporary Relevance of T. H. Marshall*. London: UCL Press.

BURKE, R. H. (ed.) (2004). *Hard Cop, Soft Cop*. Cullompton: Willan.

BUTTON, M. (2002). *Private Policing*. Cullompton: Willan.

—— (2006). *Security Officers and Policing*. Aldershot: Avebury.

CAIN, M. (1971). 'On the Beat: Interactions and Relations in Rural and Urban Police Forces' in S. Cohen (ed.), *Images of Deviance*. Harmondsworth: Penguin.

—— (1973). *Society and the Policeman's Role*. London: Routledge.

—— (1979). 'Trends in the Sociology of Police Work'. *International Journal of Sociology of Law* 7: 143–67.

CALLINICOS, A. (1989). *Against Postmodernism*. Cambridge: Polity Press.

CASTELLS, M. (1996–8). *The Information Age Vols. I–III*, Oxford: Blackwell.

CHAN, J. (1997). *Changing Police Culture.* Cambridge: Cambridge University Press.

CHATTERTON, M. (1976). 'Police in Social Control' in J. King (ed.), *Control Without Custody.* Cropwood Papers 7. Cambridge: Institute of Criminology.

—— (1983). 'Police Work and Assault Charges' in M. Punch (ed.), *Control in the Police Organisation.* Cambridge, Mass.: MIT Press.

CHESSHYRE, R. (1990). *The Force: Inside the Police.* London: Pan.

CLANCY, A., HOUGH, M., AUST, R., and KERSHAW, C. (2001). *Crime, Policing and Justice: the Experience of Ethnic Minorities: Findings from the 2000 British Crime Survey.* Home Office Research Study 223, London: Home Office.

CLARKE, R. and HOUGH, M. (eds) (1980). *The Effectiveness of Policing.* Farnborough: Gower.

—— and —— (1984). *Crime and Police Effectiveness.* London: Home Office Research Unit.

COHEN, S. (1985). *Visions of Social Control.* Cambridge: Polity Press.

—— (1997). 'Crime and Politics: Spot the Difference' in R. Rawlings (ed.), *Law, Society and Economy.* Oxford: Oxford University Press.

COPE, N. (2003). 'Crime Analysis: Principles and Practice' in T. Newburn, *Handbook of Policing.* Cullompton: Willan.

COX, B., SHIRLEY, J., and SHORT, M. (1977). *The Fall of Scotland Yard.* Harmondsworth: Penguin.

CRAWFORD, A. (2003). 'The Pattern of Policing in the UK: Policing Beyond the Police' in T. Newburn, *Handbook of Policing.* Cullompton: Willan.

—— and LISTER, S. (2004). *The Extended Policing Family.* York: Joseph Rowntree Foundation.

——, ——, and WALL, D. (2003). *Great Expectations: Contracted Community Policing in New Earswick.* York: Joseph Rowntree Foundation.

——, ——, BLACKBURN, S., and BURNETT, J. (2005). *Plural Policing: The Mixed Economy of Visible Patrols in England and Wales.* Bristol: Policy Press.

—— JONES, T., WOODHOUSE, T., and YOUNG, J. (1990). *The Second Islington Crime Survey.* London: Middlesex Polytechnic Centre for Criminology.

CUNNINGHAM, W. C. and TAYLOR, T. H. (1985). *Private Security and Police in America.* Boston: Butterworth: Heinemann.

CURRIE, E. (1998). *Crime and Punishment in America.* New York: Holt.

DAVIES, N. (1998). *Dark Heart.* London: Verso.

—— (1999). 'Watching the Detectives: How the Police Cheat in Fight Against Crime'. *The Guardian*, 18 March.

DAVIS, M. (1990). *City of Quartz.* London: Vintage.

DELSOL, R. and SHINER, M. (2006). 'Regulating Stop and Search'. *Critical Criminology.*

DENNIS, N. (ed.) (1997). *Zero Tolerance: Policing a Free Society.* London: Institute of Economic Affairs.

—— and ERDOS, G. (2005). *Cultures and Crimes: Policing in Four Nations* London: Civitas.

DIXON, D. (1997). *Law in Policing.* Oxford: Oxford University Press.

—— and MAHER, L. (2005). 'Policing, Crime and Public Health: Lessons from Australia for the "New York Miracle"'. *Criminal Justice* 5(1): 115–44.

DOWNES, D. and MORGAN, R. (2002). ' The Skeletons in the Cupboard: The Politics of Law and Order at the Turn of the Millenium' in M. Maguire, R. Morgan, and R. Reiner (eds), *The Oxford Handbook of Criminology* (3rd edn). Oxford: Oxford University Press.

DRAPER, H. (1978). *Private Police*. Harmondsworth: Penguin

DUBBER, M. (2005). *The Police Power*. New York: Columbia University Press.

ELLISON, G. and SMYTH, J. (2000). *The Crowned Harp: Policing Northern Ireland*. London: Pluto.

EMSLEY, C. (1996). *The English Police: A Political and Social History* (2nd edn). Hemel Hempstead: Harvester Wheatsheaf.

ERICSON, R. and HAGGERTY, K. (1997). *Policing Risk Society*. Oxford: Oxford University Press.

FIELDING, N. (1995). *Community Policing*. Oxford: Oxford University Press.

—— (2005). *The Police and Social Conflict* (2nd edn). London: GlassHouse.

FITZGERALD, M. (1999). *Searches in London Under Section 1 of the Police and Criminal Evidence Act*. London: Metropolitan Police.

—— HOUGH, M., JOSEPH, I., and QURESHI, T. (2002). *Policing for London*. Cullompton: Willan.

FOSTER, J., NEWBURN, T., and SOUHAMI, A. (2005). *Assessing the Impact of the Stephen Lawrence Enquiry*. London: Home Office.

FOUCAULT, M. (1979). 'On Governmentality'. *Ideology and Consciousness* 6: 5–23.

GARLAND, D. (1997). '"Governmentality" and the Problem of Crime: Foucault, Criminology, Sociology'. *Theoretical Criminology* 1: 173–214 .

—— (2001). *The Culture of Control*. Oxford: Oxford University Press.

GIDDENS, A. (1994). *Beyond Left and Right*. Cambridge: Polity Press.

GOLDSTEIN, H. (1990). *Problem-Oriented Policing*. New York: McGraw Hill.

GOLDSTEIN, J. (1960). 'Police Discretion Not to Invoke the Criminal Process: Low Visibility Decisions in the Administration of Justice'. *Yale Law Journal* 69: 543–94.

GORDON, P. (1983). *White Law: Racism in the Police, Courts and Prisons*. London: Pluto Press.

GRAEF, R. (1989). *Talking Blues*. London: Collins.

GREGORY, J. and LEES, S. (1999). *Policing Sexual Assault*. London: Routledge.

GRIMSHAW, R. and JEFFERSON, T. (1987). *Interpreting Policework*. London: Unwin.

HADFIELD, P. (2006). *Bar Wars*. Oxford: Clarendon Press.

HALL, N. (2005). *Hate Crime*. Cullompton: Willan.

HALL, S., CRITCHER, C., JEFFERSON, T., CLARKE, J., and ROBERTS, B. (1978). *Policing the Crisis*. London: Macmillan.

HARCOURT, B. (2001). *Illusion of Order: The False Promise of Broken Windows Policing*. Cambridge: Harvard University Press.

HEAL, K., TARLING, R., and BURROWS, J. (eds) (1985). *Policing Today*. London: HMSO.

HEIDENSOHN, F. (1992). *Women in Control? The Role of Women in Law Enforcement*. Oxford: Oxford University Press.

—— (2003). 'Gender and Policing' in T. Newburn (ed.), *Handbook of Policing*. Cullompton: Willan.

HELD, D. (2005). *Debating Globalisation*. Cambridge: Polity.

HILLYARD, P. (1993). *Suspect Community: People's Experiences of the Prevention of Terrorism Acts in Britain*. London: Pluto.

——, SIM, J., TOMBS, S., and WHYTE, D. (2004). 'Leaving a "Stain Upon the Silence": Contemporary Criminology and the Politics of Dissent'. *British Journal of Criminology* 44: 369–90.

HIRST, P. and THOMPSON, G. (1999). *Globalisation in Question* (2nd edn). London: Polity Press.

HOBBS, D., HADFIELD, P., LISTER, S., and WINLOW, S. (2003). *Bouncers: Violence and*

Governance in the Night-time Economy. Oxford: Clarendon Press.

HOLDAWAY, S. (ed.) (1979). *The British Police.* London: Arnold.

—— (1983). *Inside the British Police.* Oxford: Blackwell.

—— (1989). 'Discovering Structure: Studies of the British Police Occupational Culture' in M. Weatheritt (ed.), *Police Research: Some Future Prospects.* Aldershot: Avebury.

—— (1996). *The Racialisation of British Policing.* London: Macmillan.

—— and O'NEILL, M. (2004). 'The Development of Black Police Associations'. *British Journal of Sociology* 44: 854–65.

HOME OFFICE (2005). *Statistics on Race and the Criminal Justice System 2004: a Home Office Publication under section 95 of the Criminal Justice Act 1991.* London: Home Office.

HOPE, T. (2004). 'Pretend It Works: Evidence and Governance in the Evaluation of the Reducing Burglary Initiative'. *Criminal Justice* 4: 287–308.

HOUGH, M. (2003). 'Modernisation and Public Opinion: Some Criminal Justice Paradoxes'. *Contemporary Politics* 9: 143–55.

—— (ed.) (2004). 'Evaluating the Crime Reduction Programme in England and Wales'. Special Issue, *Criminal Justice* 4(3).

HOYLE, C. (1998). *Negotiating Domestic Violence: Police Criminal Justice and Victims.* Oxford: Oxford University Press.

HUMPHRY, D. (1972). *Police Power and Black People.* London: Granada.

INNES, M. (2003). *Understanding Social Control.* Maidenhead: Open University Press.

—— (ed.) (2006). 'Reassurance and the "New" Community Policing'. Special Issue, *Policing and Society* 16(2).

INSTITUTE OF RACE RELATIONS (1987). *Policing Against Black People.* London: IRR.

—— (1991). *Deadly Silence: Black Deaths in Custody.* London: IRR.

IRVING, B. and McKENZIE, I. (1989). *Police Interrogation.* London: Police Foundation.

——, BIRD, C., HIBBERD, M., and WILLMORE, J. (1989). *Neighbourhood Policing: The Natural History of a Policing Experiment.* London: Police Foundation.

JEFFERSON, T. and GRIMSHAW, R. (1984). *Controlling the Constable.* London: Muller.

——, McLAUGHLIN, E., and ROBERTSON, L. (1988). 'Monitoring the Monitors: Accountability, Democracy and Police Watching in Britain'. *Contemporary Crises* 12: 91–107.

—— and SHAPLAND, J. (1994). 'Criminal Justice and the Production of Order and Control: Criminological Research in the UK in the 1980s'. *British Journal of Criminology* 34: 265–90.

JOHNSTON, L. (1992). *The Rebirth of Private Policing.* London: Routledge.

—— (2000). *Policing Britain: Risk, Security and Governance.* Harlow: Longman.

—— and SHEARING, C. (2003). *Governing Security.* London: Routledge.

JONES, T. (2007). 'Governance and Security', in M. Maguire, R. Morgan, and R. Reiner (eds), *Oxford Handbook of Criminology* (4th edn). Oxford: Oxford University Press.

——, MACLEAN, B., and YOUNG, J. (1986). *The Islington Crime Survey.* Aldershot: Gower.

—— and NEWBURN, T. (1997). *Policing After the Act.* London: Policy Studies Institute.

—— and —— (1998). *Private Security and Public Policing.* Oxford: Oxford University Press.

—— and —— (2002). 'The Transformation of Policing? Understanding Current Trends in Policing Systems'. *British Journal of Criminology* 42: 129–46.

—— and —— (2006). *Plural Policing: A Comparative Perspective.* London: Routledge.

——, Newburn, T., and Smith, D. (1994). *Democracy and Policing*. London: Policy Studies Institute.

Jordan, P. (1998). 'Effective Policing Strategies for Reducing Crime' in C. Nuttall, P. Goldblatt, and C. Lewis (eds), *Reducing Offending*. Home Office Research Study 187, London: Home Office.

Kakalik, J. S. and Wildhorn, S. (1972). *Private Police in the United States*, (The Rand Report) (4 vols). National Institute of Law Enforcement and Criminal Justice, Washington: US Department of Justice.

Karmen, A. (2000). *New York Murder Mystery*. New York: New York University Press.

Keith, M. (1993). *Race, Riots and Policing: Lore and Disorder in a Multi-Racist Society*. London: UCL Press.

Kinsey, R. (1985). *Merseyside Crime and Police Surveys: Final Report*. Liverpool: Merseyside County Council.

—— Lea, J., and Young, J. (1986). *Losing the Fight Against Crime*. Oxford: Blackwell.

Laurie, P. (1970). *Scotland Yard*. Harmondsworth: Penguin.

Lambert, J. (1969). 'The Police Can Choose'. *New Society* 14: 364, 430–2.

—— (1970). *Crime, Police and Race Relations*. Oxford: Oxford University Press.

Lea, J. and Young, J. (1984). *What is to be Done about Law and Order?* Harmondsworth: Penguin.

Leishman, F. and Mason, P. (2003). *Policing and the Media*. Cullompton: Willan.

Loader, I. and Mulcahy, A. (2003). *Policing and the Condition of England*. Oxford: Oxford University Press.

Long, M. (2003). 'Leadership and Performance Management', in T. Newburn (ed.), *Handbook of Policing*. Cullompton: Willan.

Loveday, B. (2006). *Size Isn't Everything: Restructuring Policing in England and Wales*. London: Policy Exchange.

—— and Reid, A. (2003). *Going Local: Who Should Run Britain's Police*. London: Policy Exchange.

Lustgarten, L. (1986). *The Governance of the Police*. London: Sweet & Maxwell.

MacPherson, Sir W. (1999). *The Stephen Lawrence Inquiry*. London: The Stationery Office.

Maguire, M. (2002). 'Crime Statistics: The "Data Explosion" and its Implications' in M. Maguire, R. Morgan, and R. Reiner (eds), *The Oxford Handbook of Criminology* (3rd edn). Oxford: Oxford University Press.

—— (2003). 'Criminal Investigation and Crime Control' in T. Newburn, *Handbook of Policing*. Cullompton: Willan.

—— (2004). 'The Crime Reduction Programme in England and Wales'. *Criminal Justice* 4: 213–38.

Manning, P. (1977). *Police Work*. Cambridge, Mass.: MIT Press.

—— (1979). 'The Social Control of Police Work' in S. Holdaway (ed.), *The British Police*. London: Edward Arnold.

Marlow, A. and Loveday, B. (eds) (2000). *After Macpherson*. London: Russell House.

Marshall, T. H. (1950). *Citizenship and Social Class*. Cambridge: Cambridge University Press.

Martin, C. (1996). 'The Impact of Equal Opportunities Policies on the Day-to-Day Experiences of Women Police Constables'. *British Journal of Criminology* 36: 510–28.

Mastrofski, S. D., Parks, R. B., Reiss, A. J., Worden, R. E., DeJong, C., Snipes, J. B., and Terrill, W. (1998). *Systematic Observation of Public Police: Applying Field Research Methods to Policy Issues*. Washington, DC: National Institute of Justice.

Mawby, R. (1991). *Comparative Policing Issues*. London: Unwin.

—— (2002). *Policing Images*. Cullompton: Willan.

McBarnet, D. (1979). 'Arrest: The Legal Context of Policing' in S. Holdaway (ed.), *The British Police*. London: Arnold.

McCabe, S. and Sutcliffe, F. (1978). *Defining Crime*. Oxford: Blackwell.

——, Wallington, P., Alderson, J., Gostin, L., and Mason, C. (1988). *The Police, Public Order and Civil Liberties*. London: Routledge.

McLaughlin, E. (2005). 'Forcing the Issue: New Labour, New Localism and the Democratic Renewal of Police Accountability'. *The Howard Journal* 44: 473–89.

—— and Murji, K. (1996). 'Times Change: New Formations and Representations of Police Accountability' in C. Critcher and D. Waddington (eds), *Policing Public Order*. Aldershot: Avebury.

—— and —— (1997). 'The Future Lasts a Long Time: Public Policework and the Managerialist Paradox' in P. Francis, P. Davies, and V. Jupp (eds), *Policing Futures*. London: Macmillan.

McClintock, F. H. and Wiles, P. (1971). *The Security Industry in the UK: Papers presented at the Cropwood Round Table Conference*, July 1971. Cambridge: Cambridge Institute of Criminology.

McConville, M. and Shepherd, D. (1992). *Watching Police, Watching Communities*. London: Routledge.

——, Sanders, A., and Leng, R. (1991). *The Case For the Prosecution: Police Suspects and the Construction of Criminality*. London: Routledge.

——, —— and —— (1997). 'Descriptive or Critical Sociology: The Choice is Yours'. *British Journal of Criminology* 3: 347–58.

Miles, R. and Brown, M. (2003). *Racism* (2nd edn). London: Routledge.

Miller, J., Bland, N., and Quinton, P. (2000). *The Impact of Stops and Searches on Crime and the Community*. Police Research Paper 127, London: Home Office.

Millie, A. and Herrington, V. (2005). 'Bridging the Gap: Understanding Reassurance Policing'. *Howard Journal* 44(1): 41–56.

Morgan, R. and Newburn, T. (1997). *The Future of Policing*. Oxford: Oxford University Press.

Morris, P. and Heal, K. (1981). *Crime Control and the Police*. London: Home Office.

Mulcahy, A. (2006). *Policing Northern Ireland*. Cullompton: Willan.

MVA and Miller, J. (2000). *Profiling Populations Available for Stops and Searches*. Police Research Series Paper No. 131. London: Home Office.

Neocleous, M. (2000). *The Fabrication of Social Order*. London: Pluto.

Newburn, T. (1999). *Understanding and Preventing Police Corruption*. Police Research Studies 110. London: Home Office.

—— (ed.) (2003a). *Handbook of Policing*. Cullompton: Willan.

——(ed.) (2003b). *Policing—Key Readings*. Cullompton: Willan.

—— and Hayman, S. (2001). *Policing, CCTV, and Social Control: Police Surveillance of Suspects in Custody*. Cullompton: Willan.

——, Shiner, M., and Hayman, S. (2004). 'Race, Crime and Injustice: Strip Search and the Treatment of Suspects in Custody'. *British Journal of Criminology* 44: 677–94.

Noaks, L. and Wincup, E. (2004). *Criminological Research*. London: Sage.

Norris, C. (1993). 'Some Ethical Considerations on Field-work with the Police' in D. Hobbs and T. May (eds), *Interpreting the Field*. Oxford: Oxford University Press.

—— and Armstrong, G. (1999). *The Maximum Surveillance Society: The Rise of CCTV*. Oxford: Berg.

——, MORAN, J. and ARMSTRONG, G. (eds) (1998). *Surveillance, CCTV and Social Control.* Aldershot: Ashgate.

NUTTALL, C., GOLDBLATT, P., and LEWIS, C. (1998). *Reducing Offending.* Home Office Research Study 187. London: Home Office.

O'MALLEY, P. and PALMER, D. (1996). 'Post-Keynesian Policing'. *Economy and Society* 21: 137–55.

O'SULLIVAN, S. (2005). 'UK Policing and its Television Portrayal'. *Howard Journal* 44: 504–26.

PALMER, S. H. (1988). *Police and Protest in England and Ireland 1780–1850.* Cambridge: Cambridge University Press.

PANITCH, L. and LEYS, C. (eds) (1999). *Global Capitalism versus Democracy.* Socialist Register 1999. Rendlesham: Merlin Press.

PASQUINO, P. (1978). 'Theatrum Politicum: The Genealogy of Capital—Police and the State of Prosperity'. *Ideology and Consciousness* 4: 41–54.

PAWSON, R. and TILLEY, N. (1994). 'What Works in Evaluation Research?' *British Journal of Criminology* 34: 291–306.

PHILLIPS, C. (2005). 'Facing Inwards and Outwards: Institutional Racism, Race Equality and the Role of Black and Asian Professional Associations'. *Criminal Justice* 5: 557–77.

POLICE FOUNDATION/POLICY STUDIES INSTITUTE (1996). *The Role and Responsibilities of the Police: Report of an Independent Inquiry.* London: Police Foundation/Policy Studies Institute.

PUNCH, M. (1979a). *Policing the Inner City.* London: Macmillan.

—— (1979b). 'The Secret Social Service' in S. Holdaway (ed.), *The British Police.* London: Arnold.

—— (1985). *Conduct Unbecoming: The Social Construction of Police Deviance and Control.* London: Tavistock.

QUINTON, P., BLAND, N., and MILLER, J. (2000). *Police Stops, Decision-Making and Practice.* Police Research Paper 130. London: Home Office.

RAWLINGS, P. (1999). *Crime and Power: A History of Criminal Justice 1688–1998.* London: Longman.

RAY, L. and SMITH, D. (2001). 'Racist Offenders and the Politics of Hate Crime'. *Law and Critique* 12: 203–221.

——, —— and WASTELL, L. (2004). 'Shame, Rage and Racist Violence'. *British Journal of Criminology* 44: 350–68.

REINER, R. (1978a). *The Blue-coated Worker.* Cambridge: Cambridge University Press.

—— (1978b). 'The Police, Class and Politics'. *Marxism Today* 22: 69–80.

—— (1978c). 'The Police in the Class Structure'. *British Journal of Law and Society* 5: 166–84.

—— (1988). 'British Criminology and the State'. *British Journal of Criminology* 29: 138–58.

—— (1989). 'The Politics of Police Research' in M. Weatheritt (ed.), *Police Research: Some Future Prospects.* Aldershot: Avebury.

—— (1991). *Chief Constables.* Oxford: Oxford University Press.

—— (1992a). 'Police Research in the United Kingdom: A Critical Review' in N. Morris and M. Tonry (eds), *Modern Policing.* Chicago, Ill.: Chicago University Press.

—— (1992b). 'Policing A Postmodern Society'. *Modern Law Review* 55: 761–81.

—— (1994). 'A Truce in the War Between the Police and Academe'. *Policing Today.* 1: 30–2.

—— (2000). *The Politics of the Police* (3rd edn). Oxford: Oxford University Press.

—— (2003). 'Policing and the Media' in T. Newburn (ed.), *Handbook of Policing.* Cullompton: Willan.

—— (2007). 'Political Economy, Crime and Criminal Justice' in M. Maguire, R. Morgan, and R. Reiner (eds), *The Oxford Handbook of Criminology* (4th edn). Oxford: Oxford University Press.

—— and SPENCER, S. (eds) (1993). *Accountable Policing: Effectiveness, Empowerment and Equity.* London: Institute for Public Policy Research.

REISS, A. (1968). 'Stuff and Nonsense About Social Surveys and Observation' in H. Becker, B. Greer, D. Riesman, and R. Weiss (eds), *Institutions and the Person.* Chicago, Ill.: Aldine.

ROBINSON, C. D. (1979). 'Ideology As History'. *Police Studies* 2: 35–49.

—— and SCAGLION, R. (1987). 'The Origin and Evolution of the Police Function in Society'. *Law and Society Review* 21: 109–53.

——, SCAGLION, R., and OLIVERO, J. M. (1994). *Police In Contradiction.* Westport Conn.: Greenwood.

ROCK, P. (1973). *Deviant Behaviour.* London: Hutchinson.

ROSE, D. (1992). *A Climate of Fear: The Murder of PC Blakelock and the Case of the Tottenham Three.* London: Bloomsbury.

—— (1996). *In the Name of the Law: The Collapse of Criminal Justice.* London: Cape.

ROWE, M. (2004). *Policing, Race and Racism.* Cullompton: Willan.

—— (ed.) (2006). *Policing Beyond Macpherson.* Cullompton: Willan.

SANDERS, A. and YOUNG, R. (2003). 'Police Powers' in T. Newburn (ed.), *Handbook of Policing.* Cullompton: Willan.

SAULSBURY, W., MOTT, J., and NEWBURN, T. (eds) (1996). *Themes in Contemporary Policing.* London: Police Foundation/Policy Studies Institute.

SCARMAN, LORD (1981). *The Scarman Report: The Brixton Disorders.* London: HMSO. Cmnd 8427.

SCHWARTZ, R. D. and MILLER, J. C. (1964). 'Legal Evolution and Societal Complexity'. *American Journal of Sociology* 70: 159–69.

SCRATON, P. (1985). *The State of the Police.* London: Pluto.

SHAPLAND, J. and VAGG, J. (1988). *Policing By the Public.* London: Routledge.

SHARP, D. (2005). 'Who Needs Theories in Policing?' *Howard Journal* 44(5): 449–59.

SHEARING, C. (1996). Reinventing Policing: Policing as Governance, in O. Marenin (ed.), *Policing Change: Changing Police.* New York: Garland.

—— (2006). 'Policing our future' in A. Henry and D. J. Smith (eds), *Transformations of Policing.* Aldershot: Ashgate.

—— and ERICSON, R. (1991). 'Culture As Figurative Action'. *British Journal of Sociology* 42: 481–506.

—— and STENNING, P. (1981). 'Modern Private Security: its Growth and Implications' in M. Tonry and N. Morris (eds), *Crime and Justice: An Annual Review of Research*, vol. 3. Chicago: Chicago University Press.

—— and —— (1983). 'Private Security: Implications for Social Control'. *Social Problems* 30: 493–506.

—— and—— (1984). 'From the Panopticon to Disney World' in A. N. Doob and E. L. Greenspan (eds), *Perspectives in Criminal Law: Essays in Honour of John Ll. J. Edwards.* Toronto: Canada Law Book Co.

SHEPTYCKI, J. (1994). 'It Looks Different From the Outside'. *Policing* 10: 125–33.

—— (1995). 'Transnational Policing and the Makings of a Postmodern State'. *British Journal of Criminology* 35: 613–35.

—— (1997). 'Insecurity, Risk Suppression and Segregation: Some Reflections on Policing in the Transnational Age'. *Theoretical Criminology* 1: 303–315.

SHERMAN, L. (1992). 'Police and Crime Control' in M. Tonry and N. Morris (eds), *Modern Policing.* Chicago Ill.: Chicago University Press.

—— (1993). 'Why Crime Control is Not Reactionary' in D. Weisburd, C. Uchida, and L. Green (eds), *Police Innovation and Control of Police*. New York: Springer-Verlag.

—— (2004). 'Research and Policing: The Infrastructure and Political Economy of Federal Funding'. *Annals of the American Academy of Political and Social Science* 593: 156–78.

SHINER, M. (2006). *National Implementation of the Recording of Police Stops*. London: Home Office.

SKLANSKY, D. (2005). 'Police and Democracy'. *Michigan Law Review* 103: 1699–1830.

SKOGAN, W. (2006). 'Asymmetry in the impact of encounters with police'. *Policing and Society* 16: 99–126.

—— and FRYDL, K. (eds) (2004). *Fairness and Effectiveness in Policing: The Evidence.* Washington DC: National Academies Press.

SKOLNICK, J. (1966). *Justice Without Trial.* New York: Wiley.

—— and BAYLEY, D. (1986). *The New Blue Line.* New York: Free Press.

—— and —— (1988). *Community Policing.* Washington, DC: National Institute of Justice.

SMITH, D. (1997). 'Case Construction and the Goals of Criminal Process'. *British Journal of Criminology* 37: 319–46.

—— (1998). 'Reform or Moral Outrage—The Choice is Yours'. *British Journal of Criminology* 38: 616–22.

—— (2006). 'New challenges to police legitimacy' in A. Henry and D. J. Smith (eds), *Transformations of Policing.* Aldershot: Ashgate.

—— GRAY, J., and SMALL, S. (1983). *Police and People in London.* London: Policy Studies Institute.

SMITH, G. (2004). 'Rethinking Police Complaints'. *British Journal of Criminology* 44: 15–33.

SMITH, M. and TILLEY, N. (eds) (2005). *Crime Science.* Cullompton: Willan.

SOLOMOS, J. (1999). 'Social Research and the Stephen Lawrence Inquiry'. *Sociological Research Online* 4(1).

SOUTH, N. (1997). 'Control, Crime and "End of the Century" Criminology' in P. Francis, P. Davies, and V. Jupp, (eds), *Policing Futures.* Basingstoke: Macmillan.

—— (1988). *Policing For Profit.* London: Sage.

—— (1998). 'Control, Crime and "End of Century" Criminology' in P. Francis, P. Davies, and V. Jupp (eds), *Policing Futures.* London: Macmillan.

SPITZER, S. and SCULL, A. (1977a). 'Social Control in Historical Perspective: from Private to Public Responses to Crime' in D. Greenberg (ed.), *Corrections and Punishment.* Beverly Hills: Sage.

—— (1977b). 'Privatisation and Capitalist Development: The Case of the Private Police'. *Social Problems* 25: 18–29.

STANKO, E. (2004). Reviewing the Evidence of Hate: Lessons from a Project under the Crime Reduction Programme. *Criminal Justice* 4: 277–86.

TAMKIN, P., POLLARD, E., TACKEY, N. D. and SINCLAIR, A. (2004). *CRR Evaluation and Monitoring.* Brighton: Institute of Employment Studies.

TAYLOR, H. (1998). 'Rising Crime: the Political Economy of Criminal Statistics Since the 1850s'. *Economic History Review* 5: 569–690.

—— (1999). 'Forging the Job: a Crisis of "Modernisation" or Redundancy for the Police in England and Wales 1900–39'. *British Journal of Criminology* 39: 113–35.

TAYLOR, I. (1999). *Crime in Context.* Cambridge: Polity.

TILLEY, N. (ed.) (2002). *Analysis for Crime Prevention.* Crime Prevention Studies Series 13, Monsey, NY: Criminal Justice Press.

—— (2003). 'Community Policing, Problem-Oriented Policing and Intelligence-Led

Policing' in T. Newburn (ed.), *Handbook of Policing*. Cullompton: Willan.

TONRY, M. (2004). *Punishment and Politics*. Cullompton: Willan.

TRAVERS, M. (1997). 'Preaching to the Converted? Improving the Persuasiveness of Criminal Justice Research'. *British Journal of Criminology* 37: 359–77.

WADDINGTON, P. A. J. (1994). *Liberty and Order: Policing Public Order in a Capital City*. London: UCL Press.

—— (1999). *Policing Citizens*. London: UCL Press.

—— (2003). 'Policing Public Order and Political Contention' in T. Newburn (ed.), *Handbook of Policing*. Cullompton: Willan.

——, STENSON, K., and DON, D. (2004). 'In Proportion: Race and Police Stop and Search'. *British Journal of Criminology* 44: 889–914.

WAKEFIELD, A. (2003). *Selling Security: The Private Policing of Public Space*. Cullompton: Willan.

WALKER, N. (2000). *Policing in a Changing Constitutional Order*. London: Sweet & Maxwell.

WALKER, S. (2004). 'Science and Politics in Police Research'. *Annals of the American Academy of Political and Social Science* 593: 137–55.

WEATHERITT, M. (1985). *Innovations in Policing*. London: Croom Helm.

—— (1986). *Innovations in Policing*. London: Croom Helm.

—— (ed.) (1989). *Police Research: Some Future Prospects*. Aldershot: Avebury.

—— (ed.) (1998). *Zero Tolerance*. London: Police Foundation.

WEISBURD, D. and ECK, J. E. (2004). 'What can Police do to Reduce Crime, Disorder and Fear?' *Annals* 593: 42–65.

——, MASTROFSKI, S., McNALLY, A., GREENSPAN, R., and WILLIS, J. (2003).

'Reforming to Preserve: Compstat and Strategic Problem Solving in American Policing'. *Criminology and Public Policy* 2: 421–56.

WEITZER, R. (1995). *Policing Under Fire: Ethnic conflict and police-community relations in Northern Ireland*. Albany, NY: State University of New York Press.

WESTLEY, W. (1970). *Violence and the Police*. Cambridge, Mass.: MIT Press.

WESTMARLAND, L. (2001). *Gender and Policing*. Cullompton: Willan.

WHITAKER, B. (1964). *The Police*. London: Penguin.

WILKINSON, R. (2005). *The Impact of Inequality*. New York: New Press.

WILLIAMSON, T. (2000). 'Policing: The Changing Criminal Justice Context—Twenty-five Years of Missed Opportunities' in F. Leishman, B. Loveday, and S. P. Savage (eds), *Core Issues in Policing*. Harlow: Longman.

WILSON, J. Q. (1975). *Thinking About Crime*. New York: Vintage.

—— and KELLING, G. (1981). 'Broken Windows'. *Atlantic Monthly* 249: 29–42.

WRIGHT, A. (2002). *Policing: An Introduction to Concepts and Practice*. Cullompton: Willan.

YOUNG, J. (1986). 'The Failure of Criminology: The Need for a Radical Realism' in R. Matthews and J. Young (eds), *Confronting Crime*. London: Sage.

—— (1999). *The Exclusive Society*. London: Sage.

YOUNG, M. (1991). *An Inside Job*. Oxford: Oxford University Press.

—— (1993). *In the Sticks: An Anthropologist in a Shire Force*. Oxford: Oxford University Press.

ZEDNER, L. (2006). 'Policing Before the Police'. *British Journal of Criminology* 46: 78–96.

13

Research on the criminal courts

John Baldwin

Introduction

Since the first edition of this book was published, the climate in which empirical research on the criminal courts is pursued has significantly changed, partly as a result of the enactment in 2005 of the Freedom of Information Act. Moreover, there has been heightened public concern about justice for minority groups in the wake of the Macpherson Report concerned with the murder of Stephen Lawrence. In this second edition, I have taken the opportunity to address these matters and to examine the latest research. Although the basic structure of the essay remains unchanged, the chapter contains a new section on studies of discrimination and differential treatment. I have used the same case study, with its cautionary tale about the politics and ethics of research. It is true that those events happened many years ago and attitudes towards criminological research and researchers have undoubtedly changed in the meantime, but I believe that the lessons to be drawn remain pertinent.

The criminal courts present enticing opportunities to criminological researchers. Courts are fascinating institutions, the decisions they take are of undoubted public importance, and they sometimes provide scenes of high drama. Politicians frequently invest the courts with almost mystical powers, seeing them as occupying the front-line in the war on crime. For criminological researchers, the criminal courts have one great advantage over most other institutions within the criminal justice system: they are open to the public and no difficulties of access arise in observing them. Conducting research on the criminal courts need involve no more than turning up with a notebook, finding a convenient vantage point, and watching whatever takes place.

Although much can be learnt about the courts in this way, it will be argued in this chapter that court observation cannot in itself provide answers to many of the questions that one might wish to ask about the operation of the criminal courts. Many of these questions can only be explored with extreme difficulty. Indeed, there are certain no-go areas. It is not possible, for instance, to observe the way that sentencing decisions are reached, and researchers in this country are still prohibited by law from speaking to the people who sit on juries. More serious still, judges, lawyers, and other court personnel have proved in the past to be resistant, even downright hostile, to social research. Although attitudes may have softened somewhat in recent years, members of the senior judiciary in particular remain distinctly unenthusiastic about research, frequently viewing such endeavours as an unwarranted intrusion into matters that should be their business and no one else's.

For those of us conducting research in this climate in the past 30 years, the range of topics we have been able to examine has been severely limited and the methods we have been obliged to adopt have often been of necessity highly imperfect. Some projects have got off the ground only because researchers employed considerable ingenuity and inventiveness. Much of the research has a Heath Robinson feel to it, as researchers have devised imaginative strategies in order to overcome the access problems. Despite the recent thaw in judicial attitudes, there is no denying that studying the way that the criminal courts work remains a very tricky undertaking.

The criminal courts have, however, become more accessible to researchers. In part this is a reflection of the decline in the public standing of the courts following the many miscarriages of justice that were brought to light in the 1990s (Walker and Starmer 1993; Dennis 1993; McConville and Bridges 1994; Wasik, Gibbons, and Redmayne 1999: 563–71). One significant consequence of these revelations is that politicians and policy-makers have become more sceptical about accepting at face value what senior lawyers and judges say about how well the courts are functioning. The importance of research on the courts (and the criminal justice system in general) was acknowledged in the Royal Commission on Criminal Procedure (Philips 1981) and the Royal Commission on Criminal Justice (Runciman 1993). These Commissions, both of which were concerned with the operation of the criminal justice system, did much to change attitudes towards research. Both Royal Commissions launched extensive research programmes, opening up in the process many new opportunities for researchers. They elevated the role of academic research to new heights because they claimed to be basing many of their recommendations upon it. Although there have been many occasions on which policy change has seemed to fly in the face of research findings—and curtailment of the accused's right to remain silent is but one striking recent example (Sanders and Young 2000: 251–68; Bucke and Brown 2000)—it has nonetheless become much more common, since the Labour Government came to power in 1997, for major policy changes in the courts to be preceded by some form of evaluative exercise. Resistance to research persists in the criminal courts but times are changing. The present government's preoccupation with 'evidence-led' criminal justice policy has had the effect of providing unprecedented opportunities for criminologists. In part because of concerns that the state paymaster might be the one who calls the tune, however, some criminologists have embraced the prospects of securing the large sums of money on offer with greater enthusiasm than have others (Noaks and Wincup 2004: 26).

Describing the research experience

Although a much more professional approach to criminological research has been evident in recent years, people like myself who have been conducting criminological and related research for many years have often received precious little formal research training. I must confess that my own limited skills are in the main the result of long experience, a modicum of reading, and learning about research methods from others with whom I have collaborated. Many of us owe great debts of gratitude to Ph.D. supervisors and other colleagues who have offered advice about technical aspects of doing research and communicated their own enthusiasm for the research enterprise. This is, however, inevitably a hit-and-miss approach which tends to be reflected in the way we write about research. It is odd that, if one reads the methodology texts or research monographs, one forms only a limited impression of what it is like to carry out research. I am repeatedly struck by how scant is the information provided by many criminologists in their publications about the methods and the sampling procedures they have employed. If they bother to give such information at all, it is often relegated to a short paragraph, perhaps even to a footnote. The tendency is simply to state that 'interviews were conducted with a sample of . . .' or that 'questionnaires were distributed to . . .', and it is unusual for authors to present a copy of the questionnaires or the interview schedules they have used or to say much about the nature of the questions they have posed or the procedures they have followed. This makes critical evaluation of results extremely difficult, and most readers are, it seems, remarkably charitable in their willingness to take results on trust.

One might go further and argue that many criminologists present a misleading picture of the experience of conducting research because of their inclination to skate over the problems they have encountered. I have seen for myself how uneasy officials (whether they be practitioners, civil servants, or the representatives of funding bodies) become when researchers seek to report the details of discussions that were assumed to be off the record. This applies even when such exchanges have influenced the way that a study has been conducted or the form that a final report has taken. Given the limited published information available, it is not surprising that many people who start out on empirical research projects are taken aback when they run into difficulties that they could not have foreseen. Any researcher interested in criminal justice issues may find, for instance, that it takes months of painful and frustrating negotiation simply to get a project off the ground, if it gets off the ground at all. Even then, it may well prove impossible to conduct the study along the lines that were originally envisaged. Matters may become even more fraught when questions are raised about the publication of results. While organizations will usually tolerate critical research reports when they are kept private, many baulk at the prospect of public disclosure. There are, however, few descriptions of these common difficulties in the available literature.

Empirical and theoretical traditions

It would be misleading to imply that, because of the serious difficulties that arise in examining the work of the criminal courts, researchers have been put off studying them. Quite the opposite is true. Hundreds of criminological studies concerned with the operation of the criminal courts have been conducted in this country. But the character of this research has been increasingly determined by the interests of funding bodies rather than by researchers themselves. When surveying this huge number of disparate investigations, it is quickly apparent that most have been descriptive in nature, setting out to show how the courts (or, more accurately, particular aspects of courts' functions) operate in practice. There is nothing necessarily wrong with this since there is great public and political ignorance about the workings of the courts, and the legal mythology that surrounds them is remarkable for its endurance. But this emphasis on description, in a situation where the funding bodies increasingly call the shots, has meant that only half-hearted efforts have been made by researchers to develop theoretical perspectives in relation to the operation of the criminal courts.

Much court research in this country has been conducted in the context of an empirical and 'reformist' tradition (Low 1978) with issues examined primarily from a policy perspective. It is not difficult to understand why policy-relevant research is so much in the ascendancy. Since most of the funding for research on the criminal courts comes, directly or indirectly, from government sources, researchers have not on the whole been encouraged to engage in theoretical flights of fancy. In a discussion of the development of criminology in the 1980s, Jefferson and Shapland (1994: 268) note how, despite expansion in the size of the research community itself, financial and other pressures within the academic environment have led to the 'growth of "safe", narrowly-focused, policy-relevant research, and a decline in critical research'. This is still true today. Indeed, the tendency has become even more marked. The competition for government contracts (for which huge sums of money are often at stake), together with the pervasive pressures on university researchers to maintain a steady stream of publications to satisfy the requirements of Research Assessment Exercises, are generally enough to ensure that researchers toe the line. But, more fundamentally, funding bodies have become increasingly insistent that research on the courts be of direct value and relevance to court users and policymakers. It is, therefore, a sad, but perhaps inevitable, fact that the contours of criminological research on the courts reflect to a greater extent the demands of funding bodies, particularly when they are government departments, than the curiosity and the interests of researchers.

In so far as attempts have been made to develop theoretical perspectives on the workings of the criminal courts, three approaches which stand out as particularly promising and worthy of more sustained application may be briefly mentioned. First, variants of conflict theory have on occasion been used to explain why it is that the economically powerless are unlikely to receive a fair deal from state bureaucracies. It is suggested that courts and legal processes are likely only to reflect, reinforce, even to exacerbate inequalities and that the young, ethnic minorities, the unemployed, the dispossessed, and the poor (all of whom are over-represented amongst criminal defendants) are most likely to be disadvantaged in this situation (e.g. Box 1971; Sanders and Young 2000). Secondly, the traditional representation of the criminal process as concerned with establishing 'truth' has been challenged by authors (e.g. McBarnet 1976; McConville *et al.* 1991; Kalunta-Crumpton 1998) who see the 'truth' as being socially 'constructed' and refracted through the processes of 'interpretation, addition, subtraction, selection and reformulation' (McConville *et al.* 1991: 12). On this view, the facts of the prosecution's case are 'constructed' from competing and malleable accounts presented by the parties. Thirdly, the concept of 'court culture', originally developed in the United States (Church 1985), has been adapted to explain disparities in procedures and decision-making from court to court in this country (e.g. Rumgay 1995; Hucklesby 1997; Leverick and Duff 2002; Herbert 2004).

But such theoretical forays are rather uncommon in the literature on the criminal courts in this country. More pervasive is the large quantity of survey research that has been carried out, much of it simple fact-gathering. There is no disguising the fact that research on the criminal courts falls squarely within what Sanders (1997) has called 'administrative criminology'. It seeks in other words to provide management information primarily for use by members of the court bureaucracy, policymakers, administrators, and others to assist them in the running of the court system. The bulk of this work has emanated, directly or indirectly, from the Home Office, and even a cursory glance at the large number of Home Office reports published over the years reveals their prevailing character. Statistical tables tend to cover their pages. As many as thirty tables (or the pie charts and bar diagrams that have to some extent replaced tables) are by no means uncommon, even in short monographs. The analysis of results generally owes more to high-level statistics than to any underlying theoretical paradigm. In most of the reports, little attempt is made at assessment or criticism. An illustration of this stubbornly atheoretical approach is seen in the celebrated Crown Court study (Zander and Henderson 1993), an inquiry that was undertaken under the auspices of the Royal Commission on Criminal Justice. This was the most extensive study of the criminal courts ever undertaken in this country and was based upon thousands of self-completion questionnaires distributed to judges, prosecution and defence barristers, defence solicitors, crown prosecutors, police officers, court clerks, defendants, and members of juries. The authors make no bones about their intentions. 'It was agreed', Michael Zander writes in his introduction, 'that the report of the study would not include evaluation of the data nor recommendations. It would simply report the results' (page xvii). Like Mr Gradgrind in Dickens' *Hard Times*, the authors set out to present the facts: it is not their intention to seek to understand, explain, or assess, let alone engage in abstract or idle theoretical speculation.

Although there is a strong view within the criminological community that there are many advantages in conducting research that is closely aligned to the policy interests of government, there are nonetheless various problems that need to be recognized. In particular, issues tend to be viewed from the perspective of policymakers or court administrators rather than of those on the receiving end of judicial processes (Baldwin and Davis 2003). This raises an uncomfortable issue which is central in all criminological research: how have the 'problems' to be investigated by researchers been identified and defined? It is worth digressing to say something about this difficulty, and I shall illustrate it with reference to two of the studies in which I have participated myself. In the first (Baldwin and McConville 1977), Michael McConville and I were interested in the way that defendants in the Crown Court decided to plead guilty, and we raised doubts about the fairness of the pressures to which they were subject. We concluded that the rights of defendants were commonly infringed as efforts were made to induce them to plead guilty. We argued that the most potent pressure was exerted by defendants' own lawyers, whose arm was strengthened by the sentencing system itself. The emphasis in a good deal of the subsequent writing on this subject has, however, shifted from a preoccupation with defendants' rights to a concern about the administrative problems created by 'cracked trials', especially the way that court resources are wasted when defendants plead guilty after their cases have been listed for trial (see, further, Bredar 1992; Zander and Henderson 1993: 149–58; Royal Commission on Criminal Justice 1993: 110–14; Plotnikoff and Woolfson 1993; Auld 2001: 434–45; McConville 2002: 364–66). The important point here is that the vantage point from which 'problems' are observed and defined is critical in criminological research.

A further illustration of this difficulty emerged in a study that McConville and I conducted of the outcome of jury cases in the Crown Court (Baldwin and McConville 1979a). The question that the Home Office originally invited us to examine was whether the high rate of acquittal in the Crown Court (which was almost 50 per cent where defendants pleaded not guilty) could be justified and whether, as some prominent commentators (e.g. Sir Robert Mark 1973) were suggesting at the time, it was unreasonably high. We were, however, able to broaden the scope of the enquiry to include all jury cases and, in the final report, we expressed our concern about the numbers of wrongful convictions by juries (Baldwin and McConville 1979a: 68–87) which we viewed as a more serious evil than that of perverse acquittal. Ten years later, the revelations about the large number of miscarriages of justice, almost all of which had followed jury trials, provided an unmistakable indication that to examine the problems thrown up by juries exclusively in terms of unacceptably high acquittal rates would have been dangerously misconceived.

One might note, then, that a main difficulty with research that purports to be based on simple fact-gathering is that 'facts' are not unproblematic or self-evident realities. The 'truth' is not an objective reality waiting to be discovered but is critically influenced by those with the political power to define the nature of the 'problems' that need to be explored.

The existing research on the criminal courts

It is necessary in a chapter of this kind to delineate the main approaches that have been adopted in studying criminal courts. The following discussion is not intended to be a comprehensive review of this body of research literature (for which, see Sanders 1997; Sanders and Young 2000), and a good deal of important work will inevitably be overlooked. But it is worth attempting to identify the major landmarks in the available research on the courts and to offer a commentary on the main approaches that have been adopted. Six approaches, which do not fall neatly into watertight compartments, can be identified: the large-scale statistical surveys of courts and court users; studies concerned with 'demythologizing' criminal justice; observation of court hearings; research concerned with the pre-trial 'shaping' of cases for trial; studies of the deliberative processes of decision-makers, and the studies of discrimination, real and perceived, especially that relating to the differential treatment of people from minority ethnic backgrounds.

Statistical surveys of courts and court users

Studies are now regularly published on delays in hearing cases in the magistrates' courts; opinion polls are taken of public attitudes towards the courts and sentencers, and surveys are conducted of the reactions of court users to the standard of service provided by the courts. It is widely recognized that courts are daunting places for the uninitiated and simple consumer surveys can be very illuminating. The distinguished American scholar, Tom Church (1990: 7), once made the following perceptive observations about the low priority accorded to members of the public in the courts:

Most courts ... are organised for the convenience of judges, of court staff, and of lawyers; usually in that order. If the convenience of the public is considered at all, it comes well behind these courthouse 'regulars' ... Yet no consumer-oriented establishment could set its priorities in this way ... With the exception of the prison service and perhaps a few unrepentant social welfare organizations, I know of no organizations ... which appear to be quite as cavalier about their clientele as are the courts.

The significance of statistical surveys of court users, which are mainly carried out by the Court Service in England and Wales, should not be underestimated. The views of many thousands of respondents are systematically canvassed and much has been revealed about levels of consumer satisfaction with the service that the courts provide. In addition to these surveys, over twenty studies of the criminal courts have been published by the Home Office Research, Development and Statistics Directorate (or its forerunners). These reports deal with a great variety of questions, and the list includes—to pick a few publications on courts almost at random—studies of sentencing practices (Tarling 1979; Moxon 1988; Flood-Page and Mackie 1998); the efficacy of time limits in reducing the delays in bringing cases to trial (Morgan and Vennard 1989); mode of trial decisions (Riley and Vennard 1988; Hedderman and Moxon 1992); decisions to adjourn cases (Whittaker and Mackie 1997); and public attitudes to the courts and sentencing (Hough and Roberts 1998; Mattinson and Mirrlees-Black 2000; Chapman *et al.* 2002). Although there are inherent difficulties with policy-driven research, probably even the most grudging critic would recognize that much Home Office research has been very valuable. It is methodologically sophisticated, well informed by the relevant literature, and conducted on a larger scale than a lone researcher could possibly achieve. The esteem in which Home Office researchers are held within the criminological community is indicated by the fact that they are amongst the most frequently cited in the standard academic literature (see Cohn and Farrington 1998).

'Demythologizing' criminal justice

The many astounding revelations about miscarriages of justice of recent years led to much criticism of the criminal courts and a re-evaluation of their position within the criminal justice system. It is not, therefore, surprising that much research has sought to uncover malfunctioning in courts' operations. Many studies have indicated that a wide hiatus exists between high legal principle and the daily reality of the administration of justice in the courts—what Sanders (1997) has labelled 'gap' research. The truth is, as a generation of criminal justice researchers in this country has come to recognize, the operation of the criminal courts scarcely lives up to its own rhetoric. The criminal courts espouse certain inalienable rights and values, like the presumption of innocence, the right of the accused to be tried by a jury of peers, and the requirement that proof be established before an impartial tribunal beyond reasonable doubt. In the great majority of cases, however, these values appear to translate feebly into practice.

Research that seeks to 'demythologize' criminal justice has become a growth industry. Most of the relevant research has been highly critical in tone, as study after study has highlighted serious flaws in courts' operations. It is well established in this literature (summarized by Sanders and Young 2000: 483–549) that the criminal courts frequently do not work in the ways that the criminal law textbooks describe. Researchers have demonstrated, for example, in relation to the award of legal aid (e.g. Young *et al.* 1992), legal representation (e.g. McConville *et al.* 1994), the discontinuance of weak prosecution cases (e.g. Block *et al.* 1993; Baldwin 1997), bail (e.g. Brink and Stone 1988; Hucklesby 1997; Dhami 2004), mode of trial (e.g. Herbert 2004) and plea (e.g. Baldwin and McConville 1977; Baldwin 1985; McConville *et al.* 1994; Henham 2000, 2002) that the procedures adopted in the criminal courts fall far short of what one would expect from reading the standard legal texts. Rights of defendants, which are assumed to be absolute and non-negotiable, seem often to be based upon a very flimsy foundation indeed. The available evidence (e.g. Carlen 1976; McBarnet 1981) indicates that this disparity is likely to be even greater in magistrates' courts than in the Crown Court. 'It is no exaggeration to say', Sanders and Young (2000: 548) write, 'that magistrates' courts are crime control courts overlaid with a thin layer of due process icing'.

Observation of court hearings

Despite its immediate appeal, few criminologists have engaged in prolonged and systematic court observation. One would, for instance, be hard-pressed to find examples of this kind of research in the past ten years published in, say, the *British Journal of Criminology* and the *Howard Journal of Criminal Justice*—two mainstream British criminological journals. This is certainly not because such an approach is useless or subject to irremediable methodological flaws. Indeed, where researchers have troubled to spend time in the courts, the exercise has often produced considerable dividends. A number of studies— and some in the following list were conducted by doctoral students—were based in varying degrees upon court observation—by Bottoms and McClean (1976), Carlen (1976), McBarnet (1981), Darbyshire (1984), Rock (1993), Morgan and Russell (2000), Moore (2003), Herbert (2004) and Cammiss (2006). These are all outstanding examples of what can be achieved simply by watching the criminal courts in action. These studies have contributed in significant ways to an understanding of the influence of 'court culture' on decision-making and the importance of examining the relationships that exist between the various court actors. There have also been a number of other, small-scale but highly illuminating observational studies concerned with the way that complainants, especially those involved in rape trials, and other witnesses are treated in the courts (e.g. Adler 1982, 1987; Temkin 1987; Lees 1996).

Court observation can, however, be deceptively straightforward, and anyone who spends time in courtrooms quickly becomes aware of its drawbacks. The most obvious is that, whatever fascination courts may hold, they are nevertheless subject to lengthy periods of unrelenting tedium. Much of the business of the criminal courts is, as Bottoms and McClean (1976: 226) noted, 'dull, commonplace, ordinary and after a while downright tedious'. There are frequent periods in any court where little seems to be happening. Delays and adjournments dog the work of the courts, and the consequent administrative inertia can sap the energy and enthusiasm of even the most committed researcher. Furthermore, proceedings in courts can be extremely confusing. Much has been written about the sense of alienation that defendants experience as they confront legal processes and about the way that court procedures are much more closely attuned to the needs of the professionals than to those of defendants. The study by McConville *et al.* (1994), concerned with the organization of criminal defence practices, provides powerful evidence of this and forms part of an empirical tradition, dating back to the Bottoms and McClean study in the 1970s, which has drawn attention to the tendency of court professionals to take control of criminal cases, reducing defendants to such a passive and subsidiary position that they become malleable and acquiescent, prepared to accept the lawyer's view of matters and powerless themselves to influence the course of events. What is less often noted is that researchers are in a similar position to defendants. They are not consulted about decisions either, and they may feel a sense of exclusion, estrangement, and alienation that is comparable to that experienced by defendants. Researchers are seriously handicapped by being excluded from the significant action. Court procedures can in consequence be as baffling to them as to anyone else.

An even more serious problem with observational research is that open court proceedings present only the public face of justice. Researchers who sit in court commonly
realize, with a sense of unease, that the really important decisions in most cases are being
taken elsewhere. The sight of judges, jurors, and magistrates traipsing out of court to
consider decisions in the privacy of their retiring rooms is simply the most visible
manifestation of this. A much greater problem for researchers is that many crucial decisions are made by the parties even before the case reaches the courtroom. Much of what
happens in court is predetermined by what has happened at a number of earlier stages in
the criminal process, particularly by what has transpired in the police interrogation
room, in informal discussions between prosecution and defence lawyers (perhaps reinforced by what has happened at a pre-trial review or a Plea and Directions Hearing), or in
private exchanges between defendants and their lawyers. By the time most criminal cases
reach the courtroom, the script has already been written and agreed amongst the key participants, and the hearing itself is often concerned with little more than minor details of
the choreography. It is, then, at the pre-trial stages that cases are 'shaped' for the court,
and the result is that much judicial decision-making consists of little more than ratifying
decisions that have already been agreed between the parties in advance of the hearing.

The pre-trial 'shaping' of cases

This brings me to the fourth approach to the study of the criminal courts which involves
examining off-the-record decisions taken at the pre-trial stage. If we are to understand
decisions that are reached within the criminal courts, then the influence of pre-trial dealings needs to be taken into account. The crucial decision is the defendant's choice of
plea—a decision that is in practice just as likely to reflect the knowledge and bargaining
position of the parties as the strength of the prosecution's evidence. It has been increasingly acknowledged that judicial decision-making, including sentencing, is influenced by
the complex interplay of relations amongst various court actors and that the pre-trial
decisions taken by police officers, defence and prosecution lawyers, and defendants have
a critical bearing upon what happens in court. Although this point was made in the USA
half a century ago, it has taken a long time to dawn on researchers in this country. Any
understanding of the workings of the criminal courts is, however, incomplete without an
appreciation of the pre-trial processes that shape cases for trial.

It is important to recognize that, despite the rhetoric, the criminal justice system in this
country is a very efficient mechanism in generating a high level of guilty pleas (Baldwin
and McConville 1977; McConville *et al.* 1994). It is striking that, in many pre-trial discussions, criminal justice rhetoric is subverted and replaced by apparently diametrically
opposed values. Many years ago, Bottomley (1973: 84) presciently noted the paradox
that, whatever weight is attached to the principle of the presumption of innocence, 'once
a person has appeared in court facing a criminal charge many of the subsequent decisions
taken by the various parties concerned . . . often seem to be influenced rather by a principle of "assumption of guilt"'. While the common assumption in legal texts is that
defendants will plead not guilty and even be tried by a jury, jury trials are in practice a rare
exception. Only about one per cent of all the defendants eligible to be tried by jury are
ultimately tried in that way, and even that proportion is one that successive governments
in this country have sought to squeeze still further (Lloyd-Bostock and Thomas 2000:
89–90). Well over 90 per cent of defendants whose cases reach the criminal courts end up

pleading guilty, generally in the lower courts. In these circumstances, there is no contest, no testing of evidence, no calling of witnesses, and no open court adjudication. At the hearing itself, the prosecution's evidence tends to be dealt with only perfunctorily, and, instead of taking hours or even days to hear witnesses, cases are disposed of in a matter of minutes.

That such high proportions of defendants in the criminal courts plead guilty is extraordinary yet, until recently, scarcely merited even a mention in most legal textbooks. It would, however, be difficult to overstate the importance of the simple fact that the vast majority of defendants plead guilty. The profound legal, moral, and theoretical implications of the guilty plea continue to be the subject of debate. That so high a proportion of defendants plead guilty sometimes comes as a surprise to those unfamiliar with the subject and they ask how it can be that contested trials are so rare in courts that are committed to the principle of open court, adversarial contest. Yet pre-trial criminal procedures and the sentencing system in this country are specifically structured to induce defendants to plead guilty. The most potent pressure on defendants is the so-called discount principle in sentencing. This principle, which is well established and bolstered by a long line of decisions by the Court of Appeal—indeed now enshrined in statutory form in section 152 of the Consolidating Powers of the Criminal Courts (Sentencing) Act 2000—ensures that those who plead guilty receive a hefty reduction in their sentence. But being well established does not make the principle fair, and doubts continue to be expressed about the blanket application of the principle and whether it induces innocent as well as guilty people to plead guilty (Sanders and Young 2000: 398–436; Ashworth and Redmayne 2005: 275–96).

Formidable difficulties face researchers who seek to examine the way that guilty pleas are determined. I speak from personal experience here, and later in the chapter I shall present a case study to demonstrate how acute the difficulties can sometimes be. Guilty pleas are 'low visibility' decisions in that all the interesting exchanges take place off the record, often in hurried encounters in corridors outside the doors of the courts. As is clear from the mountain of literature on the vexed subject of 'plea bargaining' which has been amassed in the USA, guilty pleas are frequently determined in furtive bargaining sessions. Such dealings are often deliberately hidden, not just from public view but from that of the courts as well. So how can one possibly examine decisions of this kind where the participants themselves may well have an interest in keeping procedures strictly private?

There is probably no way that this can be done adequately, and researchers have had to make the best of the limited access that has been granted them. Almost thirty years ago, Michael McConville and I (Baldwin and McConville 1977) sought to examine these decisions simply by asking a sample of defendants (all of whom had indicated from the outset their wish to be tried by jury but pleaded guilty at the last minute) how they came to make what seemed on the surface a strange decision. This raises obvious methodological difficulties about whether one can accept what defendants say about their experiences, an issue which will be raised again later. In a subsequent study (Baldwin 1985), I was able to get closer to the negotiations between prosecution and defence lawyers when I was allowed to observe their exchanges (and to tape record them) at formal pre-trial reviews in the magistrates' courts. (The pre-trial review is a special procedure introduced in some courts to enable the lawyers to meet some weeks before trial to identify the issues likely to be in contention.) The exchanges between lawyers at pre-trial reviews in the magistrates' courts have also been the subject of subsequent research (Brownlee *et al.*1994; Mulcahy 1994).

No researcher has come closer to uncovering what happens in these pre-trial stages than McConville and his colleagues (1994) who persuaded forty-eight law firms throughout the country to allow them to 'shadow' solicitors as they went about their business and to observe the way they dealt with cases. Although direct observation of this kind is a time-consuming—and therefore expensive—exercise and one that is far from free from methodological problems of its own, the study nonetheless revealed much about solicitor–client interactions that could not have been uncovered by other methods. The portrayal of the criminal courts not 'as trial venues but as places where defendants can be processed through guilty pleas' (McConville *et al.* 1994: 210) has profound implications for the courts and the criminal justice system in general. The somewhat churlish complaint by Brown (1991: 108) that the sample of lawyers that was shadowed in the study was unrepresentative—when representativeness would be all but impossible to achieve in research of this kind—underlines the point that in criminological research there is a danger that even the most imaginative and revealing initiatives may be sacrificed on the high altar of an elusive methodological purity.

Studies of the deliberative processes of decision-makers

The clear implication of the above discussion is that it is simplistic, even misconceived, to view sentencing in the criminal courts in a vacuum, as if it were a stand-alone decision, uninfluenced by the way that cases are 'constructed' for trial. Sentencing decisions should be regarded as being contingent upon the way that cases are prepared for trial and examined within that broad context. The failure to do this in studies of sentencing disparities represents a significant weakness. A number of useful studies have, however, been concerned with decision-making in the courtroom, and, in this fifth category, researchers have been concerned to explore the deliberative procedures of judges, magistrates, and juries. Again, the problems that arise in studying such decision-making are formidable. As noted earlier, members of the senior judiciary in this country have generally been hostile to empirical research projects, tending in the past to regard requests to participate almost as an impertinence. But this has not meant that their decisions have not been subjected to research and, in several empirical studies, sentencing and the other decisions taken by magistrates and judges have been examined, albeit in an anonymous, statistical manner, not on a judge-by-judge basis (Hood 1962, 1992; Tarling 1979, 2006; Hedderman and Moxon 1992; Moxon and Hedderman 1994; Flood-Page and Mackie 1998; Henham 2001) or else in experimental settings (Gilchrist and Blissett 2002; Davies and Tyrer 2003; Davies *et al.* 2004; Kibble 2005a, 2005b; Lloyd-Bostock 2006). It is, however, somewhat curious that the question of sentencing disparities (in terms of race, gender, and type of courts), which has preoccupied a generation of researchers in the USA, has been largely neglected in this country. With the notable exception of the almost single-handed efforts of Roger Hood (1962, 1972, 1992), virtually all the substantial statistical research on sentencing disparities in this country has been done by researchers within the Home Office. A massive Home Office study on race and sentencing has been under discussion for over two years with tenders being invited for the project in 2004 but, at the time of writing in late 2006, no decision had been taken about whether the study would go ahead or not. Another large-scale study of sentencing was also put out to tender by the Home Office in 2004 and it has taken almost two years for a decision to be made to award the contract to researchers at the University of Cambridge.

Those researchers who have tried to go beyond the statistics and talk directly to judges have generally been frustrated. The illuminating case study provided by Ashworth *et al.* (1984) gives a good indication of the depth of judicial resistance to such exercises. Yet this distaste for research has not altogether prevented criminologists from involving sentencers in their inquiries, although it has invariably been lay magistrates rather than professional judges who have participated. One approach has been to interview samples of magistrates about the way they go about sentencing, and at least half a dozen studies have involved such interviews (see Burney 1979; Eaton 1986; Parker *et al.* 1989; Brown 1991; Rumgay 1995; and Flood-Page and Mackie 1998). As Parker *et al.* (1989: 39) argue, it is possible to 'get to the heart of the sentencing decision directly and immediately' by speaking to magistrates, and they were able in their study to use interviews with magistrates to develop arguments about the imperviousness of sentencing decisions to outside control. In a similar way, Rumgay (1995: 203) used the material she collected from extended interviews with magistrates to find out about 'the traditions and perspectives which guided the collective decision making of this disparate group of [magistrates]' and she drew a number of conclusions about the influence of 'court culture' on local sentencing patterns. It is noteworthy that several of these studies have indicated how the private views and attitudes of lay magistrates may run counter to the spirit of legislation and be reflected in sentencing decisions.

If researchers have experienced difficulties in examining the decisions taken by sentencers, these are slight when compared to the problems that arise in studying the operation of the jury system. Although a very important study has been undertaken in New Zealand which involved extensive interviews with members of juries to find out how they reached their decisions (Young *et al.* 1998; see also Findlay 2001), such a study would certainly not be possible in this country. Members of juries remain out of bounds to researchers since they are actually prohibited by law from revealing the secrets of the jury room to researchers or anyone else. Section 8 of the Contempt of Court Act 1981 states that 'it is a contempt of court to obtain, disclose or solicit any particulars of statements made, opinions expressed, arguments advanced or votes cast by members of a jury in the course of their deliberations'. Despite all the efforts that have been made to have this law changed, little willingness to give ground has been apparent. Lord Justice Auld (2001: 166), in his review of the criminal courts, for example, expressed 'grave doubt whether about intrusive research of the sort requiring amendment of the 1981 Act would be wise'. And, following a consultation exercise conducted by the Department for Constitutional Affairs (2005a), it was concluded that

[t]he Government is not opposed to amending section 8 of the Contempt of Court Act but does not believe that this should be done until there are specific and detailed questions to be answered that cannot be investigated without altering statute (Department for Constitutional Affairs 2005b: 16).

Resistance to jury research in this country is deep-rooted and difficult to explain. It is sometimes argued that we are better off not knowing how juries reach their decisions, whether they behave rationally, or whether they understand what is going at all. Some writers (e.g. Devons 1965) have even suggested that if jury deliberations were to be subjected to rigorous scrutiny, the institution would not survive. Limited dispensation has, it is true, occasionally been granted to researchers (see, e.g., Zander and Henderson 1993; Matthews *et al.* 2004) to allow them to make contact with jurors but these studies have had to skirt delicately round the question of decision-making in individual cases.

Despite the severe restrictions imposed on researchers in this country, numerous studies of jury decision-making have nonetheless been conducted (see the summaries provided by Baldwin and McConville 1979a: 4–19; Darbyshire *et al.* 2001; and Young 2003). A number of imaginative, if limited, approaches have been adopted, including re-enactments of jury trials in front of 'simulated' juries (Sealy and Cornish 1973a, 1973b; Lloyd-Bostock 2000; Finch and Munro 2005); the employment of 'shadow' volunteers to sit almost literally alongside the real jury in the courtroom (McCabe and Purves 1974; McConville 1991); and the examination of other participants' comments on the validity of juries' verdicts (Zander 1974; Baldwin and McConville 1979a; Zander and Henderson 1993: 162–72). Much of this work illustrates the point that, with sufficient ingenuity, no legal institution is truly beyond the reach of research.

Studies of discrimination and the differential treatment of ethnic minorities

The focus of recent research on the criminal courts has shifted somewhat in the past five years, reflecting government concerns following the publication in 1999 of Sir William Macpherson's report on the circumstances surrounding the murder of the black teenager, Stephen Lawrence—a racist killing in which the response of criminal justice agencies was the subject of much comment and criticism. The significant observation made in the British Crime Survey (Mirrlees-Black 2001: 3) that '[e]thnic minorities ... are less confident [than are white people] that the criminal justice system respects the rights of, or treats fairly, people accused of committing a crime' also provided considerable impetus to these developments. In the Macpherson (1999) report, a key recommendation was that a responsibility should be placed on all public bodies to review the way they treat people from minority ethnic backgrounds—a recommendation which has been taken extremely seriously in official circles. The Home Office has explicitly stated that it has 'accepted Sir William Macpherson's recommendation that it should be a ministerial priority to increase the trust and confidence in policing amongst minority ethnic communities' and it now engages in what it calls 'specific monitoring and informative assessment' on a systematic basis (Home Office 1999: ii). The Department for Constitutional Affairs has also launched a Courts and Diversity Research Programme, the agenda of which is 'specifically dedicated to examining whether, and to what extent, the court system deals fairly and justly with the needs of a diverse and multicultural society'.

In the first phase of this latter programme, four pieces of research were conducted, all of which focused in one way or another upon the question of discrimination within the court system. In what was perhaps the most important of these studies, Shute *et al.* (2005) examined perceptions of fairness and trust in the criminal justice system amongst defendants from minority ethnic backgrounds. Two other studies in this programme relevant to the criminal courts have since been conducted, one dealing with the experiences of lay magistrates from minority ethnic backgrounds (Vennard *et al.* 2004), the other by Lloyd-Bostock and Thomas, which is in train at the time of writing and concerned with ethnic diversity and the jury system. It is well known that, as court users, members of minority ethnic communities are less likely than are members of the white population to be satisfied with the treatment that they receive in court (White Paper 2002: 119) and, although some researchers have found that Asian and African-Caribbean defendants are dealt with more severely by the courts than are white defendants, the research conducted by Shute *et al.* (2005) painted a far less gloomy picture than might have been anticipated. They concluded that 'there appears to be much less evidence of perceived unfairness and a higher level of confidence among ethnic minority defendants and witnesses than was believed to exist by commentators writing a decade or so ago' (Shute *et al.* 2005: 92).

A case study in the politics and ethics of research

I have argued that, in order to understand how courts work, it is not enough simply to observe what happens in open court because so many decisions are determined by the various actors in the pre-trial stages. It is worth examining in greater detail some of the consequences for researchers who seek to investigate the controversial issue of plea nego-tiation in the criminal courts and to consider the trouble that can ensue when they insist on writing about their findings. In the mid-1970s, Michael McConville and I explored this issue in the Birmingham Crown Court, and, in the process, raised doubts about pro-cedures commonly adopted at that time in Crown Courts. We were particularly con-cerned that undue pressures were exerted upon defendants to induce them to plead guilty, and we argued that some innocent defendants were persuaded to plead guilty in court as a result of these pressures. As comparatively young men at the time, McConville and I were ill-prepared for the concerted attack that was launched on our report. It may be instructive to consider our experience as a case study of the pressures to which crim-inological researchers may on occasion be subject.

In a project that was funded by the Home Office, McConville and I were examining the outcome of jury trials in the Birmingham Crown Court. We were, however, frequently frustrated because many of the cases that the court authorities had predicted would be jury trials ended abruptly with defendants pleading guilty at the doors of the court, min-utes before the trial was due to start. As an adjunct to our jury study, we decided to try to find out why this was happening. We could not talk to the barristers concerned because the Senate of the Bar, after prolonged but fruitless negotiations with us, had refused to allow individual barristers to participate in any aspect of our enquiry. We interviewed 121 defendants who had been involved in last-minute changes of plea and asked them how they had reached what seemed on the surface a strange decision. The replies we received took us by surprise. With remarkable consistency, the defendants (including a minority who claimed to be innocent of the charges they faced) told us how they had been caught up in various out-of-court deals and how a variety of pressures had been exerted upon them, in the main by their own barristers, to persuade them to plead guilty. It seemed to us that we had stumbled upon the underhand, even shabby, side of the administration of criminal justice, at variance with textbook descriptions of criminal trials in England. Since the subject of plea negotiation had scarcely been raised in the relevant literature in this country (unlike the situation in the USA), we decided to write a book about this aspect of the research.

To say that this book was unwelcome would be a great understatement. It was considered bad form in many quarters even to raise the subject of plea negotiation, let alone discuss it in print. Months before publication of our results, McConville and I found ourselves on the receiving end of a ferocious public attack, and we became extremely unpopular amongst senior members of the legal profession and the judiciary—years later, Lord Bingham (1993: 323) described us as being 'the legal equivalent of Salman Rushdie'. In the course of the assault that was launched against us, we were subject to intense pressure from the Bar, the Law Society, and the Home Office to shelve the idea of publication of the book. For over three months, senior members of the legal profession conducted a well-orchestrated campaign in the media intended both to discredit the report (at that stage in draft form) and to raise doubts about our competence and integrity as academic researchers (Baldwin and McConville 1979b).

The first signs of trouble were evident in May 1977 after we had distributed a confidential draft of our report, *Negotiated Justice*, to interested parties for comment some months before publication. Details of our results were leaked to the *Sunday Express*, and its front-page headline, 'Do-a-deal barristers in law row', sparked off the controversy. I still remember well the sense of shock at the hostility shown by senior members of the legal profession. Sir David Napley, who was at that time the President of the Law Society and a member of the steering group appointed to advise on the research, appeared on television on the Monday evening following the *Sunday Express* leak to denounce the study. The then Chairman of the Bar went into print and dismissed the study as 'a compilation of unsubstantiated anecdotes' and as being no more than 'the tittle-tattle of the cells'. The Senate of the Bar wrote to the Home Secretary urging him to discourage publication of the book which, it was said, would be 'directly contrary to the public interest'. The Chairman of the Criminal Bar Association went even further and, in a front-page article in the *Guardian Gazette* (a leading journal for legal practitioners), accused us of being in breach of our contract with the Home Office and of breaking guarantees of confidentiality—slurs that were subsequently retracted and for which a public apology was made. The Home Secretary, who had made a lengthy statement later in May 1977 about our draft report in the House of Commons, contacted the Vice-Chancellor in our University, the late Lord Hunter, to warn him of the serious consequences to the University if the book were to be published.

Michael McConville and I, in the company of our Dean, were immediately summoned to a meeting with the Vice-Chancellor, and I can still recall with grim clarity the discussion in his gloomy room. He warned us of the risks of any precipitate move on our part to publish controversial findings of this kind. He instructed us that we were not to go ahead with publication until he had conducted an enquiry within the University to satisfy himself that the study was sound and that the conclusions drawn were reasonably based. He said that he had already contacted three Emeritus Professors and asked them to read the draft report and to comment on it. In the meantime, we were told to have no contact with the press and not to respond to any further attacks upon the study. McConville and I then had to wait for several weeks for the inquiry to be completed. It goes without saying that this was a period of great anxiety because we felt that our University careers were in the balance. In the event, the Vice-Chancellor announced that we had been 'vindicated' by the committee's inquiry and that we could after all go ahead with publication. He volunteered, albeit with subsequent misgivings, to contribute a Foreword to the book.

The point of this lengthy description is not to rake over old embers of something that happened many years ago, nor to gloat over a modest moral victory, still less to experience any frisson of pleasure from retelling a cautionary tale about the risks of engaging in criminological research. The main lesson to be derived from this experience—a lesson that is still relevant—is that seeking to challenge powerful vested interests within the judicial system is a dangerous blood sport and a determination to publish unpalatable results a high-risk activity. Seeking to tell it 'as it is' may sound fine in the methodological texts but it can prove a painful and costly undertaking, and any researcher who wishes to do so can expect to win few friends or accolades. He or she may, indeed, find that the going gets extremely tough, and public criticism, even public vilification, may be the price that has to be paid if a critical report is to see the light of day.

The sociopolitical climate in which criminological research is now conducted is, of course, very different from the research climate of the late-1970s. Almost three decades after the event, it is hard to believe that the publication of what would doubtless now be regarded as a rather innocuous academic monograph would provoke such ire from government ministers, senior judges, and leaders of the legal profession. The series of miscarriages of justice in the 1980s and 1990s, two Royal Commissions on criminal justice, and the accumulation of a huge quantity of critical research materials have made us all more sceptical about accepting claims from judges and lawyers about the operation of our criminal justice processes. Furthermore, the Freedom of Information Act, which came into force in January 2005, offers a radically different perspective to criminological researchers. Whereas researchers in the past were frequently thwarted by officials who were much more inclined to cover up than to open up, the Freedom of Information Act allows anyone to request information from a public authority and, if the public authority holds that information, to have it communicated to them. In February 2006, the Lord Chancellor described the introduction of the new Act as 'a constitutionally significant moment, comparable to reforms such as the incorporation of the European Convention on Human Rights into British law' and, although it would be naive to take at face value his claim that the Act replaces 'the opaque, secret, obstructive "need to know" with an open, transparent, statutory—and enforceable—"right to know" ', the Act nonetheless provides a telling indication of how much the political circumstances in which criminological researchers now work differ from those that confronted us 30 years ago.

But one should be wary of assuming that things have changed greatly since those days. One should certainly not think that threats, public vilification, the suppression of research findings, legal action and the like no longer occur. Criminological researchers in this country continue to experience all of these. Political interference in research remains common, and researchers who appear intransigent in the face of a sponsor's criticisms may well find that the prospects of securing future funding quickly evaporate. The consequences to those whose research proves politically unpalatable can be much more serious than this. Two researchers from the LSE have, for instance, recently reported how they were subjected to a 'torrent of high-profile attacks' from government ministers from the Home Secretary down when carrying out an assessment of the costs of Government plans to introduce identity cards (Davies and Hosein 2006). They describe the slurs, intimidation, and 'unrelenting bullying and vilification' that they encountered over an eight-month period. The authors were, incidentally, also very critical of the lack of support offered to them by members of the academic community when they were under fire.

Israel (2004: 733) has provided a long list of examples of similar experiences drawn from this country and elsewhere. He even notes a few cases where those conducting criminological research have landed up in prison. These are of course thoroughly disagreeable experiences and when they are combined with the serious risks that many criminologists run by working in potentially dangerous environments and dealing with volatile individuals, it supports one obvious conclusion: conducting criminological research remains for many a sensitive and high-risk enterprise that can seriously damage your health.

The easy option is of course to seek to reach an accommodation with critics, and, if a compromise can be reached without sacrifice of principle, then this is vastly preferable to confrontation. But in my experience this rarely is possible, and, to the extent that attempts at appeasement involve the watering down or removal of offending passages in a report, the researcher's own independent status will be violated. Appeasement will undoubtedly smooth the path to publication (and there are in the standard literature an unknown number of reports that have been emasculated in this way) but such a course quickly becomes self-defeating. It is my strong conviction that, unless researchers are prepared to resist the pressures that inhibit the free publication of results, whatever the personal costs entailed, they should not be in the business of conducting academic research. This is not to say that interested parties should be denied an opportunity to comment on the contents of draft reports. On the contrary, they have a right to do so, and researchers have a duty to pay careful heed to points that are made and, if need be, to amend drafts accordingly. However, it is vital, even axiomatic, that the content of any final report should be the researcher's responsibility and no one else's and that all pressure to discourage the publication of results be firmly resisted. But it is also axiomatic that those who are criticized in research reports have themselves an absolute right to respond, and to do so publicly if they wish. For some researchers, acrimonious public debate, in the press and in a TV studio, is as much part of the hurly-burly of academic writing as coping with unfavourable reviews and hostile rejoinders.

The experience of being on the rough end of criticisms from politicians, senior members of government, the legal profession, and judiciary is a forceful reminder that acute ethical dilemmas inevitably confront professional criminologists. While there used to be very little ethical guidance on offer from any quarter, academic researchers worth their salt nowadays are very much alive to the fact that ethical difficulties are endemic in the research enterprise. And even if they are not, then the networks of ethics committees in their universities (which have been set up to vet the research proposals of their members) will quickly draw to their attention the requirement that nothing must be done that might lead to embarrassment for the institution. In addition, a number of professional bodies have promulgated codes of practice, the three-page 'Code of Ethics for Researchers in the Field of Criminology' issued by the British Society of Criminology in 2003 being an important recent example.

Yet it is probably true to say that the moral dilemmas and choices that inevitably confront researchers are not much easier to solve than they were 30 years ago. For example, I remember finding it extremely difficult—and still do—to respond convincingly to the argument that was put forward by senior members of the Bar that Michael McConville and I, having claimed to have uncovered instances of serious miscarriage of justice, ought to reveal the identities of the individuals concerned so that matters could be rigorously investigated. The resolution of issues of this kind remains far from being clear-cut and, when confronted by them, researchers are, it seems, offered precious little guidance, whether from codes of practice or from any other source. While all professional criminologists would no doubt agree that the confidentiality of materials must be guaranteed and that respondents must be assured that their anonymity will be respected, other questions commonly arise where one cannot be so certain. Is a researcher justified, for instance, in being less than candid with respondents about the objectives of a study, knowing that full disclosure is likely to produce guarded, even distorted, responses? Is covert research permissible where seeking permission would have detrimental consequences for the study? Is a researcher ever justified in betraying confidences in order to prevent injustice, harm, injury to others, etc., say, by revealing information to the authorities about what they have observed or been told? Does the moral injunction that we do not distress, annoy, or embarrass participating organizations or individuals extend to the preparation and publication of critical reports? It is immediately clear that, while codes of conduct are helpful in resolving many ethical dilemmas and problems, they do not by any means solve all of them (Nicolson 2005). The second paragraph of the revised Code of Ethics produced in 2006 by the British Society of Criminology, for example, makes it clear that its guidelines provide 'a framework of principles', not 'a prescription for the resolution of choices or dilemmas surrounding professional conduct in specific circumstances'. In many situations, then, the resolution of ethical problems is bound to be a matter for the researcher's own conscience. As Israel (2004: 734) rightly notes, 'most of these decisions have been made quietly, with considerable difficulty and, perhaps, with little support from peers, in the face of conflicting and sometimes ambiguous advice from professional associations'.

Conclusion

Published reports almost invariably provide simpler, tidier, and more straightforward accounts of the research process than that experienced by criminologists in the field. By the time of publication, the creases have usually been ironed out of reports and the dog-fights that have taken place suppressed or forgotten. For a variety of personal and professional reasons, criminological researchers tend to be reticent about describing the problems that have arisen in the course of their investigations. Indeed, there are few accounts in the standard literature of the kind of problems that any researcher is likely to face in seeking to examine politically sensitive issues or to publish unpopular or unpalatable results.

Those of us who have had long experience of conducting research in and around the courts know something of these problems. In addition, we know how tiresome it can be to negotiate access and how disagreeable it is to encounter the hostility of certain groups to the very notion of 'research'. We have also experienced at first hand the drudgery that is involved in much academic research, the long hours spent sitting on hard benches in courts, the frustrations of wasted days, and the confrontations with disgruntled respondents. And we have found that in the end there is no guarantee whatsoever that our efforts will be applauded. Worse still, many of us have had to confront intractable problems at the publication stage and have come to accept how tough life can get when we become subject to insidious pressures to soften or distort the tenor of our findings.

This is, however, the bleak side of criminological research and, as someone who has devoted a substantial part of his working life to conducting empirical research—and earned a reasonable living by doing so—I would not in any way wish to present a picture of academic research that is negative or off-putting. There are many tangible and intangible benefits and privileges attached to conducting academic research, and for my part I have found it to be a uniquely satisfying and worthwhile activity. Criminological researchers are justified in being proud of what they do and of what they can achieve, and they are entitled to be gratified in knowing that their work is read and, on occasion, quoted. Those who have shared this experience also appreciate the fiercely addictive character of academic research and the genuine sense of excitement that attends the discovery of new knowledge.

Suggestions for further reading

Too little attention is usually paid to methodological issues in published accounts of research on the criminal courts. The following sources contain methodological discussions which are likely to be of interest to would-be researchers.

ASHWORTH, A., GENDERS, E., MANSFIELD, G., PEAY, J., and PLAYER, E. (1984). *Sentencing in the Crown Court*. Occasional Paper No 10. University of Oxford. Oxford: Centre for Criminological Research.

BALDWIN, J., and DAVIS, G. (2003). 'Empirical Research in Law' in P. Cane and M. Tushnet (eds), *The Oxford Handbook of Legal Studies*. Oxford: Oxford University Press.

BRITISH JOURNAL OF CRIMINOLOGY (2001) Vol. 41 No. 3—Special Issue: Methodological Dilemmas of Research.

JEFFERSON, T. and SHAPLAND, J. (1994). 'Criminal Justice and the Production of Order and Control: Criminological Research in the UK in the 1980s'. *British Journal of Criminology* 34: 265–90.

McCONVILLE, M. and WILSON, G. (eds) (2002). *The Handbook of The Criminal Justice Process*. Oxford: Oxford University Press.

NOAKS, L. and WINCUP, E. (2004). *Criminological Research: Understanding Qualitative Methods*. London: Sage.

SANDERS, A. (1997). 'Criminal Justice: The Development of Criminal Justice Research in Britain' in P. A.Thomas (ed.), *Socio-Legal Studies*. Aldershot: Dartmouth.

References

ADLER, Z. (1982). 'Rape—The Intention of Parliament and the Practice of the Courts'. *Modern Law Review* 45: 664–75.

—— (1987). *Rape on Trial*. London: Routledge & Kegan Paul.

ASHWORTH, A., GENDERS, E., MANSFIELD, G., PEAY, J., and PLAYER, E. (1984). *Sentencing in the Crown Court*. Occasional Paper No 10, University of Oxford. Oxford: Centre for Criminological Research.

Ashworth, A. and Redmayne, M. (2005). *The Criminal Process* (3rd edn). Oxford: Oxford University Press.

Auld, Lord Justice (2001). *Review of the Criminal Courts.* London: The Stationery Office.

Baldwin, J. (1985). *Pre-Trial Justice: A Study of Case Settlement Procedures in Magistrates' Courts.* Oxford: Blackwells.

—— (1997). 'Understanding Judge Ordered and Directed Acquittals in the Crown Court'. *Criminal Law Review* 536–55.

—— and Davis, G. (2003). 'Empirical Research in Law' in P. Cane and M. Tushnet (eds), *The Oxford Handbook of Legal Studies.* Oxford: Oxford University Press.

—— and McConville, M. (1977). *Negotiated Justice.* London: Martin Robertson.

—— and —— (1979a). *Jury Trials.* Oxford: Clarendon Press.

—— and —— (1979b). 'Plea Bargaining and Plea Negotiation in England'. *Law and Society Review* 13: 287–307.

Bingham, Lord (1993). 'Twenty-Five Years of the Institute of Judicial Administration'. *Civil Justice Quarterly* 12: 322–5.

Block, B. P., Corbett, C., and Peay, J. (1993). *Ordered and Directed Acquittals in the Crown Court.* Royal Commission on Criminal Justice, Research Study No 15. London: HMSO.

Bottomley, A. K. (1973). *Decisions in the Penal Process.* London: Martin Robertson.

Bottoms, A. E. and McClean, J. D. (1976). *Defendants in the Criminal Process.* London: Routledge & Kegan Paul.

Box, S. (1971). *Deviance, Reality and Society.* New York: Holt, Rinehart & Winston.

Bredar, J. K. (1992). 'Moving Up the Day of Reckoning: Strategies for Attacking the "Cracked Trials" Problem'. *Criminal Law Review* 153–9.

Brink, B. and Stone, C. (1988). 'Defendants Who Do Not Ask For Bail'. *Criminal Law Review* 152–62.

British Journal of Criminology (2001). Vol. 41 No. 3—Special Issue: Methodological Dilemmas of Research.

British Society of Criminology (2006). *Code of Ethics for Researchers in the Field of Criminology.* London: British Society of Criminology.

Brown, D. (1997). *PACE Ten Years On: A Review of the Research.* Home Office Research Study 155, London: HMSO.

Brown, S. (1991). *Magistrates At Work.* Milton Keynes: Open University Press.

Brownlee, I. D., Mulcahy, A., and Walker, C. P. (1994). 'Pre-Trial Reviews, Court Efficiency and Justice: A Study in Leeds and Bradford Magistrates' Courts'. *Howard Journal of Criminal Justice* 33: 109–24.

Bucke, T. and Brown, D. (2000). *The Right of Silence: The Impact of the CJPO 1994.* Home Office Research Study 199. London: Home Office.

Burney, E. (1979). *J.P.: Magistrate, Court and Community.* London: Hutchinson.

Cammiss, S. (2006). ' "I will in a Moment Give You the Full History": Mode of Trial, Prosecutorial Control and Partial Accounts'. *Criminal Law Review* 38–51.

Carlen, P. (1976). *Magistrates' Justice.* London: Martin Robertson.

Chapman, B., Mirrlees-Black, C., and Brawn C. (2002). *Improving Public Attitudes to the Criminal Justice System: The Impact of Information.* Home Office Research Study 245. London: Home Office.

Church, T. (1985). 'Examining Local Legal Culture'. *American Bar Foundation Research Journal* 3: 449–518.

—— (1990). *A Consumer's Perspective on the Courts.* Melbourne, Australia: Institute of Judicial Administration Incorporated.

Cohn, E. G. and Farrington, D. P. (1998). 'Changes in the Most-Cited Scholars in Major International Journals between 1986–90 and 1991–95'. *British Journal of Criminology* 38: 156–70.

DARBYSHIRE, P. (1984). *The Magistrates' Clerk*. Chichester: Barry Rose.

——, MAUGHAN, A., and STEWART, A. (2001). 'What Can We Learn From Published Jury Research? Findings for the Criminal Courts Review 2001'. *Criminal Law Review* 970–79.

DAVIES, M. and TYRER, J. (2003). ' "Filling in the Gaps"—A Study of Judicial Culture'. *Criminal Law Review* 243–65.

——, TAKALA, J-P and TYRER, J. (2004). 'Sentencing Burglars and Explaining the Differences Between Jurisdictions: Implications for Convergence'. *British Journal of Criminology* 44: 741–58.

DAVIES S. and HOSEIN, G. (2006). 'Hang together—or we will hang separately'. *Times Higher Education Supplement* 17 February 2006.

DENNIS, I. (1993). 'Miscarriages of Justice and the Law of Confessions: Evidentiary Issues and Solutions'. *Public Law* 291–313.

DEPARTMENT FOR CONSTITUTIONAL AFFAIRS (2005a). *Jury Research and Impropriety*. Consultation Paper CP 04/05. London: Department for Constitutional Affairs.

—— (2005b). *Jury Research and Impropriety: Response to Consultation CP 04/05*. London: Department for Constitutional Affairs.

DEVONS, E. (1965). 'Serving as a Juryman in Britain'. *Modern Law Review* 28: 561–70.

DHAMI, M. K. (2004). 'Conditional Bail Decision Making in the Magistrates' Court'. *Howard Journal of Criminal Justice*: 43: 27–43.

EATON, M. (1986). *Justice for Women?* Milton Keynes: Open University Press.

FINCH, E. and MUNRO, V. E. (2005). 'Juror Stereotypes and Blame Attribution in Rape Cases Involving Intoxicants'. *British Journal of Criminology* 45: 25–38.

FINDLAY, M. (2001). 'Juror Comprehension and Complexity: Strategies to Enhance Understanding'. *British Journal of Criminology* 41: 56–76.

FLOOD-PAGE, C. and MACKIE, A. (1998). *Sentencing Practice: An Examination of Decisions in Magistrates' Courts and the Crown Court in the mid-1990s*. Home Office Research Study 180. London: HMSO.

GILCHRIST, E. and BLISSETT, J. (2002). 'Magistrates' Attitudes to Domestic Violence and Sentencing'. *Howard Journal of Criminal Justice* 41: 348–63.

HEDDERMAN, C. and MOXON, D. (1992). *Magistrates' Court or Crown Court? Mode of Trial Decisions and Sentencing*. Home Office Research Study 125. London: HMSO.

HENHAM, R. (2000). 'Reconciling Process and Policy: Sentence Discounts in the Magistrates' Courts'. *Criminal Law Review* 436–51.

—— (2001). 'Sentencing Dangerous Offenders: Policy and Practice in the Crown Court'. *Criminal Law Review* 693–711.

—— (2002). 'Further Evidence on the Significance of Plea in the Crown Court'. *Howard Journal of Criminal Justice* 41: 151–66.

HERBERT, D. (2004). 'Mode of Trial and the Influence of Local Justice'. *Howard Journal of Criminal Justice* 43: 65–78.

HOME OFFICE (1999). *Statistics on Race and the Criminal Justice System*. London: Home Office.

HOOD, R. (1962). *Sentencing in Magistrates' Courts*. London: Stevens.

—— (1972). *Sentencing the Motoring Offender*. London: Heinemann.

—— (1992). *Race and Sentencing*. Oxford: Clarendon Press.

HOUGH, M. and ROBERTS, J. (1998). *Attitudes to Punishment: Findings from the British Crime Survey*. Home Office Research Study 179. London: HMSO.

HUCKLESBY, A. (1997). 'Court Culture: An Explanation of Variations in the Use of Bail by Magistrates' Courts'. *Howard Journal of Criminal Justice* 36: 129–45.

ISRAEL, M. (2004). 'Strictly Confidential? Integrity and the Disclosure of Criminological and Socio-Legal Research'. *British Journal of Criminology* 14: 715–40.

JEFFERSON, T. and SHAPLAND, J. (1994). 'Criminal Justice and the Production of Order and Control: Criminological Research in the UK in the 1980s'. *British Journal of Criminology* 34: 265–90.

KALUNTA-CRUMPTON, A. (1998). 'The Prosecution and Defence of Black Defendants in Drug Trials: Evidence of Claims-Making'. *British Journal of Criminology* 38: 561–91.

KIBBLE, N. (2005a). 'Judicial Perspectives on the Operation of s. 41 and the Relevance of Admissibility of Prior Sexual History Evidence: Four Scenarios'. *Criminal Law Review* 190–205.

—— (2005b). 'Judicial Discretion and the Admissibility of Prior Sexual History Evidence under section 41 of the Youth Justice and Criminal Evidence Act 1999: Sometimes Sticking to your Guns means Shooting Yourself in the Foot'. *Criminal Law Review* 263–74.

LEES, S. (1996). *Carnal Knowledge: Rape on Trial*. London: Hamish Hamilton.

LEVERICK, F. and DUFF, P. (2002). 'Court Culture and Adjournments in Criminal Cases: A Tale of Four Courts'. *Criminal Law Review* 39–52.

LOW, C. (1978). 'The Sociology of Criminal Justice: Progress and Prospects' in J. Baldwin and A. K. Bottomley (eds), *Criminal Justice: Selected Readings*. London: Martin Robertson.

LLOYD-BOSTOCK, S. (2000). 'The Effects on Juries of Hearing About the Defendant's Previous Criminal Record: A Simulation Study'. *Criminal Law Review* 734–55.

—— (2006). 'The Effects on Lay Magistrates of Hearing that the Defendant is of "Good Character", Being Left to Speculate, or Hearing that he has a Previous Conviction'. *Criminal Law Review* 189–212.

—— and THOMAS, T. (2000). 'The Continuing Decline of the English Jury' in N. Vidmar (ed). *World Jury Systems*. Oxford: Oxford University Press.

MACPHERSON, W. (1999). *The Stephen Lawrence Inquiry* (Cmnd 4262-1). London: Stationery Office.

MARK, SIR ROBERT (1973). *Minority Verdict*. London: BBC Publications.

MATTHEWS, R., HANCOCK, L., and BRIGGS, D. (2004). *Jurors' Perceptions, Understanding Confidence and Satisfaction in the Jury System: A Study in Six Courts*. London: Home Office.

MATTINSON, J. and MIRRLEES-BLACK, C. (2000). *Attitudes to Crime and Criminal Justice: Findings from the 1998 British Crime Survey*. Home Office Research Study 200. London: Home Office.

McBARNET, D. J. (1976). 'Pre-trial Procedures and the Construction of Conviction' in P. Carlen (ed.), *The Sociology of Law*. University of Keele Sociological Review Monograph.

—— (1981). *Conviction: Law, the State and the Construction of Justice*. London: Macmillan.

McCABE, S. and PURVES, R. (1974). *The Shadow Jury at Work*. Oxford: Oxford University Penal Research Unit.

McCONVILLE, M. (1991). 'Shadowing the Jury'. *New Law Journal* 141: 1588 and 1595.

—— (2002). 'Plea Bargaining' in M. McConville and G. Wilson (eds), *The Handbook of The Criminal Justice Process*. Oxford: Oxford University Press.

—— and BRIDGES, L. (1994). *Criminal Justice in Crisis*. Aldershot: Edward Elgar.

—— and WILSON, G. (eds) (2002). *The Handbook of The Criminal Justice Process.* Oxford: Oxford University Press.

——, SANDERS, A., and LENG, R. (1991). *The Case for the Prosecution.* London: Routledge.

——, HODGSON, J., BRIDGES, L., and PAVLOVIC, A. (1994). *Standing Accused: The Organisation and Practices of Criminal Defence Lawyers in Britain.* Oxford: Clarendon Press.

MIRRLEES-BLACK, C. (2001). *Confidence in the Criminal Justice System: Findings from the 2000 British Crime Survey.* Home Office Research Findings No 137. London: Home Office.

MOORE, R. (2003). 'The Use of Financial Penalties and the Amounts Imposed: The Need for a New Approach'. *Criminal Law Review* 13–27.

MORGAN, P. and VENNARD, J. (1989). *Pre-Trial Delay: The Implications of Time Limits.* Home Office Research Study 110. London: HMSO.

MORGAN, R. and RUSSELL, N. (2000). *The Judiciary in the Magistrates' Courts.* London: Home Office.

MOXON, D. (1988). *Sentencing Practice in the Crown Court.* Home Office Research Study 103. London: HMSO.

—— and HEDDERMAN, C. (1994). 'Mode of Trial Decisions and Sentencing Differences Between Courts'. *Howard Journal of Criminal Justice* 33: 97–108.

MULCAHY, A. (1994). 'The Justifications of "Justice": Legal Practitioners' Accounts of Negotiated Case Settlements in Magistrates' Courts'. *British Journal of Criminology* 34: 411–30.

NICOLSON, D. (2005). 'Making Lawyers Moral? Ethical Codes and Moral Character'. *Legal Studies* 25: 601–26.

NOAKS, L. and WINCUP, E. (2004). *Criminological Research: Understanding Qualitative Methods.* London: Sage.

PARKER, H., SUMNER, M. and JARVIS, G. (1989). *Unmasking the Magistrates.* Milton Keynes: Open University Press.

PLOTNIKOFF, J. and WOOLFSON, R. (1993). *From Committal to Trial: Delay at the Crown Court.* Law Society Research Study No 11. London: Law Society.

RILEY, D. and VENNARD, J. (1988). *Triable-Either-Way Cases: Crown Court or Magistrates' Court?* Home Office Research Study 98. London: HMSO.

ROCK, P. (1993). *The Social World of an English Crown Court.* Oxford: Clarendon Press.

ROYAL COMMISSION ON CRIMINAL PROCEDURE (Chairman: Sir Cyril Philips) (1981). *Report.* Cmnd 8092, London: HMSO.

ROYAL COMMISSION ON CRIMINAL JUSTICE (Chairman Viscount Runciman) (1993). *Report.* Cm 2263, London: HMSO.

RUMGAY, J. (1995). 'Custodial Decision Making in a Magistrates' Court: Court Culture and Immediate Situational Factors'. *British Journal of Criminology* 35: 201–17.

SANDERS, A. (1997). 'Criminal Justice: The Development of Criminal Justice Research in Britain' in P. A. Thomas (ed.), *Socio-Legal Studies.* Aldershot: Dartmouth.

—— and YOUNG, R. (2000). *Criminal Justice* (2nd edn). London: Butterworths.

SEALY, A. P. and CORNISH, W. B. (1973a). 'Jurors and their Verdicts'. *Modern Law Review* 36: 496–508.

—— and —— (1973b). 'Juries and the Rules of Evidence: L.S.E. Jury Project'. *Criminal Law Review* 208–23.

SHUTE, S., HOOD, R., and SEEMUNGAL F. (2005). *A Fair Hearing? Ethnic Minorities in the Criminal Courts.* Cullompton: Willan Publishing.

TARLING, R. (1979). *Sentencing Practice in Magistrates' Courts.* Home Office Research Study 56. London: HMSO.

TARLING, R. (2006). 'Sentencing Practice in Magistrates' Courts Revisited'. *Howard Journal of Criminal Justice* 45: 29–41.

TEMKIN, J. (1987). *Rape and the Legal Process.* London: Sweet & Maxwell.

VENNARD, J., DAVIS, G., BALDWIN, J., and PEARCE, J. (2004). *Ethnic Minority Magistrates' Experience of the Role and of the Court Environment.* London: Department for Constitutional Affairs.

WALKER, C. and STARMER, K. (1993). *Justice in Error.* London: Blackstone Press.

WASIK, M., GIBBONS, T., and REDMAYNE, M. (1999). *Criminal Justice: Text and Materials.* London: Longman.

WHITE PAPER (2002). *Justice for All* (CM 5563). London: The Stationery Office.

WHITTAKER, C. and MACKIE, A. (1997). *Managing Courts Effectively: The Reasons for Adjournments in Magistrates' Courts.*

Home Office Research Study 168. London: HMSO.

YOUNG, R., MOLONEY, T., and SANDERS, A. (1992). *In the Interests of Justice?* London: Legal Aid Board.

YOUNG, W. (2003). 'Summing-Up to Juries in Criminal Cases—What Jury Research says about Current Rules and Practice'. *Criminal Law Review* 663–89.

——, CAMERON, N. and TINSLEY, Y. (1998). *Juries in Criminal Trials.* Wellington: New Zealand Law Commission.

ZANDER, M. (1974). 'Are Too Many Professional Criminals Avoiding Conviction?—A Study of Britain's Two Busiest Courts'. *Modern Law Review* 37: 28–61.

—— and HENDERSON, P. (1993). *Crown Court Survey.* Royal Commission on Criminal Justice, Research Study No 19. London: HMSO.

14

Research on community penalties

George Mair

Introduction

In the seven years that have passed since the first edition of this chapter was written (in April 1999), there have been momentous changes in the probation service. When I originally wrote, the National Probation Service (NPS) was in the initial stages of planning and still two years away from existence. This organizational change alone has had considerable implications for research. But the restructuring of the service has taken place alongside new approaches to working with offenders, new community sentences, new partnership working arrangements, new levels of staffing, and now—a further and even more radical change—amalgamation of the NPS into a National Offender Management Service (NOMS) working much more closely (and just how closely remains a matter for conjecture) with the Prison Service. In addition, the 'old' community sentences—the probation order, the community service order, the combination order—were first renamed (as the community rehabilitation order, the community punishment order, and the community punishment and rehabilitation order respectively) and are now being phased out to be replaced, since 4 April 2005, by a new generic community order with twelve separate requirements. The boundaries between custody and community have been further eroded by the new suspended sentence order ('custody minus'), which in practice operates in exactly the same way as the community order, although it remains a custodial sentence in terms of seriousness; and by the custody plus order, which was intended to replace sentences of imprisonment of up to a year and was expected to be implemented late in 2006. As planned, custody plus would consist of a short custodial sentence of between two weeks and three months, followed by a period of community supervision of at least six months. However, the Home Office has recently announced (Home Office 2006) that its planned introduction of custody plus in autumn 2006 will not now take place; whether this is a temporary delay or a more indefinite postponement remains unclear. To complicate matters further, Fast Delivery Reports are encouraged for many of the requirements of the community order, and a national offender assessment system is in place to assess offender risk and needs (OASys). Perhaps even more disturbing than the pace and scope of change is the number of recent media and political attacks on the NPS as a result of several high-profile cases of murder where the offenders were under the supervision of probation officers. For a service that has spent most of its time in the shadows, such attention is not just unusual but unwelcome.

Seven years ago I suggested that research into community penalties might not have the immediate appeal of some criminological topics such as the police or prisons, but with its new high profile, both politically and publicly, this may no longer be the case. Major research projects (Pathfinders) have been commissioned by the Home Office to test out new approaches to working with offenders (see below); and academic debate about whether anything 'works' has intensified (see, e.g., Raynor 2003; also Burnett and Roberts 2004; Mair 2004a; and the review of these two books by Tim Chapman in the *British Journal of Criminology* 2005). Indeed, trying to keep up with the probation-related initiatives coming out of the Home Office has become a difficult task—and not just for academics. Chief Officers tend to recall how, ten years ago, they received a Home Office Probation Circular every few months; now they tend to receive communications from the Home Office (in the shape of the National Probation Directorate or NOMS) every day and many of these require action. So the probation service can no longer be said to exist on the margins of criminal justice (it shed its court welfare functions when it became the NPS); it is very much at the heart of the criminal justice process and increasingly standing in the full glare of public attention. For better or worse, the work of the probation service is no longer hidden away and one of the immediate problems for probation staff is to become accustomed to being players on a public stage.

In this chapter I shall argue that, although there has been a considerable literature focusing on the work of the probation service, most of that research has had negligible impact on policy or practice. Why should this be so? The answer is that—for the most part—the research has been fragmented, time-limited, badly focused, has concentrated on outcomes, and—despite being defined directly or indirectly by the Home Office—has rarely been an integral part of the policy process, or been successfully incorporated into practice nationally. I will return to these points at the end of the chapter.

The focus of this chapter is on research into community penalties but some editorial boundaries are necessary to make this manageable. On the one hand, I will ignore some key aspects of the work of the probation service, although this is not meant to suggest they are unimportant. For example, I will not discuss research into pre-sentence reports (PSRs, or social inquiry reports as they were previously known). However, it is important to stress that PSRs are a vital weapon in a probation officer's armoury for two reasons: first, since judges and magistrates read them regularly, they are probably the most significant tool in building up and maintaining officer credibility (and therefore agency credibility) in the courts: and secondly, the reports guide—to a considerable degree—sentencer decisions about the kinds of offenders who are sentenced to community penalties. I have noted above the increasing use of Fast Delivery Reports—a significant development, yet one that has not been subjected to any research. Nor will there be any discussion of the work carried out by probation officers with prisoners during their time in prison and while under supervision post-release, although this is becoming a topic of some significance as can be seen in the Social Exclusion Unit report 'Reducing Re-Offending by Ex-Prisoners' (2002), in a major Home Office-funded Pathfinder project on resettlement (Lewis *et al.* 2003), and in the current preoccupation with serious offences carried out by those on licence. Indeed, it should be emphasized that this is a substantial area of work; 83,400 persons were receiving pre- and post-release supervision on 31 December 2004 (Home Office 2005a), and when custody plus is implemented this figure will increase. Another area that will not be further discussed is the history of community penalties. High-quality historical research into the probation service itself remains scarce. Despite the path-breaking work of Bochel (1976), Haxby (1978), and

McWilliams (1983, 1985, 1986, 1987) and the slightly idiosyncratic study of the London Probation Service by Martin Page (1992), only Maurice Vanstone (2004) has recently addressed the history of probation. Historical studies of the origins and development of individual penalties, especially the probation order, simply do not exist (although see Mair 1991 for an account of the origins and development of senior attendance centres). Without detailed, perhaps local, studies of the evolution of community penalties we lack an important part of the context in which to understand current policy and practice.

On the other hand, two community penalties that originally had no ties with the probation service—the curfew order and the attendance centre order—will be discussed. While the curfew order is operated by whichever company has secured the tender for its operation, a curfew is also one of the requirements possible under a community order and could be imposed alongside other requirements so that probation involvement is necessary. The attendance centre order too has now become a requirement available under the community order. Both of these penalties are significant in that they present challenges to the probation service monopoly on community penalties. While the use of senior attendance centres has been decreasing (and was never a commonly used sentence) the curfew order has the potential to become a major player in the community penalty arena. Monetary penalties—still the most commonly used court sentence in this country—will also be considered briefly.

I have imposed several other arbitrary boundaries on the discussion to keep it within manageable proportions. First, only research covering adults and young adults from the age of 17 upwards will be included. Secondly, the work discussed will be UK-based. And thirdly, I will focus on the post-war period—indeed, most of the work discussed will come from the last 20–30 years.

With these considerations in mind I will first discuss more general issues that have formed the background to research into community penalties in my experience, and then move on to look at studies of specific penalties. Finally, I will revisit some key issues and suggest some possibilities for future work.

Key background issues

Who pays the piper?

For better or worse, the research agenda for community penalties has been, and continues to be, shaped by the Home Office. Using the term 'shaped' is deliberate. Researchers have always argued about just how far Home Office influence extended, and 'shaped' seems to be an appropriate word for what has—certainly in the past—usually been a fairly gentle and non-confrontational process. Recently, however, the word 'control' is much more likely to be used to describe the Home Office role, with a full awareness of the negative connotations of such a term. While it would be difficult to argue with the proposition that if the Home Office pays for research it has a right to define what it is paying for, it is equally difficult to understand why it now defines tendered projects so tightly that creativity in research design by academics bidding for the work is discouraged. Timescales seem to have been cut to the bone, and the demand for interim reports has multiplied. In the effort to control completely research projects, the Home Office seems to have ignored or forgotten the multiple problems and obstacles that can delay research for all sorts of good reasons. The assumption seems to be that the universe to be studied is immediately available, easily quantifiable, and quite controllable. As anyone who has spent any time in the field will confirm, such an assumption is—to say the least—naive. At this level alone, because of its new-found desire actively to control research more self-consciously than in the past, the Home Office has created tensions and conflict with funded researchers.

The Home Office is, of course, in a powerful position as a major funder of research. In the past, it has used its power indirectly so that funded research was carried out *almost* as a 'gentleman's agreement'. Now, research projects are subjected to a lengthy contract that researchers ignore at their peril and that gives the Home Office considerable latitude in how to deal with projects. This has implications for the research process, although I should point out that, at least as far as my own research has been concerned, these have not involved censorship in terms of unlilaterally deleting passages for purely political reasons. In the 16 years I spent working in the Home Office Research and Planning Unit (HORPU), the last ten involved in researching community penalties, my work was never subjected to such censorship. Certainly, research reports were subjected to a good deal of critical comment from colleagues in the RPU as well as from staff in the relevant policy divisions, but such comments were not the final word. Discussion and negotiation always took place and, on the whole, I think that my work was improved by the scrutiny it received. It may have been time-consuming to redraft; it may—at times—have been annoying to have to respond to policymakers who knew little about research and insisted on tinkering with carefully crafted sentences, but research reports were more tightly focused and read more clearly as a result.

How far self-censorship of some kind was involved is another matter. One should always write for one's audience; a piece for a tabloid newspaper would read very differently from an article in the *British Journal of Criminology*. With careful management and over time, one learned in the Home Office what the concerns of policymakers were and one understood how a research report should be written. If I had ever been worried about the integrity of the research being compromised, I was quite prepared to insist that my name would not appear on the title page (and the fact that Home Office reports carry authors' names is important). Only once did I feel that I *might* have to go as far as this and that was in connection with the first UK research into electronic monitoring (Mair and Nee 1990). In that case one could sense that the political pressures for a positive result from the trials were considerable, even though no pressure was directed at me. In the event, this remains the only piece of research I ever carried out at the Home Office which was commented on positively by people on both sides of the fence; those in favour of electronic monitoring as well as those against it, thought that the report backed up their positions. It had been important to me throughout the research that the published report should show the real problems confronted by the trials and the policy divisions' comments on drafts of the report did not try to obscure these problems.

Research began to be more carefully scrutinized during the Michael Howard years (indeed, his junior minister, David Maclean, even proposed closing down the HORPU altogether); more questions were asked about why projects were being proposed, what they were designed to achieve, and research reports were studied in more detail by ministers themselves. Not major problems in principle, perhaps, but such scrutiny could lead to a 'spin' being put on research, as happened with the first national study of reconviction rates for some considerable time (Lloyd *et al.* 1994), where the press release suggested that prison was the most successful sentence in terms of reconviction rates. The research said no such thing, but its publication coincided with the Howard 'Prison Works' campaign and it was hardly acceptable that the Home Secretary's own researchers should have media coverage for a study which cast doubt on this simplistic claim. It is, however, important to emphasize that the published report was not tinkered with.

'Spin' has become ever more pronounced in the past decade. As the politics of New Labour have increasingly moved to centralized control of power (despite a rhetoric emphasizing local communities and the devolution of power), the need to control government statements and thus funded research has also increased. In practice, the situation has been exacerbated by the significance of crime and law and order as political issues, New Labour's claims to follow an evidence-based approach to policy and practice, and the availability of large sums of money to be spent on research (primarily in relation to the Crime Reduction Programme). Given these factors, it is not surprising that the Home Office is exercising much greater control of its research. Delays in publication, timing publications for days when other news was planned to dominate the media, deciding on the type of publication were all used by the Home Office during the 1980s to keep research away from the public eye. Recently, however, some Home Office-funded researchers have faced the rather more serious obstacle of refusal to publish their work.

A major two-year project aimed at evaluating the new uses of electronic monitoring (costing around £270,000) was terminated six months early as a result, the researchers were informed of a major review of funded research which apparently claimed that the research was not cost-effective and did not meet Home Office aims. Despite requests for more information about this 'review,' none was forthcoming. A short report on the first, completed part of the project was requested by the Home Office and the researchers were informed that this would be published. Promised comments on the report by the Home Office were never made and the agreement to publish was reneged upon, although the researchers were told they could arrange for publication on their own as long as the version for publication was sent to the Home Office in advance (see Bottomley *et al.* 2004; Mair 2005).

Perhaps even more disturbing, given the significance of the What Works initiative for the NPS and the Home Office, the final reconviction study of the Pathfinder project on offending behaviour programmes in the probation service has never been published, despite the researchers initially being informed that it would be (for the first reconviction study, see Hollin *et al.* 2004).

It would be difficult to deny that these are examples of censorship of research into community penalties, the results of which should be made publicly available by the Home Office. If an evidence-based approach to policy or practice is to mean anything, it should surely encompass making available evidence that supports as well as fails to support the policy/practice chosen. Ironically, while the Home Office now encourages meta-analytic studies—which, to be effective, need access to all research data—it is making such studies more difficult by withholding research findings. The increased politicization of crime has led—not surprisingly—to the politicization of research.

Policy demands and the fragmentation of research

Putting the politics aside for the moment, there are two main problems with research being Home Office defined. The first is that policymakers are not adept at framing research questions. In the final analysis the research process in the Home Office is customer-driven; if a policy division cannot be persuaded to support a research project, then it is unlikely to be done. Projects can be proposed by policy divisions or by researchers; in the former case, it is difficult for the researcher to say no, while in the latter a strong case has to be made if the topic is not currently seen as important. The problem with research ideas which originate with policy divisions is that they tend to come in unresearchable terms—'we'd like to know a bit more about . . .', or 'we're having some problems with . . .'. By the time a research project has been stitched together to take account of the initial issues, it can be hard for policymakers to see how their interests are being served. This is not to argue that policy-relevant (or practice-relevant) research should be solely researcher-driven. What is really required is a much closer relationship between policymakers and researchers where the latter are treated as equals rather than (as is all too often the case) lesser beings who are called in to help solve a minor technical problem.

The recent structural change in the Home Office whereby researchers (originally part of a separate Directorate from policy divisions) were embedded in policy divisions might at first seem to help place them and policymakers on a more equal footing, but it is more likely that there will be more negative consequences. In the old structure, researchers had some collective authority by being pulled together, whereas by being part of a policy directorate they will be answerable to the policymaker who heads up that directorate. Therefore, research will be even more under the control of policymakers than in the past. Whatever power the old Research and Planning Unit or the Research and Statistics Directorate once had has been diminished. As Peter Raynor (2004: 321) has pointed out, moving correctional researchers to become part of NOMS 'hardly looks like a recipe for robust independence'.

The second problem is that research tends to be fragmented and non-cumulative. Research was planned on an annual basis in the Home Office because it was intended to be policy relevant and policy priorities can change quite suddenly. This did not mean that only projects of 12 months or less could be carried out, although the timescale for research tended to decrease over the years (the Probation Pathfinder projects, however, were for several years). The drawback was rather that research topics also changed suddenly, so that having just finished a project on a subject which had raised far more questions than it had answered and invited the development of more focused and pertinent work (as is all too often the case), one had to move to a completely different topic. Given the government emphasis on evidence-based approaches, one might reasonably expect a number of cumulative and complementary studies to be carried out to help provide an evidence-base. The organization of research in the Home Office would not seem to be conducive to providing a sound evidential base for policy and practice.

One of the more surprising things about researching community penalties from inside government was just how little basic information the Home Office had. Many of the projects carried out between 1985 and 2000 had first to find out how many examples existed 'out there'. I was amazed to discover, for example, that we first had to find out how many probation day centres there were in the mid-1980s (Mair 1988). Similar fact-finding problems were faced in studies of probation provision for drug-misusing offenders (Nee and Sibbitt 1993), of probation motor projects (Martin and Webster 1994), of community-based programmes for sex offenders (Barker and Morgan 1993), of the ways in which probation services addressed the literacy needs of offenders (Davis *et al.* 1997), and of demanding physical activity programmes for young offenders (Taylor *et al.* 1999). If such basic information is not available, it becomes impossible to begin to evaluate such programmes. The need to collect such information has implications for research; not just the fact that some kind of sample survey or full census might have to be carried out, but that as a consequence the study might take longer than envisaged and it might cover less ground than had been planned.

A similar problem that was faced in the study of the new uses of electronic monitoring (Bottomley *et al.* 2004) was a Home Office claim in the tender specification that it would be responsible for collecting and collating a complex set of data from several agencies, thereby saving the researchers considerable time. We were sceptical about whether this claim could be met and, in the event, we were proved right. We had to rearrange the research plan in order to try to collect the data—a task we had not planned for or costed. Luckily, the number of cases was so small that a more qualitative approach was needed, and the premature termination of the project obviated the requirement for the data.

These background issues which shape research are not necessarily confined to the Home Office: outside funding agencies also often want (and deserve to have) sight of research proposals and reports with the right to comment prior to publication (they may also insist on the right to deny publication); they too may find it difficult to formulate research questions; they too may not have any interest in or the ability to fund longer or follow-up studies (one of the major problems of criminological research—and this applies to other academic disciplines too—is that you get no plaudits for replication studies); and they may not have the kind of information which a researcher assumes they would hold. But the powerful position of the Home Office with regard to funding, and its increasingly coercive approach to managing research are causing academics openly to question its research strategy (see, e.g., the Special Edition of *Criminal Justice* 'Evaluating the Crime Reduction Programme in England and Wales' (2004), and *Criminal Justice Matters* (2005/6)).

Access and confidentiality

More commonplace (though rarely simple) issues for research such as access and confidentiality are also subject to the Home Office factor. Being a member of HORPU made access *in general terms* not a particular problem, but this did not mean that one thereby could study the *specific* probation areas which most needed research. Chief Probation Officers (CPOs) could easily provide reasons for not wanting researchers (perhaps especially those from the Home Office) tramping around their area. All too often the reason given was that they had recently been inspected by Her Majesty's Inspectorate of Probation (HMIP). Given the number of probation areas subjected to some kind of HMIP inspection annually this could make choosing areas for study an extremely prolonged process.[1]

---

[1] The late Graham Smith, then HM Chief Inspector of Probation, once stated that 'we would expect almost every service to be seen by us for something every year' (House of Commons 1998a), which suggests that, when local inspections/audits are included, some probation areas could well suffer from inspection fatigue.

Prior to the existence of the NPS, access to a probation area if you were not govern-ment-funded was very much left to the discretion of the CPO. When, for example, I was planning an interview study of Chiefs (funded by ESRC), I discussed the matter with the Association of Chief Officers of Probation (ACOP) who alerted Chiefs to the project. The next step involved writing personally to each CPO asking him/her whether they would be interested in participating in the research. Ultimately, a decision was made by each Chief (nine CPOSs were not interviewed for a variety of reasons—see Mair 2004b). This study was designed to be carried out before 1 April 2001; if it had been carried out after this date, the new organizational structure of the probation service would have meant getting permission from the Home Office to *contact* each CPO—and it is quite possible that the Home Office would have made any decision about Chiefs' *participation*. The centraliza-tion of probation (and its forthcoming incorporation as part of NOMS) has, therefore, made it more difficult to carry out research; Home Office control has strengthened. Indeed, it is notable that the growing data-set generated by OASys has not been made available to outside researchers, although it is used by the Home Office for planning pro-gramme provision.

Standard provisions about confidentiality were applied in Home Office research; indi-viduals would not be identified, although matters were much more vague about identify-ing probation areas. No probation area was anonymized whilst I was working in this field in the Home Office, although other researchers have felt the need—or been requested—to do this (see, e.g., May 1991; Skinns 1990). Naming areas could, no doubt, lead to indi-vidual probation staff being identified, but this was never raised as an issue as far as I was concerned. Confidentiality could obviously prove to be more problematic when it was necessary to collect names and dates of birth of offenders for the purposes of access to a national database in order to study previous criminal history and recidivism. Some pro-bation officers worried about providing such information in case it led to some kind of police action. Assurances that there were strict protocols about how such data might be used were, in my experience, always enough for the data to be supplied. However, reach-ing agreement about linking ethnic data to reconviction studies was much more prob-lematic; this was seen by probation organizations—particularly the National Association of Probation Officers (NAPO) and the Association of Black Probation Officers (ABPO)—as much too sensitive a subject to confront. While it is difficult to be sure, it is likely that with the growth of multi-agency partnerships data sharing has become less of a problem in practice, especially with protocols in place to govern such sharing.

One issue which became increasingly difficult to handle was pressure from probation services to be seen to have performed well. During the 1980s, the probation service felt more and more pressure from government to be effective, efficient, and economic, to be accountable for what it did, and to plan and target its work more appropriately (McLaughlin and Muncie 1994). The Audit Commission, which has become a significant presence in the criminal justice process, published a critical report on the probation service at the end of the decade (Audit Commission 1989). Performance indicators and national standards were introduced at the start of the 1990s. One response to all this pressure was to become defensive and if a Chief Probation Officer agreed to allow research locally there was often an expectation that the results would show the service in a positive light. This could lead to the absurd situation whereby the probation service was very keen indeed on the idea of research or evaluation in theory and in public, but when confronted with research findings which suggested that things were not going well was much less enthusiastic. The significance of performance indicators and targets has become even greater in the last five years. Performance Reports are published quarterly for the NPS with results for each area listed. The problems with such 'league tables' are too well known to rehearse here, but it should be noted that problems or difficulties specific to individual areas are ignored, and that there are financial penalties tied to certain targets. From personal experience as a Probation Board Member, there are usually 'good' reasons for decline in performance—reasons that the centre seems to be reluctant to acknowledge.

Pressure for positive results is pervasive and understandable. Many projects are set up with minimal resources and little time to operate 'normally'; researchers are asked to evaluate what are essentially pilot projects, but in the hope that a glowing report will show unequivocally positive results. Such a hope is naive, but the need to find more money is always present, and this is more likely to be forthcoming if the project is judged to be a success by a so-called 'independent' academic. It is hard to blame those who develop and work in such projects for wanting to have some job security, but it is simply not possible to conclude from the study of a *pilot* project that it is an absolute success. Not only are probation services and the like under pressure to demonstrate effectiveness, but this pressure is then transferred to researchers—a move which could have implications for the quality of research carried out, as well as leading to certain researchers being shunned in a tender if they have a reputation for not coming up with the 'right' answers.

The orthodoxy that only cognitive behavioural techniques provide the basis for effective probation work has not helped the situation. Despite the fact that the strong evidence base which its proponents claim for it does not (yet?) exist, cognitive behaviouralism has been preached as the gospel for community penalties. This raises the alarming prospect that researchers who do not subscribe to this particular credo will be marginalized in bidding for research, and even that research findings may be interpreted in such a way as to boost cognitive behaviouralist techniques or explain away any possible shortcomings. While the nonsense of 'Nothing Works' (a statement) has now been acknowledged as an empty formulation, its initial replacement by 'What Works?' (a question) should have heralded a new openness about effective approaches to community penalties. The question, however, quickly became a statement—'What Works'—which to a considerable degree foreclosed discussion. Recent research has begun to cast doubt upon some of the high expectations associated with cognitive skills programmes (see, for example, Falshaw *et al.* 2003; Cann *et al.* 2003) and it will be particularly interesting to observe the Home Office response to this.

In this section, I have discussed some of the critical issues forming the backdrop for probation research over the past 20 years. I would not wish to suggest that these issues are peculiar to researching community penalties, or that they only arise in the Home Office. They are, however, significant issues that have an (often unspoken) impact upon how research is formulated, designed, carried out, and written up. The salience of community penalties has increased greatly since the first edition of this book, so that the politics of research into this area have become more contested than they have ever been.

In the next section I will discuss some of the more important pieces of research that have been carried out into community penalties. First, the 'old' community penalties will be discussed, then more recent research associated with the What Works initiative (roughly from 1998 onwards). This discussion will concentrate on Home Office-shaped research—whether carried out by the Home Office, commissioned by it, or following in its traditions. Following this, the work of some 'mavericks' who have been responsible for important research without a great deal of Home Office input will be examined.

An overview of community penalties research

The probation order

Despite the fact that it has been the bread-and-butter work of the probation service since its beginnings, research into the basic probation order is notable by its complete absence. Probably the main reason for this is the nature of the order: most basic probation orders were rooted in one-to-one casework between a probation officer and the offender and this took place in private, behind closed doors, almost always in the probation office. It would be seen as obtrusive, perhaps threatening, and certainly as changing the dynamics of the relationship for a researcher to sit in and observe sessions of this kind. As a result, we know next to nothing about one-to-one casework in practice, a situation which is deplorable and which it is now too late to rectify.

The first significant piece of probation research (funded by the Home Office), entitled appropriately enough 'The Results of Probation' (Radzinowicz 1958), was a reconviction study, the main findings of which were as follows: adults were more likely to succeed than juveniles (success was defined as having completed the order with no reconviction during a follow-up period of three years); women were more likely to succeed than men; probation was especially effective 'in dealing with adolescent and adult first offenders'; its effectiveness decreased, however, when applied to recidivists; and 'in many of the more difficult cases the reinforcement of probation by combining it with conditions of residence has not proved to be particularly effective'. Today, such results from a reconviction study would be unsurprising, but at the time the impact of this study was considerable. Despite methodological limitations many of the findings remain relevant today.

For a ten-year period beginning in 1966, a major (and concerted) part of the Home Office research effort went into trying to discover what the key factors were in successful probation work (Folkard *et al.* 1966; Barr 1966; Barr and O'Leary 1966; Davies 1969, 1970, 1973, 1974; Sinclair 1971; Folkard *et al.* 1974; Folkard *et al.* 1976). There is little to comment on in terms of the methods used in these studies, but they do demonstrate a considerable commitment by the Home Office to conduct research into probation and how effective it might be. Unfortunately, the final report (Folkard, Smith, and Smith 1976) on this research programme which set out the results of the IMPACT (Intensive Matched Probation and After-Care Treatment) experiment was very brief, obviously disappointing ('the results showed no significant differences in ... reconviction rates ... therefore producing no evidence to support a general application of more intensive treatment'), and published immediately after the British version of 'Nothing Works' (Brody 1976). As a result, Home Office research into community penalties virtually disappeared; an examination of the two Home Office research series (Home Office Research Studies and Research and Planning Unit Papers) demonstrates just how little research into probation took place between 1976 and 1988.

By the mid-1980s, the probation service was no longer in the business of rehabilitating offenders but diverting them from custody, and the probation order was capable of having additional requirements attached to it. The publication of the Statement of National Objectives and Priorities (Home Office 1984) was the first signal that the Home Office was beginning to take a more controlling approach to the probation service, a process that culminated with the inception of the National Probation Service in 2001. Day centres became the flavour of the month, with the addition to the probation order of a condition to attend a designated centre for up to 60 days, and a detailed, long-term evaluation of one such centre was carried out by Peter Raynor (1988). In his study of the Afan Alternative project, Raynor used a variety of methods in an effort to try to capture the complexity of the phenomenon, and looked at several measures of effectiveness. His research stands as an important attempt to move away from a reliance on reconviction rates as the only measure of effectiveness for a court sentence, and to try to situate a project in its context (the beginnings, perhaps, of what we now refer to as a process evaluation). Interest in day centres was strong and a variety of studies appeared, all trying to assess how effective the centres were at diverting offenders from custody (among them Mair 1988; Vass and Weston 1990), but all facing the same methodological difficulty—how could one be certain that an offender sentenced to attend a day centre was indeed being diverted from a custodial sentence and not from another non-custodial one?

One particularly interesting study focusing on the probation order in Scotland was carried out in the late 1980s and early 1990s and involved interviewing sheriffs, offenders, and their supervising officers (social workers, as there is no probation service in Scotland) in four courts with varying uses of probation (Ditton and Ford 1994). The aim was to investigate views and attitudes about probation, how and why it was used, what the process of supervision was seen to entail, how orders ended, etc. The significance of this study lies in its pulling together the views of the three main groups involved in probation and it throws up many fascinating insights. Despite providing little methodological information this is an ambitious study that deserves to be better known.

A major Home Office study of intensive probation (Mair *et al.* 1994) which attempted to build on the work of Raynor by using various measures of effectiveness (including an assessment of the costs involved—an aspect of research which has become increasingly important, and which to do properly requires skills that most social researchers lack) as well as carrying out a process evaluation, was crippled by a loss of policy interest in the initiative and the resulting lack of support for a reconviction study. Such a study could have suggested vital links between models of intensive probation and reconviction rates—an association which is hinted at in a reconviction study of day centres (Mair and Nee 1992; for a 12 month reconviction study of one intensive probation project, see Brownlee 1995).

Drug use by offenders became an increasingly significant issue during the 1990s, and probation work with drug-misusing offenders reflected this. Two Home Office studies found wide variations in the probation response to drug misuse (Nee and Sibbitt 1993) and argued the case for a partnership approach, although few offenders completed the programme (Sibbitt 1996). The introduction of the Drug Treatment and Testing Order as part of the Crime and Disorder Act 1998 was subjected to a detailed evaluation, but despite the effort to impose greater consistency the research showed continuing variations in practice, problems in effective inter-agency working, low completion rates, and high rates of reconviction (Turnbull *et al.* 2000; Hough *et al.* 2003). The minority who successfully completed the order, however, reported considerable reductions in drug use and offending, and their reconviction rate was almost half of those who failed to complete.

Reconviction rates remain the key outcome measure for court sentences. Following the first comparative study of reconviction rates for some years that discussed the various limitations associated with using reconviction rates as an outcome measure (Lloyd *et al.* 1994), May (1999) analysed the social factors related to reconviction following a community sentence. Drug use and employment were found to be particularly relevant and probation has made efforts to tackle both of these issues (for drugs, see above, and for employment, see below). Increasingly, research has been trying to examine the association between reconviction rates and types of programme, but this is a complex topic that is not easy to unravel. Original studies (where they are carried out), describing the programmes and how they operate, tend to be published well in advance of the reconviction studies. This can mean that any relationship between the two is difficult to grasp. It is also not unusual for the reconviction study to be carried out by different (Home Office-based) researchers, which raises the question of how process and outcome can be linked satisfactorily. Reconviction studies are often published in summary form in the *Research Findings* series and it is difficult to raise complex issues in just four pages. Examples of this can be found in the case of a study of motor projects—which resulted in the issuing of Home Office guidance to probation services (Martin and Webster 1994; Sugg 1998; Home Office 1998a); and in a project studying community-based programmes for sex offenders (Barker and Morgan 1993; Beckett *et al.* 1994; and Hedderman and Sugg 1996).

More promising as a research strategy is the approach followed by Raynor and Vanstone (1994, 1996, 1997) in their detailed investigation of the STOP (Straight Thinking On Probation) programme in Mid-Glamorgan. A complex evaluation design was used to elucidate the links between the operation and organization of the programme and its outcomes. Initially promising results in terms of reconviction after 12 months were not confirmed after 24 months, although there was some evidence of a reduction in the seriousness of reconvictions for those who completed the programme.

Summing up briefly, then, we can say that research into the probation order has really been the story of research into probation with added requirements. By the end of the twentieth century we were not much further forward in knowing what was effective than we were with the 1958 report by Radzinomcz, although the definition of effectiveness has changed with the times and continues to do so (reconviction rates, however, remain the ultimate test). While innovative methods of research or evaluation are unusual to say the least, the importance of process evaluation is slowly being recognized.

The community service order and the combination order

In contrast to the probation order, the community service order (CSO) has been fairly comprehensively researched from its beginnings. To a large degree this has been because it was introduced in 1973 on a consciously experimental basis and with encouragement from its originators on the Wootton Committee (Advisory Council on the Penal System 1970) for systematic study of its workings.

The first research was carried out by the Home Office Research Unit (HORU) with the aim of assessing the viability of the scheme and the potential for national roll-out (Pease *et al.* 1975). A second HORU report was published two years later (Pease *et al.* 1977), concentrating on assessing how far the new sentence was used as a displacement from custody and rates of reconviction associated with it. It was concluded that around 45–50 per cent of those sentenced to community service were diversions from custody—a figure which has been relatively consistent in many studies of so-called alternatives to custody in the UK.

Although one cannot be certain, it looks as if the second HORU report draws its conclusions rather more firmly than the evidence suggests and it is notable that the Foreword points out that the text was edited after the departure of the authors from the Unit. Indeed, the whole official basis of the research has been questioned by Ken Pease who claimed, some years later, that the idea of the research being critical in the decision to expand CSOs nationally was simply not true; community service orders were going national whatever the research said (Pease 1983).

One key finding from the original HORU research has continued to haunt the community service order, and that is accusations of wide variations in the way in which the sentence is administered and organized (see Young 1979; McWilliams 1980; Read 1980; McWilliams and Murphy 1980; Vass 1984; Pease 1985; Skinns 1990). This is usually blamed on the deliberately ambiguous nature of the Wootton report (Wootton 1978), and is one reason why the first set of National Standards—introduced in 1989—were for community service (three years before standards for other community penalties).

Two other studies of community service are worth noting. First, that carried out by Tony Vass (1984), which covers much of the ground of earlier work but included active participant observation by the author (as an offender) in community service work placements. As a result, Vass was able to document clearly the key role of the supervision process for offenders and to show how important was the way in which the supervisor dealt with the offenders carrying out community service:

the major influence on the offender to participate in community service projects without causing disruptions is the *type of supervision* offered. The way supervisors—whether full-time, part-time, qualified or unqualified—intermingle with offenders, express their attitudes, work *with*—not above—the offender and the way they handle discontent, can determine the rate of attendance, how much pride offenders take in their work, how much effort they put in their tasks and how well they behave on site. In other words, the success or failure of a session can often be the function of the supervisor's personality and his actions (Vass 1984: 114, emphasis in original).

Vass does not go into great detail about the methodological issues involved in carrying out such participant observation, although they can be assumed to have been considerable. Today, it would almost certainly be much more difficult to get agreement to allow a researcher to participate in community service as an offender; and it would be a difficult matter to construct a suitable identity and keep it secure. The age and gender of the researcher would be important; women and older offenders are less commonly sentenced to community service which would mean that, in general, it would be easier for young males to adopt such an approach. Despite such difficulties, it is surprising that more studies using this method have not been attempted as the potential rewards are considerable.

Finally, and very much a culmination of the tradition of community service research in the UK, is the work carried out in Scotland in the second half of the 1980s by Gill McIvor and various colleagues (see McIvor 1989, 1990; Carnie 1990; Knapp *et al.* 1992; McIvor 1992a; and McIvor 1992b for a book-length study). There is nothing in this research that could be said to be methodologically innovative, but that is beside the point. What we do get is a programme of research carried out carefully and rigorously over a number of years covering key issues in community service (the kind of offenders receiving CSOs, procedural and administrative matters, the comparative costs of CSOs, the views of beneficiaries and sentencers, reconviction rates, and how far the sentence was acting to divert offenders from custody), using a variety of approaches. It is rare for such a comprehensive study to be done and is a direct result of long-term funding (from the Scottish Office, the source of funding for the Ditton and Ford work discussed above) and a real interest in issues after a sentence had moved on from its initial stage of development. McIvor's work confirmed the results of previous Community Service research and raised new questions which require further work—and that is about as much as one could expect from research.

Community service, then, has been better served in research terms than the probation order. There are several reasons for this. It was introduced in the 1970s; it does not involve any 'private' sessions between offender and probation officer; its organizational arrangements are—to a large degree—separable from other probation work (although the arrival of the combination order changed that somewhat); and the first research study defined the key parameters for study well. Innovative research (with the honourable exception of Vass), however, is lacking.

The combination order, introduced in 1992 as part of the Criminal Justice Act 1991, can be dealt with briefly. Despite the significance of a new, demanding community penalty that aimed to pull together a probation and a community service element in a single sentence, thereby requiring new organizational arrangements with the possibility of cultural tensions; and despite the relevance of the order to the present situation with the community order, no detailed study of the combination order has been published. The Home Office Research and Planning Unit carried out a research project which attempted to find out how the sentence was implemented, how it was used by the courts, and the practical issues involved in organizing and administering the sentence. The report (Mair *et al.* 1997) remains unpublished as a result of unresolved disagreements leading to lengthy delays in finalizing the report.

Other 'non-custodial' penalties

The fine remains the most commonly used court sentence. Its long-term decline *may* have been halted as its use for summary offences has recently begun to increase; however, its use as a sentence for indictable offences continues to fall (see Home Office 2005b). Even so, in 2004, 1,082,691 offenders were fined (Home Office 2005b: Table 1.2). Studies of monetary penalties, however, have not been particularly popular, have tended to rely on documentary research based on files and records, have been very much Home Office-driven and have focused heavily on the courts and their procedures—particularly enforcement (see Softley 1973, 1978a, 1978b; Softley and Moxon 1982; Newburn 1988; Mair and Lloyd 1989; Moxon *et al.* 1990; Moxon *et al.* 1992; Charman *et al.* 1996;

Whittaker and Mackie 1997; Mackie *et al.* 2003). Following the Carter report (2003) there has been a resurgence of interest in the fine—partly as a result of the size of the prison population (Mair 2004c) and particularly the unit or day fine which research has suggested is viable (Moxon *et al.* 1990). The reconviction rates associated with fines have been consistently encouraging (see, e.g., Home Office 1964; Phillpotts and Lancucki 1979; House of Commons 1998b; Jennings 2002). Despite the fact that monetary penalties remain popular, studies looking into the ways in which offenders perceive them, how they budget to pay them (or not), the reasons magistrates give for using them, and how fine enforcement procedures are perceived by offenders and applied by magistrates are rare (although it should be noted that some recent work has begun to examine some of these issues; see Mackie *et al.* 2003; Moore 2003; Raine *et al.* 2003; Raine *et al.* 2004).

Apart from the probation order, the attendance centre order is the oldest community penalty, having been introduced as a result of the 1948 Criminal Justice Act, although the first senior attendance centre (for 17–20-year-olds) did not begin operation until December 1958. There are fewer than thirty senior attendance centres in England and Wales and they play a minor role in sentencing. Partly as a result of this they have been rarely noticed. One major study has been carried out (Mair 1991), and this attempted to investigate the relationship between the policy and practice of the centres using historical material as well as a variety of social research approaches. Although senior attendance centres have been on the periphery since their introduction, it is possible that this situation might change now that they are one of the requirements possible under a community order.

A more significant sentence (because the potential to deal with a large number of offenders is much greater) is the curfew order, introduced in July 1995 on a trial basis in three areas and rolled out nationally in December 1999. Early research into the use of electronic surveillance as a tool for monitoring a curfew imposed as a condition of bail was, at best, equivocal (Mair and Nee 1990). The trials of the new sentence were subject to research by the Home Office Research and Planning Unit using tried-and-tested techniques:

Observation, formal interviews and informal discussions were carried out with the contractors; data were collected on all those sentenced to curfew orders; where possible, pre-sentence reports for those so sentenced and where a proposal for a curfew order was made were examined; and semi-structured formal interviews were carried out with 13 offenders sentenced to curfew orders, nine magistrates, three court clerks and two police representatives ... In addition, a number of informal discussions were also held with people in all these groups, except the offenders, and with 12 probation service staff (Mair and Mortimer 1996: 3–4).

In other words, there was nothing new in methodological terms although it is worth noting that the Home Office Economics Unit was drafted in to assess the relative costs of the new order. The second report on the trials (Mortimer and May 1997) focused on the 'market share' of the curfew order and involved a special 'sentencing choice' exercise for magistrates in sixteen of the twenty courts where curfew orders were an option; more sophisticated estimates of the costs and savings associated with the order were also provided. Subsequent research into aspects of electronic monitoring (Mortimer *et al.* 1999; Sugg *et al.* 2001; Walter *et al.* 2001; Walter 2002) continued to find the same kinds of problems—low take-up, poor inter-agency communication; sentencer uncertainty. As has recently been noted, there is, as yet, no clear evidence of the effectiveness of electronic monitoring:

[The research has] pointed to a range of operational problems that suggest a lack of planning and guidance by the Home Office. Perhaps even more worrying is the fact that the Home Office has signally failed to learn from its research; there is an evidence base that is reasonably clear, but little attention appears to have been paid to its message. (Mair 2005: 269–70)

As has been noted above, the most recent study of the use of electronic monitoring was terminated early by the Home Office; the findings of that research (Bottomley *et al.* 2004) are comparable to previous studies. Yet the use of electronic monitoring continues to grow; in 2004 a total of 15,142 persons were sentenced to a curfew order—almost as many as those sentenced to a community punishment and rehabilitation order (Home Office 2005b: Table 3.7). The Home Office has tightly controlled studies of electronic monitoring and it will be interesting to see the results of the current research by Mike Nellis and Stephen Shute into the use of GPS (global positioning system) monitoring. The use of curfew orders may grow even further now that they are one of the possible requirements of the community order, although it is too early for any clear indications of this.

Wider approaches

Around the mid-1990s various studies with a rather wider focus were carried out covering more general aspects of community penalties. While, for the most part, these studies were not especially methodologically innovative, they did look into aspects of community penalties that had not been addressed previously. They also demonstrated changing approaches to measuring the effectiveness of these penalties and can be seen as significant precursors of the What Works initiative

First, postal questionnaires were used to assess the satisfaction of the courts with the probation service as a result of the need to develop a performance indicator for this issue. As methods texts make clear, postal questionnaires have to be fairly simple, clearly designed, and well targeted if a reasonable response rate is desired. The two publications discussing the results of this work show response rates of over 80 per cent (May 1995) and 62 per cent (May 1997) respectively and widespread magisterial satisfaction with the probation service. The significance of sentencer confidence in probation has continued as a result of regular government claims that the courts lack such confidence, although a recent MORI mail survey conducted for the NPS continues to demonstrate positive attitudes on the part of magistrates (MORI 2003).

Secondly, one of the spin-offs of the renewed interest in the 'What Works?' question was the realization that a significant finding of much of the so-called 'Nothing Works' literature was that interventions had to be matched to individual offenders and nothing was known about how probation officers actually assessed offenders and allocated them to programmes (so-called interaction effects). Burnett (1996) was commissioned by the Home Office to research this topic and in the process interviewed 120 probation officers. Her main finding was—as might have been expected—that there were important differences amongst probation areas in how offenders were assessed and allocated. This was the starting point for a series of research studies investigating risk assessment that led to the development of a national risk/needs assessment scale—OASys (see Aubrey and Hough 1997; Raynor *et al*. 2000; Aye Maung and Hammond 2000). While there was a great deal of 'noise' from probation officers about the limitations of OASys, it looks as if it has been assimilated into mainstream probation work remarkably well (Mair *et al*. 2006). Data from OASys assessments are collected by the Home Office and are likely to play a major role in future research (whether outside researchers will be allowed access to this database remains unclear).

Thirdly, as the confidence of sentencers in community penalties became designated as a critical factor in their use during the second half of the 1990s, so interest in how such penalties were enforced became an issue. Yet another Home Office study addressed this topic (Ellis *et al*. 1996), in which probation and community service staff, magistrates, and police officers (or their civilian equivalents) were interviewed. Again—and not surprisingly—the main finding pointed to variations in enforcement practice within and between areas. The importance of enforcement was recognized by ACOP who commissioned further work into the topic (see Hedderman 1999; Hedderman and Hearnden 2000, 2001), leading to more rigorous enforcement practice. The rather simplistic equation that tougher enforcement is good has recently been questioned by research arguing that there are 'no grounds for thinking that the deterrent effect of enforcement ensures fuller compliance, and some grounds for thinking that tough enforcement can lead to low retention rates in programmes, which in turn leads to high reconviction rates' (Hedderman and Hough 2004: 163; see also Hearnden and Millie 2003, 2004).

Fourthly, alongside interest in how sentencers perceived community penalties, there was also an interest in how offenders sentenced to community penalties felt about them. Individual probation services began to take an interest in monitoring the views of 'their' offenders and the Home Office, too, realized this was an important topic. Earlier studies had used in-depth interviews with offenders (and sometimes also with their probation officers; see Day 1981; Fielding 1986; Bailey and Ward 1992) in one area. The Home Office, however, carried out a national survey of 1,200 offenders on probation or combination orders aimed at uncovering more detail about their background and circumstances and eliciting views about their supervision, their probation officers, and how helpful it all was in addressing their problems and reducing their offending (Mair and May 1997). There were difficulties with respondents failing to keep appointments which led to a lower response rate than was desirable (only 61 per cent of the effective sample of almost 2,000 were successfully interviewed), and those who could not be interviewed may well have held more negative attitudes than those who participated in the survey. Like the surveys of sentencers discussed earlier, the views about supervision and probation officers tended to be very favourable.

Finally, providing a curious link between previous studies of specific programmes such as those for motoring offenders, sex offenders, etc., there were a series of studies examining the question of getting offenders into employment. Lipsey's legendary meta-analysis (1992)—which in many ways kick-started the What Works initiative—concluded that employment was the single most effective way of reducing offending and Home Office research followed this claim (Roberts *et al*. 1997; Sarno *et al*. 2000). Both projects suggested that there was potential in focusing upon employment, but both also showed the difficulties associated with evaluating short-term projects (a Pathfinder project on employment will be discussed in the next section).

Community penalties research since 'What Works'

It is difficult to draw a hard-and-fast line between community penalties research carried out before the inception of the What Works initiative and afterwards; indeed it is difficult to be definitive about when What Works became an initiative. However, 1998 may be taken as the key year: Probation Circular 35/1998 'Effective Practice Initiative: National Implementation Plan for the Supervision of Offenders' was published (Home Office 1998b); two significant reports were published by the Probation Inspectorate (Chapman and Hough 1998; Underdown 1998); and a remarkably optimistic 'Assessment of Research Evidence on Ways of Dealing with Offending Behaviour' was published by the Home Office (Goldblatt and Lewis 1998). Despite the fact that a close reading of these texts suggested that optimism was perhaps not grounded in solid evidence (and an earlier Home Office study into cognitive behavioural approaches in probation was not especially positive; see Hedderman and Sugg 1997), the Crime Reduction Programme made considerable funding available for research in 1999 and major probation projects were designed. Peter Raynor (2004) has referred to it as the largest body of research on effectiveness ever undertaken in Britain.

The original Pathfinder projects—covering offender behaviour programmes, basic skills, and community punishment (a fourth Pathfinder on resettlement for short-term prisoners will not be considered here)—involved large-scale research studies that used a variety of methods. While there might have been expected to be some coherence about the projects, there is little sign of this. Given the significance of the results for the What Works initiative, it is surprising that publication of the results of the research studies has been haphazard with no sign of co-ordination. Results have appeared as Home Office Research Studies (Hollin *et al.* 2002), as On-Line Reports (McMahon *et al.* 2004), and as Occasional Papers (Rex *et al.* 2003). While there can be no doubt that vast amounts of data were collected and analysed, and a great deal of useful information uncovered, the bottom line, however, is that research results have been disappointing. Implementation has been poor and attrition rates for programmes have been high. Given NPS targets to reduce reconviction rates, it is particularly notable that reconviction studies for the Pathfinders have been—for the most part—absent. Hollin and his colleagues (2004) carried out a retrospective analysis of reconviction rates for offending behaviour programmes that found no difference in the reconviction rates between the experimental group and a matched comparison group. This may have been due to the high non-completion rate in the experimental group, and the rate for those who completed programmes was significantly lower. As noted earlier, a prospective analysis carried out by the researchers has not been published by the Home Office. Reconviction analyses for the other Pathfinders have not appeared.

Two further Pathfinder projects have been carried out. One, an Employment Pathfinder faced various difficulties in implementation owing to organizational problems in the areas studied; this was published as an On-Line Report (Haslewood-Pocsik *et al.* 2004) and no further results have appeared. The other, an initiative examining how programmes might be adapted to Black and Asian offenders, also found obstacles to implementation; this study was published as a Development and Practice Report (Stephens *et al.* 2004).

Since the Pathfinder projects, research has taken two routes. First, an examination of intensive supervision schemes, such as the Intensive Supervision and Monitoring Schemes (see Worrall *et al.* 2003; Homes *et al.* 2005; Dawson 2005) and the Intensive Control and Change Programme (Partridge *et al.* 2005). Once again, publication of these reports is split between On-Line Reports and Development and Practice Reports for no apparent reason. Results are what might by now be taken as expected: multi-agency or partnership work is not easy and communication is a persistent problem; implementation difficulties abound; resource issues are ever-present; effective targeting is crucial. These kinds of research results can be found in community penalties research for the previous 20 years at least, and it is surprising that the Home Office seems to have failed to learn from them. The persistent replication of results suggests that the data are reliable and valid—yet there is little evidence of any notice being taken of them.

The other route is one that might have led to rather more promising results from the Pathfinders if it had been followed prior to these projects. Case management (now offender management) has become a vital aspect of community supervision work with the increasing fragmentation of programmes and the purchaser/provider split that now lies at the heart of work with offenders. Without an effective case management system, there will be little coherence to a community order; many of the problems identified by the Pathfinder research studies might have been avoided if case managers had been in place. Partridge (2004) examined case management models and identified three models: a specialist, a generic, and a hybrid model. No one of these models was clearly superior to the others:

For each of the different models there were benefits and drawbacks for staff and offenders. However, this research has highlighted the difficulty of making direct causal links between effectiveness and models of case management. Effectiveness relates to a range of factors and it is difficult to isolate the specific impact of the model in relation to the myriad of other local and contextual factors (Partridge 2004: 49).

A National Offender Management Model (NOMM) was developed by NOMS (NOMS 2005) and another Pathfinder project, based in the North West region, was set up to test it out. The significance of getting this right is evident by the action research project that accompanied the early stages (the first few months) of implementation (PA Consultancy Group/MORI 2005). Action research, with its aim of directly influencing policy or practice (though not necessarily of questioning the goals of the policy or the grounds upon which practice has been constructed—see Kemmis (2001) for a discussion of the differences between technical, practical, and critical action research) has not been a common approach for Home Office research. Possibly the idea of 'researchers' being so closely involved with the development of policy and practice implied by the concept of action research is not welcomed by those who initiate and/or develop policy and practice. But many of the Home Office research studies that have been discussed here would benefited enormously if they had been treated as action research rather than outcome evaluations of new initiatives. The idea behind action research is, of course, to provide immediate feedback in order that the policy and practice in question can be changed for the better without waiting for a research project to be completed. This key foundation of action research is undermined somewhat, however, when we note that the NOMM is being rolled out nationally (see NOMS 2005: 22) before completion of a full process evaluation by 2006.

'Independent' research

While virtually all of the research already discussed has emanated from the Home Office either directly or via commissioning, it would be false to give the impression that government has a complete stranglehold over research into community penalties—or ever did have. Peter Raynor's study of the Afan Alternative, for example, was carried out with no formal funding whatsoever, and this was also the case with his evaluation of the STOP initiative (discussed above—Raynor 1988; Raynor and Vanstone 1994, 1996, 1997). David Smith and his colleagues carried out early research into partnership/multi-agency work and this was funded by the ESRC (Sampson and Smith 1992; Sampson *et al.* 1988). More recently, Judith Rumgay has also explored probation partnership work with reference to programmes for substance-misusing offenders in her book *The Addicted Offender* (2000). That the same tensions and problems with regard to multi-agency work appear in both studies suggests a certain intractability (or an inability to learn from empirical research), and given the significance of multi-agency work for the 'new' probation service—especially in relation to NOMS and the challenge of contestability—the need to resolve such problems is vital.

The significance of risk management and risk assessment for community penalties would be difficult to overestimate and once again, key research has been carried out outside the purview of the Home Office. Hazel Kemshall's book *Risk in Probation Practice* (1998) was the result of research over two years in one probation service—work that was, in fact, picked up by the Home Office which subsequently commissioned Kemshall to prepare a review of research on the assessment and management of risk (Kemshall 1996). Gwen Robinson, too, has examined how risk management has been implemented in a couple of probation areas (Robinson 1999, 2002). Both of these studies involved lengthy timescales (increasingly anathema to the Home Office—although it must be acknowledged that the initial Pathfinder research projects ran for several years) and also focused in-depth on one or two probation areas. The combination of several years and detailed study of one or two probation areas is not one that normally lends itself to Home Office funding.

Stephen Farrall (2002) and Sue Rex (2005) have both produced books resulting from empirical research, and each has shone light on unexplored areas that have the potential to stimulate further highly relevant work. By exploring how and why probationers desist from crime, Farrall has uncovered a serious dissonance between the views of probationers and those of their supervisors, and has called into question an over-reliance on cognitive behavioural programmes.[2] Rex examined the messages implicit in community penalties as understood by magistrates, probation and community service staff, offenders and victims. Different views suggest the need for greater coherence and this is

---

[2] Shadd Maruna's work on desistance should also be noted, although I have chosen not to discuss it here as it is concerned with exploring a 'phenomenology of desistance' (Maruna 2001: 8) rather than the work of the probation service.

especially relevant with the introduction of the community order, where the possibility of lack of coherence is all too clear.

It is important to emphasize that none of these major studies was funded by the Home Office. The ESRC funded Kemshall and Rex (and also Mair's study of Chief Probation Officers) and the Mental Health Foundation funded Rumgay. The work of Farrall and Robinson was carried out as Ph.D. research; and Farrall has followed up his sample of offenders in another work exploring the longer-term impact of probation that was funded by the Leverhulme Trust (Farrall and Calverley 2006). Home Office funding is, therefore, not necessary for high-quality, relevant research—indeed, as some of the examples mentioned demonstrate, it is possible to carry out significant research with no funding at all. Competition for research grants or Ph.D. studentships can be intense, but the relative freedom to pursue a topic in detail over several years is immensely rewarding; it can not only lead to significant research relevant to policy and practice, but can also lay the foundations for a productive career.

The salience of community penalties can also be seen by research being funded or carried out by agencies other than the Home Office. ACOP, for example, funded audits of enforcement (see above) and some work on public perceptions of probation (ACOP 1998). Both of these were carried out for defensive purposes, and the early work on perceptions was not published—rumour claimed that this was due to the findings being so negative. The NPS has also used MORI to carry out research into magistrates' and public perceptions of probation (MORI 2002, 2003), which showed that the latter were not particularly knowledgeable while the former were remarkably positive. The importance of risk assessment is further confirmed by NAPO's recent decision to fund a survey of probation officer views about OASys (Mair *et al.* 2006) in an effort to put some empirical flesh on impressionistic bones suggesting considerable discontent (an impression that was, interestingly, not confirmed by the research). The National Audit Office has become involved in examining community penalties, with a study of fine collection (NAO 2002) and an examination of the implementation and early impact of Drug Treatment and Testing Orders (NAO 2004). The latter study was partly carried out in conjunction with the Probation Inspectorate (HMIP), and while I do not propose to discuss HMIP reports here, it should not be forgotten that a great deal of material is collected and analysed by the Inspectorate annually.

It is worth repeating here the point made earlier about access. Prior to the introduction of the NPS, it was very much up to individual Chief Probation Officers to decide whether to permit access to their areas for research purposes—whether this was Home Office-driven research or work by a local academic.[3] Access is now much more in the control of the NPS (and therefore the Home Office), and it is likely to become more difficult to obtain permission to research in a probation area—especially if the proposed research is not seen as part of the Home Office agenda. Just how contestability might impact on this is not clear, nor is the influence of Regional Offender Managers (ROMs) who could have considerable power if NOMS comes fully to fruition. So-called 'independent' research has contributed hugely to our understanding of community penalties, but it is all too easy to see a threat to such research in future if Home Office backing is not secured.

---

[3] It is worth noting how productive a good relationship between a probation area and local academics can be— Peter Raynor in Mid Glamorgan, now part of South Wales, for example, or Bill McWilliams in South Yorkshire.

Conclusions

A considerable number of research studies into community penalties has been discussed (with at least as many—if not more—ignored), but the impact of all this research has been relatively minimal. In addition to the reasons given earlier for this lack of potency several others require some discussion—the relationship between research and policy (or practice), the dissemination of research, and the speed with which policy changes—and it is important to emphasize that these are closely related to each other.

Research need not always have a direct pay-off in terms of influencing policy or practice directly. Increasingly, however, with criminal justice agencies such as the probation service under pressure in terms of budget cuts, new responsibilities, and the need to be accountable, access for researchers to staff, data, or offenders cannot be taken for granted. Something has to be offered by the researcher in return for access, and often this is a vague and implicit understanding that the research will contribute to the needs of the organization. In a rather similar way, Home Office research is taken-for-granted as being policy-relevant—although how this is actually achieved is left to one side. One might flippantly suggest that it is policy-relevant simply *because* it is Home Office-commissioned research, but that only raises more questions.

The policy process involves a series of stages that can loop back to the start and research can contribute at almost any point in that process. This kind of model, however, does not seem to be recognized in the Home Office; nor, I would argue, is it recognized in the probation service. For both of these bodies, research has always been understood as something that might be used when a new policy or practice is about to be implemented in order to find out what the outcomes of that policy or practice are, with the possibility that if things are not happening as expected action could be taken. In reality, even this simplistic model of the research and policy relationship is rarely achieved. As we have seen, the Home Office research into community service was never *intended* to influence the decision to make community service available on a national basis; Home Office research into intensive probation (an initiative seen as having significant implications for national practice) was marginalized because it was decided to introduce the combination order *before* intensive probation was evaluated; and successive studies of electronic monitoring have found similar problems without any action to try to resolve these. If research is to continue in its role of servant to policy/practice (and I have argued that, in fact, it should be seen as equal partner), then precisely what it can contribute needs to be hammered out and clarified anew for every project. The relationship between research and policy or practice is too important to be left to vague, ambiguous understandings that have never been spelled out.

As for the dissemination of research, this is in an even more nebulous state than clarifying the research and policy relationship (but is, of course, closely related to it). It is little wonder that research has such a limited impact upon policy or practice when its results are hardly ever formulated or disseminated in such a way as to make them easily accessible to those who make policy or practice. The lessons of community penalties research are set out with other researchers in mind, not with a view to influencing how probation officers do their work. The increasing use of Executive Summaries, and the introduction by the Home Office of brief distillations of larger studies in the *Research Findings* series, are steps towards making research more accessible to busy non-researchers, but neither translates the results of research into practice recommendations. And even if this were the case, any such recommendations would have to be backed by advice on how they might be implemented and then subject to further research. Academic researchers themselves may not be the most appropriate people to translate the results of their work into nostrums for practice, and others may have to be involved if this is to be done effectively. But, given the fact that so much research into community penalties is grounded on basic ideas about practice, about how such penalties 'work', it is—in one sense—wasted research if results are not actively related to practice. Interestingly, the Home Office now publishes *Development and Practice Reports*, but just how these differ from its other publications is unclear. And there are, as I have argued earlier, problems with having different types of report published in different formats. In addition, what appears to be the increasing use of consultants to carry out research that would previously been done by academics does not bode well for dissemination; and, as I write (September 2006) the Home Office is in the third month of a 'pause' in publishing its research. If government is—as it claims to be—committed to an evidence-based approach to policy and practice, then at least it needs to publish the findings of its research in a timely and accessible fashion.

The difficulties posed by the relationship between research and policy, and the dissemination of research, are exacerbated by the speed of policy change. Twenty years ago, policy with regard to community penalties was relatively slow-moving but since 1998 it has accelerated rapidly and new initiatives are announced before earlier policies are properly bedded down (e.g. the creation of the NPS and its subsequent succession by NOMS). For research to have an impact, it has to be applied to a recognizable landscape; if this has changed as a result of policy development, then research will be outdated. This has always been a problem for policy-oriented research, but with what seems to be a lemming-like rush to change policy and practice for its own sake by New Labour, research is left behind.

Since the first edition of this book a number of other, new issues have emerged to complicate further community penalties research:

1. In its search to find out 'What Works', the Home Office now favours (possibly as a result of its interest in the ideas of the Campbell Collaboration) randomized control trials as the 'gold standard' for outcome research. This means that other approaches to measuring outcome are marginalized, as are process evaluations—with the latter being vital in order to interpret outcomes.

2. While it remains unclear about precisely what contestability will involve, it is certainly likely that agencies and organizations other than the NPS will become providers of community penalties and that this will mean having to negotiate with these (possibly for-profit) agencies to carry out research.

3. In relation to the previous point, trying to unravel which parts of a community order contribute to the success or failure of the order will become even more difficult (and we never did unravel how and why a simple probation order 'worked').

4. With the advent of regionalization and the power of Regional Offender Managers (ROMs), the landscape for research may change again. Should we be looking at individual probation areas, the NPS as a whole, or at a regional level? What scope will ROMS have for commissioning research independently of NOMS?

For the most part, research into community penalties in the UK has followed fairly mundane paths and has had little direct, immediate impact upon policy or practice. The methodologies adopted have been predictable, although they have been applied competently and carefully. Indeed, there may not be very much scope for radically novel approaches; the basic tools of social research have not changed dramatically over the years, they have simply been refined. While innovation simply for its own sake is not necessarily a good thing, neither is the Home Office insistence that randomized control trials should be used wherever possible (Friendship *et al.* 2004). It should be emphasized that it is not as a result of 'bad' research that we know so little. It is much more to do with assuming that we know more about the basics of community penalties than we actually do, with pressure to evaluate the outcomes of penalties before we know what they are doing and for whom they are doing it, and with small-scale, limited, fragmented research studies carried out in a vacuum. It is, in short, to do with the lack of a centrally planned, strategic, long-term programme of research which is deliberately targeted and plugged into practice or policy whenever appropriate. While it cannot be denied that there is a considerable Home Office interest here, the increasingly tight grip of research by the Home Office is not helpful. The politicization of community penalties may have led to an explosion in research, but more does not necessarily mean better. The creation of the NPS and the emergence of NOMS are likely to lead to even greater Home Office control over research. A rhetorical insistence upon evidence-based policy and practice is in practice the use of selected, acceptable evidence that fits the received Home Office vision.

This should not be greeted as a statement of gloom and despair. On the contrary, the need for challenging, 'independent' research that questions the new 'certainties' is greater than ever. Researchers may need to explore alternative sources of funding, but with the current significance of community penalties this might be less difficult than it has been in the past. We still know little about the organization of probation services and how that relates to the delivery and outcomes of penalties, or how individual probation officers justify what they do and how they do it, to name only two subjects that would seem to be highly relevant to improving the effectiveness of community penalties. The need for more holistic, joined-up studies is pressing with the advent of the community order and NOMS. A greater willingness to address the politics of community penalties as part of the research agenda is required; the wider context is at least as important as a narrow-minded obsession with simplistic notions of effectiveness. Following orthodoxies blindly has never led to positive developments; the task of research is to ask questions, to throw up contradictory findings, and these lead to new ways forward. Research into community penalties is well-placed to do this—but is the Home Office ready to listen?

Suggestions for further reading

Virtually all of the research worth reading has been mentioned, although issues regarding the effectiveness of community penalties are covered usefully in two edited collections: James McGuire's *What Works: Reducing Reoffending* (Chichester: John Wiley 1995) and George Mair's *Evaluating the Effectiveness of Community Penalties* (Aldershot: Avebury 1997). Good introductions to the work of the probation service can be found in: Wing Hong Chui and Mike Nellis (eds) *Moving Probation Forward: Evidence, Arguments and Practice* (Harlow: Pearson Longman 2003); Peter Raynor and Maurice Vanstone *Understanding Community Penalties* (Buckingham: Open University Press 2002); and Anne Worrall and Clare Hoy *Punishment in the Community: Managing Offenders, Making Choices* (2nd edn) (Cullompton: Willan 2005). The essays contained in *Community Penalties: Change and Challenges* (Cullompton: Willan 2001) edited by Tony Bottoms, Loraine Gelsthorpe, and Sue Rex address key issues for the future of probation. The *Handbook of Probation* (Cullompton: Willan 2007) edited by Loraine Gelsthorpe and Rod Morgan is likely to become an important source for the study of community penalties.

There is no alternative to reading the various research studies discussed in this chapter and reflecting critically on them. Many research methods texts are available—my only advice would be never to fall into the trap of thinking that you have to follow their bloodless prescriptions to the letter in order to produce a perfect piece of research. For better or worse, life is a much more messy business.

I would like to thank Roy King and Emma Wincup for helpful comments on the first draft of this chapter; and Peter Raynor and Tony Vass for lending me copies of their books on the Afan Alternative and community service respectively.

References

ACOP (1998). *Re-branding the Probation Service*. London: ACOP.

ADVISORY COUNCIL ON THE PENAL SYSTEM (1970). *Non-Custodial and Semi-Custodial Penalties*. London: HMSO.

AUBREY, R. and HOUGH, M. (1997). *Assessing Offenders' Needs: Assessment Scales for the Probation Service*. Home Office Research Study No. 166. London: Home Office.

AUDIT COMMISSION (1989). *The Probation Service: Promoting Value for Money*. London: HMSO.

AYE MAUNG, N. and HAMMOND, N. (2000). *Risk of Re-offending and Needs Assessments: the Users' Perspective*. Home Office Research Study No. 216. London: Home Office.

BAILEY, R. and WARD, D. (1992). *Probation Supervision: Attitudes to Formalised Helping*. Belfast: Probation Board for Northern Ireland.

BARKER, M. and MORGAN, R. (1993). *Sex Offenders: A Framework for the Evaluation of Community-Based Treatment*. London: Home Office.

BARR, H. (1966). *A Survey of Group Work in the Probation Service*. Home Office Studies in the Causes of Delinquency and the Treatment of Offenders 9. London: HMSO.

—— and O'LEARY, E. (1966). *Trends and Regional Comparisons in Probation*. Home Office Studies in the Causes of Delinquency and the Treatment of Offenders 8. London: HMSO.

BECKETT, R., BEECH, A., FISHER, D., and FORDHAM, A. S. (1994). *Community-Based Treatment for Sex Offenders: An Evaluation of Seven Treatment Programmes*. London: Home Office.

BOCHEL, D. (1976). *Probation and After-Care: Its Development in England and Wales*. Edinburgh: Scottish Academic Press.

BOTTOMLEY, K., HUCKLESBY, A., MAIR, G., and NELLIS, M. (2004). *Electronic Monitoring of Offenders: Key Developments*. London: NAPO.

BRODY, S. (1976). *The Effectiveness of Sentencing: A Review of the Literature.* Home Office Research Study No. 35. London: HMSO.

BROWNLEE, I. D. (1995). 'Intensive Probation with Young Adult Offenders: A Short Reconviction Study'. *British Journal of Criminology* 35: 599–612.

BURNETT, R. (1996). *Fitting Supervision to Offenders: Assessment and Allocation Decisions in the Probation Service.* Home Office Research Study No. 153. London: Home Office.

—— and ROBERTS, C. (eds) (2004). *What Works in Probation and Youth Justice: Developing Evidence-based Practice.* Cullompton: Willan.

CANN, J., FALSHAW, L., NUGENT, F., and FRIENDSHIP, C. (2003). 'Understanding What Works: Accredited Cognitive Skills Programmes for Adult Men and Young Offenders'. Home Office Findings 226. London: Home Office.

CARNIE, J. (1990). *Sentencers' Perceptions of Community Service by Offenders.* Edinburgh: Scottish Office Central Research Unit.

CARTER, P. (2003). *Managing Offenders, Reducing Crime.* London: Strategy Unit.

CHAPMAN, T. (2005). 'Review of G. Mair (ed.), What Matters in Probation and R. Burnett and C. Roberts (eds) What Works in Probation and Youth Justice'. *British Journal of Criminology* 45: 785–90.

—— and HOUGH, M. (1998). *Evidence Based Practice: A Guide to Effective Practice.* London: HMIP.

CHARMAN, E., GIBSON, B., HONESS, T., and MORGAN, R. (1996). 'Fine Impositions and Enforcement Following the Criminal Justice Act 1993'. Home Office Research Findings No. 36. London: Home Office.

CRIMINAL JUSTICE 4: (3). Special issue 'Evaluating the Crime Reduction Programme in England and Wales'.

CRIMINAL JUSTICE MATTERS 62. Winter 2005/06. 'Uses of Research'.

DAVIES, M. (1969). *Probationers in their Social Environment.* Home Office Research Study No. 2. London: HMSO.

—— (1970). *Financial Penalties and Probation.* Home Office Research Study No. 5. London: HMSO.

—— (1973). *An Index of Social Environment.* Home Office Research Study No. 17. London: HMSO.

—— (1974). *Social Work in the Environment.* Home Office Research Study No. 21. London: HMSO.

DAVIS, G., CADDICK, B., LYON, K., DOLING, L., HASLER, J., WEBSTER, A., REED, M., and FORD, K. (1997). *Addressing the Literacy Needs of Offenders under Probation Supervision.* Home Office Research Study No. 169. London: Home Office.

DAWSON, P. (2005). *Early Findings from the Prolific and Other Priority Offenders Evaluation.* Home Office Development and Practice Report 46.

DAY, P. (1981). *Social Work and Social Control.* London: Tavistock.

DITTON, J. and FORD, R. (1994). *The Reality of Probation: A Formal Ethnography of Process and Practice.* Aldershot: Avebury.

ELLIS, T., HEDDERMAN, C., and MORTIMER, E. (1996). *Enforcing Community Sentences.* Home Office Research Study No. 158. London: Home Office.

FALSHAW, L., FRIENDSHIP, C., TRAVERS, R., and NUGENT, F. (2003). 'Searching for "What Works": an Evaluation of Cognitive Skills Programmes'. Home Office Findings 206. London: Home Office.

FARRALL, S. (2002). *Rethinking What Works with Offenders: Probation, Social Context and Desistance from Crime.* Cullompton: Willan.

—— and CALVERLEY, A. (2006). *Understanding Desistance from Crime: Theoretical Directions in Resettlement and*

Rehabilitation. Maidenhead: Open University Press.

FIELDING, N. (1986). *Probation Practice: Client Support under Social Control.* Aldershot: Gower.

FOLKARD, M. S., LYON, K., CARVER, M. M., and O'LEARY, E. (1966). *Probation Research: A Preliminary Report.* Home Office Studies in the Causes of Delinquency and the Treatment of Offenders 7. London: HMSO.

——, FOWLES, A. J., McWILLIAMS, B. C., McWILLIAMS, W., SMITH, D. D., SMITH, D. E., and WALMSLEY, G. R. (1974). *IMPACT Intensive Matched Probation and After-Care Treatment: Volume 1 The Design of the Probation Experiment and an Interim Evaluation.* Home Office Research Study No. 24. London: HMSO.

—— SMITH, D. E. and SMITH, D. D. (1976). *IMPACT: Volume 2 The Results of the Experiment.* Home Office Research Study No. 36. London: HMSO.

FRIENDSHIP, C., STREET, R., CANN, J., and HARPER, G. (2004). 'Introduction: the policy context and assessing the evidence', in G. Harper and C. Chitty (eds), *The Impact of Corrections on Re-Offending: a Review of 'What Works'.* Home Office Research Study No. 291. London: Home Office.

GOLDBLATT, P. and LEWIS, C. (1998). *Reducing Offending: an Assessment of Research Evidence on Ways of Dealing with Offending Behaviour.* Home Office Research Study No. 187. London: Home Office.

HASLEWOOD-POCSIK, I., MERONE, L., and ROBERTS, C. (2004). *The Evaluation of the Employment Pathfinder: Lessons from Phase 1 and a Survey for Phase II.* Home Office Online Report 22/04.

HAXBY, D. (1978). *Probation: A Changing Service.* London: Constable.

HEARNDEN, I. and MILLIE, A. (2003). *Investigating Links between Probation Enforcement and Reconviction.* Home Office Online Report 41/03.

—— and MILLIE, A. (2004). 'Does Tougher Enforcement Lead to Lower Reconviction?'. *Probation Journal* 51: 48–58.

HEDDERMAN, C. (1999). *ACOP Enforcement Survey: Stage 1.* London: ACOP (available at *http://www.kcl.ac.uk/icpr/*).

HEDDERMAN, C. and HEARNDEN, I. (2000). *Improving Enforcement: the Second ACOP Enforcement Audit.* London: ACOP (available at *www.sbu.ac.uk/cpru*).

—— and —— (2001). *Setting New Standards for Enforcement: the Third ACOP Audit* (available at *http://www.kcl.ac.uk/depsta/law/research/icpr/publications/acop3.shtml*).

—— and HOUGH, M. (2004). 'Getting Tough or Being Effective: What Matters' in G. Mair (ed.), *What Matters in Probation.* Cullompton: Willan.

—— and SUGG, D. (1996). 'Does Treating Sex Offenders Reduce Reoffending?'. Home Office Research Findings No. 45. London: Home Office.

—— and —— (1997). 'The Influence of Cognitive Approaches: a Survey of Probation Programmes' in *Changing Offenders' Attitudes and Behaviour; What Works?* Home Office Research Study No. 171. London: Home Office.

HOLLIN, C., McGUIRE, J., PALMER, E., BILBY, C., HATCHER, R., and HOLMES, A. (2002). *Introducing Pathfinder Programmes into the Probation Service: an Interim Report.* Home Office Research Study No. 247. London: Home Office.

——, PALMER, E., McGUIRE, J., HOUNSOME, J., HATCHER, R., BILBY, C., and CLARK, C. (2004). *Pathfinder Programmes in the Probation Service: a Retrospective Analysis.* Home Office Online Report 66/04.

HOME OFFICE (1964). *The Sentence of the Court.* London: HMSO.

Home Office (1984). *Probation Service in England and Wales: Statement of National Objectives and Priorities.* London: Home Office.

—— (1998a). 'Probation Circular 72/1998: Motor Projects'. London: Home Office.

—— (1998b). 'Effective Practice Initiative: National Implementation Plan for the Supervision of Offenders'. Probation Circular 35/1998. London: Home Office.

—— (2005a). *Offender Management Caseload Statistics 2004.* Home Office Statistical Bulletin 17/05. London: Home Office.

—— (2005b). *Sentencing Statistics 2004 England and Wales.* Home Office Statistical Bulletin 15/05. London: Home Office.

—— (2006). *Rebalancing the Criminal Justice System in Favour of the Law-Abiding Majority: cutting crime, reducing reoffending and protecting the public.* London: Home Office.

Homes, A., Walmsley, R. K., and Debidin, M. (2005). *Intensive Supervision and Monitoring Schemes for Persistent Offenders: staff and offender perceptions.* Home Office Development and Practice Report 41. London: Home Office.

Hough, M., Clancy, A., McSweeney, T., and Turnbull, P. J. (2003). 'The Impact of Drug Treatment and Testing Orders on Offending: Two-year Reconviction Results'. Home Office Findings 184. London: Home Office.

House of Commons (1998a). *Third Report from the Home Affairs Committee—Alternatives to Prison Sentences: Volume I Report and Proceedings of the Committee.* London: The Stationery Office.

—— (1998b). *Third Report from the Home Affairs Committee—Alternatives to Prison Sentences: Volume II Minutes of Evidence and Appendices.* London: The Stationery Office.

Jennings, D. (2002). *One Year Juvenile Reconviction Rates: July 2000 cohort.* London: Home Office.

Kemmis, S. (2001). 'Exploring the Relevance of Critical Theory for Action Research: Emancipatory Action Research in the Footsteps of Jurgen Habermas' in P. Reason and H. Bradbury (eds), *Handbook of Action Research.* London: Sage.

Kemshall, H. (1996). *Reviewing Risk: A Review of Research on the Assessment and Management of Risk and Dangerousnes.* London: Home Office.

—— (1998). *Risk in Probation Practice.* Aldershot: Ashgate.

Knapp, M., Robertson, E., and McIvor, G. (1992). 'The Comparative Costs of Community Service and Custody in Scotland'. *Howard Journal* 31: 8–30.

Lewis, S., Vennard, J., Maguire, M., Raynor, P., Vanstone, M., Raybould, S., and Rix, A. (2003). *The Resettlement of Short-Term Prisoners: an Evaluation of Seven Pathfinders.* RDS Occasional Paper No. 83. London: Home Office.

Lipsey, M. (1992). 'Juvenile Delinquency Treatment: a Meta-analytic Inquiry into the Variability of Effects' in T. D. Cook, H. Cooper, D. S. Cordray, H. Hartmann, L. V. Hedges, R. J. Light, T. A. Louis and F. Mosteller (eds), *Meta-Analysis for Explanation: a Casebook.* New York: Russell Sage Foundation.

Lloyd, C., Mair, G., and Hough, M. (1994). *Explaining Reconviction Rates: A Critical Analysis.* Home Office Research Study No. 136. London: HMSO.

McIvor, G. (1989). *An Evaluative Study of Community Service by Offenders.* University of Stirling: Social Work Research Centre.

—— (1990). 'Community Service and Custody in Scotland'. *Howard Journal* 29: 101–13.

—— (1992a). *Reconviction among Offenders Sentenced to Community Service.* University of Stirling: Social Work Research Centre.

—— (1992b). *Sentenced to Serve: The Operation and Impact of Community Service by Offenders*. Aldershot: Avebury.

McLaughlin, E. and Muncie, J. (1994). 'Managing the Criminal Justice System' in J. Clarke, A. Cochrane, and E. McLaughlin (eds), *Managing Social Policy*. London: Sage.

McMahon, G., Hall, A., Hayward, G., Hudson, C., Roberts, C., Fernandez, R., and Burnett, R. (2004). *Basic Skills Programmes in the Probation Service: Evaluation of the Basic Skills Pathfinder*. Home Office Online Report 14/04.

McWilliams, W. (1980). 'Selection Policies for Community Service: Practice and Theory' in K. Pease and W. McWilliams (eds), *Community Service by Order*. Edinburgh: Scottish Academic Press.

—— (1983). 'The Mission to the English Police Courts 1876–1936'. *Howard Journal* 22: 129–47.

—— (1985). 'The Mission Transformed: Professionalisation of Probation between the Wars'. *Howard Journal* 24: 257–74.

—— (1986). 'The English Probation System and the Diagnostic Ideal'. *Howard Journal* 25: 241–60.

—— (1987). 'Probation, Pragmatism and Policy'. *Howard Journal* 26: 97–121.

—— and Murphy, N. (1980). 'Breach of Community Service' in K. Pease and W. McWilliams (eds), *Community Service by Order*. Edinburgh: Scottish Academic Press.

Mackie, A., Raine, J., Burrows, J., Hopkins, M., and Dunstan, E. (2003). *Clearing the Debts: the Enforcement of Financial Penalties in Magistrates' Courts*. Home Office Online Report 09/03.

Mair, G. (1988). *Probation Day Centres*. Home Office Research Study No. 100. London: HMSO.

—— (1991). *Part Time Punishment? The Origins and Development of Senior Attendance Centres*. London: HMSO.

—— (ed.) (2004a). *What Matters in Probation*. Cullompton: Willan.

—— (2004b). 'What Works: a view from the Chiefs' in G. Mair (ed.), *What Matters in Probation*. Cullompton: Willan.

—— (2004c). 'Diversionary and Non-supervisory Approaches to Dealing with Offenders' in A. Bottoms, S. Rex, and G. Robinson (eds), *Alternatives to Prison: Options for an Insecure Society*. Cullompton: Willan.

—— (2005). 'Electronic Monitoring in England and Wales: Evidence-based or Not?'. *Criminal Justice* 5: 257–277.

—— Burke, L., and Taylor, S. (2006). ' "The Worst Tax Form You've Ever Seen"? Probation Officers' Views about OASys'. *Probation Journal* 53: 7–23.

—— Crisp, D., Sibbitt, R., and Harris, J. (1997). *The Combination Order*. Unpublished report to the Home Office.

—— and Lloyd, C. (1989). *Money Payment Supervision Orders: Probation Policy and Practice*. Home Office Research Study No. 114. London: HMSO.

——, ——, Nee, C., and Sibbitt, R. (1994). *Intensive Probation in England and Wales: An Evaluation*. Home Office Research Study No. 133. London: HMSO.

—— and May, C. (1997). *Offenders on Probation*. Home Office Research Study No. 167. London: Home Office.

—— and Mortimer, E. (1996). *Curfew Orders with Electronic Monitoring*. Home Office Research Study No. 163. London: Home Office.

—— and Nee, C. (1990). *Electronic Monitoring: The Trials and their Results*. Home Office Research Study No. 120. London: HMSO.

—— and —— (1992). 'Day Centre Reconviction Rates'. *British Journal of Criminology* 32: 329–39.

Martin, J. P. and Webster, D. (1994). *Probation Motor Projects in England and Wales*. London: Home Office.

Maruna, S. (2001). *Making Good: How Ex-Convicts Reform and Rebuild their Lives*. Washington, DC: American Psychological Association Books.

May, C. (1995). *Measuring the Satisfaction of Courts with the Probation Service*. Home Office Research Study No. 144. London: Home Office.

—— (1997). 'Magistrates' Views of the Probation Service'. Home Office Research Findings No.48. London: Home Office.

—— (1999). *Explaining Reconviction Following a Community Sentence: the Role of Social Factors*. Home Office Research Study No. 192. London: Home Office.

May, T. (1991). *Probation: Politics, Policy and Practice*. Buckingham: Open University Press.

Moore, R. (2003). 'The Use of Financial Penalties and the Amounts Imposed: the Need for a New Approach'. *Criminal Law Review*, January: 13–27.

MORI (2002). *Perceptions of the National Probation Service*. London: National Probation Service.

—— (2003). *Magistrates' Perceptions of the Probation Service*. London: National Probation Service.

Mortimer, E. and May, C. (1997). *Electronic Monitoring in Practice: The Second Year of the Trials of Curfew Orders*. Home Office Research Study No. 177. London: Home Office.

—— Pereira, E., and Walter, I. (1999). 'Making the Tag Fit: Further Analysis from the First Two Years of the Trials of Curfew Orders'. Home Office Research Findings No. 105. London: Home Office.

Moxon, D., Corkery, J., and Hedderman, C. (1992). *Developments in the Use of Compensation Orders in Magistrates' Courts since October 1988*. Home Office Research Study No. 126. London: HMSO.

—— Sutton, M., and Hedderman, C. (1990). *Unit Fines: Experiments in Four Courts*. Research and Planning Unit Paper 59. London: Home Office.

—— Hedderman, C., and Sutton, M. (1990). *Deductions from Benefit for Fine Default*. Research and Planning Unit Paper 60. London: Home Office.

National Audit Office (2002). *Collection of Fines and Other Financial Penalties in the Criminal Justice System*. London: National Audit Office.

—— (2004). *The Drug Treatment and Testing Order: Early Lessons*. London: National Audit Office.

Nee, C. and Sibbitt, R. (1993). *The Probation Response to Drug Misuse*. Research and Planning Unit Paper 78. London: Home Office.

Newburn, T. (1988). *The Use and Enforcement of Compensation Orders in Magistrates' Courts*. Home Office Research Study No. 102. London: HMSO.

NOMS (2005). *The NOMS Offender Management Model*. London: NOMS.

PA Consultancy Group/MORI (2005). *Action Research Study of the Implementation of the National Offender Management Model in the North West Pathfinder*. Home Office Online Report 32/05.

Page, M. (1992). *Crimefighters of London*. London: Inner London Probation Service.

Partridge, S. (2004). *Examining Case Management Models for Community Sentences*. Home Office Online Report 17/04.

——, Harris, J., Abram, M., and Scholes, A. (2005). *The Intensive Control and Change Programme Pilots: a Study of Implementation in the First Year*. Home Office Online Report 48/05.

Pease, K. (1983). 'Penal Innovations' in J. Lishman (ed), *Social Work with Adult Offenders*. Aberdeen: University of Aberdeen Press.

—— (1985). 'Community Service Orders' in M. Tonry and N. Morris (eds), *Crime and*

Justice: An Annual Review of Research Volume 6. Chicago, Ill: University of Chicago Press.

—— BILLINGHAM, S., and EARNSHAW, I. (1977). *Community Service Assessed in 1976*. Home Office Research Study No. 39. London: HMSO.

—— DURKIN, P., EARNSHAW, I., PAYNE, D., and THORPE, J. (1975). *Community Service Orders*. Home Office Research Study No. 29. London: HMSO.

PHILLPOTTS, G. J. O. and LANCUCKI, L. B. (1979). *Previous Convictions, Sentence and Reconviction*. Home Office Research Study No. 53. London: HMSO.

RADZINOWICZ, L. (1958). *The Results of Probation*. London: Macmillan.

RAINE, J., DUNSTAN, E., and MACKIE, A. (2003). 'Financial Penalties as a Sentence of the Court'. *Criminal Justice* 3: 181–97.

——, ——, and —— (2004). 'Financial penalties: Who Pays, Who Doesn't and Why Not?'. *Howard Journal* 43: 518–38.

RAYNOR, P. (1988). *Probation as an Alternative to Custody*. Aldershot: Avebury.

—— (2003). 'Evidence-Based Probation and its Critics'. *Probation Journal* 50: 334–45.

—— (2004). 'The Probation Service "Pathfinders": Finding the Path and Losing the Way?'. *Criminal Justice* 4: 309–25.

—— and VANSTONE, M. (1994). 'Probation Practice, Effectiveness and the Non-treatment Paradigm'. *British Journal of Social Work*, 24: 387–404.

—— and —— (1996). 'Reasoning and Rehabilitation in Britain: The Results of the Straight Thinking on Probation (STOP) Programme'. *International Journal of Offender Therapy and Comparative Criminology* 40: 272–84.

—— and —— (1997). *Straight Thinking on Probation (STOP): the Mid-Glamorgan experiment*. Probation Studies Unit Report No. 4. University of Oxford Centre for Criminological Research.

——, KYNCH, J., ROBERTS, C., and MERRINGTON, S. (2000). *Risk and Need Assessment in Probation Services: an evaluation*. Home Office Research Study No. 211. London: Home Office.

READ, G. (1980). 'Area Differences in Community Service Operation', in K. Pease and W. McWilliams (eds), *Community Service by Order*. Edinburgh: Scottish Academic Press.

REX, S. (2005). Reforming Community Penalties. Cullompton: Willan.

——, GELSTHORPE, L., ROBERTS, C., and JORDAN, P. (2003). *Crime Reduction Programme—An Evaluation of Community Service Pathfinder Projects: final report 2002*. RDS Occasional Paper. London: Home Office.

ROBERTS, K., BARTON, A., BUCHANAN, J., and GOLDSON, B. (1997). *Evaluation of a Home Office Initiative to Help Offenders into Employment*. London: Home Office.

ROBINSON, G. (1999). 'Risk Management and Rehabilitation in the Probation Service: Collision and Collusion'. *Howard Journal* 38: 421–433.

—— (2002). 'Exploring Risk Management in Probation Practice: Contemporary Developments in England and Wales'. *Punishment and Society* 4: 5–25.

RUMGAY, J. (2000). *The Addicted Offender: Developments in British Policy and Practice*. Basingstoke: Palgrave.

SAMPSON, A. and SMITH, D. (1992). 'Probation and Community Crime Prevention.' *Howard Journal* 31: 105–119.

—— STUBBS, P., SMITH, D., PEARSON, G., and BLAGG, H. (1988). 'Crime, Localities and the Multi-Agency Approach'. *British Journal of Criminology* 28: 478–93.

SARNO, C., HEARNDEN, I., HEDDERMAN, C., HOUGH, M., NEE, C., and HERRINGTON, V. (2000). *Working their Way out of Offending: an Evaluation of Two Probation Employment Schemes*. Home Office Research Study No. 218. London: Home Office.

SIBBITT, R. (1996). *The ILPS Methadone Prescribing Project*. Home Office Research Study No. 148. London: Home Office.

SINCLAIR, I. (1971). *Hostels for Probationers*. Home Office Research Study No. 6. London: HMSO.

SKINNS, C. D. (1990). 'Community Service Practice'. *British Journal of Criminology* 30: 65–80.

SOCIAL EXCLUSION UNIT (2002). *Reducing Re-offending by Ex-Prisoners*. London: Office of the Deputy Prime Minister.

SOFTLEY, P. (1973). *A Survey of Fine Enforcement*. Home Office Research Study No. 16. London: Home Office.

—— (1978a). *Compensation Orders in Magistrates' Courts*. Home Office Research Study No. 43. London: HMSO.

—— (1978b). *Fines in Magistrates' Courts*. Home Office Research Study No. 46. London: HMSO.

—— and MOXON, D. (1982). *Fine Enforcement*. Research and Planning Unit Paper 12. London: Home Office.

STEPHENS, K., COOMBS, J., and DEBIDIN, M. (2004). *Black and Asian Offenders Pathfinder: Implementation Report*. Home Office Development and Practice Report 24. London: Home Office.

SUGG, D. (1998). 'Motor Projects in England and Wales: An Evaluation'. Home Office Research Findings No. 81. London: Home Office.

——, MOORE, L., and HOWARD, P. (2001). 'Electronic Monitoring and Offending Behaviour: Reconviction Results for the Second Year of Trials of Curfew Orders'. Home Office Research Findings No. 141. London: Home Office.

TAYLOR, P., CROW, I., IRVINE, D., and NICHOLS, G. (1999). *Demanding Physical Programmes for Young Offenders under Probation Supervision*. London: Home Office.

TURNBULL, P. J., McSWEENEY, T., WEBSTER, R., EDMUNDS, M., and HOUGH, M. (2000). *Drug Treatment and Testing Orders: Final Evaluation Report*. Home Office Research Study No. 212. London: Home Office.

UNDERDOWN, A. (1998). *Strategies for Effective Offender Supervision: Report of the HMIP What Works Project*. London: Home Office.

VANSTONE, M. (2004). *Supervising Offenders in the Community: a History of Probation Theory and Practice*. Aldershot: Ashgate.

VASS, A. A. (1984). *Sentenced to Labour: Close Encounters with a Prison Substitute*. St Ives: Venus Academica.

—— and WESTON, A. (1990). 'Probation Day Centres as an Alternative to Custody: A "Trojan Horse" Examined'. *British Journal of Criminology* 29: 255–72.

WALTER, I. (2002). *Evaluation of the National Roll-Out of Curfew Orders*. Home Office Online Report 15/02.

——, SUGG, D., and MOORE, L. (2001). 'A Year on the Tag: Interviews with Criminal Justice Practitioners and Electronic Monitoring Staff about Curfew Orders'. Home Office Research Findings No. 140. London: Home Office.

WHITTAKER, C. and MACKIE, A. (1997). *Enforcing Financial Penalties*. Home Office Research Study No. 165. London: Home Office.

WOOTTON, B. (1978). *Crime and Penal Policy: Reflections on Fifty Years Experience*. London: Allen & Unwin.

WORRALL, A., MAWBY, R. C., HEATH, G., and HOPE, T. (2003). *Intensive Supervision and Monitoring Projects*. Home Office Online Report 42/03.

YOUNG, W. (1979). *Community Service Orders*. London: Heinemann.

15

Doing research in prisons

Roy D. King and Alison Liebling

Introduction

Both of us have spent a lot of our professional lives inside prison walls, doing prisons research. Most of this has been in England (King 1972; King and Morgan 1976; King and Elliott 1978; King and McDermott 1989, 1990, 1995; Liebling 1992; 1995; 1999; Liebling and Price 2001; Liebling 2004; Liebling *et al.* 2005) but substantial periods have also been spent in Scotland (Bottomley *et al.* 1994), the United States (King 1987, 1991, 1999), Australia (OICP 2004) and in Russia (King 1994; King and Piacentini 2004). In this chapter we offer our reflections on the process of doing research in prisons.

Our remarks are directed primarily to those embarking upon prisons research for the first time, whether as doctoral students, novice researchers whose first rung on the ladder of a research career involves working on a prisons project, or post-doctoral applicants for their first prisons research contracts. But we hope they may also be of interest to undergraduate or postgraduate students whose courses address penological questions, or afford them opportunities, however limited, for placements in prisons. We would also like to address some of our comments to those supervising prisons research. In this revised edition the format of the chapter remains much the same. As before, we begin with some brief remarks on the growth and scale of prisons research, and then consider the politics of getting prisons research funded, up and running, and published. We have, of course, updated these sections to take account of the many developments since the first edition was published. Combining our experience of prisons research, and after consulting our past and present students and colleagues, we have greatly expanded the number of nostrums on the process of doing research from what was contained in the first edition. Space has dictated that these are presented largely in the form of detailed lists of dos and don'ts, but since many of these detailed recommendations can be derived from the original ten nostrums, first timers are urged to read these in the context of what was said in the original chapter (King 2000). It remains a highly selective and personal account and we shall finish with some of our reasons for thinking that prisons research is important and worthwhile.

The growth and scale of prisons research

In many parts of the world prisons remain secret places: in extreme cases they are off limits even to the relatives and lawyers of the prisoners held inside, let alone researchers. That is no longer the case in Britain which probably now leads the English-speaking world, which in turn probably leads the rest of the world, in terms of research in prisons. Although many of the early developments in the sociology of prisons, especially in theoretical and conceptual terms, came from the USA, and although many other English-speaking as well as European jurisdictions have invited or allowed researchers inside, it is in the UK that the strongest tradition of prisons research by academics has developed. This did not happen overnight.

The report compiled by the Labour Research Department on the evidence of suffragists and conscientious objectors (Hobhouse and Brockway 1922) was received with hostility by the Prison Commissioners. In the dying days of the Commission, however, Sir Lionel Fox, and his successor Sir Arthur Peterson, gave their backing to the pioneering case study of Pentonville (Morris *et al.* 1963). This change of heart came about in the context of what Garland (1994) has described as the emerging governmental project which saw major government support for criminology as an administrative aid through the establishment of the in-house Home Office Research Unit and as a scientific discipline through the foundation of the Cambridge Institute of Criminology. Fox was a believer in the policy benefits that would flow from soundly based criminological knowledge, and these were days of great expectations about the potential of an administrative criminology. The Morrises said little about the origins of their research, although Fox initially proposed a *comparative* study of Pentonville and Maidstone. Had it taken place this would have demonstrated sufficient contrast in conditions between 'local' and what were then called 'regional training' prisons to have helped in at least two areas of Fox's policy agenda—the development of remand centres to take untried prisoners out of local prisons and the need for a prison-building programme to improve physical facilities. At about the same time the Prison Commission invited the Tavistock Institute of Human Relations to appraise the implementation of the 'Norwich system'—the introduction of associated dining on the landings for some prisoners previously fed in cells, a longer working week for prisoners (much longer than they work today), and an early version of using prison officers as personal officers—at Bristol local prison (Emery 1970). The price of harnessing this research resource was, unevenly but inexorably, a new level of openness about what goes on in prisons. In any event in the years since then a tradition of criminological research in prisons has been built up, generating a sizeable group of academics with a detailed, first-hand knowledge of what goes on inside prisons which one rarely finds in other countries.

In a reflexive account such as this we make no attempt to list all the studies, still less to review them systematically. For now it will suffice to sketch in the terrain. There have been studies based on work carried out in individual local, training, or high-security prisons for men at Pentonville (Morris *et al.* 1963), Bristol (Emery 1970) Birmingham (Sparks 1971), Durham (Cohen and Taylor 1972), Albany (King and Elliott 1978), Grendon Underwood (Genders and Player 1995), the Wolds private prison (Bottomley *et al.* 1997), Manchester Strangeways (Carrabine 2004) and Wellingborough (Crewe 2005a); comparative studies that have examined open and closed prisons (Jones and Cornes 1977) or prisons of the same type (Liebling 2004), prisons from different security categories (King and McDermott 1995) and high-security prisons (Sparks *et al.* 1996; Drake 2007); and studies based on Dover borstal for young male offenders (Bottoms and McClintock 1973), on Cornton Vale prison for women in Scotland (Carlen 1983, Dobash *et al.* 1986), on young offender institutions more generally (McAllister *et al.*

1992) and comparative studies of women's prisons in England (Smith 1996; Bosworth 1999). There have also been a number of studies of special topics from conditions for remand prisoners (King and Morgan 1976) to the state of race relations (Genders and Player 1989; McDermott 1990); from suicide and self-harm (Liebling 1992, 1999; Liebling *et al.* 2005) to studies of the mental health of prisoners (Gunn *et al.* 1978; Gunn *et al.* 1991); from absconding from open prisons (Banks *et al.* 1975) to evaluations of special security units and units for difficult prisoners (Walmsley 1989; Bottomley 1995; Cooke 1989; Bottomley *et al.* 1994); from the impact of incentives and earned privileges (Liebling *et al.* 1997; Bottoms 2003) to the effectiveness of prison work and vocational training (Simon and Corbett 1996; Cheliotis, under review); and from studies of prison staff (Colvin 1977; Marsh *et al.* 1985; Liebling 2001; Liebling and Price 2001; Crawley 2004) to the processes of decision-making in Scottish and English prisons (Adler and Longhurst 1994; Padfield *et al.* 2003). There have been studies of the use of the media in prisons (Jewkes 2002), the transition into custody for young offenders (Harvey 2006), the operation of temporary release (Cheliotis 2005) and the drugs economy in prison (Crewe 2005b). There have even been a few studies which have taken an internationally comparative approach with the prison experience in the Netherlands (Downes 1988; Resodihardjo 2006) and the USA (King 1991). The majority of these studies have been funded by the Home Office or its Scottish equivalent—some have been funded in whole or in part by ESRC or its predecessor SSRC. Some have been directly funded by the Prison Service, and a handful by the Carnegie Trust and the Nuffield Foundation. At least one was unfunded (Cohen and Taylor 1972). The list is illustrative, not exhaustive. We are all too aware that we have not included any of the studies done in-house by prison psychologists, for example, or the occasional research done by serving probation officers and medical officers and other members of staff, or accounts by former prisoners, and no doubt there are others which we have neglected. We shall return to some of these studies later when we consider some methodological issues in doing research in prisons.

The politics and economics of prisons research

Although there has been a considerable opening up of the closed world of British prisons this is not to say that access is by any means guaranteed, or that funding is easy to come by, or that the results of research will always be welcomed. If crime is a political issue, so too is punishment. It is also an economic issue: not only do different forms of punishment cost money, but researchers require reasonable levels of support if they are to do their research well. One of the crucial issues for concern here is that the Home Office is *both* gatekeeper as far as access is concerned *and* principal funder of research, which also means that it has considerable control over what is published and when. In the circumstances it is hardly surprising that researchers sometimes have precarious relationships with officialdom: to put it no higher, most researchers will have experienced some degree of ambivalence in their dealings with the Home Office. It is also true that officials will have experienced some degree of frustration in their dealings with researchers, but the relationship is far from symmetrical with real power resting largely in the hands of officialdom.

Ever since Cohen and Taylor (1972) published their appendix criticizing the Home Office-funded study of pyschological deterioration amongst long-term prisoners (carried out by their colleagues at Durham), there have been some criminologists who regard almost everything done with Home Office funding or approval as necessarily tainted. The reality is much more complex and nuanced than that. Compared to Western Europe or the United States, let alone Russia or Eastern Europe, it is remarkable that in England and Wales, a sometimes irritating relationship has evolved between officials and the research community which, in spite of all the difficulties, has fostered a reasonably steady flow of good quality research, which is building a cumulative base of knowledge and understanding.

There have certainly been situations where researchers have found themselves at least temporarily sidelined, where access has been denied, where publication of results has been suppressed or delayed (Bottomley *et al.* 1997), or self-censored for fear of libel-suits (Sim 1990), and where inappropriate policies have been based ostensibly upon independent research findings (as with the closure of Barlinnie following the press misrepresentation of the report by Bottomley *et al.* 1994; see Sparks 2003). But there have also been instances of fruitful collaboration between policymakers and researchers (following King and Morgan 1980, and see the discussion in King and McDermott 1995: 3–15, as well as much of the work done by Alison Liebling and colleagues); where policymakers have welcomed adverse research findings exposing the consequences of past policies (King and McDermott 1989); and where important scientific research has been carried out in the most unpromising of political circumstances (for example when Sparks *et al.* 1996 were able to address the problem of *social order* in prisons in a climate when politicians, though not necessarily officials, were looking for easy answers on the *control* of prisoners).

It is, of course, necessary to cultivate contacts to some degree in order to gain access, but this does not mean that one automatically buys in to an official agenda or that one has to restrict the research to the officially constructed version of 'the problem'. In fact the 'official agenda' has not always been very clear. It certainly is not as monolithic as is often assumed and politicians and their official advisers can sometimes be in conflict. Michael Howard's deputy, David Maclean, wanted to close down the Home Office Research and Planning Unit because even 'in-house' research was seen as subversive. The Home Secretary at the time of writing (John Reid) has declared a 'moratorium' on the publication of research, while he reviews all the activities of the Home Office (*Daily Telegraph*, 2 July 2006). Even where politicians, policy advisers, and research managers see eye to eye their intentions can still fall foul of the micropolitics at institution level where co-operation may be withheld. Nevertheless, the research agenda has become more centralized, culminating in the current drive to marshal research to policy needs through the determination to support only evidence-based practice (Home Office 1998) and particularly practices thought to reduce reoffending. This can mean that crucial questions of how prisons function, how and why they differ, how cultures can subvert intentions, and how prisoners feel, risk being neglected. However, research managers have to work together with outside academics who are not always political dupes, but themselves players of politics, sometimes with considerable skill. Researchers can also play to their own agendas once access has been provided, or on occasion use the denial of access to political effect. They can also attract funding from elsewhere, at which point access is normally permitted. Our point is that this is a two-way process and getting access and funds need not mean that one automatically loses any sense of independence, scholarly judgement, or personal integrity. In this complex relationship, it is important to maintain a sense of irony, as well as relativism: for what happens in this country may be a great deal less tainted than what happens elsewhere.

Gaining access

The process of gaining access for research has been revised, formalized, and to some extent, streamlined since the first edition of this chapter went to press, so we shall describe the current procedure and its strengths and limitations below. The guidance for gaining access is contained in a Prison Service Order: Research Applications (PSO 7035) available on the Prison Service website, under 'Research'.

There is a single form for all research requests, but there are several routes for research applications to follow, depending on the number of establishments to which access is sought. The application form includes instructions, the criteria used for reviewing applications, and a series of questions about the aims and objectives of the research, the reason for undertaking the study, the key research questions, the potential benefits, the methodology and timetable, ethical issues, reasons for the choice of establishment(s), the number of staff and prisoners involved, and the contact time involved. The procedure excludes undergraduates, and some co-ordination of research requests goes on, so that individual prisons do not become over-researched. In a new climate of managerialism and financial stringency, the major concern of senior managers has arguably shifted from control over information to anxiety about the resource implications of a research presence. Nevertheless, the new system is intended to encourage applications from a wide range of individuals and research teams.

It is possible for a small-scale study in a single prison to be arranged through direct contact with the prison governor concerned, whose approval will in any case be needed before the research can be carried out. In this case, the form should be sent to the Governor concerned, often after some informal contact has taken place. In many cases, the Governor will pass the form to the prison psychologist for a view. This can cause difficulties, especially for applications where the study has been designed to deal with sociological issues. Where an applicant requests access to several prisons, a number of possibilities arise. If they are all within one Prison Service Area, the application goes to the Area Psychologist. Where a number of Areas are involved, the application goes to Planning Group, in Prison Service Headquarters. Where the project is National Strategic Research (that is, funded by the Home Office or likely to be sent to Ministers) the application goes to RDS-NOMS. At present, there is no such formal procedure for access to private prisons, so these requests are handled on an individual basis, often via the prison Director.

Access for research students

One important element in gaining access will be the track record in prisons research of the research director/supervisor and the university department concerned. In alphabetical order Bangor, Cambridge, Hull, Keele, LSE, and Oxford have probably had the most consistent commitment to research of this kind, but the situation changes with the mobility of academic staff, and this is not to suggest that access would be denied to would-be researchers who had not previously been involved in prisons research. The acceptance of research proposals will also depend upon the perceived importance of the topic, and a trade-off between the possible benefits and the possible demands of having a researcher around. Two approaches are likely to have a good chance of success: research which links to self-contained emerging areas of policy where policy divisions have not yet been able to find a place in the larger official research programme (as with Smith 1996; Tait in progress) and fairly narrowly defined pure research which offers further exploration of promising leads which have emerged from earlier research (as with Ahmad 1996). Prison officials will probably see Ph.D. research as potentially the least threatening—if only because work conducted as an apprentice is bound to be limited in scope, take a long time to complete, and unwelcome findings may be easier to dismiss. There seems now to be some official recognition that Ph.D., MPhil/MA students may provide a useful—and cheap– resource to undertake exploratory studies of various issues. This is an area of significant growth.

Access for independently funded research

With the right credentials, a viable research proposal, and the prospect of some funding of one's own from a Research Council or some other body there is a reasonable chance of a researcher being granted access providing the topic of research is not too currently controversial. It will help if the researcher has a track record, or the backing of someone with a track record. As with Ph.D. research, it is sometimes possible to get small projects off the ground by making direct contact with prison governors first. It is one of the ironies of the prisons research world that on the ground, staff are often quite enthusiastic about research, whereas those in control of the access procedures can be more cautious. Decision-makers will want to consult policy divisions to see that the research could have some useful pay-off, but with no funding at stake there is likely to be a greater acceptance of longer-term outcomes based on more theoretical exploration and development work. They will also want to consult line managers to ensure the research is not too disruptive. Since the research would be *additional* to the official research agenda the decision may depend more upon whether there are reasons *against* doing the research.

To talk about seeking access on the basis that one *has* independent funding is, of course, an oversimplification. In reality one would be most unlikely to get ESRC or other independent funding unless one had already demonstrated at least a high probability of access. But access can never come with a cast-iron guarantee. Would-be prison researchers should understand that there can be many reasons for saying 'no' or 'not here' or 'not now' which do not always involve 'big' politics. As often as not, the problems may derive from the micropolitics of institutions.

Prisons can be volatile places and prior agreement in principle can be undermined right up to the last moment by local tensions, which may mean a change of research location. This need not be a problem in a large system where the numbers of institutions can allow considerable scope for substitutability, but if one needs access to a more or less unique institution this can be crucial. In a rare case of completing fieldwork early King and McDermott asked that their ESRC-funded research be extended from male prisons to include the women's prison at Holloway. At the time Holloway was at the centre of one its periodic controversies and the Prison Service indicated that, for local political reasons, it could not be made available as a research location. They decided that none of the other women's prisons offered would be an adequate comparator for the men's local prison at Birmingham, and chose instead to take advantage of a unique opportunity to use the remaining time for a quick glimpse at the impact of 'Fresh Start' in the five existing research sites. They were criticized by one commentator for not including women's prisons in the first place, and by another for not withdrawing from the research process altogether in the face of such a rebuff from the Home Office. It is important in such circumstances for researchers both to be flexible in making the best of their opportunities and to have the courage of their convictions.

Access and Home Office—National Offender Management Service Funding

It is a very different matter if one is seeking to do prisons research and one needs funding from the Home Office (or now, the National Offender Management Service). Indeed in these circumstances not only are questions of funding and access inseparable, but issues concerning ownership and publication of the results are also likely to be negotiated at the same time. When the Home Office is paying the piper it not unreasonably expects to call the tune (although it has been quite difficult in practice for officials to control *how* the tune is played). The question now becomes one not of whether there are political reasons *against* the research, but whether there are political reasons *in favour*—although the way in which such matters may be determined has changed dramatically over the years.

Newcomers to the field of prisons research are now most likely to become involved in bidding for Home Office funding in response to invitations to tender for a given research project in which the aims, objectives, methodology, access to institutions, timing, and reporting procedures have already been closely specified. Researchers, now known as 'contractors', are invited to compete on costs, on methodology, and on likelihood of supplying the most valuable research report, to good time. However, their 'customers' in policy divisions, who have already determined the parameters of the research required, are not necessarily bound to accept the lowest bid. Rather, they reserve the right to choose, presumably on the advice of Home Office-RDS research managers, the bid which offers best value bearing in mind other matters including the track record of researchers.

It has not always been this way, and it may be helpful before returning to current problems to see how Home Office-funded research has developed. In the early days ministers and their officials might have been vaguely aware of the potential value of research but not known what research offered the best prospects, or how to go about it. In these circumstances it was possible for individual academics, perhaps with the backing of a prison governor, and often with a direct line into the Home Office at a high level, to get particular projects accepted as relevant to policy needs. For example, in 1967, Roy King was able, with the mentorship of the late John Martin, to respond to governor David Gould's invitation to monitor the opening of his new prison, Albany, and to evaluate the effectiveness of its training regime. In fact it was already too late to research the opening of Albany, but with the agreement of Gould, and the support of Martin, he set about persuading the Home Office Research Unit that what was really needed was a comparative study of several prisons which would describe and, if possible, measure prison regimes, using Albany as a pilot to develop measuring techniques. He argued that it would be vital to be able to describe and measure regimes, since too many studies of the effectiveness of treatment at that time failed to describe just what variables were supposed to produce the treatment effects (or lack of them). The Prison Department (as it then was) was then committed to a policy of treatment, training, and rehabilitation and claimed that its allocation policies were intended to send prisoners to prisons where they would get the treatment they 'needed'—but no one had yet seen this as a priority area for research. Tom Lodge, then Director of the Research Unit, readily agreed and the *Prison Regimes Project* was funded with access to five prisons.

The subsequent history of this research did not run smoothly. The preliminary findings were presented to the Home Office Research Unit in 1972. They showed that it was possible to measure prison regimes in various ways and that statistically significant differences could be demonstrated. However, the research team found little evidence of anything which resembled treatment, training, or rehabilitation programmes: the principal differences between prisons were in the 'hotel functions'—the food service, the sanitary conditions, the crowding, and so on—and the way these differences were distributed made no sense to prisoners or staff. The research team did not have the protection of a steering group intended to keep the project on the right lines, and they were asked by Lodge's successor to justify their results in ways that rather undermined the confidence of the research team. The third and final stage of the project was never approved and the findings of the comparative study were not written up at the time. However, 15 years later in a quite different climate it was possible to resurrect those findings to demonstrate how prison regimes had further deteriorated over the period since security and control had become such important issues (King and McDermott 1989). These findings were now welcomed by officials since they spoke to a different agenda—already recognized pre-Woolf (Home Office 1991)—in which the Prison Service needed resources to deal with overcrowding and to improve and maintain standards to counterbalance the concerns with security and control. The lesson is that in research it sometimes pays to take a longer view.

Nevertheless, it is important to stress that there was never any interference in the conduct of the research and the absence of a steering group gave the researchers free rein. The relationship with Albany was maintained over several years and close and co-operative relationships were established. It was possible to explore the way in which both staff and prisoners developed strategic ways of doing or spending time, and also to attempt an analysis of the breakdown of order once Albany had become a dispersal prison—none of which had played any part in the original proposals. When this part of the research was finally published (King and Elliott 1978) it contained a strong critique of dispersal policy, and for several years thereafter King was not able to regain access to high-security prisons. In 1983 he therefore turned his attention to maximum security prisons in the USA—access to which, in sharp contrast, was provisionally agreed in trans-Atlantic telephone calls to the Federal Bureau of Prisons and the Minnesota Department of Corrections. By the time he returned, security and control issues were back on the research agenda following the *Report of the Control Review Committee* (Home Office 1984), and access opened up once more. (Some years later, however, in a supreme irony, King was denied access to the Federal ADX facility in Florence, Colorado by the very authority that had previously given him access to the Federal Control Unit at Marion, Illinois, despite being armed with independent funding from ESRC and the public support of Richard Tilt, the then Director of the Prison Service for England and Wales. Nothing, it seems, can be taken for granted in the field of prisons research.)

Other research (Bottoms and McClintock 1973) has had similar beginnings to the Albany study, and it may still be possible to convince officials of the need for major research initiatives in this way, although increasingly the Home Office has developed priorities for its annual round of research on the basis of bids from its customers in policy divisions. An example of one priority area identified by the Prison Medical Service, but which nevertheless remained in the future programme of research for several years, was the need for research on the therapeutic prison at Grendon Underwood. The relative proximity of the Oxford Centre for Criminological Research to Grendon and professional links between the two institutions led to the submission of successful proposals (Genders and Player 1995). A similar symbiosis has developed between Cambridge and HM Prison Whitemoor—a dispersal prison which has now played host to several Cambridge-based research projects either at the initiative of successive governors (Liebling and Price 2001), or in discussions with the Cambridge Prisons Research Centre (Liebling 2002; Drake 2007).

To some degree, and at different periods, the wider Home Office research agenda has been influenced by periodic consultation exercises with the academic research community, either to comment on the existing programme or to help identify the general directions it might take in the future. But the contemporary scene has arguably become dominated by the NOMS-inspired return to reconviction studies. Prisons research has not loomed large in general Home Office consultations, although academics have sometimes had an input when a crisis has enabled the Prison Service to obtain priority for particular projects in which it had an interest. One such opportunity occurred following the *Report of the Control Review Committee* (Home Office 1984) which emphasized the need for research. Tony Bottoms, John Gunn, and Roy King were appointed to the Research and Advisory Group (RAG) which was concerned with implementing the recommendations of the CRC, especially the small unit strategy to deal with control problem prisoners, but also the circumstances in which control problems arose in the dispersal prisons. At this time King was about to undertake the ESRC-funded *Security, Control and Humane Containment* project, for which members of the CRC had given substantial backing and effectively guaranteed access, not least because it might throw light on some of these issues through a possible comparison between Gartree, then still a dispersal prison, and Oak Park Heights in Minnesota (King 1991).

RAG took the view that there were two important strands for RAG-sponsored research to pursue from which wider lessons might be drawn. The first was to compare a 'successful' dispersal prison (such as Long Lartin or Wakefield which had survived without riots or serious disturbances) with an 'unsuccessful' one (such as Albany or Gartree which had been plagued with riots and disturbances). Albany and Long Lartin thus became the sites in a Home Office-funded study (Sparks *et al.* 1996) whose sociological importance far transcended the simplistic origins just described but which may not have reached its practitioner audience perhaps because of its theoretical weight. The second was to regard the small units as quasi-experiments in which careful description and detailed analysis of staff–prisoner interactions might offer useful lessons about what could be done to promote greater order throughout the dispersal system. This strand was altogether less successful, in large part because of the way it was funded as a series of often retrospective consultancy exercises in which the consultants could do little more than rehearse the obvious whilst regretting they had no opportunity to pursue the more interesting issues (Bottomley 1995).

In recent years, however, the preferred mechanism for allocating research budgets has been for policy divisions, increasingly in discussion with ministers, to agree priorities, develop research briefs and for these to be put out to tender. We now return to a consideration of the advantages and disadvantages of these arrangements. On the one hand it has to be said that the process looks fairer and more transparent as well as more systematic than heretofore: it is also clearly more businesslike. On the other hand it can be argued that to some extent these advantages are more apparent than real, and that serious questions have to be raised about whether this system succeeds in getting the best research done or even getting reasonable, let alone best, value for money. Nevertheless, it is important to say that many of the criticisms we raise have to do with practicalities rather than larger political concerns. In good faith they could be met by revisions to existing procedures.

First, it is by no means clear that all interested researchers are made aware of the opportunity in time to prepare a realistic tender. If the Home Office is genuinely interested in opening up research opportunities to the widest audience it needs both to ensure that all media are used to advertise tenders—the press, the Internet, letters to all Departments of Criminology, and so on—and that much longer and more realistic lead times are provided for the preparation of proposals and start dates for the research. As things stand 'inside track' researchers, working in institutions where it is possible to retain researchers who are able to switch activities at short notice, are considerably advantaged. Indeed, if unofficial reports are to be believed, it still happens that individual researchers are telephoned and invited to 'tender' for projects which may not be advertised at all.

Secondly, there seems little point in being business-like when scientific research does not proceed, and cannot proceed, in accordance with business principles, but marches instead to the sound of a different drummer. The present system undoubtedly encourages researchers to overlook the sometimes massive methodological problems which have been inherent in research specifications attached to tender documents and to say that they will deliver what manifestly cannot be delivered within the scope of the time limits and the funding available. Some successful tenders have simply repeated the words of the customer's tender specification as though they had come from the pen of the researcher. Such tenders, as their authors know, would get short shrift if they were submitted as research proposals to the ESRC. In fact it cannot be in the real long-term interests of either customers or contractors for both parties to collude in a process which ignores intractable methodological issues. The best protection for contractors and researchers alike has been to build an element of peer review into all tender decision-making. This has started to develop, and certainly peer review is now used at the reporting stages of completed research projects.

The net effect of having wider advertising and peer review has been to broaden and strengthen the research base emerging from inside or commissioned by the Home Office, and has made it more likely that the discussions which take place around research projects include methodological rather than 'handling' issues.

Sometimes the Prison Service has put research out to tender in a two-stage process. First, researchers are invited to bid to undertake a literature review on the subject. Only when the outcome of the review is known are researchers invited to bid for the resultant research in those areas where previous research has failed to come up with the answers. There is an obvious and artful economy in organizing matters in this way which inhibits the widening of research agendas once access has been granted. But the treating of the two stages as though they were independent is a kind of legal fiction, because the winners of the first contract could hardly avoid placing themselves in pole position for winning the second (Price and Liebling 1998; Liebling and Price 1999). In the interests of maintaining a continuing research commitment from academe to the changing needs of the prison system, the Prison Service has developed innovative research funding procedures for one leading prison researcher (a co-author of this chapter). It supplied the required 30 per cent of outside funding to secure a four-year ESRC Research Fellowship for Alison Liebling (1994–8) and then the 50 per cent necessary to support a Leverhulme Special Research Fellowship (1998–2000). When Alison Liebling secured a permanent job at the University, the Prison Service agreed to continue to pay its ongoing contribution (amounting to around £18,000 per year) to enable her to build up a prisons research centre. The aim of the centre was to cultivate a new generation of prisons researchers who would be able to conduct increasing quantities of high quality, the-oretically-informed research. Research proposals were required in the usual way, and even the most jaundiced observer would have to say that this imaginative, but still quite modest, funding arrangement has been very productive. The Centre is now thriving, having attracted large research grants from outside the Prison Service (e.g. Nuffield and the ESRC), with a staff of three and six linked Ph.D. students (one of whom, Harvey, has contributed to this volume). Independent reviewers agree that this kind of long-term and coordinated effort has produced work of the highest scientific quality.

Neither of us can speak to the problems associated with getting materials published, because neither of us has experienced serious problems (with a few, historic exceptions involving mainly delays). It is more likely that we would receive acerbic remarks of 'offence taken', or that alternative explanations for negative findings might be offered (which are sometimes helpful). King submitted the text of his only Home Office-funded study to the Research Unit and to prison staff and prisoners for comment (as a matter of courtesy since there was no contractual requirement). It took a long time to get comments back but no strings were attached and many comments were helpful. After carefully considering the dis-agreements which remained he decided to stick to his version and publish anyway. Colleagues have expressed irritation about publication, not so much about censorship but about their reports being Crown copyright, the resultant format of publication, and the often inordinate delay. In today's climate it would be folly to take a publish-and-be-damned attitude if one wanted to gain future research contracts, but there is also a fairly open culture, in which carefully defended 'bad news' is accepted as useful in a performance-improvement climate. It seems likely that in the contract-awarding process officials probably have a fair idea of what 'line' different researchers may take. Diplomacy, care, and consideration make it pos-sible to 'get away with' expressing otherwise unpalatable truths. These are, some would argue, good research or writing skills to develop in any case. Perhaps the strongest argument for inde-pendently funded research is that it puts the matter of who owns the results beyond question.

It should be stressed that initial access is only the first hurdle. In fact negotiating and renegotiating access takes place on almost a daily basis once the research is under way— but that brings us to the research process itself.

The process of prisons research

Roy King first tried to set out as explicitly as possible his views on the process of 'doing research in prison' in the context of his report on Albany (King and Elliott 1978, ch. 2). As well as trying to be transparent about what they did, he tried to deconstruct at some length what had really happened methodologically in the studies of Pentonville by Morris, Morris and Barer (1963) and of Durham by Cohen and Taylor (1972)—for neither of these monographs devoted any detailed discussion to methodology—although Cohen and Taylor (1977) returned to these matters in a famous reflexive account after the Albany book had gone to press. He also reviewed the two other extant studies at that time by Bottoms and McClintock (1973) and by Emery (1970) and concluded that it was possible to classify research by the justifications for the roles claimed by the investigators: *independent* (Morris *et al.*), *officially sponsored* (Emery) *mutual prisoner and research interest* (Cohen and Taylor), *mutual staff and research interest* (Bottoms and McClintock). King argued that all these approaches were viable, though each brought its own problems in the way it was likely to be understood by research participants. He advocated an alternative model whereby the researcher was open and explicit about a research problem and sought help from both staff and prisoners to throw light on it. Alison Liebling has written about doing prisons research in Liebling 1999 and 2001. Both articles address the emotional and practical realities of prisons research, and the political entanglements and mixed loyalties that can quickly develop.

In the first edition of this chapter King set out ten nostrums for doing research in prisons—as follows:

1. You have to be there.
2. You have to do your time.
3. You should not work alone unless you have to.
4. You have to know why you are there.
5. You must always remember that research has costs for staff and prisoners.
6. You must know when to open your mouth and when to keep it closed.
7. You must do whatever you have to do to observe but do not go native.
8. You should triangulate your data collection wherever possible.
9. You must strike a balance between publicity and anonymity.
10. You should try to leave the site as clean as possible.

Each was set out at some length, and woven into them was advice about the establishment of a research role that carried credibility with both staff and prisoners, as well as some sobering lessons of what happens when things go wrong. In the years since the first edition there is much that has changed. Prison staff are generally more 'research-literate', and the organizational context now includes eleven private prisons as well as a 'public sector prison service'. The procedure for gaining access has become more formal, and standardized and funding sources more varied, with small charities, as well as large research organizations having an active interest in the operation of prisons. There is, at least at establishment level, a relative openness to research, and at headquarters, a (vested) interest in outcomes; so that far more research is being conducted. There are also new pressures and constraints as official research agendas have become more explicitly tied to a narrowly defined policies. Moreover, there is now far more internal information-gathering for the purposes of auditing performance and so on.

It was tempting to expand on that original exposition to take account not just of the impact of the above changes on the research process but also the different experiences of the co-author and our various students and colleagues. In the end we resisted that and instead would encourage new readers to revisit the original chapter for virtually all of it remains appropriate advice. In reality the ten nostrums contained many elements of advice of what to do and what not to do in different settings. We have therefore decided to develop a more extensive and detailed list of dos and don'ts by way of guidance on how to prepare for a research application and for the fieldwork, as well as what to do in the field, and how to leave it. It should be noted that in compiling such a list we did not always find ourselves in complete agreement—for example, Liebling is more open to the possibility of researchers carrying keys, and about them going native, but more cautious about identifying prisons than was King in the first edition. We include these issues in a short list of dilemmas towards the end. But we would expect that most experienced prison researchers would accept the great majority of the propositions below Some of these are technical, some are behavioural, and others are about the general attitude researchers should in our view adopt whilst entering, occupying and leaving the field.

A. Preparation

Dos

1. Discuss the research in advance with 'insiders' if possible.

2. Cultivate good relationships with the local area psychologist (and other informal contacts).

3. Prepare an ethics strategy (including seeking consent, assuring confidentiality, and protecting participant well-being).

4. Have contingency plans, and be flexible.

5. Get the language right, in questionnaires. Call staff what they want to be called (e.g. standard grade officers), pilot survey instruments, and interview questions.

6. Work out an effective transcribing strategy, from the start, so you don't get behind. Investigate the latest technology—but test it out first, before committing yourself or calculating the time involved.

7. Consider using Appreciative Inquiry (a focus on best or peak experiences) as part of the overall research strategy. It can be more creative than standard problem-focused research approaches, and it has (in our view) both ethical and emotional strengths (see Liebling *et al.* 1999, 2004, ch. 3).

8. Be aware of and sensitive to constraints (e.g. of the prison day—it can be short).

9. Make sure you know how your tape recorder works, and where the batteries go (for example, there is often one hidden in the small microphone).

10. Remember that where taping interviews cannot be done, try to write as close to verbatim accounts as soon as possible.

11. Accept that there will be times when you cannot take notes, or you have to turn off the tape recorder. These times are still informative and useful.

12. Ask for a written letter from the security department to give you permission to bring a tape recorder in and out. Carry this letter at all times.

13. Consider engaging staff and prisoners actively in the research process (e.g. in the development of interview questions).

14. Prepare a brief, eye-catching research summary, with names and contact details included for wide distribution.

B. In the field

Dos

1. Listen.

2. Always be ready to explain as fully and truthfully as possible what you are doing and why.

3. Check stories (triangulate). Don't be 'taken in', but take all accounts seriously. Remember that the same events can be perceived differently and that perceptions may explain actions.

4. Keep full notes, including your immediate reflections on and feelings about what you have observed.

5. Be considerate, and friendly.

6. Recognize the vulnerability of prisoners (and some staff) in their role as 'the researched', and your own power as 'the researcher'.

7. Handle information very carefully—protect identities, be cautious, and diplomatic.

8. Respect the safety concerns of staff—they will feel responsible if anything goes wrong.

9. Respect 'stakeholders'—and remember to talk to specialists (workshop instructors, education staff, IMB members, and so on, as well as staff and prisoners).

10. Go to parties if invited, but leave the notebook behind.

11. Wind down, discuss everything with your supervisor, and find outlets for pent-up emotion outside the field.

Don'ts

1. Say much—retain your neutrality; try not to take sides.

2. Intervene, except in very exceptional circumstances.

3. Allow others to speak for you about the research. Always explain it in your own words, and act quickly to correct any false impressions that may be given outside your control.

4. Take things in or out of the prison.

5. Make quick friendships with prisoners.

6. Ignore staff.

7. Have affairs (with prisoners or staff).

8. Regard people as obstacles, or be overdemanding.

9. On the other hand, don't be too weak: don't give in to 'unreasonable constraints', like feeling there are areas you cannot visit.

10. Leave notes or questionnaires lying around.

11. Ask staff to collect or distribute questionnaires.

12. Fixate on your research questions, or overdetermine the answers.

13. Continue once compassion fatigue sets in.

14. Restrict the research to the most vocal prisoners or staff.

15. Rush your interviews.

16. Take unnecessary risks—check prisoners' psychological states with staff, and ask your supervisor if joint interviews seem to be called for in exceptional cases.

17. Use judgemental language—let the data speak for themselves.

18. Raise expectations of either staff or prisoners about things (including their participation in the research) which you cannot deliver.

C. Leaving the field

Dos

1. Provide feedback (if appropriate, at several stages) but be honest, fair, and diplomatic, and stress the provisional nature of the emerging findings.

2. Recognize that prisons change as you write up your time-bound account.

3. Thank people by letter afterwards.

Don'ts

1. Leave problems behind for subsequent researchers to pick up.

2. Forget to honour any undertakings you gave to individuals in the course of the fieldwork.

D. Mistakes and dilemmas

We include below some examples of dilemmas as topics for reflection, and discussion with supervisors. The novice researcher should be aware that even the most experienced prison researchers sometimes make consequential mistakes.

1. Be wary of colluding in disrespectful treatment. If staff use prisoners as examples, and talk about them in your presence, attempt to engage them in a more respectful conversation at the time, or shortly afterwards.

2. Be cautious about offers to lodge with staff and governors. This can be extremely valuable, but it is potentially difficult, especially if views of reality differ, if bad news emerges, and is likely to undermine prospects of maintaining a 'neutral' position in the eyes of staff and prisoners.

3. A dilemma that needs constant work, and for which formal mechanisms need to be devised within the prison service, is the difficulty of pursuing sociological approaches in situations where psychologists are principal gatekeepers.

4. What is to be done when conditions of access are unreasonable. For example, there is a requirement in the access form at the moment that 'behaviour that may be against the disciplinary code' should be reported. This is impossible to fulfil if the research touches on drug use, trade, or many other subjects.

5. Consider carefully the question of whether or not to use keys: there are advantages and disadvantages (see Sparks *et al.* 1996: Liebling 1992: 249–50 ch. 5, fn 2, and King 2000).

6. Every researcher has to develop a position on the circumstances when one steps outside the research role. If one sees disturbing incidents or outrageous acts or comes into possession of certain types of information, these will raise the question of how and when to respond (i.e. there may be exceptions to B2).

7. Using inducements—it is good practice to thank prisoners and staff for their time, but even making biscuits available in focus group discussions can be hazardous (some have foil wrappers, questions arise as to who gets the best chocolate ones, etc.). In what circumstances is it appropriate to reward respondents financially?

8. Should prisons be identified? There are arguments for and against. If a finding is interesting enough, it might well 'carry the project' without needing to be located in a particular, named establishment. On the other hand, identities can usually be rumbled by the well informed, and sometimes it is important to 'revisit' a prison with a familiar history.

9. How close should you get? (Brief spells of going native may be inevitable). Discuss regularly within the team or with supervisors and colleagues.

E. Supervising Ph.D. students and research assistants

1. Do some fieldwork alongside your student/research assistant to begin with. Fully discuss interview technique and structure, and the difficulties of observation, as well as the adequacy of the notes.

2. Conduct one or two joint interviews at the early stages, as above.

3. Read and respond quickly to full fieldwork notes, and debrief. In this way you can advise on dilemmas before they become mistakes, and anyway this is an informative and enjoyable process.

4. Participate when political issues arise—i.e. when requests arise for feedback at high-level management meetings. Don't leave junior researchers to handle such situations alone.

5. Encourage joint working across projects, and regular discussions among Ph.D. students.

6. Keep the fieldwork to a realistic plan, and encourage 'time out' if it gets too stressful or the student/research assistant is getting too close for comfort.

Conclusion

We hope it will be clear that we have found the process of doing research in prisons endlessly fascinating. Sometimes the subject matter is delicate or difficult to deal with and the process of collecting data can be arduous and exhausting. The current sentencing climate makes additional emotional demands on prisoners and upon staff, and therefore upon researchers, that can sometimes seem overwhelming. Returning from a bout of prisons research can sometimes be a confusing experience, as the voices and problems of staff and prisoners continue to echo in our heads, as we try to disengage from the inside, and return to a free life. Sometimes these adjustments take time, and require talk. So why then do we continue with this line of research? First, prisons are endlessly interesting as institutions. They are places where the best and worst aspects of human nature can appear in a moment. They pose complex problems of power, justice, authority, and care in a particularly concentrated way. Prisons and their uses, flaws, possibilities, are politically important, and criminologically, they have much to teach us about the possibilities and pitfalls of punishment and reform.

The study of the prison raises, and sometimes addresses, issues of crucial importance. There are always more questions to ask. Why are some prisons so much better than others? Is it possible to improve seemingly entrenched cultures in the oldest, most traditional prisons? How has managerialism shaped the experience of prison life, for prisoners and for the practitioners of criminal justice? Are private prisons different, and if so, why? How is it possible for prisoners to survive in the most extreme conditions of overcrowding or prolonged solitary confinement in a world virtually devoid of stimulation? How is it possible for managers and staff to plan and carry out regimes that subject prisoners to an all-encompassing authority without abusing that authority? And how can staff daily go through the grind of locking, unlocking, escorting, searching, and supervising, without themselves becoming demeaned by the process, or taking a delight in the humiliation or torture of their charges? What happens when they do? What are the conditions under which things go wrong? How is it that, despite the obvious divisions, most prisons, most of the time, remain in a tolerable state of order without staff and prisoners, or prisoners and prisoners, constantly at each other's throats?

These are challenging intellectual questions in their own right. But there is no shortage of intellectual challenges, and for us it is also important to believe that even partial answers could make some modest difference to the human condition—otherwise one might as well do something more profitable for a living. We are no longer so sanguine about the capacity of our research, or anyone else's for that matter, to make much of a difference as we might have been at the outset. As one rather notorious prisoner once told Roy King after he had explained the intention behind his research that the Home Office would 'look at your results, find the one thing they can screw us with and they will implement that—the rest will stay on a dusty shelf'. As the years go by it may be that we have become content with making smaller and smaller differences—or that we increasingly realize, as others have before us, that the exterior conditions that shape prison population size, structures of accountability, and the moral status of prisoners, should also be the focus of our criminological attention.

Suggestions for further reading

There are a few detailed discussions on the doing of research in prisons, and the following are essential reading: *Albany: Birth of a Prison—End of an Era* (ch. 2) by Roy D. King and Kenneth W. Elliott (1978); 'Talking about Prison Blues', by Stan Cohen and Laurie

Taylor in *Doing Sociological Research*, edited by Colin Bell and Howard Newby (1978); *Prisons and the Problem of Order* (Appendix A) by Richard Sparks, Anthony E. Bottoms, and Will Hay (1996); *Suicide in Prison* (ch. 5) by Alison Liebling (1992), and 'Doing Research in Prison: Breaking the Silence', by Alison Liebling, in *Theoretical Criminology* (1999). There is also an interesting chapter on methodology in Genders and Player's account of *Grendon: A Study of a Therapeutic Prison* (1995) (ch. 2) and a discussion about 'taking sides' by Alison Liebling in the *British Journal of Criminology* 2001.

References

ADLER, M. and LONGHURST, B. (1994). *Discourse, Power and Justice: Towards a New Sociology of Imprisonment.* London: Routledge.

AHMAD, S. (1996). *Fairness in Prison.* Unpublished Ph.D. thesis. Cambridge University.

BANKS, C., MAYHEW, P., and SAPSFORD, R. (1975). *Absconding from Open Prisons.* London: HMSO.

BOSWORTH, M. (1999). *Engendering Resistance: Agency and Power in Women's Prisons.* Aldershot: Dartmouth.

BOTTOMLEY, A. K. (1995). *CRC Special Units: A General Assessment.* London: Home Office Research and Planning Unit.

—— JAMES, A., CLARE, E., and LIEBLING, A. (1997). *Monitoring and Evaluation of Wolds Remand Prison, and Comparisons with Public-sector Prisons in Particular HMP Woodhill.* Hull and Cambridge: A Report for the Home Office Research and Statistics Directorate.

—— LIEBLING, A. and SPARKS, R. (1994). *The Barlinnie Special Unit and Shotts Unit.* Edinburgh: Scottish Prison Service.

BOTTOMS, A. E. (2003). 'The retical Reflections on the Evaluations of a Penal Policy Initiative', in L. Zedner and A. Ashworth (eds), *The Criminology Foundations of Penal Policy: Essays in Honour of Roger Hood.* Oxford: Oxford University Press.

BOTTOMS, A. E. and McCLINTOCK, F. H. (1973). *Criminals Coming of Age.* London: Heinemann.

CARLEN, P. (1983). *Women's Imprisonment: a Study in Social Control.* London: Routledge & Kegan Paul.

CARRABINE, E. (2004). *Power, Discourse and Resistance: A Genealogy of the Strangeways Prison Riot.* Aldershot: Ashgate Publishing.

CHELIOTIS, L. K. (2005). The prison furlough programme in Greece: Findings from a Research Project in the Male Prison of Korydallos. *Punishment and Society* 7: 201–15.

—— (under review) Reconsidering the Effectiveness of Temporary Release: a Systematic Review of the Literature.

COHEN, S. and TAYLOR, L. (1972). *Psychological Survival: The Experience of Long-Term Imprisonment.* Harmondsworth: Penguin Books.

—— and —— (1977). 'Talking about Prison Blues' in C. Bell and H. Newby (eds), *Doing Sociological Research.* London: Allen & Unwin.

COLVIN, E. (1977). *Prison Officers: A Sociological Portrait of the Uniformed Staff of an English Prison.* University of Cambridge Ph.D. thesis.

COOKE, D. J. (1989). 'Containing Violent Prisoners: An Analysis of the Barlinnie Special Unit'. *British Journal of Criminology* 29: 129–43.

CRAWLEY, E. (2004). *Doing Prison Work: The Public and Private Lives of Prison Officers.* Cullompton: Willan Publishing.

CREWE, B. (2005a). 'Codes and conventions: the terms and conditions of contemporary inmate values', in A. Liebling and S. Maruna (eds), *The Effects of Imprisonment.* Cullompton: Willan Publishing.

CREWE, B. (2005b). The prisoner society in the era of hard drugs. *Punishment and Society* 7: 457–81.

DOBASH, R. P., DOBASH, R. E., and GUTTERIDGE, S. (1986). *The Imprisonment of Women.* Oxford: Basil Blackwell.

DOWNES, D. (1988). *Contrasts in Tolerance: Post-war Penal Policy in the Netherlands and England and Wales.* Oxford: Clarendon Press.

DRAKE, D. (2007). *A Comparison of Quality of Life, Legitimacy and Order in Two Maximum-Security Prisons.* Cambridge University: Unpublished PhD Thesis.

EMERY, F. E. (1970). *Freedom and Justice Within Walls: The Bristol Prison Experiment.* London: Tavistock Publications.

GARLAND, D. (1994). 'Of Crimes and Criminals: The Development of Criminology in Britain' in M. Maguire, R. Morgan, and R. Reiner (eds), *The Oxford Handbook of Criminology.* Oxford: Oxford University Press.

GENDERS, E., and PLAYER, E. (1989). *Race Relations in Prisons.* Oxford: Clarendon Press.

—— and —— (1995). *Grendon: A Study of a Therapeutic Prison.* Oxford: Clarendon Press.

GUNN, J., ROBERTSON, G., DELL, S., and WAY, C. (1978). *Psychiatric Aspects of Imprisonment.* London: Academic Press.

—— MADEN, T., and SWINTON, M. (1991). *Mentally Disordered Offenders.* London: HMSO.

HARVEY, J. (2006). *Young Men in Prison: Surviving and Adapting to Life Inside.* Cullompton: Willan Publishing.

HOBHOUSE, S. and BROCKWAY, A. F. (1922). *English Prisons Today.* London: Labour Research Department.

HOME OFFICE (1984). *Managing the Long-Term Prison System: The Report of the Control Review Committee.* London: HMSO.

—— (1991). *Prison Disturbances April 1990, Report of an Inquiry by the Rt Hon. Lord Justice Woolf (Parts I and II) and His Honour Judge Stephen Tumim (Part II).* Cm.1456, London: HMSO.

—— (1998). *Crime Reduction Programme Prospectus.* London: Home Office Research, Development and Statistics Directorate.

JEWKES, Y. (2002). *Captive Audience: Media, Masculinity and Power in Prisons,* Cullompton: Willan.

JONES, H. and CORNES, P. (1977). *Open Prisons.* London: Routledge & Kegan Paul.

KING, R. D. (1972). *An Analysis of Prison Regimes.* Unpublished Report to the Home Office, University of Southampton.

—— (1987). 'New Generation Prisons, the Prison Building Programme, and the Future of the Dispersal Policy' in A. E. Bottoms and R. Light (eds), *Problems of Long-Term Imprisonment.* Aldershot: Gower.

—— (1991). 'Maximum Security Custody in Britain and the USA: A Study of Gartree and Oak Park Heights'. *British Journal of Criminology* 31: 126–52.

—— (1994). 'Russian Prisons after Perestroika: End of the Gulag?'. *British Journal of Criminology, Special Issue,* 34: 62–82.

—— (1999). 'The Rise and Rise of Supermax: An American Solution in Search of a Problem?' *Punishment and Society: the International Journal of Penology* 1: 163–86.

—— (2000). 'Doing Research in Prisons' in R. D. King and E. Wincup (eds), *Doing Research on Crime and Justice* (1st edn). Oxford: Oxford University Press.

KING, R. D. and ELLIOTT, K. W. (1978). *Albany: Birth of a Prison—End of an Era.* London: Routledge & Kegan Paul.

—— and MCDERMOTT, K. (1989). 'British Prisons 1970–1987: The Ever-deepening Crisis'. *British Journal of Criminology* 29: 107–28.

—— and —— (1990). ' "My Geranium is Subversive" Notes on the Management of Trouble in Prisons'. *British Journal of Sociology* 41: 445–71.

—— and —— (1995). *The State of Our Prisons.* Clarendon Studies in Criminology. Oxford: Clarendon Press.

—— and MORGAN, R. (1976). *A Taste of Prison: Custodial Conditions for Trial and Remand Prisoners.* London: Routledge & Kegan Paul.

—— and —— (1980). *The Future of the Prison System.* Farnborough: Gower Press.

—— and PICACENTINI, L. (2004). The Russian Correctional System During the Transition, in W. A. Pridemore (ed.), *Ruling Russia: Law, Crime and Justice in a Changing Society.* Lanham, MD: Rowman & Littlefield.

LIEBLING, A. (1992). *Suicides in Prison.* London: Routledge.

—— (1995). 'Vulnerability and prison suicide', *British Journal of Criminology* 35: 173–87.

—— (1999). 'Doing Research in Prison: Breaking the Silence?' *Theoretical Criminology* 3: 147–73.

—— (2001). 'Whose Side are We On? Theory, Practice and Allegiances in Prisons Research' in E. Stanko and A. Liebling (eds), *Researching Violence: Methodological and Ethical Issues, British Journal of Criminology Special Issue,* 472–82.

—— (2002). 'A "liberal regime within a secure perimeter"? Dispersal Prisons and Penal Practice in the late Twentieth Century' in A. E. Bottoms and M. Tonry (eds), *Ideology, Crime and Criminal Justice: a Symposium in Honour of Sire Leon Radzinowicz.* Cullompton: Willan.

—— (2004). *Prisons and their Moral Performance: A Study of Values, Quality and Prison Life.* Oxford: Oxford University Press.

——, DURIE, L., STILES, A., and TAIT, S. (2005). 'Revisiting prison suicide: the role of fairness and distress', in A. Liebling and S. Maruna (eds), *The Effects of Imprisonment.* Cullompton: Willan Publishing.

——, ELLIOT, C., and PRICE, D. (1999). 'Appreciative Inquiry and Relationships in Prison'. *Punishment and Society: The International Journal of Penology* 1/1: 71–98.

—— MUIR, G. and ROSE, G. (1997). *An Evaluation of Incentives and Earned Privileges: Final Report to the Prison Service.* Cambridge: Institute of Criminology.

—— and PRICE, D. (1999). *An Exploration of Staff–Prisoner Relationships at HMP Whitemoor.* Prison Service Research Report, No 6. Cambridge: Institute of Criminology, University of Cambridge.

—— (2001). *The Prison Officer.* Leyhill: Prison Service and Waterside Press.

MARSH, A., DOBBS, J., and MONK, J. (1985). *Staff Attitudes in the Prison Service.* London: Office of Population and Censuses.

MCCALLISTER, D., BOTTOMLEY, A. K., and LIEBLING, A. (1992). *From Custody to Community: Throughcare for Young Offenders.* Aldershot: Avebury Publishing.

MCDERMOTT, K. (1990). 'We Have No Problem: The Experience of Racism in Prison'. *New Community* 16: 213–28.

MORRIS, T., MORRIS P., and BARER, B. (1963). *Pentonville: A Sociological Study of an English Prison.* London: Routledge & Kegan Paul.

OICP (2004). 'Office of the Inspector of Custodial Services, *Annual Report.* Perth: OICP Press.

PADFIELD, N., LIEBLING, A., and ARNOLD, H (2003). 'Discretion and the release of life sentence prisoners', in L. Gelsthorpe and N. Padfield (eds), *Exercising Discretion: Decision-making in the Criminal Justice System and Beyond.* Cullompton: Willan Publishing.

PRICE, D. and LIEBLING, A. (1998). *Staff-Prisoner Relationships: A Review of the Literature.* Unpublished Report to the Prison Service.

RESODIHARDJO, S. (2006). *Crisis and Change: Understanding the Crisi-reform Processes in Dutch and British Prison Services.* Amsterdam: Vrije Universiteit.

SIM, J. (1990). *Medical Power in Prisons: The Prison Medical Service in England 1774–1989.* Milton Keynes: Open University Press.

SIMON, F. and CORBETT, C. (1996). *An Evaluation of Prison Work and Training.* A Report for the Home Office Research and Statistics Directorate, Brunel University.

SMITH, C. (1996). *The Imprisoned Body: Women, Health and Imprisonment.* Unpublished Ph.D. thesis. Bangor: University of Wales.

SPARKS, R. (2003). 'Out of the Digger: The Warrior's Honour and the Guilty Observer', *Ethnography—Special Issue: In and Out of the Belly of the Beast: Dissecting the Prison.* 3: 556–82.

SPARKS, R., BOTTOMS, A. E., and HAY, W. (1996). *Prisons and the Problem of Order.* Clarendon Studies in Criminology. Oxford: Clarendon Press.

SPARKS, R. F. (1971). *Local Prisons: The Crisis in the English Penal System.* London: Heinemann.

TAIT, S. (in progress). 'Officer Culture and Care for Prisoners in One Men's and One Women's Prison'. Cambridge University PhD Thesis.

WALMSLEY, R. (1989). *Special Security Units.* London: HMSO.

PART V

SOME RECENT CASE STUDIES

16

Cybercrime and online methodologies

Matthew Williams

Introduction

Criminologists collect primary data from a myriad of sources via a range of methods. The choice of source and research instrument is most typically driven by key research questions. In relation to data sources criminological research like most social science can be considered 'multi-sited'. Researchers rarely rely upon one source or site for data collection when seeking to answer research questions. For example, ethnographies have become increasingly selective, distancing themselves from bounded holistic representations. Such representations, while arguably once achievable, are now hindered by field sites that are not only influenced by the local but also events and forces quite distant (Giddens 1990). The traditional notion of the field-site is subject to erosion due to political, economic, and cultural forces that shape local contexts (Gupta and Ferguson 1997). The multisited nature of criminological research also impacts upon the choice of method. Each field site exhibits distinct characteristics that provide challenges and affordances to the types of method chosen to collect primary data. In contemporary criminology the Internet has become an additional field that researchers can consider as part of their multi-sited research enterprise. At the most pedestrian level crimino-logical researchers utilize the Internet as a vast information retrieval system particularly in early stages of research such as literature reviewing (sourcing academic and grey literature) and obtaining up-to-date information on government web sites (such as the latest prison population figures and police service strength statistics). While the 'democratic' and speedy distribution of secondary information over the Internet has aided criminological researchers, few have taken the opportunity to collect primary data online. This chapter delineates the experiences and methodological dilemmas of planning and conducting primary criminological research within online field sites. The chapter specifically draws upon experiences of researching cybercrime and its control via online interviewing and online participant observation.

Cybercrime

Cybercrime and cyber deviance are rapidly becoming an increasingly relevant component of contemporary criminological research (see Wall 2003, 2001; Wall and Williams forthcoming, Williams 2006, Grabowsky and Smith 1998). The Internet and its associated technologies can facilitate existing criminal entrepreneurship while also creating new forms of online deviance yet to be rationalized in legal discourse. Theoretical, empirical, and technical aspects of cybercrime have been the focus of study for researchers within a variety of disciplines. Of the claims made across writings one overarching commonality remains constant that the Internet and its constituent technologies distanciate time and space (Giddens 1990). This process both facilitates criminal enterprise while also serving to complicate its control. Over the past decade industry victimization surveys[1] evidence how cyber criminals utilize networks of computers to commit multiple frauds in compressed periods of time over vast distances. The same surveys illustrate how private companies, governments, and domestic Internet users are ill-prepared for the array of threats they face online. Further, the ability of cyber criminals to transcend traditional geographic boundaries presents criminal justice systems across the globe with their greatest challenge. The increasing ubiquity of Internet and our dependency on communication at-a-distance leaves us exposed to the actions of sophisticated hackers, online fraudsters, and abusers. This chapter examines the ways in which some of these 'harms' and crimes can be researched in their native online environment.

Online field sites

Previous qualitative Internet research has been conducted in numerous settings (for examples, see Baym 1995a; 1995b; 1998; Correll 1995; Denzin 1999; Hine 2000; Paccagnella 1997; Turkle 1995). Both Baym (1995a; 1995b; 1998) and Correll (1995) conducted what they considered an ethnography of Internet use, by following participants through real-time discussions, to email exchanges and face-to-face interviews. Both researchers claimed to have studied and represented the 'enduring practices' of their participants through which their online community became meaningful. In a similar process Turkle (1995) refused to use online interview data unless it was accompanied by an interview in the off-line setting, fearing a lack of authenticity would result if the identities of participants were not verified. The common thread through these studies is the stress placed on the meanings of different sites of investigation. For both Baym (1995a; 1995b; 1998) and Correll (1995) the meaning of community could only be understood if the ethnographer 'travelled' experientially with the participants through the varying technological settings. Similarly, Turkle's (1995) fears over the reliability of her data were quashed only by visiting another site of investigation frequented by her participants. The importance of these seemingly distinct field sites has a resonance with the multisited nature contemporary criminology. While 'the Internet' can become a primary criminological research site, the actual range of technologies that constitute the Internet and go to inform an analysis are diverse. Web pages, newsgroups, email discussion lists, blogs, wikis, chat rooms, and graphical online communities are but a few of the potential research sites available to the online researcher. The online spaces that constituted the field sites in my research included a graphical online community (Cyberworlds), associated newsgroups,

---

[1] See the UK Government's Information Security Breaches Survey and the US Federal Bureau of Investigation and Computer Security Institute's Computer Crime and Security Survey.

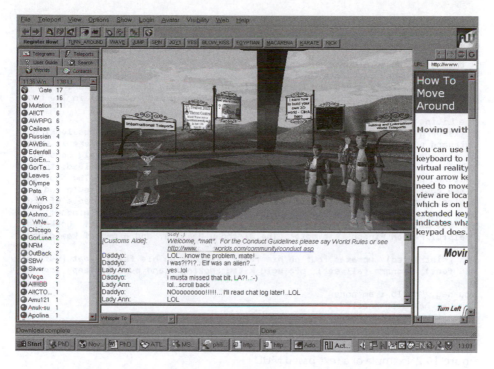

Figure 16.1 Example of an online graphical environment

web pages, and an email distribution list. Via these technologies I was able to observe community members in their natural online environment and interview them in order to answer my research question: what is the prevalence and nature of online deviant activity and how is it best regulated within online graphical communities?

The environment of cyberworlds

Cyberworlds is one of a handful of graphically represented three-dimensional virtual reality online social spaces that forms part of the Internet (see Figure 16.1). These online arenas can be described as second-generation multi-user domains (MUDs); less technologically advanced methods of one-to-many text-only online communication first developed in the late 1970s[2] (see Figure 16.2, overleaf). MUDs were first designed by programmers as gaming arenas, much like an online version of the classic role-playing game 'Dungeons and Dragons'. In traditional MUDs action, description and communication takes place purely through text. Users have to rely on their imagination to create the environment that is being described to them. Cyberworlds takes advantage of broadband network communications, meaning much more information can be transmitted in shorter periods of time. This allows for information to be represented by more that just simple text. A graphical window allows a user to see themselves represented as an avatar—a three-dimensional persona. Via this interface users can locate each other and navigate around their three-dimensional environment. Text still functions as communication, and is

---

[2] MOOs (object orientated MUDs) are another type of one-to-many text-only online social spaces.

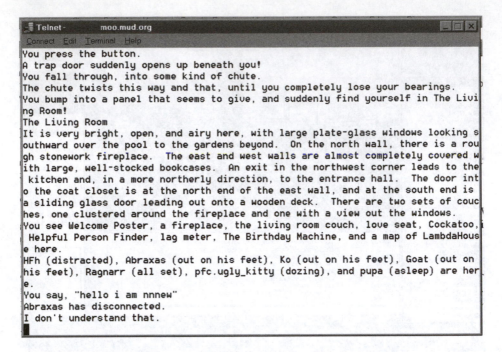

Figure 16.2 Example of a text-based MUD

essential to the maintenance of the 'community', but it has become relegated, where visual components now represent action and description. Cyberworlds and other 'advanced' MUDs have grown in popularity over the past ten years due to the level of social and 'physical' immersion they provide to the user. Essentially, they are the closest domestic technology to more elaborate and expensive Virtual Reality platforms.

Over decades, as increasing numbers of people became connected to computer networks, gaming spaces transformed into more general social spaces, providing an escape from the 'real' world. MUDs and the social networks they harbour have been the subject of much research in media and communications disciplines (see Jones 1995, 1997, 1998 for an overview). Many studies have focused upon the substantive issues of race, gender, and sexuality within MUDs and other associated technologies (such as Newsgroups and Internet Relay Chat). The effects of anonymity and disembodiment, experienced by each MUD user, have forged much of what is now understood of online social experience (see Kramarae 1998, Danet 1998, Poster 1998, Dietrich 1997, Shaw 1997). However, graphical MUDs, like Cyberworlds, have received little academic attention. While the concept of deviance within online communities has been considered within some academic articles (see Mackinnon 1997 and Reid 1999), few have theorized or attempted to collect empirical data on more advanced forms of online communication that in essence increase the bandwidth of sensory perception, allowing for unprecedented forms of virtual criminality. The combined features of these new graphical environments—the use of avatars, buildings, informal and formal community rules, and so on—compound to create an environment where unprecedented acts of online deviance can develop and mature, providing a fertile ground for the study of online deviant activity. This activity and the reactions it evoked from community members became the focus of online observations and interviews in my study.

Online participant observation

Participant observation has traditionally been the nexus of ethnographic enquiry (Hammersley and Atkinson 1995). In part this convention has much to do with maintaining authenticity in the final product; 'the convention is to allow the field-worker's unexplicated experience in the culture to stand as the basis for textual authority' (Van Maanen 1988: 47). The need for authenticity, as in all research projects, was paramount in my study. With this in mind prolonged periods of time were spent among the community members of Cyberworlds in order to observe and experience life in a virtual setting. Over a period of approximately six months observation was carried out on a daily basis. It became rapidly apparent that conducting observation within a graphical virtual environment was far removed from the practice in an off-line setting. The online setting proved to attenuate and exacerbate certain aspects of participant observation which are discussed in the following sections.

Ethics of online access

Realizing that participant observation involved becoming part of a group or community negated the possibility of simply 'hanging around' in Cyberworlds. A process of acceptance had to occur, where those observed and questioned in the setting would feel comfortable and trusting. Informing those observed involved posting an automated message in the text box indicating that a researcher was carrying out fieldwork. In some cases individuals felt uncomfortable with the intrusion and voiced their concern, whereupon the appropriate decision to observe was made. In other situations, when community members were notified of the planned observation, some left the environment of their own free will. Yet this posed clear problems with the rights and freedoms of online community members. In response one might have decided to adopt the ethical guidelines for conducting participant observation in the off-line world, taking refuge in the idea that what is being researched is 'public'. However, what is considered private and public in online communities can vary greatly from the terrestrial world. Research has highlighted the disinhibiting effect of computer-mediated communication, meaning members of online communities, while acknowledging the environment as a 'public' space, often use it to engage in what would be considered 'private talk' (Joinson 1998). The ephemeral nature of Internet interactions, including anonymity, a reduction in social cues, and the realization of time space distanciation (Giddens 1990), leads individuals to reveal more about themselves within online environments than would be done in offline equivalents.

The harvesting of textual and visual data within online environments is unethical in respect of the blurred boundary between public and private discourse within online communities. Some early studies that aimed to investigate computer-mediated communication perceived it ethical simply to take data from chat rooms and newsgroups without gaining consent from participants, based on the understanding that these forums were in the public domain. The data used in my study were collected on the basis that those observed were aware and had no reservations over its use for academic purposes. Yet achieving complete informed consent is difficult in any setting. Informing every community member of the research intentions and delivering full information proved impractical. Moreover, given the rate at which individuals arrived at and left the environment, attempting fully to inform everyone would have seriously hindered the study and disrupted the flow of community chat (it is more than likely that I would have been ejected for 'flooding'). Further, it is possible that those observed did not take the opportunity to voice their objections. Some may not have read the automated message, while others may have simply felt it inappropriate to object. Either case may have meant informed consent was not fully achieved. In an attempt to negate these ethical concerns the collection of textual talk was constrained to areas deemed public spaces within Cyberworlds. Data were not collected from the more private settings such as online homes or churches. Additionally, those who wanted to engage in private or sensitive conversation could have used the *whisper* feature, preventing anyone in the setting from witnessing their textual interaction. Once the ethical concerns were satisfactorily met by the safeguards put in place, observation began. The following reflexive account details the experiences of the first days of observation within the Cyberworlds environment.

First days in the virtual field

My first steps into Cyberworlds were temporarily halted by my *Immigration*, a process, I discovered, was not as gruelling as its off-line equivalent. Prompted by a dialogue box asking '*Who would you like to be today?*' I typed in a pseudonym, upon which I was assigned a '*temporary tourist visa*'. Later I discovered that for a nominal fee I could become a *citizen* of Cyberworlds, bestowing me with a selection of rights that were absent to those with tourist status. Upon reflection, the process of *Immigration* and the act of creating an online persona prompted me to recall Goffman's (1955) notions of 'personal front' and 'impression management'—how might I identify myself to fellow world *tourists* and *citi-zens*? Might those I talk to take me more seriously if I were a *paying citizen* rather than an every day *tourist*? While there are parallels with off-line forms of ethnography, it became clear that the setting afforded the researcher with the ability to be completely covert amongst those researched. Covert note-taking, data collection, even video recordings—processes deemed challenging in traditional fieldwork—were possible while maintaining the ignorance of those researched, even if ethically dubious. Following the completion of *Immigration*, feeling somewhat perplexed by the notions of *tourists, citizens*, and the thought of 'travelling' somewhere without actually leaving the office chair, I took my first step onto fertile 'virtual' grassland. Subsequently, I was informed that my first point of entry was called *Ground Zero*, the area at which all *tourists* and *citizens* enter the world known as *The Gateway*. This world, like the other hundred or so in Cyberworlds, is experienced in three modes of representation. The more conventional of these modes are the use of typed words (synchronous chat) and web pages, modes of communication ubiqui-tous on the Internet. More unfamiliar is the mode of communication that allows both *citizens* and *tourists* to visualize themselves (as avatars) and their three-dimensional envir-onment on-screen (see Figure 16.3, opposite).

Figure 16.3 A researcher's view of cyberworlds

Moving away from the restrictions of text-based-only environments, participants in the community are able to walk about the landscape and experience it visually, allowing individuals to achieve a feeling of being present somewhere removed from their actual physical location. The very first instance I 'landed' at *Ground Zero* I noticed that I was standing in what seemed like a grand central station to other worlds within this universe. Above my avatar's head was a large grey structure acting as some kind of shelter, under which twenty or more other avatars were standing, running, and what seemed like floating or flying. The very first person to talk to me was the *Immigration Officer* followed by two others with the names *StockQuoteBot* and the *Customs Aide*

Immigration Officer: Welcome to the Cyberworlds Gateway! Please note that whispers are currently disabled for tourists while in the Gateway.

[StockQuoteBot]: *Hi Mat01. Ask me for stock quotes! Whisper HELP or 0:symbol to me, e.g., whisper 0:MSFT :-)*

[Customs Aide]: Welcome, Mat01. For the Conduct Guidelines please say World Rules or see *http://www.Cyberworlds.com/conduct.html*

(Fieldnotes 22-10-99)

I quickly typed back, 'cheers Immigration Officer', hoping for some kind of initial contact and response. I got one, but in a different way than expected. Another tourist was quick to inform me that the *Immigration Officer* was not in fact a real person, but an automated message, and more to my surprise both *StockQuoteBot* and *Customs Aide* were forms of artificial life known as bots. These artificial life forms had been created by the *citizens* of Cyberworlds, with the aim of helping newcomers with frequently asked questions (FAQs).

Recognizing that I had just made my first cyber *faux pas* in being polite to a 'non-human' I quickly set out to chat with something that had 'meat in the machine'. I began to notice that everything I typed into the text box appeared above my avatar's head, allowing everyone in the world to see exactly who says what. Such an identification system seemed essential considering the rapid speed at which textual communication appeared to erupt onto my screen. Transitions in talk seemed to take little notice of relevance points, so much so that the researcher is presented with a 'messy text' (Denzin 1999). This mode of communication, in tandem with interacting with the visual representation of self and others in talk can create a disorienting effect upon the researcher. Further complicating the communication process, I noticed that certain avatars looked different; some simply looked either male or female, while others resembled animals and other less animated objects. Not only did they look different but many were moving, as if making gestures to other avatars. I recall seeing characters distinctly waving, and others shaking their heads in what seemed like disagreement. Tying the action to the written text seemed impossible unless directly engaged in conversation.

Following several visits to *The Gateway* I decided to pay my dues and become a *citizen*. This allowed me not only to join in discussions in newsgroups outside of the Cyberworld's software, but also to change my avatar's appearance—an ability deemed central to developing an online persona within the community. More so, having the ability to alter the avatar's appearance allowed for the mimicking of others in the setting, a salient consideration while trying to 'fit in' and gaining the trust of other community members (Hammersley and Atkinson 1995). I found others more forthcoming in conversation and I began to learn more detailed histories about Cyberworlds and how it was run. I began to discover that other worlds could be visited via *teleports*—booths found littered all around *The Gateway*. Annual events took place such as awards ceremonies that attracted hundreds of guests. *Citizens* would build towns of their own on public land. Online weddings, birthdays, and funerals were regular occasions. Yet, of more interest were the acts of virtual vandalism and *avabuse* (online harassment through text and avatar movement) which had increased over previous years calling for the institution of formal rules of conduct, including the introduction of formal social control under the guise of the *Peacekeeper Core*. This core and the community rules it enforced became central to my study.

Methodological dilemmas of observing virtual space

There are few systematic ways of conducting participant observation. This is often made apparent in the teaching of the method, where frustrated students often feel cheated as no prescribed set of instructions are delivered and concluding remarks usually echo the notion that the only way to learn how to observe is actually to go out into the field. This perspective was certainly applicable to the first days of observation within a virtual environment. Having conducted participant observation in several off-line settings, it was hoped that learnt conventions and rules of thumb could be applied to the online field. However, several conventions had to be adapted to suit the technology that mediated social interaction. Yet concerns over whether the observations taken were adequate enough to portray an authoritative final product were mirrored in the online setting. The timing of observation was an important factor in designing the research. Given its international membership, visitors frequented Cyberworlds at different times, with Americans dominating the social scene most early evenings. Initially, therefore, collecting 'adequate' observational data became an exercise of timing. It was thought that visiting a setting devoid of conversation would be fruitless. However, the job of the ethnographer is not to seek out the unusual and exotic, but to observe the mundane aspects of online life in tandem with the former. During the early days of the study there was the feeling that the observations were a product of a *flâneur*, an urban spectator wandering the virtual streets in search of spectacle (Tester 1994). Upon this realization modes of observation were altered, recognizing that virtual wedding ceremonies and similar exotic spectacles did not characterize the way of life in Cyberworlds. More time was then spent observing the setting, including both busy and less chaotic periods. Yet knowing when to leave and enter the field became a testing problem. The feeling that something important may be missed if the setting was left too early frequently plagued the observational process. Nonetheless, as Hammersley and Atkinson (1995) suggest, even though the temptation to observe everything is overwhelming, there has to be a point at which the writing up of field notes and analytical memoranda take precedence. Moreover, in the virtual setting, entering and leaving the field in an apparently chaotic manner seemed to mirror the behaviour of other community members, further entrenching the experience of virtual life.

Questions of adequacy expanded beyond complex temporal significance. In a similar vein to Bruyn (1966) and his notion of 'subjective adequacy', other elements of observation came under scrutiny, further assisting the continual process of reflexivity. The physical surroundings in Cyberworlds became an important feature of observation, given the importance of the visual element in the research. The notion of *place* then played both a part in the research and in the lives of Cyberworlds community members. How avatars would interact with buildings and similar objects, how they navigated through three-dimensional virtual space, and how they related to the physical presence of other avatars during social interaction became focal points for observation. Further, in relation to deviance online, the notions of place, ownership, and citizenship become integral in understanding cases of virtual vandalism. How avatars used their physical presence during acts of harassment or avabuse also became pivotal in understanding deviant behaviour in online graphical environments. During each period of observation the scene would then be set, with field-notes detailing the physical setting, ranging from what advertisements were on the billboards that day to the appearance of those avatars present. Taking detailed notes of observations has been described as the ethnographer's raison d'être (Fielding 1993). It became clear that deciding what worlds to observe, where to place my avatar, and in what direction to look would significantly influence what observational data of Cyberworlds I would collect. It was decided to keep observations contained to the two most established and populated worlds in Cyberworlds (the Gateway and CW). In most cases an overt but distanced approach was adopted, allowing for minimal interference and wide visual scope for observation. Detailed field notes could then be taken at the computer desk.

Language became another important facet of observation. Speech bubbles that appeared above avatars' heads allowed interlocutors to remain conspicuous. Tying what was said in text with body language was made less complicated by this convention. The unique textual patterns identified during interaction, such as the use of emoticons,[3] turn-taking conventions, and the use of contractions proved difficult to grasp at first, but became an important source of data for interpreting the life and character of the people studied. The use of language within the computer-mediated setting ultimately shaped several theoretical underpinnings of the study. Understanding how language was used to harass or defame victims online and how such uses differed from and mirrored off-line cases proved essential in developing an aetiology of online deviance and harm (Williams 2001).

Gaining what Bruyn (1966) termed *intimacy* with the group studied became a dual process. Allowing those observed to become familiar with the researcher and vice versa was a gradual achievement. However, there were periods of observation that were jeopardized by events quite distant from Cyberworlds, which had divisive effects both upon reactions to the research and within distinct groups in the community. A man convicted of homicide in Kansas was said to have been a member of Cyberworlds, where he made initial contact with one of his victims (CNN.com 2000). While the community was not accountable for its members' actions outside of Cyberworlds, the fact that such an individual was attracted to and used such technology to find his victim generated many ethical and moral debates. It can be imagined that anyone researching deviance and criminality online would have been looked upon with some degree of suspicion at this point. Several of those questioned about the murder and its impacts upon the community became hypersensitive and uncomfortable. Some actually reacted quite fervently feeling as if they were being interrogated. It was at this point in the research where the notion that online and off-line lives are linked at multiple levels became most apparent. Not only did the homicide in Kansas prove to be an example of reciprocity but it also suggested the need for a multi-sited and reflexive ethnography.

The second part of the dual process of gaining intimacy with the community involved entering a different set of *social circumstances* and observing both 'front' and 'backstage' behaviour (Goffman 1971). Becoming familiar with the 'backstage' official aspect of Cyberworlds required interviews with both Gatekeepers and Peacekeepers. The perception of a Cyberworlds community and culture were unfolded at both levels, allowing for a more authoritative understanding of the linkages between the official and grass-roots aspects of the setting. Monitoring decision-making at both levels also allowed for the observation of Bruyn's final category—*social consensus*. How the community operated at both the official and grass-roots level allowed for a certain familiarity with the online culture evident within Cyberworlds. In particular, issues of social control highlighted a disparity in *social consensus* within the community, with Peacekeeper interest duelling with the community masses. This *social dissensus* proved very useful in appreciating the often conflict-ridden relationship between the community members and the agents of social control.

While participant observation formed a major part of the research process, other methods were used to elicit further data from respondents. Gupta and Ferguson (1997: 37) posit that 'talking to and living with the members of a community are increasingly taking their place alongside reading newspapers, analysing government documents, observing the activities of governing elites, and tracking the internal logic of transnational development agencies and corporations'. Similarly, Hammersley and Atkinson

---

[3] The use of ASCII (American Standard Code for Information Interchange) characters to convey emotion online (such as :-) for happy and :-(for sad).

(1995: 158) write 'In many instances…ethnographers need to take account of documents as part of the social setting under investigation'. In recognizing that the study focused on deviance within online settings, a method was needed that allowed for the systematic probing of participants in an interview setting. It was decided that the established method of group interviewing, or the focus group, was to be engineered to operate within the online environment in order to elicit further detailed and focused narrative from the members of Cyberworlds.

Online focus groups

In combination with online participant observation the focus group method was chosen to elicit data from Cyberworlds' community members. Focus groups allowed for a systematic questioning and probing of participants that was unavailable in participant observation. The more systematic inquiry allowed for a refinement of ideas, thus permitting more developed and sensitive theory building. Questioning during the focus group exercise also allowed for the mapping of linkages between Internet mediums used by participants, tracing networks of significance and meaning.

Online focus group composition and access

Identifying and gaining access to populations for research purposes is very often the first hurdle to overcome. Researching Internet populations is no exception. Indeed the similarities between on and offline research are numerous, such as ascertaining what kind of population is required for the research, and what criteria the population must meet. Taking advantage of existing social groups online is by far the most common and successful method of recruiting participants. Notably medical sociology and health research has taken advantage of the 'captive populations' online, characterized by health and illness support networks (Murray 1997, Stewart *et al.* 1998). However, the same had not been done for more exploratory ethnographic research that is devoid of such a rigid and defined population. My research did not have a cohesive pre-existing sample or group for recruiting purposes. While the population of Cyberworlds was definable by membership of an online community, their membership and social bonds were far more fluid and turbulent than those found in online health-support networks. The individuals who frequented the online community did so for varying reasons and motives. This made recruiting a population for more exploratory ethnographic research online problematic. To overcome this stumbling block, sampling conventions from online survey research were adopted. Taking a similar approach to Witmer *et al.* (1999) a suitable population base had to be identified, guided by the research aims. It was found that newsgroups presented an opportunity to draw from a large and varied database of potential focus group participants. The newsgroups identified met the research criteria in being both a technical and social support network for the online community being studied. Essentially this method allowed for the canvassing of a very large proportion of the population of Cyberworlds. Emails were then sent to over one thousand individuals inviting them to take part in the focus group.

In evaluating this approach to recruitment Witmer *et al.* (1999) discovered newsgroups to be useful in attaining a population sample for two reasons: (i) they represented a broad demographic range of end users, and (ii) they were easily accessible and allowed publicly posted email addresses to be drawn for a sample. At first glance these two points support the use of newsgroups for research canvassing but there still remains an important ethical issue. While it remains an established understanding that newsgroups are a public medium intended for public consumption, the emerging recognition that these spaces are being used for private discourse calls into question the usability and accessibility of this medium for research purposes. Indeed, Witmer *et al.* (1999) found a hostile response from several of those canvassed and many objected to receiving 'junk mail'. In my own study several respondents were concerned with the infringement of privacy resulting in many of the responses demanding to know how their email addresses were obtained.

The issues presented by 'canvassing' large static Internet populations for research purposes highlights yet another area of concern for the researcher. The ease at which populations can be identified and recruited for research purposes online, while being a blessing for many market research projects, can mean that these groups become over-researched. The problems this may generate are clearly dependent on the individual research project's aims and focus. Yet generally, it can be ascertained that of the one billion or so global Internet users, many may become nonchalant towards the myriad questionnaires, interviews, and focus groups they are asked to partake in on a weekly basis (CIA 2005). Indeed on several occasions I encountered other researchers online. Only a few days into the research an entire class from an American university entered the community in a practical session of online participant observation, while the previous evening a master's student from a university in the UK was gathering chat data for a thesis. It would be naive to assume such an invasion upon a social setting would not affect respondents' behaviour. Further, issues of access are altered in this light. As is commonly known, gaining access to a setting is sometimes a hierarchical process, first gaining approval from the so-called gatekeeper, followed by ground-level negotiations with the actual research participants. While this process was adhered to in my study, it became apparent that many other researchers had conducted their fieldwork without such safeguards. Granted, many of these individuals may have been students, yet the status of the researcher cannot negate the ethical dilemmas of 'harvesting' data.

As these dilemmas hinder research online, so do the problems of response rates. In tandem with off-line recruitment it is recommended that more individuals be approached for the focus group than are needed to make up a viable number. Reasons for this include possible group atrophy and no-shows (Morgan 1997). One benefit of the online environment is the relative ease and speed at which a researcher can identify and contact a large group of individuals. With this advantage and the relative inexpense of sending emails, Witmer *et al.* (1999) were able to canvass over five hundred possible respondents for their research. Similarly I had access to over one thousand possible respondents. Yet such voluminous numbers do not guarantee good response rates. Witmer *et al.* (1999) received an overall response rate of those wishing to participate of 21 per cent, whilst the rate for my study was a mere 6 per cent. The difference can probably be accounted for by the fact that Witmer *et al.* (1999) were disseminating online questionnaires, which involve less commitment and time, whereas the participants in my study were involved in the research for over two months. Moreover, Witmer *et al.* (1999) required a statistically viable sample, whereas such concerns were less important for my research.

Although I have argued that statistical representativeness was of little importance in my research, this did not mean group size and composition could be ignored. Most research texts advocate group sizes between six and eight participants, warning if a group is too large moderation and transcription becomes complex (Morgan 1997). Such concerns have to be recast when engineering focus groups in asynchronous online settings. The method of communication and mediation alters drastically from off-line to online environments where conversation becomes digitized, making transcription redundant and mediation less problematic. This ultimately means that groups can be larger allowing for longer and more involving discussion, often resulting in threading.[4] Murray (1997) opted for the conventional off-line number of participants for the asynchronous online focus group (6–8) but later acknowledged that a larger group may have yielded richer and more detailed discussion. This assumption was corroborated in Robson's (1999) research on inflammatory bowel disease sufferers; with an asynchronous online focus group subscription of 57 respondents Robson encountered threading in discussions, with multiple topics simultaneously discussed. Further, the larger number ensured that participants remained open, responsive, and familiar with each other which encouraged a hands-off approach with minimal guidance and questioning from the researcher.

Asynchronous online focus groups

The online focus group utilized in my study incorporated asynchronous technologies. The discussion list program *Majordomo* was utilized to mediate discussion between group members. Discussion lists are email-based discussion groups, with a single central email address to which contributions are sent before they are automatically bounced off to the inboxes of those subscribing to the list. Although lacking the visual niceties of newsgroup threads, distribution lists have the user familiarity of email, and a number of administration options that make them particularly attractive for research purposes. Subscription to the list was closed off, allowing strict control over who could take part in the discussion, and who had access to information about the discussion and its subscribers. Contributions were sent in digest form, whereby individual emails were pooled and sent out as a single compiled email at specified intervals. The list was also moderated, allowing for information such as identifying header information to be removed. Moderation also allowed for message threads to be organized and interjections enabled prompts or questions to be asked in a similar manner to a 'real-life' focus group moderator. Distribution lists proved relatively straightforward to set up and run, requiring no specialist software or expertise, and were similarly easy for research participants to contribute to.

Ethical issues of online research

The speed, ease, and low cost of computer-mediated social research makes it an appealing option. However, the ethical considerations of online participant observation and online focus groups must temper the enthusiastic rush to have a go. In the increasingly

---

[4] The simultaneous conduct of multiple topics of conversation.

regulated space within which researchers practise their craft the online environment poses unique challenges. To ensure online research designs pass through University and other ethical committees, established guidelines and procedures must be revisited, reframed, and anticipated carefully. Such considerations must take account of both codes of conduct relating to behaviour in computer-mediated communities, and the codes of conduct relating to the practice of social research.

The acceptable behaviour of Internet users is governed by a combination of service providers' acceptable use policies (AUPs) and codes of conduct. Acceptable use policies are contractual agreements made between users and service providers that, to some degree, define how the user can use the network. Largely similar in what they cover, these outline what is and is not allowed on the particular network, usually with a strong emphasis on responsible use of the network and not affecting the availability of the network to others. Informal codes of conduct developed naturally by online communities as the Internet grew and developed. These outline standard practices for the various services available over the Internet (email, newsgroups, IRC, etc.) and define what is acceptable behaviour within these areas. These codes are known as netiquette and should be required reading for anyone new to the Internet. These codes of conduct along with civil rights and cyber rights issues are continually being discussed, developed, and defended by the online community through organizations such as Computer Professionals for Social Responsibility (CPSR), the Electronic Frontier Foundation (EFF), and the Association of Internet Researchers (AoIR 2002). Beyond broader general netiquette guides many Internet communities, such as Cyberworlds, have created their own specific set of rules or guidelines that apply just to that particular group.

When planning my online social research, these considerations were combined with requirements of ethical guidelines regarding social research. However, while social science guidelines may be more familiar to social researchers, they needed rethinking in their application in an online context. Seeking consent from those who are recruited for an online focus group was relatively straightforward and comparable to eliciting consent in more traditional situations. Ostensibly the idea of the confidentiality of identifying information in any written report of the research seemed fairly straightforward. However, the risk of deductive disclosure was very real in the research, and was carefully anticipated during the planning of the online focus group.

In computer-mediated communications, complete anonymity is almost impossible to guarantee, as information about the origin of a computer-transmitted message is, for most users, almost impossible to remove. While the absence of anonymity in research does not mean researchers cannot guarantee confidentiality to research subjects, in computer-mediated research this is also more difficult to achieve, especially in online focus groups. Traditional procedures for storage of data and anonymizing participants are complicated in a medium where the original data is routinely available to other participants. Any research quoting or explicitly referring to an article posted in any kind of group discussion necessarily permits some level of identification of the author of that message by others in the group. If discussions are set up in a way that disguises the headers of a message, this identification need only be confined to the username chosen by the author, but if headers are left on, the situation is comparable to sending off-line focus group participants home with a full transcript of the discussion together with the names and addresses of all those present. The known or foreseeable risks of participating in any research project must be outweighed by the potential or probable benefits of the research findings, but the ability to do this can be undermined in a setting where the research process and data can be so easily shared by others.

Analysing online data

Reservations about online communications and research often focus on the lack of non-verbal data such as setting, expression, movement, phatic noise,[5] and the like. Text-only online data is 'all-inclusive text', making it harder to identify its constituent elements. These elements are easily distinguishable in conventional face-to-face interactions, allowing them to become primary targets for analysis. In traditional off-line settings, the convention is to see these separate elements contributing to a whole meaning. By impos-ing such separation on the all-inclusive text of online data, while delineation is less rigid, it is useful to tease out these elements in order to counter arguments about the depth-lessness of textual online communication. To this end three features can be identified that have comparable characteristics with accepted off-line data categories:

1. Form—comparable to 'context' in off-line research. Email, web-board messages, chat rooms and the like all have particular background expectancies and shared understandings in the way, for example, a school or hospital setting does in off-line research.

2. Style—comparable to non-verbal cues in off-line research. The conveyance of meaning through idiomatic forms of expression, for example emoticons, line width, use of capitals, colour, and font.

3. Content—comparable to the verbal elements of off-line data—the words partici-pants use to express themselves.

All three elements have considerable bearing on where online research might take place, how research is conducted in these settings, and what kind of analyses are used. For example, setting up a focus group within a chat room holds quite distinct challenges from holding a focus group over a distribution list. The kinds of data generated in both settings are also significantly different. Data collected in a chat room will exhibit features associ-ated with synchronous forms of textual communication. Overly stylistic content, dis-rupted adjacency,[6] overlapping exchanges, and topic delay all have to be contended with during mediation and analysis. Asynchronous modes, such as email, are less likely to be littered with stylistic responses, with more focus on content, fostering more considered narratives. It is important to maintain these stylistic characteristics when (re)-presenting the data, in order to retain the respondent's communication style and identity (Markham 1998). Emoticons, contractions, run-on sentences, and spelling errors are all retained in the data extracts found in my research. While both synchronous and asynchronous modes of communication are viable for research purposes, the kinds of data produced

---

[5] Language used more for the purpose of establishing an atmosphere, such as 'gee', 'hmm', and 'ahh'.

[6] Temporal lag between responses characteristic of many synchronous and asynchronous online communi-cations.

are sufficiently different to warrant careful consideration when planning the use of online focus groups.

Conclusion

Criminology has a history of fixating on certain types of delinquency. Researching the types of delinquency that break the criminological mould becomes the duty of researchers working on the fringes of the discipline. While online deviance currently dwells within this fringe, the centripetal force emerging from the pervasiveness of information communications technologies within society will ensure its central location within the discipline in decades to come. However, today the use of the Internet for research by criminologists remains largely parochial. Those few researchers that do venture into online social spaces to collect primary data face nascent methodological challenges on paths yet to be trodden. Non-physical social spaces, time–space distanciation, disinhibited research participants, and the ephemeral nature of Internet-based communication are but a few of the methodological quagmires with which criminologists must deal when collecting online data. The apparent ubiquity of the Internet means that criminological researchers will at some point need to engage with these issues and re-engineer their off-line methods to deal with the challenges and possibilities which online field sites present.

References

Association of Internet Researchers (AoIR) (2002). Ethical Decision Making and Internet Research: Recommendations from the AoIR Ethics Working Committee www.aoir.org/reports/ethics.pdf [Accessed 04/09/2003].

Baym, N. (1995a). 'The Emergence of Community in Computer-Mediated Communication' in S. Jones (ed.), CyberSociety. Newbury Park, CA: Sage.

—— (1995b). 'The Performance of Humor in Computer-Mediated Communication'. Journal of Computer-Mediated Communication, 1: 2. http://www.ascusc.org/jcmc/vol1/issue2/baym.html [Accessed 03/04/98].

—— (1998). 'The Emergence of Online Community' in S. Jones (ed.), Cybersociety 2.0. Newbury Park, CA: Sage.

Bruyn, S. (1966). The Human Perspective in Sociology: The Methodology of Participant Observation, Englewood Cliffs, NJ: Prentice-Hall.

CIA world fact book (2005). http://www.odci.gov/cia/publications/factbook/rankorder/2153rank.html [Accessed 04/07/2006].

CNN.com 06/08/2000 www.cnn.com/2000/US/06/08/barrel.bodies.02/ [Accessed 20/08/2000].

Correll, S. (1995). 'The Ethnography of an Electronic Bar: The Lesbian Café'. The Journal of Contemporary Ethnography 24(3): 485–96.

Danet, B. (1998). 'Text as Mask: Gender, Play, and Performance on the Internet' in S. Jones (ed.), CyberSociety 2.0. Newbury Park, CA: Sage.

Denzin, N. K. (1999). 'Cybertalk and the Method of Instances' in S. Jones (ed.), Doing Internet Research. London: Sage.

DIETRICH, D. (1997). '(Re)-fashioning the Techno-Erotic Woman: Gender and Textuality in the Cybercultural Matrix' in S. Jones (ed.), *Virtual Culture: Identity and Communication in Cybersociety.* London: Sage.

FIELDING, N. G. (1993). 'Ethnography' in N. Gilbert (ed.), *Researching Social Life.* London: Sage.

GIDDENS, A. (1990). *The Consequences of Modernity.* Polity Press: Oxford.

GOFFMAN, E. (1955). 'On Face-Work: An Analysis of Ritual Elements in Social Interaction'. *Psychiatry* 18: 213–31.

—— (1971). *The Presentation of Self in Everyday Life.* Harmondsworth: Penguin.

GUPTA, A. and FERGUSON, J. (1997). 'Discipline and Practice: "The Field" as Site, Method, and Location in Anthropology' in J. Ferguson and A. Gupta (eds), *Anthropological Locations: Boundaries and Grounds of a Field Science.* Berkeley: University of California Press.

GRABOWSKY, P. N. and SMITH, R. G. (1998). *Crime in the Digital Age: Controlling Telecommunications and Cyberspace Illegalities.* New Brunswick, NJ: Transaction Publishers.

HAMMERSLEY, M. and ATKINSON, P. (1995). *Ethnography: Principles in Practice* (2nd edn). London: Routledge.

HINE, C. (2000). *Virtual Ethnography.* London: Sage.

JOINSON, A. N. (1998). 'Causes and effects of disinhibition on the Internet' in J. Gackenbach (ed.), *The Psychology of the Internet.* New York: Academic Press.

JONES, S. (1995). *Cybersociety: Computer Mediated Communication and Community.* Newbury Park, CA: Sage.

—— (1997). *Virtual Culture: Identity and Communication in Cybersociety.* London: Sage.

—— (1998). *Cybersociety 2.0: Revisiting Computer Mediated Communication and Community.* Newbury Park, CA: Sage.

KRAMARAE, C. (1998). 'Feminist Fictions of Future Technology' in Steve Jones (ed.), *Cybersociety 2.0.* Newbury Park, CA: Sage.

MACKINNON, R. C. (1997). 'Punishing the Persona: Correctional Strategies for the Virtual Offender' in S. Jones (ed.), *Virtual Cultures: Identity and Communication in Cybersociety.* London: Sage.

MARKHAM, A. (1998). *Life Online: Researching Real Experience in Virtual Space.* Newbury Park, CA: Sage.

MORGAN, D. (1997). *Focus Groups as Qualitative Research* (2nd edn), Newbury Park, CA: Sage.

MURRAY, P. (1997). 'Using virtual focus groups in qualitative health research'. *Qualitative Health Research* 7(4): 542–9.

PACCAGNELLA, L. (1997). 'Strategies for ethnographic research on virtual communities'. *Journal of Computer Mediated Communication* 3(1). *http://www.ascusc. org/jcmc/vol3/issue1/paccagnella.html* [Accessed 12/01/98].

POSTER, M. (1998). 'Virtual ethnicity: tribal identity in an age of global communications', in S. Jones (ed.), *Cybersociety 2.0.* Newbury Park, CA: Sage.

REID, E. (1999). 'Hierarchy & Power: Social Control in Cyberspace' in P. Kollock and A. Smith (eds), *Communities in Cyberspace.* London: Routledge.

ROBSON, K. (1999). 'Employment Experiences of Ulcerative Colitis and Crohn's Disease Sufferers'. Unpublished Ph.D. thesis. Cardiff: University of Wales.

SHAW, D. F. (1997). 'Gay Men and Computer Mediated Communication: A Case Study of the Phish.Net Fan Community' in S. Jones (ed.), *Virtual Culture: Identity and Communication in Cybersociety.* London: Sage.

STEWART, F., ECKERMANN, E., and ZHOU, K. (1998). 'Using the Internet in Qualitative Public Heath Research: A Comparison of Chinese and Australian Young Women's Perceptions of Tobacco Use'. *Internet*

Journal of Health Promotion. http://www.monash.edu.au/heath/IJHP/1998/12 [Accessed 03/12/2000]

Tester, K. (1994). *The Flâneur.* London: Routledge.

Turkle, S. (1995). *Life on Screen: Identity in the Age of the Internet.* London: Weidenfeld & Nicolson.

Van Maanen, J. (1988). 'An End to Innocence: The Ethnography of Ethnography' in J. Van Maanen (ed.), *Representation in Ethnography.* Thousand Oaks: Sage.

Wall, D. (ed.) (2001). *Crime and the Internet.* London: Routledge.

—— (ed.) (2003). *Cyberspace Crime.* Aldershot: Ashgate.

—— and Williams, M. (forthcoming) *Understanding Cybercrime.* Milton Keynes: Open University Press.

Williams, M. (2001). 'The Language of Cybercrime' in D. S. Wall (ed.), *Crime & the Internet.* London: Routledge.

—— (2006). *Virtually Criminal: Crime, Deviance & Regulation Online.* London: Routledge.

Witmer, D. F. Colman R. W., and Katzman S. L. (1999). 'From Paper-and-Pencil to Screen-and-Keyboard' in S. Jones (ed.), *Doing Internet Research.* London: Sage.

17

Ethnographic research and the licensing courts

Philip Hadfield

Background

In Britain, any sustained attempt to respond to violent street crime and antisocial behaviour has to address the issue of alcohol misuse. This is particularly apparent in relation to contemporary urban nightlife, in which the socially and culturally embedded restraints, which act to deter excessive consumption in other settings, are often absent. Attempts to control the consumption of alcohol—and thus alcohol-related crime—through placing restrictions upon the availability of drink are an archaic component of urban governance. At a local and national level, alcohol availability is shaped by licensing and market demand; with the former used to control the latter. Where licensing interventions are lax, or absent, bar and club developments respond to consumer pressure, with little concern for the broader public good (Hadfield 2006).[1] In the absence of a major reform in our cultural attitudes to drink, effective use of the licensing system at least allows local authorities, the police, and local residents to play their part in the creation of sustainable night-time cities (Plant and Plant 2006).

Close reading of ethnographies of place, combined with theory and research in the mostly statistically-driven or mixed-method tradition of 'environmental' criminology, reveals how people's routine encounters in urban space and time form the building blocks of a criminogenic social setting (Hadfield and contributors 2004). This analytical fusing sensitizes us to the understanding that it is not the criminal justice system, but rather, planning and licensing law—the mundane tools of municipal regulation—which determine both where and when alcohol-related crime and disorder might typically occur, and where and when it might not. At issue here is what one might term the 'administrative governance of crime', a topic long neglected by criminologists.

This chapter recounts my attempts to explore the social organization of licensing litigation, which may be regard as one isolated—but criminologically important—mode of administrative governance. In particular, the chapter describes some of the research processes which underpin my doctoral thesis and its subsequent development in the book

---

[1] Sections of this chapter have previously appeared, in different form in *Bar Wars: Contesting the Night in Contemporary British Cities (2006)*. The research that forms the basis of both that book and this chapter was initially funded by a three-year studentship from the Economic and Social Research Council (R42200034167). I remain grateful to the Council for its support.

Bar Wars: Contesting the Night in Contemporary British Cities. The chapter begins with an examination of the ways in which external pressure and circumstance conspired to draw the research into new and unforeseen directions; directions which were highly politicized, media-saturated, and adversarial. Through the lens of Chicagoan notions of 'moral work' and 'career', the chapter then provides a reflexive account of how fieldwork experiences and dilemmas served to reshape not only my analysis, but also aspects of my identity.

Beginnings

My doctoral research arose in response to a previous study of the night-time economy on which I had worked with my supervisor, Dick Hobbs, and others.[2] The subsequent Ph.D. project sought to respond to various unanswered questions and emergent lines of enquiry from that study. Initial fieldwork explored work-related risk within a nightlife context. Although this proved to be a rewarding topic of investigation, I found that many of my informants had other—for them—more pressing, concerns. A broad range of public sector agencies, businesses, community groups, individuals, media, and political interests were becoming actively engaged in the governance of our cities after dark. All of these interests were struggling with the issue of how to comprehend, manage, and prevent a range of problems associated with hedonistic excess in the night-time public realm. Pointedly, these interests were also struggling with *each other*, the appropriate uses and meanings of night-time public space being issues of deep-seated contestation.

Most saliently, conflict had broken out between sections of the pub trade and drinks industry on one side, and a number of police forces, residents' groups, and local authorities on the other. Although there were often issues of significant disagreement within these two camps, the main thrust of contention arose in response to a constant pressure by business interests to open up the night for the business of pleasure and consequent moves by their opponents to re-impose more restrictive approaches to licensing. Feelings were running high on all sides. Local skirmishes fuelled and mirrored the broader battles occurring at a national level in the debates that raged over impending legislation widely understood to be ushering in a new era of '24-hour drinking.' This contestation of the night in contemporary British cities became the major focus of my research.

It was within this context that the dissemination of findings from my earlier research began to attract the attention of crime prevention practitioners and other interested parties from across the UK. Police, local authorities, and leisure corporations began to approach members of the research team with requests for assistance in the form of consultancy work. My supervisor encouraged me to respond positively to these requests in order to enhance my contextual knowledge, establish valuable links with key gatekeepers, and broaden my fieldwork. The majority of enquiries involved requests for me to appear as an expert witness in licensing trials.

My first experiences of licensing litigation were a revelation; the new data exerting a powerful influence over my emergent understandings. It quickly became apparent that my

---

2 Economic and Social Research Council (ESRC) Violence Research Programme award no. L133251050, culminating in the book, *Bouncers: Violence and Governance in the Night-time Economy* (Hobbs *et al.* 2003).

consultancy activities—especially the role of expert witness to the licensing courts—afforded unrivalled opportunities to conduct ethnography. This approach involved the use of participant observation, wherein the researcher places his or her self at the heart of the research setting and seeks to experience and record events as they unfold. Participant observation is informed by a pragmatist epistemology, wherein the analytical spotlight is directed toward interpretation of the meanings and understandings of social actors as revealed through social interaction (Atkinson and Housley 2003, Rock 1979). Formal deductive reasoning and a-priori speculations are largely eschewed in favour of generative processes of empirical investigation. Inferences remain tentative and fluid, being posited only as they emerge *from the data*, to be repeatedly adapted and refined via an evolving process of analytic induction (Becker 1958, Znaniecki 1934). Knowledge is regarded as primarily grounded in one's personal engagement with the enacted environment; thus, ontological claims are necessarily modest, cautious, and context-bound. Although attention may be drawn to the broader 'conditions of action' that are considered, in some ways, to shape those environments, ethnographic analyses have a tendency to emphasize particularities of process and action within discrete social settings. In so doing, the ethnographer displays his or her allegiance to an intellectual tradition which regards social science's proclivity to generalize with unease—at the least, in so far as such generalizations are not supported by the fine-grained analysis of related social interaction.

Peculiarities of the licensing trial

One seemingly universal feature of trial settings is that proceedings are conducted in accordance with a set of regulations which control the content and form of testimony, thereby delimiting interaction. In discharging their administrative functions, licensing authorities and the courts are required to act fairly and in accordance with the rules of natural justice. Natural justice maxims provide that decisions should be free from bias, partiality, personal advantage, commitments, or interest. The twin pillars of natural justice are the right to have one's case heard by an independent and impartial tribunal and the right of both sides to have their views heard before a decision is reached. More specifically, natural justice affords each side the right to know the case made against them and the opportunity to 'test' and correct such assertions. In order to uphold natural justice, most trials and tribunals are governed by rules of procedure which stipulate the approved means for introducing evidence, ruling on admissibility, examining witnesses, and so on. However, the procedural rules of the administrative tribunals in which I participated departed in many ways from those of the criminal courts explored by previous ethnographers.

English administrative tribunals are required to act quasi-judicially, which involves, at a minimum, deciding each case on its merits, taking into account all relevant considerations, and observing basic tenets of fairness and impartiality. In criminal and some civil trials, rules of evidence are used to control the content of the testimony that may be introduced. In determining licence applications, administrative decision-makers enjoy a broader discretion in governing the conduct of hearings and they do not apply strict rules of evidence. There were, for example, no strict rules as to the timetable for disclosure of documentary evidence and witness statements. These matters were often simply agreed between the parties in advance of the trial. Although a distinctly adversarial approach is adopted and each party calls evidence in support of their case, 'hearsay' evidence is admissible[3] and there is no burden of proof. This means that no party has anything to 'prove'—it is up to the committee/justices/judge to decide disputed issues on the 'balance of probabilities', according to the persuasiveness of the evidence they have heard.[4]

In jury trials, the Crown Court Bench Specimen Directions offer guidance to the judge on the adducing of expert evidence. These instructions give a clear sense of how the court proposes to limit the potential influence of expert evidence. No comparable directions are issued in the licensing courts. This permits counsel to build up their own experts or diminish their opponent's, free of any of the guidance used in jury trials. Indeed, in licensing cases, lawyers are able to refer to people as 'experts' who would never qualify to give evidence in criminal trials, for example, ex-police officers acting as 'licensing consultants.'

The adversarial tradition regards the opportunity to participate in a live oral hearing as fundamental to fair procedure (Ellison 2001; Langbein 2003). Despite the relaxed rules of evidence in licensing trials, the predilection for oral testimony remains strong and the bench may indicate their intention to accord less weight to documentary and audiovisual evidence that cannot be verified by the presence of a supporting witness. The oral tradition employs cross-examination as its primary technique for assessing the credibility of witnesses and unearthing evidence that might otherwise have been omitted or suppressed. The English administrative trials in which I partook were constituted mainly as gladiatorial struggles between partisan teams of professionals, with relatively limited involvement by lay people.

The research process

My fieldwork did not focus entirely upon the courts. I also interviewed a wide range of persons whose work, residence, or consumption choices brought them into contact with the night-time economy, and conducted extended periods of observation in and around licensed premises. These settings were, by nature, open to the public and therefore presented no formal barriers to participation. By contrast, access to the private domain of pre-trial meetings and correspondence, barristers' chambers, police stations, and the offices of local authorities and business executives arose only as a result of my 'utility' to such parties. Sampling of research sites was, for the most part, externally task-oriented and informants were accessed by the snowballing of personal introductions, with no pretence to statistical representation.

I appeared as an expert witness in licensing trials on twenty-six occasions and attended a further ten trials simply to observe. The trials were conducted in Magistrates' Courts and Crown Courts throughout England and Wales. My participation in trial-related

---

[3] Under the 'hearsay rule', a statement, whether of fact or opinion, is not normally admissible as evidence where it is made otherwise than by a person giving oral testimony in court. Similarly, persons cannot give evidence as to what they heard another person say about an event; they can only give evidence as to their own experience or knowledge.

[4] In criminal cases the prosecution bears the burden of proof and the standard of proof is higher, being that of 'beyond reasonable doubt'.

activities involved three main tasks: pre-trial briefing, the preparation of witness state-ments, and the presentation of oral testimony.

The process would begin following an approach by a client's solicitor. Once commis-sioned, I would begin to correspond with counsel and other legal professionals in relation to the preparation of each case. My first task would be to examine bundles of documents containing witness statements and other relevant information, such as previous judg-ments, architectural plans, promotional material, radius maps, crime statistics, and let-ters of correspondence. I would be required to dissect these documents and provide counsel with my response in the form of confidential briefing notes. This task involved the critique of arguments constructed by our opponents, the aim being to inform the preparation of witness cross-examination. On many occasions, I would be called to meetings attended by other witnesses. At these events, team strategies for the fighting of each case would be devised.

My main contribution was to prepare and present a written statement (described by lawyers as a 'proof of evidence report'). Very little of this trial-related work was conducted in the region in which I lived (north-east England), therefore the research for each case would typically involve one or two weekends away from home in the town or city in ques-tion. It would be necessary for me to visit the relevant site and its surrounding area on a Thursday, Friday, or Saturday night, in order to observe activities during apposite periods of time. In the case of new licence applications from branded chain operators, I was also required to spend one or more evenings in an existing 'unit'. This would typically require the planning of further weekends in other areas. Where applications had been made sim-ply to *vary* the licence of an existing premises (typically, by extending its trading hours, or increasing its physical capacity), I would simply visit the venue and its environs.

In the course of my visits to over fifty high-street premises, over a four-year period, I developed a systematic observation schedule to assist in the recording of detailed field notes. I became attuned to those aspects of the social and physical environment indicated by the research literature, and by my own experience, to be associated with alcohol-related crime and other forms of urban 'stress.' In relation to licensed premises this would include issues such as the concept of the business; the availability of food; levels of com-fort; customer occupancy levels; age, social profile, and intoxication level of patrons; behaviour of bar and door staff; and drinks pricing policies. Issues recorded in sur-rounding public space included the number, density, size, and terminal hours of the vari-ous premises; availability of transport; location of taxi ranks and fast-food outlets; direction and density of traffic and pedestrian flows; noise levels; general profile and demeanour of the crowds; policing strategies; incidents of littering and street fouling; and the extent of street lighting and CCTV coverage.[5]

Events were recorded in chronological order as each night progressed. To appear unobtrusive, for personal safety reasons, and most importantly, simply to make the task less onerous, I employed friends to assist me. The evenings would begin at around 7–8 p.m., usually with attempts to buy a meal, and run through until around 3.30 a.m. the fol-lowing morning (or as late as 5 a.m. in Central London) when the streets began to clear. In a few cases, where an area was new to me, I was accompanied by police officers or local

---

[5] These various physical, social, and managerial factors and their relationship to the constitution of crime risk are discussed in Hadfield and contributors (2004).

authority personnel. Officers would sometimes be in uniform and on other occasions would wear plain clothes. These 'authority figures' would answer my questions and impart local knowledge, whilst showing me the 'circuit', the key hot spots, and all the major venues.

Time on the streets and in licensed premises undoubtedly exceeded that spent within the licensing courts, permitting considerable opportunity for observation in a wide variety of settings. Yet, unlike Hobbs (1988), who was able to combine research in the pub with pleasurable socializing, I often found fieldwork in licensed premises and night-time public space to be hard, tiring, and frustrating. I was away from home, among strangers and tasked with the detailed recording of almost everything I witnessed; accounts that might later be tested in a court of law. Drinking (very much) was therefore not an option I could realistically explore. Indeed, spending almost every weekend evening in this environment impacted adversely on my social life and was a source of worry for my family. Despite such drawbacks, my nocturnal movements remained something of an adventure. They provided an exciting element of regress to my pre-academic self, a 'holiday from academic rituals . . . an opportunity to get away from books, papers, essays, seminars, and sedentary pontificating on the ills of the world' (Punch 1978: 325).

In court, my primary tasks were to submit testimony under oath and present myself for cross-examination. As I was often the only objection witness to have direct experience of the premises and its surroundings, my evidence was sometimes of central importance to a client's case. It was essential that I pay close attention to the evidence and cross-examination of other witnesses, particularly those of our opponents. On occasion, I would be asked to sit next to, or directly behind, counsel in order to make myself available for whispered questioning and the passing of hastily written notes in relation to unfolding events.

As a fully-fledged participant, my experience of the courtroom was quite different to that of non-participant observers such as Bottoms and McLean, who recall their experiences of the criminal trial as 'dull, commonplace, ordinary, and after a while downright tedious' (Bottoms and McLean 1976: 226). By contrast, my experience developed into one of excitement, nervous trepidation, intense concentration, and personal challenge. Periods of tedium did occur, but these involved time spent in court corridors and canteens waiting for postponed hearings to begin. The majority of cases proceeded slowly and at a pace determined only by court insiders and other legal professionals (see Rock 1993). In their concern to appear fair, magistrates and judges were often loath to assert much influence over the pace of events. Laborious and repetitive submissions were used tactically in order to restrict opportunities for participation by time-pressured witnesses. When scheduling the presentation of their party's evidence, counsel would give precedence to the needs of busy professional witnesses such as police officers and hospital consultants. Such witnesses had to arrange time away from work in order to attend, and their co-operation and good will had to be preserved. Control over my own use of time had to be subordinated to the dictates of the court and the strategies adopted by counsel. I fulfilled counsel's expectations with good humour as they enabled me to 'earn as I learned' (Saunders 1997), observing every twist and turn of events.

My field roles were strategically adapted to the requirements of each setting. In some instances—for example, when observing licensed premises for the purposes of a pre-trial report—my role had to be covert in order to avoid provoking actions by the researched that would have disrupted the naturalism of the setting. It was especially important for my purposes to prevent the possibility of compensatory behaviour that might have obscured more routine and deviant social practices. I therefore attempted to participate as a legitimate and unobtrusive observer. On other occasions, for example, when requesting interviews, my role was overt and my purposes explicit. In my role as an expert witness, I told clients I was conducting a study of the regulation of nightlife and made no secret of my interest in the social practices of litigation and courtroom interaction. However, to have sought the express permission to observe from every participant in every trial would have unduly compromised the research. Trials were public spectacles and those present would, in all likelihood, have inferred that, like others engaged in copious note-taking (including legal professionals and journalists), I intended to relate matters to a broader audience.

My analyses of the licensing trial are undoubtedly partial as I have sought to rely upon note-taking and informal interview methods, employed in the course of my own participation. My evolving and inductive approach to analysis involved the coding of data into categories based upon my interpretations of social interaction in situ and may have painted a different picture from that elicited by other methods such as formal retrospective interviewing. More fundamentally, the validity of my data, like all sociological research, remains open to question. I cannot know what impact my presence had upon the settings, or how typical, or atypical the views and behaviours of my (opportunity) sample may have been. I will never know if, or to what extent, informants sought purposely to adapt their actions and interactions in my presence. In conducting field research, ethnographers (and social scientists in general) have always trod an epistemological minefield, and I was no exception.

My personal attributes exerted a major influence over the character of fieldwork relationships. I am a white male who grew up in the north-west of England, my social class of origin is the 'petite bourgeoisie',[6] and my age during the research period was early-mid thirties. Of course, researchers are not merely passive observers or scribes, but active participants in the research process (Van Maanen *et al.* 1989). This is an issue of epistemological concern (Miller and Glassner 1997). In the interview context, for example, 'the story is being told to a particular person; it might take a different form if someone else were the listener' (Riessman 1993: 11). I had considerable work experience as a disc jockey, which undoubtedly assisted me in establishing rapport with workers in licensed premises, allowing me to empathize with their stories and respond appropriately. I found my age to be an asset, as I was still young enough to mingle unobtrusively with the late-night crowds, yet also had sufficient experience and credentials to be taken seriously as an expert witness. My value to the courts stemmed, in part, from my ability to get 'close to the action.' I often felt like a colonial anthropologist, tasked with reporting and interpreting the mores and rituals of the (ignoble) savage. Licensing trials were dominated by white male upper-middle-class legal professionals. For me, issues of intersubjective interpretation therefore revolved around 'class work' much more so than gender or race.

---

[6] Petite bourgeoisie: a group of ambivalent status, who tend to share the economic privileges of the middle classes, but are culturally and socially more akin to the respectable working classes than to middle-class professionals, bureaucrats, or administrators (see Savage *et al.* 1992).

This was because, with few exceptions, black and ethnic minorities were simply absent from the courtroom, whilst women tended to play supporting, rather than key, roles.[7]

Becomings

The first time I gave evidence was at the Crown Court in Leeds in 2001. I had rarely set foot in a court of law and my naivety made me easy meat for counsel who took some delight in misconstruing my words and exposing my 'incompetences'. My experiences matched those described by Shuy (1993: 201) who warns that:

Expert witnesses who submit to examination and cross-examination should expect to be treated in ways quite unfamiliar to what they are used to in an academic setting. For example, they can expect ridicule of various types. They can expect to be submitted to the temptation to get angry. They can expect loaded questions... The expert witness is in a language game and must be alert at all times for traps.

As requests for court work began to mount, I resolved to 'get my act together' in order that such humiliations might be avoided. In attending trial and spending time with lawyers, business executives, and crime prevention practitioners, I found it necessary to adapt my usual comportment in order to construct a more appropriate professional persona. In the absence of formal training, I learned how a witness was expected to behave through 'the more indirect means of observation and imitation' (Becker 1963: 48). I listened attentively to the cross-examination of other witnesses and the way in which testimony was received. I overheard the conversations of lawyers as they passed judgment on witnesses' performance and asked each counsel I worked with for an assessment of my strengths and weaknesses. In becoming accustomed to courtroom convention, I learned to 'save face' by managing my fear and adopting the necessary emotional fortitude.

Sensitivity to the social adaptations of self and others is a cornerstone of Chicago School interactionism, wherein:

The social self is not an entity, it is a process. Selves and identities are never fixed. Processes of socialization or enculturation do not have a determinate end-point. Socialization is not viewed... as the preliminary to some final state. The processes of becoming—of the flux of identity and biography—are the very stuff of social life (Atkinson and Housley 2003: 89).

Following the seminal work of Becker (1963), Glaser and Strauss (1971), and Goffman (1968), the concept of social 'career' has been central to interactionist accounts of

---

[7] I did not encounter any female licensing applicants, nor did I encounter applicants from black and ethnic minorities. Only four female expert witnesses were observed and women comprised around a third of all police witnesses and approximately half of all lay witnesses; the vast majority being residents, together with a small number of supporters of the application. In the Magistrates' Courts, a significant minority of district judges and magistrates were female, with Crown Court benches having a much lower proportion of female judges and magistrates. Only twice did I encounter a female advocate, and only once, a black male advocate.

individual and organizational experience (Crawford 2003). Interactionist notions of career differ from those of everyday use by encompassing not only individual (and collective) development within an occupational sphere, but also more general forms of social progression and status passage (see Goffman 1968: 119; Becker 1963, Glaser and Strauss 1971). Such approaches informed my analysis of how those witnesses who repeatedly participated in licensing trials moved, by a process of enculturation, from the state of 'real people'—typified by lawyers as one of naïvety and performative 'incompetence'—to the level of consummate 'professionals' who had learned how to behave and participate effectively within an adversarial setting (Hadfield 2006: ch. 8). By nurturing a reflexive awareness of such processes of becoming, I became attuned to the effects of social career transition, not only amongst my informants, but also within my self.

Competent courtroom performance involved, at a minimum, the ability to translate verbal and written testimony into 'evidence'—a mode of discourse understandable and useful to courtroom actors. As is often the case with the dissemination of social research to lay audiences, submitting evidence required 'simplification that renders a complex world in blacks and whites' (Walker 2001: 1, and see Shuy 1993: 201). My accounts had to be stated clearly, in a form that was largely stripped of academic jargon. I also had to acquire presentational skills. First of all, I learned to dress appropriately. My normal casual and somewhat creased attire was replaced by a black or navy blue suit, shiny shoes, a crisp and well-pressed shirt, and bright, but sober, silk tie. I learned the formal decorum of the courts and how to interact in an appropriate manner. As with my fieldwork in licensed premises and on the streets, much of my courtroom activity was conducted many miles from home. In the south-east of England I found myself attempting to neutralize my Northern accent by adopting my own mutant variety of 'received pronunciation.' As well as learning how to talk, I also had to learn when to keep my mouth shut. In court, conversation among observers was strictly prohibited, and even in the 'backstage' arena of the corridor, restaurant, or briefing room, unnecessary chat was often unwelcome. Lawyers had to concentrate and continually re-organize their case; nervous witnesses had to be briefed.

Most importantly, I had to learn how to present and defend my report. With experience, I became more cautious, robust, even tempered, and assertive. Once confident enough to resist counsels' attempts to cut short or misconstrue my words, I began to use my new speech opportunities to display the breadth and depth of my knowledge; draw upon supportive evidence from other witnesses, and to launch my own 'counter-attacks.' Following Goffman (1968), my progression from real person to professional witness may be understood as a 'moral' career path. The career displayed moral components to the extent that it involved ongoing processes of induction and fluid transformations of identity which influenced the ways in which I judged and categorized the actions of self and others. Like Becker's marihuana users, I found that once basic lessons of performance had been learnt, my affective responses to the task were dramatically transformed. Trials acquired a new and more positive meaning, becoming exciting and challenging struggles rather than humiliating ordeals: 'what was once frightening and distasteful becomes, after a taste for it is built up, pleasant, desired, and sought after' (Becker 1963: 56). Of course, the experience of delivering oral testimony remained stressful, but my biography and identity had moved on. I now had a feeling of preparedness, a fine-tuned sense of danger, and the ability to take appropriate remedial action. The scales of interaction were no longer so lop-sided: I had learned to play the game.

Tensions arose in attempting to occupy the dual role of researcher and consultant. Most profoundly, my research was shaped and informed by the requirements of my sponsors. This was perhaps most apparent in the creation of somewhat unusual research situations in which covert methods were required and the clients of one's legal opponents were—at the same time—the subjects of one's investigation. This is not to say that the lawyers who commissioned me were simply interested in 'digging the dirt', or that they sought to prevent me from offering the court what I considered to be a fair and balanced view, it is rather to acknowledge that certain professional protocols, such as the obtaining of subjects' informed consent, were effectively foreclosed to me.

As I discuss elsewhere (Hadfield 2006: ch. 8), experienced consultants used sophisticated oratory and omission to obscure bias and accomplish credibility and persuasion before the court. This was not an element of the role that I wished to emulate. Most of the evidence I presented involved the presentation of detailed descriptions of events witnessed at first hand. Opposing lawyers took it upon themselves to emphasize certain elements of my testimony—whilst ignoring others. This said, as an active participant, and the subject of cross-examination, it was not possible for me to avoid the fray. I had stated my case and was obliged to defend it. Having published work which firmly apportioned some of the blame for alcohol-related crime and disorder at the feet of the pub and bar chains, I was, and was known to be, sympathetic to objection arguments. It could be argued that these preconceptions prevented me from conducting objective, and therefore 'good' social research.[8] However—following Becker's (1967) seminal reflections on the 'taking of sides'—recent decades have seen a growing recognition of the inescapably normative and political dimensions of the research process (Smith 1998, Stanley and Wise 1983). It would have been difficult, if not impossible, for me to accept a commission from an industry client in the face of well-researched opposition by crime prevention practitioners. Although, in cross-examination, opposing counsel continually sought to question my integrity, it would have only been in accepting such a commission that more forceful issues of professional ethics may have arisen. In actuality, the adversarial system encouraged both sides to somewhat overstate their case. Yet, the evidence presented by opponents often did offend my own interpretations of the matter. In such circumstances, it was not possible to remain dispassionate. As an integrated team member, I had invested time and effort into each case and successful outcomes gave rise to considerable personal satisfaction. My reluctantly accepted access opportunity had become a sought-after game of strategy; a battle of wills.

Conclusion: lessons from the research process

As Baldwin (in **Chapter 13**) notes, a serious problem facing those conducting observational research is that open court proceedings present only the public face of justice. In equal measure, the observation of licensing trials reveals only the public face of the

---

[8] This view is commonly associated with positivism and also with Weber (1949), who argued that social research should and could be value-free.

administrative governance of crime. What non-participant observers cannot see is the way in which the evidence and arguments of the parties are shaped in preparation for trial. My role as a direct participant afforded access to the hidden processes through which opposing parties strategically sought to construct their competing and malleable accounts. In particular, I was able to explore the peculiar forms of strategic interaction adopted by protagonists in their efforts to present their own arguments in a favourable light, whilst, at the same time, attempting to discredit the counter-arguments of their adversaries. It became apparent that ethnography could provide a rarely glimpsed view of differentially and asymmetrically assigned skills, resources and capacities, and the ability of protagonists to deploy them in interaction. I have argued elsewhere that—in relation to licensing litigation, at least—these factors may be understood as vital elements in the constitution and exercise of power (Hadfield 2006: ch. 9).

As described above, participatory engagement in the courtroom was not initially sought or planned, but rather, was something that was thrust upon me as the price to be paid for an otherwise unattainable quantity and quality of research access. Introductions from my consultancy clients were invaluable in helping me to gain the trust and co-operation of new informants within their own organizations and beyond. As my insight deepened, it became increasingly apparent that something very important was going on. Licensing litigation was playing a fundamental role in shaping not only the 'night-time high street' and its related crime patterns, but also the wider public life and economic development of Britain's towns and cities. These findings had a profound effect upon my analysis, prompting me to reflect upon the challenges of devising a more fully democratic approach to the adjudication of licensing matters.

The choice to adopt such a 'hands-on' approach and to work alongside one's informants in an adversarial trial setting may not be appealing to all academics. Some may question whether I went 'native', or strayed too far from the supposedly attainable path of impartiality. What was clear was that if I wanted to participate in an adversarial trial system, I too would need to be adversarial. These were special circumstances. At issue was not merely a pressure to adhere to the indigenous ethics of a specific research setting, but the very normative framework of a legal tradition (English common law), which regarded the 'truth' as best revealed by the robust submission of 'both sides of the question'. To participate in a trial—rather than to merely observe it—inevitably involves the taking of sides, at least, to the extent that one allows one's evidence to be introduced (and subsequently 'used') by one or other of the parties.

Participation in the day-to-day dramas of the licensing courts undoubtedly enhanced my work in relation to both its empirical validity and theory development through analytical induction. By the end of the research, I had established links with key protagonists; social actors who occupied centre-stage in the contestation of the night, at a time of radical upheaval and transformation. This was a better vantage point from which to analyse my data than I would ever have contemplated attaining at the outset of my research. I would never have achieved this level of insight by rigidly adhering to academic protocol, or imposing my own pre-conceptions on the shape of the project. My method was to remain flexible, willing, and curious; to embrace the on-going process of my becoming.

References

ATKINSON, P. and HOUSLEY, W. (2003). *Interactionism: An Essay in Sociological Amnesia*. London: Sage.

BECKER, H. (1958). 'Problems of Inference and Proof in Participant Observation'. *American Sociological Review* 23: 652–60.

—— (1963). *Outsiders: Studies in the Sociology of Deviance*. New York: The Free Press.

—— (1967). 'Whose Side are We On?', *Social Problems* 14: 239–48.

BOTTOMS, A. and McLEAN, J. (1976). *Defendants in the Criminal Process*. London: Routledge & Kegan Paul.

CRAWFORD, G. (2003). 'The Career of the Sport Supporter: The Case of the Manchester Storm'. *Sociology* 37(2): 219–37.

ELLISON, L. (2001). *The Adversarial Process and the Vulnerable Witness*. Oxford: Oxford University Press.

GLASER, B. G. and STRAUSS, A. L. (1971). *Status Passage*. London: Routledge.

GOFFMAN, E. (1968). *Asylums: Essays on the Social Situation of Mental Patients and Other Inmates*. London: Penguin.

HADFIELD, P. (2006). *Bar Wars: Contesting the Night in Contemporary British Cities*, Oxford: Oxford University Press.

——, with contributions by COLLINS, J., DOYLE, P., and MACKIE, K. (2004). 'The Prevention of Public Disorder' in P. Kolvin (ed.), *Licensed Premises: Law and Practice*. London: Tottel.

HOBBS, D. (1988). *Doing the Business: Entrepreneurship, Detectives and the Working Class in the East End of London*. Oxford: Clarendon.

——, HADFIELD, P., LISTER, S., and WINLOW, S. (2003). *Bouncers: Violence and Governance in the Night-time Economy*. Oxford: Oxford University Press.

LANGBEIN, J. (2003). *The Origins of Adversary Criminal Trial*. Oxford: Oxford University Press.

MILLER, J. and GLASSNER, B. (1997). 'The "Inside" and "Outside": Finding Realities in Interviews' in D. Silverman (ed.), *Qualitative Research: Theory, Method and Practice*. London: Sage.

PLANT, M. and PLANT, M. (2006). *Binge Britain: Alcohol and the National Response*. Oxford: Oxford University Press.

PUNCH, M. (1978). 'Backstage: Observing Police Work in Amsterdam'. *Urban Life* 7(3): 309–35.

RIESSMAN, C. (1993). *Narrative Analysis*. Newbury Park, CA: Sage Publications.

ROCK, P. (1979). *The Making of Symbolic Interactionism*. London: Macmillan.

—— (1993). *The Social World of an English Crown Court*. Oxford: Clarendon Press.

SAUNDERS, C. (1997). 'Earn as You Learn: Connections between Doing Qualitative Work and Living Daily Life'. *Qualitative Sociology* 20(4): 457–64.

SAVAGE, M., BARLOW, J., DICKENS, P., and FIELDING, A. (1992). *Property, Bureaucracy and Culture*. London: Routledge.

SHUY, R. (1993). *Language Crimes: The Use and Abuse of Language Evidence in the Courtroom*. Oxford: Blackwell.

SMITH, M. J. (1998). *Social Science in Question*. London: Sage.

STANLEY, L. and WISE, S. (1983). *Breaking Out: Feminist Consciousness and Feminist Research*. London: Routledge & Kegan Paul.

VAN MAANEN, J., MANNING, P., and MILLER, M. (1989). 'Series Editors Introduction' in J. Hunt, *Psychoanalytic Aspects of*

Fieldwork. Qualitative Research Methods Series no. 18, Beverley Hills, CA: Sage.

WALKER, D. (2001). *Heroes of Dissemination*. Swindon: ESRC.

WEBER, M. (1949). *The Methodology of the Social Sciences*. Glencoe, IL: The Free Press.

ZNANIECKI, F. (1934). *The Method of Sociology*. New York: Farrar & Rinehart.

18

An embedded multimethod approach to prison research

Joel Harvey

Introduction

When we want to understand a person, it is always important to understand him or her not in isolation but within his or her wider world. That is true whether we want to understand a person in wider society or within the smaller world of the prison. Even psychology, which had embraced individualism, 'now recognises the importance of social context and situation in making sense of the phenomena once studied in sterile laboratory settings' (Haney 2005: 75). Yet research in prison which has taken a predominantly psychological perspective has perhaps not caught up with the contextual revolution that has taken place within the discipline of psychology as a whole. Of course, prison sociological studies have long taken a contextual approach to understanding prison life, including the classic studies by Clemmer (1940) and by Sykes (1958). More recently, Drake (forthcoming) in her comparative study of two maximum security prisons in the UK has emphasized the importance of taking a historical-contextual approach to prison research. But how can we then make sure that we have understood the *psychological* experiences of prisoners within this wider context? This was what I had to work out when I set about trying to understand the psychosocial experience of imprisonment for young men aged between 18 and 21. I focused not only on the successful adaptation of young men to prison life but also on the difficulties that they faced. An important aspect of this work was a study of self-harming behaviour in prison (see Harvey 2006).

I chose what I called an *embedded multimethod approach*. The approach was *embedded*, because I was continually based in one prison for ten months, in order to get to know the full social world of the individuals whose psychosocial experiences I wanted to understand. The approach was *multimethod*, because I used a range of both qualitative and quantitative methods of research, in order to understand the experience of the prisoners from as many perspectives as possible. The combination was a practical necessity, because using so many different methods required a long involvement with one institution. Moreover, the combination allowed not only cross-sectional research designs but also a longitudinal one.

This chapter describes my fieldwork in more detail and the practicalities and benefits of an embedded multimethod approach. I developed my embedded multimethod fieldwork in a pilot study at HM YOI Brinsford, a young offender institution in the

Midlands, UK.[1] I then carried out my main fieldwork, using this approach, at HM YOI Feltham over ten months between July 2002 and May 2003. Feltham is the largest young offender institution for London and the south-east. To locate the individual within the microsocial context of their day-to-day lives in this complex and large institution, a wide variety of methods over a long period seemed necessary.

Choice of prison and gaining access

It is first important to give careful consideration as to which prison to choose for field-work. I chose one young offender establishment from the sixteen within England and Wales (see Solomon 2004). The issue of access has been discussed in previous literature on fieldwork research (Lee 1999; see King 2000; Smith and Wincup 2002). The main reason for choosing Feltham was a practical one: I could gain access. My doctoral supervisor, Professor Alison Liebling, arranged a meeting, which both my supervisor and I attended, with the deputy governor and governor at Feltham. We explained the proposed research and the prison granted access following these discussions. Why was access granted in my case? Feltham had had a turbulent history, and the governor might have thought that my research would document some of the positive changes that he had introduced, or suggest to others that the prison had nothing to hide. More personally, I had been involved in the evaluation of a project called the *safer locals programme* full-time for five months and had visited Feltham, which was one of the pilot sites for that project; the familiarity helped. (Locals are a type of prison that accept men and young offenders directly from court. These prisoners are either on remand or have been sentenced.)

It is necessary to be pragmatic, but it is also necessary to consider how well the chosen prison will allow for the research questions to be answered. Is the most relevant population accommodated there? What regimes and programmes are in operation? Each prison is unique and no prison is representative of the whole prison estate. For example, Feltham is also the largest remand centre for young offenders in London and the south-east and so offered a diverse population to interview. I particularly wanted to study young prisoners on remand, in order to interview lots of people after their first arrival. On the other hand, working in a remand centre such as Feltham also meant that the attrition rate among my longitudinal participants was likely to be high. A compromise must be reached between practicality and the needs of intellectual enquiry.

I also had to gain access to different parts of the establishment. A prison is a complex world and internal obstacles can easily prevent the researcher from carrying out a project efficiently. Gaining access is an ongoing business and as Lee (1999) states, 'an often implicit process, in which the researcher's right to be present is continually renegotiated' (p. 122). Preliminary contacts with the principal officers whom I had met on previous visits (for the evaluation of the safer locals programme) made this negotiating process smooth. On the first day I met the suicide prevention co-ordinator, and I was given a desk

---

[1] During the six weeks I spent at HM YOI Brinsford, seventeen prisoners took part in a social network analysis, seventeen interviews were carried out with people during their first few days in custody, and fourteen interviews were carried out with people who had recently been on, or were then on, an F2052SH form (for prisoners identified as being at risk of suicidal behaviour). I also facilitated two focus group discussions and carried out detailed observations of the reception area, visiting time, association, life on the first night centre, and attended two F2052SH case conferences.

in the office of the outreach team managed by him. I was granted keys and a password for the LIDS system, the computer database of all prisoners. This privileged access gave me a tremendous amount of freedom to carry out my research within the prison. Soon after arrival, I was taken to the induction unit, Kingfisher, to meet the staff who worked there; a good rapport with them was vital, as my study involved interviewing prisoners at the earliest phase of entering custody. I had what Lee would call 'sponsors' in my fieldwork setting, people who act as a 'bridge', or 'guides' who 'map a way for the researcher through unfamiliar social and cultural terrain' (Lee 1999: 131).

An embedded approach

Next, what are the advantages to the researcher of being based in only one prison? There are of course advantages in comparing prisons, but there are also advantages in embedding oneself in one place, which have been highlighted by researchers carrying out ethnographic research. An ethnography 'involves prolonged observation of the group, typically through participant observation in which the researcher is immersed in the day-to-day lives of the people or through one-to-one interviews with members in the group' (Creswell 1998: 58). My research was not an ethnography in that the ultimate aim was not to trace or study cultural practices. Nevertheless, it did share many aspects of that approach, in that I spent a prolonged period of time in the day-to-day lives of one group of people, and that I conducted one-to-one interviews. Being attached to a prison is a prerequisite to understanding the dynamics of life there and the social relationships that lie therein. Without this constant presence I would have lost much of the richness of the research and gained only a superficial picture of life at the prison. As Hammersley and Atkinson (1997) stated, 'it is only through watching, listening, asking questions, formulating hypotheses, and making blunders that the ethnographer can acquire some sense of a social structure of the setting and begin to understand the culture of the participants' (1997: 100). So in Feltham, through extended contact I began to understand particular people, interactions or events in their wider social world, as I might not have done on a briefer visit.

An important gain from being embedded in one prison was local knowledge about the regime and the structural aspects of the prison, which could provide a contextual account of prisoners' adaptations. Being present allows the researcher to understand the subtleties in social interaction: for example, how to appreciate humour and banter in the prison, the tone of which might be hard for a researcher who has just arrived in the prison to gauge). An understanding of the *language* of the prison is also developed which helps when interviewing and generally interacting with others within the prison. It is through prolonged presence that the researcher begins to understand the interpersonal dynamics among staff members and between staff and prisoners and to sense the dynamic *emotional climate* of the prison. Indeed, as Sztompka (1999) stated, it is by looking at the 'fabric or tissue of which the social field is made, the culturalist perspective directs attention to a specific category of social bonds: the world of "soft" interpersonal relationships' (Sztompka 1999: 4).

Finally, being embedded allows the researcher to observe events and conversations that may not have been covered by his or her original research questions but that prompt further enquiry and shape further reflections. For example, I observed members of staff supporting a prisoner who had recently self-harmed. If I then interviewed him, I asked not only about support in general but also about the instance that I myself had observed. Sometimes such prisoners would report that they did not perceive that they had been supported, and so I decided to explore further the discrepancy between the help actually offered and the perceptions of it. The research itself takes on a more dynamic feel and thus departs from a purely deductive or purely inductive approach. As in Layder's (1998) adaptive theory approach, an embedded approach to research in prison allows the researcher to test initial hypotheses and to test, in later months of the fieldwork, the new hypotheses that emerge from *being there*.

Being present for a long period of time also has some simple practical benefits: the embedded researcher can learn the best times to interview prisoners or how to work with officers more easily, without intruding upon the difficult job they have to do. For example, I could sense from entering a wing whether something had happened there and whether it would be unsuitable to interview at that time. Nor did I feel rushed to complete interviews in one full session, and so I could wind down an interview at any time and resume it at a later time that day. I did not intrude upon prisoners' association, education, or work, but could work around the regime.

This leisurely pace is particularly important when dealing with sensitive topics, such as the experience of the first few days in prison, family contact, friendships, and self-harm, where individuals would sometimes be experiencing psychological distress. As the field-work progressed I became more aware of the ethically meaningful implications of being present in one prison. I knew to whom an individual could speak if he did feel distressed, and I could inform prisoners about these options (e.g. the outreach team). Although my role was not that of adviser or counsellor, I was able sometimes to start the process of seeking support with the individual's consent. I learned to trust particular members of staff and knew that they would speak to a prisoner if I asked them to do so.

Personal contacts with the suicide prevention co-ordinator and other members of the outreach time were very helpful in moving from 'physical' to 'social' access to the members of staff (Cassell 1988). They worked as what Lee would call 'patrons': 'someone who simply by associating with the researcher, helps to secure the trust of those in the setting' (1999: 131). These contacts developed over time were, importantly, supportive to me: being a sole researcher in a prison can be emotionally and physically difficult at times (see King 2000), and officers and the outreach team were very encouraging. Because I was present for a substantial period of time, the staff perhaps began to trust me more. In a way I had become invisible to them: they would talk freely and would not be uneasy about my presence. The presence of a researcher can be threatening to those who work within a prison, who might fear interference or surveillance from authorities or outsiders, and it takes time to earn trust and respect from staff and prisoners.

Yet the researcher has to perform a delicate balancing act between observing and fitting in. Being continually present, I did become accepted to some degree as part of the estab-lishment; but on the other hand, I remained a Ph.D. student and this gave me some distance from the fieldwork setting. I did not 'go native' as I was never completely part of the institution. I was encouraged by my supervisor to make regular trips back from West London to Cambridge for supervision and these ensured that I remained attached to the institution of the university too. I was, and felt, accepted within the prison but I never felt that I belonged there. Being accepted enabled me to understand this world a little better than I might otherwise, but distance enabled me to keep different perspectives on it.

Being embedded within one prison allows the researcher to test the ecological validity of his or her findings. I developed a model of adaptation and due to the fact that I had developed a contextual understanding of the prison environment I was able to see whether the model made ecological sense. Did it reflect the adaptation experiences of young men within this specific environment? There is time to refine the researcher's interpretation of the prison and to compare it with the interpretations of prisoners and staff. If I could not make sense of their interpretations, I had time to ask additional questions of them or to alter my own perspective. Yet although my understanding of prison life was dynamic, as I too was embedded in the prison my own perspective provided a relatively constant context, against which to compare each prisoner's experiences. This allowed me to get closer to *why* particular prisoners experienced the *same* environment but in different ways.

A multimethod approach

In order to answer my research questions, I decided to employ a number of different methods. I employed observations in key areas in the prison and at adjudications, segregation, visits, education, pre-release courses, and case reviews. I shadowed prisoners from reception to the induction unit and observed daily life on each of the wings, sometimes from the time of 'unlock' to 'bang-up' at night. Such observations provide a background to more systematic qualitative and quantitative research. My multimethod analysis included social network analyses, semi-structured interviews, and quantitative measures. The design was both longitudinal and cross-sectional. Utilizing different methods allowed for data triangulation, which is 'the checking of inferences drawn from one set of data sources by collecting data from others' (Hammersley and Atkinson 1997: 230).

Short longitudinal study

In order to understand the transition into prison and adaptation within the first month, I undertook a short longitudinal study of certain prisoners over time. Each day I was in the prison I would randomly select prisoners to take part in the research from a computerized list. Such a longitudinal design is fairly novel in research in prisons in the UK. It allows the researcher to monitor change over time in a way that a cross-sectional design cannot. It allows the development of narratives as well as statistics. As mentioned above, there are problems with attrition in a fast-moving prison: of the seventy participants interviewed, I followed up forty after 10 days and twenty-eight after 30 days. However, there are benefits in the depth of information gleaned: the longitudinal researcher may build up trust with participants; because they know that the researcher is coming back, they are more willing to invest in the process. Of course, being interviewed, even three times, is not equivalent to a therapeutic engagement—although there are a few similarities, in the importance of listening. The information is fuller, and perhaps more ethical, in that the interview is not just a one-off enquiry into a stranger's personal life without any follow-up.

On a practical note, it is imperative to interview only in a private interview room. I also offered each person a carton of blackcurrant juice and some chocolate biscuits as an appreciation for his help. I obtained consent to record the interviews on mini-disc: this piece of equipment had less feel of the police-station, where tape-recorders are used, and prompted much discussion of its cost—a good ice-breaker! Interviews need to be structured carefully. In the first part, the interviewer should gather background-demographic information such as prior custodial history, ethnicity and sentence status, in order to put the prisoner at ease. I only broached more sensitive questions (about prior self-harm, drug problems, psychiatric treatment) later in the interview, when it seemed a more appropriate time to do so. I also used a number of quantitative measures, on Likert scales. Using such measures also requires sensitivity and sometimes help, as nearly a third of young men in prison have deficits in basic skills in literacy and numeracy (Prison Reform Trust 2006: 20).

What measures should be used? For my longitudinal study, I used measures that had been used in prisons beforehand, such as the prison locus of control scale devised by Pugh (1994) and items on outside social support taken from the study of the Office of National Statistics on psychiatric morbidity among prisoners (Singleton *et al.* 1998). I also used items, with permission, from previous research aimed at 'measuring the quality of prison life' (Liebling 2004) and from the evaluation of the safer locals programme (Liebling *et al.* 2005). All but one of the measures devised had good internal reliability.

Within each interview, I also asked questions about each prisoner's social networks, his level of support from people outside prison, about seeking support, and his experiences so far in prison. There is a challenge in asking people to recall their experience over the past month or even over the past three days, when those days have been as chaotic and traumatic as the first few days in prison can be. My strategy was to ask the prisoner to imagine that I was wearing a virtual reality head mask and that I was following him from court until this present moment, so that I could see what he saw, think what he thought, and feel what he had felt, from being arrested to the present interview.

These interviews therefore produced both quantitative data, from the measures, and qualitative data, from the transcriptions of the semi-structured interviews. Interestingly, the quantitative data did not reveal any changes over time; however, changes were clear from the qualitative data-analysis, and it was from them that I developed a model of adaptation. Different research methods will be sensitive to different aspects of the topic, and it is the advantage of the multimethod approach that it allows the researcher to balance different methods.

Cross-sectional study of particular groups

As well as taking random samples of whoever is in the prison, the researcher can also sample a group with or without some particular characteristic. To focus on a particular group, it is also important to understand that group's experiences within the context of other people's experiences and the world of the prison as a whole. The multimethod approach allows those comparisons.

This type of study can be difficult within just one prison: unless the researcher is present for a long period, he or she may not encounter enough members of the relevant group. Selecting such a specific group is logistically difficult—frustrating at times—and being embedded in the fieldwork setting for a long time was essential to getting the numbers. At Feltham I carried out a cross-sectional matched control study comparing twenty-five individuals who had self-harmed with twenty-five who had not. Because I was based in the office of the outreach time, each day I checked the records to discover whether anyone had self-harmed and then ask those people if they wanted to take part. I interviewed the relevant people within three days of the incident of self-harm, in order to see the dynamic nature of distress. Yet my contact with the outreach team ensured that their more important work was taken care of before my secondary research.

I then chose from the current prison roll the other participants, matched to the self-harming participants on the following variables: length of time in prison (current term, measured from their date at reception in Feltham), first time in prison or not, sentence status (remand, convicted but unsentenced, and sentenced) and ethnicity. As it was somewhat difficult to find a perfect match on length of time in prison, I allowed one week's leeway; again practicalities must be balanced with methodological rigour if the researcher is to complete the study. In a way, finding these matched controls allows the researcher to try to control for some contextual factors or elements of the larger social group (those factors or elements that he has picked out), in order to explore why some individuals react to contexts in different ways. For example, the early entry phase is difficult for most prisoners, but why do *some* prisoners respond with self-harm? Self-harm is commoner among white prisoners, but why only among *some* white prisoners? The researcher can pinpoint more precisely from matched controls what the differential experiences are within the wider social world.

Cross-sectional survey

It is helpful, too, to get an even broader perspective on the particular experiences and the particular groups on which the researcher focuses. In Feltham I wanted to understand the wider patterns of help-seeking behaviour among the prisoners generally, not only among the newer arrivals and the prisoners who had self-harmed. To do so I drew on a cross-sectional questionnaire survey of support seeking among a sample of 182 prisoners. Even with the large-scale and anonymous use of questionnaires, however, being embedded was helpful. I distributed the questionnaires to each prisoner over five lunchtime lock-up periods in a week. Before I did so I spoke to the prisoners who were on exercise, explaining who I was and asking them if they would take part; I then handed them a questionnaire when they were on their way back to their cell with their meal and told them that I would pick up the questionnaires before they were unlocked for the afternoon regime. This initial face-to-face contact dissipated the impersonal feel of research with questionnaires and perhaps prompted my reasonable response rate. (I handed out 254 and had 182 returned, a response rate of 71.6 per cent.)

Designing the questionnaire must be given a lot of thought. Unlike a semi-structured interview transcribed verbatim, there is no room for thematic analysis of responses. I did leave some room for comments at the end, which gave participants some freedom in choosing what to talk to me about. However, the main purpose of using a questionnaire is to analyse systematic data at an aggregate level. My questionnaire was a modified version of the questionnaire used by Hobbs and Dear (2000) designed to ascertain how willing prisoners were to seek help for both practical and emotional problems from a range of members of staff. As with the measures I used in the longitudinal aspect of the research, there are benefits in using modifications to scales already available. However, there are also risks that the wording of the questions will be interpreted in different ways or will be completely misunderstood. The literacy problems are again one obstacle of which the researcher must be mindful: I endeavoured to keep the language as plain as possible and explained the purpose of the research in person.

Questionnaire data allows for inferential quantitative data analysis. It is useful to consider this quantitative data alongside data gathered from in-depth one-to-one interviews.

Social network analysis

The final method by which I tried to understand how the individual prisoners related to their wider social world was a social network analysis on particular prison wings. A social network analysis allows the researcher to move beyond the level of the individual and analyse individual behaviour in the social context of the small groups around him. The researcher analyses 'specific relationships and then determines how those relationships are organised or structured and how that structure has an impact on individual lives. They describe the structured environment of individuals, organisations and societies' (Trotter 2000: 211). To my knowledge, this was the first time a 'whole-network' social network analysis had been carried out in prisons in the UK. Yet the method of analysis lends itself to being used in prisons, given that groups of people are confined together in one institution which inevitably means that most of the face-to-face ties and interactions are contained within the microcosm of the prison.

In a social network analysis, a network consists of a set of actors and a set of relational ties among the actors, which are depicted in a sociogram or sociograph. A sociogram is 'a picture in which people (or more generally, any social unit) are represented as points in two-dimensional space, and relationships among pairs of people are represented by lines linking the corresponding points' (Wasserman and Faust 1999: 11–12). Actors in a network are represented with 'nodes' (vertices or points) and the relational ties among the actors are represented with 'lines' (edges or arcs). These relational ties can be directional or non-directional in nature, can be signed, and can be multiple. A directional relation is one where 'the ties are oriented from one actor to another' (Wasserman and Faust 1999: 122). Considering a friendship, for example, person A may state that person B is his friend but it does not necessarily follow that person B will state that person A is his friend. For these relationships to be valued, though, we must look for 'signed relations' which are given a positive value number by both participants. The social network analysis allows participants to give 'the additional information of a valence: a positive or negative sign' (Wasserman and Faust 1999: 137); and this sign will denote whether an individual likes or dislikes someone. From the data it is possible to see how popular a particular individual is within a wing and to analyse his position within the context of the network as a whole. The sociograms are also represented in the form of a matrix which contains exactly the same information as a graph. It is useful to present the information in this form, especially when it comes to analysing the data using computer software such as UCINET 6.0.

Some prisons engage in their own network analysis for security purposes: the members of staff complete observational reports of interactions, for the purpose of intelligence (King and McDermott 1990). More generally in network analysis, data are gathered from questionnaires in three different formats (Wasserman and Faust 1999). First, there is a distinction between rosters or free recall. Either an actor can be given a complete set of other actors to whom he or she must specify a relationship, or he can be given free reign and is simply asked to name as many people as possible who fit a predetermined relationship tie. Secondly, he can be told to specify a fixed number of alters or to list as many as they wish. Finally, there is a distinction between ratings and complete rankings: participants can rate other actors by assigning a value to them (i.e. present or not, or a positive or negative value) or they can rank the other actors in a specific order.

In my own research, I carried out social network analyses on three wings. One of these wings was measured on two occasions, thus allowing for gathering some longitudinal data on the dynamic nature of social tie formation. In order to compare whether different populations of prisoners affected how networks were formed, I studied two 'normal' units and one which tended to be where the staff placed prisoners who had psychological difficulties or who could not speak English as their first language. (I could only study one side of each wing in each analysis, as in Feltham the wings were divided in half by gates.) The researcher has to carry out each social network analysis quite quickly, while the network remains stable, before people move to different units or prisons. This meant that I had to carry out each network analysis over one weekend, as there was no movement on a Sunday.

I spoke with each prisoner individually in a private room and explained the study and asked him whether he would take part. After the basic background and demographic questions, I presented a roster of the surnames of everyone on the wing and asked him to identify as many people as he talked to ('free choice') and to rate them on a number of questions on a five-point Likert scale. The questions were things such as 'I consider him to be a mate of mine' or 'Since I've been here he has helped me out with a personal problem'. I also asked him to indicate whether he knew the people from outside prison, from a previous time in prison and so on. Each of these questions yields out-degree and in-degree scores. An out-degree is a value that indicates how many people an individual nominates. For example, if an individual states that they are friends with three others individuals they will have an out-degree score of three. An in-degree is a value that indicates how many people nominate a particular individual. For example, if four people state they are friends with a particular individual then he will have an in-degree score of four.

These paired measures thus allowed me to assess the reciprocal ties that were important for my study of the wider social world of the prisoners. In order to correlate this wider context with their individual psychological experiences, I also asked each participant to complete the measure of psychological distress which I had used in other parts of my multimethod analysis. Layder's (1998) adaptive theory approach highlights the multilayered nature of social reality and the need for different levels of analysis. Through a social network analysis the researcher is able to analyse social life in the prison at a structural level and can begin to understand the individual's psychosocial experience within this wider web of relationships.

Ethical considerations

When carrying out any research project, it is important to take into account any ethical considerations. Doing so protects the individuals who are involved in the research and it allows researchers to reflect on their own positions within the research process (Smith and Wincup 2002). The British Psychology Society's (2000) Code of Conduct, Ethical Principles, and Guidelines raise a number of ethical considerations for researchers. These include consent, deception, debriefing, confidentiality, withdrawing from the investigation, protection of the participant from harm, and giving advice.

Before entering the field and carrying out interviews, one of the important ethical questions to ask is the appropriateness of the research methods, especially when the topic is a sensitive one. A multimethod analysis allows for a variety of methods, to fit the needs not only of the researcher but also of different participants. For example, it could be argued that quantitative research techniques are inappropriate when dealing with people who are emotionally distressed: these methods may be inherently insensitive, asking difficult personal questions and only allowing people to express how they feel with a small tick on a scale. Accordingly, here, a qualitative-based study may be deemed more appropriate: interviews allow people to discuss how they are feeling and allow the interviewer to be more attuned to how distress is experienced even within the interview setting. Yet what is most important for ethical research is not necessarily the method per se that is used, but the manner in which the method is used. A sensitive researcher might assist someone completing a questionnaire with greater care than an insensitive person might interview him. What is essential is the quality of the interaction during the interview: there must be privacy, respect, and a non-judgemental attitude.

Another important ethical issue to consider during the interview is that of control or power. Within the interview interaction there is an imbalance of power. I was asking people to disclose personal information about themselves while simultaneously revealing very little about myself. It is important to ensure that the individual has been given the opportunity to have his say. Lee (1999) noted that 'where the format of the interview is not rigidly specified by prior standardization, it is possible to see the exercise of power in the interview as a two-way process' (1999: 110). Although I wanted to cover a number of different topics within the interview I tried to ensure that the interviewees felt that they could talk about what was important to them. I asked them if there were any questions that I had not asked which they felt were important, thus allowing them to have some input into the interview schedule. Also, by reminding them that I was grateful that they were helping me with my research, this brought about some sense of control to participants. In fact, many would mention to me that the main reason for them agreeing to take part was that it was to help someone with their 'college course'.

At the start of each interview session I firstly ensured that the individual consented to taking part. This consent is particularly difficult to ensure in a prison, because there may always be an element of the prisoner feeling obliged to take part, given the compulsoriness of much of the regime (Moser *et al.* 2004). Bearing this feeling of obligation in mind, I emphasized that participation was voluntary and that the prisoners could leave at any time. All but two individuals wanted to talk about their experiences at Feltham; the need to be listened to was pressing. I also emphasized that the prisoners could ignore particular questions if they wanted, to manage any possible distress. Lee (1999) noted that 'interviewing about sensitive topics can produce substantial levels of distress in the respondent which have to be managed during the course of the interview' (1999: 106). I checked that people were happy to continue talking about particular topics and gave them the chance to talk about something else if they wanted to. I also had to be careful where to position the very sensitive topics within the interview schedule and to decide whether or not it was appropriate to continue down a particular line of questions, given possible discomfort on their part—or my ability to manage that, as I was not trained as a clinical psychologist or other healthcare professional. Yet the interviewer needs confident engagement because, as Lee (1999) suggested, when interviewers are uncomfortable about raising a sensitive or embarrassing issue or question, this unease can impact upon the data.

Of course, confidentiality and trust were important. Lee (1999) argued that in order to develop trust the researcher needs privacy, a non-condemnatory attitude, and confidentiality: 'within this framework, researchers can lead those studied to confront, in a fundamental way, issues which are deep, personally threatening, and potentially painful' (1999: 98). Confidentiality is especially important within the prison, which is by definition a low-trust environment (Liebling 2004). Despite this distrust, I often experienced what I would call ironic disclosure: while prisoners told me that they did not trust anyone nor ever reveal personal information, they would then subsequently disclose personal life events to me, someone whom they had never met before. On the one hand, because I was embedded in the prison, the prisoners did know me to some extent. On the other hand, I could always tell them that I was independent from the prison authorities, build up some rapport, and ensure them of confidentiality. My social remoteness, or independence from the institution, may have enabled individuals to disclose their experiences. Lee (1999) confirmed that there may be a curvilinear relationship between disclosure and intimacy: 'the recipients of intimate details about one's life are most likely to be either those standing in a very intimate relation to oneself, or those who are socially remote' (1999: 113). The embedded researcher manages to be both familiar and distant.

However, there was one way in which, for ethical reasons, I had to consider whether and how to become an even more active participant in their world. Some prisoners revealed to me that they had thoughts of suicide. Most of them were on an open F2052SH form, the form then used to monitor prisoners at risk of self-harm, and therefore the staff knew about this suicidal ideation; however, some had told no one except me. On one occasion, after a lengthy interview, one individual revealed that he had 'stashed' a razor blade in his cell; he was suicidal and had attempted to hang himself on several occasions. In response, I explained that although the interview was confidential he had told me something that was of concern and that I would like to tell a member of staff about the razor blade. Yet I asked him to whom he would prefer me to speak and he named a nurse, to whom I later passed on the information. The following day I went back to see him to reassure him that everything else in the interview was confidential. Although on this occasion I did strain the trust of this one interviewee, if I had ignored his disclosure, he might have interpreted this as an uncaring response. Moreover, any interview needs to end with a debriefing, in order to find out how the participant experienced the interview. The British Psychological Society's (2000) Code of Conduct, Ethical Principles, and Guidelines state that researchers 'should discuss with the participants their experience of the research in order to monitor any unforeseen negative effects or misconceptions' (2000: 10). At the end of the interview session I did so. Also, because I was embedded in the prison, I knew how to direct the person to the relevant member of staff to deal with any practical or emotional concerns. This is just one way in which an embedded multimethod approach is an ethical one.

Conclusion

In this chapter I have argued that an embedded multimethod approach allows the researcher to use different methods to tap different aspects of social reality and allows for this data to be triangulated. Through being embedded within one institution the researcher can be more confident that the findings would make sense for the participants concerned and do reflect the realities experienced by the prisoners. Moreover, because this approach encourages the researcher actively to reflect on his or her findings, it allows for ideas to be developed and then tested throughout the course of the fieldwork. The researcher can combine general and substantive theory and can begin to test new theoretical ideas during the fieldwork. The research is therefore carried out in a holistic manner, so that the social context becomes integral to the research process.

References

BRITISH PSYCHOLOGICAL SOCIETY (2000). *Code of Conduct, Ethical Principles and Guidelines.* Leicester: British Psychological Society.

CASSELL, J. (1988). 'The Relationship between the Observer to Observed when Studying Up' in R. G. Burgess (ed.), *Studies in Qualitative Methodology: Volume 1: Conducting Qualitative Research.* Greenwich, CT: JAI Press.

CLEMMER, D. (1940). *The Prison Community.* New York: Holt, Rinehart & Winston.

CRESWELL, J. W. (1998). *Qualitative Inquiry and Research Design: Choosing Among Five Traditions.* London: Sage.

DRAKE, D. (forthcoming). *A Comparison of Quality of Life, Legitimacy and Order in Two Maximum Security Prisons.* Unpublished Doctoral Dissertation, University of Cambridge.

HAMMERSLEY, M. and ATKINSON, P. (1997). *Ethnography: Principles and Practice.* London: Routledge.

HANEY, C. (2005). 'The Contextual Revolution in Psychology and the Question of Prison' in A. Liebling and S. Maruna (eds), *The Effects of Imprisonment.* Collumpton: Willan.

HARVEY, J. (2006). *Young Men in Prison: Surviving and Adapting to Life Inside.* Collumpton: Willan.

HOBBS, G. S. and DEAR, G. E. (2000). 'Prisoners' Perceptions of Prison Officers as Sources of Support'. *Journal of Offender Rehabilitation* 31: 127–42.

KING, R. D. (2000). 'Doing Research in Prisons' in R. D. King and E. Wincup (eds), *Doing Research on Crime and Justice.* Oxford: Oxford University Press.

—— and McDERMOTT, K. (1990) ' "My geranium is subversive". Notes on the Management of Trouble in Prisons'. *British Journal of Sociology* 41: 445–71.

LAYDER, D. (1998). *Sociological Practice. Linking Theory and Social Research.* London: Sage.

LEE, R. (1999). *Doing Research on Sensitive Topics.* London: Sage.

LIEBLING, A. (1992). *Suicides in Prison.* London: Routledge.

—— (2004). *Prisons and Their Moral Performance. A Study of Values, Quality and Prison Life.* Oxford: Oxford University Press.

——, TAIT, S., DURIE, L., STILES, A., and HARVEY, J. (2005). *Evaluation of HM*

Prison Service's Safer Local Programme. Report submitted to HM Prison Service.

MOSER, D. J., ARNDT, S., KANZ, J. E., BENJAMIN, M. L., BAYLESS, J. D., REESE, R. L., PAULSEN, J. S., and FLAUM, M. A. (2004). 'Coercion and Informed Consent in Research Involving Prisoners'. *Comprehensive Psychiatry* 45: 1–9.

Prison Reform Trust (2006). *Bromley Briefings Prison Factfile April 2006.* London: Prison Reform Trust.

PUGH, D. N. (1994). 'Revision and Further Assessments of the Prison Locus of Control Scale'. *Psychological Reports* 74: 979–86.

SINGLETON, N., MELTZER, H., GATWARD, R., COID, J., and DEASY, D. (1998). *Psychiatric Morbidity Among Prisoners in England and Wales.* London: ONS.

SMITH, K. and WINCUP, E. (2002). 'Some Reflections on Doing Feminist Research in Criminal Justice Institutions' in T. Welland and L. Pugsley (eds), *Ethical Dilemmas in Qualitative Research.* Aldershot: Ashgate.

SOLOMON, E. (2004). *A Lost Generation: The Experiences of Young People in Prison.* Prison Reform Trust: London.

SYKES, G. (1958). *The Society of Captives.* Princeton, N.J.: Princeton University Press.

SZTOMPKA, P. (1999). *Trust: A Sociological Theory.* Cambridge: Cambridge University Press.

TROTTER, R. T. (2000). 'Ethnography and Network Analysis: The Study of Social Context in Cultures and Societies' in G. L. Albrecht, R. Fitzpatrick, and S. C. Scrimshaw (eds), *Handbook of Social Studies in Health and Medicine.* London: Sage.

WASSERMAN, S. and FAUST, K. (1999). *Social Network Analysis: Methods and Applications.* Cambridge: Cambridge University Press.

19

Researching bullying in the classroom

Darrick Jolliffe

Introduction

A large proportion of research on bullying and victimization has involved administering questionnaires to school students in a classroom (e.g. Smith 2004). Many other studies in which children and youth are the research subjects have also used school children in classrooms as their major source of data (e.g. Beinart *et al.* 2002; Wikstrom 2002). Obviously classrooms hold appeal for those conducting certain types of social research. Schools, by their very nature, provide a high number of 'captive' subjects, who when in a classroom setting are seated at a desk with pen or pencil to hand. Moreover, the problem of obtaining respondents of certain ages or age groups can be completely solved by targeting specific year groups (e.g. Shenton 2004). Another benefit of using school children as research subjects is that the children attending a school often reflect the racial and socioeconomic composition of the neighbourhood and community in which they exist. Obtaining this level of diversity by other methods of data collection would likely prove difficult, and this diversity is crucial in assisting researchers in making generalizations about the research findings.

In addition to the above benefits, most researchers will have attended school as youngsters, and therefore have a familiarity with this research setting which might not apply to others, such as young offenders institutions. However, successfully undertaking research in school classrooms is hardly a straightforward endeavour. Obtaining access to the schools and the students in the classroom, data collection, and maintaining a relationship with the school after data collection has taken place all pose unique challenges. This chapter will specifically focus on the issues of both physical and social access while outlining the interactive research process that finally resulted in a successful investigation of 720 Year 10 students from three schools in Hertfordshire.

Conceptual development

The original aim of my Ph.D. was to undertake a comprehensive investigation of the psychological construct of empathy and its relationship to offending. Empathy is usually defined as the ability to experience or understand another persons' emotions (Cohen and

Strayer 1996), and for many years empathy has been theoretically linked to aggressive and criminal behaviour. The theory suggests that the diminished ability to feel or understand the emotions of others means that those with low empathy have fewer internal constraints on their behaviour. An individual with low empathy simply does not experience the fear, pain, and distress which occurs in others as a result of their own behaviour. In fact it has been suggested that those with low empathy may fail to connect their actions and the consequences of their actions to the emotional responses of others (Hare 1999).

Given the strong theoretical relationship between empathy and various forms of antisocial behaviour, it is not surprising that 'a lack of empathy' has been used to explain the actions of those who are aggressive or antisocial. For example, a lack of empathy is an oft-cited facet of psychopathy, a constellation of psychological and behavioural traits which significantly increase ones' propensity for violent criminal behaviour (Hare 1999). A lack of empathy was also cited as a feature of low self-control by Gottfredson and Hirschi (1990) in their influential theory of the causes of criminal behaviour. A significant element in programmes for the rehabilitation of criminal offenders, especially those involved in violent and sexual offending, is also predicated on the notion that offenders have low empathy. For example, Mulloy *et al.* (1999: 16) state that 'increasing empathy is often seen as the key to reducing the likelihood of offending against others. Some form of empathy training is, therefore, a common treatment component of those convicted of crimes such as assault, robbery, murder, and sexual assault'.

However, there has been a lack of empirical support for the basic premise of the theoretical relationship between empathy and offending. That is, research studies have not consistently shown that offenders had significantly lower levels of empathy when compared to a group of non-offenders. Some studies did find evidence of low empathy among offenders (e.g. Burke 2001), while others did not (Hayashino *et al.* 1995), and still others found that offenders had high empathy (Fisher *et al.* 1999). This apparent contradiction between theory and empirical evidence was to be the point of departure of my Ph.D. research.

It was suggested to me that the best way to investigate this issue further was to undertake a systematic review and meta-analysis. Although at that time I knew nothing about the procedures involved with this method of literature review, I was directed to the work of Lipsey and Wilson (2001) whose highly accessible account I would strongly recommend to anyone considering undertaking systematic reviews and meta-analyses. Systematic reviews are a method of literature review which aims to reduce the bias of more typical narrative literature reviews. Narrative reviews summarize the literature, but do not describe how fully, accurately, or precisely the material has been reviewed. Alternatively, systematic reviews employ rigorous methods for locating, appraising, and synthesizing evidence from prior studies. They have explicit objectives, explicit criteria for including and excluding studies, and they are reported with the same level of detail that characterize high-quality research (e.g. Farrington and Petrosino 2001). Meta-analysis is a form of survey research based on research reports rather than subjects. Using the quantitative information available in the original reports, an effect size is derived for each study and these effect sizes are summarized to determine the mean effect of the relationships (Lipsey and Wilson 2001).

Systematically reviewing and quantifying the relationship between empathy and offending in this way proved extremely useful. Overall, the results suggested that low empathy was related to offending, but importantly, the strength of this relationship was dependent on the methodological features of the study (see Jolliffe and Farrington 2004). For example, the relationship between low empathy and offending was stronger for younger as opposed to older offenders, and stronger for violent as opposed to mixed offender groups. Most importantly, however, the relationship between low empathy and offending was strongly related to how well the offender and non-offender groups were matched on various characteristics. When offenders and non-offenders were matched on intelligence and socio-economic status there was little difference in empathy between these two groups.

In addition to providing unique insight into the possible mechanism between low empathy and offending, the systematic review also allowed for the identification of a number of gaps and problems in the current research on low empathy and offending. While there were several problems (e.g. some of the questionniares used to measure empathy were of limited value), the most important of these was that in every study that was reviewed individuals were classified as offenders based on convictions, and in all but one case these individuals were incarcerated. The problem with using incarcerated populations to assess the level of empathy of offenders is that if offenders were found to have low empathy, it would be impossible to determine if this low empathy might have contributed to the offending, or if this low empathy had resulted from incarceration in an 'unempathic' environment (Grounds and Jamieson 2003). Using the less stringent criterion of criminal convictions as the measure of offending is also problematic. First, convictions are a diluted measure of who has committed offences because not all of those who commit offences are arrested, and not all of those arrested are convicted. Secondly, using convictions likely results in the failure to count many offences that have taken place. Some estimates have suggested that to determine the actual number of offences an individual has committed every conviction should be scaled up by a factor of five (West and Farrington 1977). Thirdly, using current convictions to classify offenders into offending groups (e.g. violent or non-violent offenders) results in significant contamination of offender groups because those convicted of a non-violent offence may have a history of acting violently, and those convicted for violence may have a history of non-violent offending (see Farrington 1998). Given the limitations of these official measures of offending it was surprising that no studies had compared self-reports of offending to levels of empathy.

Self-reports of offending involve asking individuals to report if they have committed a specified offence in a set time period (usually the past 12 months), and if so, how many times. Self-reports can be administered by interview or other non-anonymous methods, but research has suggested that anonymous questionnaires might provide more accurate information (Kulik *et al.* 1968). The major limitation on the accuracy of self-reports is honesty since not all people will be willing to disclose socially undesirable behaviour. Furthermore, self-reports rely on an individual's memory, and there is evidence to suggest that the most prolific offenders have a distinct tendency to under-report offences (Farrington 2001). Even with these limitations, however, researchers have generally concluded that self-reports are a valid measure of offending with most populations (Farrington 2001; Jolliffe *et al.* 2003).

Clearly, the relationship between empathy and self-reported offending was an interesting and under-researched topic. Having decided to collect information about self-reported offending and levels of empathy I immediately thought of schools as a potential setting to collect data. Like many researchers, I presumed schools would provide easy access to a large sample of research subjects. I also foresaw additional benefits of using school-aged children. First, I thought that school-aged children would likely be involved in a fair amount of offending as research evidence has suggested that ages 14–17 are the peak ages of involvement in offending (Loeber *et al.* 2003). Secondly, I thought this might be an important age in terms of levels of empathy as the systematic review and meta-analysis suggested empathy differences were especially prominent among young people who committed offences (Jolliffe and Farrington 2004).

Getting access

I set out developing my questionnaire and concurrently attempting to get access to schools for data collection. Being located in the city of Cambridge, and attending the University of Cambridge I naively assumed that the Local Education Authority (LEA) would be happy to have me undertake research in their schools. I contacted the Cambridge LEA by phone and was told to compose a letter detailing my research and stating specifically what I wanted from the schools.

While I will not reproduce this letter here, mostly out of embarrassment, I would suggest that the letter I produced would be a good illustration of how not to make contact with those who hold access to potential research sites. The letter described the study of empathy and self-reported offending and why I was interested in undertaking the research, but it did not demonstrate any research competence. By failing to describe clearly how I intended to collect the data within the boundaries of the schools' day-to-day operations I had made it easy for them to turn me away. The letter of rejection that I received also made specific reference to the school's concern about hosting research on self-reported offending as there was 'no appreciable offending at schools in Cambridge'.

After this setback I tried approaching three head teachers at schools in Cambridge through contacts at the Institute of Criminology. While I had tried to refine my approach, in each case the schools appeared to have no interest in taking part in the research. One head teacher suggested that their school was contacted by various university researchers about once a week hoping to use their students for research purposes, and that if access was granted to all of these requests there would be no classroom time for teaching the students. This comment suggested to me that being located within easy reach of one of the most research-oriented universities in England, the schools in Cambridge might be suffering from research fatigue. For this reason I thought it best that I look to another locality to conduct my research.

By this point a number of months had passed, and while I had at least assessed that I wouldn't be able to conduct my research in Cambridge, I was no closer to conducting the research. Fortunately for me there was expertise available in the Institute of Criminology upon which I could call for advice in the form of colleagues engaged on a large-scale study which involved data collection from school students in a nearby city. Although these researchers did not have much of a problem in gaining access—because their study began with both Home Office and LEA approval—they had accumulated a great deal of experience in dealing with the hierarchy at schools, and therefore were in a position to help me refine my approach. They made a number of useful suggestions such as offering the schools something, say a research report or classroom assistance, in exchange for access to the students, but they also confirmed what had already been alluded to by the Cambridge LEA, namely, that a study of self-reported offending was not an attractive prospect for schools. Publicity about findings of high levels of self-reported offending could irreparably damage a school's reputation. It might be possible to allay this fear somewhat by reassuring the head teacher that all information would be kept strictly confidential, but it was becoming clear that focusing on another topic, of more relevant interest to the schools might help me gain access. Most importantly these colleagues suggested that I study school bullying in addition to self-reported offending, since all schools in England and Wales are required to dedicate time to the topics of bullying and victimization every year. My research could then be 'sold' as a way of providing the schools with a report of their bullying and victimization, which I would subsequently be able to use for research purposes. Since I then knew little or nothing about bullying and victimization but would need to appear knowledgeable about the subject in future discussions with LEAs and schools I set about reviewing the literature on bullying and victimization, as well as trying to figure out how I might be able to incorporate this topic into my Ph.D.

At times bullying has been considered a relatively harmless, if endemic, part of school life, but it is now recognized as a serious issue with considerable negative consequences for both victim and bully. Bullying as a topic for systematic research was introduced to the western world by the influential work of Olweus (1978) which described a number of studies of bullies, and victims of bullying in schools in Stockholm in the early 1970s. Almost thirty years after this seminal publication, international research has resulted in the accumulation of a great deal of knowledge about certain aspects of school bullying. Most importantly, this research has suggested that bullying in school is remarkably common. Over half of school children have been victimized at one time or another and over half have taken part in bullying (Farrington 1993). Consistent relationships between bullying and age, and bullying and gender have also been identified: bullying is more common among younger (primary school) children than older (secondary school) children (Whitney and Smith 1993), and males are much more likely to be involved in bullying compared to females (Olweus 1993).

Victims of bullying consistently report physical and psychological distress, and often report being afraid to go to school because they fear further victimization (Mellor, 1990). In the longterm victims have been found to have low self-esteem and high depression many years after leaving school (Olweus 1993). The behaviour of bullies may escalate to more serious criminal acts, possibly because the pleasure of bullying reinforces their aggressive tendencies (Farrington 1993). Furthermore, in one study 60 per cent of school bullies were later found to have been convicted of a criminal offence up to age twenty-four (Olweus 1991). Not only does there appear to be continuity in bullying and victimization from primary to secondary school (e.g. Farrington 1993), but there is also evidence to suggest that adults who were school bullies or victims of bullying are more likely to have children who also become school bullies and victims (Farrington 1993).

The bulk of bullying research has been carried out with the goal of assessing the prevalence of bullying and victimization in specific schools before and after a bullying intervention programme has taken place. Interestingly, many of the intervention studies have demonstrated that bullying and victimization can be reduced, but not completely eradicated and Smith (2004) has suggested that there may be a small group of hardcore bullies with specific social or psychological characteristics that make them resistant to change.

However, the individual, family, social, and contextual factors associated with bullying, and also those associated with victimization, have been the subject of much less research. This was somewhat surprising given the obvious conceptual link between bullying and juvenile delinquency, a topic for which there is much information about the factors correlated with its genesis (e.g. Loeber *et al.* 2003). A Ph.D. research project examining the factors associated with school bullying and victimization was shaping up in which I could incorporate my interest in the relationship between low empathy and antisocial behaviour, and possibly make a useful contribution to knowledge regarding bullying. However, I was still no closer to getting access to schools to conduct this research.

I decided to persist in contacting LEAs rather than individual schools because the stamp of approval from an LEA would facilitate access to a greater number of schools more quickly than approaching one school at a time. A new letter was composed describing my interest in conducting a review of bullying and victimization in a number of schools for research purposes, and this was sent to two nearby LEAs. Within a week both had responded positively and while I attempted to meet with both it was only possible to meet a representative from the Hertfordshire LEA. I attended the meeting well prepared to discuss bullying and victimization and to discuss what I could provide to the schools and the LEA. The enthusiasm of the LEA representative was a welcome, and much needed, contrast to my earlier experiences. Most crucially I was provided with the names of fifteen head teachers who were thought to be interested in bullying and thus potential hosts for the research, and several suggestions as to how to make the research as unobtrusive as possible and therefore more attractive to the schools. For example, it was suggested that the first period in the morning, when the students were in their home form, would be the best time to conduct the research. Also, it was suggested that I focus only on only one year group, rather than several, because that would be logistically much easier to organize. I was advised that Year 10, comprising 14–15 year olds, would be more appropriate than Year 11 children who would be preparing for examinations, and that the best time to study them would be late in the school year, in May or June when there would be fewer other demands on their time. Finally, it was suggested that the quicker I could get in the school, get my data collected, and get out again, the better it would be for the school. Ideally, I should have all the questionnaires completed by all the Year 10 students in all of the classrooms in a single class period of 45–60 minutes. For all those wise suggestions I remain deeply grateful.

Completing the questionnaires in a single session obviously made sense from a research perspective as well since it would eliminate the possibility that one group of students who had previously completed the questionnaire would 'prep' others who would be completing it later. However, some schools in Herftfordshire had over ten classes of particular year groups, suggesting that I would need to have help administering the questionnaire. I immediately considered the possibility of using classroom teachers as research assistants, a procedure used in other research conducted in a classroom (e.g. Beinart *et al.* 2002). This idea was not well received. I was informed that head teachers would have a hard time selling the research to their staff if it involved extra work on top of the inevitable timetable complications that accompanied the research. It was therefore agreed that I would bring research assistants with me to each school, one for each class. The researcher would be responsible for the data collection but the teacher would remain in the class to control student behaviour (if necessary), help any students with special needs, and also, because all classrooms needed the presence of a qualified teacher, for insurance purposes.

Using research assistants to help collect the data introduced an additional complication but it would definitely speed up the research process. I then had to find research assistants. First I approached my Ph.D. colleagues, but many were busy collecting their own data or otherwise unable to help. I then approached the Institute's M.Phil. students who were eager for practical research experience. Although I am sure that many of them would have helped me out for free I thought it only fair that they receive some remuneration for their assistance. This was especially the case because they would be travelling for about two hours in total before contributing an hour of their time to conducting the research. Some of them bravely agreed to drive their own cars as well, since I would only be able to take a maximum of six other people in my vehicle. The research assistants were briefed on the background to the research project, and given a copy of the research instrument to allow them to get familiar with it in case students or staff had any questions.

With a research topic and procedure completely different from when I started out I now began to contact my list of ten potential schools. Most head teachers were difficult to get hold of, but I found that immediately before and immediately after the school day were the most successful times. Out of ten head teachers I was able to speak to nine, and managed to arrange meetings with seven. I travelled to the seven different locations in and around Hertfordshire over a period of three weeks meeting head teachers in person, 'selling' the research, and providing them with a copy of my proposed questionnaire. Five head teachers agreed to let me administer questionnaires at their schools, and dates for data collection were agreed. Unfortunately, two schools dropped out before data collection could be undertaken, leaving three schools. However, before I could collect data from the students at these three schools I needed to obtain parental consent for them to take part in the research.

In the 2004 version of the ethical guidelines published by the British Educational Research Association, there is no reference to a specific minimum age of research subjects whereby a legal guardian's consent should be obtained. However, the ethical guidelines of the British Psychological Society suggest that for children under the age of 16, obtaining a legal guardian's consent is good practice. At the time this research was conducted parental consent could be obtained with a passive consent procedure. A parental consent form, containing a description of the research and a tear-away section to be signed if the legal guardian did not wish their children to be involved was provided to the head teacher for distribution to all Year 10 students. Head teachers found this procedure to work well, and were happy to communicate the information about who was not to take part in the research (according to their parent's wishes) to the appropriate form tutor, and also arrange for other activities for this minority of students.

Another consideration was whether to use anonymous or non-anonymous questionnaires. A benefit of using non-anonymous questionnaires from a research standpoint was that people who were absent on the day the questionnaire was administered might be able to fill in the questionnaire at a later date. This would help to establish the response rate, and therefore assess the generalizability of the findings. Also, given that those who are the most antisocial report attending school less regularly, and that victims of bullying report truanting to avoid further bullying (Farrington 1993), this might have increased the validity for some of the key points of investigation. From an ethical perspective a non-anonymous questionnaire would have meant that the researcher would have been in a position to draw the school's attention to those individuals who reported being bullied so that they might be helped.

In the end, however, I decided to use anonymous questionnaires. This was because it was suggested to be the least problematic from an ethical standpoint for the schools, as no names or class lists would need to be released. Also, this method gives individuals the freedom to report socially undesirable information without fear of repercussion, and therefore increase the validity of the reports (e.g. Kulik *et al.* 1968). Another benefit of this method was that the data could be analysed and published in the future without requiring further permission from the students, something that would have been required for non-anonymous data.

In the time leading up to the data collection I refined the questionnaire, trying to reduce the number of items and scales that were included so that it could be completed by the students in the single time period allotted. The bullying and victimization questions were based on those used in a large-scale study of bullying and victimization in England (Whitney and Smith 1993). This included asking about whether the child was involved in bullying either as a bully or a victim. Also, these questions enquired about the frequency of bullying and victimization as well as the place where this most commonly took place, the form the bullying or victimization usually took and the typical parental and teacher response. All of these facets of bullying and victimization were of particular interest to the schools. In line with the original goal of my Ph.D. I also wanted to measure empathy and self-reported offending. Surprisingly, with the focus of my research being bullying and victimization neither the representative at the LEA nor any of the seven head teachers saw a problem with asking a few self-reported offending questions. These questions were based on those administered as part of a large-scale Home Office study (Flood-Page *et al.* 2000) and were chosen to represent a number of different categories of offence. I also included additional personality measures such as those designed to assess impulsivity, alexithymia, and a global personality inventory. A pilot study conducted with a small number of Year 10 students, to whom I had access through family connections, suggested that the wording on a number of these items needed to be changed to suit a younger audience. One member of the pilot study was used to assess the appropriateness of the alterations that were subsequently made. Lastly (although they appeared first on the questionnaire), questions regarding basic sociodemographic background such as gender, race, living circumstances, and parental occupation were included. I was keen to ask about the typical parental supervision that the child received and also about parental criminal history as I knew both of these to be important criminological variables. However, parental criminal history was judged by all of the head teachers to be potentially problematic so it was removed from the questionnaire.

Data collection

The days in which data collection took place were always unbelievably hectic. The research assistants and I needed to travel approximately one hour away from Cambridge through rush-hour traffic, have the correct number of questionnaires, pencils and pens, and then find the appropriate classroom. There was a significant potential for things to go wrong because the timing was so tight. A missed turn or a flat tyre and my research would have been set back significantly.

Upon arriving in the classroom the research assistants were required to hand out the questionnaires, but not allow the students to start until they had been read the instructions. These instructions described the purpose of the research and informed the student that the questionnaire they were about to complete was completely anonymous and so there was no reason why they should not answer the questionnaire as honestly as possible. Upon completing the questionnaire they were asked to place it within the envelope provided. The instructions also made the students aware that they were not required to take part in the research, and if they decided to take part they could withdraw at any time without penalty.

The last point of the instructions was to make the students aware of a prize draw for music store vouchers for which they would be eligible to enter as a reward for completing the questionnaire. Research has shown that the more difficult research subjects tend to be the more interesting ones (Farrington *et al.* 2006) and it was decided that a draw for music store vouchers might increase the students motivation to complete the questionnaire quietly and without assistance from others in the classroom. It was hoped that this might increase the response rate and the validity of the data. A post-it note with a unique number was attached to every questionnaire, and upon completing (or attempting to complete) it the student removed and retained the post-it note. A random draw of numbers was conducted before we left the school and those with the matching numbers on the post-it note were provided with the music vouchers by the head teacher. This provided a useful incentive to the students and most unruly behaviour could be brought back in line by the threat of taking away that person's post-it note number.

After the time period was up all the research assistants returned the completed questionnaires to me and made a verbal report about how the data collection had taken place. In most cases it had gone smoothly but there were occasional problems. One research assistant noted that the classroom teacher had filled in the questionnaire posing as a 14 year-old and tried to include it in the pile of completed questionnaires. In another case a student had used the self-reported offending items as a prompt to engage with the research assistant in a threatening manner. This incident was dealt with well by the research assistant in question by assertively directing the student to complete the questionnaire or not as they chose, but that further aggressive behaviour would be directly reported to the head teacher. I was concerned that the classroom teacher appeared to have no control over the students in this particular class, and from that point on I instructed any research assistant who felt nervous or threatened to leave the room and return to our meeting point.

In addition to dealing with some aggressive behaviour from students, the researchers were also prepared to deal with being personally approached by a student about being the victim of bullying. There was a chance that completing the questionnaire might have prompted some students to seek help, and the researcher, removed from the school environment, might have appeared a suitable person to approach. Researchers were all given the Childline helpline number to pass on to the student, and were also required to report this to the classroom teacher. While no students came forward, this could have presented a challenging ethical concern, especially if the student requested help, but did not want the school staff to be notified.

Maintaining the relationship

It is important to try to maintain a relationship with the schools after data collection has taken place. This is done not just with a view to assisting the schools which provided the data, but also to facilitate future research in schools. A bad experience with a researcher in one school could potentially close the door to many schools for future researchers.

After collecting data from the schools I had over 300 questionnaires to enter into a computer package and analyse. After the delays in getting access to schools I was keen to make up time, and the reports that I promised the schools regarding their levels of bullying and victimization were pushed to the back of my mind. However, when the data was coded and I had 365 completed questionnaires, and what I thought to be a wealth of data, I knew I owed the schools a debt. I set about writing a report for each of the three schools as promised. The reports included information about the amount of bullying and victimization, where it tended to take place, and the typical response of parents and teachers to victimization and bullying. The report then compared this information to that available from a national survey of bullying (Whitney and Smith 1993), and the strategies which have proven useful to combat bullying (Rigby 1996). The reports were sent to the schools two months after the data collection had taken place and were well received by the head teachers and staff.

Some months after I completed the report I was contacted by one school which wanted more information about bullying and victimization by females, and another which wanted me to give a brief talk about bullying. While I found it difficult to find the time to undertake this additional work I always did my best to meet their requests because without their help I would have had no data at all.

In hindsight, maintaining this relationship with the schools was very fortunate. Subsequent analyses of my data showed that I did not have enough subjects to make my analysis powerful enough to detect empathy differences between offenders and non-offenders. Moreover, because of the low number of female bullies I would have little to contribute to this important topic. It was clear that another wave of data collection was needed. Several months after my initial data collection I again contacted the head teachers at the three schools. All agreed to have me back and a second wave of data collection was carried out at the same time of year as the first, with all of the new Year 10 students. When the second wave of data collection was completed I had 720 completed questionnaires, and although I was certain that I wouldn't be conducting future research at the schools, I provided all three with another report on bullying and victimization which also included some year-on-year comparisons to examine how patterns of bullying and victimization had changed.

What would be done differently?

Given my description of how I conducted this research it is fair to ask what I would have done differently if I were doing it again. First, I would have spread the net wider at the beginning of the research. Instead of waiting and expecting to get access to the Cambridge LEA I should have contacted five or six LEAs in the hope of finding at least one that was amenable to the research. On the same theme once I had made contact with the LEA I would have asked for information about many more potential schools that I could include in the research than I actually intended to use. For example, if I had been given twenty potential schools as opposed to ten, and if my hit rate for data collection was the same (30 per cent) then I would have had collected data from six schools, plenty of data in one set of data collection.

Once I had met with the head teachers, and they had agreed to take part in the research, I would have made two dates to collect data rather than just one. Having a single date from the school to collect the data put the research under unnecessary pressure. Any small incident such as a broken down car, traffic, a research assistant not showing up, had the potential to cause that school to be missed completely. A back-up date even if never used would have helped reduce the stress and also reduce the opportunity for missing a school.

Conclusions

Reflecting back on the entire procedure I am amazed at how challenging it was to conduct a study in school classrooms. Unfortunately, I think that there is a trend towards making it more difficult for researchers to conduct this sort of research. While this is an understandable response based on the current pressures that schools face, it would be a shame to lose such a potentially rich source of data. That is not to suggest that the doors of all schools should be opened to all wanting to do research, but merely that researchers should be given the opportunity to explain to LEAs and head teachers why their research might be useful, and how it could be conducted with a minimum disruption to the students and staff. Given the efforts of those at the Hertfordshire LEA, the head teachers at the three schools and the 720 students, I now consider it my duty to use the information that they have provided me to contribute in whatever way I can to our understanding of these problems. To date I have published three academic papers based on these data (Jolliffe and Farrington 2006a, 2006b; 2007), and I expect to contribute at least two more in the future. None of this would have been possible without the efforts of my advisers and respondents.

I would like to thank the staff and students at the participating schools for making this research possible. I would also like to thank Roy King and Emma Wincup for their helpful comments and suggestions.

References

Beinart, S., Anderson, B., Lee, S., and Utting, D. (2002). *Youth at Risk: A National Survey of Risk Factors, Protective Factors and Problem Behaviour Among Young People In England, Scotland and Wales.* London: Communities that Care.

British Educational Research Association (2004). *Revised Ethical Guidelines for Educational Research 2004.* www.bera.ac.uk

British Psychological Society (2006). *British Psychological Society Ethical Guidelines.* www.bps.org.uk

BURKE, D. M. (2001). 'Empathy in Sexually Offending and Nonoffending Adolescent Males'. *Journal of Interpersonal Violence* 16: 222–33.

COHEN, D. and STRAYER, J. (1996). 'Empathy in Conduct-disordered and Comparison Youth'. *Developmental Psychology* 32: 988–98.

FARRINGTON, D. P. (1993). 'Understanding and Preventing Bullying' in M. Tonry (ed.), *Crime and Justice* 12: 381–458. Chicago: University of Chicago Press.

—— (1998). 'Predictors, Causes, and Correlates of Male Youth Violence' in M. Tonry and M. H. Moore (eds), *Youth Violence*. Chicago: University of Chicago Press.

—— (2001). *What Has Been Learned From Self-Reports About Criminal Careers and the Causes of Offending?* London: Home Office. Online Report (*http://www.home-office.gov.uk/rds/pdfs/farrington.pdf*).

——, COID, J. W., HARNETT, L., JOLLIFFE, D., SOTERIOU, N., TURNER, R., and WEST, D. (2006). *Criminal Careers up to age 50 and Life Success up to age 48: New Findings from the Cambridge Study in Delinquent Development*. Home Office Research Study. London: Home Office.

—— and PETROSINO, A. (2001). 'The Campbell Collaboration Crime and Justice Group'. *Annals of the American Academy of Political and Social Science* 578: 35–49.

FISHER, D., BEECH, A., and BROWNE, K. (1999). 'Comparison of Sex Offenders to Nonoffenders on Selected Psychological Measures'. *International Journal of Offender Therapy and Comparative Criminology* 43: 473–91.

FLOOD-PAGE, C., CAMPBELL, S., HARRINGTON, V., and MILLER, J. (2000). *Youth Crime: Findings from the 1998/99 Youth Lifestyles Survey*. Home Office Research Study 209. London: Home Office.

GOTTFREDSON, M. R. and HIRSCHI, T. (1990). *A General Theory of Crime*. Stanford, CA: Stanford University Press.

GROUNDS, A. and JAMIESON, R. (2003). 'No Sense of an Ending. Researching the Experience of Imprisonment and Release among Republican Ex-prisoners'. *Theoretical Criminology* 7: 347–62.

HARE, R. D. (1999). 'Psychopathy as a Risk Factor for Violence'. *Psychiatric Quarterly* 70: 181–97.

HAYASHINO, D. S., WURTELE, S. K., and KLEBE, K. J. (1995). 'Child Molesters: An Examination of Cognitive Factors'. *Journal of Interpersonal Violence* 10: 106–16.

JOLLIFFE, D. and FARRINGTON, D. P. (2004). 'Empathy and Offending: A Systematic Review and Meta-analysis'. *Aggression & Violent Behavior* 9: 441–76.

—— and —— (2006a). 'Development and Validation of the Basic Empathy Scale'. *Journal of Adolescence* 29: 589–611.

—— and —— (2006b). 'Examining the Relationship between Low Empathy and Bullying'. *Aggressive Behavior* 32: 540–50.

—— and —— (2007). 'Examining the Relationship between Low Empathy and Self-reported Offending'. *Legal and Criminological Psychology* (in press).

——, ——, HAWKINS, J. D., CATALANO, R. E., HILL, K. G., and KOSTERMAN, R. (2003). 'Predictive, Concurrent, Prospective and Retrospective Validity of Self-reported Delinquency'. *Criminal Behaviour and Mental Health* 13: 179–97.

KULIK, J. A., STEIN, K. B., and SARBIN, T. R. (1968). 'Disclosure of Delinquent Behaviour under Conditions of Anonymity and Nonanonimity'. *Journal of Consulting and Clinical Psychology* 32: 506–9.

LIPSEY, M. W. and WILSON, D. B. (2001). *Practical Meta-Analysis*. Thousand Oaks, CA: Sage.

LOEBER, R., FARRINGTON, D. P., STOUTHAMER-LOEBER, M., MOFFITT, T. E., CASPI, A., WHITE, H. R., WEI, E. H., and BEYERS, J. M. (2003). 'The Development of Male

Offending: Key Findings from 15 years of the Pittsburgh Youth Study' in T. P. Thornberry and M. D. Krohn (eds), *Taking Stock of Delinquency: An Overview of Findings from Contemporary Longitudinal Studies*. New York: Kluwer Academic/Plenum Press.

MELLOR, A. (1990). *Bullying in Scottish Secondary Schools*. Edinburgh: Scottish Council for Research in Education.

MULLOY, R., SMILEY, W. C., and MAWSON, D. L. (1999). 'The Impact of Empathy Training on Offender Treatment'. *Focus on Corrections Research* 11: 15–18.

OLWEUS, D. (1978). *Aggression in the Schools*. Washington, DC: Hemisphere.

—— (1991). 'Bully/victim Problems among School Children; Basic Facts and Effects of a School based Intervention Program' in D. J. Pepler and K. H. Rubin (eds), *The Development and Treatment of Childhood Aggression* 411–48. Hillsdale, NJ: Lawrence Erlbaum.

—— (1993). *Bullying at School*. Oxford: Blackwell Publishers.

RIGBY, K. (1996). *Bullying in Schools and What to do About it*. London, UK: Jessica Kingsley.

SHENTON, A. (2004). 'Information-seeking Research in Schools: Opportunities and Pitfalls'. *ASLIB Proceedings: New Information Perspectives* 56: 180–6.

SMITH, P. K. (2004). 'Bullying: Recent Developments'. *Child and Adolescent Mental Health* 9: 98–103.

WEST, D. J. and Farrington, D. P. (1977). *The Delinquent Way of Life*. London: Heinemann.

WHITNEY, I. and SMITH, P. K. (1993). 'A Survey of the Nature and Extent of Bullying in Junior/middle and Secondary Schools'. *Educational Research* 35: 3–25.

WIKSTROM, P. O. (2002). *Adolescent Crime in Context: A Study of Gender, Family Social Position, Individual Characteristics, Community Context, Life-Styles, Offending and Victimisation*. Unpublished Report. University of Cambridge: Institute of Criminology.

Index